CAMBRIDGE LIBRARY COLLECTION

Books of enduring scholarly value

History

The books reissued in this series include accounts of historical events and movements by eye-witnesses and contemporaries, as well as landmark studies that assembled significant source materials or developed new historiographical methods. The series includes work in social, political and military history on a wide range of periods and regions, giving modern scholars ready access to influential publications of the past.

The World's Cane Sugar Industry

H. C. Prinsen Geerligs (b.1864) was a Dutch microbiologist and Director of the Sugar Experiment Station in Java, an important research centre at the heart of the sugar industry. A leading expert in the production of sugar and the workings of the international market, Geerligs presents a detailed and comprehensive history of the industry, from its ancient origins through to the early twentieth century. Developing into a global industry during a time of great turbulence, the story of sugar interweaves with the history of slavery and colonial expansion, and into an age where science revolutionised production methods. As well as detailing the survival and growth of the industry through wars, piracy, conquest and social change, this book includes detailed country-by-country studies of the state of the industry in 1912 when the book was first published. A fascinating portrait of industrial and commercial history from an expert eyewitness.

Cambridge University Press has long been a pioneer in the reissuing of out-of-print titles from its own backlist, producing digital reprints of books that are still sought after by scholars and students but could not be reprinted economically using traditional technology. The Cambridge Library Collection extends this activity to a wider range of books which are still of importance to researchers and professionals, either for the source material they contain, or as landmarks in the history of their academic discipline.

Drawing from the world-renowned collections in the Cambridge University Library, and guided by the advice of experts in each subject area, Cambridge University Press is using state-of-the-art scanning machines in its own Printing House to capture the content of each book selected for inclusion. The files are processed to give a consistently clear, crisp image, and the books finished to the high quality standard for which the Press is recognised around the world. The latest print-on-demand technology ensures that the books will remain available indefinitely, and that orders for single or multiple copies can quickly be supplied.

The Cambridge Library Collection will bring back to life books of enduring scholarly value (including out-of-copyright works originally issued by other publishers) across a wide range of disciplines in the humanities and social sciences and in science and technology.

The World's
Cane Sugar Industry

Past and Present

H.C. Prinsen Geerligs

CAMBRIDGE
UNIVERSITY PRESS

CAMBRIDGE UNIVERSITY PRESS

Cambridge, New York, Melbourne, Madrid, Cape Town, Singapore,
São Paolo, Delhi, Dubai, Tokyo, Mexico City

Published in the United States of America by Cambridge University Press, New York

www.cambridge.org
Information on this title: www.cambridge.org/9781108020299

© in this compilation Cambridge University Press 2010

This edition first published 1912
This digitally printed version 2010

ISBN 978-1-108-02029-9 Paperback

THE WORLD'S
CANE SUGAR INDUSTRY

PAST AND PRESENT

NGELOM MILL IN JAVA.

THE WORLD'S
CANE SUGAR INDUSTRY

PAST AND PRESENT

BY

H. C. PRINSEN GEERLIGS

Late Director of the Sugar Experiment Station, Pekalongan, Java.

AUTHOR OF

" *Cane Sugar and its Manufacture,*"
" *Chemical Control in Cane Sugar Factories.*"

NORMAN RODGER

ALTRINCHAM

(MANCHESTER)

—

1912

PREFACE

AT a time when, through the co-operation of numerous factors, a new epoch of prosperity for the cane sugar industry has begun, the opportunity seems to have arrived to bring together in a coherent survey the past, the present, and the probable future of the cane sugar industry in the different countries of production.

The various causes which have contributed to animating with new vitality an industry, which by many writers was already considered to be dying out, are still fresh in the mind of the reader. One may mention here only the most conspicuous of these, viz., the Brussels Convention, the conquest of Formosa by the Japanese, the tariff privileges granted by the United States to the former Spanish colonies, and, last but not least, the great advance of science in the province of sugar cane cultivation and cane sugar manufacture—all of which has occurred during the last twenty years.

I, personally, felt inclined to tackle this important subject, the more so because, first of all, I myself have been an eye-witness of the decline, and then the revival, of the cane sugar industry; and, further, because, as well through my own observations as through regular correspondence with authorities on the subject in well-nigh every cane sugar producing country, I am able to draw on the most reliable information concerning that industry in every part of the world where it is found.

Apart from the private information which I gratefully acknowledge here, I found many interesting data in the ARCHIEF VOOR DE JAVA SUIKER INDUSTRIE, in the INTERNATIONAL SUGAR JOURNAL, and in all the other periodicals quoted in the list on page iv., and in the various sources of reference mentioned at the end of each chapter.

I further beg to offer my thanks to MESSRS. J. H. DE BUSSY, of Amsterdam, who enabled me to study so many a valuable and original book in their well-stocked reading room; and to MR. ALGERNON E. ASPINALL for his courtesy in allowing me to reprint the beautiful maps of Barbados, Trinidad, and Jamaica from his POCKET GUIDE TO THE WEST INDIES.

I make use of this opportunity cordially to invite my readers to write to me and draw my attention to any errors or omissions which have struck them when reading the book. All of these will be thankfully considered in a future edition.

H. C. PRINSEN GEERLIGS.

Wanningstraat 17,
    Amsterdam,
        1st July, 1912.

LIST OF PERIODICALS CONSULTED IN THE COMPOSITION OF THIS WORK.

Agricultural News.
American Sugar Journal and Beet Sugar Gazette.
Archief voor de Java Suiker Industrie.
Australian Sugar Journal.
Boletin Official de la Secretaria de Agricultura, Industria y Comercio.
Bulletin Agricole.
Centralblatt der Zuckerindustrie.
Cuban Review.
Deutsche Zuckerindustrie.
Hacendado Mexicano.
Indische Mercuur.
International Sugar Journal.
Journal des Fabricants de Sucre.
Licht's Wochenberichte.
Louisiana Planter.
Planters' Monthly.
Revista industrial y agricola de Tucuman.
Revue Agricole de la Réunion.
Sucrerie Indigène et Coloniale.
West Indian Bulletin.
West India Committee Circular.
Willett & Gray's Weekly Statistical Sugar Trade Journal.
Zeitschrift des Vereins für die Zuckerindustrie.

CONTENTS

Part I.

General History of the Cane Sugar Industry.

Contents.

Part II.

The Condition of the Cane Sugar Industry in the Different Countries of Production.

ASIA.

Contents.

Contents.

Contents

Contents.

AUSTRALASIA.

I

APPENDIX.

INDEX.

LIST OF ILLUSTRATIONS IN THE TEXT

LIST OF PLATES

LIST OF MAPS AND DIAGRAMS

NOTES :—

(1) The maps of BARBADOS, TRINIDAD, and JAMAICA are reproduced from Aspinall's " Pocket Guide to the West Indies," by kind permission of the Author.

(2) The map of Formosa is reproduced by permission of His Majesty's Stationery Office, from British Consular Report, No. 3863 (1907) on Formosa.

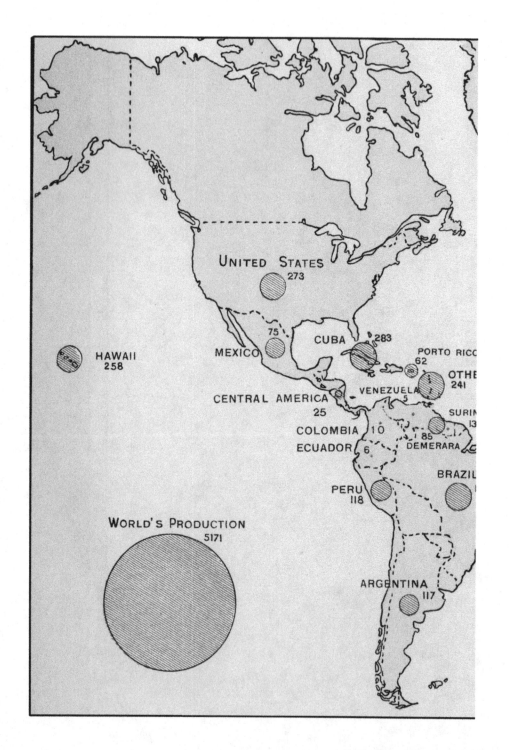

United States
273

75

CUBA

283

PORTO RICO
62

OTHE
241

HAWAII
258

MEXICO

VENEZUELA

SURIN
13

5

CENTRAL AMERICA
25

COLOMBIA   10

85

DEMERARA

ECUADOR   6

BRAZIL

PERU
118

WORLD'S PRODUCTION
5171

ARGENTINA   117

World's Pr

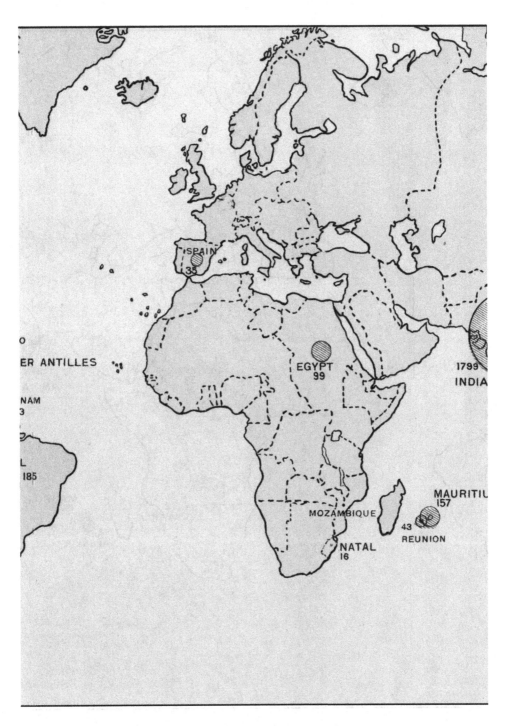

oduction of Raw Sugar in the different
during 1900.

Expressed in Thousands of Tons.

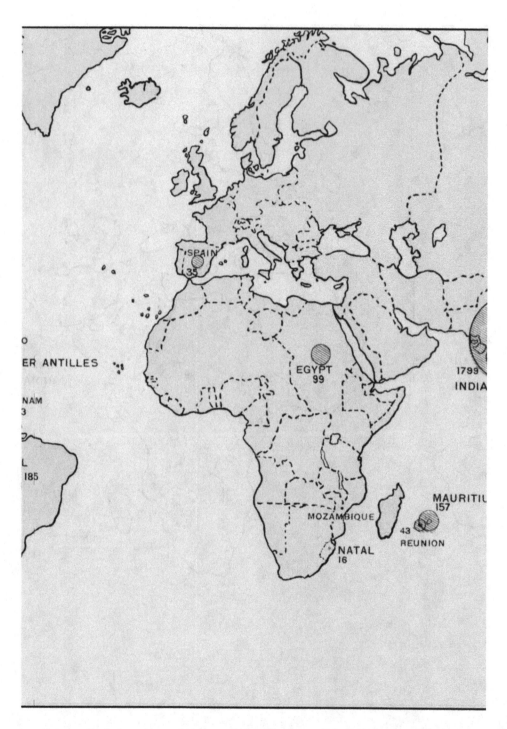

roduction of Raw Sugar in the different
during 1900.

Expressed in Thousands of Tons.

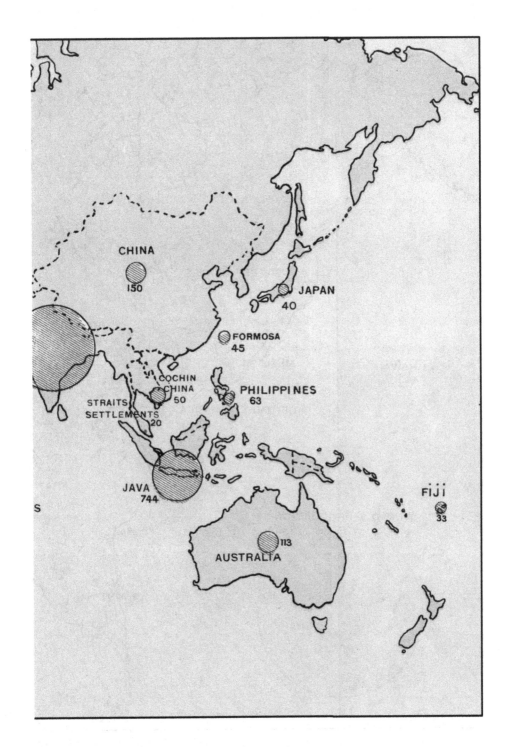

Countries

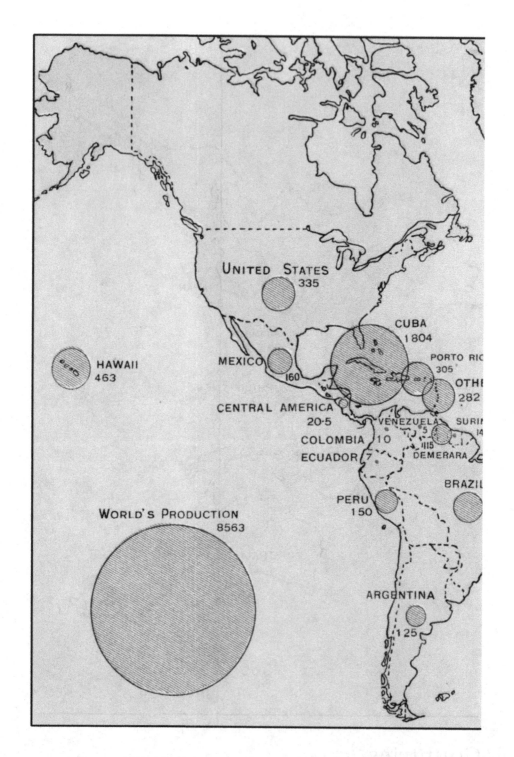

UNITED STATES
335

CUBA
1804

HAWAII
463

PORTO RICO
305

MEXICO
160

OTHE
282

CENTRAL AMERICA
20·5

VENEZUELA
5

SURIN
14

COLOMBIA 10

ECUADOR 7

115

DEMERARA

BRAZIL

PERU
150

WORLD'S PRODUCTION
8563

ARGENTINA
125

World's Pr

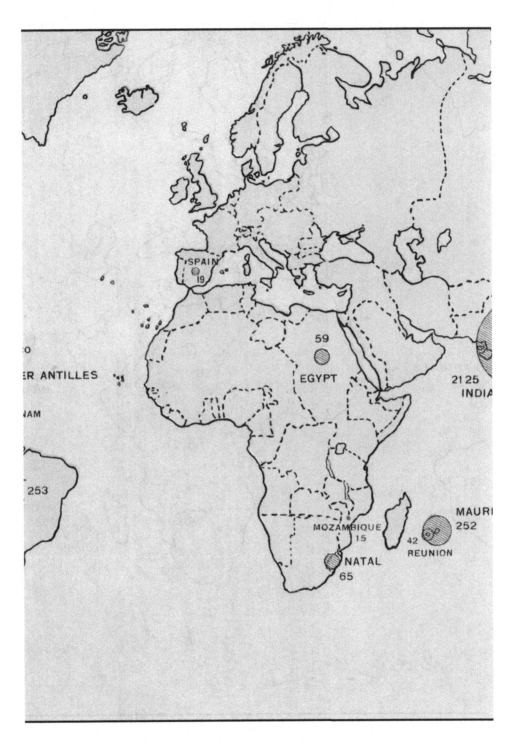

oduction of Raw Sugar in the different

during 1910.

Expressed in Thousands of Tons.

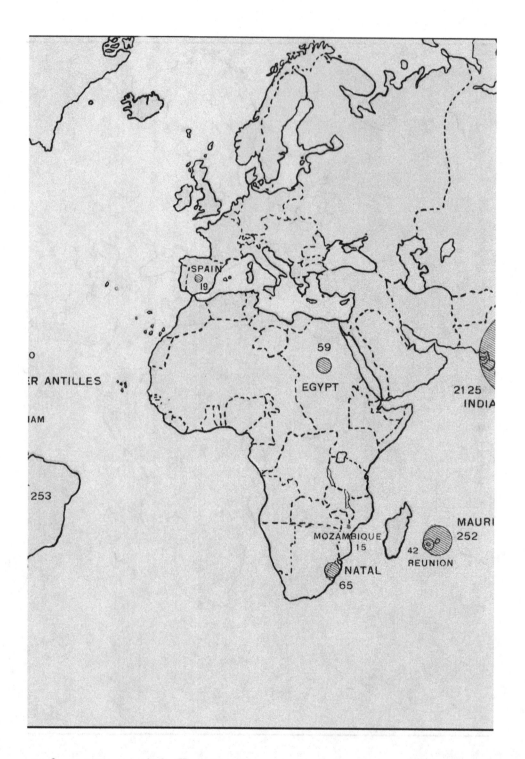

oduction of Raw Sugar in the different
during 1910.

Expressed in Thousands of Tons.

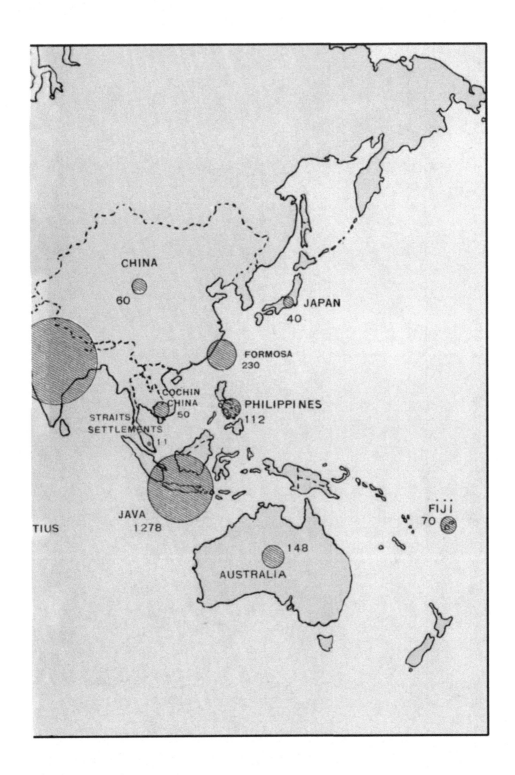

CHINA
60

JAPAN
40

FORMOSA
230

COCHIN
CHINA
50

PHILIPPINES
112

STRAITS
SETTLEMENTS
11

JAVA
1278

FIJI
70

AUSTRALIA
148

TIUS

Countries

PART I.

General History of the Cane Sugar Industry.

PART I.

General History of the Cane Sugar Industry.

———

CHAPTER I.

General Survey of the History of the Cane Sugar Industry from the Beginning till the Introduction of the "Continental System."

In all probability the sugar cane originally came from India, more especially from the banks of the Ganges. We cannot be absolutely certain of this, as at the present day sugar cane in its wild state is not found anywhere.

The probability, however, of its originating from India is very strong, as only the ancient literature of that country mentions sugar cane, while we know for certain that it was conveyed to other countries by travellers and sailors.

According to Hindu mythology, sugar cane was created by the famous hermit Vishva Mitra to serve as heavenly food in the temporary paradise which was organized by him for the sake of Raja Trishanku. This prince had expressed his wish to be translated to heaven during his lifetime, but Indra, the monarch of the celestial regions, had refused to admit him. In order to meet his wish, Vishva Mitra prepared a temporary paradise for him, but when a reconciliation between the two rajas was brought about, the paradise was demolished and all its luxuries destroyed except a few, including sugar cane which was spread all over the land of mortals as a permanent memorial of Vishva Mitra's miraculous deeds.

We find sugar cane mentioned in the Atharva Veda, one of the latter

3

General History of the Cane Sugar Industry.

portions of the sacred books of the Hindus, from which we quote the following :

> " Paritwâ paritantu néxunâgâmawidwisé Yathâ mâm kaminyaso yathâ man nâpagâ assah."
>
> " I have crowned thee with a shooting sugar cane, so that thou shalt not be averse to me."

The fellow-travellers of Alexander the Great, and afterwards writers who made use of their notes, tell us of a reed growing in India which produced honey without the aid of bees.

We also find sugar cane repeatedly mentioned as a tribute to the Emperor of China from the Indian border provinces, which also accounts for sugar cane having spread as far as the East.

Although sugar cane was known in ancient times, we do not come across any regular statement of sugar being made from cane at any period previous to 300—600 A.D. It is a fact that Greek and Roman authors, such as Strabo, Dioscorides, Pliny, and others, refer to a kind of honey made from cane which grows in India, and some substance, " saccharon," which, also in the East, is obtained from cane ; but on closer examination it does not appear to have been sugar, being in some cases manna, and in others " tabaschir," a gelatinous silica which sometimes forms in the joints of some species of bamboo.

The first kind of sugar mentioned was simply concentrated cane juice, called " gur " in India and known under the name of " gud " in Sanskrit, which (although we cannot be certain of it) points to the fact of " gur " having been known in India even in prehistoric times.

We do know that in A.D. 627, at the time of the Conquest of Dastagerd in Persia, sugar was among the spoils taken by the Byzantines, and also that, according to the Pen-tsao-kang-mu, a famous encyclopedia written in 1552 by Si-Shi-Tjin, the Emperor Tai Tsung (627—650) sent people to Behar, in India, in order to learn he art of sugar manufacture.

From that time the art of making sugar out of cane spread rapidly, being considerably aided by the vast trade renaissance of the seventh, eighth, and ninth centuries.

It was not restricted merely to evaporating the juice to dryness, but the Arabs and Egyptians soon learnt how to purify raw sugar by re-crystallization, and to make a great variety of sweetmeats out of the purified sugar.

Marco Polo, who visited China during 1270-1295, and other western travellers after him, mention a great many sugar factories in South China where sugar could be freely bought at low prices.

Although the Chinese had soon learned how to prepare a light-coloured kind of sugar by draining off the raw molasses, the proper art of refining seems to have been brought to China by people from Cairo subsequent to Marco Polo's time

General History of the Cane Sugar Industry.

The Mohammedan writers, who refer to the sugar industry in India, mention a great many kinds that, about the end of the thirteenth century, were prepared from the evaporated cane juice by re-dissolving, clarifying it with milk, and then either concentrating it to solid matter, or crystallizing it into candy.

Further, we find that sugar cane was taken to Sicily by the Arabs in 703, and Sicilian sugar conveyed to Africa in 900. Sanutus writes in 1300 that sugar cane was produced not only in the dominions belonging to the Sultan, but also in the Christian countries of Cyprus, Rhodes, and Sicily.

The Crusaders found extensive sugar cane plantations in Tripoli, Mesopotamia, Palestine, Syria, Antioch, etc.

As early as 755, sugar cane was taken to Spain by Abdurrahman, and it was especially on the south coast of Andalusia that it was cultivated, so that as far back as the year 1150 Spain could boast of a flourishing sugar industry, commanding an area of no less than 75,000 acres.

The Arabs and Chinese introduced sugar cane not only to the above-mentioned countries, but also to the coast of the Mediterranean and the Indian Ocean, consequently to Tunis, Morocco, Gambia, Madagascar, Siam, Sunda Islands, the Philippines, Formosa, and Japan, and it flourished wherever it was cultivated.

In all the countries mentioned, however, any regular sugar industry was out of the question ; the cane was cultivated simply for the purpose of supplying local wants, while before 1400, with the exception of China, a proper sugar industry was carried on only in the countries round the Mediterranean.

The Crusaders looked upon sugar cane cultivation as a profitable venture, and therefore interested themselves in it, making Tyre an important centre of the sugar trade. Both the administration of King Baldwin's dominions and the different knighthoods founded extensive sugar cane plantations in Palestine, in Antioch, in Syria, and in Cyprus, and greatly improved the sugar industry in those parts.

Egypt continued producing large quantities of very good sugar, which met with a ready demand in all the markets round the Mediterranean. In Sicily the sugar industry, which was in a flourishing state during the Norman Conquest, gradually dwindled to such an extent that the Emperor Frederic II thought it expedient to send to Tyre for two capable sugar manufacturers in order to revise the almost forgotten art of sugar manufacture.

This sugar industry soon developed, a result partly due to the influence of the instructors, and partly to the fact that the government began henceforward to patronize agriculture. Discord and war, however, soon had a disastrous influence on the political affairs of the island, and about 1400 A.D. the sugar industry was entirely abandoned. But after the restoration of order under King Alfonso (1410—1418) prosperity returned, so that even in

General History of the Cane Sugar Industry.

1418 much sugar was being exported from Palermo. a great many sugar cane plantations and mills being found in 1450 in Sicily.

At the same time a sugar industry flourished in Spain, and was also taken up in the south of France, where many of its inhabitants had acquired a thorough knowledge of cane cultivation and sugar manufacture, through constantly coming into contact with their Spanish neighbours and through their participation in the Crusades.

Consequently, all the countries round the Mediterranean were cane sugar producing countries in the thirteenth and fourteenth centuries : Spain, France, Calabria, Sicily, Cyprus, Rhodes, Asia Minor, Egypt, Tripoli, Tunis, Morocco all taking part, more or less, in the sugar industry. The sugar that was not needed for their own consumption was chiefly exported viâ the Italian ports of Venice, Pisa, and Genoa. The Crusaders who, when in the Far East, had become accustomed to sugar, wished to continue its use after their return home, and thus developed a brisk trade between the Italian towns and Northern Europe, both by land and by sea.

The sugar was sold in the form of loaves, square blocks, or powder. The small loaves were wrapped up in palm leaves, two at a time, with one base lying against the other, sewn up in cloth, and marked with the seller's trade mark.

Sometimes the loaves were packed in barrels, and the open spaces filled in with dried cane leaves. Another way of packing was to knock the top off the sugar-loaf and to put the truncated cones, thirty-six of them together into a chest in two layers, while the open spaces, which were left, were filled in with the broken–off tops. Finally, the chest was wrapped up in cloth and the vendor's trade mark affixed.

Only the inferior kind of sugar was packed up in chests like this ; it went by the name of *cassonade*, which means simply " packed in wooden boxes." Later on, however, the name was also given to any inferior grade of sugar, so that in course of time it has become the general term for inferior sugar.

Then there was sugar powder, which was obtained from inferior sugar loaves crumpled to powder, and this also was sent away in chests and barrels. Finally, there was sugar candy in a variety of tints between clear white and brown.

The sugar industry in the countries round the Mediterranean flourished up to the end of the fifteenth and the beginning of the sixteenth centuries. Syria lost much of its importance as a sugar trade centre when, after the fall of Acre in 1291, the Crusaders had to give up their conquests in Asia Minor ; but Tyre and Beirut, Antioch and the Jordan Valley all continued producing large quantities of sugar, while Damascus and Tripoli became sugar refining centres. Cyprus, still tributary to Venice, extended its industry considerably, and every year sent large supplies to the mother-town ; while Egypt, too, still produced considerable quantities of sugar.

6

General History of the Cane Sugar Industry.

All this prosperity, however, suddenly and unexpectedly came to an end. In 1453 Constantinople was taken by the Turks, in 1461 Trebizonde followed, and soon after the other commercial towns of Asia Minor and all Genoa's colonies on the Black Sea were also conquered, so that the trade relations between Europe and Asia Minor were no longer what was previously the case. Moreover, the entire industry was much restricted during the Turkish sovereignty, and the manufacture of sugar soon declined. In 1517 the Turks attacked and conquered Cairo, and made Egypt a Turkish province, which step had an equally fatal effect on the sugar industry there.

In 1532 Rhodes, and finally in 1571 Cyprus, were taken from the Venetians and added to the Turkish dominions ; by this time, however, the sugar cultivation in these islands had already lost much of its importance, while the industry of Sicily had quite dwindled away, so that within one hundred years the once flourishing sugar industry of the Mediterranean was condemned to extinction.

As early as 1419 the Portuguese had taken the sugar cane to Madeira, where it grew up luxuriantly and developed so quickly that the island soon produced unheard-of quantities of sugar, which were taken to Italy by Portuguese seafarers. In 1444 the Azores were captured and colonized by the Portuguese ; between 1456 and 1462 the Cape Verde Isles followed ; San Thomé, Principe, and Annobon in the Gulf of Guinea were acquired in 1496, while in the same year the Spanish colonized the Canary Islands, and assisted in the establishment of sugar cultivation. Favoured by the mild and moist climate of these islands, the cane grew luxuriantly, and was produced at so little cost, with the help of African negro slaves, that the price of sugar fell considerably, and both Cyprus and Sicily were obliged to abandon competition, so that in 1570 the sugar industry of these Mediterranean islands ceased to exist.

When the Portuguese West African colonies began to flourish, Bartholomew Diaz sailed round the Cape of Good Hope, and in 1490 Vasco de Gama reached Calicut by the unbroken sea route, the result of which was that Venice lost its ascendancy as a trade centre, and the Portuguese distributed Indian goods as well as those coming from their own colonies, consequently opening up new routes for the world's trade.

Still greater changes in the history of cane sugar were brought about by the discovery of America, and the colonization of that vast territory—first by the Spanish and the Portuguese, and later by the Dutch, the English, and the French. In consequence of the colonization of Brazil, the Antilles and Guiana, the production of sugar increased so rapidly that the latter, which up to now had been a very costly article, only to be indulged in as a medicine or as a luxury by the very rich, became in quite a short time an article of common consumption.

Although previously the annual production of the principal sugar centres was only some thousands of hundredweights, it was now possible to state the production in thousands of tons.

The enormous progress in production was caused not only by the great abundance of fertile land in a favoured climate, but also by the cheap labour in the form of negro slaves obtained from the countries on the Gulf of Guinea.

Throughout the history of the cane sugar industry in tropical countries the labour problem has influenced the whole production. When plenty of labour is to be had, and soil and climate allow of sugar cultivation, cane sugar production can flourish, while a decline immediately sets in when in any way labour becomes scarce.

We shall repeatedly come across instances of this fact in the second part of this volume, when dealing with the industry in the different countries of production, and this influence is so great that at the present time a few islands would suffice to produce all the sugar needed for the world's consumption if the lack of the necessary cheap labour did not limit their power of production.

For this very reason Christopher Columbus's first attempt, made on his second journey in 1493, to introduce sugar cane cultivation in San Domingo resulted in loss for the time being. When, however, the Portuguese and the Spanish, in imitation of what they had done in their own colonies on the West Coast of Africa, took negro slaves from the Gulf of Guinea to America, the industry was placed on a firmer footing, and spread to an unprecedented extent. The aborigines of most islands disappeared soon after the conquest by foreigners, and for the greater part were replaced by negro slaves from Africa, who established their race in all the West Indian islands and the adjoining parts of the Continent of America.

Up to the first half of the fifteenth century hardly any slavery existed in Christian countries; it only occurred in Mohammedan lands.

Even in 1442 Henry the Navigator sent Moors, who were taken prisoners, back to their own country, but later on, when it appeared to what account they might be put, he began to deal differently with them. In the year 1481 the Portuguese built three fortresses in Africa, namely, on the Gold Coast, on an island in the Gulf of Guinea, and at Loango, and from these sent slaves to the American possessions. In 1502 negro slaves were used in the mines by the Spanish in Hispaniola (now San Domingo), and Charles the Fifth granted the Genoese the privilege of importing every year as many as 4,000 into Cuba, Jamaica, and Porto Rico. But, quite independent of this monopoly, the import of slaves greatly increased, and even in 1772 it amounted to 74,000, supplied by the following nationalities :—

38,000 by the British.
20,000 ,, ,, French.
4,000 ,, ,, Dutch.
2,000 ,, ,, Danes.
10,000 ,, ,, Portuguese.

General History of the Cane Sugar Industry.

They hailed from Gambia, Sierra Leone, Las Palmas, the Gold Coast, Whydah, Lagos, Benin, Boma, New Calabria, Cameroons, Loango and Benguela, that is from the entire West African Coast, and were distributed all over the American and West Indian countries, so that a mixed population of Americans, Africans and Europeans sprang up.

In Brazil, which in 1500 was discovered by Pinzon and by Cabral, sugar cane was imported from Madeira, and in a very short time the sugar industry there attained to considerable importance. In 1590 there were thirty-six mills in Bahia, and sixty-six in Pernambuco, which numbers continued increasing, so that in 1600 the export from Brazil amounted to 60,000 chests of sugar, each containing 500 lbs. At that time Brazil belonged to Spain, which in 1580 had annexed Portugal and the Portuguese colonies. Because of the truce with Spain the Dutch, who more than once had coveted the rich Portuguese colony, were compelled to suspend their plans of conquest till hostilities were resumed. When in 1621 the armistice had come to an end, the West Indian Company, which was just founded, made up its mind to conquer Brazil, in which attempt it succeeded in 1629, when Pernambuco was taken, and consequently the whole of Brazil fell to the Dutch. It was at this time that a great many sugar mills and plantations were destroyed, but the governor, Joan Maurits, succeeded in resuscitating the sugar industry to the extent that during the years 1636—1643 a total of 159,148 chests, each containing 500 lbs. of white sugar, 49,903 chests of muscovado, and 218,220 chests of brown sugar were exported. In the year 1640 Portugal regained its independence, and although a treaty guaranteed the possession of Brazil by the Dutch, the Portuguese, helped by the English, instigated a rebellion which ended in the Dutch being expelled in 1654, whereupon in 1661 Brazil was acknowledged a Portuguese possession under an indemnity of eight million guilders, paid to the Dutch West Indian Company.

In 1665 the Portuguese government committed a serious mistake in banishing the 20,000 Dutchmen who then lived in Brazil; and it was a twofold error, because, in the first place, a great number of quiet and industrious citizens were driven away, and, secondly, because the latter settled in the neighbouring Caribbean Islands, where they introduced the sugar industry, and consequently became in the long run formidable rivals of Brazil.

Meanwhile, it was impossible for Portugal to regain her former importance, and a great many measures taken by her only tended to favour the Portuguese without at all developing the resources of their country. Moreover, gold mines were discovered in 1725 in the province of Minas Geraes, which caused the regular trade in field and factory to decline, as many labourers found work at the gold mines instead. The sugar factories could not stand these successive blows, and a great many of them were deserted, with the result that the sugar exportation fell rapidly.

After some time it recovered more or less, especially when, at the end of the eighteenth century, a new cane, *Otaheite* (now known as *Bourbon*), was introduced, which contained much more sugar. Still, Brazil has never since attained its former importance in the sugar world.

In the year 1625 the island of St. Christopher (now St. Kitts) was occupied by both the English and the French, and planted with sugar cane. Further, the French conquered Guadaloupe and Martinique in 1635, and the English took Barbados in 1627, and Jamaica in 1656. Sugar cane cultivation was introduced in all these islands, but the people there did not know how to prepare good and durable sugar, till in 1655 the Dutch manufacturers, who had been driven away from Brazil, came to settle there and put their knowledge and experience, gained in Brazil, into practice.

After the French had successively occupied and deserted San Domingo, France took permanent possession of this island in 1697, and it is from this time that the flourishing state of the sugar industry there dates ; for a century it was one of the first among the cane sugar exporting West Indian islands. On the whole the French colonies flourished more than the English, which was partly owing to their more rational way of working, and partly to the more liberal French trade policies. Because of the cruel way, however, in which the French treated their negro slaves a rebellion broke out in 1791, in which, within a very short time, almost the entire white population was massacred or expelled, and sugar plantations and mills were destroyed and burnt, so that San Domingo lost its ascendency, and has ever since been of little importance in the sugar world.

After the fall of this sphere of activity, the other countries became more prominent, especially Jamaica, which made the most of her opportunity, and succeeded in doubling her yearly output in some twenty or thirty years, so that at the end of the eighteenth century this island was first among the sugar producing West Indian islands.

San Domingo's fall was also an incitement to Cuba to extend her sugar cultivation.

Owing to her subjection to Spain, Cuba's sugar industry had to submit to all sorts of restricting stipulations until 1772, after which date, however, they ceased ; and henceforward the manufacture and export of sugar gradually increased in quantity, and after 1791 expanded at such a rate that even in 1802 it amounted to 40,800 tons.

The Dutch colonies, St. Eustatius and Curacao, and the Danish islands, St. Croix, St. John, and San Thomé, also profited by this general prosperity ; and, especially during the American War of Independence, became increasingly important, not so much through producing sugar as through being good trade centres for the smuggling of sugar in those stirring times.

In the meantime the sugar industry had also got a firm hold in the other countries on the continent of South America, with the exception of Brazil. In 1634 French people who were engaged in sugar cultivation settled in Cayenne, and in 1640 in Surinam. This cultivation did not amount to much for the first hundred years, even after the conquest of

General History of the Cane Sugar Industry.

Surinam, Demerara, Essequibo, and Berbice by the Dutch, owing to the scarcity of labourers; consequently, the importation of slaves on a large scale was thought necessary for developing the sugar production in these parts.

This want of labour was gradually supplied, and when the hostilities with the French, who had continually disturbed the peace of the colony, had come to an end, the manufacture of sugar began to flourish, and in the year 1750 Surinam produced the maximum quantity of 12,300 tons of sugar, a quantity never again realized in the eighteenth century. Essequibo, Berbice, and Demerara also supplied some sugar, but disturbances prevailed, while lack of capital and lack of enterprise, together with careless financial management, prevented any sound development of the industry. Through continuous wars the colonies fell to the French, then again to the English, then reverted to the Dutch; but in the end, with the exception of Surinam, they remained English possessions.

Finally, sugar was grown in Peru, Argentina, Chile, Mexico, Louisiana; also in Trinidad, which was taken by the English in 1792, but at the time of which we speak this was of little consequence for the world's trade, as all the sugar produced was used for local consumption.

According to Reesse, in his book on " De Suikerhandel van Amsterdam," page 225, the exportation of American colonies and countries during the last years of the eighteenth century amounted to the following quantities (expressed in Amsterdam pounds and tons):—

	Amsterdam Pounds		Tons
French Colonies (1788)	188,350,000	..	93,045
English ,, (1781—1785) ..			
yearly average ..	157,953,000	..	78,029
Danish Colonies (1768)	41,600,000	..	20,550
Cuba (1790)	28,325,800	..	13,993
Brazil (1796)	69,384,000	..	34,276
Dutch Colonies (1785) .. .	18,000,000	.	8,892

Owing to the large supplies of sugar from the Antilles and Brazil, the sugar industry in Madeira, the Cape Verde Isles and Canary Isles had been outrivalled, and sugar from these islands gradually disappeared from the sugar markets. This was also the case with the sugar industry in the Islands of the Gulf of Guinea, which previously in their turn, shortly after the commencement of the great voyages of discovery by the Portuguese and Spaniards in the fifteenth century, had destroyed the sugar industry of the countries lying on the Mediterranean.

Sugar cane was also introduced by the French to the Isle de France (now Mauritius) and Bourbon (now Réunion), and at about the end of the eighteenth century people began to export sugar to Europe from this part of the world.

Finally, Eastern Asia should not be omitted from the list of important sugar producing countries. On their first voyages the ships of the Dutch East Indian Company carried Formosan, Bengal, and Siamese sugar to Amsterdam, where it was sold at such a profit that they kept on importing it. In order to be able to send still larger consignments of sugar, the Company had sugar cane planted in Java itself, but before the plantations had had time to spread, the price of sugar (in 1642) fell so considerably, in consequence of the large Brazilian harvests, that the profits dwindled away, and it was necessary to reduce the imports of sugar from the East. During the time that elapsed between the beginning of planting in Java and the disbanding of the East Indian Company, the sugar production of this island experienced enormous fluctuations. In 1710 a 14,000,000 lb. harvest was reaped ; between 1742 and 1748 absolutely nothing ; from 1751 to 1760, 6,000,000 lbs. a year, which quantity by no means came up to the amount exported by the Dutch West Indian colonies. The sugar was sent both to the Netherlands and to Persia, Japan, and other countries. The English East Indian Company exported large quantities of sugar from British India (" gur " as well as crystals) ; while, moreover, a fair amount of Chinese, Formosan, and Indian sugar was sent to New York, where, in consequence of fiscal restrictions, importations from the East Indies were less onerous than from the much nearer West Indian colonies.

It was a very bad time for the development of the cane sugar industry when, during the last years of the eighteenth and the first years of the nineteenth centuries, France (first alone, but later on in combination with her allies) was at war with Great Britain. The larger part of the hostilities took place in West Indian waters, where the French and British fleets not only destroyed each other, but where also a great number of laden merchant ships were captured, with consequent loss to sugar planters and merchants. East Indian sugar, too, was often captured by privateers or men-of-war, while, on the other hand, the French Government enacted all sorts of restricting stipulations in order to deal a serious blow to British trade.

When, in the end, Great Britain reigned supreme at sea and succeeded in preserving trade relations with the Continent, in spite of Napoleon's effort to crush them out, the French Emperor in 1806 had recourse to what is known as the " Continental System," which eventually dealt a disastrous blow to the cane sugar industry.

Literature :
Sayid Muhammad Hadi. *The Sugar Industry of the United Provinces of Agra and Oudh.*
F. O. von Lippmann. *Geschichte des Zuckers.*
G. Washington Eves. *West Indies.*
J. J. Reesse. *De Suikerhandel van Amsterdam.*

CHAPTER II.

General Survey of the History of the Cane Sugar Industry from the Introduction of the " Continental System " down to the Present Day.

Much to his regret, Napoleon did not succeed in humiliating his greatest enemy, Great Britain, and had to give up his intention of attacking this country when, in 1805, Nelson destroyed the French fleet off Trafalgar, consequently preventing the landing of the French in England. As the struggle was not to be brought to an end by fighting, Napoleon tried to isolate his enemy by prohibiting all commercial intercourse between England and the Continent, which for the greater part was submissive to him. In 1806 the Berlin decree was issued, according to which all trade communication with Great Britain was forbidden, and all colonial and British goods were confiscated. In answer to this move, England prohibited ships of any nationality from approaching French harbours on the penalty of confiscation ; whereupon Napoleon, in his turn, by the Milan decree, confiscated any ship that had either submitted to English examination or had paid dues in English harbours.

In short, the one party endeavoured to outdo the other in confiscating goods and forbidding any intercourse ; so that the importation of sugar was hindered, and prices went up to a figure that was previously unknown. It is true that the Trianon decree later on allowed colonial products to enter, but only under high import duties, so the price of these articles was not conducive to any widespread distribution, and only wealthy people could afford to use sugar.

Napoleon did not conceal from himself the fact that this want of sugar was most inconvenient to his subjects, but, in the first place, he was sure trade would hit upon a means by which sugar might be brought from the East to the West of Europe viâ the land route (Constantinople and Vienna) ; secondly, he cherished great expectations as regards substitutes for cane sugar, which might be produced in Europe and supply a much-felt want. Such were the sugar produced from grapes and from beetroot—while strenuous endeavours were also made to extract sugar from apples, pears, plums, quinces, mulberries, chestnuts, figs, sorghum and maize stalks, and from the sap of the nut and maple trees ; but only from the two first-mentioned sources could sugar be produced on a large and industrial scale.

In the year 1747 Marggraf, in a communication to the Royal Academy of Science and Literature in Berlin, had shown that various kinds of beetroot, the sweet taste of which was already known, contained sugar that could be extracted and crystallized in a fairly simple way. Other plants which had

13

a sweet taste also contained sugar, although in a less degree, but it was found that in many cases it did not crystallize out, but remained as syrup, no matter how long it was kept.

This discovery of crystallizable sugar occurring in plants that thrive in a European climate was for a long time considered a mere laboratory demonstration without any practical importance, till in 1786 Achard began to occupy himself with beetroot cultivation on his estate, Caulsdorf, near Berlin. He planted beetroot there in the hope of finding a species rich in sugar, and at the same time containing few impurities destructive to the yield; but, because of a fire which burnt down his house, as well as through financial difficulties, it was not till 1799 that he made his result known. The King of Prussia, Frederick Wilhelm III, took a great interest in this beetroot sugar manufacture, and after he was convinced of the truth of Achard's information, he bought, in 1801, the Crown land, Cunern, in Silesia, for experimenting on a large scale, and provided Achard with the necessary means for the erection of a sugar factory. Moreover, the king contributed towards the erection of further sugar factories round Berlin, in Pomerania, and in Silesia, by means of funds and advice, while he held out premiums to any farmer or manufacturer who should work up more than twenty tons of beetroot a year.

Although the war calamities and defeats from which the Prussians suffered after 1806 hindered the development of the sugar industry, yet the manufacture advanced so far that in 1810 it was possible to declare that this industry had proved itself a success when properly conducted; consequently, the experiments at Cunern were discontinued. Hence, in 1812, this experimental farm was turned into a school for the sugar industry, but, unfortunately, in 1813 it was destroyed by the ravages of war.

Achard's important experiments caused much surprise all over Europe, especially in France, the more so as Achard, being of French origin had communicated with several French savants, and, as a result, had had his method of working officially examined by the Physical Section of the Paris Academy, who judged favourably of it. Notwithstanding this, since capitalists hesitated to risk money on building sugar factories, only two were constructed, one near Paris and one at St. Ouen, both of which, however, soon failed for want of adequate knowledge and through working with a very inferior kind of beetroot, the beetroot sugar manufacture thus coming to an entire standstill for some years. But although the industry had come to a temporary stop, the possibilities were not overlooked; and it is from this time that a number of documents date, which show how much the French had the idea of a national sugar industry at heart, and how everywhere, although on a small scale, people fervently looked forward to the realization of this hope.

As, however, the manufacturing branch of the industry had given negative rather than positive results, a great many scholars, especially Proust and Parmentier, became interested in the preparation of sugar on a large scale from grapes. Although it had long been known that a saccharine substance

14

could be obtained from grape must by evaporating and cooling the residue, it remained for the chemist Proust to point out in a lucid *memoire* the profit obtainable from the manufacture of sugar from grapes. So we must look to him as the real pioneer of this industry.

It also stood Proust in good stead, that shortly after the publication of his *memoire* the " Continental System " was started, in consequence of which cane sugar could only be imported at great expense and danger, the demand for a substitute thus becoming great. About the same time the chemist Parmentier had published an official report, in which he advised his countrymen not to manufacture beetroot sugar in France, as the French soil would not allow the production of beetroots containing sugar.

Further, the extraction of sugar from must was greatly stimulated by the fact that the vine abounded in France, and brief instructions were issued by the Government for preparing syrup and sugar from must for domestic use. Where there was a dearth of sugar it was a great convenience for the inhabitants of the vine-growing countries to be able themselves to produce sugar easily from grapes, so this native sugar industry began immediately to flourish.

Napoleon was greatly pleased to see the results of the attempts at sugar production within the boundaries of his empire, hoping that such sugar might supersede the cane sugar imported from America. He consequently ordered his subjects to apply themselves vigorously to the manufacture of this substance, in order to extend its consumption to districts outside the vine-growing provinces.

Proust succeeded in obtaining a solid sugar from concentrated syrups, while Fouquet was able to work this into white sugar, which, though not crystallizing in the same shape as cane sugar, corresponded in colour and consistency to it. As a reward they received by Imperial decree sums of money amounting to 100,000 francs in Proust's case, and 40,000 francs in that of Fouquet, on condition that factories for grape-sugar should be founded with the money in the south of France, and their factory secrets should be divulged.

A few months later Napoleon disposed of a sum of 200,000 francs, to be divided among twelve factories that should produce the greatest amount of sugar out of grapes in proportion to the quantities manufactured. A minimum weight of 10,000 kg. was necessary for those competing for the prize.

Parmentier, who had greatly exerted himself in the manufacture of sugar from grape-must, and had done what he could in the way of giving hints and instructions about that manufacture, finally wrote a memorandum dealing with the best way in which to prepare this kind of sugar on a large scale, which monograph contained much information for manufacturers.

The committee appointed to distribute prizes reported that, in 1811, 2,000,000 kg. of syrup and 500 kg. of sugar had been prepared from grapes, but that only three establishments, whose yearly output of prepared sugar and syrup exceeded 10,000 kg. were entitled to a prize. Consequently, only three prizes of 16,666·66 francs each were awarded, and further a premium of 12,000 francs to a fourth manufacturer who had prepared 4,500 kg.

The greatest apprehensions were entertained as to this national industry when in 1814, owing to Napoleon's downfall and the revocation of the "Continental System," cane sugar was freely imported again, and owing to its low price dealt a deadly blow to the manufacture of grape sugar.

Although people expected great things of the grape sugar industry, their feeling towards beetroot sugar production had now greatly changed. The primary dislike for this industry was largely due to the influence of Parmentier, who advocated the cause of sugar manufacture from grapes; but the enterprise and the never-ceasing activity of those in favour of the beetroot sugar industry led ultimately to Napoleon contributing generously towards the manufacture of sugar from this plant. Thus in 1811 Napoleon ordered 32,000 hectares to be planted with beetroot—to be equally distributed over the several provinces—four schools were to be founded in which sugar manufacture was to be taught, while on January 1st, 1813, all further importation from the East and West Indies was prohibited.

In 1812 the number of sugar schools was increased to five, the pupils of which obtained scholarships, and the area devoted to beets amounted to 100,000 hectares. Further, 500 licences for the manufacture of beetroot sugar were granted in France—that is, at least one in each department. Each licensee was obliged to erect a factory, which was supposed to yield at least 10,000 kg. of sugar in the campaign of 1812–13, and in case one of them was to improve the manufacture or increase its output the licence was extended, on condition that no duty or excise should be raised on its produce during the time of the licence. Finally, the decree also contained restrictions as regards the foundation of four Imperial factories, which were to deliver up 2,000,000 kg. of sugar in 1812–13, and of a small factory on the Crown land, Rambouillet, with a capacity of 20,000 kg. of sugar.

In consequence of this decree no fewer than 338 licences were taken out in 1812, four of which fell through, so that in the campaign 1812–13 334 sugar factories must have been working on French soil, which, according to a report by the Minister of the Interior, turned out 7,000,000 lbs. of sugar. The largest among the factories was that of Crespel-Dellisse, founded at Lille in 1810, where Spanish prisoners of war were employed as labourers. Many of them had been used to working in the colonies, where they had come into contact with the sugar industry, so that their knowledge and experience stood the French enterprise in good stead.

In Austria, too, some factories were built in the nineteenth century, which, because of the high price of sugar, yielded large profits during the time of the " Continental System."

Consequently, a promising beetroot sugar industry, soon capable of supplying the wants of Europe, sprang up in 1813 all over Germany, France, and Austria. But in 1814, when Napoleon had to abdicate, the " Continental System " was abolished, and colonial sugar was admitted again into Continental harbours. On account of this, the price of sugar fell so rapidly that it was impossible for the new beet sugar industry to compete with cane sugar ; hence, nearly all the factories which had just been opened were closed again.

However, an industry which had experienced such a rapid rise, thanks to the patronage and support of Frederick Wilhelm of Prussia and the Emperor Napoleon, and which had developed through the industry and devotion of the entire population, was not destined to go to ruin just because of the great change produced by Napoleon's fall. On the contrary, it was realized that although the majority of the factories could not possibly have obtained good results, there were others where the manufacture of beetroot could be turned into profit, even where American sugar had free access. Acting up to Napoleon's commands, beetroots had been planted all over the country, machinery had been erected in great haste, and work had been begun without the slightest knowledge or experience being obtained, and attempts had even been made to manufacture sugar from roots which had gone bad. This, of course, led to the factories producing either no sugar, or such a bad type that the enterprise resulted in a financial failure, and from 1814 onwards people were generally disposed to distrust the beetroot sugar industry. However, Chaptal, the Director-General of Commerce and Industry in France, kept drawing the Prefect's attention to the beetroot sugar industry, while the chemist De Dombasle of Nancy, published a paper in which he gave definite instructions for the rational manufacture of beetroot sugar. In 1815 there were still about a hundred sugar factories in France, and the average yearly output of beetroot sugar amounted to 1,000 tons during the years 1816—1821. This industry derived great profit from the fact that the importation of sugar from abroad was heavily taxed, while the inland sugar was free from duty. In 1821, 49·5 francs duty was placed on every 100 kg. raw sugar from the French colonies, and 70 francs on white sugar—while sugar from other parts was taxed 90 francs, which amount increased to 125 francs in 1819. Later on the surtax was increased on foreign sugar, while an extra duty was paid on sugar imported in foreign ships. As in spite of these differential duties, the French still complained, the refining of French colonial sugar intended for export was made possible by a drawback of 120 francs per 100 kg. (restitution of duty) being given on refined sugar when exported. Since this, however, was also the case with exported home-grown sugar, on which no duty had been paid, the State paid an export premium of 120 francs per 100 kg. beet sugar. One can imagine that on account of this fiscal arrangement it was not long before new sugar factories sprang up and old ones were extended ; and that by 1836 about one-third of the sugar refined in France was beetroot sugar. But the payment of the premium was a great loss to the Exchequer, and that was why, in 1840, the French Government proposed to buy up all the existing beetroot sugar factories for the sum of

40,000,000 francs, and to tax the inland sugar at the same rate as the colonial sugar. This plan fell through, and, instead, beetroot sugar and cane sugar were equalized in 1843. This was most detrimental to the home industry, and von Lippmann tells us in his *Geschichte des Zuckers* that if it had not been for the cane sugar industry suffering severely on account of the abolition of slavery, the beetroot sugar industry might have been utterly ruined by this measure.

After 1836 the sugar industry in Germany made great progress ; the Germans succeeded in getting more sugar out of the beet, consequently the production became more and more profitable. The following table shows the steady progress of the production :—

| Year. | No. of Factories. | Production. | | Yield on 100 beetroot. |
		In quintals of 50 kg.	In tons.	
1836/37	122	28,162	1,383	5·51
1837/38	156	153,552	7,540	5·51
1840/41	145	284,102	13,951	5·88
1841/42	135	314,817	15,459	6·13
1844/45	98	259,360	12,736	6·67
1846/47	107	402,518	19,881	7·14
1848/49	145	717,154	35,217	7·27
1850/51	184	1,066,979	52,396	7·25

In Austria the beetroot sugar industry was again taken up in 1831 ; there were a great many factories in existence by 1840, while in 1854 the amount of sugar prepared in the country itself was equal to that imported from abroad ; hence, towards the latter half of the nineteenth century—that is about fifty years after the beetroot sugar industry had been introduced—it had been generally adopted in Europe, and was likely to become a formidable rival to the colonial cane sugar industry.

During the first decades following the revocation of the " Continental System," this competition was hardly noticeable. The sugar consumption in Europe increased so rapidly that the beet sugar produced in European countries did not supply the increased demand, and in spite of its home production, rather more than less cane sugar was being imported into Europe. But the cane sugar industry was not restricted to the same place during the first part of the nineteenth century, and America practically lost the monopoly of the sugar importation into Europe, which had been hers during the eighteenth century.

This was partly due to the abolition of slavery in most of the European colonies, and partly to the development of the cane sugar industry in other non-American countries, such as British India, Java, etc. Indeed, the first of these two causes had an exceptionally great influence on the cane sugar industry in the majority of cases, and brought some of them to the verge of utter ruin. The sugar industry was so dependent upon slavery that the abolition of the latter jeopardized its existence, and it was not till some twenty or thirty years later that it became accustomed to the new state of affairs. Unfortunately, this transition period coincided with an artificial and continuous extension of the new beet sugar industry, which, supported by bounties and privileges, tried to supplant cane sugar everywhere ; consequently, the second half of the nineteenth century, especially the last fifteen years, was most unprofitable for the cane sugar producers.

The long-planned abolition of slavery became in the period 1825—1850 a settled fact in most of the colonies under European government, while the other colonies and republics set their negroes at liberty, either at that time or else a little later on.

In 1776 the first motion for the abolition of slaves was submitted to the British Parliament, and in 1787 a society for the suppression of slavery was founded in England, of which Wilberforce and Clarkson were the ruling spirits. The agitation against slavery was ever after persevered in, the result being that in 1807 a bill introduced by Lord Grenville was passed, prohibiting all further slave-trading in British territory. Those, however, who were slaves at that time remained so. On August 1, 1834, the entire system of slavery in the British colonies and possessions was abolished ; the owners of the liberated slaves received an indemnification of £20,000,000, while, as a measure of transition, it was resolved that the quondam slaves should become apprentices of their former owners up till 1838—and up till 1840 in the case of agriculturists ; and that the slaves should not be free to go where they chose till after that time. The sum of £20,000,000 was divided among the West Indian colonies, the Cape, and Mauritius—the first-mentioned receiving £16,500,000 sterling, while Mauritius and the Cape came in for the remainder.

Although the indemnification was much appreciated, it could not buy back the labourers so necessary for the sugar industry. The liberated slaves, in many cases, refused to work, and in many of the islands they left the plantations in great numbers, in consequence of which the necessary work could not be done, and the production of the British colonies in the West Indies dropped considerably, their sugar exportation decreasing from 17,000 tons to 8,000, On the other hand, the production of the other West Indian islands where slavery was still in full force increased, and in order to grant the British colonies some compensation a special import duty was placed on sugar produced in countries where slaves were still kept. But in 1846 this difference in prices was much reduced, to be entirely done away with in 1848, from which time onwards sugar was admitted to England on the same terms, whether imported from colonies where slaves were still at work, or from those where the work was done by other labourers.

Slavery was abolished in the French colonies in 1848, at the time of the Second Republic; in the Dutch West Indian colonies in 1863; in Porto Rico in 1873; in St. Thomas in 1876; while in Cuba not until 1880. The different states of the American continent likewise eventually abolished slavery, this leading to a turning point in the sugar production of these countries. Since slavery had never been of much consequence, either in Asia or Australia, the sugar production there gradually developed and filled the gap caused by a decrease in American production.

Though there was a decrease in the number of labourers, the cane sugar industry did not all at once dwindle. Fields once planted with the cane sugar, as a rule yield year after year crops which only gradually diminish in quantity.

At the time of the abolition the fields had been planted and cared for, while the roads and dykes were in a sound condition, so that during the following years nothing needed to be done but harvesting the crop. Later on, however, some necessary steps were omitted, old exhausted plots which were ready for ploughing-up, and which ought to have been planted anew, were kept in constant cultivation for want of labourers, and consequently yielded poor harvests. The roads, reservoirs and dykes gradually got into a bad state, through not being kept in repair, while both cultivation and manufacture were little improved.

Attempts were certainly made to supply the want of labour by the importation of indentured coolies from other parts, for which Chinese, free negroes and British Indians were chosen; but in most cases the supply was too expensive and of too little avail to fill up so great a deficit of labour. Even in colonies such as Demerara and Trinidad, where the immigration of British Indians has given comparatively the best results, the amount of available labour is not sufficient to do the same amount of excavation and dyke building which, in the times of slavery, had been done with much more primitive implements than those that are now at our disposal.

The same fact was noticeable all over America and in the African islands. Both the British West Indian islands, as well as Surinam, Demerara, Cuba, Brazil, Louisiana, Peru, Mauritius, Réunion, etc., suffered from lack of labour and before one had got used to this new state of affairs, and had learned how to do the work with a limited labour supply, the cane sugar industry in the emancipated countries had an anxious time of it. In some countries they imported labour; in others they either divided up the plantations into smaller plots, which lower class planters had to work, or sold the plantations piecemeal; in short, all sorts of means were tried, but during this time of difficulty the cane sugar industry could not properly develop, and was left far behind by its reviving competitor, the beet sugar industry, as is shown by the following table of the world's sugar production from 1852 to 1903*:—

Year.	Beetroot Sugar.	Cane Sugar.	Total.	Per cent. Cane Sugar.
	Tons.	Tons.	Tons.	
1852/53	202,810	1,260,404	1,463,214	86·0
1859/60	451,584	1,340,980	1,792,564	74·3
1864/65	529,793	1,446,934	1,996,727	73·5
1869/70	846,422	1,740,793	2,586,915	67·3
1874/75	1,302,999	1,903,222	3,206,221	59·4
1880/81	1,820,734	2,027,052	3,847,786	52·7
1883/84	2,485,300	2,210,000	4,695,300	47·0
1884/85	2,679,400	2,225,000	4,904,400	45·4
1885/86	2,172,200	2,300,000	4,472,200	51·4
1886/87	2,686,700	2,400,000	5,086,700	47·1
1887/88	2,367,200	2,541,000	4,908,200	51·7
1888/89	3,555,900	2,359,000	5,914,900	40·0
1889/90	3,536,700	2,138,000	5,674,700	37·7
1890/91	3,679,800	2,597,000	6,276,800	41·2
1891/92	3,480,800	3,501,900	6,982,700	51·6
1892/93	3,380,700	3,040,500	6,421,200	47·3
1893/94	3,833,000	3,561,000	7,394,000	48·2
1894/95	4,725,800	3,531,400	8,257,200	42·7
1895/96	4,220,500	2,839,500	7,160,000	39·6
1896/97	4,801,500	2,841,900	7,643,400	37 2
1897/98	4,695,300	2,868,900	7,564,200	38·0
1898/99	4,689,600	2,995,400	7,785,000	38·5
1899/00	5,410,900	2,880,900	8,291,800	34·7
1900/01	5,943,700	3,646,000	9,589,700	38·0
1901/02	6,800,500	4,079,000	10,880,500	37·5
1902/03	5,208,700	4,163,900	9,372,600	44.4

But that the cane sugar industry was eclipsed by the more recent beet sugar industry was not altogether due to the abolition of slaves, nor to want of interest or enterprise among the owners; other causes contributed to it, which are of so much account in the history of the cane sugar industry during the latter half of the nineteenth century and the first years of the twentieth, that we shall deal with them more fully here.

When about 1830 the sugar industry in Germany began to revive after its decline at Napoleon's fall, foreign sugar was much more heavily taxed

* Very varying figures as regards the total cane sugar harvest are repeatedly met with, and these can only be explained by the fact that sometimes the total production of a country is given and sometimes only its export. This is clearly shown by the fact that British India, which produces over 2,000,000 tons of sugar does not appear on the older statistical lists, while every beet sugar producing country is mentioned for its full production without deducting what is used for its own consumption.

than inland produce, so that gradually inland sugar was exclusively used, and the revenue from sugar duties became less and less. Since this loss was made up for by an increase in the duty on home-grown sugar, colonial sugar was no longer at such a great disadvantage. But the latter became scarce, and the quantity of sugar produced at home so much exceeded the amount required for the German consumption that it became even possible to export sugar. The basis for the levying of the duty on beet sugar was a combination of the weight of the roots, and their assumed rendiment of sugar, which latter might have been exact at the outset, but which, through an improved system of working in the factories, and especially through better raw material, gradually produced a much lower figure than was really the case. So the amount of sugar produced at the factories much exceeded the estimated quantity, and as the excess of weight was exempt from duty, although it fetched the full price *plus* excise when sold, the manufacturers enjoyed a considerable premium. When exported to other countries the duty was returned, but it was calculated according to the actual quantity exported, so that if a factory exported all its sugar, a much greater amount of excise was returned than was originally paid, in which case the premium would obviously have been paid by the Exchequer. As long as the export from Germany remained insignificant, this premium was of little consequence; but the situation altered when, after 1875–6, the export rapidly increased, as may be judged from the following table:—

Year.	Metric tons.	Exportation per cent. on Production.
1875/76	56,121	—
1876/77	60,354	21·75
1877/78	96,778	25·60
1878/79	138,077	32·40
1879/80	134,486	32·85
1880/81	283,904	52·54
1881/82	314,410	52·43
1882/83	472,551	56·58
1883/84	595,814	63·38
1884/85	673,727	59·99

Through this exportation, and the restitution of excise only partly paid, the exporting manufacturers became the richer, whereas the country got less and less of the excise money. The import duties on sugar, which used to amount to 12½ million marks in 1871–72—and later on to 7 million—now only brought in 1½ million marks. The home consumption increased from more than 200,000 to about 400,000 metric tons.   The duty on raw material in 1871–72 realized 36 million marks, in 1872–73 almost 51 millions, in 1873–74 more than 56 millions, in 1884–85 as much as 166·4 millions.   The restitution of excise, on the other hand, increased still more, that is from 3½ millions during the first years after 1870 to 96·3 and 128·5 millions respectively during the periods 1882–83 and 1884–85.   The remainder of import duty and excise which finally fell to the Exchequer, after the drawbacks had been paid on exportation amounted to the following figures :—

1881/82	.. ..	..	58,456,658 marks.
1882/83	.. .	..	67,286,890 ,,
1883/84	.. ..	..	47,788,316 ,,
1884/85	.. ..	..	39,368,907 ,,
1885/86	.. ..	.	24,500,000 ,.
1886/87	.. ..	..	33,600,000 ,.
1887/88	.. ..	..	14,670,000 ,,

It goes without saying that such a state of affairs could not last, and that the Treasury could not possibly go on disbursing the amount of duty on home consumed sugar almost entirely on drawbacks on exported goods, so measures were taken to increase the excise, and to diminish the bonus on export which led to a more favourable difference for the Exchequer, but left the evil itself untouched.

In Austria-Hungary duty was levied according to the size of the diffusers and the number of times they could be filled (not according to the number of times they actually were filled).   In order to gain as much sugar as possible above the " quota," the manufacturers tried their best to work with extremely small diffusers at an enormous rate, so that, though there may have been a little more sugar left in the slices, the profit on the untaxed sugar would be more than sufficient to cover twice or several times this loss.   When sugar was exported the full amount of excise was returned, and that is why they exported as much sugar as they possibly could, so that in 1875–76 there was an excess of 135,556 florins paid as restitution of excise over and above the total amount received by the State.   So the exporters received more in the way of a disguised export-bounty than the entire inland excise had amounted to.

This, of course, was only the case with exports, hence everything was done to increase the amount.   The surest way to attain that end was to lower the price at which sugar was sold to foreign countries ; consequently, the exporters did not pocket the premium in full, but gave part of it to foreign buyers to secure their custom, that it might end in their retaining the bounty. It was a good thing that just at this time of forced production and exportation the daily consumption of sugar increased considerably, both in England and the United States, so that during the first years the surplus was entirely disposed of ; this state of affairs, however, did not last long, and was upset by the tremendous crisis of 1884–86, when the price fell to about half the former amount.

France, during the second half of the nineteenth century, could boast of a considerable sugar export trade, and although she had to have recourse to foreign and colonial importation, which sugar was used as raw material in the Paris refineries for the famous French loaves, a considerable surplus for export was left, till, in the first years following 1880, this surplus was super-seded by a deficit, the import exceeding the export trade, and soon surpassing the former surplus. Owing to the slight difference between excise and import duty (the surtax), it became even possible to import, with profit, German sugar into France.

In 1883–84 no less than 125,000 metric tons of sugar were imported from abroad ; and their own produce and that from their colonies amounted to 474,000 and 76,000 tons respectively, while the sugar for their own consumption amounted to only slightly over 400,000 tons ; but of the 125,000 tons of imported sugar, 47,000 came from Germany and 15,000 from Austria, and it was especially this invasion of German sugar, together with the sudden fall in price, that stirred up the hostile feeling of the French, who had not got over their defeat of 1870–71. All at once the surtax was increased to put an end to a further influx of foreign sugar, but as this did not appease the French, nor give them back their former export trade, disguised export bounties were resorted to.

As a basis of taxation a certain *rendement* of sugar out of the beetroot was fixed, on which duty had to be paid ; the excess of product used to be exempted from taxation, but eventually became lightly taxed, when the Exchequer was too pressed to dispense with it.

The fixed quantity of sugar to be obtained from beetroot, which formed the basis, was repeatedly raised as circumstances required it, and the excess was at one time exempted from duty and then again lightly taxed, which regulation for a long time formed the standard according to which the French sugar was taxed. It goes without saying that owing to an improved system of manufacture in the factories and a better condition of raw material, the excess product was very often a considerable one, so that a handsome premium was allotted to the manufacturers, which gradually increased as more work was done and a better product turned out. This, of course, resulted in an unprecedented extension of the sugar industry, and also in the long-desired return of a sugar exportation trade. Urged on by these examples, each European beet sugar producing country drew up its legislation in such a manner that open and disguised bounties on sugar exported were allotted, and it was in their own interests that producers tried their very best to send as much sugar as possible to foreign markets, in order to secure the export premium. Consequently, the sugar production was unnaturally stimulated, so that the price of sugar fell at the end of 1883, much to the detriment of all countries concerned.

General History of the Cane Sugar Industry.

This lowering of prices, on the whole, affected the cane sugar industry much more than that of beet sugar, because the latter was more in touch with the interests of the European market, and the parties concerned in all European countries knew how to obtain the support of their governments, whereas those interested in the colonial industry hardly had a say in the matter.

The respective European governments were rather anxious to get rid of these once approved bounties, and when, in 1886, Lord Salisbury convened a meeting in London, in order to agree to a general abrogation of the bounties, which would have been most beneficial to the colonial sugar industry, the realization of this prospect seemed a not unlikely contingency.

While the smaller countries, as well as Austria and Germany, agreed to the gradual abolition of bounties, France, on the contrary, having just adopted as basis for its taxation scheme the Meline system—which was based on the exemption of excedents—was opposed to this plan. For the rest, the British consumers were greatly pleased with the existing state of affairs, and did not think it wise to interfere for the sake of their colonies. Great Biitain, which was not a sugar-producing country though a great consumer of sugar, was doubtless the very best market for sugar exported by the principal producing countries; and, being compelled to dispose of their produce abroad, the exporters offered their goods to the British market even below cost price, just for the sake of the bounties held out to them. Owing to the rivalry among the continental producers, the British consumers, especially the preserve manufacturers who were in the habit of using enormous quantities of sugar, got as much sugar as they wanted at a price at which it was impossible for them to produce it themselves. One can imagine that they wished this advantageous, though abnormal, condition to continue, and that they did not approve of measures put forward by their own Government to put an end to the system for the sake of the West Indian colonists. Both through their own opposition and through that of France, the London Conference resulted in nothing, and things remained as they were, in spite of an unnatural production and many defects.

To put an end to the fact that the return of the excise swallowed up a substantial part, if not the whole, of the revenue and left little or nothing for the Exchequer, a duty was levied on sugar consumed in Germany from which the sugar for export was exempted, so that there was no need to give restitution; at the same time finished product instead of raw material was being taxed.

This kind of excise was something one could rely upon, and amounted to 40 or 50 million marks for the whole empire, a small sum considering the enormous consumption. The amount of excise levied, however, on raw material was absorbed by the excise restitution on exports, which, because of the new system rather increased, the country itself thus deriving little benefit from the several kinds of taxation.

In 1890 the German Government made up its mind to strip the sugar industry of all its privileges, in order to swell the Exchequer with the full amount of taxation. A new law was adopted, and it was resolved that from 1895 all bounties should be stopped, but a fixed export bounty in money should be allotted by way of transition, as had been done in Austria, when some time ago they had adopted the finished product instead of the raw material as basis for taxation. In 1891 a law was brought into force according to which a direct export bounty was granted, amounting to 1·25 marks per 100 kg. of raw and refined sugar up to 98° polarization, and to 2 marks per 100 kg. of sugar of at least 99½°. In 1895 these bounties were to be reduced, to be entirely done away with in 1897, so that by that time all export bounties on sugar were to be a thing of the past.

Unfortunately, at this very time agriculture went through a crisis, in consequence of large supplies of American cereals being exported at such a low price that European competition was killed for the time being. It became necessary to find a substitute for corn, and as beetroot was the very thing to take its place, the lowering of corn prices necessarily led to a further extension of the beet sugar cultivation. This in its turn was followed by an unprecedented fall in sugar prices, compared with which that of 1884 was a mere trifle.

In these circumstances the German Government could not possibly pass any measure to lower, much less to abolish, the bounties, all the more as none of the other countries seemed inclined to follow their example ; this latter attitude may be looked upon as a sure sign that a decrease in German exportation would mean an extension of the export trade of other countries, without leading to any improvement generally. At the request of the farmers, the proposed restriction in output of 1895 was deferred, and through the so-called " Antrag Paasche " it was doubled, so that the export bounty was raised to 2·50 marks per 100 kg. for raw sugar and 3·55 marks per 100 kg. for refined sugar. This heavy bounty, called a " Kampfpramie," was meant to favour the export sugar still more, and consequently to compete with that of other countries in the hopes of leaving Germany finally in full possession of the trade. It was also meant to send up the cost so considerably that it would become impossible for any country to go one better, and in this way they would be obliged by co-operation to abolish bounties altogether. The result was quite different from what was expected, for instead of forcing them to give in, the raising of the German bounties induced their rivals to follow their example, and raise their own bounties by a similar amount; so that eight months after the German law was enacted nothing had been gained, only a greater amount of money was withheld from the Exchequer of the producing countries, to be bestowed on foreign consumers, or even on the Exchequers of foreign countries.

In 1897 the United States raised, besides a fixed duty, an extra tax on sugar ; this extra taxation was aimed at the bounty system, and corresponded with the bounties in amount, all the money derived from bounties allotted by the governments of the several European countries thus going to swell the Treasury of the United States, an example which British India imitated some two years later.

The Austrian and German producers, apart from the profit made by the export bounties, which was greatly reduced by the low price sugar fetched in the world's markets, enjoyed an extra profit by the introduction of the so-called " Cartel " (or " Kartell "), in imitation of the Russian *Normirovka*.

The Russian Government fixes the quantity of sugar required every year for inland consumption, which quantity may be sold by the manufacturers as their contingent. Next, the amount of sugar to be kept in reserve, and to be sold when the price exceeds the amount stipulated by the Government Committee (that is 4·30 roubles per pood in winter, or 4·45 roubles in summer) is fixed. If the production exceeds the quantities destined for home consumption and reserve, sugar may be exported, in which case the exporter gets the duty at the rate of 1·75 roubles per pood returned, or is allowed to sell the remainder in his own country ; but the duty in this case is doubled, and consequently amounts to 3·50 roubles per pood. If it comes to this, exportation becomes much more profitable, and as the fixed price is rather high for the interior, one can easily afford to lose on the export and sell sugar more cheaply, without running the risk of loss. There is another inducement for the manufacturers to produce much sugar, namely, the stipulation that the contingent in the profitable inland sugar market shall increase as the total produce of the factory becomes more, for which reason also a large production yields a greater profit. All these are reasons for providing the foreign markets with cheaper sugar, at the expense of the home consumer, though the manufacturer profits by it. Perhaps this was simply done for the purpose of keeping the sugar prices at home at one level, and of enabling the producers to supply the home market without being dependent on international supplies, and not for the purpose of extending the sugar exportation. It, however, had that result ; and an import duty of 3 roubles gold per pood (which put an end to the importation of foreign sugar, and made abnormally high prices at home possible) greatly contributed to this.

All this system was brought about in Russia by government interference, whereas in Germany and Austria the co-operation of manufacturers achieved the same results. As early as 1890 the Austrian refiners had formed a Confederation or Cartel, in order to exploit the high surtaxes, by bringing for the time being the production of refined sugar in line with the consumption. Later on the contingent of sugar to be taken to the home market was fixed for every refinery belonging to the Cartel. But owing to the lowering of prices, and the promotion of other competing refineries, the temptation to sell more than was stipulated proved to be too much for them, so that in 1894 the first Cartel was dissolved.

In 1898 a new association consisting of manufacturers and refiners was founded, their principal stipulation being that the raw sugar manufacturers were only to sell their product to refiners who belonged to the Cartel ; that as regards their contingent in the home sugar trade they were not allowed to sell white sugar, while as regards the sale of the remainder to markets abroad, they could please themselves. The supply of refined sugar for the home market was contingented amongst the refiners, in return for which privilege they had to allow a fixed price of 30 kronen per 100 kg of raw sugar, the market price of which was paid by the buyer and the difference by the Cartel, which obtained the funds by simply raising the price of white sugar at home. Should the Cartel be the only seller, and the importation of foreign sugar become impossible on account of the high surtax (the difference between taxes levied on imported and inland sugar), the consumers would have to approve of these prices, and pay them as long as the difference between the world's price and the price fixed by the Cartel was lower than the surtax.

This profit was turned into a fund, through which the parties concerned who had not yet acceded were brought into line, either by a temporary lowering of prices when a factory was about to produce white sugar, or by buying up shares in the recalcitrant enterprises. The remainder was used for paying the difference between the market price (with 22 kronen as minimum) and 30 kronen, while what was then left fell to the refiners as Cartel profit.

The share in the profit for the raw sugar manufacturers amounted to :—

16,200,000 kronen in 1897/98		
15,100,000	,,	,, 1898/99
15,700,000	,,	,, 1899/1900
20,600,000	,,	,, 1900/01

The Cartel profit for raw sugar manufacturers and refiners, is calculated per 100 kg. refined sugar, which is taken to equal 110 kg. raw sugar, as follows :—

Price of refined sugar for the interior per 100 kg.	..	kr. 85·00
Raw sugar 110 kg. at kronen 22	kr. 24·2	
Refining cost and profit	,, 7·56	
Excise	,, 38·00	
		,, 69·76

Nett profit of Cartel	kr. 15·24

With a market price of 22 kronen so much is added that the fixed price of kronen 30 is arrived at ; consequently 110 kg.
at kronen 8 .. .. ,, 8·80

Leaving a nett Cartel profit for the refiners of.. . .. kr. 6·44

Whenever the raw sugar manufacturers receive 8·80 kronen, the refiner's share in the entire Cartel profit amounts to 6·44 kronen, from which, of course, the expenses, sometimes rather high, are not deducted.

General History of the Cane Sugar Industry.

Chiefly in imitation of Austria, Germany also founded a Cartel, which fixed 12·75 marks as minimum fixed price per 50 kg. : that is, exactly the same as in Austria. The Cartel again pays to the raw sugar manufacturers the difference between the market price and the fixed price, together with the 10 per cent. extra for the reduction of raw sugar to its equivalent of refined sugar, like as in Austria 110 parts of raw sugar = 100 parts of refined.

If, for instance, the price of raw sugar in Magdeburg is 10·60 marks per 50 kg., the Cartel pays to the combined raw sugar factories for each 50 kg. sugar leaving the refineries: 12·75 − 10·60=2·15+10 per cent = 2·36 ; this has to be divided among the raw sugar factories according to their contingent. Suppose that price should continue for a year, and the consumption amount to 13,500,000 quintals of 50 kg., then the sum to be divided among the combined raw sugar manufacturers would be 31,927,500 marks ; and should the entire production have come up to 37,000,000 quintals, the German raw sugar manufacturers would receive—as Cartel profit—a premium of 85 pf. per quintal of 50 kg. on their whole production as long as they did not exceed their contingents.

The disguised as well as the open bounties absorbed each year such an amount of money that every country suffered from them, and desired most fervently to see them abolished. It is impossible to quote the exact amount, as in some cases a specially low railway tariff or a conveyance by subsidized steamers was considered as a bounty. This made the United States alter the amount of the countervailing duties continually, so as to correspond with that of the bounty. At first, for instance, the contingenting of Russia sugar was not looked upon as a disguised premium in the United States, and, consequently, no countervailing duty was levied on it, while the same sugar when imported into British India, where such taxes were also levied, was taxed extra at Rs. 3.11.0 per cwt., afterwards reduced to Rs. 2.7.4. per cwt. for refined sugar. Later on, America started to tax Russian sugar heavily ; and the following table shows how much was to be paid as additional duty on European sugar when imported into the United States, according to the decree of 12th December, 1898 :—

Austria-Hungary	0·252	cents. per lb.
Denmark ..	0·136	,, ,, ,, refined
France	0·978	,, ,, ,,
Germany .	0·270	,, ,, ,,
The Netherlands	0·322	,, ,, ,,
Russia	0·627	,, ,, ,,

Raw sugar was meant when not otherwise specified. Although not all the data were given which made alterations repeatedly necessary, this table shows the amount at which bounties were fixed, and the heavy tax they levied on the producing countries.

General History of the Cane Sugar Industry.

To receive a much-coveted article below cost price was very welcome to the countries to which the sugar was destined, and it must seem strange that the governments of these very countries should insist on putting an end to that state of affairs, while, on the other hand, countries which spent most on the bounties opposed the proposed change with all their might.

Let us, therefore, first see what happened in the countries to which sugar was exported.

In the United States there had long been an endeavour to produce as much sugar as would supply their own wants, and that is why nothing was left undone to improve the beet sugar cultivation, and to obtain sugar from sorghum and maple, as well as cane. The maple sugar industry did not progress much, while people were greatly disappointed in sorghum cultivation. In the south the cane sugar industry slightly increased, although its production of about 250,000 tons in 1900 did not greatly exceed that of 1890—which amount could not possibly supply their enormous wants. In 1875 a reciprocity treaty with Hawaii was signed, in which exemption of import duty was mutually granted, so that Hawaiian sugar could enter America free of taxation. The duty on imported raw sugar was not high at that time, but was ultimately abolished by the McKinley tariff, after having been repeatedly lowered. In order to satisfy the manufacturers at home, a premium of 2 cents. per lb. was promised on sugar manufactured in America; but Hawaii, not belonging to the United States, was out of it. This premium, however, soon appeared to be too much for the Treasury, so that as early as 1894 the Wilson tariff fixed the import duty at 40 per cent. of the value, with an extra duty of 0.1 per cent. per lb. for bounty-fed sugar. The reinstitution of this duty had a twofold result: first, it got rid of the payment of bounties; secondly, it secured a better revenue to the Treasury. As the prices fell considerably just at that time, the revenue was not great, while a general lowering of the prices of corn and cotton was to be feared; this all led to a strong wish for the extension of their sugar cultivation.

The result was a general tendency in favour of the raising of the import duty, which was expressed by the Dingley tariff of 1897, with its import duty of 0·95 to 1·825 cents per lb. of raw sugar, and 1·05 cents per lb. of refined.

In spite of all these duties, the Hawaiian sugar came in freely: first, because of its reciprocal treaty; and later on, after 1898, through the annexation of the Hawaiian Islands, in virtue of which all the privileges of the sugar grown in the States were enjoyed. This was not the case with sugar from Cuba, Porto Rico, and the Philippines, which counties had also come under the rule of America, but were not treated in quite the same way as their own producers as regards sugar importation. It was nothing new to see the Hawaiian Islands so highly favoured; this really dated from a time when the United States produced little sugar herself, and thought an increased sugar importation from these islands rather expedient for her own wants. After a struggle it was decided to levy 15 per cent. of the value of the Dingley tariff on Porto Rican sugar, but in 1901 the importation from that island entered altogether free of duty.

On Cuban sugar a reduction of 20 per cent. of the import duty was allowed, and on Philippine sugar a reduction of 25 per cent., so that the several parties in America were satisfied.

The Dingley tariff was responsible for another new measure exclusively directed against the European continent, which was to the effect that over and above the fixed duty an additional duty would be raised on all bounty-fed sugar, to an amount corresponding with that of the bounty; hence, the bounty allotted by any European government on the exportation of white sugar to America was gladly accepted by the Customs of the United States, without its having been of any use to the country which had issued the bounty.

That the bounties were not abolished till five years later shows the mutual feelings of jealousy which existed between the European States.

The cane sugar industry likewise suffered during the struggle between the beet sugar producing countries just mentioned. That it was not altogether ruined is due to the fact that the producers could not think of any article that was a little more profitable, so that they were obliged to stick to this kind of sugar, however hard they were put to it to make ends meet.

The British West Indian Islands were the worst off of all, and their inhabitants continually asked the mother-country for help and support.

When Joseph Chamberlain, in 1895, became Colonial Secretary, one of his first acts was to appoint a Royal Commission on the West Indies, which, in January, 1897, began its inquiries and published the results in a full report the same year.

The facts elucidated were much more serious than had been expected. Through their isolation the islands were marked out for sugar production only, and as the price of sugar went down at such a rate that it could only be produced at a loss, their condition became deplorable and ruin imminent. The Commission proposed, firstly, to establish agriculture on a small scale by letting out small plots of land to negroes and coolies, and so encourage them to grow other crops than cane; secondly, to improve the means of conveyance between the islands, and so lead to a better export trade in fruit to New York and London; and, finally, to borrow the necessary funds for the foundation of central factories. The cost was estimated at a lump sum of £90,000, besides a yearly sum of £27,000 for ten years, and of £20,000 during the next five years.

This report of the Commission gave rise to much controversy, and it was clearly not only sympathy with the population of a part of the empire that counted in the matter. The West Indian Islands are close to North America, and are, no doubt, favourably situated as regards trade facilities with the States. As they are British colonies, their produce is so heavily taxed on entering the States that competition is out of the question. No

31

wonder, then, that the West Indian planters have often wished to be American citizens, that their distress might come to an end. The United States, if it were so inclined, could easily persuade the British colonies to join the Union, and that is partly what the British Government wished to prevent.

Consequently, Chamberlain declared himself willing to make any sacrifice, and even to exceed the amount proposed by the Commission. In 1898 subsidies were granted, which soon proved inadequate to bring about permanent changes for the better, as the capitalists, warned by the bad reports as to a steady decline in the islands, shrank from further risking their money, and the local governments economized on what they could—all of which made matters worse.

British India, too, had come to its turning point. The sugar cultivation in that country must be considered as a branch of native industry, and each village produces a sufficient quantity of sugar to supply its own wants, which sugar the Hindus and Mahommedans preferred to the cheaper imported brands, because they thought the latter were prepared with the aid of animal blood, or charcoal from oxen or pigs' bones, a product they were not allowed to use.

Refined sugar was comparatively little used in the huge Indian Empire; the few refineries which refined the jaggery or sugar imported from the neighbouring countries, including the supplies of white sugar from Mauritius, were all they wished for. White sugar from Europe, however, was offered at such low prices and of such good quality that the native confectioners and manufacturers of sweets and sorbets dropped their religious scruples, and, without mentioning it to their customers, began to use more and more refined sugar, often mixed with the ordinary home-made sugar for fear of being found out. This, of course, led to a considerable importation of cheap refined sugar, while most of the inland and Mauritius sugar did not find buyers, much to the detriment of Indian refiners. Although the discontent of the big refiners could not bring the Government to take measures on their behalf, the distress of the inland producers finally induced the Government to act. These sold their produce, on which money had been advanced, to the many sugar bakeries, but as the latter had still sugar left over from the preceding harvest, they preferred to use it up first, instead of advancing money again. The second-rate agriculturist in India (who had gone through many a time of famine and epidemic, and only a short time ago had survived the invention of artificial indigo, and the discovery of huge sources of petroleum which had deprived him of a considerable means of income derived from his indigo and oil-seed plantations) could not possibly afford a further retrenchment, and it was almost certain that the payment of taxes would soon become an impossibility, and thus affect the revenue of the State.

Besides this, the Mauritius planters complained of the invasion of European refined sugar into India. This unfortunate island had suffered much from great drought, hurricanes, pestilence and cattle-plague, and had hardly known how to bear up under it. As Australia no longer bought their produce, their sugar went chiefly to India, but this source of demand also was threatened with extinction, in which case South Africa could be their only market.

Both in India and in Mauritius there was a great desire for levying countervailing duties in the first-mentioned country, as was done in America. This wish was soon complied with, thanks to Chamberlain's influence, so that at the beginning of 1899 the resolution for enforcing these taxes was passed, and immediately became law.

Yet the law did not answer the purpose, for much European refined sugar was still imported, especially from Austria and Germany, as the producers from these countries still made enough profit by their Cartels to bear the increased taxation.

However, in 1903, a new special duty was levied on the two kinds of sugar, a duty covering the actual Cartel profit, and quoted at Rs. 3.3.9 per cwt. Austrian sugar, and at Rs. 2.13.9 per cwt. German sugar. This fresh taxation, of course, prevented all further importation of these kinds of sugar.

The increase of the German bounties in 1897 had not resulted exactly as anticipated, viz., in making matters so much worse that the condition might become unbearable to others. On the contrary, it had led to an ever-increasing amount of sugar being exported and a regular swelling of foreign Exchequers, without restricting them in any way as regards their exchange of other goods.

Much against their wish, however, the representatives had been obliged to agree to a further increase in the bounties ; but every now and then they expressed the wish to abolish the bounties by general agreement ; the respective governments had already the right to reduce them as soon as occasion offered itself.

When they were busy increasing the bounties, the Austrian and German Governments by mutual agreement sounded France as to the possibility of an entire and simultaneous abolition of all the bounties. It was France's wish only to do away with the direct bounties, leaving the indirect ones, which lay in the untaxed excedent, untouched.

That the United States looked upon the indirect bounties as genuine ones, and not as affairs of internal administration, is proved by the fact that in Washington the German bounty was considered to be 2·40 marks, the Austrian 2·47 kronen, and the French 10·82 francs. Should England, as had been repeatedly suggested, adopt the levying of countervailing duties, France would suffer from it, so that she was wise to give in, in case the competing nations should make a start at taking their international agreements seriously.

General History of the Cane Sugar Industry.

This proved to be so, when in 1898, at the invitation of the Belgian Government, a conference was held in Brussels, where Germany, Austria, Belgium, Great Britain, the Netherlands, France, Russia, Spain, and Sweden were represented. France, however, had demanded that the inland excise affairs should not be discussed, while the other countries set up as a taxation basis the quantity of sugar actually produced, so that a disguised bounty like that of the French could not possibly exist any longer. As regards this difference in opinion, neither party could gain its own, and on June 1, 1898, the Conference was adjourned, it being left with Belgium to summon the members again as soon as the preliminary negotiations, which would take place under Belgium's mediation, had gone so far that unanimity would be possible.

As we mentioned before, in 1899 British India, strongly influenced by the British Government, had levied countervailing duties, which were taken all round as a hint of what the mother-country could do too, when conferences were of no avail. It was not unexpected, as the government measures in the West Indies had led to nothing, and also as the British Government, which in its war in South Africa wanted the support of the colonies badly, would do anything to please them. After much negotiation, another conference was held in December, 1901, in Brussels, but things had changed in the meantime.

The German and the Austrian sugar Cartels had been much discussed, and it had been proved that the high surtax enabled the Germans and Austrians to get such high prices in their own market, even when the direct bounties were abolished, that their overproduction became excessive, and their large exports forced down prices in outside markets. Belgium and Great Britain therefore insisted on a considerable decrease in the surtax to the extent that, though foreign sugar might be kept out of the country, it would not leave enough margin to make the formation of Cartels profitable. Austria and Germany did not approve of this, and it looked as if the conference would again prove abortive, when the British Government declared that should this conference result in nothing, they would lay before Parliament a proposal either to prohibit bounty-fed sugar altogether, or to take other measures, and they pointed out how in British India a measure had already been considered to the effect that an extra duty on German and Austrian sugar would be levied, to an amount equal to that of the Cartel profit.

This declaration put an end to all opposition, and on 5th March, 1902, the Convention was signed by the representatives of Germany, Austria, Belgium, Spain, France, Great Britain, Italy, The Netherlands, Sweden, and Norway. The Convention, which may be found *in extenso* in Appendix I, was to the following effect :—

The countries agreeing to the Convention pledged their word to abolish all direct or indirect bounties on the production or exportation of sugar from the date of issue, and not to grant new ones during the term of the Convention.

34

General History of the Cane Sugar Industry.

The sugar factories, refineries, and factories where molasses are separated out, will be considered bonded warehouses, and be superintended by Custom-house officers.

The maximum surtax or difference between import duty and excise is to amount to 6 francs per 100 kg. of refined sugar, and 5 50 francs per 100 kg. of raw sugar. All sugar coming from countries where bounties are granted on the production or exportation of sugar is to be specially taxed, the extra duty to be not less than what the bounty amounts to. At the same time, any country will have the right to prohibit the importation of such kind of sugar. The countries joining the Convention pledged themselves to allow each other's own colonial sugar to enter at the lowest import duty when premiums are not granted. Spain, Italy, and Sweden might do as they liked as regards their sugar legislature, as long as they do not export any sugar, but agree to modify their laws within a year according to the spirit of the Convention, as soon as the Permanent Committee can prove that they export sugar. The Convention was enforced on the 1st of September, 1903, and was to remain in force for five years. Unless notice was given by one of the participants within twelve months before the date of expiration, the Convention was implicitly understood to be prolonged for another year.

Moreover, a Permanent Commission was appointed, whose duty it was to see that none of the contracting countries granted bounties ; and, if granted in other countries, to ascertain to what extent they were given in order to fix the sum to be levied as an extra import duty by the Convention countries. These sums are now and then made known, and the most recent list of them is to be found in Appendix II.

Thus, after a lengthy struggle, the die was cast, and the bounty system abolished ; and, strange to say, through the help of the country that during the last years preceding the Convention had enjoyed exceptional profits, simply owing to the fact that the sugar was sold in their market below cost price. One can easily imagine that the wholesale sugar consumers in England— such as jam, biscuit and chocolate manufacturers—were not pleased with this change in affairs, and that at the following election the sugar policy of the government was used as a weapon against them. In 1906 the Conservatives were turned out of power, and as the Liberal Government enjoyed the support of the opponents of the Convention, it was thought necessary to comply with their wishes. On 6th June, 1907, the Foreign Secretary informed the Permanent Committee that he considered the restriction of the sugar importation incompatible with his policy and with the interests of the English consumers and manufacturers, so that he could not continue taxing those kinds of sugar heavily which were declared to be bounty-fed. As long as the other contracting countries would not interfere with Great Britain's policy of not increasing the duties on these bountied sugars, His Majesty's government would be pleased

35

to continue as a participant in the thus modified Convention ; but should they in this case consider England as no longer belonging to the Convention, she would be only too pleased to withdraw.

Although the Convention had ceased to answer its original purpose, the contracting countries, which were joined by Peru, Switzerland, and Luxemburg, were so satisfied with its results that they did not wish to have them put an end to by a possible dissolution, and that is why, on 28th August, 1907, they agreed to prolonging the Convention for another five years, to begin on 1st September, 1908. Their conditions would remain the same, with the one exception that Great Britain should be exempted from the obligation laid down in Art. 4 of the Convention, namely, that an extra duty amounting at least to the bounty money was to be levied on bounty-fed sugar when imported into Convention countries.

Russia, too, joined the Convention in September, 1908, under the reservation that she should not have to alter her fiscal legislature and her present excise regulations, nor increase the profits to be gained by the sugar manufacturers from the way in which the selling price at home should be fixed. On the other hand, Russia pledged herself not to export more than 1,000,000 tons during the next five years to countries other than Finland, Persia, and the remaining neighbouring Asiatic countries which could be reached by land ; this restriction was enforced on 1st September, 1907.

The thus modified Convention was prolonged to September, 1913, by agreement on the part of all the contracting countries, and on the 15th March, 1912, was again extended till 31st August, 1918, on almost the same terms as the 1908 Convention, the difference being that Russia was allowed to export 1,650,000 tons in the seven years between September 1st, 1911, and August 31st, 1918,

The Convention put an end to all pressure on the part of the sugar manufacturers to export sugar at any price, and many a government availed itself of the fact that an export bounty need no longer be levied to lower the inland sugar excise ; Germany, France, and Belgium reduced theirs considerably, in consequence of which the consumption price went down at such a rate and so much more sugar was used that the total amount of excise had soon risen again to what it used to be, and in some cases actually surpassed the old figure.

The increased home consumption, of course, reduced the desire for exportation, so that both the measures taken in the leading European sugar producing countries, i.e., the enforcing of the Convention and the excise reduction, limited the exportation of cheap sugar to the foreign and especially British markets.

This result was most favourable to the cane sugar industry, in the first place because sugar was no longer being exported below its prime cost ; and, secondly, because the whole trade had got on a firmer footing. During the conflict among the European powers as regards the sugar exportation, one was never sure of what measures were to be taken next to promote the exports of one country or other, and of their influence on the sugar prices. This was the reason why people did not wish to risk their money and interests in the cane sugar industry of those countries which did not enjoy bounties, nor to sink money in ultra-radical improvements which might prove to be a failure on account of the world's price having been lowered in the meantime.

But people were set at ease after the Convention had come into force, and they were certain that the European powers had abolished all their bounty systems, and did not entertain the slightest wish to re-introduce, them. Everywhere factories were re-installed and new enterprises set on foot, so that from 1st September, 1903, a new period began for the cane sugar industry.

The hard times this industry has experienced have not been without a beneficial result, inasmuch as the planters and owners had been taught how to be prepared for a struggle.

Up to 1880 the cane sugar industry had been carried on in haphazard style, both economically and technically. Most of the owners of the sugar factories lived well up to the income accruing from their possessions, and did not invest much money on improving conditions; in fact, as a rule, they were prone to spend all their income without thinking of a proper reserve fund. Consequently, they were absolutely unprepared for the struggle for existence when luck changed and hard times began for them. Much to their credit, this condition did not continue long; they tried their utmost to improve the canes and the sugar production, and left no stone unturned to lower the prime cost of sugar by a more economical and rational production. Java was leading in this respect; after 1884 new capital was largely invested in sugar enterprises and in founding and keeping up experimental stations; everything was done for the practical application of science to this industry. Moreover, all those interested in this branch of industry tried with success to place the sugar cultivation on a firm footing through strict and economical management and cordial co-operation. They also succeeded in getting their undertakings fully equipped with the newest and best machinery and means of conveyance to be had, while leaving an ample reserve fund for untoward circumstances, that they might be more equal to the occasion than they were in 1884.

The results of the application of science in this industry have far surpassed the greatest expectations, so that when the Brussels Convention was signed Java had already reorganized the cane sugar industry to such an extent that immediate profit was yielded, while the other cane sugar producing countries had still to go through a transition period before they could enjoy the benefits resulting from the abolition of bounties.

The example set by Java was universally followed, and now experiment stations and testing grounds and laboratories, for the benefit of planters and

General History of the Cane Sugar Industry.

manufacturers, are to be found in every sugar producing country; and it is a fact that the cane sugar industry of the present day knows far better how to turn to account any given area than it used to do before the crisis.

But this great improvement in the quantity of cane sugar produced is also in part due to altered politics of certain countries and colonies.

During the last years of the nineteenth century the Spanish colonies, Cuba, Porto Rico, and the Philippines, suffered greatly from internal troubles, which caused the cane sugar production, of Cuba especially, to fall to an incredible small quantity, while the development of this industry in other less harassed countries had practically come to a standstill.

When in 1898 peace was signed in Paris, Spain lost almost all her colonies, having to part with Porto Rico and the Philippines, which became possessions of the United States; Cuba was declared an independent state, but was glad to sign a reciprocal treaty with the great Republic, according to which either country allowed the other a rebate of 20 per cent. on import duties. A short time after the annexation Porto Rican sugar could enter the United States exempt from import duties, which privilege was also practically granted to the Philippines in 1909, so that sugar from these countries was highly favoured and this, of course, told on the improvement of their sugar industry.

In their war with China, the Japanese conquered Formosa, where, soon after the annexation, they began to extend the cane sugar industry, so that a modernized sugar cultivation sprang up in these parts.

As Formosa is a part of the Japanese Empire, her sugar when imported into Japan pays no import duty, except the consumption duty, thus enjoying a great advantage over foreign sugar, which is subject to both duties.

Australia, Natal, and the American republics tax foreign sugar heavily, while on inland sugar a much smaller, if any, duty is paid; this, of course, has led to a considerable change as regards sugar protection in quite a short time.

Before the Brussels Convention had come into existence, the much priviledged and protected beetroot sugar industry towered over the suffering and unprotected cane sugar cultivation, on which full import duties had to be paid when exported to foreign markets. Nowadays we see the reverse. With the exception of Russia and the United States, hardly any beetroot sugar producing country of importance subsidizes its home industry whereas a great many cane sugar producing countries now support their industry by means of differential import duties, surtaxes, and direct governmental assistance, as will be shown in subsequent pages of this book. Owing to the above-mentioned advantages the cane sugar industry, in its turn, predominates nowadays, but it will not be able to oust the beetroot sugar manufacture, especially as an evergrowing consumption draws on both kinds of sugar, and, consequently, gives both of them a chance to spread and flourish. To how great an extent

General History of the Cane Sugar Industry.

both branches of the industry have developed since the Brussels Convention can be seen from the following table (in which also a column is entered which does not include the British Indian industry, and this for the sake of comparison with the table on Page 21, which likewise omits the Indian output). It shows that neither industry is inferior to the other, a state of equilibrium which is not likely to cease.

World's production of sugar in tons in the years after the Brussels Convention :—

Year.	IncluRing British India.				Not including British India.			
	Total.	Cane Sugar.	Beet Sugar.	Per cent. Cane Sugar	Total.	Cane Sugar.	Beet Sugar.	Per cent. Cane Sugar
1903/04 ..	—	—	—	—	10,080,000	4,234,000	5,746,000	42·0
1904/05 ..	12,022,000	7,144,000	4,878,000	59·4	9,654,000	4,776,000	4,878,000	49·5
1905/06 ..	14,007,000	6,834,000	7,173,000	48·8	12,083,000	4,910,000	7,173,000	40·9
1906/07 ..	14,799,000	7,691,000	7,108,000	52·0	12,349,000	5,241,000	7,108,000	42·4
1907/08 ..	13,861,000	6,866,000	6,995,000	49·5	11,745,000	4,750,000	6,995,000	40·5
1908/09 ..	14,582,000	7,654,000	6,928,000	52·4	12,709,000	5,781,000	6,928,000	45·8
1909/10 ..	14,981,000	8,303,000	6,588,000	55·7	12,766,000	6,177,000	6,589,000	48·3
1910/11 ..	16,687,000	8,115,000	8,572,000	48·6	14,587,000	6,015,000	8,572,000	41·2
1911/12 .. (estimate)	15,449,000	8,648,010	6,801,000	56·0	13,349,000	6,548,000	6,801,000	49·0

Literature:

Em. Legier. *Histoire des Origines de la Fabrication du Sucre en France.*
Paasche. *Zuckerindustrie und Zuckerhandel der Welt.*
Stein. *Zuckererzeugung und Verbrauch der Welt.*
Max Schieppel. *Zuckerproduction und Zuckerpramien.*
The West India Committee Circular.

PART II.

The Condition of the Cane Sugar Industry in the different Countries of Production.

Asia.

I.

BRITISH INDIA.

I.—Planted Area and Total Production.

It is a most difficult, nay, an almost impossible, task to collect exact data relating to the area planted with sugar cane in the British Indian Empire, and the quantity of sugar obtained from it. First of all, this empire contains districts where statistical accounts are very much neglected; secondly, the sugar cane cultivation is not under the management of large undertakings, but is everywhere carried on on a very small scale, so that any exact estimation of the area becomes an impossibility.

Moreover, the planted sugar cane is by no means destined to be used exclusively for the preparation of sugar; a considerable portion of it is sold for chewing purposes, while what is left is turned into sugar in a very primitive way. Supposing the statistics of the planted area to be exact, it would not give us a clear idea as to what portion is destined for sugar preparation, for one never can know beforehand, or later on, how much of the cane grown there is used for direct consumption, and how much is ground and made into sugar.

We should not forget this when the figures of the cane-planted area in British India are being considered, and when the results of some years differ greatly from those of other years. This does not point in the least to a great difference in planting, but rather to a difference in opinion between the individual estimates.

Asia.

The cane sugar cultivation is chiefly carried on in the following provinces: 1, Bengal; 2, Eastern Bengal and Assam; 3, United Provinces of Agra and Oudh; 4, Punjab; 5, the North-West Provinces; 6, Madras; 7, Bombay and Sind; 8, the Central Provinces and Berar; 9, Burma; and 10, the Rajput States. From these the six first mentioned have furnished useful statistical data for years, as for some time has Bombay, too; while those of the other parts are most deficient and unreliable. Fortunately, the percentage of the provinces which afford useful data amounts to a high figure in the total area planted with cane for sugar manufacture, so that their ratio between planted area and finished production may easily be taken as the average for British India.

According to the average statistics derived from five years' observation, 1904–5 to 1909–10, the quantity of seven out of the ten provinces amounts to no less than 98·5 per cent of the total cane planted area, and that of the first-mentioned six (*i.e.*, excluding Bombay and Sind) to 95·4 per cent., so that the results of the rest are not likely to influence much the average figure.

Making allowance for the above-mentioned uncertainties, and arriving at an average from unknown figures, we obtain the following figures for the total cane-planted area in acres in British India :—

1890/91	....	2,758,000
1891/92	. .. .	3,100,000
1892/93	....	2,798,000
1893/94	..·	2,897,000
1894/95	....	2,764,000
1895/96	....	2,930,000
1896/97	....	2,651,000
1897/98	....	2,648,000
1898/99	....	2,755,000
1899/00	.... .. ·.	2,693,000
1900/01	....	2,599,000
1901/02	. . ....	2,474,000
1902/03	. .. .	2,358,000
1903/04	....	2,280,000
1904/05	....	2,244,000
1905/06	....	2,110,800
1906/07	....	2,366,000
1907/08	... . ..	2,681,000
1908/09	....	2,219,700
1909/10	....	2,157,000
1910/11	....	2,164,000
1911/12	.·..	2,370,000

The area divided over the different provinces was, as far as could be fixed, as follows :—

Year.	Bengal.	Eastern Bengal and Assam	United Provinces of Agra & Oudh.	Punjab	North-West Provinces.	Madras	Bombay and Sind.	Central Provinces and Berar.	Burma.
1902/03	659,700	42,044	1,151,929	320,258	26,478	59,903	56,471	24,814	16,272
1903/04	645,400	40,555	1,089,660	330,767	27,224	54,740	59,251	19,397	13,108
1904/05	638,000	44,869	1,212,729	333,231	26,000	64,369	59,116	23,465	11,213
1905/06	421,600	201,500	1,220,716	172,700	26,003	60,700	58,882	—	12,710
1906/07	424,500	199,900	1,386,700	257,600	28,600	52,500	49,090	—	—
1907/08	436,200	171,000	1,481,700	391,800	35,200	49,000	74,300	—	—
1908/09	375,100	169,200	1,119,400	365,600	27,500	43,700	83,500	—	—
1909/10	351,600	170,700	1,037,600	411,700	30,600	43,200	81,600	—	—
1910/11	346,600	177,400	1,059,500	388,000	32,700	47,200	80,100	—	—
1911/12	340,600	179,300	1,340,600	292,500	31,500	60,000	87,400		

As regards these figures, we may make the following remarks : --

Bengal. The considerable decrease noticeable as regards the figures of planting since 1905 is only apparent, and solely due to the dividing up of Bengal into two parts, by which fourteen districts were attached to Assam. That is why the cane-planted area of Bengal has lost about 200,000 acres, while that of Assam and Eastern Bengal has gained by the same amount.

Agra and Oudh. Of these two provinces, the former is by far the more important for the sugar cane cultivation, as in this province alone about 950,000 acres are planted with sugar cane. The United Provinces are respon-sible for half of the total cane-planted area in British India, so that this territory is surely the most important for cane cultivation.

Punjab. In the year 1905–6 we notice a sudden decrease in the number of acres planted with cane, which decrease we shall also find in the sugar production. The source from which we derive these figures, " The Agricultural Statistics," does not explain the point any further, but as the figures for the following years revert to the original amount, this falling off is either only apparent or only temporary ; we need, therefore, not consider it any further.

Bombay and Sind. A sudden temporary decline is to be noticed here, too, during one of the years. For the year 1905–6 we find for Bombay the figures 56,333 acres, and for Sind 2,549 ; while both of them fall to 49,090 in 1906–7, to rise again soon after. Although the cane-planted area in this province is not extensive, the sugar production is of considerable importance, as much more sugar is yielded per acre on irrigated land than in other parts of India.

Central Provinces and Berar. There are no reliable statistics to be had from these parts, but it is known that in 1904–5, 21,390 acres were planted with cane in the Central Provinces, and 2,076 in Berar.

Burma. The cane cultivation is chiefly met with in Lower Burma. Here in 1905–6, which was an average year, 10,439 acres were planted with cane while 2,281 acres represented the Upper Burma harvest.

Independent Inland States in Rajputana and Central India. The joint cane-planted area of the States of Mysore, Jaipur, Gwalior, Bikanir, Marwar, Tonk, Alwar, Kishangarh, Bharatpur, Jhalawar, and Kotah amounted to about 40,000 acres, out of which Gwalior planted some 5,221, Jaipur 645, Bharatpur 459, Tonk 340, Kotah 320, and Alwar 220 acres ; while as to the rest we have no specified lists.

The total sugar production of British India comes to figures that vary greatly in the different statistics given, which is not to be wondered at if we realize that the cultivation of sugar cane and the manufacture of sugar rests for the greater part with very small owners, so that it becomes a kind of home industry. The produce when prepared is chiefly used for local consumption, and what is left is consumed in the country itself, so that any exact production statistics are an impossibility. The best figures are provided by the six first-mentioned provinces at the beginning of this chapter, yet we suspect them to be too low.

According to these statistical accounts, 2,307,618 acres are said to have yielded from 1898—1906 for these six provinces an average of 1,988,211 tons of raw sugar (*gur*, jaggery, or evaporated cane juice), or less than 0·9 ton per acre (2,250 kg. per hectare).

This does not tally with other lists, which on the whole give higher amounts. According to different statements, the production amounts to the following : —

Provinces.		Maunds* per acre.	Tons per acre.	Kg. per Hectare
Bengal		—	1½—3	3718—5024
United Provinces.	Meerut	36	1·32	3320
	Benares	35	1·29	3244
	Rohilkhand	34	1·25	3145
	Allahabad	28	1·07	2671
	Oudh	30	1·10	2766
	Agra	22	0·85	2136
	Average	33	1·21	3043
Central Provinces		30—40	0·7—2·2	1767—5533
Rajputana		—	1·10—1·47	2766—3697
Bombay		—	3·1	7796
Madras		—	2—2¼	3718—6290
Burma—first quality soil		—	1·3	3269
„ second „ „		—	0·9	2263

* Maund = 82 28 lbs. = 37·35 kg.

These figures no doubt hold good for very successful plantations, and, consequently, they are too high for the average. For this reason the true amount will be between the two.

According to the official statistics, the sugar production of the six provinces, to which that of Bombay is added later on, amounts to the following in tons of raw sugar or gur :—

Year.	Bengal.	Eastern Bengal and Assam	United Provinces of Agra & Oudh.	Punjab.	North-West Provinces.	Madras.	Bombay.	Total.
1899/1904 average	492,300	—	957,800	230,400	23,200	95,500	—	1,799,200
1904/05 ..	444,900	189,800	1,184,400	238,300	22,600	90,000	—	2,169,000
1905/06 ..	452,300	162,700	884,800	89,000	22,800	114,500	—	1,725,300
1906/07 ..	419,300	193,500	1,264,600	212,800	32,800	100,400	121,874	2,345,200
1907/08 ..	407,800	175,300	916,700	238,700	32,200	92,000	184,200	2,046,900
1908/09 ..	255,900	174,900	844,200	265,600	30,100	81,000	221,200	1,872,900
1909/10 ..	309,400	198,800	955,200	334,000	33,100	81,800	213,000	2,125,300
1910/11 ..	367,700	195,800	1,042,900	262,600	35,700	87,100	226,000	2,217,800
1911/12 ... (estimate)	393,400	215,200	1,259,300	176,600	31,900	110,700	203,300	2,390,400

If we suppose these statistics to stand for 98·5 per cent of the total cane planted area (since Bombay is represented also), the total production for the whole of British India would amount to about 2,400,000 tons of raw sugar, which no doubt is too low. From other statistics we obtain a figure of 3,411,000 tons, to which is added 543,000 tons of palm sugar, so that the production in the parts spoken of must come to no less than 4,000,000 tons. How far more exact this very high figure is than the lesser one just mentioned is difficult to say, but as all the sugar is used for home consumption and, consequently, is of no importance for the world's trade, we do not think it necessary to trouble ourselves about it further. Although we consider the official figures too low, we shall adhere to them, in order not to quote figures which differ from other statistics.

II.—Cane Cultivation.

(a) Tillage and Manuring.

It is easy to imagine that in such an extensive territory as British India the cultivation methods in the different parts of the country do not always correspond, being based on the results of meteorological circumstances, the quantity of water available, the condition of the soil, etc. On the whole, however, there is a similarity that enables them to be condensed into a short survey.

As a rule, cane is planted in India as an annual only, and ratoons are seldom grown, while cane is planted again on the same soil after some years' interval; manuring is accomplished by means of stable dung, or garbage from the towns, or with the crushed oil cakes left as a residue from producing oil. The cane is planted from February to April, and is reaped from the middle of January up till the beginning of April the following year. The cuttings are sometimes taken from the middle of the stalk, and sometimes from the top; they are cut with three eyes, and are soaked for some days before they are planted.

Three different methods of cultivation exist: the first method consists in leaving the soil fallow for a whole year after the spring harvest, beginning the ploughing after the first spells of rain and continuing till the planting time commences. The second method is mostly applied to soil irrigated by means of canals, in which case the ground is left fallow during the winter time after an autumn harvest; then ploughing is begun directly after the harvest is reaped, and is repeated sometimes as much as forty times; then the soil is levelled, the manure is spread, and the furrows are dug. In the third type of cultivation the soil is ploughed after a spring harvest, and immediately prepared for the reception of the cane cuttings.

Then, where irrigation is possible, the soil is thoroughly moistened during the planting time, and constantly watered afterwards, till the plants have attained to their full height; the soil is kept loose, and the young plants are banked up, while drainage is carried out in the rainy season. From July till October dry leaves are wound round the cane stems in order to ward off attacks from jackals, wild boars, and mice, and also as a shelter from the wind, which at this time generally blows severely from the direction of the Gulf of Bengal.

In January and February the harvest is begun, and lasts till the end of March or the beginning of April. When no ratoons are kept, which is generally the case, the cane is dug out and loosened with a pull from the roots. Only in the district of Poona is much ratoon to be met with, but even then only first ratoons, while in the other parts ratooning is an exception. For the ratooning the cane is cut off with a sharp knife and the stump covered with leaves, which are burnt in April. After a month, when the young shoots have budded, the soil between the old plants is loosened, the cane being treated as ordinary plant cane. As the ratoon ripens sooner than the planted cane, the next crushing season the ratoons are dealt with first, and then the new planted cane is ground. The cane that is not kept for ratooning is dug out altogether, and not cut off at harvest time.

In British India much irrigation is carried out with river water, as well as with well water, which is led across the country in canals that get narrower and narrower as they proceed. Soil where no irrigation is available is first planted with cane, after it has lain fallow for a whole year, and been ploughed repeatedly during that time. In this case the planting is done during the

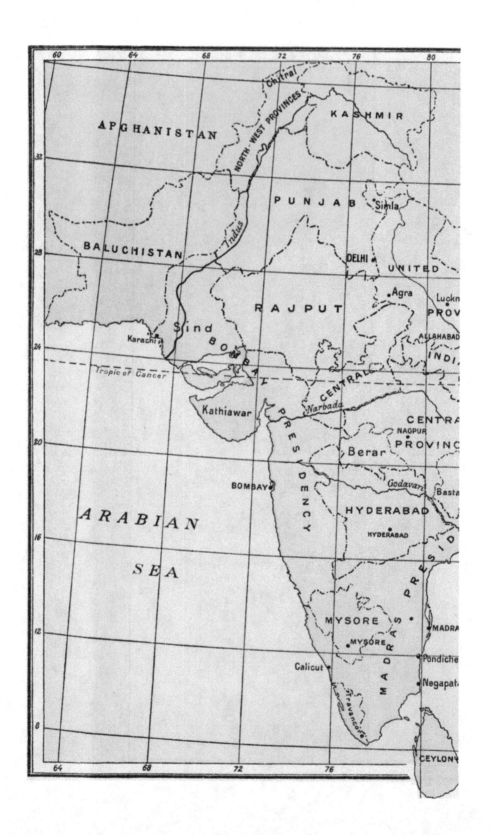

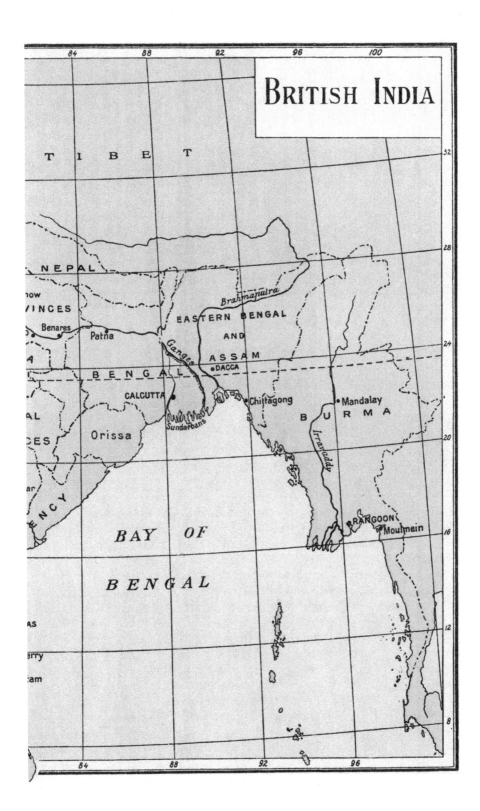

BRITISH INDIA

months of November, December, and January, and cow dung is used for manuring in quantities of 50 to 200 maunds per acre (4,500 to 18,000 kg. per hectare, or 4,100 to 16,400 lbs. per acre). As soon as the cane has grown up, the soil is covered with leaves to prevent evaporation, and to supply the want of irrigation water in the best possible way.

(b) Cane Varieties, Diseases and Pests.

According to the use to which cane is put, *i.e.*, whether it is to be used for direct consumption, or as raw material in sugar manufacture, a great variety of canes exist in British India which can, however, be placed under three different heads, namely, the *Ukh*, the *Ganna*, and the *Paunda*.

The *Ukh* cane species occur most frequently; they are chiefly planted for the manufacture of sugar, and used by the lower classes only for chewing. They have a hard rind and a hard internal tissue, are thin and rather short. The leaves are small and narrow, while the stalk is scantily provided, and this only on a few of the lower joints, with aerial roots. A great many joints are hollow when the cane is ripe, while the fibrovascular bundles extend all through the hollow space. The buds lie hidden, and generally are little developed. Being hard, this kind of cane is little subject to diseases and the attacks of parasites and wild animals.

The *Ganna* cane species are exclusively cultivated as an article for direct consumption as a dainty, except in Meerut, Rohilkhand, Gorakhpur, and Benares Divisions, where they are also used for sugar manufacture. They are generally taller and thicker than the Ukh kinds, and their leaves are longer and broader too. The rind, as a rule, is hard, but the interior is soft, and there is no inner cavity. Although this kind of cane is very juicy, it is not so rich in sugar as the first-mentioned species, and the sugar prepared from it is not of the same quality. As the Ganna cane species are so much softer, they are more subject to attacks from animal pests than the Ukh sorts, and they are also more liable to infection with *Colletotrichum falcatum*. That is why their planting has been considerably reduced during the last twenty years, especially in the district of Meerut, where both kinds of cane were planted simultaneously, and where it was noticeable how much more capable the Ukh cane was of resisting attacks from parasites and other enemies than the other kind.

The introduction into India of the *Paunda* cane species dates from more recent times. They are almost exclusively planted for direct consumption, and, as a rule, in the neighbourhood of large towns. These kinds of cane require much care and heavy manuring in their cultivation, and therefore they are not thought fit for profitable sugar production. The stalks are tall and thick, and have a hard rind and a very soft internal tissue without any cavities; their leaves are long and broad, and the aerial roots all along the stems are much developed.

Seedling cane is not met with in British India, which cannot be wondered at when we realize the primitive stage at which cane sugar cultivation stands there.

To the list of animal enemies met with belong wild boars, jackals, mice, white ants, borers (*Diatraea saccharalis*, *Chilo simplex*, and *Chilo auricilia*, *Scirpophaga auriflua*, and *Scirpophaga excerptalis*, as well as *Nonagria uniformis*), beetles and grasshoppers. The parasitic types of fungi which do most harm in British India are *Thielaviopsis aethaceticus* (pineapple disease, or black rot), *Colletotrichum falcatum* (red smut), *Trichosphaeria sacchari* a very common parasite, *Ustilago sacchari* (smut), *Sphaeronoema adiposum*, and some kinds of *Cercospora* and *Leptosphaeria*, which cause diseases in the leaves. Then there is a phanerogamic parasite, namely, the *Striga lutea*, a kind of broom-rape which vegetates on the cane roots, and sometimes is capable of destroying an entire cane harvest. This parasite is so harmful and so difficult to exterminate that the cane growers take good care not to plant cane where the *Striga* occurs.

Finally, the climate is anything but reliable, and the spells of drought are sometimes so long that the cane is the worse for it ; that is why the crop of 1908-9 was a failure. The low cane soil suffers much from inundations in the rainy season, while the sugar cane in the western districts of the United Provinces experiences much harm from severe frost.

***

III.—Sugar Manufacture.

According to the most reliable sources, the art of preparing sugar from cane came originally from India ; the plant itself had long been known, and so had the use of its juice as a luxury ; but the art of evaporation to a solid substance is an Indian invention of about the seventh century and was spread all over the then known world.

Among the Mohammedan authors there is a certain Ibn-i-Batuta, who, travelling in different parts of India at the end of the thirteenth century, mentions in his *Safar-namah* the cultivation of several kinds of cane, but does not go into particulars. The author of the *Makhzan-ul-Adviyya*, who is an authority on medicinal plants, and also lived at the time of the Mohammedan period in the Indian history, divides the sugar cane into three kinds, *i.e.*, paunda, a white, and a red type of cane. According to him the best white cane is found in Bardwan and Murshidabad, in Patna,. Gorakhpur, and Oudh ; and the best red cane in Rajmahal, Agra, etc. Further, a number of sorts of cane sugar are given, which go by different names ; although many of those names have been altered since, most of the undermentioned preparations are still manufactured in exactly the same way as described by the ancient author, which shows, first of all, to how high a degree the manufacture of sugar rose in India already at so early a period; and, further, it points to the conservative spirit among the inhabitants of that country, who have clung to old traditions and customs.

These sorts are distinguished as follows:—

1. *Qand-i-siyah*. The solid product obtained by evaporating cane juice to dryness.
2. *Shakar-i-ahmar* or *Shakar-i-tari*. The product obtained by concentrating the juice considerably longer than No. 1, and by rubbing the cooled dry substance to powder.
3. *Shakar-i-safed*. Sugar obtained by refining raw sugar.
4. *Nabat-i-safed*. The product obtained by purifying *Shakah-i-safed* with milk or albumen.
5. *Shakar-i-sulaimáni*. Obtained by refining No. 4 more thoroughly.
6. *Qand*. Obtained by boiling No. 5 in water, and crystallizing its syrup out into conical moulds.
7. *Ibluj* or *Qand-i-mukarrar*. Obtained by a further solution of *Qand*, and of re-crystallizing its syrup out in oblong moulds.
8. *Nabat-i-sanjari*. Obtained by refining *Qand-i-mukarrar*.
9. *Shakar-i-tabarzad*. Obtained by boiling *Qand* with a tenth of its weight of milk till it becomes solid.
10. *Faniz* or "drops." Obtained by dissolving product No. 3 (*Shakar-i-safed*) with water and milk, and by skimming it off.

Although the modern way of preparing sugar is sometimes applied, the original processes are much more adhered to, and, consequently, demand a fuller description.

The simplest way of extracting cane juice is to put the cane, cut up into pieces, into a kind of stone or wooden mortar, and to crush it with a pestle driven by oxen, while the juice runs into an earthenware vessel put under an opening in the mortar wall. In former times the mortar was made by sawing through a rather big tamarind tree about 3 ft. above the ground, and excavating its stump, but as the right sort of trees was not always to be found in the right spot, cut logs were also used after they had been hollowed and buried into the earth for some length. Later on, similar mortars were made of stone, and were considered a most desirable possession, so that it was a long time before they were supplanted by the iron-roller mills. The accompanying illustrations show amply the way in which this kind of mill works.

The pestle is a two-armed lever, whose point of support lies on the **edge** of the mortar, so that the cane is crushed between the mortar wall and the pestle. A couple of oxen are put on the yoke, and are driven round, while the driver stands on the extremity of the yoke in order to increase the pressure or puts some stones on it instead. (Fig. 1.)

The first improvement was the mill with two vertical wooden rollers, the longer of the two having a frame at the top connected with a capstan to which the oxen are attached. Both the rollers are provided with grooves and corresponding teeth, so that when one is put into motion the other is also turned round. The cane stalks are then placed between the turning cylinders, and the juice is pressed out of them. In the end these again were superseded by mills with two or three iron cylinders and gear wheels, which are called Behea mills, after the place where they were first introduced.

These mills express much more juice from the cane than the older mortar and pestle mills, but to show how far this kind is from perfection we may as well quote a few figures from the work of Saiyid Muhammad Hadi, " The Sugar Industry of the United Provinces of Agra and Oudh," which states the returns obtained through these Behea mills.

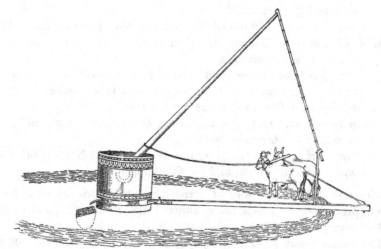

FIG. I. STONE MILL IN THE EASTERN DISTRICTS OF AGRA.

District.	Species of Cane.	Average percentage of juice from cane expressed by a	
		2 Cylinder Mill used by the Cultivator.	3 Cylinder Behea Mill.
Fyzabad	Sarauti	52·27	62·50
Farukhabad	Chin	56·33	61·06
Unao	,,	50·01	58·11

The results of a great many experiments on several kinds of cane gave figures varying between 50 and 60 per cent., so that these can be considered the average for the quantity of juice to be obtained from cane in India.

British India.

From the cane juice a great variety of sugar is prepared which, however, either belongs to the *gur* or the *rab* brands.

For the preparation of *gur* the juice flowing out of the mill is strained first through a coarse sieve, in order to prevent the pieces of coarse fibre from passing through, and later on is caught in an earthenware pot which is sunk in the earth. As soon as this pot is filled the contents are scooped out by means of cans and placed in a number of vessels, which are put by in readiness beside a furnace. While the juice is settling all sorts of dirty matter rise, floating to the surface to be skimmed off. This is a very superficial way of purifying, and does not amount to much considering the dirtiness of the vessels, which are seldom or never cleaned, in which the juice has to stand for a considerable time, in addition to which there is loss caused by inversion. The furnace (Fig. 4), as a rule, consists of three pans, though sometimes only of one single pan. It is a very simple contrivance of one or more shallow iron dishes sunk into the ground with a wall of bricks and tiles round it. The evaporation is carried on through a subterraneous bagasse furnace, which keeps heating the pan, some other fuel being sometimes added. In a great many cases the juice is only purified by being skimmed off. The juice is treated first in the first pan, and when the scum be-

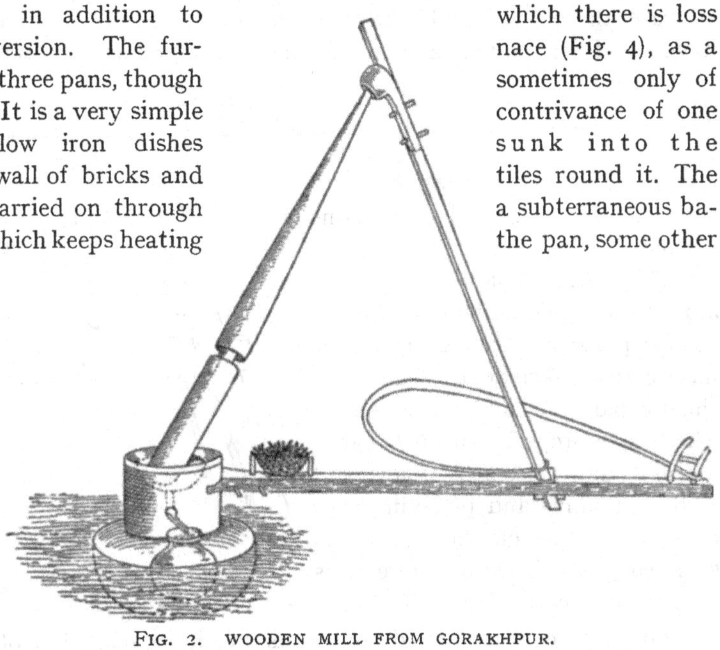

FIG. 2. WOODEN MILL FROM GORAKHPUR.

gins to float on the surface after having been boiled, the clean juice is transferred to the third pan, being left the e to concentrate, the process being finished by means of the second pan. Generally some milk-of-lime, Glauber's salt, crude soda ash, or some *Hibiscus esculentus* root extract is added as a purifying agent. A mixture of anchusa leaf extract, soda, and alum is used to give it a better colouring. The scum, which as a result of the purifying process floats on the top, is skimmed off with a spoon, and kept in a basin to be used as food for animals, and sometimes even for poor people.

When the juice under concentration becomes yellowish-brown, it is constantly stirred, and as soon as bubbling becomes active a little of the substance is rolled between finger and thumb to a ball in order to judge of its consistency. When it remains moderately soft after cooling, the concentration is considered

53

sufficient, and the boiling process is stopped. With some kinds of *gur* the hot mass is scooped out into earthenware moulds where it is left to cool, and turn hard ; with other kinds it is kneaded first with wooden pestles in an earthenware dish, and then, after being sufficiently cooled to be touched, kneaded into balls or flattened on a cloth-covered mat and cut into triangular pieces. To prevent the hot mass from sticking to the hands, the latter are first dusted with wood ashes. The sundry balls and pieces are put aside to dry in baskets, and when dry they are fit for consumption.

When soft and well crystallized, *gur* is well suited for refining, but when solidified into a hard mass, it can be used for direct consumption only, while extremely hard and burnt *gur* never goes through the refining process at all In case the cane should have been fallen, unripe, or if its juice should have stood for too long a time, the quantity of reducing sugar it contains is so

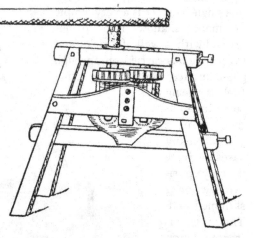

considerable that it never can become a dry sugar, but remains viscous.

For the preparation of *rab* almost the same method is followed as for preparing *gur*, except that more care is taken about cleanliness, the iron pans then amounting to five. These are properly cleaned every morning, and more attention is paid to the skimming and purifying process, while the clarified juice is strained through cloth before it is evaporated to dryness. The con-

FIG. 3.   BEHEA IRON ROLLER MILL.

centration is not conducted so far as in the preparation of *gur*, so that a thinner product is struck into the cooling vessels.

To promote a better crystallization it is well stirred in the pots in which it is scooped, and within a few days changes into a moist, rather soft substance, which is sold together with the pot in which it is crystallized, and the latter has therefore to be broken into pieces in order to get at the contents.

As *rab* is a semi-liquid mixture it is difficult to convey, and, consequently, its use is restricted to the immediate neighbourhood of the place where it is prepared. *Gur*, however, being a hard, solid matter, is easily sent long distances. *Gur* is used partly for direct consumption and partly for refining purposes, while *rab* is almost exclusively employed for refining.

A very primitive and simple way of refining is achieved by packing the *rab* in sacks and getting a man to keep trampling on them, whereupon the syrup, called *shira*, runs out, and a moist, whitish sugar, *putri*, is left, which may be further refined.

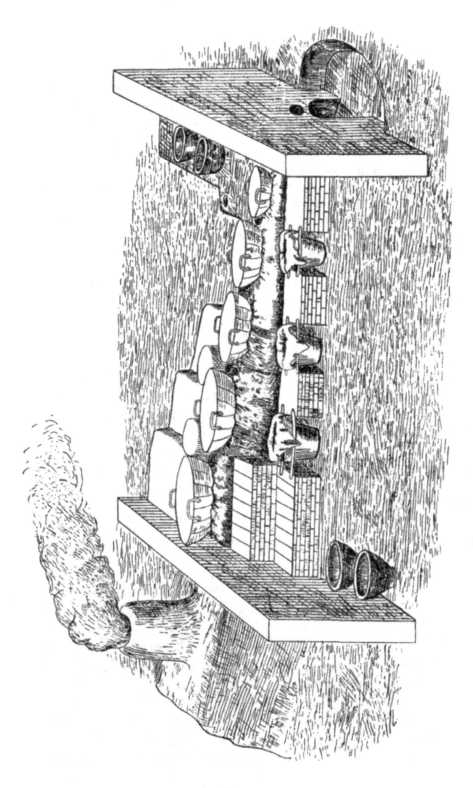

FIG. 4. FURNACE FOR BOILING CANE JUICE INTO RAB.

Sacks of *rab* are sometimes piled up on a floor covered with mats and provided with little holes ; the syrup, trickling out of the sacks, soon collects into a little well in the floor, while the process of draining off the molasses from the raw sugar is greatly helped by placing big pieces of baked earth on the top of the bags. Only half of the quantity of *rab* is turned into *putri* or *shakar*, while half of this again is lost when refined to *chini*, or white sugar.

With this treatment the drained *rab* is put into pots which have an opening at the bottom, and are covered with a layer of wet water-plants, *Hydrilla verticillata.* The water it contains trickles over the sugar crystals and dissolves the adhering syrup, which runs out through an opening at the bottom. After four or five days the plants are taken away, and the light-brown sugar (*pachni*) is scraped off the surface, when a fresh layer of plants is placed again on what is left, which process is repeated till all the syrup has drained out. The sugar obtained in this way is in this form used for several purposes, or left to dry in the sun, and kneaded by human feet in order to give it a lighter colour.

This method, modified in many ways, is applied to both *rab* and *gur*, and its result, as a rule, is a more or less purified sugar. The syrup that first drains off is either used for sweetening food, or is distilled after fermentation, while the sugar syrup which is obtained later on, and which is richer in sugar through some sugar being dissolved in it, is evaporated to dryness, and worked up to a second kind of *rab*. The *pachani*, or *kacha*, or *kacha qand* obtained through this process is sometimes dissolved again, clarified with skimmed milk, skimmed off and strained through blankets and worked up to white sugar (*pucka chini*) loaves (*qand*), or candy (*misri*), so that the scheme is as follows :—

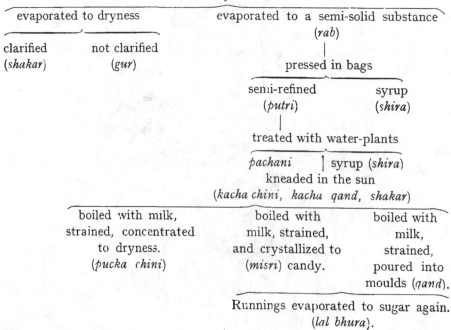

Cane juice

evaporated to dryness — evaporated to a semi-solid substance (*rab*)

clarified (*shakar*) — not clarified (*gur*)

pressed in bags

semi-refined (*putri*) — syrup (*shira*)

treated with water-plants

pachani | syrup (*shira*)
kneaded in the sun
(*kacha chini, kacha qand, shakar*)

boiled with milk, strained, concentrated to dryness. (*pucka chini*) — boiled with milk, strained, and crystallized to (*misri*) candy. — boiled with milk, strained, poured into moulds (*qand*).

Runnings evaporated to sugar again. (*lal bhura*).

British India.

Through the primitive draining off and covering methods, much sugar is lost, and that is why the Assistant-Director of Land Records and Agriculture at Allahabad, Saiyid Muhammad Hadi, has tried to prepare *rab* in a more rational way ; much sugar is now being prepared according to the so-called Hadi process.

The difference is that the heating apparatus is constructed on much more practical lines, and that one can easily regulate the fire, so that there is less chance of burning or of the juice decomposing.

Further, the cooled *rab*, or massecuite, is no longer separated into crystals and molasses through the covering and draining-off process for the sake of further purification, but in a handworked centrifugal. As can be seen, the modifications brought about by the Hadi process are not in the least radical, but the native sugar manufacture in British India is still at such a primitive stage that a little improvement like this affects the yield of white sugar from *rab* considerably.

The following figures may show what heavy losses are suffered from the primitive refining methods of *gur* and *rab*.

The analyses of some raw and semi-refined sugars are as follows :—

	Polariza-tion.	Glucose.	Ash.	Water.	Un-determined.	Nett.
Gur	71·80	10·65	3·76	8·50	5·29	42·35
,, . .	76·20	6·48	5·94	7·48	3·90	40·02
Rab .. .	80·20	5·30	1·76	9·40	3·34	66·10
Putri	82·30	6·10	1·60	7·34	2·66	68·20

The nett yield by these figures is the trade yield calculated by deducting from the polarization the percentage of the glucose, and five times the percentage of ash, and does not refer to the actual amount of white sugar obtained from it. This is considerably less, and depends on the raw material. According to Hadi, the buyers distinguish three kinds of *rab* as regards quality, and the following productions on 100 parts of original raw sugar are obtained as the average figure :—

Products.	1st class.	2nd class.	3rd class.
1st class of sugar	28·00	22·00	16·00
2nd ,, ,, ...	5·33	3·00	4 00
Syrup	62·00	70·00	74·50
Loss	4·67	5·00	5·50

Asia.

On an average a yield of only 20 to 33 per cent. of sugar from *rab* is obtained when working in the old way ; while a yield of 40 per cent is easily arrived at when the work is done with centrifugals according to the Hadi process.

The production of sugar from the same quantity of raw material is sure to increase gradually, but as British India adopts new ideas slowly, it will take some time before each factory possesses centrifugals.

In spite of due encouragement from the Government, and the improved prices, the modern methods of sugar industry do not spread. In 1896 there were 236 sugar factories and refineries in India, while in 1900 the number had dropped down to 203, employing 5,000 people ; and, consequently, could not possibly have been of much importance. According to *Financial and Commercial Statistics*, which since 1904 do not record factories employing fewer than 25 employees, there were in the year 1904 only 28 large sugar refineries in India, with 4,612 employees.

Considering the small sugar production per acre, and the loss of raw sugar through injudicious methods of purification, one might expect a sugar enterprise with plenty of funds, and carrying on the cane sugar cultivation according to modern methods, to do well. Results, however, fall short of these expectations, as no increase in the number of enterprises, working after European methods, is to be noticed, although the Brussels Convention has made competition with beetroot sugar easy; while their financial results are not promising either.

Classified according to the provinces, the factories are as follows :—

In BENGAL.

Sakri	Production 200 tons.
Bara Chakia ..	,, 2,000 ,,
Cossipore Refinery	Refines chiefly Java sugar.
Ottur	Production 2,500 tons.
Soeraha	,, 800 ,,
Burgohah	Has stopped work.
Japaha	Production 1,200 tons.
Kotchandpore ..	Refines palm sugar.
Pursa	Production 1,200 tons
Tarpore	Refines palm sugar.
Marhourah .. .	Production 12,000 tons, works with carbonatation plant
Maharajganj ..	Melts 20 tons of *gur* a day.

In the UNITED PROVINCES OF AGRA AND OUDH.

Cawnpore Sugar Works	Refines exclusively *gur*.
Purtabpore	Production 1,200 tons.
Rosa	Refines *gur* and *rab*.

In the PUNJAB.

Punjab Sugar Works.

British India.

In the NORTH-WEST PROVINCES.
Peshawar Sugar Manufacturing Co
  In BOMBAY.
Poona Sugar Works.
Gaewar Sugar Works.
  In MADRAS.
Aska.
Samalkot.
East India Distilleries and Sugar Factories, Ltd.
Gorihiduor.
Petai.
Podanur.
Bellary.

The East India Distilleries and Sugar Factories, Ltd. has sugar works in Nellikam, Coimbatore, and Tinnevelly. They grind cane during the crushing season, and at other times they refine cane and palm sugar.

These factories and refineries were originally founded for the purpose of manufacturing sugar out of sugar cane, but in most cases it seems an impossibility to get enough cane to work on steadily. The land in India is divided up into such little plots and belongs to so many owners that joint cane plantations do not exist, so that the raw material has to be conveyed from places at some distance, and only in small quantities. Owing to the indifference of farmers this raw material, as a rule, is of a very inferior kind, and is not likely to be improved by the slow methods of transport in vogue. As the supply of cane leaves much to be desired, the manufacturers have been compelled to work up *gur* and *rab* as well for the sake of constant work, and this, again, has given rise to difficulties.

First of all, there is only a slight difference in price between the raw material *gur* and the white sugar obtained from it ; moreover, among the orthodox Hindu population there is a dislike for sugar prepared in the European way, so that the *chini* made according to native methods fetches a far higher price than the sugar refined in the big sugar works. The British India manufacturers are at a great disadvantage all round : first, in comparison with foreign competitors who have access to a far better and cheaper kind of raw material ; and, secondly, when compared with their native rivals, who, although they have to use the same raw material, get much higher prices for their produce.

The fact is, *gur* is generally used either as food as it is, or for baking purposes, and it does not deteriorate in value should it contain much glucose or its colour be dark through caramelization, which conditions mean loss to the sugar refiner.

The European breweries do not think it a disadvantage when *rab* contains glucose or is caramelized, so that a bad kind of raw material realizes the same as a better kind, in consequence of which the refiner pays too much for the inferior sort.

As regards refining sugar, the modern refiner is better off, his loss being less severe than that of the native manufacturer, who must make shift with primitive implements. The latter, on the other hand, has hardly any installation costs, and does all the work himself, together with his family; he can, moreover, gain his livelihood in another way, and can stop his refining business when prices become unprofitable, which a big undertaking cannot.

The sale price of native refined sugar is considerable, being much higher than either the sugar prepared in up-to-date refineries or imported produce; and will, no doubt, continue to be so as long as religious and caste prejudices are so strong against foreign sugar.

Animal charcoal is used for refining operations, and the ancient legends about clarification with ox-blood still prevail. Hence the Hindus are much opposed to the consumption of sugar thus prepared, and wish to take nothing but *chini* sugar, which they think free from these admixtures.

Then there is the difficulty lest sugar worked up by the lowest caste should be consumed by people of the superior castes to their defilement.

The native refiners have realized for some time that it would be far more profitable for them to use European beetroot or Mauritius and Java cane sugar as a raw material than the much more expensive *putri* or *pachani*, which is got with great difficulty from *rab* or *gur*. Consequently, this kind of sugar is greatly supplemented by the once-despised foreign sugar, which is nowadays much used by the devout high-caste native, who, of course, is ignorant of the fact. The confectioners, too, have recourse to imported sugar for the preparation of their sweetmeats, being sure of its better effect.

Thus the native refiner can make use of a better and cheaper material than his European colleagues in British India. All these reasons go far to show how it is possible for a gigantic empire such as British India to prepare and refine a large amount of sugar in an irrational and primitive way, and, in addition, import a good deal of white sugar, modern economical methods being scarcely employed at all.

IV.—Prime Cost, Importation and Transportation. Excise and Duties levied.

The prime cost of an acre planted with cane varies much as regards the different districts.

Watts, in his " Commercial Products of India," quotes the following figures for prime cost and profit :—

British India.

Rupees per acre of cane.

	Prime cost.	Profit.
Bengal	160	—
United Provinces	66—158	—
Central Provinces	164	38
Bombay	420	120—150
Madras	150	90
Burma	90	—

while Hadi has the following specified statements of a number of treatments applied in the districts of Agra and Oudh :—

DISTRICTS	Ploughing		Seed.	Cost of Sowing.	Hoeing and Weeding.		Irrigation.			Manure	Rent.	Total.
Name of Tract.	Num-ber.	Cost.			Num-ber.	Cost.	Source of	Number of Water-ings.	Cost.			
		R a. p.	R a. p.	R. a. p.		R. a p.			R. a. p.	R a. p.	R. a. p.	R. a. p.
Meerut	14	10. 8.0	8 0.0	2. 8.0	8	10. 0.0	canal	6	18. 0. 0	5. 0 0	12. 0 0	66. 0.0
Agra	18	9. 0.0	10. 0.0	2. 6 0	6	13. 8.0	well and canal	5	20 14.10	8. 0.0	8.12.0	72. 8.0
Rohilkhand.. ..	15	15. 0.0	12. 0.0	2. 4.0	5	11. 4 0	,,	4	18. 0. 0	9 0.0	13. 8.0	8'. 0.0
Allahabad . ..	15	15 0.0	11. 0.0	2. 8.0	4	5. 0.0	well	4	16 0. 0	6. 0.0	12. 0.0	67. 0.0
Bundelkhand ..	9	6.12.0	12. 0.0	2. 8.0	5	11 4.0	,,	4	20. 0. 0	8. 0.0	7. 8 0	68. 0.0
Benares	16	8. 0.0	10. 0.0	3. 0 0	11	9. 4.0	,,	5	20. 0. 0	6.12 0	10. 0 0	67. 0 0
Gorakhpur	20	15. 0.0	9. 6.0	2. 4.0	14	15.13.0	,,	4	12.18.10	7. 4 0	12. 4.0	74.12.0
Lucknow	15	15. 0.0	9. 0.0	3. 0.0	10	12. 0.0	,,	4	18. 0. 0	10. 0.0	18. 0 0	80. 0.0
Fyzabad..	17	'7. 0.0	9. 0.0	3. 0.0	10	6. 0.0	,,	5	15. 0. 0	9. 0 0	13. 0.0	72. 0.0

The same author also quotes the cutting, crushing, and grinding cost per acre of cane in the same districts, but with hired labour —

	R. a. p.
40 men for cutting, stripping, and carrying to the mill, 2 annas per head	5 0 0
Hire of an iron mill at 8 annas per day during fifteen days.. .	7 8 0
Hire of bullocks for the same period at 8 annas each . .	15 0 0
Hire of the boiling pan, 2 annas a day	1 14 0
Wages of the man who keeps the mill supplied with cane and feeds it, at 2 annas a day	1 14 0
Wages of the labourer who feeds the furnace, at 2 annas per day, or 1¼ seers of gur	1 14 0
Earthen vessels	0 8 0
Fuel in addition to bagasse	2 0 0
Oil	0 6 0
Total	36 0 0

1 rupee = 16 annas.   1 anna = 12 pies   1 rupee = 1s. 4d.

The total expenses consequently amount to 70 + 36 =: 106 rupees for the product of an acre, which is reckoned to be one ton, so that the prime cost in the above case for *gur* is £7 1s. 4d. per ton, or 7s. 1d. per cwt.

This prime cost is fairly high, and figures provided by the manager of Rosa factory mention 6s. 2d. as the price of *gur* per cwt., and 6s. 6d. as the price of *rab* per cwt., while *putri* fetched 8s. 9d. per cwt. Although these prices do not come up to those quoted by Hadi, they are still so high, considering the inferior quality of the product, that it shows us clearly how difficult it is for those engaged in this industry to produce out of this inferior kind of raw material a refined sugar that can compete with a corresponding foreign produce.

Besides the very considerable home product, British India also imported a great amount of foreign sugar, which during the last ten years has been derived from the following countries, and is reckoned in cwts. :—

	1901/2*	1902/3	1903/4	1904/5	1905/6	1906/7	1907/8	1908/9	1909/10	1910/11
Beetroot Sugar.										
Austria-Hungary	2,257,928	888,018	299,259	1,441,240	2,340,717	1 617 160	703,265	1,918,158	782,773	714,093
Germany	577,139	145,666	7,205	176,488	712 440	2,001.316	51,879	3 071	51,537	8,206
United Kingdom†	94,150	157,388	51,865	50,452	177 682	88,264	12 932	—	—	—
Other countries ..	6,979	266,445	194,408	48,308	201 565	116,700	11,799	22,610	23,702	2,496
Total	2,936,196	1,457,517	552,737	1,716,488	3,432,404	3 823 580	806,875	1,943,839	858,012	724,795
Cane Sugar.										
Mauritius	1,759,203	1,915,664	2 616,655	1.823,675	2,015,476	2,310,023	2,690,193	2,514.440	2,435 560	2,923,983
China	182,767	568,601	348,898	285 027	189,628	51,279	7,340	6,384	22,094	129,373
Java	446,686	573 666	1 335,548	2,091,508	1,685,391	3,304,366	6,593,699	6,172,089	7,815,745	8,758 715
Straits Settlement	63,056	207,987	229,993	211,040	150,868	38,938	12,933	—	—	962
United Kingdom ⎱	94,151	157,388	51 865	50,452	177,682	88 265	11,787	804	3 114	—
Other countries ⎰	83,198	106,512	368,872	351,163	176,920	114,286	12,104	25,777	1,288	1 428
Total	2,629,061	3,529,678	5,485,378	4,833,309	4,265,644	5,907,152	8,238,026	8 719,444	10,277,801	11,814,361
General Total ..	5,566,257	4,987,195	6,038,115	6,547,397	7,698,048	9,780,682	10,044,901	10,663,283	11,136,813	12,589,156

Only 500,000 to 600,000 cwts. of the total amount is raw sugar from Java and Mauritius ; the rest is white sugar.

The sugar importations were not extensive till 1871-72, when they amounted to 562,559 cwt. ; in 1881–82 they were as much as 982,266 cwt. ; while for 1801–92 we have 2,734,491 cwt. This was principally cane sugar from Mauritius, but in 1895–96 the competition with beetroot sugar, chiefly from Germany, became noticeable. In the same year the total amount imported was 2,730,693 cwt., 57 per cent. of which was Mauritius sugar, while the rest came from Germany and from various cane-sugar producing countries. It is a fact that in 1890–91 the importation from Germany just for once amounted to 700,000 cwt., but during the four following years it never exceeded 275,000 cwt., to rise suddenly to 718,000 cwt. in 1905-6. The next year Austria-Hungary,

* The statistical year in British India is from April 1st to March 31st.
† The importations from the United Kingdom are reckoned to be half cane sugar and half beetroot sugar, and that is why an equal amount of these two kinds is given in many years.

too, exported great quantities of sugar, so that these two countries are together responsible for 880,000 cwt. In 1896–97 British India's total importation amounted to 2,861,400 cwt., while the year after it had increased to 4,608,630 cwt., which, although other countries provide more than they used to do, comes chiefly from Germany and Austria-Hungary. Both the Dingley tariff in the United States and the competition with the French sugar on the English markets induced the exporting firms of these countries to find new outlets for their produce, and so British India got the benefit of this surplus of foreign sugar. To put a stop to this influx a law was passed in March, 1899, which entitled the Government to raise, besides the 1894 import duty of 5 per cent., equivalent duties on bountied sugar to the amount of the bounty. The following year there was a decrease in sugar imports from 4,077,499 to 3,360,862 cwt., the German as well as Austrian supplies being less ; indeed, Germany disappeared altogether from the lists. This decrease is not altogether due to the countervailing duties, as the amount imported by countries which are exempted from this duty either remained what it was, or went down. The then prevailing high sugar prices, together with a famine in the west part of India, must have caused the consumption to be reduced considerably, while there might have been much sugar left in stock from the year preceding. When, in the following year, the condition of the sugar trade improved, Germany and Austria-Hungary came in again for a rather large amount, and it may be seen from current statistics that while Mauritius imported 2,085,156 cwt., the figures of Germany and Austrian importation were respectively 1,321,330 and 201,980 cwt. The countervailing duties thus had not had a lasting influence, if any. In 1901–2 the importation of Austrian sugar had increased to 2,257,928 cwt. ; while of the 577,139 cwt. sent by Germany no doubt some came from Bohemia, being transhipped viâ Hamburg, as the countervailing duty on German sugar is a little less than that on Austrian (Rs. 1.4.7 German ; Rs. 1.7.4 Austrian). This practice was, however, put a stop to when it became necessary to send with the imported sugar certificates of origin.

It was proved at the Conferences held preparatory to the Brussels Convention that much profit was made in Germany and Austria, apart from bounties, through the concentration of the sale by the Cartels. The latter enabled the producers to keep sugar at a high price at home, so that they could export sugar below prime cost, and yet realize on the whole a fair profit. In order to annul this artificial competition, the Indian Government passed a bill in June, 1902, that an extra duty should be levied to the amount of the Cartel profit—namely, of 3.3.9 rupees per cwt. on Austrian sugar, and of 2.13.9 rupees on German sugar. On German sugar, for instance, a fixed duty of 5 per cent. of the value, a countervailing duty of 1.4.7. rupees and a Cartel tax of 2.13.9 rupees per cwt. was paid, while for Austrian sugar we find 5 per cent. of the value + 1.7.4 + 3.3.9 rupees per cwt.

The effect of these duties was at once noticeable, the more so as they were levied immediately after the law was enacted. Of the year 1901–2 three months had passed, so that for that period the law was in force only during nine months, and yet we notice a decrease in importations, from Austria only 888,018 cwt., and from Germany only 14,566 cwt. Half of the amount of Austrian sugar had come in in April, and neither German nor Austrian sugar was imported after September, but the other countries, especially the Netherlands and Belgium, supplied more than they usually did. A greater quantity of cane sugar was also imported, principally from the Straits and Hong Kong, as the sugar mentioned in the statistical accounts of China is nothing but sugar from Java and the Philippines refined in Hong Kong.

When, in September, 1903, the Brussels Convention was signed, by which all bounties were abolished and the surtaxes were reduced to such an extent that any Cartel profit was out of the question, the high countervailing and additional duties disappeared too, and the import duty in every country was fixed at 5 per cent of the value, with the exception of bounty-fed sugar from countries not belonging to the Convention countries. Consequently, the importation of European refined beetroot sugar increased, and had risen in 1905-6 to the same height as in the best year before. During the time, however, when beetroot sugar had become practically excluded from importation, Java began to supply large quantities, partly raw sugar and partly white, the so-called " superior sugar " (above No. 25 D.S.), and in spite of an increase in the importation of Austrian sugar, Java has held its own in the import trade with British India, and its supplies have increased during the last few years ; while Hong Kong's exports have gone down.

The import duty as we know amounts to 5 per cent of the value, which is fixed according to the following scale (dating from January, 1909) :—

		Per cwt.	
		R	a.
Sugar, crystallized beetroot	.. ..	10	0
,, ,, and soft from China	.. ..	11	0
,, ,, from Java No. 21 D.S. and higher	. ..	10	0
,, ,, ,, ,, No. 16—20 D.S.	.. .. .	9	0
,, ,, ,, ,, No. 15 D.S. and lower	..	8	0
,, ,, ,, Mauritius No. 16 D.S. and higher	..	9	8
Molasses from Java	.. ..	2	4
,, ,, other countries ..	.. ..	3	0

No excise is levied in British India on its own produce.

As regards the *specification of imported sugar* throughout the empire, the several kinds of beetroot sugar are found from November till May, while the cane sugar supplies are distributed over the whole year, though the period from August till November is their special season. Bombay, Karachi, Calcutta, and Madras are the harbours through which it is imported. In 1906-7 Bombay received more than 2,000,000 cwt. of sugar, of which Bombay Presidency got 843,000, the Central Provinces 367,000, the United Provinces 358,500, and Rajputana and Central India 241,500 cwt. Karachi imported 1,863,000 cwt., which was chiefly sent to the Punjab, while Sind received only 355,000 cwt. The remaining 1,508,000 tons were not destined entirely for the Punjab, but were for a large part conveyed across the frontier to Afghanistan and Kashmir. In the Punjab the imported produce can be sold at a lower price than sugar from the other provinces. This is because transit by railroad is very inexpensive, the railway companies having in any case to run their trains empty from the seaport town to the interior to fetch goods hundreds of miles distant, so they think it more profitable to transport sugar at the same time, be the freight tariff ever so low.

Calcutta imported 1,250,000 cwt. in 1906–7, out of which East Bengal and Assam received 573,000 ; Bengal, 363,500 ; and the United Provinces 235,500. The importation of Madras finally amounted to only 111,400 cwt. in the same year, which was consumed in the neighbouring country.

The sugar imports in cwts. during the last three years for the different provinces have been as follows :—

E

1908-9.

Month.	Beetroot Sugar. Bengal.	Bombay.	Sind.	Madras.	Burma.	Total.	Cane Sugar. Bengal.	Bombay.	Sind.	Madras.	Burma.	Total.	General Total.
April	34,823	41,722	95,977	4,149	20,992	197,663	130,283	118,807	50,838	158	6,074	306,160	503,823
May	40,098	45,356	155,487	4,467	4,744	250,155	29,004	253,929	18,996	2,069	144	304,142	554,294
June	19,568	51,264	129,374	1,765	45	202,016	86,094	83,929	36,391	3,569	287	210,270	412,286
July	85	9,132	4,171	775	59	14,222	300,334	119,924	57,470	10,538	30,293	518,559	532,781
August	123	23,407	4,119	51	74	27,774	289,418	67,945	292,794	1,102	39,347	690,606	718,380
September	447	79,399	13,124	55	148	93,173	752,683	229,638	167,844	18,799	54,517	1,223,481	1,316,654
October	12,087	34,325	40,643	608	189	87,852	879,840	357,160	232,271	16,135	80,927	1,566,333	1,654,185
November	96	59,040	122,011		208	184,461	616,047	378,171	312,761	11,544	66,603	1,385,126	1,569,587
December	21,318	20,262	147,280	3,106	147	192,608	287,669	187,490	151,432	23,551	70,058	720,200	912,808
January	49,718	40,515	153,485	7,761	1,280	252,759	373,653	290,968	170,101	570	59,653	894,945	1,147,701
February	46,290	26,058	133,911	8,273	4,883	219,415	179,301	206,182	23,789	3,141	26,042	438,455	657,870
March	34,670	70,126	100,645	12,154	4,331	221,926	247,295	163,714	29,324	437	20,218	460,988	682,914
Total	308,917	501,606	1,100,131	46,270	37,100	1,994,024	4,222,655	2,457,857	1,544,011	91,613	404,163	8,719,265	10,713,289

1909-10.

Month.	Beetroot Sugar. Bengal.	Bombay.	Sind.	Madras.	Burma.	Total.	Cane Sugar. Bengal.	Bombay.	Sind.	Madras.	Burma.	Total.	General Total.
April	77,099	86,057	105,768	18,876	5,103	202,903	144,480	67,450	21,725	3,850	7,483	244,988	537,891
May	68,391	25,572	59,235	13,939	2,045	169,182	145,360	214,579	70,466	1,430	1,608	433,443	602,625
June	9,676	39,459	55,768	7,874	147	112,924	64,511	127,332	29,819	7,971	1,428	231,061	343,985
July	211	4,505	4,230	1,032	70	10,048	381,437	257,923	222,530	46,362	16,758	925,010	935,058
August	200	214	91	37	68	610	593,113	288,311	148,096	27,786	60,207	1,117,513	1,118,123
September	167	349	1,090	73	163	1,852	655,176	497,117	554,528	22,150	19,227	1,748,198	1,750,049
October	130	251	72	44	134	631	383,138	387,641	388,790	25,994	76,918	1,262,481	1,263,112
November	167	9,035	12,117	3,086	102	24,507	840,827	230,912	160,279	15,972	101,337	1,373,327	1,397,834
December	6,104	12,854	17,633	4,835	105	41,531	343,439	217,929	113,761	14,921	49,432	739,482	781,013
January	19,129	15,390	20,297	4,168	95	59,079	427,632	258,053	112,868	13,800	27,011	839,364	898,443
February	13,227	10,262	5,045	1,549	114	30,197	285,786	206,626	43,371	235	56,750	592,768	622,965
March	15,483	12,193	85,041	2,926	98	115,741	320,225	248,145	143,716	4,165	77,723	793,974	909,715
Total	209,984	216,141	366,387	58,439	8,244	859,205	4,584,924	3,002,018	2,009,949	184,636	495,882	10,275,409	11,136,814

British India.

1910-11.

Month.	Beetroot Sugar.						Cane Sugar.						General Total.
	Bengal.	Bombay	Sind.	Madras	Burma.	Total.	Bengal.	Bombay.	Sind.	Madras.	Burma.	Total.	
April ..	77,099	86,057	105,768	18,876	5,103	292,903	144,480	67,450	21,725	3,850	7,483	244,988	537,891
May ..	4,482	525	10,049	1,055	107	16,228	75,772	384,697	148,570	3,850	3,383	616,272	632,500
June ..	113	174	137	541	137	1,102	163,114	168,518	30,229	3,848	800	366,509	367,611
July ..	128	247	44	48	63	530	344,317	95,574	224,958	29,737	19,941	714,527	715,057
August ..	151	142	21	26	67	407	450,049	73,126	69,299	14,857	27,586	634,917	635,324
September ..	75	202	86	44	58	465	1,117,415	547,489	285,468	35,857	51,682	2,037,911	2,038,376
October ..	214	103	165	40	73	595	943,920	454,319	399,018	53,977	56,032	1,907,266	1,907,861
November ..	229	1,139	191	65	55	1,679	640,989	286,504	255,533	45,742	59,223	1,287,991	1,289,670
December ..	6,118	27,370	98,380	1,260	93	133,221	467,421	341,154	121,340	4,972	33,584	968,471	1,081,692
January ..	7,767	40,664	86,299	1,549	1,134	137,413	391,872	237,191	105,620	59,092	69,729	863,504	1,000,917
February ..	22,908	44,928	115,185	7,924	197	191,142	302,265	302,041	138,690	17,311	29,477	789,784	980,926
March ..	25,979	40,285	110,065	5,578	179	182,086	226,615	368,493	115,604	2,032	72,955	785,699	957,785
Total ..	145,363	241,836	526,390	37,016	7,266	957,871	5,268,229	3,326,556	1,916,054	275,125	431,875	11,217,839	12,175,700

The figures tabulated above do not tally perfectly with the statistics mentioned on Page 62, and data are not available to account for the small discrepancies.

67

Of the British Indian provinces the Punjab is the greatest consumer of imported sugar ; then follow Bombay, the United Provinces, Eastern Bengal and Assam, the Central Provinces and, last, Bengal ; which shows that districts which have an important home industry have, as a rule, foreign imported sugar placed on their markets.

The sugar *exportation of British India* is not of much importance, though it used to be of far more consequence. In 1851 India exported 1,607,508 cwt., 1,506,051 of which went to the United Kingdom ; in 1861 these figures had gone down to 845,961 and 696,012 respectively. This was almost entirely refined sugar, but when the British refining industry made some progress, the exportation of raw sugar increased, to be followed by a period of gradual decrease. This also refers to white sugar.

Exportation of Sugar from British India in cwt.

	Raw Sugar.		Refined Sugar.
1877/78	366,997	..	477,128
1878/79	—	..	51,053
1882/92 (average)	1,145,685	1888/89	34,523
1892/04 ,, ...	733,654		
1904/05	192,890		
1905/06	230,498		
1906/07	164,299		
1907/08	198,843	..	20,564
1908/09	174,538	..	20,725
1909/10	123,440	..	21,402
1910/11	175,095	..	26,732

V—The Future.

It has repeatedly been pointed out by various people that should the cultivation and manufacturing methods in India be only slightly improved and modernized, the country would not only be able to supply its own wants, but would also rank among the sugar exporting countries. This has been said so often, and yet the planted area remains stationary, and the production per acre does not increase, whereas the imports do. No doubt there are important and insurmountable difficulties which prevent the immediate extension and improvement of the cane cultivation. What these are and whether they are the outcome of conservatism or of poverty among the native population, of too much dividing-up of property, or of lack of co-operation it is hard to tell, and we do not see any promise of a radical change in the near future

Consequently, there is every reason to believe that British India, in spite of its gigantic sugar production, will remain for some time to come a sugar importing country, to whose markets beet as well as cane sugar will continue to be taken.

Literature :
Reports of the Netherlands Consuls of Bombay and Calcutta.
Agricultural Ledger.
Imperial Gazetteer for India.
Sir George Watt. *Commercial Products of India.*
Newlands. *Sugar : A Handbook for Planters and Refiners.*
Agricultural Statistics of India.
Agricultural Journal of India.
Saiyid Muhamad Hadi. *Sugar Industry in the United Provinces of Agra and Oudh.*

II.

STRAITS SETTLEMENTS.

On the Malay Peninsula, in the Province Wellesley, opposite the island of Penang, and in the native State of Perak, a sugar industry is to be found which used to be of more importance than it is now, as it is slowly but steadily being supplanted by the cultivation of rubber.

Between the years 1890 and 1900 the sugar industry in these parts was at its best, when in different spots ground was opened up and planted with sugar cane, to be worked up into sugar in numerous factories by Europeans and Chinese.

The first European sugar manufacturers who settled in the Malay Peninsula were Frenchmen from Mauritius, who, in the nineteenth century, started cane plantations opposite the Isle of Penang, and constructed factories, which were abandoned when the ground round them became exhausted and covered with weeds. Later on British from Demerara appeared on the scene, and laid out the plantations in the manner they were used to in their former country, being induced to do so because of the similarity between it and Demerara as regards the condition of the soil.

As a matter of fact, all the plantations are to be found near rivers and creeks, which are nothing but hollows in the plain not yet filled in by the deposits of the sea, being simply sea creeks. They do not discharge fresh water from inland, but are filled with tidal water, which is, of course, subject to ebb and flow. The entire low coast is intersected by these creeks, which wind through the country in all directions, and divide it up in a number of little islands. It is a very moist climate, and because of its proximity to the

69

equator there are no distinctly defined monsoons, but the amount of rain is spread rather regularly all over the year, as the following table for 1905 shows :—

				mm.		inches
January	..	.	.	163	..	6·5
February	..	..	..	149	..	6·0
March	..	..	..	363	..	14·0
April	..	.	..	169	..	6·6
May ..	..	..	..	160	..	6·25
June ..	..	..	..	230	.	9·2
July ..	.	..	..	109	..	4·3
August	..	..	..	221	..	8·7
September	..	..	..	254	..	10·0
October	..	..	..	350	..	13·75
November	.	..	.	126	..	5 0
December	..	..	.	224	..	8 8
Total	..	.	.	2,518 mm.		99·1 ins.

The average annual temperature is about 25°C. (77°F.), varying but little for the different months.

There are no rivers to speak of, and irrigation is altogether out of the question, so that cultivation is absolutely dependent on the rain ; this, however, on account of the equal distribution of the rainfall is no drawback. The jungle land is given by the Government in " quit rent " to the farmers at a low rate. In this way one can obtain immediate possession of extensive tracts of land, but the places where Malay natives have settled down are precisely marked off and excluded from the transaction. The first part of the cultivation process is to provide the creeks with dykes to prevent salt water from coming in at high tide It is a much simpler plan to shut off these creeks from the sea through a " stop off," or dam, as near the sea as possible, which saves the erection of dykes along the creeks and their by-streams It is quite safe to do this, as they are only in contact with the sea, and do not carry any water from the land. Only in case of Malay compounds lying on the creek in an inland direction can such a damming off be brought about by the promise of indemnification, as the sea-fisheries suffer much from it, if they are not altogether stopped on that account. After the sea water has been barred from the land, the jungle is cut and the trees and weeds burned or carried away, and ditches are dug throughout the land by way of drainage canals. Near the sea these ditches end in a sort of wooden lock, with a moveable gate which is fixed at the top, but can open seaward at the bottom. During ebb the water being higher in the canal than outside pushes the gate open, and flows into the sea. When, on the contrary, the sea water comes rushing up in time of flood tide, it pushes the gate shut, and is thus barred from spreading over the land. Besides this network of drainage canals, a number of wide canals is dug for navigation, and this also forms a coherent network which, however, does not communicate with any of the drainage canals. These canals for navigation are so deep that a well-laden barge can easily pass along, so that all the necessary sugar cane can be transported by water. When the newly laid out land has been rid of its superfluous saline content by the rains, shallow furrows are dug, 120 ft. in length, at distances of 6 ft. apart, wherein cane tops are planted, which soon grow up and do not require manuring for the first year or so. A year after the planting is done the cane is cut, and fresh cuttings are planted again in the same fields in such a manner that the new rows lie between the old ones. Weeding is practised, and efforts are made to keep down the "lalang" (*Imperata arundinacea*), the roots of which grow to an intertwined mass, and to prepare the soil for cane cultivation again. In case of lack of labour for this purpose, the field is abandoned altogether, and a fresh plot is taken up, so that cane cultivation in the Straits has often caused a field which was originally arable land to be turned into a "lalang" field, which only after much toil and labour can be made fit for cane cultivation again. The great drawback of cane cultivation in Malay Peninsula undertakings is lack of labour. The natives do not wish to do a regular day's work, and that is why the planters have to employ labourers from other countries.

Indentured Javanese are mostly employed in digging work, and British-Indian coolies, chiefly from Madras, are used for field and factory work. These immigrants leave their country under a three years' indenture, and earn from fifteen to twenty dollar-cents (one Straits dollar = 2s. 4d.) a day, and when doing piece-work they make more, as well as getting free housing and other privileges. When their time of indenture is over they may go on serving as free labourers, and then, of course, receive higher wages, or receive more money through piece-work.

The importation of indentured coolies is carried on in the face of great difficulties, and so it is very hard to have the entire plantation under one's own management. In order to meet these difficulties in some way, the planters have adopted another system besides that of planting under their own management. They provide Chinese labourers with plots of fresh soil, the trees on which are cut, and which have the necessary dykes and partitions. Each Chinese contractor gets a plot of two orlong* ($2\frac{2}{3}$ acres), and if they work in co-operation, as is often the case among the Chinese, the combined workers receive so many times that area as the number of workers amounts to. The management procures the cane cuttings, and further advances them implements and some money each month on credit. As soon as the cane is ripe, according to the management's judgment, it is cut by the Chinese and taken to the mill to be crushed, either at their own expense or at that of the mill owner.

* 1 orlong = $1\frac{1}{3}$ acre = 0·535 hectare.

Asia.

The payment is 1·5 dollar-cents per gallon of juice, which money they receive after the money advanced has been deducted. Proper control should, of course, prevent the money advanced from exceeding the value of cane, and should see to the work being done under a manager's supervision. This system has given good results, but it is necessary to take good care not to be altogether dependent on the Chinese farmers ; for that reason it is not wise to dispose of all the land in this way, but rather to keep some portion under European management. As a rule, one proceeds in the following way : the new land is given to Chinese farmers, who plant cane on it during three consecutive years without manuring ; then the factory itself plants cane on it year after year, without letting it lie fallow or be planted alternately with other crops, but with the aid of manure. Finally, the "lalang" has to be dug out, or a fresh start is made, abandoning the old soil altogether, which is used by Chinese tapioca growers after they have succeeded in rooting out the weeds by untiring efforts.

The canes that are planted are White or Chinese, Ribbon, Purple, or Bourbon Cane (imported from Martinique). The White cane is grown by the Chinese labourers in preference to other kinds, because it grows to a great height and weight, and contains plenty of juice that is easily extracted, so it is most profitable to them, as they are paid according to the amount of juice extracted.

Both Ribbon and Purple canes are stunted in growth, and are subject to disease, and their sugar quality is low, and yet the greater part of the plantations consist of this kind. The Bourbon cane is tall, heavy, and rich in sugar, and not very liable to disease. Borers are seldom met with, but a kind of large beetle does occur, which tunnels the cane from bottom to top. The old beetles lay their eggs on a manure heap, and through the compost they gain access to the cane, so that the hatched insects, which are not cane enemies by nature, are induced to attack cane.

The cane on the whole is short, and its juice poor, which is due to the low soil, the scanty tillage, the little sunshine, and the steady rain. On the best plantations no greater cane yields than 43,500 to 52,200 kg. per hectare, or 17·3 to 20·75 tons per acre, are realized.

The cost of an acre of cane is about $52, so that a ton of cane on the field costs $2·40, which, together with transport expenses, costs the factory $2·56 to $3·20.

The Europeans manufacture a kind of white sugar, and obtain 7·5 per cent. of sugar on the weight of cane. The Chinese work up the cane juice to concentrated juice, like the British-Indian *gur*, and, of course, in this way realize a greater quantity, as all the impurities of the juice remain in the sugar and add to the weight.

In the year 1896 there were three European factories in the British Province Wellesley, and one in the State of Perak, besides a great many Chinese undertakings, most of which were equipped with steam power.

Cochin China.

The total cane planted area was estimated at 14,200 acres, or 5,670 hectares, in 1898, and its total production at 15,000 tons. This increased up to the year 1900, and amounted to 7,500 tons for Wellesley, and to 13,000 tons for Perak ; but since rubber has become so much more profitable than sugar, a great part of the land destined for cane cultivation has changed considerably. In the first place, rubber does not require quite so much manual labour as sugar cane, and the work is easier, so that it is not so difficult to get labour for rubber as for cane fields. Moreover, rubber yields far more profit than sugar ever will do ; and so, taking things as they are, the sugar industry of the Straits Settlements is not likely to revive. In Wellesley three European factories are still working, two of which grow sugar cane as a catch crop between rows of rubber trees, but will give this up when the latter grow up well. The Chinese plantations in the provinces have all stopped working. The yearly sugar production amounts at the present moment to 7,500 tons, all of which, except what is required for local consumption, is sent to England ; but this is sure to diminish in quantity. In Perak there are three Chinese sugar works, with a yearly output of 4,000 tons, but these, too, are gradually giving up sugar cultivation, in consequence of which the once promising sugar industry of the Malay Peninsula will have died out in a very short time.

III.

COCHIN CHINA.

In the extensive French colonies of Cochin China, Annam, and Tonkin a kind of impure, brown, raw sugar is prepared by the native population on a large scale for their own consumption, but is very seldom exported ; and it is said that in Annam especially the land is extremely suitable for cane cultivation. It is impossible to get at the exact figures as regards the extension of this industry, but the yearly output is estimated at 50,000 tons of raw brown sugar.

One hundred and ninety-two tons of sugar were imported into France from Indo-China in 1897, but no figures of the French imports are available for the other years.

IV.

CHINA.

ALTHOUGH China during many centuries has cultivated sugar cane and prepared cane sugar, this has never got past the stage of a home industry, and sugar is still being prepared in the same primitive and wasteful way as it was done centuries ago. Farmers often plant sugar cane on a small scale, and what is not wanted for direct consumption is sold to small manufacturers, who prepare sugar from it in a very simple way. The cane is ground between vertical wooden or stone rollers, which are turned by cattle, and the cane has to go through three times before being crushed sufficiently. The juice is put into the boiling pans, of which there are five as a rule, and, as has been explained before, the juice is scooped from one pan into another as evaporation proceeds. The rawest form of sugar is the concentrated and cooled cane juice, from which a white sugar is gained by draining off and covering. For this purpose the brown sugar is put into casks with perforated bottoms, and is covered up with a layer of grass which is kept moist. The moisture from the grass gradually trickles down, penetrates the sugar, washes the brown syrup from the crystals, and carries it away through the holes in the bottom, while the moist soft white sugar is left as a residue. The syrup is used for sweetening food or baking cakes, while the sugar, when dried in the sun, forms the commercial article. This sugar is also melted again in hot water, and slowly re-crystallized to candy. One can easily imagine that this most primitive and yet expensive mode of preparation no longer holds its own in competition with the far superior factory methods of the adjacent countries, and though the sugar consumption in China increases, it is the foreign countries which profit by this expanding demand, while the inland industry rather decreases.

Since the sugar industry in China, as has been pointed out, is a home industry, the produce of which is consumed in the immediate neighbourhood of its manufacture, we cannot very well give the exact figures of its output, but when we go through the export figures of Chinese sugar to other Chinese harbours, we see a gradual decrease in the quantity of sugar exported by China, a fact which benefits Hong Kong, Java, Japan, and even Europe.

The principal producing districts are:—

I. SWATOW.

The sugar cane here chiefly grows in the Prefecture of Chao Chow Fu and its sugar, consisting of brown, white and candy sugar, is mostly exported to the northern harbours of China, i.e., Shanghai, Newchang, Tientsin, Chinkiang, and Hankow, while only a small portion is transhipped to Hong Kong Siam, and the Straits Settlements.

China.

The sugar exported by Swatow for the last few years has been as follows—in piculs of 133·13 lbs. and in tons:—

Year.	Brown.		White.		Total.	
	Piculs.	Tons.	Piculs.	Tons	Piculs.	Tons.
1891 ..	826,888	49,613	831,647	49,899	1,658,535	99,512
1892 ..	625,708	37,542	563,287	33.797	1,188,995	71,339
1893 ..	544,700	32,682	470,126	28,208	1,014,826	60,890
1894 ..	457,969	27,478	464,488	27,869	922,457	55,347
1895 ..	690,518	41,431	630,640	37,838	1,321,158	79,269
1896 ..	701,231	42,074	625,854	37,551	1,327,085	79,625
1897 ..	704,270	42,256	629,780	37,868	1,334,050	80,124
1898 ..	789,298	47,358	667,465	40,048	1,456,763	87,406
1899 ..	1,028,218	61,693	796,910	47,815	1,825,128	109,508
1900 ..	846,261	50,776	531,023	31,861	1,377,284	82,637
1901 ..	814,402	48,864	572,198	34,332	1,386,600	83,196
1902 ..	640,264	38,416	449,010	26,941	1,089,274	65,357
1903 ..	590,974	35,458	421,025	25,261	1,011,852	60,719
1904 ..	591,974	35,518	473,563	28,414	1,065,537	63,932
1905 .	492,991	29,579	311,496	18,690	804,387	48,269
1906 ..	325,821	19,599	231,443	13,807	557,264	33,406
1907 ..	573,337	34,400	316,845	19,011	890,182	53,411
1908 ..	481,244	28,875	346,231	20,774	827,475	49,649
1909 ..	297,018	17,821	198,221	11,893	495,239	29,714
1910 ..	612,619	38,288	220,510	13,783	833,129	42,071

Owing to the heavy competition of Hong Kong and Java sugars in the Yangtse Valley and the harbours of North China, the formerly large Swatow exportation has sunk to a low figure.

It may be taken for granted that about 22,000 acres are planted with cane in Swatow, and that about 2,000 mills are engaged in sugar manufacture. These work, on an average, 100 days every year, and yield between 600 and 1,000 piculs of sugar in harvest time. In the districts of Cheng-hai cane is being bought by the sugar manufacturers from the planters, but in other districts where the plantations are more scattered each cane planter in his turn hires the mill and grinds his own sugar cane.

The cane is planted in early spring, and is cut ten to twelve months later ; then three ratoon crops are reaped, each of which takes a year   Finally, the

75

roots are dug out, and the soil is planted with other crops. Oil cakes of soja beans are used as manure.

2. AMOY

In the districts of Tungan and Chang Chow most of the planting is done. The better kinds of sugar are exported to the northern harbours of China, to Tientsin and Shanghai, and the inferior kinds to Foochow, Ningpo, Cheefoo, and Newchang.

The last-mentioned harbour exports much less than it used to do, for while in 1896 its exportation amounted to 278,761 cwts., in 1906 it had gone down to 79,352 cwts., no doubt in part owing to the competition of Java, Hong Kong, and Japanese sugar. In 1909 the exportations of sugar amounted to 79,478 cwts., and in 1910 to as much as 123,322 cwts

3. CANTON, KOWLOON, LAPPA.

The principal sugar producing districts used to be Waichow, Tsinshing, and Fungkow, but in consequence of bad crops, rebellion, and internal commotions the sugar production in these provinces has deteriorated, and they have ceased to be the important producers of yore. Formerly large quantities of sugar were exported from Waichow to Hong Kong, but this is no longer the case, and their only exportation of sweetstuffs is that of the sugar cane itself, which is sold as a dainty. The export trade in 1905 amounted to 7,336 cwts. of sugar, in 1906 only to 67, while in 1900 it was still 160,000 cwts

4. KIUNGCHOW IN THE ISLAND OF HAINAN.

Sugar is being produced in the Island of Hainan, South China, with Kiungchow as an export harbour. This sugar, as well as the sugar brought from the opposite peninsula, Leichow, is transhipped in steamers to Macao and Hong Kong.

The exportation of raw sugar amounted to :—

174,501 cwts. in 1897.	192,752 cwts. in 1901.
120,041 ,, 1898.	294,803 ,, 1902.
175,548 ,, 1899.	68,028 ,, 1909.
104,752 ,, 1900.	194,507 ,, 1910.

5. CHUNKING, IN THE PROVINCE SZECHUAN.

In addition to the provinces of the sea coast already mentioned, much cane is planted and sugar produced in Central China, on the banks of the Yangtse-Kiang. Here, too, manufacture is carried on as a home industry, and though the quantity of sugar produced may be very large, it is not possible to know the exact figures. The quantity of sugar exported to foreign parts is known ; but as this is only an inconsiderable portion of the total production, we might just as well leave it unmentioned. The kind of sugar is again of a light brown colour, or fine crystal sugar made white through draining off the molasses.

Besides its own sugar, which, although we cannot quote the exact figures, seems to decrease instead of increasing, China demands more sugar, which is imported from abroad, viz., brown sugar from Java and the Philippines ; white crystal and second sugar from Java ; and refined sugar from European countries, Hong Kong, and Japan.

The import figures, both in piculs and in tons, have been for the last twenty years as follows :—

Year.	Piculs.	Tons.	Year.	Piculs.	Tons.
1891 ..	290,035	.. 17,402	1901 ..	2,564,787	.. 153,867
1892 ..	531,614	.. 31,897	1902 ..	4,473,222	. 268,393
1893 ..	1,549,297	.. 92,958	1903 .	3,169,914	.. 190,195
1894 ..	1,823,890	. 109,433	1904 ..	3,708,800	.. 222,528
1895 ..	1,483,217	.. 88,993	1905 ..	4,496,164	.. 367,770
1896 ..	1,636,129	.. 98,168	1906 .	6,575,742	.. 394,544
1897 ..	2,298,427	.. 137,905	1907 ..	5,095,100	. 305,706
1898 ..	1,813,202	.. 108,792	1908 ..	4,129,080	.. 247,745
1899 ..	2,077,959	.. 124,677	1909 ..	5,485,765	.. 329,196
1900 ..	1,291,289	.. 77,474	1910 ..	4,255,543	.. 255,333

Literature :
C. Kraay. Sugar number of *De Indische Mercuur.*
British and American Consular Reports.
Imperial Maritime Customs Report.

V.

JAPAN.

IN the several islands which form part of Japan proper, sugar cane is cultivated and cane sugar prepared in a primitive way, which branch of industry has developed during the last few years. The principal sugar cane cultivating tract is found in the Riu-Kiu group, which extends to 24° N. Lat In 1902 the islands Okinawa, Miyako, and Jajeyama, all belonging to the same group, produced 19,788 tons of sugar, which quantity in 1908 rose to 26,377 tons. Then the Oshima Islands, south of Hondo, have a yearly output of 7,500 tons, and some sugar is grown in the northern islands, so that we can fix 40,000 tons for the local sugar production of Japan.

The sugar produced is brown, and is prepared from juice in a very primitive way, and is used entirely in the island of its production, or is transported to Kagoshima and Osaka.

We may expect some change for the better in this very primitive state of affairs, as a company with a capital of 2 million yen* has been floated, called the " Okinama Seito Kabushiki Kaisha," in order to plant sugar cane

* 1 yen is about 2s 1d.

in the Riu-Kiu Islands, and to work it up according to modern practice. We do not possess any more details about this scheme, but as the Riu-Kiu Islands are not far from Formosa, where the sugar industry flourishes, it is quite possible that in these islands, too this branch of industry will do well, and contribute towards the realization of the Japanese economic ideal, *i.e.*, to become independent of foreign countries as regards their sugar supply.

It has not attained to this ideal state yet, but the island of Formosa has produced increasing quantities of sugar during the last five years; while we notice a steady decrease in the importation of foreign sugar into Japan, which the following statistics show, and which during the present and future years may become still more pronounced :—

Country of origin.	1900	1901	1902	1903	1904	1905	1906	1907	1908	1909	1910
China	655,996	352,504	223,008	267,954	271,489	117,402	114,044	81,211	111,972	110,626	9,460
Hong Kong	1 217,947	1,473,012	411,708	260.834	347.880	111 976	46,414	62,820	75.877	46,004	27,277
Philippines	358,675	534,776	239 477	572,198	336,046	62,221	89,073	269 548	211,772	93,684	6,831
The Netherlands	—	4,251	569	—	—	—	—	—	—	—	—
United States	668	1,176	1,450	2,799	2 558	5,142	6,109	6 116	19,155	4,454	5,596
Hawaii	—	—	1,995	2	—	—	—	—	—	—	—
Germany	479,118	1,192,828	539,549	451,398	166,106	42,923	263,584	65,050	29,820	434	31
Great Britain	1,692	7,116	675	23	11	—	—	—	—	—	—
Australia	4,212	—	84	—	—	—	—	—	—	—	—
Austria-Hungary	439,162	560,850	177,952	422,243	28,072	845	55,659	32,394	6,326	1	—
Belgium	13,969	45,616	22,917	89,365	—	—	6,482	8	—	—	—
British India	3,173	4,557	26	—	3	—	—	—	—	—	—
Dutch India	447,991	390.287	475,191	1,830,766	2,642,161	1 822 672	3,186,910	2 690,383	2,868 903	1,986,028	1,954,101
France	171	454	454	206	285	—	—	—	—	—	—
Russia	2,833	17,270	299	25,379	310,165	2,540	8	166	—	—	—
Other Countries	420,678	342,778	555 358	316	27	1,752	17,849	88,689	5,256	278	150
Total piculs	4,045,785	4,928,075	2,651,212	3,923,488	4,104,753	2,168,473	3,786.127	3,296.885	3 323,541	2.241,507	2 003,446
In Tons	242,747	295,685	159,073	235,409	246 285	130 108	227,168	197,783	199,412	134,490	120,207

The following table shows the imports into Japan from Formosa, and also the total imports :—

Year.	Importations from				Total.	
	Foreign Countries.		Formosa.			
	Piculs.	Tons.	Piculs.	Tons.	Piculs.	Tons.
1905	2,168,473	130,108	707,722	42,463	2,876,195	172,571
1906	3,786,127	227,168	1,090,079	65,405	4,876,206	292,573
1907	3,296,385	197,783	942,280	56,537	4,238,665	254,320
1908	3,323,541	199,412	1,035,356	62,121	4,358,897	261,533
1909	2,241,507	134,490	2,097,466	125,848	4,338,973	260,338
1910	2,003,446	120,207	3,099,616	185,977	5,103,082	306,184

Japan.

The whole of this quantity is not consumed in Japan itself, for Japan exports a considerable amount of refined sugar. This exportation first became considerable after the war with China, and now yearly increases, as the following figures show —

Exports in tons of refined sugar and candy from Japan.

	1904	1905	1906	1907	1908	1909	1910
Refined sugar	1,030	14,831	50,610	14,803	17,145	29,249	41,481
Candy ..	374	392	454	422	399	146	148
Total ..	1,404	15,223	51,064	15,225	17,544	29,395	41,629

The refined sugar is chiefly exported to China and Korea, while the exportation to other countries is of little account.

In 1907 the Japanese refineries began to work up Formosan sugar on a large scale ; the Kolagashi Refiners' Group melted 40,593 piculs (2,436 tons) of the total of 3,000,000 piculs (100,000 tons), which is the quantity usually melted in all the Japanese refineries.

The reason why in the years preceding 1907 a comparatively small quantity of Formosan sugar was worked up in the refineries is to be found in the fact that this sugar generally was a brown concrete sugar, which was used for direct consumption, while the raw cane sugar from Java was more suitable for refining purposes. As Formosa is exporting more and more crystal sugar, a greater portion of it is being refined, which means a gradual decrease in the Java sugar importation.

Import duty has to be paid on foreign sugar imported into Japan, which was levied until 16th July, 1911, as follows (in yen per picul) :—

		General tariff.	Conventional tariff.
1.	Sugar below No. 8 D.S. ..	1·65	.. —
2.	Sugar from 8—15 D.S. ..	2·25	.. —
3.	Sugar from 15—20 D.S. ..	3·25	.. 0·748
4.	Sugar No. 20 and higher ..	3·50	.. 0·827

After the termination of the commercial treaties the import duty became levied as follows :—

1.	Sugar below No. 11 D.S.	..	..	2·50
2.	Sugar from 11—15 D.S.	..	..	3·10
3.	Sugar from 15—18 D.S.	..	..	3·35
4.	Sugar from 18—21 D.S.	..	..	4·25
5.	Candy	..	..	7·40
6.	Other kinds of sugar ..	..	..	4·65

Asia.

When sugar imported from abroad is used for direct consumption, the import duty is levied in full. But should the sugar be refined in Japanese refineries, and its produce be used for consumption in Japan, then the Government refunds a sum of 1·45 yen per picul sugar below No. 8, and a sum of 1·95 yen per picul sugar from Nos. 8 to 15. This amount of money refunded is limited to 1,000,000 piculs, but 1 yen per picul is to be allowed on any excess above this quantity. The subsidy for the year 1910-11 to refiners in this way is estimated at 2,830,000 yen, or £288,896. When directly consumed, their own and Formosan sugar enjoys a privilege of 1·65 and 2·25 yen, according to its quality, and when refined a privilege of 1·65 yen — 1·45=0·20 yen or 2·25 — 1·95 = 0·30 yen per picul. One can understand that foreign sugar is used as much as possible for refining, while Formosan sugar is used for direct consumption. As Formosa is gradually producing more and more sugar, the amount of sugar gained will exceed the demand of unrefined sugar for consumption, and, consequently, the refineries will use a steadily increasing quantity of Formosan sugar for melting. It was decided to cancel the drawback of foreign raw sugar refined in Japan on 1st April, 1912, on the ground that the new Customs tariff which came into force in July, 1911, will give sufficient protection against the competition of foreign sugar ; but we shall be surprised if the Japanese refiners, who have much to say in the matter, are not indemnified in some way or other for the loss.

Besides the import duty on foreign sugar, Japan raises a consumption duty or excise on all sugar consumed in the country, which consequently, has to be paid on imported as well as on native sugar.

This nowadays (in yen per picul) amounts to :—

I. Sugar below No. 8 D.S. :
    (a) Brown sugar in barrels 2
    (b) Unrefined sugar, except centrifugalled
        or sugar other than refined, which has
        been manipulated, or made partially
        or entirely by modern machinery .. 2·50
    (e) All others 3
II. Sugar No. 8—15 D.S. 5
III. Sugar, No 15—28 D.S. 7
IV. Sugar, No. 18—21 D.S. 8
V. Sugar above No. 20 D.S. 9
VI. Candy, crystal, or sugar cubes.. 10

At the present time one pays on foreign refined sugar a total of 0·827 + 10 = 10·827 yen per picul, and on foreign sugar below No. 8, 1·65 + 3 = 4·65 yen per picul duty when used for consumption. It follows that all these duties have caused sugar to be very expensive, and have also led to a system of protection which aims at enabling Japan, in conjunction with Formosa, eventually to supply her own wants in sugar.

TAIWAN OR FORMOSA.

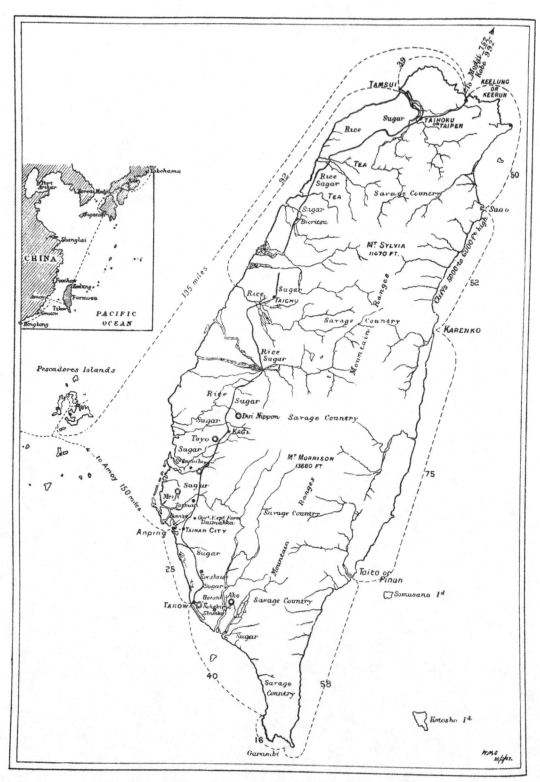

For the rest, it will depend upon legislature whether Japanese refineries, strengthened by high home prices, shall come out first in the struggle with sugar refined in Hong Kong, in the Yangtse Valley, and with Russian sugar in Manchuria. As long as the present high protection holds good, Japan will be able to supply the above-mentioned markets with refined sugar, and even extend the scope of her exportations ; but should the Government as is said, reduce its protection, it may be possible yet for Japan to produce enough refined sugar for home consumption, but exportation abroad will be out of the question then.

Literature :
Report of the Netherlands Consul at Kobe.
British and American Consular Reports.

VI.

FORMOSA.

ALTHOUGH Formosa forms part of the Japanese Empire, and is politically united with it, her sugar industry is of quite a different character to that of the other Japanese islands, and for that reason we propose to treat of it separately.

The Island of Formosa (Taiwan) lies in the China Sea between 21° 45′ and 25° 38′ N. Lat. and 120° 10′—122° E. Long. ; it is separated from the mainland by the Straits of Formosa. Its entire area covers 13,504 sq. miles. A mountain range runs through the island from north to south, which is flanked by two subsidiary ranges. The highest peak of the middle range is 13,600 ft. high, and that of the western range 9,290 ft. The highlands are rather rough, and are covered with woods, but in the south-west there is an extensive plain, which is well suited for agriculture, and here sugar is being cultivated.

The west coast is richer in bays and harbours than the east coast, so that most of the towns are built on the former. Its climate is almost tropical, and dependent on the monsoons ; the month of February is the coldest, with an average temperature of 51·6° F. (10·9° C.) on the coast, and the month of July is the hottest, with an average temperature of 72·5° F. (22·5° C.). The rainfall is very considerable, and in 1898 amounted for the town of Kelung to no less than 206 ins.

Formosa, together with the Pescadores, on 1st October, 1905 had a population of 3,039,751 inhabitants—57,335 of which were Japanese, 8,973 Chinese, 163 of other nationalities, 2,492,784 of Chinese origin from Fukin,

397,195 Chinese from Kantung, 506 from other parts of China, and 46,432 semi-civilized and 36,363 uncivilized savages. Of the latter about 35,076, or almost the entire number, live in the wild mountainous district of Taito, while the half-civilized tribes are found all over the islands.

The population of the Pescadores at the date given was 56,327, 2,083 of which were Japanese.

As Formosa is very narrow, being not more than seventy-seven miles wide, its rivers are short, and only the Dakusui and Tamsuikei are navigable. The network of railway, on the other hand, which, of course, is restricted to the western part of the island, is extensive, and joins the towns of Tainoku with Kelung, and with Tainan and Takao.

Besides these public railways, there are extensive light railways on the plantations for the transportation of cane and sugar, amounting in all to 220 miles; they also connect the plantations with the main line.

The sugar industry in Formosa dates from a long while back; we find it mentioned that in 1622 the Dutch East Indian Company sent a cargo of 796 piculs (48 tons) of Formosan powder sugar to the Netherlands, which dispatch was now and then followed by others, till the flourishing state of the sugar cultivation in the West Indian colonies made the importation of East Indian sugar less profitable, and drove the Formosan sugar out of the western markets. In spite of this, the sugar industry in Formosa spread so that during the last years of Chinese dominion the sugar production amounted to 60,000 to 80,000 tons every year. The greater part of this consisted of a soft brown finely-grained sugar, while only a small portion of the production was the so-called " white sugar." The latter kind was obtained by draining off the syrup from brown sugar, or by claying, and, consequently, was by no means the white sugar of the present day.

When, in 1895, Formosa became part of the Japanese Empire, there were about 1,000 small factories, which were all worked by buffaloes and prepared brown or clayed sugar. Half this sugar was used for home consumption, and the rest was exported to China and Japan by Chinese traders.

The species of cane that was mostly cultivated was a green variety that yielded little juice, but which had the advantage over a red type that was also grown in Formosa of never dying off, however much it was neglected, which was usually the case. This kind of cane, called " Tekchia." is reckoned to yield on an average 8 tons per acre (20,000 kg. per ha.) each crop. About 45 per cent of juice on the cane was obtained, while the rendement of moist brown sugar was 6 per cent for the green sort of Tekchia, and 8 per cent for the red kind, i.e., an average of 9½ cwts. per acre (1,200 kg. per ha.).

Although the Japanese had seized the Island of Formosa, they found subduing it no easy task, as the inhabitants did not at all like the idea of coming under Japanese rule. First of all they founded a kind of republic, which, after a heavy struggle, was suppressed by the Japanese; and only in 1898 did the Japanese get possession of the island. In 1902 another armed rebellion was suppressed ; but since then there has not been any further disturbance.

Not till 1900 could the Japanese authorities find time to think of repairing the damage done by the war, and of developing what resources the island could boast of ; but then they set to work with a zest which may be realized from the rapid way in which the sugar industry began to flourish. In June, 1902, a law was promulgated for the encouragement of sugar cultivation, in consequence of which a Sugar Bureau was established in Tainan, to superintend all affairs dealing with the sugar industry. The first work done by this office was to send out young Japanese students to countries where the sugar industry was at a high degree of development, especially in Germany, Java, and Hawaii, in order to study the industry thoroughly, and to report what might be of use for Formosa. At the same time, other varieties of cane were imported from foreign countries, planted in different places, and their peculiarities studied.

The experimental station for the new cane was founded at Daimokko, and it was not long before some of the new species appeared to excel the cane planted hitherto in Formosa. The Striped Tanna and the Lahaina varieties yielded a very satisfactory product, but required great quantities of irrigation water and constant care, circumstances which were against their retention. The Rose Bamboo, imported from Hawaii, on the contrary, could stand a rougher treatment and an unsatisfactory water supply, and yet yield an output gratifying in all respects, so that the planting of this kind of cane was strongly recommended by the Sugar Bureau.

Apart from this, sugar factories which were founded obtained during five years a Government subsidy of 6 per cent. yearly on the *paid-up capital*, or a lump subsidy of 20 per cent. on the value of factory and installation. There were other cases in which promoters borrowed machinery from the Government for five years, which meant that the Government paid for the machinery and claimed the money from the hirers only after five years had elapsed. The cane planters could also get land on very moderate terms, and even manure was gratuitously provided by the Government, on condition that the planters pledged themselves not to leave off sugar cultivation for the following five years. On 1st April, 1911, most of these privileges were withdrawn.

When these restrictions were being planned, the Taiwan Seito Kaisha (Taiwan Sugar Company) was founded in 1900, with a Government subsidy of 60,000 yen for each of the first five years. The capital amounted to 500,000 yen, and it was meant to work up purchased cane and export the sugar. This factory was ready in November, 1901, and began to grind, but the Chinese farmers soon appeared to be unwilling to sell cane to the factory, so they resolved to plant cane for themselves. This led to an increase of the capital to 1 million yen. The company reckoned on producing 30 tons of sugar each day during the 150 crushing days, which would mean an output of 4,500 tons each crushing season ; but the first year, 1902, realized only 20,000 piculs, or 1,200 tons.   This factory was favourably situated on the railway, halfway between Takao and Tainan, and, moreover, was privileged in only having to pay half of the tariff for having its goods conveyed by the State railway.

At the same time, two factories belonging to Chinese were started through the assistance and pressure of the Government, both situated near Tainan. Chiefly owing to difficulties experienced when sugar cane was bought, and also because they were not conversant with the modern kind of machinery thrust upon them, and, finally, because of quarrels with the experts of the Sugar Bureau, these two factories yielded little result, and all efforts to improve the sugar industry proved of no avail.   The Chinese farmers refused to sell their cane to the manufacturers, and chose to grind it in their own buffalo mills in the old primitive way, so that the Government's plans to turn Formosa into a second Java fell through.   The natives, too, refused to plant the new kind of cane, although the tops for planting could be had gratis, and although they were provided with manure and irrigation facilities, and enjoyed a subsidy if they would only plant a better kind of cane than the rubbish they were hitherto wont to use.

When all their efforts for encouragement, guidance, and instruction were opposed by the distrust and conservatism among the natives, the Japanese Government took stronger measures, and in June, 1905, issued a set of ordinances to the following effect :—

Anyone wishing to erect a modern sugar factory must first obtain permission from the Director of the Sugar Bureau, who will mark out the district within which the applicant is to be allowed to buy sugar cane, and where no other sugar works may be started.   Anyone planting sugar cane in that district is under obligation to sell it to the factory, and is not free to export it outside the district, nor to use it for any other purpose, so that the factory enjoys the monopoly of buying all the sugar cane planted there.   On the other hand, the factory is bound to take all the cane planted in the district, and is not free to refuse a part of the planting should the supply exceed their wants.   Cane planters are not allowed to grind their cane in their own buffalo mills, unless permitted to do so, and as the Sugar Bureau means to promote modern methods of sugar cultivation, these licences are not easily granted.

In some districts which have no cane cultivation of their own, large extensions of soil may be ceded free of cost to sugar undertakings.   The only condition stipulated is that the factory should really work at a certain time with a capacity, arranged beforehand.   When this is the case the land becomes the property of the factory as soon as it is entirely cultivated ; but should the concession not be acted on in good time, it is cancelled, and the factory has to be pulled down.

These restrictions immediately influenced the industry for the better, for at the present day fifteen big companies, with a paid-in capital of more than £2,500,000 sterling, manufacture sugar in the modern way in the Island of Formosa.

Formosa.

In 1908 only two buffalo mills existed out of the 1,000 which were in use at the time of Japan's conquest of this island. There were, however, 50 factories worked by steam, which ground 40 to 200 tons of cane every twenty-four hours; and 11 big sugar works, 7 of which have a capacity of 1,200 tons of cane per twenty-four hours, and 4 a capacity of 500 to 1,000 tons.

During 1909, 1910, and 1911 a great many new factories were added, while for 1912 some more are under construction. At the present time (1911) 29 big factories are in working, and 9 are under construction, all of them brand new, excellently fitted out, and equipped with the latest and most economical machinery by British, American and German firms. In November, 1910, it was announced that no more charters would be granted for the time being for the formation of sugar manufacturering companies, nor for the extension of existing mills, the object being to check the expected over-production of sugar in the island in excess of the demands of Japan for direct consumption and for refining, pending the opening of foreign markets. No period has been fixed for this limitation, which is, however, officially stated to be a temporary measure.

All the land on the west side set apart for the sugar industry is divided among the big companies, while on the east side there are some 10,000 acres available for the sugar cane cultivation, which the Sugar Bureau is willing to dispose of should there be parties eager to apply. As the advantages on the east coast for navigation are few as compared with the west, plenty of ground remains to be disposed of, nobody having as yet applied for it.

This change in the state of affairs has, of course, been opposed by the native farmers, so that the cane planted area of a district has, as a rule, gone down in the year following the allotting of ground to a factory; but as soon as the farmers found that the produce of the cane sold to a factory exceeded that of other crops, they gradually fell back again on cane cultivation, the more so as it was advantageous owing to the Government's premium for planting Rose Bamboo cane.

If the manufacturers are alive to their own interests, pay well for the cane, and advance money to the planters in order to help them through the bad time when the cane is still in the field, then the supply of cane will be so abundant that there is more chance of the factory being too small to hold it than of the raw material supply being insufficient. One should not forget that though the manufacturers have the monopoly as regards buying cane, the planters are not forced to plant it, so that should the factory offer too low a price the planters grow other crops than cane, and as the factory cannot import cane from other parts it cannot work at its full capacity, which, of course, must mean great loss to an industrial undertaking. For this very reason the cane price is kept high enough to be profitable for the planter, while it has to be approved of by the Government as well.

Asia.

The factories built during the last four years have been erected without any subsidy or help from the Government, which shows the satisfactory state of affairs in Formosa, and the independent position of the manufacturers.

In order to support the planters and to extend the Rose Bamboo cane cultivation, the Sugar Bureau provides manure to a value of 20 yen gratuitously for each koh* planted with this kind of cane, on condition that the planter himself puts 25 yen worth of manure (that is 45 yen in all) into the ground. The manure can be bought at net cost from the Sugar Bureau, and paid for after the harvest is reaped, and no interest will be charged.

In consequence of these favourable stipulations, the cultivation of Rose Bamboo has much improved, and this kind of cane now forms 75 per cent. of the total plantation, which will soon consist of this variety altogether. While the average production of the old variety of cane used to amount to 8 tons to the acre with a rendement of 6 per cent. of brown soft sugar, the average output of Rose Bamboo per acre is 14 tons, 11 per cent. of which is turned into centrifugal sugar : that is 30 cwts. of crystallized sugar against 9½ cwts. of an inferior product of times past, which fetched only two-thirds the price.

Owing to the energy of the Sugar Bureau, the produce per acre has become five times as much as it used to be, both to the profit of the planter and that of the manufacturer ; while the Government, through the consumption duty, has also benefited by it.   In 1909 60,987 koh, or 169,018 acres, land were planted with sugar cane in Formosa ; while the figures for 1910 are 90,000 koh, or 220,512 acres.

Irrigation in Formosa is still very primitive, and the plantations have to depend chiefly on rain.   Fortunately, the two monsoons in the south are fairly regular, and one can be sure of much rain during the period from June to September, and of a dry period between the months of November and April, so that cane can grow from January till October, and ripen afterwards.   The climate of the north is not nearly so favourable, and that is why most of the small and all the big sugar undertakings are found crowded together in the south.

The native farmers plough the land most unsatisfactorily with wooden ploughs, but the more modern undertakings employ steam ploughs, which turn over the soil thoroughly.   The cane grows for one year, and is planted afresh every year, without keeping ratoons.   The crushing season begins in November, and is over in May or in June at the latest, so that it amounts to 150 grinding days.

The plant of the old-fashioned factories, as is everywhere the case with primitive installations, consists of a battery of open pans placed over an open fire, together with earthenware pots, in which the massecuite is cooled and clayed, the product consisting of a soft fine brown or whitish sugar.   The

---

* 1 koh = 2·45 acres or 0·9915 hectare.

modern factories are up-to-date with crushers, mills, clarifiers, filter-presses, quadruple effects, vacuum pans, crystallization-in-motion plant, centrifugals and sugar dryers.   Their produce is centrifugal sugar, colour No. 15—16 D.S., chiefly for exportation while the exhausted molasses is sold to the natives.

Bagasse is used as fuel, to which Japanese coal, delivered at the factory for £1 15s. per ton, is added if necessary.

The factories nowadays generally pay 3 yen (6s. 2½d.) per 10 piculs* cane, and obtain about 11 per cent. of sugar out of it, so that a picul of sugar costs 2·73 yen in raw material.   When we allow 1 yen for manufacturing cost, and 0·50 yen for other expenses, and another 0·50 yen for transportation, etc., then the price of the sugar at the factory will come to 4·73 yen = 9s. 9½d. Add to this 5 yen for consumption duty (which is very seldom paid in full), the cost price increases to 9·73 yen = £1 0s. 1½d. per picul.   As the price in Japan, however, is as high as 13 yen, it is evident that when transport costs and other expenses are deducted, a considerable profit is still left to the sugar manufacturers.

The amount of 3 yen per 10 piculs paid to the planters comes to 70 yen per acre, at a production of 234 picul (14 tons) per acre ; whereas the planters, when they had worked up the cane to brown sugar in their old-fashioned way, would never have made more than 48 yen net profit, and had they treated the old Tekchia cane, certainly not more than 24 yen per acre.   Although the manufacturers are able to obtain more profit, the planter is none the worse for this new system as his gain also increases, which is simply due to a greater amount of raw material yielded by the same area, and to a better production of better paid sugar, achieved with very little more trouble and expense.

At the time of the Chinese dominion the sugar trade of Formosa rested entirely with Chinese and British merchants.   The Chinese Government raised an export duty of 18 cents (4½d.) per picul, and the sugar was sent to China and Japan, where it was consumed.

During the years 1897—1901 the exportation amounted to 34,000 tons on the average from Anping only, while that from Kelung was of little importance.

In 1901 both consumption duty and import duty were raised on sugar in Japan, and as Formosa forms part of the Japanese Empire, the sugar sent straight to Japan for consumption was exempted from import duty.

For this reason it was easy for Formosan sugar to supplant imported brown and white sugar for consumption, and as their own country people had less difficulty in importing sugar than foreigners had, the trade in Formosan sugar soon fell into the hands of Japanese merchants in Yokohama and Kobe, and the Chinese had to withdraw.   The importation into Japan was further promoted by an import duty on sugar destined for foreign countries of 0·50 yen (1s. 0½d.) per picul.

* 1 Japanese picul = 133·33 lbs. or 60·5 kg.

Later on, in 1906, this was changed into 0·45 yen per picul brown sugar, and 0·50 yen per picul white sugar, but as no Formosan sugar was exported, this export duty did not at first amount to much.

As, however, sugar manufacturers looked for foreign markets for Formosa sugar, they raised an agitation, in consequence of which the export duties were abolished in November, 1910.

The original consumption duty raised in 1901 was increased in 1906—a year of trouble—and also in 1908, and was modified again in 1909.

The amounts were, in yen per picul, as follows :—

	1901	1906
Sugar below No. 8 D.S.	1·	3·
„ from 8—15 D.S.	1·6	5·50
„ from 15—20 D.S.	2·2	8·50
„ above 20 and candy	2·8	10·

In 1909 there was a different kind of classification, and the consumption duty was levied as follows :—

Class I. Sugar below No. 8 D.S. :

Brown sugar in barrels	2 yen
Other kinds	3 „
„ II. Sugar between No. 8 and 15	5· „
„ III. „ „ No. 15 and 18	7 „
„ IV. „ „ No. 18 and 20	8 „
„ V. „ above No. 20	9 „
Candy, crystal sugar, cubes	10 „

In April, 1911, the duty on the sugar from Class I. was changed as follows :—

(a) Brown sugar in barrels ..   .. 2·00 yen
(b) Unrefined sugar, except centrifugalled 2·00   „
(c) All others ..   .. 3·00   „

When imported into Japan for direct consumption, the Formosan sugar enjoys the full protection of the Japanese import duty, and when imported for refining purposes that of the difference between the import duty and the drawback. There have been complaints about too low a classification of the consumption duty on Formosan sugar by the Customs officers, who reckon Formosan sugar to belong to a lower class for the payment of duty than should be the case. How far there is cause for these complaints, and how far this cause, if any, will continue to exist it is difficult to say ; but even without this privilege the Formosan sugar has a great advantage over other kinds of sugar when imported into Japan proper, and so it becomes clear

KOHEKIRIN MILL IN FORMOSA.

Formosa.

that so long as Japan is able to take it up, the entire Formosan sugar exportation is bound for Japan, and only the surplus will be sent to other countries. In 1911 some 10,000 tons of Formosan sugar have actually been shipped to other places than Japan, *e.g.*, to China, Korea, Canada, and Hong Kong ; but as the 1912 crop will be rather short, owing to hurricanes that befell the cane in August, it is very improbable that such exportation will take place in 1912 as well.

It is difficult to get the exact figures for the total production of Formosan sugar, as nobody knows for certain how much of the brown sugar prepared in the second-rate factories is consumed in the island itself. It is easier to get at the figures of exportation, which show that a rapid increase in the sugar production has been brought about by Japan's promotion of the sugar trade The figures are as follows :—

Formosan Sugar in tons.

1901/02	..	..	..	46,893
1902/03	..	..	..	32,992
1903/04	..	..	..	58,968
1904/05	..	..	..	49,565
1905/06	..	..	..	63,359
1906/07	..	..	..	81,448
1907/08	..	..	..	68,450
1908/09	..	..	..	122,000
1909/10	..	..	..	160,000
1910/11	..	..	..	256,950

Of the 256,950 tons sugar produced in 1910/11, 59,000 tons were brown sugar, and the rest centrifugal sugar. The first-mentioned sugar exceeded the quantity exported in former years, as almost all Philippine sugar is now sent to the United States because of the exemption from import duty there, so that there is more room for Formosan sugar in Japan. For this reason a number of licences was taken out a couple of years ago for the foundation of small factories for brown sugar, which may lead to an increase in the quantity at which it is now estimated.

The main increase, however, is due to the improved production of crystal sugar. There is a constant addition of newly installed factories, while the existing ones increase their production by turning their capacity to better account, so that the importation of Formosan crystal sugar annually improves, and may continue to do so.

According to the Dutch Consul's report at Kobe, there were in 1910 15 big sugar estates existing in the island of Formosa, 8 of which ran a number of factories installed on the most modern plan, while the other 7 were hastening to build factories for the rapid preparation of centrifugal sugar. Besides the tracts marked out by the Sugar Bureau as fields of operation for the big estates with their modern factories, there are still a number of old-fashioned sugar factories, which, provided with new machinery, manufacture exclusively brown sugar.

The modern estates are capitalized as follows, and have the number of factories mentioned either already at their disposal, or else under construction :—

Name.	Capital in million Yen.		Number of Factories.	Production in Piculs 1909-10.	In Tons.
	Nominal.	Paid-up.			
Taiwan Seito Kaisha ..	10	6·9225	5	650,000	39,000
Meizi Seito Kaisha ..	5	2·5	3	150,000	9,000
Toyo Seito Kaisha ..	5	2·5	2	150,000	9,000
Ensuiko Seito Kaisha ..	5	1·5	3	240,000	14,400
Takasago Seito Kaisha ..	2·5	0·625	1	—	—
Dai Nippon Seito Kaisha ..	12	4	2	200,000	12,000
Niitaka Seito Kaisha ..	5·5	1·25	4	—	—
Hokko Seito Kaisha ..	2·5	—	1	—	—
Rinhogen Seito Kaisha ..	2·5	2·5	1	—	—
Formosa Sugar Dev. Co. ..	0·8	0·8	1	100,000	6,000
Shinko Seito Kaisha ..	0·6	0·6	1	70,000	4,200
Shinchiku	0·3	—	1	—	—
Bain & Co.	0·3	0·3	1	40,000	2,400
Cada Seito Kaisha	0·2	0·2	1	—	—
Byoritsu	0·5	0·125	1	—	—
				1,600,000	96,000

According to the same authority, the total grinding capacity of the modern undertakings amounted to 10,400 tons per twenty-four hours for the crushing season 1909/10 ; but this was increased to 17,000 tons of cane for the year 1910/11, so that this latter season yielded the already-mentioned quantities of 197,480 tons of crystal, and 59,000 tons of soft sugar. The construction of more factories is under way, so that, if the weather had not been too unfavourable, in the year 1911/12 Formosa would have produced an amount of sugar equal to that required by Japan for supplying her own wants, in addition to her own production of 1,000,000 piculs (60,000 tons).

It is certain that Formosa will not be satisfied with this success, and will aspire after greater things, and endeavour to export her produce to other countries, either as raw sugar or as sugar refined in Japan.

We must not lose sight of the fact that the success achieved is greatly due to the Government's powerful patronage, and the preferential treatment accorded to Formosan sugar in Japan. The industry may, of course, lose all these privileges before long, in which case the present state of affairs may change altogether ; but we must not forget how in Europe at the time of the sugar bounties refined sugar could be exported to foreign countries by the levying of a high surtax and a clever co-operation of sugar refiners and merchants.

The possibility of a great export trade in Formosan sugar depends on Japanese inland politics, so that we cannot say anything certain about it. We may predict, however, that Formosa will produce after 1912 a quantity of sugar large enough to supply Japan's wants, and for the rest we must leave things to the future.

Literature :

Summary of the Administration in Taiwan (Formosa).
Report of the British Consul at Tamsui, 1909.
Report of the Netherlands Consul at Kobe, 1910.
British, German and American Consular Reports.

VII.

THE PHILIPPINES.

I.—Geographical Conditions, Population and Modes of Communication.

THE group of islands called the Philippines lies in the Pacific Ocean, south-east of the Chinese Empire, between 4° 10′ and 21° 10′ N. Lat., and 116° 40′ and 126° 53′ E. Long.   It consists of no fewer than 3,140 different islands, greatly varying in size, which in all cover 127,853 sq. miles of land.

The names and areas of the principal islands are as follows :—

Mindanao	46,721 sq. miles
Luzon	44,235 ,,
Samar	5,448 ,,
Palawan	5,037 ,,
Panay	5,103 ,,
Negros	4,854 ,,
Leyte	4,214 ,,
Mindoro	4,108 ,,
Cebu	1,782 ,,
Masbate	1,732 ,,
Bohol	1,614 ,,

But we must not forget to mention that these numbers stand for the combined areas of the bigger and the neighbouring islands. As a whole, the Philippines group is intersected by mountain ridges of a volcanic nature, which continue under the sea, and join the different islands coherently together. The islands possess some fifty volcanoes, active and partly extinct, while the country is always subject to earthquakes. The highest volcanoes are Apa, near Davao Bay in Mindanao (10,331 ft.), and Mayon, on Luzon, (8,970 ft.).

The coasts of the island are much indented, and are rich in favourable landing places. The principal harbour is Manila, in Luzon, with a splendid bay, which is sheltered from the fiercest typhoons by a breakwater, and, consequently, is a safe port for large ships in the worst weather. The bay is so deep that ocean vessels with full cargo can advance as far as the Pasi River. Other important harbours are those of Cebu and Iloilo, while the numerous islands can point to many other ports which are noted for their navigable rivers. Both owing to the mountainous nature and the considerable rainfall of these islands, a great many rivers exist which are of considerable width but of only moderate length.

The streams descending from the mountains carry along the disintegrated deposit of volcanic stones, and fill the hollows between the mountain ridges with them, so that broad valleys of very fertile soil are created, which form the banks of the river. In many cases the rivers inundate the surrounding country in the rainy season, and cover it with a layer of mud, which occurrence stops all traffic on the spot when it is raining. The Rio Grande de Mindanao, which with its numerous tributaries drains the extensive inland, is one of the principal rivers, and joins the sea at the port of Cotta Bato, on the Celebes Sea. Further, there is in Mindanao the Agusan River ; in Luzon the Cagayan River, which flows out at Aparri into the Chinese Sea ; and the Panay River, in Panay ; and many others. The three first-mentioned are navigable to a great distance from their mouths, but only for small steamers.

Although the Philippine Islands are in the tropics, their meteorological conditions vary so much that it is impossible to give any general data as regards climate. On the whole, one can describe the sea coast climate as moderate between November and the beginning of March, fairly hot in March, July, August and September, and extremely hot in April, May and June. The nights, however, are always cool. The temperature in the mountains, of course, is lower than at the coast, and greatly depends on the elevation above sea level, so that fixed data are out of the question. The average monthly temperature varies between 25° C. in January and 28·3° C. in May. The yearly rainfall is on an average 74 ins., 50 of which fall in the months of July, August, September, and October, and the rest during the other eight months.

The Philippines.

The monthly mean temperature for a period of twenty years is for Manila as follows expressed in degrees Centigrade :—

Year.	Jan.	Feb.	March	April	May	June	July	Aug.	Sept.	Oct.	Nov.	Dec.	Mean
1883 ..	25·2	25·6	27·7	28·2	28·7	27·1	26·7	27·4	26·5	26·5	26·0	24·1	26·6
1884 ..	23·6	24·7	26·4	27·8	28·2	27·0	26·3	26·5	26·6	26·6	25·9	24·3	26·2
1885 ..	24·6	24·4	26·1	27·3	28·5	28·3	27·3	27·1	27·6	27·3	26·4	25·2	26·7
1886 ..	25·2	24·7	26·4	28·3	28·5	27·5	27·0	27·5	27·1	26·6	26·0	24·9	26·6
1887 ..	25·2	25·3	26·7	27·7	27·7	27·6	27·1	27·3	26·3	26·4	26·1	25·4	26·6
1888 ..	24·9	25·2	27·5	28·7	29·2	27·8	26·1	27·2	27·6	26·3	26·5	26·0	26·9
1889 ..	25·8	26·4	27·5	29·4	30·3	28·7	27·5	27·3	27·5	27·1	26·5	24·0	27·4
1890 ..	25·6	25·9	27·3	27·9	27·9	27·3	27·3	27·4	26·5	26·1	25·4	25·2	26·6
1891 ..	24·6	25·0	26·7	28·6	29·8	27·6	26·8	26·6	26·8	27·4	26·3	25·5	26·8
1892 ..	25·3	26·0	27·1	28·0	28·8	28·1	27·3	27·0	26·7	27·1	25·8	25·0	26·9
1893 ..	24·1	25·4	26·5	28·3	27·8	27·7	27·3	27·7	26·6	26·5	25·7	25·4	26·6
1894 ..	24·7	25·0	26·6	28·2	28·0	27·7	27·2	27·3	26·8	26·9	25·6	25·0	26·6
1895 ..	24·7	25·1	26·7	28·3	28·0	27·8	27·5	27·1	26·9	27·5	25·8	25·1	26·7
1896 ..	24·6	25·8	27·2	28·4	27·6	28·0	27·3	26·4	27·2	27·2	26·4	25·3	26·8
1897 ..	25·7	26·3	27·7	29·0	29·4	29·5	27·5	27·1	27·2	27·3	26·8	25·5	27·4
1898 ..	25·5	26·2	26·3	27·9	28·2	27·6	26·7	27·3	27·2	26·9	26·1	25·7	26·8
1899 ..	25·3	25·0	25·7	27·9	28·1	27·5	27·0	27·0	27·3	27·0	25·8	25·7	26·6
1900 ..	25·1	26·0	27·5	28·9	29·8	28·3	27·7	27·4	27·5	27·2	26·5	25·5	27·3
1901 ..	25·3	25·2	26·6	28·4	28·9	28·3	27·6	26·8	27·7	27·0	26·4	25·0	26·9
1902 ..	25·4	24·0	26·7	28·1	28·8	28·2	27·2	27·0	26·7	28·8	26·1	25·8	26·7
Average	25·0	25·4	26·8	28·3	28·6	27·9	27·1	27·1	27·0	26·9	26·1	25·2	26·8

The period of rainfall for the different places depends on their position as regards the mountain ridges, which stop the trade-winds, and so force them to yield up their moisture. That is why on the west coast of the islands they have dry weather from November till May, and a rainy season from June till October. On the east coast, on the other hand, the period between November and May is noted for its rainfall, but during the months between June and October there is not nearly so much rain as on the west coast. This refers to the mountainous parts of the islands, while in the plains, which are exposed to wind and not sheltered by mountain ranges, they have a very regular rainfall.

The Philippine Islands are not far away from the typhoon area, which makes the Chinese Seas unsafe. The typhoons usually come on between the months of April and October, especially in September. An up-to-date and well-established observatory in Manila foretells their approach through barometric indications derived from a great number of stations, and warns all the harbours that shipping may be aware of the impending danger. On land the typhoons do hardly any damage, and are not nearly so disastrous in their effects as the hurricanes are in Mauritius or in the islands of the Caribbean Sea.

The population of the Philippine Islands, according to the census of 1903, amounted to 7,635,426, 6,987,686 of whom were Christians and the rest Mohammedans and heathen; the density is, therefore, only 60 per sq. mile. The population is densest in the province of Ilicos Sur, with 414, and in the provinces of Cebu and Pangasinan with 337 inhabitants per sq. mile; while the extensive island of Mindanao has only 15 inhabitants per sq. mile.

Besides the old-established railway from Manila to Dagapan, about 720 miles of railway have been constructed in the Philippine Islands during the last few years, to connect the best harbours with the most fertile part of the interior; 430 miles of them are constructed in the isle of Luzon, and about 300 miles in the Viscaya group, namely, Cebu, Negros, and Panay. In Negros the port of Escalente, in the north, is connected with San Juan de Ilog harbour, on the west coast, viâ the richest sugar country of the Philippines. In Cebu the Danao railway runs through densely populated parts along the east coast for 80 miles southward; while in Panay the important harbour of Iloilo, in the south, is connected with the ports of Capiz and Batan, in the north, by a main line of 95 miles and a branch line of 20 miles.

The isle of Luzon is, however, developing the most extensive railway system. First of all, on the most southern peninsula a railway is being constructed from Pasacoa to Albay with branch lines through the principal hemp-producing parts of the island. From Manila there is already a railway running to Dagapan, which is being extended in a northern direction to Loagag. Then a smaller line goes from Dagapan to the summer resort of Baguio, situated at a height of 5,000 ft.; and, finally, Manila is going to have some more railway connections with the interior, and a main line in a southern direction to Cavite, Batangas, and Laguna on the south coast. All these lines are either finished or under construction, and will soon bring the principal productive parts of these populous islands into touch with the harbours in a convenient and inexpensive way.

After the Americans took possession of the Philippines, not only the railways, but also the main roads were taken note of and improved, as their condition under Spanish rule left much to be desired, especially in the rainy season.

Although sugar cane is used everywhere on the inhabited islands of the Philippine group as a dainty, a regular sugar industry only exists in the islands of Negros, Cebu, Luzon, and Leyte, covering 250,000 acres of ground, and producing 207,219 tons of sugar for export in 1911.

II.—History of the Cane Sugar Industry.

The sugar cane itself and the art of preparing sugar therefrom was most probably introduced into the Philippine Islands by the Chinese, as many of the names of implements and the customs there in use point distinctly to a Chinese origin.   When Magellan, in 1521, discovered these islands, he already found a sugar industry in existence on a small scale, but entirely similar to the Chinese system, and its product likewise similar to the Chinese product, which fact points undoubtedly to the Chinese origin of this branch of industry.

Pope Alexander VI., in 1493, in order to prevent discord between the rivals Spain and Portugal, divided the world into two parts, and, according to the treaty of Tordesillas of 1494, allotted to Portugal all the newly discovered, as well as the unknown countries, east of the meridian, which passes 470 miles west of the Cape Verd Isles ; while Spain got everything lying west of this line.   Charles the Fifth sent out the Portuguese Ferdinand Magellan, who had enlisted with the Spanish, to navigate in a western direction, reach the Moluccas, and take possession of them, as they lay west of the dividing line. On this expedition round the southern point of America, Magellan discovered the Philippine Islands, to which, however, no further attention was paid till 1564, when a Spanish expedition set sail from Mexico, and in 1565 claimed these islands in the name of the King of Spain.   It took some time before the possession was sufficiently confirmed, but, apart from a short period of British dominion between the years 1762 and 1764, the Philippine Islands continued under Spanish rule till 1898, when they fell to the United States. In the year 1896, in consequence of the Spanish oppression, revolutionary outbreaks were prevalent, but were forcibly suppressed by the Spanish Government.   The insurgents invoked the help of the Americans, who were then waging war with Spain.   This led to the destruction of the Spanish fleet in the harbour of Manila in 1898, and to the final conquest of that town by the Americans on August 13th of the same year.   It was, however, not the wish of the revolutionaries to substitute an American government for a Spanish, and so they proclaimed an independent national government, but were soon driven out by the Americans, who had taken possession of the group of islands.

During the Spanish régime not much attention was paid to the development of the resources of these islands ; the Spaniards were keener on building churches and convents than on the construction of roads or the development of the means of livelihood and the facilitation of industry.   The religious Orders had become increasingly powerful, and were the proprietors of considerable plots of land, which they allowed the natives to cultivate.   These Orders were far from desirous to suppress the population ; they were kind and considerate, and aimed at nothing but the welfare of their protégés ; but they could not be expected to achieve great things, nor to take a broad view in business matters ; consequently, the state of the industry remained most primitive.

Asia.

That the general state of the country was not bad appears from the fairly rapid increase in population, which from 667,612 people in 1591 rose to 7,635,426 in 1903—a tenfold increase was thus attained in 400 years. In 1871 the newly-appointed Governor-General claimed both corvée and taxes, which caused much anger and friction among the population, and, in conjunction with many other grievances as regards despotism and incapacity on the side of the Spanish rulers, led to the loss of the Philippine Islands in the end.

The Philippines were not of any importance as a sugar producing country till after 1849, in which year the island Negros, by command of the Spanish Governor-General, was placed under the jurisdiction of the religious Order of the Recoletos, one of the three communities of the Minorites. The governor encouraged the sugar industry very much, and was unexpectedly assisted by an increase in sugar prices through the Crimean war, so that it became profitable to cultivate sugar for export purposes in Negros, Luzon and Cebu.

In spite of the bad roads, the unskilfulness of the sugar planters, the lack of capital, and the primitive mills and factory installations, the sugar exportation rapidly gained in importance to reach during the last years of the Spanish Government, in 1893, its greatest output of 261,686 tons. Through a financial crisis in consequence of a fall in the price of silver, and later on through friction and turbulence, the industry went down in 1901 to as low as 52,274 tons, but has since gradually increased to 207,219 tons in 1911.

Immediately after the United States had taken possession of the Philippines, they tried hard to promote the well-being of the islands. They improved the sanitary conditions everywhere, looked after transportation facilities and harbours, began to construct an extensive railway system, put the education of the natives on a sound basis, and opened up possibilities for getting credit cheaply, all of which measures will perforce influence the sugar industry for the better when once this influence becomes felt. Up to then the greatest obstacles to a rapid development of the sugar industry had been the poverty of the manufacturers and their dependence on money-lenders, and a lack of good roads. All the sugar factories are small, and installed in a primitive and uneconomical way, and are in the habit of losing enormous quantities of sugar through the very bad system of juice extraction and evaporation in open pans, and curing in earthenware pots. It is not only that the manufacturers are unable to obtain their sugar in a more rational and profitable way, but they are also much in debt to the sugar buyers in the seaport towns, so that large sums must be deducted for interest from the price of sugar provided before there can be any thought of profit.

On the west coast of Negros, the seat of the large sugar estates, there are no seaports for ships, so that the sugar from each factory has first to be taken to Iloilo in small sailing vessels, to be there laded into steamers. By constructing a railway on Negros the object is to put the sugar districts in direct communication with the harbours of the island, and, consequently, to avoid the difficulty of re-loading.

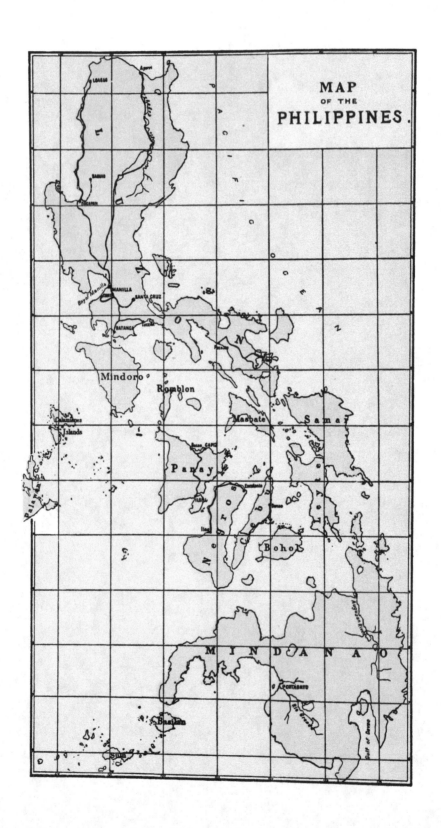

MAP
OF THE
PHILIPPINES.

The Philippines.

Although the American Government has put some funds at the disposal of native peasants as credit, this has had hardly any effect : first of all, because the sums advanced were not far-reaching enough ; and, secondly, because the Filipinos feel too much the pressure of money-lenders to avail themselves without restraint of this State assistance ; and we must not forget, either, the national dislike for all that is new.

Besides the indirect help, the Government of the United States, in 1902, allowed a drawback of 25 per cent. of the import duties on all sugar imported into the territory of the United States from the Philippine Islands.

This has not been of much avail, as, to judge from the figures representing the exportation of Philippine sugar, only very little has been imported into the States since. As a matter of fact, the sugar is of such inferior quality and is so impure that only a few of the American refiners can handle it, and then only in small quantities together with a much larger amount of better raw sugar. Most of the Philippine sugar is sent to the neighbouring countries of China and Japan, where the far less fastidious population like to eat it in the raw state.

This privilege, therefore, has not led to much, and that is why, in 1909, it was extended by a clause to the effect that each year the quantity of 300,000 tons of sugar was to be allowed to be imported exempt from duty into the United States, but that full import duty had to be paid on all sugar above that quantity. A restricting stipulation has been added to prevent some first-rate manufacturer from establishing gigantic factories in the Philippine Islands, grinding his cane very early, sending the sugar in fast steamers to America, and thus getting his sugar imported free from duty ; while the less enterprising native manufacurers, who lag behind, would enjoy none of these privileges.

According to this stipulation, only those estates will be privileged that are likely to export less than 500 tons sugar a year, while those that wish to exceed the amount of 500 tons will be considered last. Further restrictions involve a thorough investigation as regards the identity of the privileged exporter to ensure that he who comes in for protection shall have produced the sugar himself, and not act as a go-between for a leading manufacturer. The object is clear : the small manufacturer is always to have the first benefit of free importation. As the existing production, however, only forms two-thirds of the quantity allowed free from duty, and a good kind of sugar (basis 96°) is much more welcome to the American refiners than the present universally manufactured Philippine mat-sugar, we may suppose that should large factories be erected according to modern methods, they will be able to import their sugar exempt from import duty into the United States, and it will be some time before the American industry in the Philippines will increase sufficiently to attain to or even exceed the limit of 300,000 tons allowed by America.

Most of this imported sugar will, no doubt, be sugar polarizing 96°, and it will be a long time before the conservative small manufacturer will produce this kind on such a large scale that his part in the importation of sugar into the United States can be so considerable as to cause uneasiness to the central factories that may be established later on.

Up to three years ago there was a restriction which made it difficult for American concerns to start large sugar establishments in the Philippines. This restriction was to the effect that a single person was not allowed to occupy more than 40 acres, and a company to occupy more than 2,500 acres; according to American ideas it was an impossibility to found a proper sugar enterprise on so small a tract of land. This seems to be no longer a restriction, as the Government sells larger plots of ground, which, when the Americans took possession of the islands, belonged to religious Orders, and have since been bought from them. In a similar manner an agent of an American corporation bought in 1909 no less than 55,000 acres of friar land in the isle of Mindoro for the sum of $361,000; and Hawaiian sugar planters have bought 20,000 acres from the Calamba convent in the province of Laguna, in Luzon, in order to establish a sugar undertaking on that spot, which by rail and boat is connected with Manila.

The corporation just mentioned has already formed a company named the Mindoro Development Company, which has built a sugar factory on the site. So we may expect great things of the Philippine Islands in the near future.

III.—Cane Cultivation and Sugar Manufacture.

In the Philippines it is the custom to burn the trash, and to plough up the soil immediately after the cane is reaped, or as soon as the weather permits. This is chiefly done with inefficient wooden ploughs, although gradually superior American iron ploughs have been introduced, allowing of a better tillage. After the big lumps have been broken by a harrow, the furrows are dug 6 ins. deep, and at 30—60 ins. distance from centre to centre. All this happens in the months between November and April in soil that has just been planted with cane; in the case of tilling fallow land the work is begun in July or August, in order to have everything ready for the time of planting. For planting purposes one takes the white tops of the cane, in most cases first soaked in water in order to germinate better. Generally the cuttings are planted at 16 ins. distance from each other, so that an acre will hold 10,000 of them. The sets are laid into the furrows sloping slightly, so that a very little of one end peeps out of the soil; four or five weeks after planting the weeding and banking are done, but manuring is out of the question.

In July, at the time of the rain monsoon, some more banking and weeding is carried out, this concluding the field activities, so that nothing is left but harvesting.

Cane is not planted afresh every year, but allowed to ratoon. In some parts nothing else but first ratoons is kept; but in case of a rich and deep soil one can reap as many as eight crops before planting afresh. The plant cane is usually reaped from eleven to fourteen months after it has been planted, and the ratoon always after one year.

The variety of cane mostly planted in Luzon is a white or yellowish sort, while the Morada, or Purple Cane, is exclusively planted in Negros. Only a little white and black cane is found in some places in this island.

Of parasites, grasshoppers and a species of coco-beetle are most to be feared; while an epidemic among the water buffaloes, which are used both for ploughing and driving mills, greatly contributed towards a considerable decline in the sugar industry in 1901.

The planters have much difficulty in getting regular labour. They recruit labourers from the other islands, but are obliged to advance money before these are willing to come, while the legal security is not great, and the trustworthiness of the borrower not high, either; so that breach of contract and loss of the money advanced is frequently experienced, and, of course, impedes any regular progress of affairs.

Plant cane is reckoned to yield 2·5 tons of sugar per acre; first ratoon 2·0 tons; second ratoon 1·75 tons; third ratoon 1·5 tons; fourth ratoon 1·25 tons. A field that does not yield more than 0·8 ton sugar per acre is not thought fit for ratooning, and has to be planted again. It also depends, of course, on the small or large supply of labour, on the amount of land, etc., as one sooner thinks of planting again with an abundance of labour and land, than when there is a scarcity of both.

Considering the smaller production of first and second ratoons, one can safely reckon half of the total product to be supplied by plant cane, and the other half by the first and subsequent ratoons.

The prime cost of cane, of course, has much to do with the production per acre, and also with the type and the fertility of the soil. Allowing 40 centavos de peso Philippino (10 pence) for day wages, the cost of an acre of plant cane amounts to 18·72 pesos (from the burning over of the field to the cutting), not reckoning cost of cattle, implements and superintendence. When calculated in the same way, the cost of an acre of first and second ratoon amounts to 9·65 pesos, so that an average acre of cane in the field comes to 14·32 pesos, for tillage and seed. Allowing a yield of 24 piculs[*] sugar per acre, the cultivation of a picul sugar is reckoned to cost 60 centavos (1s. 3d.).

In cutting the cane much care is not taken, so that tall cane stumps often stick out of the ground, which, naturally, causes direct loss. The bigger estates have at their disposal portable rails with trucks, or a fixed railroad with movable sidings, while the smaller ones transport the cane by means of bullock or carabao (water-buffalo) carts of 30 piculs capacity. The cutting of the cane comes to 12·5 to 20 centavos per picul sugar, and the transport to the mill costs 10—25 centavos per picul sugar, varying with the distance to be covered.

* 1 Philippine picul = 63·28 kg. or 137½ lbs.

The installation of the factories is rather primitive. In 1907 in the Philippine Islands 1,075 little factories were found—528 working with steam, 470 with carabaos or human power, and 77 with water power. The number of carabao mills steadily diminishes, and will soon become nil, while water mills are only limited to the very unimportant little factories in the interior, where mountain streams yield a very inexpensive supply of power. The majority of the factories grind 50—60 tons, or 800—1,000 piculs, cane a day in a single mill, without second crushing, so that the loss of sugar in bagasse is very considerable, and the bagasse is so moist that it is unfit for fuel without being dried in the sun.

Evaporation in vacuum pans, and the use of centrifugals, are not known in the Philippine factories, the juice being clarified with a little lime and evaporated to dryness in a battery of five or six hemispherical pans or " cauas."

The following diagram gives a clear idea of what the installation of such a factory is like :—

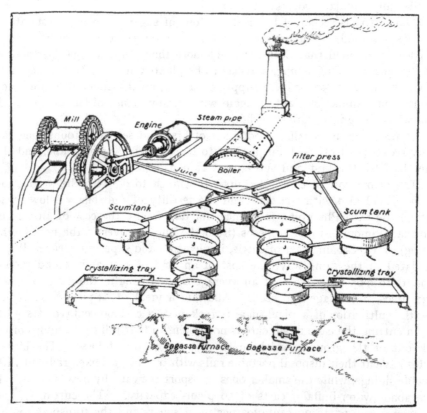

FIG. 5. SCHEME OF A PLANT TO MAKE SUGAR FROM CANE JUICE IN THE PHILIPPINES.

There are generally two distinct batteries built over separate furnaces, having only the No. 5, or juice-receiving " caua " in common. The two batteries are fired through a separate furnace, and the furnace chambers converge into one under the boiler, which, moreover, can be heated from the side too. The juice coming from the mill is freed from the suspended particles of bagasse by being strained through a cloth or wire screen, and then comes into a " caua," where it is warmed up to 70 or 80° C., some of the lighter impurities rising to the surface in the form of a froth, which is skimmed off and thrown into the scum-tanks at one side. From time to time, as required, juice is ladled with a kerosene tin into the smaller " cauas," where it is mixed with lime. In Nos. 3 and 2 the first violent ebullition occurs, and the impurities that float to the top are steadily skimmed off and thrown into the scum-tanks. The juice, left by the scum, tends to flow back, and the remainder now and then flows to a strainer, from which the extracted juice returns to the mill juice tanks. When the juice is properly concentrated, the thick mass is quickly ladled into wooden crystallizers, where it is stirred with a spade till it coagulates to a soft crystalline substance, when it is ready for transportation.

Philippine sugar is classified commercially under two main headings, which are subdivided again into numbers.

Sugar that polarizes above 80° is called " Superior," and is subdivided as follows :—

No. 1 from 87—88·9° (or higher) average 88° polarization.
No. 2 ,, 85—86·9° average 86° polarization.
No. 3 ,, 80—84·9° ,, 82·5° ,,

The difference in price between grades has ordinarily been 25 centavos per picul, but since Philippine sugar is now more and more bought for shipment to New York this simple and harmonious scale of prices is disturbed. According to the New York basis of 0·1 cent gold per lb. for each degree difference in polarization, the difference in price between Nos. 1 and 2 would be 56 centavos per picul, and between Nos. 2 and 3 98 centavos per picul.

When large purchases of " Superior " are made, and nothing special is stipulated, ½ of No. 1 quality, ¼ of No. 2, and ⅝ of No. 3 may be reckoned, the price for assorted being midway between Nos. 2 and 3, and its average polarization 84°. Of late years rather more No. 1 has been produced, so that 26 per cent. No. 1, 18 per cent. No. 2, and 56 per cent. No. 3 is nearer the figure, the average polarization of the lot coming to 84·4°.

Besides the " Superior " sugar, there is :—
" Humedo " (wet) from 76—79·9° polarization.
" Corriente " (current) from 70—75·9°.

" Humedo " is quoted at about 1 peso less than No. 3, while " Corriente " has no fixed ratio to the other grades. The relative amount of these two grades produced is rather difficult to estimate, since much is mixed together and sold to Chinese buyers as " wet " sugar, regardless of its polarization ;

while the better grade of "humedo" is frequently worked off by blending it in small quantities with No. 3 superior. Climatic conditions during different years also affect the proportion of low-grade sugars, but generally it varies between 10 and 20 per cent. of the total production. The average production consists of 85 per cent. superior of 84° polarization, and 15 per cent. of wet at 75° polarization, with an average polarization for the whole of 82·6°.

Manufacture, as is seen, is most primitive, and although all the molasses are kept in the product, so that no loss is suffered as regards this waste substance, the sucrose loss from material to finished product in Iloilo amounts to no less than 44 per cent., classified as follows :—

In the bagasse	25·0 per cent.
In the scum skimmed off in the boiling process	5·0 ,,
By inversion, caramelization, etc.	2·5 ,,
Burned, spilled, stolen, and unaccounted for	10·0 ,,
Tare, loss of weight in transport, etc. ..	1·5 ,,
	44·0 per cent.

The cane as ordinarily ground in the mills averages 14·75 per cent. of sugar, so the yield in sucrose on the weight of the cane amounts to 8·26 per cent., or almost exactly 10 per cent. of raw sugar polarizing 82·6. This does not hold good for all parts of the islands, but we may reckon an average of something between 9 per cent. and 11½ per cent.

The manufacturing cost of a picul of sugar may be estimated at 63 centavos per picul, when it is done under a single management. If, on the other hand, as is sometimes the case, the grinding, the sugar boiling, and the bagasse drying are each done by different people, who have to share in the profit, manufacture costs 72 centavos per picul. Then the sugar has to be carted to the lorcha (a small flat-bottomed schooner), which carries it to the ports of exportation. Next, commission amounting to 2 per cent. has to be paid, so that for extra expenses we may calculate 53 centavos per picul.

Hence the net cost of sugar is estimated generally, per picul, to be as follows :—

Ploughing, planting, and caring for cane sugar until it is ready for cutting	0·60 pesos
Cutting the cane and carting it to the mill	0·32 ,,
Manufacture	0·63 ,,
Shipping, and placing on market ..	0·53 ,,
	2·08 pesos

The Philippines.

This does not include cost of buffaloes, implements, machinery, survey, interest on capital, working capital, but only states the cost price in wages and all direct expenses. Herbert S. Walker, in his essay on the sugar industry in the isle of Negros, gives an estimate of the other expenses, and arrives at a rate of interest of 10 per cent. on fixed and working capital, and 10 per cent. depreciation per annum—an additional cost of sugar at the coast of 4·15 pesos per picul. On the other hand, most of the planters are not able to raise money at 10 per cent. interest, but have to pay considerably more, so that the cost price of that kind of sugar polarizing 82° exceeds 4·15 pesos (8s. 8d.). In the case of the few planters using their own capital, if no interest is charged on this, the cost of production, including all amortization and maintenance expenses, would be reduced to 3·38 pesos per picul.

This leaves a fair profit, as sugar in Manila and Iloilo brings per picul in pesos (in November, 1909) :—

	Per picul.	Per ton.
Superior No. 1	7·50 ..	118·59
,, No. 2	7·25 ..	114·63
,, No. 3	7·00 ..	110·68
,, average (assorted) ..	7·12 ..	112·66
Humedo (wet)	5·62 ..	68·96
Corriente (current)	4·00 ..	63·24

On the New York market the price quoted for Iloilo " Assorted " is practically constant at 1 cent gold per lb. less than that of 96° centrifugal, so that the price of Philippine sugar is to be inferred from the New York quotations. In 1907 there were in all 1,075 small factories, classified as follows :—

Island.	Province.	Number of Factories	Driven by Steam.	Driven by Cattle.	Production in Pesos.	Average production in Pesos.
Luzon	Pampanga	194	131	48	758,691	3,911
,,	Bulacan	38	3	35	83,070	2,186
,,	Tarlac and Capiz ..	35	12	21	62,206	1,777
,,	Bataan	18	10	—	46,520	2,584
,,	La Laguna	23	10	13	40,551	1,763
,,	Cavite	15	—	13	27,452	1,830
,,	Batangas	8	1	7	16,063	2,008
,,	Pangasinan	4	2	2	8,354	2,089
,,	La Union	3	2	1	6,600	2,200
,,	Miramis	3	—	3	6,586	2,195
	Carried forward	331	171	143	1,056,093	22,543

Island.	Province.	Number of Factories	Driven by Steam.	Driven by Cattle.	Production in Pesos.	Average production in Pesos.
	Brought forward	331	171	143	1,056,093	22,543
Luzon	Sorsogon	4	—	4	6,350	1,588
,,	Rizal	3	—	3	6,190	2,063
,,	Nueva Ecija	4	—	4	5,219	1,305
Negros	Negros Occidental	531	291	194	4,644,398	8,747
,,	,, Oriental	38	32	6	325,611	8,569
Panay	Iloilo	62	26	36	372,399	6,006
,,	Antique	14	2	9	26,018	1,858
Cebu	Cebu	69	59	63	149,268	2,163
Leyte	Leyte	9	1	8	11,460	1,273
	Total	1,075	528	470	6,603,006	6,142

The estates employed in all about 45,247 labourers. The largest of all in that year was Talisey, in Negros, which produced 300 piculs, or 20 tons, of sugar each day.

The entire exportation of sugar, dating from the year when it became important down to the present day, is given, together with the names of the countries of destination, in the following table (the figures indicate metric tons) :—

Year.	United Kingdom.	Cont. Europe.	Australia	United States.		Canada.	China, Japan, etc.	Total.
				Atlantic Ocean.	Pacific Ocean.			
1849	11,545		6,094	5,593	—	—	—	23,232
1850/54	13,952		9,616	8,048	935	—	—	32,551
1855/59	21,369		14,040	6,967	1,903	—	—	44,279
1860	27,231		10,976	13,204	4,342	—	—	55,753
1861	26,666		18,550	4,885	2,626	—	—	52,727
1862	37,603	1,162	28,413	6,482	4,160	—	2,922	80,742
1863	26,886	819	15,424	3,422	4,786	—	23,672	75,009
1864	41,854	429	1,794	6,346	9,043	—	4,319	63,785
1865	20,292	939	11,543	4,290	8,202	—	9,910	55,176
1866	29,417	685	3,607	5,365	8,234	—	7,528	54,836
1867	31,715	1,788	7,617	6,156	5,111	—	12,172	64,559
1868	51,216	660	6,061	11,601	2,753	—	1,789	74,080
1869	32,055	437	7,202	21,497	7,546	—	90	68,827
1870	40,547	2,307	7,156	19,039	4,100	—	5,063	78,212

Year.	United Kingdom.	Cont. Europe.	Australia.	United States. Atlantic Ocean.	Pacific Ocean.	Canada.	China, Japan, etc.	Total.
1871	34,744	3,592	8,737	34,121	6,240	—	31	87,465
1872	52,773	2,766	7,277	24,418	7,801	—	491	95,526
1873	35,266	4,468	13,649	27,412	8,409	—	134	89,338
1874	41,637	2,545	7,924	37,038	14,178	—	540	103,862
1875	63,074	1,777	7,703	41,693	11,855	—	87	126,188
1876	49,352	1,549	974	59,467	19,066	—	22	130,430
1877	55,406	2,528	—	55,138	9,179	—	160	122,411
1878	46,572	3,133	1,681	47,109	16,892	—	2,639	117,926
1879	69,151	2,168	—	53,237	2,839	—	7,409	134,804
1880	69,818	4,490	575	97,908	5,048	—	2,909	180,748
1881	108,909	9,532	3,120	80,419	4,949	—	4,488	211,417
1882	66,162	3,162	1,559	75,907	2,081	—	2,122	150,993
1883	56,309	9,214	—	140,656	8,874	—	183	215,236
1884	18,721	8,073	—	77,191	12,437	—	6,503	122,925
1885	33,292	4,175	—	147,997	4,829	—	22,498	212,791
1886	26,448	5,442	—	130,883	4,000	—	19,012	185,785
1887	29,887	4,510	89	118,997	4,500	—	21,165	159,146
1888	35,155	4,629	86	74,064	34,293	10,500	26,529	185,256
1889	54,874	5,123	—	112,223	17,819	14,728	14,160	218,927
1890	40,041	3,926	5	35,482	5,145	26,883	36,042	147,520
1891	48,819	2,337	—	60,022	—	36,570	18,712	166,464
1892	73,837	3,032	—	61,542	—	32,575	76,218	247,686
1893	98,572	4,344	—	61,103	—	19,610	78,057	261,686
1894	61,139	4,119	—	36,420	—	20,465	72,176	194,313
1895	92,212	4,009	200	40,593	—	19,022	74,887	230,929
1896	39,312	3,547	—	78,489	—	20,135	88,430	229,913
1897	47,037	1,775	—	15,223	—	9,130	128,928	202,093
1898	46,780	180	—	27,997	—	—	105,863	180,820
1899	17,967	2	—	22,105	—	—	52,980	93,054
1900	12,748	—	—	2,100	—	—	47,896	62,744
1901	27	—	—	1,975	—	—	50,272	52,274
1902	5,912	—	—	2,550	—	—	83,610	92,072
1903	—	—	—	33,805	—	—	55,755	89,560
1904	4,350	—	—	20,893	—	—	58,740	83,983
1905	500	—	—	42,930	—	—	61,563	104,993
1906	—	—	—	—	11,726	—	112,657	124,383
1907	11,663	—	—	8,698	2,002	—	99,615	121,978
1908	10,944	—	—	45,969	—	—	85,535	142,448
1909	—	—	—	50,223	—	—	77,065	127,288
1910	—	—	—	84,681	12,932	—	18,733	116,346
1911 .. .	—	—	—	168,461	17,700	—	21,058	207,219

The import duty in the Philippine Islands has been since 5th August, 1907, as follows :—

Raw sugar, $3·72 (American) per 100 kilos.
Refined　　$4·22　　,,　　,,　,,　　,,

but as no sugar is being imported into the islands, this duty counts for nothing.

Then there is an export duty of 5 cents (American) per 100 kilos on all sugar not bound for the States. Sugar destined for other Philippine Islands or for American harbours is exempted from it.

IV.—Future.

As regards the prospect of the cane sugar industry in the Philippine Islands, all forebodings point to gigantic progress in the near future, which may be caused either by improvement and development of the existing undertakings, or by the establishment of large central factories, with American capital, either on land now occupied by the Philippine population, or else on newly prepared soil. This follows when we consider that it was actually possible to produce sugar that could compete with others in the world's market, at a time when machinery was most primitive and uneconomical, and when irrigation and agriculture and means of transportation left much to be desired, and the manufacturers were poor and much in debt, while the product was burdened with an export duty in its own country, and handicapped by import duties in almost every country of destination.

The American Government has established at Iloilo, in Panay, a Sugar Bureau, where the different kinds of cane are being examined, and where the best manuring methods will be investigated. Then there is a bank for the native producer to get credit from at little cost, which guarantees him against excessive interest, and enables him to turn the produce of his land to a better account. As we saw, the actual production cost of sugar treated in a primitive way was quite low, and we can therefore guess what it will be when well-selected cane varieties are properly planted, manured, and kept in irrigated land ; when cane is carried by railways to an economically working central factory, where it will be worked up to centrifugal sugar ; when it is sent to America in fast steamers ; and when it enters free and enjoys a premium of no less than 1·685 cents per lb. for sugar basis 96° over sugar from other sources which have no special treaty with the United States.

There is land and irrigation water in abundance, but labour is scarce, as the country is as thinly populated on the average as Cuba. Now that the latter, however, in spite of its small number of inhabitants and lack of irrigation, has a greater yearly output of sugar than any other country in the world, it does not seem to interfere with the important extension of the sugar industry, while we should not lose sight of the fact that each of the two bigger islands, Luzon and Mindoro, covers a slightly larger area than, for instance, Cuba does, so that it is not unlikely that considerable areas will be planted with sugar cane.

Besides the Filipinos, the American firms are sure to benefit by these facilities—no doubt far more so. Through the purchase of 55,000 acres of friar land in Mindoro and elsewhere by American sugar magnates, and of 20,000 acres in Luzon by Hawaiian planters, they have begun to turn to account the treasures which the soil of the Philippine Islands offers to the sugar industry ; and, encouraged as it is by the protection of the United States, it may have, in the end, a future such as we dare not yet put down in figures.

BOOKS OF REFERENCE—

Literature :

Hamilton M. Wright. *A Handbook of the Philippines.*
Bulletins of the U.S. Department. of Agriculture.
British Consular Reports.
Report of the Philippine Commission for 1906.
Herbert S. Walker. *The Sugar Industry in the Island of Negros.*

VIII.

JAVA.

I.—Geographical Location, Climate and Area planted with Cane.

THE island of Java is situated in the Indian Ocean, between 105° 12′ 37″ and 114° 36′ 4″ E. Long. and between 5° 52′ 30″ and 8° 46′ 51″ S. Lat.

Its total area, not including Madura, amounts to 48,688 sq. miles ; its greatest length measures 657 miles, while its breadth varies from 13 to 50 miles. It is narrowest in the western, middle, and eastern parts, while broader stretches of land lie between.

The north coast is low and muddy, and broken up by several unimportant bays, which, though in the dry season they may serve as sheltered landing places, during the wet monsoon are unsuitable as roadsteads.

The road of Soerabaja only is an exception, while the seaport of Tandjong Priok is an artificial one on the muddy coast land. At Rembang the flat north coast is broken up by steep limestone mountains, east of which stretches again the alluvial plain. The south coast is steep, and in some places rocky. Sometimes dune formation is met with ; in most cases, however, it is surrounded by steep cliffs, while the heavy breakers which generally prevail on that part of the coast make the navigation of sea-going craft an impossibility. The sheltered harbour of Tjilatjap alone is an excellent sea-port, and the only natural port in the entire island

As regards the orography, one can divide Java into three parts, which are separated by dividing lines running south of Cheribon and Semarang. Of the entire western part, the north coast is almost wholly taken up by the alluvial plain, which sometimes stretches across one-third of the entire width, while the centre and the south parts consist of extensive highlands. Towards the centre of Java the mountainous land becomes very narrow, and there are alluvial tracts on the north as well as on the south coast that do not attain in width to the former. In East Java one finds in the north two low and broad limestone mountain ranges, while a similar chain runs along the greater part of the south coast. Through the longitudinal axis of the island, or very close to it, goes a range of volcanoes, some of which are not active, while the others emit smoke or sand, and are repeatedly in eruption.

Java possesses a great many rivers, the direction of flow of which is influenced by that of the principal mountain chain or to the general slope of the country. Most of these rivers break up the north coast, and others, the smaller ones, the south coast. Although the slope is chiefly northward, the principal rivers, though running parallel with the limestone mountains in East Java, have a more northern or north-eastern direction. That is why the two principal rivers in the east part of Java, the Solo and the Brantas, are larger than those in the west, which flow from the mountains, where they rise, straight into the sea. Besides the two big rivers, we ought to mention the Tji Manoek, the Tji Taroem, the Tji Tandoei, and the Serijoe river as being available for navigation, while all the others are important from an agricultural point of view, as they supply the water for irrigating the arable land. Owing to the heavy rainfall in Java, and the short course of the rivers, the effluence of the rivers varies for the different seasons. While many of the rivers during the dry season contain but little or no water, in the rainy monsoon they often change into roaring mountain torrents, which devastate the country by over-flowing their banks. On the occasion of these inundations very large quantities of products of disintegration of rocks or matter emitted from the volcanoes are carried along, and are partly deposited on the land and partly carried out as mud to sea. The deposal of this fine kind of disintegrated mud has given rise to the alluvial plains along the river beds and on the north coast, and as this formation still goes on the coast gradually extends in a northern direction, and the mouths of the rivers get shallow, so that the harbours must be kept at their proper draught by dredging. The deposit of matter emitted by volcanoes and spread by inundation is less profitable than the disintegrated products, as the coarse pieces of lava will cover the arable land, and will not form a fertile layer for some years, when the disintegration process will be sufficiently advanced.

The amount of silt in the river water greatly varies according to the season, and to the soil the river passes through. There are times when only a few milligrams of mud are found per litre, while at other times the water contains 1 grm. of silt per litre or more.

Java lies altogether in the tropics, and has a fairly constant annual temperature ; a considerable amount of moisture and rain, with little wind, prevails. The average annual temperature for the whole of Java is 25·94° C., and the difference between the warmest and coolest months is not more than 1° C., as the warmest months, May and October, have an average temperature of 26·39° and 26·37°, and the coolest, January and February, one of 25·35° and 25·39° respectively. Neither the day differences nor the hourly differences during the same day amount to much. In the most extreme case, the greatest deviation during the years from 1866 to 1905 observed at Batavia was 13·5° C., and in the least case no more than 0·9° C.

The average figures for Batavia between 1866 and 1900 were as follows :—

Observations at Batavia, 6° 11′ 0″ S. Lat. 107ᵛ 7′ 19″ E. Long.

	Tem— perature.	Absolute Moisture.	Relative Moisture.
January	25·40	20·94	87·1
February	25·43	21·10	87·5
March	25·86	21·22	85·9
April	26·30	21·51	85·0
May	26·44	21·31	83·6
June	26·03	20·66	83·1
July	25·77	19·73	80·8
August	26·01	19·21	77·7
September	26·36	19·54	77·5
October	26·48	20·07	79·0
November	26·20	20·55	82·0
December	25·68	20·69	84·8
Average	26·00	20·54	82·8

Asia.

and in some sugar cane cultivating areas we find :—

Observations made at Kagok (Pekalongan Resiaency), 109° 12′ 30″ E. Long.,
6° 95′ 10″ S. Lat., the altitude of the instruments above the sea level being 151 ft.

Average Temperature.

Year.	Jan.	Feb.	Mar.	Apl.	May.	June	July.	Aug.	Sept.	Oct.	Nov.	Dec.	Average
1889 ..	26·9	26·8	26·8	27·5	27·3	26·4	26·0	26·2	26·5	27·3	27·1	26·8	26·8
1890 ..	26·8	26·3	26·5	26·7	26·2	25·9	25·6	25·4	26·2	26·4	26·3	26·2	26·2
1891 ..	26·2	25·9	26·3	26·6	26·6	25·9	25·3	25·4	27·0	27·9	26·9	27·0	26·4
1892 .	25·7	26·2	26·4	26·2	26·2	26·0	25·8	26·0	26·5	26·7	26·1	26·2	26·2
1893 ..	25·4	25·4	25·9	26·4	26·5	26.0	25·9	26·2	26·6	26·8	26·3	26·0	26·1
1894 ..	25·7	25·7	25·9	26·3	25·9	25·4	25·5	25·7	26·3	27·3	26·3	26·2	26·0
1895 .	25·6	25·9	26·1	26·5	25·6	26·2	25·5	25·5	26·8	27·1	26·8	26·1	26·2
1895 ..	26·1	25·9	26·2	26·2	26·3	25·6	25·5	26·1	26·8	27·9	27·6	26·4	26·4
1897 .	26·9	26·2	26·9	27·0	26·9	26·9	26·2	26·2	27·3	28·0	27·2	26·8	26·9
1898 .	26·2	26·4	26·4	26·6	26·6	26·1	25·8	26·0	26·7	26·9	26·7	26·5	26·5
Average ..	26·1	26·1	26·3	26·5	26·5	26·1	25·7	25·9	26·7	27·2	26·7	26·4	26·5

Average Relative Moisture of the Air.

Year.	Jan.	Feb.	Mar.	Apl.	May.	June	July.	Aug.	Sept.	Oct.	Nov.	Dec.	Average
1899 ..	83	85	84	83	82	84	80	74	76	76	77	77	81
1890 .	80	82	83	80	82	82	79	77	73	76	80	81	80
1891 ..	82	81	82	81	74	77	69	65	63	64	72	79	74
1892 ..	86	85	86	86	80	78	79	78	73	78	81	80	81
1893 ..	85	87	84	82	84	84	79	76	79	77	88	83	82
1894 ..	87	87	85	82	82	81	76	59	77	75	80	87	80
1895 ..	87	88	85	84	84	86	87	78	69	73	78	86	79
1896 .	87	89	88	88	81	75	72	68	65	67	75	86	76
1897 .	84	88	85	84	78	74	77	69	67	74	77	80	79
1898 ..	84	87	83	84	81	85	78	78	77	77	78	82	81
Average ..	85	86	84	83	81	81	78	71	72	74	79	82	79.3

Java.

Observations at Pekalongan. 109° 40' 26" *E. Long.*, 6° 52' 39" *S. Lat.*
Altitude of instruments above the level of the sea, 13 *ft.*

Average Temperature.

Year.	Jan.	Feb.	Mar.	Apl.	May.	June	July.	Aug.	Sept.	Oct.	Nov.	Dec.	Average
1902 ..	26·49	25·91	26·43	27·96	27·47	26·68	25·94	26·33	26·75	27·92	28·70	27·54	27·01
1903 ..	27·73	26·67	27·07	27·36	27·71	26·78	26·39	26·83	27·30	27·81	26·99	26·10	27·02
1904 ..	26·07	25·93	26·56	26·83	26·70	26·39	26·16	26·29	26·99	27·38	26·83	26·29	26·54
1905 ..	26·64	26·07	27·26	26·90	27·05	27·10	25·93	26·19	26·86	27·82	27·56	27·53	26·91
1906 ..	26·41	27·25	27·10	27·02	27·28	26·71	26·82	26·88	26·88	27·43	26·47	26·42	26·89
Average ..	26·67	26·64	26·69	27.21	27·14	26·73	26·25	26·50	26·96	27·67	27·31	26·98	26·87

Average Relative Moisture of the Air.

Year.	Jan.	Feb.	Mar.	Apl.	May.	June	July.	Aug.	Sept.	Oct.	Nov.	Dec.	Average
1902 ..	90	91	89	83	79	78	79	79	75	74	71	82	80·8
1903 ..	83	88	84	85	85	82	85	79	80	80	83	86	83·3
1904 .	89	88	86	84	84	86	86	83	82	84	85	88	85·4
1905 ..	86	87	84	85	84	83	81	80	80	79	89	84	83·5
1906 ..	89	86	85	85	84	83	83	82	84	81	87	88	84·6
Average ..													

Observations at Pasoeroean during the years 1901-06.

Average Temperature.

Year.	Jan.	Feb.	Mar.	Apl.	May.	June	July.	Aug.	Sept.	Oct.	Nov.	Dec.	Average
1901 ..	27·3	27·1	27·1	28·2	27·8	27·5	26·7	26·8	27·4	28·7	29·0	28·0	27·60
1902 ..	27·7	26·6	27·2	28·0	27·8	27·3	26·8	27·0	26·9	28·2	29·3	28·6	27·62
1903 ..	28·5	27·4	27·6	27·2	27·6	27·1	27·1	27·4	28·0	29·0	28·7	26·6	27·72
1904 ..	27·2	26·9	26·6	27·4	27·3	27·1	26·7	27·1	27·7	28·7	28·7	27·9	27·44
1905 ..	27·3	26·7	28·0	27·5	27·5	27·4	26·8	26·4	27·6	28·8	29·2	29·2	27·70
1906 ..	27·1	28·1	27·9	28·1	28·0	27·0	27·2	27·8	28·5	29·3	27·8	28·0	27·90
Average ..	27·52	27·13	27·40	27·70	27·67	27 23	26·89	27·08	27·68	28·78	28·78	28·05	27·65

Asia.

Relative Moisture.

Year.	Jan.	Feb.	Mar.	Apl.	May.	June	July.	Aug.	Sept.	Oct.	Nov.	Dec.	Average
1901 ..	80·3	81·3	82·0	75·3	70·7	76·0	75·3	67·0	61·7	62·0	67·7	75·3	72·88
1902 ..	76·3	80·3	78·0	70·3	71·0	69·0	65·0	65·0	63·0	62·3	62·7	73·0	69·60
1903 ..	75·0	80·0	80·3	79·3	76·0	71·0	67·3	63·7	63·0	63·7	70·5	81·5	72·60
1904 ..	77·0	80·0	80·3	76·0	76·0	73·0	70·7	66·7	64·3	64·3	67·6	73·4	72·49
1905 ..	78·0	81·3	76·7	78·7	76·3	70·0	67·3	67·8	65·0	61·0	64·3	70·0	71·37
1906 ..	82·3	78·7	77·7	76·0	73·7	70·0	69·0	65·0	68·3	64·0	74·7	75·3	72·89
Average ..	78·15	80·27	78·83	75·93	73·95	71·50	69·10	65·87	64·22	62·89	69·58	74·75	71·97

The rainfall varies greatly for the whole year in different parts of the country. As a rule, it rains more in the west than in the east, and there is also more rain in the mountains than in the plains. From May to September the east monsoon or dry season prevails, while the west monsoon, or rainy season, extends from November till March. Between the monsoons there are intervening periods, which are distinguished by great heat and an oppressive atmosphere. The monsoons begin and end later as one goes further eastward, so that the foregoing months are not to be considered as limits of these periods for every place.

For a great many stations in these parts of the plain which are fit for cane cultivation, the average rainfall in inches of a great many years has been as follows :—

	Stations.	Jan.	Feb.	Mar.	Apl.	May.	June	July	Aug.	Sept.	Oct.	Nov.	Dec.	Total
North Coast.	Cheribon ..	17·13	14·65	14·69	7·95	5·28	4·33	2·72	0·87	1·18	2·44	6·06	14·80	92·10
	Semarang ..	14·61	14·13	8·90	7·36	5·04	3·35	3·11	2·56	3·70	5·39	7·28	10·47	85·90
	Soerabaja ..	12·09	10·98	10·39	6·58	4·45	3·50	2·01	0·83	0·55	1·57	4·57	9·65	67·17
	Pasoeroean ..	9·06	10·39	7·95	5·12	3·03	2·44	1·10	0·24	0·16	0·51	2·24	6·61	48·85
	Probolinggo	9·25	9·69	6·10	3·98	2·52	1·77	0·79	0·39	0·16	0·47	2·44	6·46	44·02
	Beznoeki ..	12·80	11·81	7·09	3·39	2·17	1·54	0·98	0·24	0·12	0·28	2·24	7·60	50·26
Low land in the interior.	Banjoemas ..	13·35	11·50	13·35	10·04	7·68	5·55	4·06	2·99	3·66	12·17	17·13	17·95	119·43
	Djokjakarta	13·78	12·48	12·91	8·15	5·39	3·90	1·89	1·22	1·50	3·74	9·57	13·90	88·43
	Soerakarta ..	12·87	12·95	11·81	8·03	4·88	3·86	2·24	1·85	1·81	4·06	8·78	10·51	83·65
	Madioen ..	12·44	10·91	10·12	8·82	5·08	2·99	1·61	1·06	1·22	2·64	7 87	9·61	74·37
	Djember ..	14·65	15·24	14·37	8·98	6·22	4·37	2·95	2·17	3·07	6·30	11·26	14·17	103·75
	Sitobondo ..	10·67	8·66	6·30	2·36	1·97	1·14	0·63	0·16	0·16	0·75	2·05	5·79	40·63

The barometric readings in Java do not vary much all through the year. During the forty years between 1866 and 1905 the average reading at Batavia was 758·77 mm. (30 inches), with a maximum of 764·41 and a minimum of

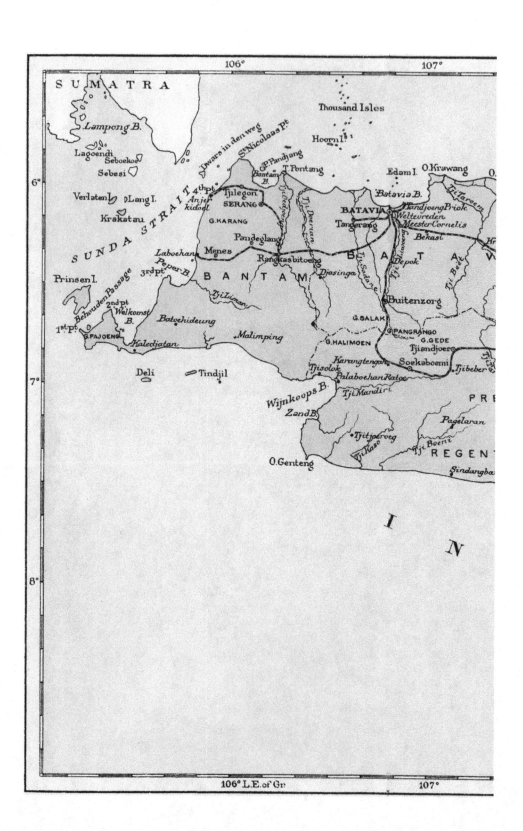

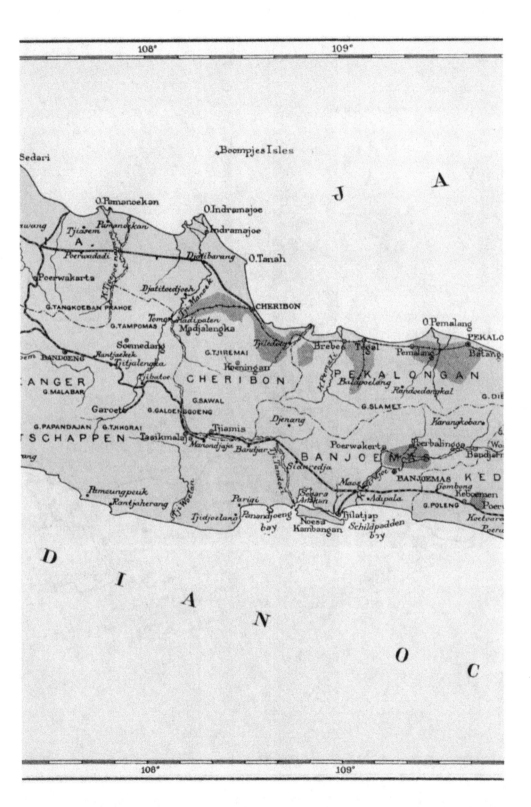

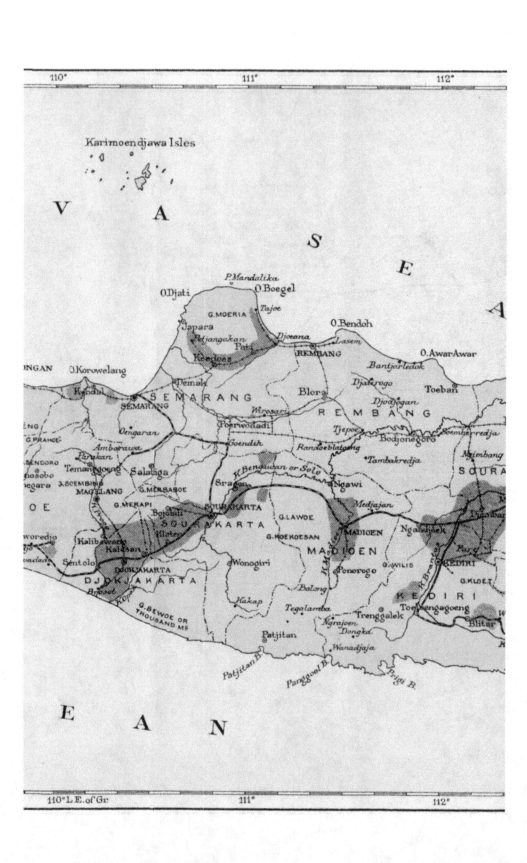

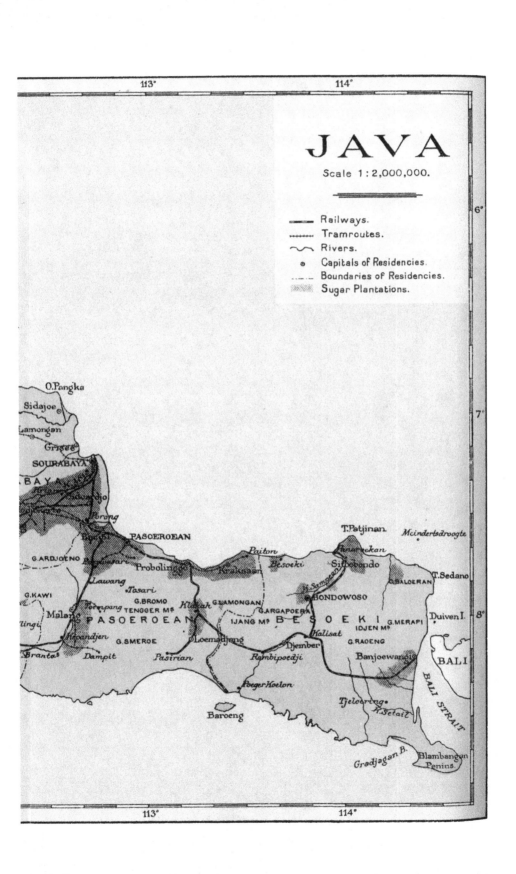

JAVA

Scale 1 : 2,000,000.

Railways.
Tramroutes.
Rivers.
Capitals of Residencies.
Boundaries of Residencies.
Sugar Plantations.

Java.

752·39.   The greatest variance observed in one day did not amount to more than 5·56 mm. (0·25 ins.) ;   the smallest 1·40 mm.

As may be seen from these lists, Java does not suffer from cyclones, which in other countries often cause great havoc.

The population of Java, including Madura, amounted to 30,098,008 on 31st December, 1905, and, leaving the island of Madura out, to 28,604,719. These are divided as follows :—

Natives	28,227,983
Europeans.	64,305
Chinese	292,108
Arabs	17,562
Other foreign Orientals	2,761
	28,604,719

The population has increased marvellously, in spite of a considerable emigration to other parts of the Archipelago, while except that of a few Europeans, Chinese, and other Orientals, no immigration has taken place. The figures representing the censuses of 1824–62 only showed from 6 to 13 million inhabitants ; but the later censuses of Java and Madura have realized the following figures :—

1880	19,794,559
1885	21,467,445
1890	23,914,564
1895	25,697,701
1900	28,746,638
1905	30,098,108

Java is intersected with a network of well-kept roads, both footpaths and cart roads.   Owing to the direction of the mountain chains, the traffic goes better along the island than from north to south ; although here, in this latter respect, the roads are numerous, too, and each of the mountains is traversed by a main road that connects the north and south of the island.

Right through the island from west to east, from sea to sea, runs a railway, which at many points has branch lines which run to the coast northwards and southwards.   Further, in addition to this, there is a network of well-developed tramways, which connect all parts of the country with the main line.

For the rest, there is a splendid connection with the several harbours across the sea through the mail and steamship service, which makes it quite easy to send goods from one place to another, so that no single district is cut off from the outer world.

Asia.

The sugar industry is only carried on in Mid and East Java, the western boundary being formed by the Tjimanoek, although some small plantations are met with west of this river. In Mid Java the entire northern plain from the Tjimanoek to the limestone mountains of Rembang is given up to the sugar industry, and from the sea up to the foot of the middle mountains cane plantations are found. In the corresponding plain south of the central mountains an important sugar industry is met with, which, however, begins more to the east, because in the south the mountains stretch further in an eastern direction than they do in the north. In East Java the sugar industry is most prominent in the extensive valley of the Brantas, further, in the alluvial north coast of the narrow eastern streak of that island and in the tableland between the volcanoes in the residencies of Madioen and Kediri. On the map the cane sugar centres are indicated by shading.

The cane planted area for the harvest of 1910 amounted to 314,335 acres which are divided over the different residencies, and to which, for the sake of comparison, are added the figures of some previous years.

Area Planted with Cane for Crop in Hectares.

Crop 1911. 135,780 hectares = 335,591 acres, divided as follows :—

Residencies.	1895	1900	1905	1910	1911
Cheribon	5,901	6,901	7,779	9,019	9,114
Pekalongan	7,287	8,762	9,984	10,759	11,060
Bagelen and Banjoemas	2,443	2,731	3,605	4,707	6,345
Djokdja	5,972	5,588	7,335	10,716	11,062
Solo	5,769	6,406	7,018	8,248	9,015
Semarang	7,372	7,804	8,105	8,636	8,990
Rembang	750	—	—	—	—
Madioen	2,410	3,321	3,894	4,446	4,803
Kediri	6,251	8,744	12,288	17,625	19,493
Soerabaja	16,891	19,806	23,806	26,253	26,358
Pasoeroean	12,887	13,584	14,710	20,143	22,766
Bezoeki	5,019	5,602	6,906	6,709	6,774
Total hectares	79,152	89,248	105,430	127,261	135,780
Equal to acres	195,505	220,440	260,412	314,335	335,591

These figures stand for the number of hectares that have been planted with cane for one of the harvests, and as no cane in Java is kept from the preceding year, but every year yields a new crop, they also represent the number of reaped hectares of this planting.

114

The actual area taken up by the sugar industry covers much more ground, as more than a year is required for the whole vegetation period, and the sugar cane cultivation in Java generally demands triennial change. Each acre of actually planted cane requires altogether three acres of available ground, so that the planting alone makes $3 \times 314,335 = 943,005$ acres of ground necessary. Further, nurseries are needed for the cultivation of cuttings, while the factory buildings and compounds require ground as well, so that we can reckon that 1,000,000 out of the 10,000,000 acres of arable land in Java, or 10 per cent, is given up to the sugar cane cultivation, two-thirds of which is not occupied by cane, for the moment being planted with other crops.

In the following list one finds expressed the sugar production and the number of factories of each residency of recent years, the former in piculs of 61·76 kg. and metric tons of 2,200 lbs. :—

Residencies	1899			1904			1909			1911		
	Piculs	Tons	Factories	Piculs	Tons	Factories	Piculs	Tons	Factories	Piculs	Tons	Factories
Cheribon	827 706	51,093	15	1.138,298	70,265	12	1,456.222	89,890	13	1,578,035	96,099	12
Pekalongan ..	1,225,545	75,651	15	1,780,656	109 917	15	1,983,452	122,435	15	2,048,207	126,377	15
Bagelen and } Banjoemas }	381,200	23,531	5	539,187	33,283	5	659,589	40,715	5	1.074,778	66,379	7
Djokdja	782,200	48,284	13	1,210,789	74 740	15	1,621,374	100,085	18	1,997,847	124,114	18
Solo	861,200	53 160	16	1,053 313	63,785	15	1,283,992	79,259	16	1,535 687	95 258	16
Semarang	1,008,200	62,235	14	1,375,805	84,926	14	1,524,857	94 127	12	1,620,285	100,934	2
Rembang	—	—	—	—	—	—	—	—	—	—	—	—
Madioen	420,734	25,971	6	566,259	34,954	6	740,846	45.731	6	851,930	52,600	6
Kediri	1,199,843	74,033	15	1 998 396	123.358	17	2,484,579	158,369	19	3,172.725	196 953	21
Soerabaja	2,852,091	176 055	39	3,919 504	241,945	39	4,030,852	248.787	38	5,240,894	317 448	38
Pasoeroean ..	1,593,805	98,383	31	2,177,897	134,438	29	2,667 499	164.660	29	3,512,061	218,143	29
Bezoeki	739,785	45,666	13	895,427	55,273	12	939,557	57 997	11	1,173,353	72,165	11
Total	11,891,809	734,062	182	16,635,531	1,026,884	179	19,392,319	1,197,005	182	23,745,802	1,466,569	185

II.—The History of the Java Cane Sugar Industry.

Since times immemorial sugar cane has been planted in Java, where it was introduced by Chinese or Hindus, who regarded the cane as a dainty, and probably squeezed out the juice and evaporated it to dryness on a small scale. The Chinese traveller, Fahian, who visited Java in 424, mentions the presence of sugar cane in the island, so that, considering the many commercial relations between Java and China, India and Arabia, there is no doubt as to the knowledge of evaporating the juice to a soft brown sugar existing on the island, as well as in the countries it traded with.

That a sugar industry in its present-day form should have already been in existence when the Dutch arrived at Jakatra (a sugar industry the produce of which was divided into sugar and molasses) is an erroneous supposition originating from a misinterpreted fact by van Gorkom, and by other authors who imitated him, as regards the occurrence of arrack-distilleries in the above place.*

During the first years following the conquest of Jakatra, which gave the Dutch a firm footing in Java, nothing much was done for the encouragement or extension of the sugar industry, because the East Indian Company was mainly a commercial undertaking more intent on the carrying on of trade in Eastern produce than on the production of any commodities by itself.

The sugar which was transported by the Company to its fatherland during the first years after its existence consisted of the produce of China, Formosa, Siam, and Bengal, and not till after 1637 did the first shipment of Java sugar take place. In that very year the exportation of Bantam sugar amounted to as much as 10,000 piculs (618 tons), and as the sugar profits were very tempting, and the foreign article was not always to be had, the Company resolved to erect sugar cane mills on their property in the neighbourhood of Batavia, and to establish a sugar industry of their own.

The Company allotted ground to Chinese sugar manufacturers and bestowed a great many privileges on them, e.g., a licence for cutting free firewood for the sugar manufacture out of the woods, etc., on condition that the entire produce should be delivered to the Company at a price to be fixed by itself. These prices were 6, 5, and 4 rijksdaalders† respectively per picul for first, second, or third quality; but the next year 1 rijksdaalder was deducted from each class. The Company kept changing the terms, the quantities to be delivered, and the prices, so that the sugar industry was ever in a state of uncertainty, and the number of factories and the quality of their output were not two years running the same. Moreover, the industry suffered from wars, disturbances, and diseases among the canes and the cattle which were used both for ploughing and for driving the mills, and from lack of labour. In the year 1648 the sugar harvest in the Company's territory amounted to 2,000 piculs (124 tons), which in 1652 had increased to 11,712 piculs (723 tons), as the Brazilian disturbances created a greater demand for Eastern sugar in Europe. When the West Indies on the other hand began to supply more sugar, the period of prosperity came to an end again for the time being;

---

* Although nowadays in Java arrack is almost exclusively prepared from the molasses remaining from the sugar manufacture, this substance should not be considered as the sole raw material of this liquor, so that the existence of arrack distilleries does not imply the presence of sugar factories. Arrack was originally a beverage made from rice, and in China a good deal of it is manufactured from glutinous rice; but palm wine and cane juice would do just as well for its preparation, so that the distilling of arrack out of molasses dates from a much later period than its manufacture from malted rice, palm wine, or similar juices, and the arrack distilleries do not go far to prove the existence of a sugar industry.

† 1 rijksdaalder = 4s. 2d.   1 Java picul = 61·76 kg. or 136 lbs. avoird.

while the Bantam war, about 1660, likewise prevented the development of the sugar industry. In 1652, 20 sugar mills were working, but in 1660 only 10 of these were in use, while the other 10 had discontinued operations. After peace was concluded with Bantam, in 1684, owing to the ever-growing power of the Company a better state of affairs began ; in 1710 as many as 130 sugar mills were working, and the sugar industry spread to Bantam, Cheribon, and Japara. The commercial politics of the Company were not consistent with any large production of Eastern goods. There was nothing they feared so much as an abundance of any product, and a reduction in price in consequence of it, so acting up to this the Company prohibited the erection of any more sugar factories, and stipulated that no mill was to be allowed to yield more than 300 piculs (18 tons) sugar yearly, so that a maximum product of 40,000 piculs (2,470 tons) was fixed. This quantity, however, was not realized by a long way, as in 1745 the number of sugar factories in the territories surrounding Batavia had fallen to 65. The Company then fixed on 70 as the maximum number of these factories, which was raised to 80 in 1750. However, the number of factories actually grew less, but their output increased, so that in 1779 only 55 supplied in all 100,000 piculs (6,176 tons) sugar to the company, exclusive of the molasses, which they were free to sell to other people.

In 1795 the East Indian Company was dissolved, and Java came under the direct management of the Batavian Republic, which was afterwards called the Kingdom of Holland, and when that kingdom became part of France, it became French too ; but in 1811 it was seized by England, only to be returned to the Netherlands in 1816.

During all this period the restrictions as regards the sugar industry kept changing. The manufacturers' complaint during the management of the East Indian Company had always been the same, namely, that they were obliged to deliver all their produce to the company, which in its turn did not feel any obligation as regards taking a fixed quantity of sugar, so that the business was most uncertain, as the planters could never prepare for any pre-arranged production. In order to remedy this, it was decreed in 1797, that the factories in the surroundings of Batavia should produce 15,000 baskets (of 375 lbs.) of sugar, and were to be free to dispose of any excess production at their own risk. The share of every mill in the contingent quantity of sugar was fixed according to the condition of the mills, the condition of the crops, etc.

For the north and east coast also similar regulations were fixed. In 1794 there were in these parts 31 sugar factories, which together were capable of producing 2,000,000 lbs. of sugar, an amount they wished to increase till 4,000,000 lbs. should be reserved for the Government, and another 1,000,000 lbs. be left for sale to outsiders. For this purpose the owners of the existing and the new mills were to receive untilled plots of ground for plantation purposes, and the Government was to advance money to the amount of half the expected harvest, the price of which was fixed at 4½ rijksdaalders per picul, first quality. The proposed regulations, however, were not brought into force, so that the production of that part of the island never realized more than 2,000,000 lbs. In the surroundings of Batavia this system had good results, the more so as the Government kept supporting the manufacture of sugar by raising the advances and the sugar prices. The sugar production of Java consequently rose during the first years of the nineteenth century, to be followed by a time of marked decline. The unfavourable political situation in Europe, Holland's forced alliance with France, and the activity of the British privateering hampered the free intercourse of trade so much that Java sugar had to lie stored up in the island, any transportation being out of the question. The Government still lived in the hopes of peace being restored in the future, and in spite of the existing large stock-in-trade, it kept encouraging the manufacturers to remain working, in order that when the war should cease, the industry might not be found in an inactive state.

As the Government's stock of sugar yearly increased, and as it was no longer thought desirable to have so much capital lying inactive, the Governor-General Daendels in 1809 abandoned the policy hitherto followed, and granted the manufacturers freedom to dispose of their goods ; but, as ill-luck would have it, the sugar cultivation became free just at the time when selling the produce became an impossibility. The British occupation during the years 1811–16 confirmed that state of affairs. We may safely call this a complete check for the industry, for we see that in 1813 the total Java production amounted to only 10,000 piculs (618 tons), a figure that in 1816 had gone up only to 20,000 piculs (1,235 tons).

After these colonies in 1816 had reverted to the Netherlands, the new government provisionally maintained the system of a free sugar industry ; but the sugar manufacturers had suffered so severely that although they were certain of getting their crop sold, their business remained stagnant. When in 1826 Governor-General du Bus de Guisignies came to Java, the entire sugar production did not exceed 19,795 piculs (1,223 tons). This statesman started advancing money once more, and knew how to encourage the sugar production so much that in 1830, at the end of his term of office, the production had risen to 108,640 piculs (6,710 tons). He was succeeded by Governor-General van den Bosch, who was provided with well-nigh absolute power, and among other things was especially instructed to take measures to make Java produce for the mother-country. These measures include one known by the name of the " Cultural System," which, as regards the sugar industry, consisted of the following regulations : —

The native population of the districts suited for sugar growing was to give up one-third of its arable land for the planting of sugar cane, to be disposed of as necessity required, so that the entire third need not be taken into cultivation. Further, the native population was to till the fields, supply fuel, draught and ploughing cattle, and in this way was exempted from corvée duty.   All labour was to be paid out of the money the given produce fetched, from which the requisite land tax was to be deducted first.   In order to work up the cane to sugar, sugar contracts were drawn up with private parties who received loans in money for the erection of factories.   The contracting parties were to deliver all their produce to the Government at a fixed price, and were allowed to redeem the money advanced by means of sugar supplies.

In the beginning the profits for the State and for the sugar manufacturers were meagre ; in fact, the transaction even resulted in loss during the first years the system was tried, and it was not without some trouble that private individuals were won over to the idea of entering into sugar contracts.   Later on the regulations were revised and improved, the manufacturers being allowed to dispose of part of the sugar at their own risk, so that their interest in a profitable manufacture became keener ; there was thenceforward a change for the better noticeable in the state of affairs, and the Java sugar industry gradually became a profitable business, both for the Exchequer and for the manufacturer.   When, by 1870, the sugar manufacture was settled on a sound basis, it was considered time for the Government to withdraw from any direct participation in the production, and so new regulations were made as follows :—

The direct interference of the State with the sugar industry was restricted to the growing of the cane.   This made it necessary for the Government to dispose of part of the land and the labour of the population, on condition that a proper price should be paid both for ground and labour, and that when the crop in the field was given to the contractor he should provide for the further tending, cutting, and transportation of the cane out of his own purse, without any assistance from the Government.   Beginning with 1879, the original plantations stipulated by contract were to be diminished by one-thirteenth every year, so that in 1891 the connection of the Government with the sugar cultivation and industry was to come to an end.   The manufacturers could freely dispose of the sugar they produced, and pay as rent for the land they were planting on with the aid of Government intermediary up till 1891 a fixed price for the cane, and, further, a fixed premium, which is reckoned on the basis of production during the years 1864–69.   On the private plantations a fixed premium of 25 guilders (or £2 1s.) per bouw* is due to the Government.   In order to come to the assistance of industry which was not in prosperous circumstances the premium on the private-grown cane was done away with in 1886, and the premium on the Government plantations was reduced to half between the years 1887 and 1891, on condition that the payment of the other half should be postponed till the years 1892–96.

Just at the time these new regulations were introduced, Java was struck by two calamities, which brought the sugar industry to the verge of ruin.   The enormous beetroot sugar production referred to in the first part of this volume caused the price of sugar to go down considerably in 1882–84, so that it eventually fell below net cost price.   At the same time a mysterious disease, which

* 1 bouw = 500 sq. Rhineland rods = 1·74 acres.

has not been explained in spite of careful and continuous investigations on the part of several able botanists and plant pathologists, attacked the cane plantations, and did great harm. Noticed first in 1884, in the western part of the island, this disease (called *sereh*) spread eastwards, and caused a considerable decrease in production everywhere. The sugar manufacturers, oppressed by the two evils, did not lose courage ; they put considerable capital into their industry, and invoked the aid of science to help them to improve their cultivation and manufacturing methods. Three experimental stations were founded for the purpose of combating the *sereh* disease, which have done good work outside their original scope, and which have given useful information as regards planting and manufacturing methods, chemical analysis, and control, and even now as regards mechanical installations of factories. Capital was provided by the Dutch capitalists and invested in the calamity-stricken industry, science was practically applied, and the estates were managed in an economical, rational, and energetic manner. This praiseworthy combination of energy, science and capital not only saved the Java sugar industry from utter ruin, but also placed it among the foremost cane sugar-producing countries, so that for years Java has been an example to other countries, who recognize it to be expedient to carry on the cane sugar industry in a scientific manner.

So much active power and rational application of science was sure to be crowned with success, and it is due to these circumstances that the Java sugar industry, in the dark days just before the Brussels Convention, was never destitute, but could hold its own, unprotected as it was. Even during the last years of the nineteenth century the planted area increased so much that the Government began to fear that arable land for other articles of food would fall short, and therefore took measures to stop the extension of the cane plantations. As that fear soon appeared to be without foundation, the extension, as will be seen, went on regularly, and is still going on.

A statement of the total production in metric tons, from the early years following the introduction of the Cultural System down to the present time, shows the steady and uninterrupted growth of this production :—

1840	.. ..	47,040	1851	.. ..	120,345
1841	.. ..	45,901	1852	.. ..	76,007
1842	.. ..	51,128	1853	.. ..	111,727
1843	.. ..	56,436	1854	.. ..	112,094
1844	.. ..	63,421	1855	.. ..	103,963
1845	.. ..	90,962	1856	.. ..	125,101
1846	.. ..	87,647	1857	.. ..	106,157
1847	.. ..	82,738	1858	.. ..	132,824
1848	.. ..	89,931	1859	.. ..	133,682
1849	.. ..	105,126	1860	.. ..	136,153
1850	.. ..	86,519	1861	.. ..	136,889

1862	145,047	1887 375,784
1863	131,799	1888 355,334
1864	140,224	1889 332,997
1865	137,893	1890 399,999
1866	142,290	1891 406,800
1867	133,049	1892 422,000
1868	178,784	1893 479,660
1869	182,461	1894 530,963
1870	152,595	1895 .. . 581,569
1871	190,866	1896 534,390
1872	209,299	1897 586,299
1873	199,068	1898 725,030
1874	201,502	1899 762,447
1875	193,634	1900 744,257
1876	237,870	1901 803,735
1877	245,814	1902 897,130
1878	224,689	1903 944,798
1879	233,302	1904 1,055,043
1880	216,179	1905 .. . 1,039,178
1881	279,207	1906 .. . 1,067,798
1882	292,005	1907 1,210,127
1883	324,704	1908 1,241,885
1884	394,247	1909 1,247,260
1885	380,046	1910 1,278,420
1886	356,022	1911 1,466,569

III.—Cane Cultivation.

Cane cultivation, as a rule, is carried on in Java on land which is not the planter's property, but is rented by him either for a single crop or for a comparatively small number of years ; though sometimes he gets it on perpetual lease. Nearly all the cane ground by the sugar factories is planted under their own management, and only a very small part is bought from native growers, so that the manufacturers are cane planters as well, and both agriculture and manufacture are controlled by the same people.

Most of the sugar factories get their arable land by voluntary agreement with the population, i.e., they hire land for one harvest only from " dessas," or villages, round the factories, and work them under estate control with their own labourers. They never hire more than is wanted for their immediate needs, but leave the rest to the owners, who use it for rice and other crops. According to the civil regulations, it is forbidden to hire more than one-third of the arable land belonging to a dessa ; moreover, a maximum planting area has been fixed for every factory, which cannot be exceeded when hiring. When people wish to found a new factory or extend the plantation of an existing one, permission from the Governor-General is first required and only granted when it is sufficiently proved that the step will not be detrimental to the economical interests of the native population : which are, that enough ground shall be left for the cultivation of articles of food, and that there is sufficient irrigation water for both the cultivation of these articles and of cane.   In Djocdjakarta and Soerakarta, the so-called Principalities, hiring has more the character of perpetual leasing ; extensive stretches of land are hired from the native princes for a number of years at a time, and plots of that land selected for cane cultivation.   The remaining land is given to the native population, who grow food crops on their own account in return for payment in money, in produce, or in labour.   Finally, a few sugar estates are established on long leases, where the land is ceded to the estate for seventy-five years on payment of annual rent.   In this case there of course results a large surplus of ground, and suitable plots for cane cultivation have to be selected.

While in one case only such ground as is wanted for cane cultivation that very year is hired, in the two other cases large plots of ground are partly cultivated with cane, and partly grown with other crops, either by the estate itself or by natives at their own expense or joint account.

The planting is exclusively done on irrigated land, and a triennial rotation of crops is practised.   In some parts where the soil is scarce, one meets with a two-year rotation, and in other places a four-year is met with ; but a triennial one is the rule, and in every case cane is planted after a rice crop.   The following scheme approximately indicates the succession of crops, although it is not an exclusive example.   Sometimes tapioca or some other crop is planted instead of rice, so that then only one rice crop finds its place between two cane harvests.

September..	cane crop.
September to November	beans, maize, etc.
November to April	rice.
April to November	fallow, beans, indigo, etc.
November to April	rice.
April to September of the next year	cane, etc.

As soon as the rice is reaped, the field operations are begun.   The land, for months together, has been saturated with water ; all sorts of reducing processes have taken place there, and oxygen is altogether wanting.   In order to make this soil fit again for cane, it should be exposed to sun and wind.   For this purpose, first, a deep ditch which carries off the water, and also serves to supply irrigation water later on, is dug.   Then the plot is divided up into pieces of one-tenth or one-twelfth of a bouw through cross ditches, and, finally, the furrows are dug in which the cane is to be planted.   These generally measure 30 ft. in length by a little more than I ft. in depth, and are placed at a distance of 4 or 5 ft. apart. Their width is 1 or 1½ ft., and the displaced earth is piled up between the furrows. In some places where the condition of the ground allows it, ploughing is first done, and afterwards the digging of furrows with spades is commenced. When the plot is " open " it looks like a network of trenches, which remain in that position during five or six weeks exposed to the sun. The wet clods become dry, crumble up, assume a lighter colour, and in the end a light-grey, powdery soil instead of a lot of wet, cold, black clods is obtained. During the drying-up, and also after the planting of the cane, grass has to be repeatedly weeded away, which becomes especially necessary when the cane is not yet well developed. As soon as it is full grown, however, it will produce shade which will cause the weeds to wither. When the land has been in this condition for some time, the soil is thoroughly loosened again in the furrows where the cuttings are planted directly or in holes.

The cuttings are put in the loosened subsoil in the furrows, then covered with a layer of earth and irrigated repeatedly every four or five days. As the planting time happens to be in the dry monsoon, it is thus necessary to irrigate the cane plantations. In most cases the irrigation installation is already ready for use, as the same fields used for rice cultivation serve as cane plots. These installations, ditches, and canals are hired together with the land, while the irrigation water is given by the Government, according to a plan of division drawn up beforehand, which allows for the size of the plantations of sugar cane, the extent of those of the native population, and the amount of disposable water. As the latter is not always adequate, the sugar factories often have large pumping stations for the irrigation of their land, when should the quantity of water from the canal supply not prove sufficient the water pumped up is used.

Manuring is done either simultaneously with the planting, or later on, and sometimes at both times, to an average amount of £4 3s. 4d. each bouw, or £2 6s. 8d. per acre. Manuring is almost exclusively carried on with nitrogenous compounds, sulphate of ammonia, oil-cakes (*boengkil*) from arachis nuts, kapok-seed, castor beans or cotton-seed, bat-dung, but most of all with sulphate of ammonia. Potash and phosphoric acid are seldom applied, the former almost never, and phosphoric acid in the form of superphosphate and basic slag only in combination with great quantities of ammonium sulphate on soils rich in lime, which are found in the residencies of Djokdja, Solo, and Semarang. The silt yearly deposited by the rivers contains so much potash and phosphoric acid in combination with other elements, but which are set free by disintegration processes, that the cane, as a rule, does not want any more ; and experiments have shown us that any increase in the quantity of potash and phosphoric acid in most cases does not lead to any better cane and sugar production.

As the cane grows up it is banked with loose soil, which up to that time has been heaped up between the rows. Finally, good care is taken by the time the heavy rains of the west monsoon are due that the cane is entirely banked up, and stands on fairly high banks, so that the rain water can run off instead of being forced to collect round the roots of the cane. As soon as the cane has ripened, which takes from eleven to fifteen months according to the kind of cane and the state of the weather, it is reaped and then dug out as deep as the root.

Ratoons, as known in most cane sugar producing countries where, in many cases, they are most profitable, are not grown in Java, but every year the past year's crop is reaped, and nothing is kept for a following harvest. This is due to the fact that the first and following ratoons yield so much smaller a crop that, owing to the heavy rent and the small amount of disposable land, it becomes an absolute necessity to obtain as much cane sugar as possible from the little area of land; while labour in Java is so abundant and cheap that it pays well in the end to spend more money on labour connected with the yearly planting.

As compared with most of the other cane-growing colonies, where land is abundant and cheap, and labour is scarce and expensive, Java, with its 30,000,000 inhabitants, wants the land badly for the cultivation of articles of food, so that the ground disposable for cane growth becomes costly and very limited. On the other hand, this extensive population offers an ample supply of cheap and readily accessible labour, which counterbalances the first-mentioned disadvantage. This explains why it is advisable to proceed in Java quite differently from the manner in which they work in Cuba, and why it is necessary in Java to obtain as much cane, and from the cane as much sugar, as possible through intensive tillage, manuring, careful up-keep, and constant care; whereas in other countries the quantity of cane produced by a unit of area does not count so much, as there is an abundance of ground to be got for little money.

In the years preceding 1850 a kind of white cane was planted, until a sugar manufacturer from Cheribon, Gonsalves, noticed that a kind of dark red cane, which for centuries had existed among the plantations, yielded far more sugar than the white cane, but at the same time was harder and not so easy to crush. He had cuttings of that cane collected and planted in a sequestered spot in his ground, and showed the Government officials, who up to that time had objected to the planting of this dark variety, how much more sugar was to be had from it than from the white cane. The difference was considerable, and it soon appeared that the new cane had not only the advantage of a larger yield in sugar, but was also less susceptible to damage by heavy rains, as well as by drought, while it would thrive in both light and heavy soils. It was not long before the Black Cheribon cane, as it was called, was being planted everywhere in Java, and this, no doubt, greatly contributed towards increasing the sugar production. But this favourable state of affairs was not destined to last long. In 1882 a planter from the most westerly district of Java noticed that part of his cane did not grow more than a few feet high, and formed a bunch of shoots and leaves, while yielding no well-developed cane stalks. The following year the same thing happened in the more easterly plantations, the new disease spreading further, till, in 1892, it had gone so far as the Bali Straits. Only the mountainous regions and the interior were exempt from the disease, and have continued so owing to very severe quarantine laws. Because of the shape assumed by the plants that were struck with the disease, it went by the name of *sereh*, as the canes resembled clods of Citronella grass (*Andropogon schoemanthus*; Javanese *sereh*).

The phenomena of the disease in its worst phase are absolute stagnation of growth, together with the sprouting of buds and aërial rootlets after the first months of vegetation; in case the disease should be less serious, stagnation only occurs after the cane has attained to a certain height, so that the financial loss is then not so ruinous as with a more severe attack. At any rate, a decrease in the quantity of cane to be reaped cannot fail to be noticed, but as the plant does not die, the sugar content remains satisfactory, and the yield of sugar from the same weight of *sereh*-stricken cane is not less than that from cane in a sound condition. It appeared that ratoons suffered much more from the disease than plant cane, and that when tops of attacked cane were planted the disease showed itself in a far more severe form than was the case with tops from sound cane; finally, that cane planted from sound sets in infected soils did not become attacked by *sereh* till after two generations. A first measure taken against the fatal disease was to avoid planting cuttings out of infected plots, so new fields were planted with cuttings coming from the more easterly uninfected regions. There was a regular transportation of cuttings from east to west, which the Government assisted by lowering the freight charges on the State railways, and in 1888 and 1889 even by transporting the seed free of cost along their lines; but as the disease spread more and more eastward the need of this plant-seed increased while the supply diminished, so that this assistance was only of temporary avail. With the aid of the experiment stations, which were established in the meantime, cane varieties were obtained from all parts of the world within reach in order to try and find a variety which would be able to withstand *sereh*, and possess the same good qualities as the Black Cheribon cane does. At the same time, nurseries were laid out in remote spots in the mountains in order that fresh and sound plant-seed might always be available. The planters also did their utmost to keep the *sereh*-free districts immune from it by means of disinfection and quarantine, and they began to start extensive scientific experiments in order to discover the nature and the propagation of the disease.

Among the newly imported varieties there were some that, although not altogether immune from *sereh*, were fairly resistant to it: such varieties as the Loethers, Muntok, Canne Morte or Yellow Fiji cane, etc.; but however welcome these might have been at a time when the sugar industry was much pestered by untoward circumstances, they could not now altogether supplant the Black Cheribon cane. Some sorts did give adequate returns, but were not so rich in sugar ; others were sensitive as regards the soil, and required either a light or a heavy soil, or could not stand much moisture, so that the new varieties could not be entirely substituted for the Black Cheribon. As long as fresh supplies of plant cane were provided from the mountain nurseries, and not more than one generation was planted, while ratoons were never kept, *sereh* could easily be avoided, and good crops obtained. But although the yields were satisfactory the expense caused by the renewing of plant-seed was so heavy that this method had soon to be given up. For one bouw of cane in the field would take as many as 40 piculs of cuttings, which cost 2s. per picul in the mountainous regions where they were raised, and, delivered in the field, perhaps 3s. 4d., so that a bouw of new cane cost £6 13s. 4d. in tops from mountain nurseries, and supposing this to yield 100 piculs of sugar, no less than 12 per cent. of the cost of production would be wanted for plant-seed. As only part of the plots was planted with tops from mountain nurseries, and the rest with tops from the cane field itself, the average cost of plant-seed became less, but about 1900 it was estimated at the average price of 10d. per picul sugar.

The discovery of the propagation of cane through seed, made by Soltwedel in Java in 1887, and by Harrison and Bovell in Barbados in 1888, independently of one another, revived the hope of obtaining a better species of cane.

As *sereh* was attributed by many people to a weakening in consequence of the continuous asexual propagation, it was evident that if this supposition was right *sereh* would not attack the new kinds of cane obtained from seed. But this was not the case, and it appeared that cane raised from seed was as well susceptible to *sereh* as cane from cuttings. Wakker, Moquette, Bouricius, Kobus, and others, through their scientific crossing experiments, succeeded in producing new varieties of cane which were not susceptible to *sereh* disease, and which were both heavy in weight and rich in sugar. These kinds, after they had been reared from seed, were propagated through cuttings, and are now reproduced all over the cane plantations. The cultivation of new species is still in progress, and even now in Java there are a great many cane varieties which have gradually supplanted the old Cheribon cane. A heavy blow was dealt to the latter cane by the so-called *dongkellan* disease, which caused much of the Black cane to die all over Eastern Java, and thereby contributed greatly to the wholesale substitution of that kind of cane by the seedling canes. Some of these latter ripen early, some late ; some prefer a light soil, others a heavy one ; some are proof against drought, others can stand much moisture ; in short, there is so much choice that every manufacturer can choose a special kind to suit a special time of the season, and a special part of his plantation, and always provide the mills with fresh ripe cane. There is still a necessity to keep on special nurseries for cuttings, but as these need not be in distant parts the cost of carriage to the fields has become considerably less.

Experiments destined to select from a number of cuttings those richest in sugar through chemical selection as regards sugar content and through physical selection, as regards specific weight, and to plant them, relying on hereditary reproduction of the high qualities, have ultimately proved useless in spite of a short period of apparent success.

Besides the *sereh*, the cane suffers greatly from infectious diseases caused by parasitical fungi. Some of these attack the roots, others the stalks, or leaves and leaf-sheaths, but only a few of these diseases are highly injurious, namely, the *Pineapple* disease or Black Rot, caused by *Thielaviopsis aethaceticus*, and the Red Smut brought about by *Colletotrichum falcatum*. The first-mentioned fungus possesses highly resistant spores, and once it gets a hold in the fields it is most difficult to exterminate. It sometimes occurs on the ends of cuttings, and penetrates them till it has got at the young plant, which generally dies soon after. To prevent this, the cutting is soaked in Bordeaux mixture, which renders the penetration of the moulds an impossibility. This disease is only dangerous to the very young cane plants. As soon as these have reached the stage of no longer being dependent on the seed, but possess their own roots, the danger is past.

On the other hand, the other disease mentioned, Red Smut, only threatens the grown-up cane plant. The slightest wound serves as an opening for the penetration of the fungus *Colletotrichum*, which develops and attacks the cane.

It is rather remarkable that really pernicious disease germs, such as smut and others, cause so little damage to the cane, while fungi, on the other hand, though harmless in themselves, do so much damage. This may be explained by the fact that the crop is dug out and planted anew every year, so that the dangerous diseases have no time to spread or get a firm hold. Yet the large open wound surfaces of the cuttings give ample scope to the development of facultative parasites, which find everything in readiness for them.

As soon as the cane has attained to some height, it may be attacked by animal enemies. We need only mention termites or white ants, boring caterpillars, beetle-larvæ, beetles, and mice. There are plenty of others which, however, do not accomplish any great mischief. Grasshoppers, usually so pernicious in tropical countries, cause little damage in Java for want of a desert where they can quietly mature, and then attack the plantations in great swarms. The caterpillars, especially the boring variety, are by far the most dangerous and injurious, while the leaf-eating caterpillars do very little harm. Five kinds of borers have been discovered up to now, all of which attack cane in their special way.

Owing to improved varieties of cane, rational treatment and manuring of the fields, and extremely punctilious superintendence, the cane production per unit of area has considerably increased during the last sixteen years, as the following statistics dealing with the production of the different residencies will show :—

RESIDENCIES.	1893/4.		1894/5.		1895/6.		1896/7.	
	Piculs per Bouw.	Tons of 2,240 lbs. per acre.	Piculs per Bouw.	Tons of 2,240 lbs. per acre.	Piculs per Bouw.	Tons of 2,240 lbs. per acre.	Piculs per Bouw.	Tons of 2 240 lbs. per acre.
Bezoeki	824	28·564	900	31·198	831	28·807	934	32·377
Probolinggo ..	832	28·941	903	31·225	734	25·444	861	9·854
Pasoeroean ..	666	23·187	723	25·063	669	23·191	706	24·473
Soerabaja ..	857	29·718	897	31·095	785	27·213	883	30·609
Kediri	848	29·397	1037	35·948	884	30·649	957	33·175
Madioen	664	23·018	821	28·460	701	24·300	781	27·074
Rembang ..	—	—-	591	20·487	229	7·962	372	13·890
Japara	688	23·850	858	29·743	743	25·756	815	28·253
Semarang ..	619	21·458	798	27·663	639	22·151	752	26·068
Solo	705	24·439	835	28·946	787	27·282	845	29·293
Djokdja	827	28·668	986	34·180	946	32·793	1030	35·705
Banjoemas .. } Bagelen .. .. }	593	2c·556	885	30·679	788	27·317	1016	35·220
Pekalongan ..	870	30·158	912	31·874	815	28·253	952	33·001
Tegal	840	29·119	962	33·357	811	28·114	875	30·332
Cheribon ..	694	24·058	813	23·183	771	26·727	800	27·732
East Java* ..	808	28·010	891	30·887	775	26·866	868	30·097
Middle Java ..	721	24·994	878	30·436	804	27·871	903	31·302
West Java ..	788	27·317	895	31·026	801	27·767	858	29·743
Average ..	782	27·108	888	30·783	789	27·351	875	30·332

RESIDENCIES.	1902/3		1903/4		1904/5		1905/6	
	Piculs per Bouw.	Tons of 2 240 lbs. per acre.	Piculs p·r Bouw	Tons of 2 240 lbs. per acre.	Piculs per Bouw.	Tons of 2 240 lbs. per acre.	Piculs per Bouw.	Tons of 2,240 lbs. per acre
Bezoeki	1126	38·566	1106	38·339	1056	36·606	1072	37·160
Pasoeroean ..	971	33·660	1095	37·959	1098	38·063	1093	37·889
Soerabaja ..	1033	35·809	1137	39·414	1097	38·028	1077	37·334
Kediri	1166	40·419	1203	41·702	1189	41·217	1202	41·667
Madioen	929	32·204	924	32·031	1027	35·601	996	34·526
Semarang ..	980	33·972	1067	36·988	985	34·156	1039	36·017
Solo	988	34·250	1088	37·716	1060	36·745	1079	37·403
Djokdja	1043	36·156	1112	38·547	1129	39·137	1142	39·587
Banjoemas .. } Bagelen .. .. }	1239	42·950	995	34·492	1042	36·121	1172	40·627
Pekalongan ..	1043	36·156	1109	38·443	1164	40·350	1104	38·270
Cheribon ..	959	33·244	886	30·713	1010	35·012	994	34·457
East Java* ..	1050	36·398	1114	38·617	1106	38·339	1102	38·200
Middle Java ..	1034	35·844	1075	37·265	1052	36·467	1099	38·097
West Java ..	1009	34·977	1018	35·290	1105	38·305	1058	36·676
Average ..	1039	36·017	1089	37·750	1092	37·854	1094	37·924

* The division of Java into west, middle and east Java does not tally with the one given on Page
Solo, Djokdja, Bagelen, and Banjoemas to Middle ; and Madioen, Kediri, Soerabaja, Pasoeroean and
were Japara with Semarang, and Tegal with Pekalongan ; that is why since 1900 the production of the

Java.

1897/8		1898/9		1899/1900		1900/1		1901/2	
Piculs per Bouw.	Tons of 2,240 lbs. per acre.	Piculs per Bouw.	Tons of 2 240 lbs. per acre.	Piculs per Bouw.	Tons of 2,240 lbs. per acre.	Piculs per Bouw.	Tons of 2,240 lbs. per acre.	Piculs per Bouw	Tons of 2 240 lbs. per acre.
1052	36·467	1033	35·809	1012	35·081	1017	35·255	942	32·654
907	31·441	871	30·193	938	32·516	891	30·887	835‡	28·946
808	28·010	840	29·119	854	29·604	799	27·697		
1047	36·295	1031	35·740	998	34·596	939	32·550	921	31·927
1113	38·582	1045	36·226	1058	36·676	870	30·158	961	33·313
928	32·170	860	29·819	804	27·861	747	25·895	782	27·108
370	13·826	—	—	—	—	—	—	—	—
946	32·793	903	31·302	991	34·353	894	30·991	858	29·743
1011	35·047	912	31·614	893	30·956	826	28·633		
1027	35·631	955	33·106	996	34·526	747	25·895	898	31·130
1098	38·063	946	32·793	1092	37·854	882	30·574	988	34·250
1190	41·563	993	34·422	1063	36·849	771	26·727	1089	37·750
993	34·422	836	28·980	1048	36·330	1074	37·230	1071	37·126
1039	36·017	916	31·753	1008	34·943	971	33·660		
962	33·347	833	28·876	803	27·836	835	28·946	860	29·819
999	34·630	978	33·903	972	33·694	901	31·233	902	31·267
1042	36·121	947	32·828	1019	35·324	829	28·737	932	32·307
1001	34·700	868	30·097	938	32·516	927	32·135	981	34·007
1001	34·700	949	32·897	979	33·937	888	30·783	922	31·961

1906/7		1907/8		1908/9		1909/10		1910/11	
Piculs per Bouw.	Tons of 2,240 lbs. per acre.	Piculs per Bouw.	Tons of 2,240 lbs. per acre.	Piculs per Bouw.	Tons of 2 240 lbs. per acre.	Piculs per Bouw.	Tons of 2,240 lbs. per acre.	Piculs per Bouw.	Tons of 2,240 lbs. per acre.
1202	41·667	1182	40·794	1142	39·587	1123	38·929	1209	41·910
1086	37·646	1143	39·622	1110	38·478	1117	38·731	1154	40·020
1169	40·523	1172	40·627	1170	40·558	1157	40·118	1326	45·966
1114	38·617	1302	45·133	1207	41·841	1138	39·448	1186	41·113
1087	37·681	1145	39·692	1156	40·073	1044	36·191	1167	40·464
1054	36·537	1222	42·360	1193	41·355	1123	38·929	1142	39·587
1192	41·320	1296	44·926	1174	40·697	1143	39·622	1199	41·559
1194	41·390	1341	46·486	1214	42·084	1163	40·315	1238	42·915
1115	38·652	1362	47·213	1238	42·916	1112	38·547	1176	40·766
1027	35·601	1234	42·707	1235	42·912	1156	40·080	1230	42·638
1001	34·700	1064	36·884	1098	38·063	990	34·318	1130	39·171
1135	39·345	1192	41·320	1164	40·350	1133	39·275	1224	42·430
1143	39·612	1298	44·996	1200	41·598	1140	39·518	1193	41·345
1016	35·220	1156	40·073	1172	40·627	1081	37·473	1185	41·078
1118	38·756	1213	41·977	1172	40·627	1126	39·033	1210	41·945

108. In sugar circles Cheribon and Pekalongan are supposed to belong to West Java ; Semarang, Bezoeki to East Java. ‡ In 1900 the residencies Pasoercean and Probolinggo were united, so component parts of the united residencies is no longer given separately.

Asia.

To judge from the above table, it is clear that no fixed cost price of cane can be set down, as the cane production per unit of area varies greatly, and the cost of the different operations for the different parts of the country is not the same either. From a great many annual reports of sugar factories we may infer, however, that the net cost price of cane in the field—that is, without cutting and carting wages, but including the items of land rent, cutting, cultivation, manuring and wages—amounts to 4d. to 5d. per picul, or from 5s. 4d. to 6s. 11d. per ton. Higher and lower figures may occur, but most of the data at our disposal for 1909 vary between these two values.

In the *Archief voor de Java Suikerindustrie*, 1908, on page 830, we find the average cost of cane for 1901–1905, on one of the best managed sugar estates in Java, specified as follows :—

	£	s.	d.	£	s.	d.
European employés	2,620	18	4			
Native labour	1,561	0	0			
Rent of land	3,515	10	0			
Cultural expenses	15,330	11	8			
Watching expenses	425	8	4			
Manure	5,943	8	4			
Premiums for killing vermin	430	13	4			
Disinfection of tops	70	15	0			
				£29,898	5	0
Import of cuttings	590	13	4			
Various expenses	166	18	4			
Seedling nurseries in the plain	137	15	0			
				895	6	8
Various costs for bridges and roads				215	16	8
Mountain nurseries				4725	8	4
				£35,734	16	8

The average planted area amounted for those years to 1,345 bouws = 2,358 acres, so that the total cost of sugar cane in the field per bouw amounted to £26 11s. 8d. (£15 3s. 1d. per acre), or 4s. 9d. per picul cane (6s. 7d. per metric ton), not including interest, management, taxes, and other expenses.

IV.—Manufacture.

The manufacture of sugar from sugar cane in Java has attained to great perfection, and may serve as an example of a well managed and well controlled business. The ample investment of funds in the newest machinery, the activity of the sugar experiment stations, the adequate training of sugar chemists and factory chiefs—all these have contributed towards making the Java sugar industry a model one, of which it may rightly be proud.

In other works by the author the manufacture and the methods of control have been fully dealt with, so that it may suffice here to refer but briefly to them. It need only be pointed out that as a method for juice extraction mill crushing is exclusively employed ; as a rule, a crusher or a shredder is used with three or sometimes four mills, and usually maceration with water and with last mill juice. The juice is generally clarified with a little lime, sometimes followed by a neutralization with sulphurous acid ; while some factories which prepare white sugar apply the double carbonatation process. Evaporation and boiling is exclusively done *in vacuo*, all massecuites are cooled in motion and separated into sugar and syrup in centrifugals. Centrifugal sugar is dried in a revolving roller by means of hot air before being packed into bags and baskets.

According to the figures of the *Mutual Control of Javan Sugar Factories*, the extraction and losses of sugar have been during the last ten years as follows :—

Year.	Sucrose on 100 parts of Cane.	Sucrose in Juice on 100 parts of Cane.	Sucrose extracted in Juice on 100 parts of Sucrose in Cane.	Sucrose obtained on 100 parts of			Sucrose lost on 100 parts of Cane in			Total.
				Cane.	Sucrose in Cane.	Sucrose in Juice.	Bagasse.	Filter cake.	Molasses & undetermined	
1899	13·99	12·63	90·3	11·27	80·58	89·23	1·36	0·10	1·26	2·72
1900	12·26	11·04	90·1	9·62	78·53	87·15	1·22	0·10	1·32	2·64
1901	12·68	11·44	90·2	10·21	80·51	89·25	1·24	0·09	1·14	2·47
1902	13·43	12·22	91·0	—	—	—	1·21	0·09	—	—
1903	12·40	11·23	90·6	9·94	81·07	89·58	1·17	0·09	1·08	2·35
1904	13·04	11·92	91·4	10·77	82·58	90·35	1·12	0·10	1·05	2·27
1905	12·66	11·54	91·2	10·33	81·69	89·51	1·12	0·09	1·12	2·33
1906	12·38	11·26	90·9	9·98	80·64	88·74	1·13	0·09	1·18	2·40
1907	13·11	11·96	91·2	10·75	82·00	89·91	1·15	0·10	1·11	2·36
1908	12·30	11·19	91·0	10·05	81·73	89·63	1·11	0·09	1·05	2·25
1909	12·16	11·07	90·7	9·89	81·33	88·38	1·09	0·10	1·08	2·27
1910	12·54	11·43	91·2	10·26	81·82	89·76	1·11	0·10	1·07	2·28

The yields of sugar from cane in the different residencies during the last fifteen years have been as follows :—

Residencies	1897	1898	1899	1900	1901	1902	1903	1904	1905	1906	1907	1908	1909	1910	1911
Bezoeki ..	9·48	9·40	9·74	8·76	9·84	9 97	8·95	9·37	9·33	9·21	11·29	9 43	9·52	9·21	10 1
Probolinggo*	9·73	10·29	10·26	9·47	9·77	} 10 38	11·13	10 46	10·05	9·93	11·49	9·80	9·74	9 95	9·5
Pasoeroean..	10·35	10·54	10·94	10 09	10 34										
Soerabaja ..	10·23	10·17	10 89	9·40	9·92	10·71	10·29	10 56	10·54	10·09	12·49	9 80	9·93	10·42	10·4
Kediri	8 98	9 61	10 58	8·43	8 71	10·15	8·92	9·9	9·14	8 91	11 61	8·98	8.93	9·55	9·7
Madioen ..	11·16	11·39	11·84	10·56	11·07	11·27	10·79	12·14	11 20	11·26	12·63	10·70	10·76	11·00	10·8
Rembang ..	11·76	9 35	—	—	—	—	—	—	—	—	—	—	—	—	—
Japara* ..	11·20	11·11	11·69	10·86	10 88	} 11·47	10·59	11·58	11·22	10·61	11 97	10·88	10·85	11 00	11·3
Semarang ..	9·84	9 76	10·95	10·53	10·79										
Solo ..	10·54	10·25	10 89	9·32	10·60	11 12	9·95	10·86	10 31	9·87	12·64	9·76	9·83	10 06	10·2
Djokdja .	10·23	10·17	11.17	9·01	10·53	10·79	10 01	11·01	10 71	10·46	13·34	10·53	9 60	10 04	10·4
Banjoemas ..	} 10·19	9·95	11·19	9·12	10·32	10·75	9·92	10 72	10·44	9·88	11 57	10 03	9·83	10·57	10·2
Bagelen															
Pekalongan*	10·06	10·37	12·25	10·81	11·08	} 11·42	10·66	11·78	11·11	10·63	11·69	10·91	10 93	11·00	10 7
Tegal	10 22	10 58	12 00	10·68	11·20										
Cheribon ..	9·71	10·18	10·72	10 74	10·72	11·01	10·66	11·86	10·87	10·58	11·54	10·67	11·06	11 29	10·9
East Java ..	9·90	10 09	10 68	9·29	9·71	10 47	9 84	10·39	10·05	9·78	11·95	9 62	9·26	10·09	10·1
Middle Java	10·47	10 83	11 20	9·55	10·63	11 07	10·12	10·97	10·72	10 26	12·52	10·34	10·05	10·87	10 5
West Java	10·00	10·89	11 52	10·72	11 00	11·26	10·66	11·79	11·02	11·25	11·63	10·85	10·74	11·11	10·8
Average ..	10·06	10·21	10·94	9·57	10·16	10·77	10 03	10·74	10·37	10·04	12·03	10·00	9·97	10·33	10·26

In these statistics the yield of sugar is calculated by taking the quantity of first sugar and second sugar for the full weight, to which is added half of the black stroop weight. If on 100 cane 8·39 per cent. white sugar, 0·37 per cent. refining crystals, 1·80 per cent. second sugar, and 0·38 per cent. black stroop are yielded, the *rendement* is calculated as follows :—

$$
\begin{aligned}
\text{White sugar} \quad && 8 \cdot 39 &= 8 \cdot 39 \\
\text{Refining crystals} \quad && 0 \cdot 37 &= 0 \cdot 37 \\
\text{Second sugar} \quad && 1 \cdot 80 &= 1 \cdot 80 \\
\text{Black stroop} \quad && 0 \cdot 38 \div 2 &= 0 \cdot 19 \\
\hline
\text{Total rendement} \quad && &10 \cdot 75
\end{aligned}
$$

A most instructive lot of figures is to be gleaned from the statistics of Government plantations between the years 1840 to 1888, and from the statistics of the *Archief voor de Java Suikerindustrie* from 1903 up to now, which clearly shows the extraordinarily high degree in which the sugar production of the same area has increased during the last sixty years.

The increase of sugar production per bouw dates from 1872, when the sugar manufacture was no more interfered with by the Government, and the sugar needed no more to be passed over to the State warehouses, but could be freely disposed of. It became, therefore, profitable to the manufacturers to try and increase the output of their land, as everything which they produced went to

* See footnote on page 128.

their benefit, whereas in former years their interest in the production was very small.

During the years from 1840 to 1872 the production per bouw of the Government's plantations amounted to :—

1840/44	..	..	23·38	piculs,	or	0·809	tons per acre	
1844/49	..	..	30·54	,,	,,	1·058	,,	,,
1850/54	..	..	33·58	,,	,,	1·163	,,	,,
1855/59	..	..	38·89	,,	,,	1·347	,,	,,
1860/64	..	..	43·25	,,	,,	1·499	,,	,,
1865/70	..	..	49·74	,,	,,	1·723	,,	,,

This rose to an average of 65·28 piculs during the years 1872/76, and amounted in

1877	..	..	to	67·62	piculs, or	2.343	tons per acre	
1878	..	..	..	64·38	,,	,, 2·231	,,	,,
1879	..	..	..	62·08	,,	,, 2·152	,,	,,
1880	..	..	..	60·30	,,	,, 2·090	,,	,,
1881	..	..	..	75·12	,,	,, 2·605	,,	,,
1882	..	..	..	75·28	,,	,, 2·609	,,	,,
1883	..	..	..	84·27	,,	,, 2·920	,.	,,
1884	..	..	..	92·75	,,	,, 3·215	,,	,,
1885	..	..	..	87·42	,,	,, 3·030	,,	,,
1886	..	..	..	89·74	,,	,, 3·110	,,	,,
1887	..	..	..	97·99	,,	,, 3·396	,,	,,
1888	..	..	..	94·00	,,	,, 3·258	,,	,,

After 1888, the Government's sugar production was so much reduced that the production figures per bouw as regards this cultivation do not give any satisfactory indication of the total production. Not till 1893 were any figures of production compiled by private cultivators to be relied upon ; these figures were first published in the *Archief voor de Java Suikerindustrie*, and have since been continued.

From them we gather that after the great improvement during the years following 1872, there followed a period of stagnation during the *sereh* years *circa* 1890, which, however, for reasons mentioned above, was followed by a sharp revival that is still in progress, and the end of which is not to be expected for some time yet.

RESIDENCIES.	1893/4. Piculs per Bouw.	1893/4. Tons of 2,240 lbs. per acre.	1894/5. Piculs per Bouw.	1894/5. Tons of 2,240 lbs. per acre.	1895/6. Piculs per Bouw.	1895/6. Tons of 2,240 lbs. per acre.	1896/7. Piculs per Bouw.	1896/7. Tons of 2,240 lbs. per acre.
Bezoeki	81·0	2·808	83·35	2·891	83·55	2·887	88·0	3·050
Probolinggo ..	85·05	2·946	89·3	3·095	76·55	2·655	83·9	2 908
Pasoeroean ..	71·1	2·464	79·35	2·755	72·10	2·500	73·1	2·534
Soerabaia ..	88·65	3·070	89·75	3·110	84·75	2·940	90·35	3·132
Kediri	79·15	2·740	88·15	3·055	82·0	2·842	85·45	2·962
Madioen	79·95	2·770	90·15	3·125	80·25	2·783	87·1	3·020
Rembang ..	40·55	1·405	56·1	1·945	21·6	0·749	43·85	2·906
Japara	75·10	2·602	87·45	3·033	84·15	2·919	91·25	3·162
Semarang ..	67·20	2·330	77·85	2·697	68·4	2·371	73·75	2·555
Solo	72·85	2·500	78·6	2·725	82·95	2·874	89·2	3·092
Djokdja	90·05	3·120	96·45	3·345	99·1	3·436	105·35	3·642
Banjoemas ..	56·7	1·955	} 83·55	2·895	83·25	2·885	103·55	3·591
Bagelen	69·95	2·420						
Pekalongan ..	93·85	3·250	91·2	3·161	86·8	3·009	95·7	3·317
Tegal	95·75	3·318	97·7	3·386	89·85	3·114	89·45	3·100
Cheribon ..	71·05	2·462	81·7	2·832	80·3	2·783	77·55	2·687
East Java* ..	82·35	2·850	86·85	3·012	81·13	2·812	85·93	2·977
Middle Java ..	76·15	2·636	85·63	2·967	86·26	2·989	94·54	3·275
West Java ..	85·75	3·005	90·24	3·127	86·52	2·998	85·69	2·970
Average ..	81·15	2·812	86·94	3·012	83·29	2·887	88·16	3·057

RESIDENCIES.	1902/3. Piculs per Bouw.	1902/3. Tons of 2,240 lbs. per acre.	1903/4. Piculs per Bouw.	1903/4. Tons of 2,240 lbs. per acre.	1904/5. Piculs per Bouw.	1904/5. Tons of 2 240 lbs. per acre.	1905/6. Piculs per Bouw.	1905/6. Tons of 2,240 lbs. per acre.
Bezoeki	100·8	3·494	100·8	3·494	98·6	3·418	98·8	3·425
Pasoeroean ..	99·2	3·439	103·6	3·590	110·4	3·827	108·5	3·761
Soerabaia ..	106·35	3·674	110·5	3·830	115·7	4·012	108·6	3·765
Kediri	104·0	3·605	120·1	4·167	108·7	3·768	107·1	3·713
Madioen	100·3	3·476	119·8	4·156	115·1	3·992	112·2	3·890
Semarang ..	104·0	3·605	123·7	4·292	110·5	3·831	110·3	3·823
Solo	97·55	3·380	112·7	3·907	109·2	3·785	106·6	3·695
Djokdja	104·45	3·620	122·4	4·247	121·0	4·198	119·5	4·145
Banjoemas ..	} 123·0	4·268	106·6	3·695	108·8	3·772	115·8	4·016
Bagelen								
Pekalongan ..	101·1	3·505	130·6	4·534	129·3	4·488	117·4	4·072
Cheribon ..	102·25	3·485	105·0	3·640	109·8	3·806	105·1	3·644
East Java ..	103·25	3·580	115·7	4·012	111·2	3·855	107·7	3·733

* See note on page 128.

Java.

1897/8.		1898/9.		1899/1900.		1900/1.		1901/2.	
Piculs per Bouw.	Tons of 2,240 lbs. per acre.	Piculs per Bouw.	Tons of 2,240 lbs. per acre.	Piculs per Bouw.	Tons of 2,240 lbs. per acre.	Piculs per Bouw.	Tons of 2,240 lbs. per acre.	Piculs per Bouw.	Tons of 2,240 lbs. per acre.
98·95	3·430	100·6	3·487	88·7	3·074	94·95	3·290	94·85	3·287
93·30	3·234	89·6	3·106	88·8	3·078	87·1	3·020	86·6†	3·002
85·30	2·956	91·85	3·183	86·35	2·993	82·7	2·866		
106·55	3·676	112·3	3·883	93·95	3·257	93·1	3·228	98·8	3·425
107·05	3·709	110·5	3·814	89·25	3·097	75·75	2·625	97·7	3·386
105·75	3·641	101·9	3·534	85·0	3·946	82·7	2·866	88·15	3·055
34·5	1·196	—	—	—	—	—	—	—	—
104·95	3·639	105·6	3·661	102·75	3·559	96·85	3·357	98·35	3·408
98·7	3·421	99·85	3·461	93·65	3·246	89·15	3·090		
105·25	3·641	104·1	3·609	92·95	3·221	79·25	2·746	99·6	3·453
111·7	3·850	105·65	3·662	98·3	3·307	92·85	3·218	106·65	3·680
118·3	4·093	111·25	3·858	96·95	3·362	79·65	2·760	117·3	4·068
103·0	3·570	102·55	3·552	113·25	3·935	119·05	4·129	122·4	4·247
109·95	3·812	109·85	3·806	107·55	3·729	108·75	3·772		
97·9	3·393	89·1	3·089	86·2	2·988	89·55	3·103	94·75	3·383
100·9	3·500	104·4	3·619	90·3	3·130	87·55	3·034	94·55	3·276
107·65	3·711	105·35	3·642	97·4	3·376	88·15	3·055	103·3	3·580
104·0	3·605	100·05	3·467	100·7	3·490	101·95	3·532	110·5	3·814
103·15	3·571	103·95	3·601	93·75	3·249	90·1	3·124	99·35	3·443

1906/7.		1907/8.		1908/9.		1909/10.		1910/11	
Piculs per Bouw.	Tons of 2,240 lbs. per acre.	Piculs per Bouw.	Tons of 2,240 lbs. per acre.	Piculs per Bouw.	Tons of 2,240 lbs. per acre.	Piculs per Bouw.	Tons of 2,240 lbs. per acre.	Piculs per Bouw.	Tons of 2,240 lbs. per acre.
113·0	3·918	111·4	3·862	108·7	3·768	113·5	3·920	122·5	4·247
114·9	3·984	112·0	3·883	108·1	3·748	111·1	3·870	110·1	3·812
125·0	4·348	114·9	3·984	116·2	4·030	120·6	4·180	138·5	4·801
116·1	4·027	116·9	4·054	107·8	3·897	108·8	3·773	115·5	4·004
126·3	4·383	122·5	4·250	125·4	4·352	114·8	3·980	125·9	4·364
119·6	4·149	132·4	4·597	129·5	4·495	123·5	4·280	130·0	4·506
126·4	4·387	126·5	4·390	115·4	4·002	115·0	3·986	121·7	4·220
133·7	4·642	141·4	4·912	116·6	4·044	116·08	4·018	128·1	4·40
115·7	4·012	136·6	4·744	121·8	4·226	117·6	4·076	120·1	4·163
117·1	4·062	134·7	4·677	135·0	4·688	127·2	4·408	131·4	4·555
115·4	4·002	113·6	3·939	121·4	4·212	111·8	3·876	122·9	4·260
119·5	4·145	114·7	3·977	112·0	3·883	114·4	3·990	123·5	4·281
125·2	4·345	134·3	4·663	120·7	4·187	118,2	4·098	125·3	4·343
115·9	4·019	125·0	4·338	128·9	4·474	121·7	4·219	127·6	4·423
120·3	4·173	121·3	4·208	116·8	4·051	116·3	4·033	124·1	4·302

† See note on page 129.

Asia.

The kind of sugar shipped from Java has recently gone through some changes. During the years 1894 to 1902 sugar was almost exclusively delivered as raw sugar Nos. 11—14*, and 5 to 8 per cent. black stroop or sack sugar. The second sugar was melted and worked up to raw first again, while only a few factories prepared white sugar. After 1902, when Java gradually lost the American market and was directed to the British-Indian and the Chinese markets, white first and second sugars were prepared in larger quantities, so that these two kinds together represented in 1910 and 1911 more than one-third of the total production. The second sugar, at first hardly even in demand, was later produced in lighter colours, whereupon it more readily found buyers, and latterly has fetched such a price and been so much in demand that in 1906 more than 7 per cent. of the total production consisted of this brand. This was followed, however, by a reaction, and the percentage of second sugar fell, although it still accounts for 5 per cent. of the export trade. The black stroop up to 1898 represented 8 per cent. of the production, till through the introduction of processes involving the returning of molasses during the first strike, the quantity of sack sugar produced has dropped considerably, and is still decreasing. In percentage of the total production, the relation of the quantities of each kind has been for the last fifteen years as follows :—

Superior Sugar.—A crystallized sugar as white as possible and whiter than No. 25 Dutch Standard. It is sold according to type of sample, without reference to the polarization.

First Sugar No. 18 and higher : very light-coloured crystallized sugar, which corresponds in colour with that of the numbers of the Dutch Standard. It is sold according to sample, without reference to polarization.

First Sugar, No. 15 to 17.—Also going by the name of European Assortment. A light-coloured crystallized sugar corresponding in colour with that of the samples of the Dutch Standard Nos. 15 to 17. The basis of polarization is 98.0.

First Sugar, No. 12 and higher or so-called American Assortment, or refining crystals. A moist, dark-coloured, and well-crystallized type of sugar corresponding in colour with samples of the Dutch Standard Nos. 12 to 14. The basis of polarization is 96.5.

Red Sugar or Gula Merah.—A dark-coloured kind of sugar, corresponding in colour with samples of the Dutch Standard Nos. 8 to 10. It is prepared from syrup with first molasses, and sold according to sample without having to attain a certain polarization.

Superior Second Sugar.—A fine-grained white kind of sugar, which is delivered according to sample without having to attain a certain polarization.

Second Sugar No. 14,—A light-coloured, finely-grained sugar. It need not attain a certain polarization.

Centrifugalled Sack Sugar —A dark after-product of the same colour as No. 8 of the Dutch Standard. It is viscous, and sticks together ; no special analysis is wanted, but at least 80 polarization is expected. It must come up to a good saleable quality.

Ordinary Sack Sugar.—Sticky magma of fine crystals and adhering molasses obtained by draining oft in mat bags. It is not sold by polarization, but has to be of a good saleable quality, while a polarization of 72—75 is expected.

ASSORTMENT.	1896	1897	1898	1899	1900	1901	1902	1903	1904	1905	1906	1907	1908	1909	1910	1911
Sack sugar ...	8·2	7·8	5·5	5·0	4·7	4 8	6·4	5·2	4·2	4·4	4·6	3·6	3·3	3·2	3·1	2·2
Gula merah ...	—	—	—	—	—	—	0·2	0·1	—	—	0·3	0·1	0·1	—	—	—
10—13 D.S. ...	—	11·8	—	—	—	—	—	—	—	—	—	—	—	—	—	1·7
11—14 D.S. ...	—	36·0	65·4	16·2	—	—	—	—	—	—	—	—	—	—	—	0 2
12—14 D.S. ...	58·4	14·6	13·1	67·2	81 8	81·2	76·1	71·8	75·8	74·2	60·2	56·8	59 2	40 5	31·8	27·0
13 D.S. and higher	—	0·1	0·1	—	—	—	—	—	—	—	—	—	—	1·6	—	—
14 D.S.	—	0·6	—	—	—	0·4	—	—	1·2	—	—	0·7	—	—	—	—
15 D.S.	31·6	16·0	3·3	1·0	4·2	—	—	—	—	—	—	—	—	—	—	0·1
15—17 D.S. ...	—	9·2	10·8	8·3	5·3	8·2	11·8	14·3	6·4	4·8	5·6	2·4	1,5	0·7	—	—
16 D.S.	0 5	1·7	0·5	0·2	1·4	2·5	1·1	3·5	5·3	5·5	14·0	13·5	13·1	24·8	30·2	33 4
16 D.S. and higher	—	0·1	—	0·3	0·2	0 4	0·9	0·8	1·1	—	2·3	1·4	0·8	0·4	—	—
18—19 D.S. ...	0·3	0·1	—	—	—	—	0·4	—	0·8	0·9	0·6	0·8	0·2	0·2	—	—
19—20 D.S. ...	0·8	—	—	—	—	—	—	—	—	—	—	—	—	—	—	—
20 D.S.	—	—	0 6	0 8	0 9	—	—	—	—	—	—	—	—	0·3	—	—
20 D.S. and higher	—	1·7	0·4	0·7	1·0	—	—	—	—	0·3	0·8	2·1	2·5	0·2	—	0·2
Superior	0·2	0·3	0·3	0·3	0·5	2·5	3·1	4·3	5·2	8·5	11·6	18·6	19·3	28·1	34·9	35·2
Total	100	100	100	100	100	100	100	100	100	100	100	100	100	100	100	100

The prime cost of sugar, first of all, depends on the class which is produced, on the cost price and the quality of the cane, on the distance between the factory and the harbour, and also on the factory installation. Generally speaking, it may be taken that the manufacture of superior sugar costs 1s. more than the brown sugar, basis 96·5, and that of sugar Nos. 18—20 6d. more per picul—that is allowing for the diminished *rendement*. But these figures, of course, vary.

According to van den Berg, the cost price of sugar during the years 1885–88 was, not including interest on the fixed capital or floating capital, or loans :—

	Per picul.	Per ton.
1885	f 8.17	£11 6s. 0d.
1886	f 7.72	£10 11s. 8d.
1887	f 6.68	£9 3s. 2d.
1888	f 6.67	£9 2s. 10½d.

When allowing an average interest of f 0.88 per picul or £1 4s. 2d. per ton, we come to f 7.55 or £10 7s. per ton as the cost price of sugar during 1888. Engelberts calculated this figure for the years *circa* 1900, and his calculation on the returns of 111 factories, or 60 per cent. of the total number which produced 7,835,700 piculs, or 60 per cent. of the total Java crop, gave the following data :—

Asia.

	All over Java.		Examined Factories.
Number	185	..	III
Piculs cane per bouw	979	..	1055
Piculs sugar per bouw	93·69	..	102·23
Rendement	9·57	..	9·69

The factories which procured the figures were considered the best, in which case the sugar cost ƒ 5.64* per picul or £7 14s. 7½d. per ton, including all expenses of management, planting, manufacture, shipping, or conveying to the harbour, maintenance of factory, machinery, buildings, interest on floating capital, and commission on the sale of the produce. This does not include expense of new machinery for the extension of the factory installation or of new transportation plant for the transport of cane, or the interest on the capital and debts. If one reckons, as van den Berg did, ƒ 0.88 per picul or £1 4s. 2d. per ton, for interest and administration expenses, the cost price will amount to ƒ 5.52 per picul or £7 11s. 4d. per ton.

H. 's. Jacob published at the same time a specification of the prime cost of sugar, estimated for 212 factories during the years 1899—1902, and arrived at the following figures :—

	Per picul.	Per ton.
1899	ƒ 5.50	£7 10s. 8d.
1900	ƒ 6.27	£8 11s. 11d.
1901	ƒ 6.24	£8 11s. 0d.
1902	ƒ 5.59	£7 13s. 2d.

This includes interest on floating capital, but no interest or mortgage on fixed capital, which really should be added to be exact.

The amount of £7 10s. 8d. is specified by him as follows :—

	Per picul.	Per ton.
Employés	ƒ 0·50	£0 12s. 5d.
Agriculture.. ..	ƒ 2·00	£2 15s. 8½d.
Transport of Cane..	ƒ 0·60	£0 16s. 6½d.
Fuel	ƒ 0·07	£0 1s. 11d.
Wages	ƒ 0·14	£0 3s. 10d.
Sundries	ƒ 0·07	£0 1s. 11d.
Packing	ƒ 0·16	£0 4s. 4½d.
Transport of Sugar	ƒ 0·31	£0 8s. 7d.
Maintenance ..	ƒ 0·32	£0 8s. 9d.
Diverse expenses ..	ƒ 0·17	£0 4s. 9d.
Commission ..	ƒ 0·27	£0 7s. 6d.
New machinery ..	ƒ 0·59	£0 16s. 2d.
Interest	ƒ 0·30	£0 8s. 2½d.
Total	ƒ 5·50	£7 10s. 8d.

* ƒ stands for florin or guilder = 1s. 8d.

Java.

The yearly reports of the different joint stock companies give various figures as the cost price of sugar on the several estates, which vary so much as regards the class of sugar, the distance from the seaport, the interest on capital due, the produce, etc., that it is impossible to quote any fixed amount as cost price. Generally speaking, we may consider H. 's. Jacob's figures still to hold good, so that the cost price of the sugar Nos. 11—13 D.S. comes to ƒ 5.50 per picul or £7 10s. 8d. per long ton, including all expenses except interest on the capital.

V.—Import and Export Duties, Consumption, Exportation, Places of Destination.

Sugar entering into the Dutch East Indies is not subject to a special sugar duty, but, like all other articles of food, is taxed with an import duty which since the recent rise has been fixed at 12 per cent. of the value. Previous to 1884 an export duty of 3d. was paid per cwt. of sugar, which in 1884 was lowered to 1½d. It was suspended, however, from July 1, 1887, till July 1, 1892, and was abolished in 1898.

The consumption of cane sugar of European standard is not great, and amounts to about 50,000 tons every year for the entire archipelago. This does not seem much for a population of 40,000,000 people who are very fond of dainties and sweet things ; but we should remember that besides the sugar industry carried on by European methods there is also a flourishing native sugar industry, which produces an unknown but considerable amount. All over the island sugar is being prepared on a small scale from sugar cane and palm trees, which is much in demand in all the markets in the Dutch Indies, and almost entirely supplies the want of sugar among the native population. The sugar produced in the European sugar works is chiefly consumed by the Europeans, Chinese, and wealthy natives, while the bulk of the inhabitants like to stick to the sugar prepared from cane and palms in the orthodox way, and prefer evaporated juice to crystals. Part of the crystallized sugar recrystallized to candy is, however, also in demand by the natives.

The greater portion by far of Java sugar is exported to foreign countries During the years previous to 1880 a fair amount of this sugar was sent to the Netherlands, but when that country itself began to produce an increasing amount of beetroot sugar, and consequently wanted no cane sugar from the colonies, the demand for cane sugar to be worked up in Holland ceased to exist, and, with the exception of the occasions when there has been a dearth of beetroot sugar, Java sugar has not been refined in Holland since.

From that time a great amount of Java sugar went to England, and soon after the United States also became a regular buyer ; but when the latter began to supply its wants with sugar from its own colonies, and from countries with which it had entered into reciprocal treaties, Java had to look out for some other market—and so sugar has been exported to Hong Kong, too. During the last few years the exportation of brown sugar to Japan, and especially of white sugar to British India, has become of increasing importance, as the statistical data clearly show

Shipments of Java Sugar from July 1st—June 30th.

TO	1890/91.		1891/92.		1892/93.		1893/94.		1894/95.		1895/96.	
	Piculs.	Tons.	Piculs.	Tons.	Piculs.	Tons.	Piculs.	Tons.	Piculs.	Tons.	Piculs.	Tons.
Europe	3,204,565	197,918	3,548,164	219,139	2,612,804	161,370	1,740,890	107,520	2,167,169	133,847	5,052,659	312,059
America	1,368,875	84,542	1,001,184	61,834	1,605,817	99,177	2,424,642	149,749	2,284,249	137,990	1,922,542	118,739
Australia	530,045	32,736	797,282	49,241	821,470	50,735	773,657	47,782	538,228	33,245	247,179	15,266
China	1,308,543	80,816	1,623,220	100,252	1,745,440	107,800	2,798,597	172,845	2,445,582	151,042	2,328,615	143,818
British India	71,084	4,390	85,454	5,278	66,298	4,095	82,333	5,085	124,541	7,692	90,707	5,595
Singapore	336,879	20,806	186,445	11,515	325,168	20,083	355,194	21,937	495,059	30,575	—	—
Timor Deli	612	38	192	12	207	13	79	5	185	11	140	9
Japan	—	—	—	—	—	—	—	—	—	—	—	—
Singapore for order	—	—	—	—	—	—	—	—	—	—	—	—
Total	6,820,603	421,246	7,241,941	447,271	7,194,227	443,273	8,175,292	504,903	8,005,073	492,402	9,935,672	613,640

TO	1896/97.		1897/98.		1898/99.		1899/1900.		1900/01.		1901/02.*	
	Piculs.	Tons.	Piculs.	Tons,	Piculs.	Tons.	Piculs.	Tons.	Piculs.	Tons.	Piculs.	Tons.
Europe	4,834,095	298,560	342,997	21,183	1,059,620	65,442	263,292	16,261	179,065	11,059	3,004,034	182,395
America	1,007,610	62,232	4,847,054	299,354	6,570,706	405,807	8,162,944	504,143	5,987,704	369,800	2,233,100	135,584
Australia	303,208	18,726	525,469	32,453	41,034	2,534	218,730	13,509	1,162,993	71,826	1,368,639	83,100
China	1,652,592	102,066	2,436,083	150,452	2,464,411	152,202	2,251,030	139,024	2,267,136	140,018	3,132,538	190,196
British India	82,340	5,085	90,898	5,614	144,014	8,277	208,265	12,862	290,402	17,935	368,849	22,395
Singapore	294,904	18,213	486,381	30,039	390,703	84,130	384,517	23,748	547,282	33,800	480,239	29,156
Timor Deli	142	9	95	6	47	3	62	4	20	1	—	—
Japan	4,302	260	20,000	1,235	307,382	18,984	372,600	23,012	509,725	31,481	845,926	51,369
Singapore for order	30,047	1,855	—	—	—	—	—	—	—	—	—	—
Total	8,209,240	507,006	8,749,977	540,336	10,967,917	677,379	11,861,440	732,563	10,944,327	675,920	11,433,325	694,190

* Time 1st May, 1901—30th April, 1902.

Java.

Shipments of Java sugar from 1st May—30th April.

TO	1902-03 Piculs	1902-03 Tons	1903-04 Piculs	1903-04 Tons	1904-05 Piculs	1904-05 Tons	1905-06 Piculs	1905-06 Tons
Europe	26,869	1,650	554,279	34,109	1,273,508	78,653	154,379	9,534
Port Said f.o.	227,423	14,045	1,400,425	86,492	2,437,986	150,573	6,399,761	394,701
Delaware Breakwater f.o.	6,132,015	378,721	1,540,451	95,140	4,143,175	255,887	486,822	30,067
Boston	—	—	181,843	11,231	274,191	16,934	—	—
Vancouver f.o.	175,368	10,831	261,820	16,170	346,110	21,376	93,514	5,776
Barbados f.o.	321,542	19,859	960,685	59,533	120,217	6,807	—	—
Azores f.o.	81,921	5,060	115,553	7,136	390,330	24,107	115,310	7,122
United States	—	—	—	—	87,524	5,406	—	—
Australia	1,273,508	78,563	1,187,396	73,335	230,578	14,241	295,808	18,269
Hong Kong	3,192,367	197,169	3,861,534	238,493	2,809,562	173,552	2,403,473	148,441
China	—	—	9,697	599	24,011	1,483	17,845	1,102
Japan	1,111,961	68,676	2,474,508	152,829	1,950,229	120,448	2,127,952	131,424
British India	490,435	30,290	1,174,138	72,516	1,564,447	96,622	1,420,737	67,746
Singapore f.o.	667,960	41,254	759,420	46,903	657,912	40,624	1,075,372	66,416
Total	13,701,369	846,213	14,479,749	894,286	16,299,780	1,006,693	14,581,963	900,598

TO	1906-07 Piculs	1906-07 Tons	1907-08 Piculs	1907-08 Tons	1908-09 Piculs	1908-09 Tons	1909-10 Piculs	1909-10 Tons	1910-11 Piculs	1910-11 Tons
Europe	277,473	17,754	471,179	28,483	63,662	3,932	453,111	27,983	1,111,515	72,355
Port Said	557,738	34,447	2,844,738	175,695	1,984,785	122,582	3,329,970	205,663	3,032,269	187,276
Delaware Breakw. f.o.	2,157,458	133,247	2,225,491	137,449	4,866,569	300,750	103,080	6,366	—	—
Vancouver f.o.	282,359	17,439	199,110	12,297	190,361	11,757	301,475	18,619	392,304	24,229
United States	449,975	27,791	148,315	9,160	564,175	34,844	41,176	2,534	336,858	20,805
Azores f.o.	163,249	10,082	129,681	8,009	—	—	—	—	—	—
Hong Kong	2,389,861	147,601	2,311,606	142,768	2,621,818	161,927	3,523,416	217,610	3,364,032	207,767
China	379,029	23,409	221,611	13,687	136,083	8,405	229,997	14,199	372,874	23,029
Japan	3,124,963	193,001	3,303,395	204,022	1,787,649	110,407	1,546,334	95,503	2,015,852	124,501
British India	2,427,550	149,929	5,169,130	319,251	5,057,601	312,662	6,320,739	390,376	7,215,223	445,621
Australia	654,165	40,402	90,587	5,595	456,060	28,167	1,317,831	81,391	346,034	21,371
Singapore f.o.	1,113,111	68,747	617,306	38,126	206,059	12,726	237,433	14,664	894,607	55,252
Diverse	—	—	—	—	—	—	27,251	1,603	7,241	447
Total	13,986,931	863,849	17,722,149	1,094,541	17,937,795	1,107,859	17,431,723	1,076,600	19,148,819	1,182,653

VI.—Future.

Java's sugar production has steadily improved since 1890, when the *sereh* disease and the consequence of the sugar crisis had been overcome by a powerful economical and judicious management.

Something peculiar strikes us in the figures of production, namely, that the weight of the sugar produced will all at once rise after some years' interval, to remain almost stationary during the following years, and then experience a period of considerable increase again. Thus the years 1894, 1898, 1904, 1907 and 1911 are marked by a sudden rise, while the production of the intermediate years was stationary.

There is not the slightest reason why we should expect the end of progress yet. The production of sugar per unit of area is ever rising; the rational methods of labouring, manuring, and treatment of the soil, together with the selection of those kinds of cane that thrive best in the respective soil, and a shortened campaign through improved methods of juice extraction and manufacture, have contributed to a steadily increasing crop per acre, and that while the sugar content of the cane has slightly dropped, as the figures on page 132 have shown.

Great things are to be expected when the cross-fertilization of cane varieties for the sake of new species of cane is successfully accomplished; attention will be paid not only to a high cane produce, but also to a satisfactory sugar content. Then there is the experience that a high sugar content always goes together with a superior purity, so that, in consequence of an increase of sugar content in cane juice, the yield of sugar improves for the following two reasons: first of all, because the juice contains more sugar; and, secondly, because this increased amount of sugar yields a greater percentage of rendement through the purer condition of the juice. So there is every reason to believe that the sugar production per unit of area will increase, and that the cane planted area of Java will grow larger, too. Everywhere bigger stretches of ground are being prepared for cane and rice cultivation through a new irrigation system, and although a period of five years has been stipulated as the interval before newly irrigated land should be let to cane sugar factories, still, in the end, more arable land for cane growing will be at their disposal, and the industrialists will not be long availing themselves of it. Sugar cane is also planted on jungle land after it has been carefully made fit at great expense, and the ever-recurring flow of applications for licences to build new sugar factories shows how little the spirit of enterprise slackens. So we cannot but expect either a steady or a sudden extension of the Java sugar industry, if we base our hopes on the quick rate at which it has improved since 1890.

Java.

Whenever, owing to changed circumstances, one of the markets, where Java sugar used to be imported, was lost to that industry, the Java manufacturers, as a rule, were energetic enough to plan the exportation to another market, and to take good care to prepare such kind of sugar as was most in demand, so that the Java product has always been thought much of, and has come up to the highest expectations.

As energy, enterprise, knowledge, and science are all to the fore in Java, we may hope for the best results in the future.

Europe.

I.

SPAIN.

SPAIN is the only European country where sugar cane is still cultivated on a commercial scale, and this cultivation is restricted to that part of Andalusia which lies between Almeria and Gibraltar, it being the only part of the peninsula where climatological circumstances allow the sugar cane to thrive.

A high average temperature and a total lack of frost are only to be met with in Spain on the Mediterranean coast, where in the irrigated parts of the country, especially on the alluvial stretches of land in the midst of the valleys, sugar cane cultivation is carried on.

Three kinds of cane are planted in Spain: the white, red, and striped; and the particular species is chosen according to the nature of the soil. The white cane only thrives on well-manured soil of a good quality; its average sugar content may attain to 15 per cent. of the weight of cane, but its yield is low, and seldom amounts to more than 15 to 18 tons per acre. Plant cane takes a year to ripen, but first and subsequent ratoons take two years. The red cane thrives best on ground with a deep and moist layer of earth; it is stronger than the white cane, and demands good manuring. In the best of circumstances the cane yield will amount to 32 tons per acre, and, as compared with white cane, the ratoons of this variety also ripen in one year. As long as good care is taken to manure every year with readily assimilable fertilizers, one is sure to reap crops from the same canes for five years running. Although its yield exceeds that of the white cane, the sugar quality of the red cane is lower, and becomes more so as it is cultivated further east of Gibraltar. In the Malaga Plains the sugar content of cane runs to 13—14 per cent., with 0·5—1·2 per cent. reducing sugars. The striped cane corresponds with the red as regards productiveness of cane and other circumstances, but is most inconsistent in its yield of sugar.

These three kinds of cane are planted in the same way. The land is laid out with cane after it has born different crops such as wheat, barley, maize, or sweet potatoes for at least three years. In January and February the soil is ploughed deeply, while large quantities of stable dung (12 to 16 tons to the acre) are put into the soil. In March the furrows are dug, about $3\frac{1}{2}$ ft. apart from each other, 12 in. deep, and 8 in. wide, which are hollowed out with spades and dressed with manure when former supplies are thought insufficient. Besides stable dung, superphosphates, sulphate of ammonia,

SUGAR FACTORY SAN NICOLAS IN SPAIN.

Chili saltpetre, basic slag, and sometimes fish guano coming from the sardine and tunny fisheries, are also employed. Basic slag is generally given before the ploughing is done, while the fish guano, superphosphate and two-thirds of the sulphate of ammonia are laid in the furrows just before the planting, and the rest of the ammonia and the Chili saltpetre is used as a top dressing when the plants are banked up.

For planting, the tops of the cane are used, from which the youngest still colourless joints are removed. Two parallel rows are planted in every furrow, this necessitating a large quantity of seed material, viz., 9,800 lbs. per acre. This may be explained by the fact that in the comparatively cool climate of Andalusia they cannot rely upon the formation of secondary stalks, so that enough primary stalks must be provided for. Moreover, a great many of these die when a cold or wet spell of weather immediately follows the planting. The seed is covered with a thin layer of earth and watered, so that the soil gets fairly moist; this degree of moisture is kept up, by means of irrigation water, as long as possible till the end of the period of vegetation. Occasionally, as the growth of cane proceeds, the cane is banked. Then the field is made quite level with a hoe, or better still with a plough, and, finally, the cane is banked for the last time, so that the rows now stand slightly elevated and banked earth and shallow gutters alternate where the rows used to be, the whole forming a connected system. The irrigation water is admitted, and flows slowly through the entire gutter system all over the field, following the natural slope of the ground. During the summer the land is irrigated every ten or fifteen days, and about 40,000 gallons of water per acre are used each time.

The cane ripens in March, when it is cut and worked up; the grinding season lasts till May. The cane is cut close to the ground with knives, and after being cleaned is taken to the factory. The leaves are conveyed to the stables, where they serve as straw for the cattle, while the rest is burnt, this operation at the same time destroying the parasites. Some more manuring is done, either with stable dung or guano; the earth between the rows is loosened by means of a plough; and the cane plants left in the ground are now so much shortened that only two nodes are left on each stalk. This is done to prevent too big a formation of secondary stalks which are unlikely to keep alive, so that now only the budding shoots come up, instead of the primary stems of the year before. Then the young shoots are covered, manured, and irrigated, and cut after a year in the same way as explained above, which process is repeated so long as the field yields a satisfactory crop.

As may be seen from the above, the mode of cultivation is very expensive; a most intensive treatment and manuring are necessary for the little part of Spain that is fit for cane cultivation in order to yield a profitable crop.

The manufacturers pay a very high price for the cane, namely, 40 pesetas per ton of cane delivered in the field (£1 11s. 8d. per ton).

The factories can be divided in two groups: the " trapiches " and the

" fabricas." The former are insignificant undertakings which grind only a little cane, and concentrate the juice to table syrup, which is sold in tins. The fabricas are large undertakings which prepare as their first product pilé sugar, white powdered sugar as their second, yellow sugar as their third and fourth product, and, finally, work up the molasses into alcohol. The factories, as a rule, are well arranged, and a kind of bagasse diffusion is generally in operation, which gives very satisfactory results. The bagasse that enters the diffusion battery with a content of 7 per cent. sugar and 70 per cent. water leaves it again with a content of 0·30—0·40 per cent. sugar, and 85—87 per cent. water, part of which is first expressed in mills, and afterwards the moist bagasse is dried on a concrete floor in the sunshine. The juice is sulphitated, made slightly alkaline with lime, heated, and clarified in the usual way. The clarified juice is filtered over animal charcoal, and the mud through bag filters. The dry mud from the filters is used as fodder for cattle. The syrup is again filtered over animal charcoal, and afterwards boiled to a fine-grained masse-cuite in the boiling pan and centrifugalled in the form of pilé, which, when broken into little pieces, is used for direct consumption. The first molasses are boiled to a fine-grained white sugar, and the second molasses made into a dark, soft kind of sugar.

The cane, as we said, costs 40 pesetas per ton, to which must be added 6 pesetas for transport from the field to the factory, and 14 pesetas for manufacturing expenses. A ton yields 209 lbs. of sugar, so that the production cost of sugar in Spain is not less than 63 pesetas per 220 lbs., or about £1 5s. per cwt.

In the time when Spain still possessed her cane sugar colonies, which were accorded a preference by the mother country over the European beet industry, the condition of the cane sugar manufacture in Spain was not what could be described as a favourable one, and its yearly output only amounted to 35,000 tons. The importation of sugar came to the following quantities in tons :—

Year.	Spanish Colonies.	Other Countries.	Total.
1893	23,776	1,679	25,455
1894	41,332	1,262	42,594
1895	46,005	924	46,929
1896	36,808	923	37,731
1897	28,036	28	28,064
1898	8,668	14	8,682
1899	9,000	299	9,299
1900	103	354	457
1901	24	71	95
1902	8	56	64

Spain.

The Spanish colonies used to send much sugar to the mother country and, as one can imagine, the inland sugar industry had ample scope to improve when, after the war with the United States, these colonies were lost, and, consequently, were deprived of all further protection from Spain.

In 1892 the duty on sugar was fixed as follows :—

	Pesetas per 100 kg.
Foreign sugar	50·
Sugar from Spanish colonies	33·50
Excise on sugar produced in Spain ..	20·

As regards the last item, a rendement of 5 per cent. from both beetroot and cane was taken as the basis for taxation.

In 1899, that is after Spain had lost her colonies, the import duty went up to 85 pesetas and the excise to 25, so that a surtax of 60 pesetas was allowed, which on the one hand prevented the importation of foreign sugar, but on the other promoted strongly the inland industry. By this means the beetroot sugar industry was exclusively benefited, and the production of cane sugar has rather diminished than increased since 1899. With the aid of the capital flowing back from the lost colonies, extensive stretches of land were planted with beetroot, especially in Andalusia, and a large number of factories was built which realized enormous profit. Thus tempted, an ever-increasing number of speculators invested money in the beetroot sugar cultivation, so that it was not long before the country could supply its own wants, and this was soon followed by over-production, as any exportation was an impossibility.

In 1903 there were 50 beetroot sugar factories, 32 large cane sugar factories, 15 mills for syrup preparation, 11 refineries, and 2 factories for sorghum sugar and glucose. Prices, however, fell afterwards to such a degree that they could not cover the very considerable cost of production in Spain ; hence a period of great loss followed the short and glorious period of great profit. It is from this difficult time that there dates the Society of Sugar Producers, formed after lengthy negotiations. It went by the name of *Sociedad General Azucarera de España*, and included 43 beetroot sugar factories, 13 cane sugar factories, and 13 mills. It was decided to go on working with 40, and eventually with 35, factories ; and in order to simplify the management, the country was divided into four zones (Central, Andalusia, North-East, and North-West) ; then the distribution of seed and manure was arranged among the beetroot producers, and a company was started for the sale of molasses.

In this way the *Sociedad* expected to have the production well in hand, and to keep it in correspondence with requirements ; for the rest, they thought of improving the sugar quality of the beetroot by providing a good kind of seed, and, consequently, of lowering the cost of production, which would bring in its train a sound and lasting period of prosperity. This, however, was not so easy as it seemed to accomplish. First of all, a number of factories, especially cane sugar works, were left out of the society, and then a great many former proprietors founded competing factories with the money derived from the first sale of their property to the *Sociedad* ; so that, notwithstanding the stopping of a number of factories belonging to the *Sociedad General*, the Spanish production exceeded the consumption, which excess in 1904 amounted to one-third of the total yearly consumption. An attempt to export to England failed through a protest from the Belgian Government, based on the Brussels Sugar Convention, which compels the signatories to levy a penal duty on bounty-fed sugar from countries which, like Spain, have not submitted to the Convention.

After much negotiation between the *Sociedad General*, the free factories, and the Government, they came to an agreement in 1907, according to which the consumption duty was raised to 35 pesetas per 100 kg.* (220 lbs.), and the erection of new sugar factories was prohibited within a radius of fifty miles of each existing factory. Factories which have not been working for five consecutive years are considered as non-existing. Further, the Government, in deliberation with the factories themselves, fixes the production of each factory for every year in accordance with its capacity. Should a factory exceed the fixed amount of production, the excess quantity will be put to account the next year.

In 1910 there were in Spain 21 factories and 13 mills for cane sugar, 3 factories and 2 mills of which had not been working for some time.

In the 18 factories and 11 mills—11 of the factories belong to the *Sociedad General*—188,660 tons of cane were ground, which produced 18,851 metric tons of sugar. The total production since 1900 has been as follows :—

Year.	Sociedad factories.			Free factories.			Total.		
	Tons of Cane.	Tons of Sugar.	Per cent.	Tons of Cane.	Tons of Sugar.	Per cent.	Tons of Cane.	Tons of Sugar.	Per cent.
1900	—	—	—	356,182	34,548	9·70	356,182	34,548	9·70
1901	—	—	—	295,403	27,998	9·47	295,403	27,998	9·47
1902	—	—	—	226,329	16,979	7·50	226,329	16,979	7·50
1903	—	—	—	205,298	21,677	10·56	205,298	21,677	10·56
1904	148,480	12,558	8·45	112,551	9,617	8·54	261,031	22,175	8·49
1905	144,726	13,642	9·42	164,426	15,177	9·23	309,152	28,820	9·32
1906	80,656	6,765	8·36	105,060	8,957	8·52	185,917	15,722	8·45
1907	96,007	7,100	7·38	109,386	8,993	8·22	205,393	16,093	7·83
1908	52,621	5,818	11·56	74,839	8,240	11·01	127,460	14,058	9·05
1909	131,529	10,423	7·91	119,474	11,246	9·36	251,003	21,669	8·63
1910	67,803	7,784	11·48	120,865	11,067	9·16	188,668	18,851	9·92

* This was raised to 37·5 pesetas on 1st August, 1911.

Spain.

The crop for 1911 amounted to 18,000 tons.

Of the 7,701 tons of molasses produced in 1908, 7,175 were worked up into brandy, 333 were consumed as human food, and the rest was used as cattle fodder.

As may be seen from the steadily decreasing figures of production, the cane sugar industry in Spain has much to contend with. The area for cane plantations is small, and the climate is not very favourable for this branch of industry, so that it means great expense and no little trouble to obtain any satisfactory crops. It is a fact that a very high surtax keeps the inland price high, too, but this again hinders the consumption, so that Spain is not likely to consume more than the present quantity of fully 100,000 tons. This amount nowadays is being produced by the existing beet sugar and cane sugar factories, while a number of beet sugar factories are not at present in operation, but in case of an eventual shortage of sugar are sure to take up work again in order to make up for the deficit. Most of the Convention countries are closed to bounty-fed sugar from Spain, so that Great Britain only comes in for the export trade, and it will be most difficult considering the high production cost, to arrange the exportation in such a way that a probable loss may be fully compensated by the high inland price of sugar. We can assume from this that any extension of the Spanish cane sugar industry is most unlikely.

Literature :

Paul Bouvier. *La Culture de la Canne à Sucre en Espagne.*
Reports of the Commercial Attaché to his Britannic Majesty's Embassy in Madrid.

North America.

I.

THE UNITED STATES OF AMERICA.

THE only portion of the United States situated on the Continent of America where sugar cane is cultivated is the territory round the Gulf of Mexico— Louisiana, Texas, Florida, and Georgia, the first of which is by far the most important. Both in Louisiana and Texas, the cane is worked up to sugar in well-installed factories, while in both these and the other States much cane is crushed and the juice evaporated to a thick syrup, to be used for direct consumption. In Louisiana the cane production occurs in the south, especially along the banks of the Mississippi, the Bayou Teche*, and the Bayou La- fourche, while there are many cane sugar factories to be met with along the rivers in the western and southern parts outside those States. The greatest width of the Sugar Belt, from west to east, *i.e.*, from Calcasieu to Jefferson, amounts to 186 miles, while its greatest length, from north to south, *i.e.*, from Rapides to Terrebonne, is 125 miles. In Texas the sugar industry is located near the sea in the south, while in South Georgia and in North Florida it is distributed throughout the districts.

As the cane sugar producing region of the United States falls outside the tropics, a real winter time with frost is there experienced, so that the sugar industry has to make allowance for climatological circumstances that are unknown in most of the other cane cultivating countries.

Some meteorological data collected in 1905 from many of the stations are given below. We may add that these data vary very little for other years :—

---

* Bayou is the name given to slowly running, shallow, wide, and marshy rivers, which form branches of the Mississippi in the delta-territory formed by that river.

Station.	Parish.	Height above sea level in ft.	Temperature in degrees Centigrade.					Rainfall in inches.					Number of rainy days	Direction of the wind.
			Average for the year.	Maximum.	Date.	Minimum.	Date.	Total.	Maximum in one month.	Month.	Minimum in one month	Month.		
Abbeville	Vermillion	—	19·63	37·4	9·6	− 8·8	14·2	80·20	16·10	June	2·10	Oct.	131	S.E.
Alexandria	Rapides	77	18·97	39·6	25·8	− 6·6	14·2	78·42	14·21	Apl.	1·91	Sep.	135	S.
Baton rouge	E. Baton rouge	58	—	37·4	8·9	− 9·3	14·2	—	—	—	—	—	—	E.
Burnside	Ascension	20	19·47	35·7	25·8	− 8·2	14·2	75·80	12·38	Feb.	3·69	Aug.	117	—
Cherreyville	Rapides	64	—	36·3	9·6	−10·0	13·2	—	—	—	—	—	—	S.
Donaldsonville	Ascension	33	—	39·0	25·8	− 8·8	14·2	79·62	9·32	Feb.	3·78	Aug.	107	N.E.
Franklin	St. Mary	10	19·91	36·3	20·8	− 7·2	14·2	90·90	11·70	June	3·89	Oct.	133	S.E.
Grand coteau	St. Landry	93	19·47	35·7	9·6	−10·0	14·2	95·82	13·89	Apl.	3·29	Oct.	89	N.
Houma	Terrebonne	—	19·63	35·7	8·6	− 8·2	26·1	83·93	11·62	Oct.	3·74	Jan.	129	S.E.
Lafayette	Lafayette	22	—	36·3	9·6	—	—	82·04	18·52	June	2·09	Aug.	113	N.
Lake Charles	Calcasieu	22	—	36·3	12·6	− 9·3	14·2	67·40	9·61	Apl.	0·08	Oct.	89	E.
Lawrence	Plaquemines	—	—	—	—	− 7·2	13·2	—	—	—	—	—	—	S.E.
Melville	St. Landry	45	18·75	36·3	25·8	− 9·3	14·2	81·75	18·90	Apl.	1·62	Oct.	103	N.
New Iberia	Iberia	15	19·63	33·0	8·6	− 8·2	14·2	81·38	12·75	June	2·85	Oct.	111	E.
New Orleans	Orleans	8	20·13	34·6	25·8	− 7·7	14·2	80·07	14·43	Dec.	3·62	Nov.	127	
Opelousas	St. Landry	83	19·05	36·3	12·6	− 9·3	14·2	84·54	12·69	Feb.	1·78	Oct.	119	
Port Eads	Plaquemines	2	—	33·0	20·8	− 2·2	26·1	—	—	—	—	—	—	S.E.
Reserve	St. John Baptist	—	19·71	40·7	15·7	− 7·2	14·2	74·62	7·83	Sep.	3·02	Nov.	88	
Schriever	Terrebonne	—	—	37·4	15·7	− 7·7	14·2	—	—	—	—	—	—	

North America.

As may be seen from the list, all the sugar producing districts lie in the plain, as the highest elevation above sea level does not exceed 83 ft. A dry time is not known in these parts, for even during the month which is most deficient in rain, a rather considerable quantity falls; while the local rainfall of about 80 ins. is more than sufficient for the growth of the sugar cane. During the months December to February the frost may be heavy enough to cause the cane to freeze up; hence the planters must be on their guard to take such measures as will reduce the damage to a minimum. During the autumn Equinox hurricanes from the Gulf of Mexico are known to blow across Louisiana, and cause havoc to the cane fields, which havoc is all the more considerable as the cane has just reached its greatest height at this time of the year, and, consequently, can least withstand the violence of the storm.

Sugar cane was introduced into Louisiana in 1737 by the Jesuits, but the manufacture of sugar did not become of any importance till 1796, when an able manufacturer introduced a practical way of preparing sugar. This method was then very primitive, as the mills were driven by oxen or horses, and a good deal of sugar was lost in the bagasse and during the working up of the juice. During the early years of the nineteenth century the production did not amount to much, but it gradually improved, so that in 1823, the first year from which we have exact data, it yielded more than 15,000 tons, and did not stop long at that figure. Though the cane planted area and the yield of sugar expanded, the number of sugar plantations decreased, which means that the average area of the individual estates increased. In 1830, there were 691 sugar plantations, with a population of 36,000 negro slaves; while the figures for 1840 amounted respectively to 668 and 50,670. Later on the large plantations got into difficulties, but the number in 1853 reached its maximum figure of 1,500, with an average area of 198 acres each. At this time, when slavery prevailed, the cane cultivation and sugar manufacture were in the hands of the same people, but after the Civil War the industry was almost reduced to beggary, and the slaves were set free; the old system could not possibly be kept up when the industry eventually revived, so from this time onward planting and manufacture were separated in the bulk of cases. Under the new conditions only a comparatively small number of manufacturers worked up the cane that had been grown by a great many farmers, and this led to the system of central factories now generally found in Louisiana. The large plantations lease stretches of land measuring 25 to 60 acres to farmers who plant sugar cane for the factory at their own expense. Both the black and white populace take the land on lease, and this system is such a success that the centralization of the manufacture of cane sugar grown on extensive tracts of ground is still in vogue. In 1888–89 there were as many as 776 sugar factories in operation, which produced 144,878 tons of sugar; in 1898–99 the number of factories had gone down to 347, whereas their production had increased to 245,511; while in 1910 the number of factories amounted to 214, and their production to 325,000 tons of sugar.

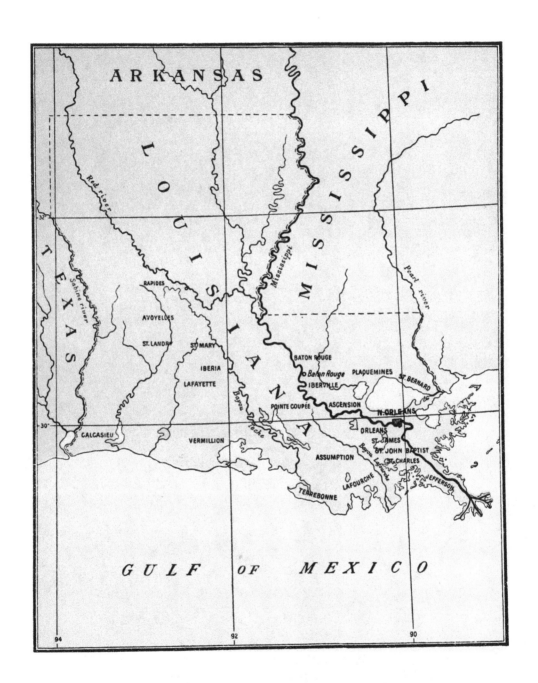

LOUISIANA

The United States of America.

In 1890 21 factories worked in the districts of Lower Terrebonne and Little Caillou Bayou, which have now been supplanted by one single large factory. The latter grinds not only the cane from the same area as was crushed by the 21 factories together, but from some extra 2,000 acres of land that hitherto had not been planted with cane. In Texas there are 9 factories, which between them grind the cane from 37,000 acres; they produce besides sugar a large quantity of light and dark syrups for table use.

For the rest, many plans are being entertained for the foundation of new plantations in the neighbourhood of the town of Brownsville, some of which plans have already been carried out, so that the production in Texas promises soon to become an important one.

As in Louisiana, the temperature does not become favourable for the growth of cane till March, and as frost may be expected as early as December it is necessary for the planters to do all they can to promote a quick ripening of the cane, and to have the crop cut before it can be blighted by frost. They generally plant cane once every three years on the same soil; first the plant-cane and first ratoons are reaped, after which maize is sown, and finally a species of large pea (*Vigna sinensis*) is sown directly the maize crop is gathered. At the end of the summer the pea-vines are ploughed, together with the maize stubble, into the earth, and four weeks afterwards the furrows are dug, at distances of 6 ft. to 6 ft. 8 ins. from each other. The cane is planted during the first days of October, if the state of the fields allow. For that purpose whole cane stalks are placed in two rows in the furrows, for which 8,000 lbs. cane per acre are allowed. The cane is then covered with a layer of loose earth from 5 to 6 ins. thick, and in this way it is protected from the frost which does not penetrate to that depth. Should one not be ready to plant, at the right time—that is, should the winter season have begun before the ground is in proper condition—the cane which is to be used for seed is cut, covered with dry leaves, and is put into furrows in order to protect it against frost. As soon as the spring arrives this cane is planted, while the covering layer of earth is for the greater part removed from the cane that was planted in the autumn, in order to promote the shooting out of buds and the budding of young sprouts. Manuring is carried on with stable dung, cotton-seed meal, kainite, phosphates, and nitrates, while sufficient drainage is constantly ensured. At the end of November the cane cutting is begun, while the dry leaves and the pieces of cane which remained in the field are burnt for the twofold purpose of killing the vermin and of preventing the drainage canals from getting obstructed by this rubbish. As long as no frost is expected the cane is kept in the field, to be reaped as it is wanted for grinding; but as soon as the Meteorological Department prophesies a " cold wave," which may be detrimental to the standing cane, they make haste to get it cut. The cane is cut close to the ground, and the stalks are placed lengthwise in the plant-rows, and then covered with the dry cane leaves to be protected from frost This treatment is called " windrowing," and is only applied when frost is expected. During the cold winter season cane thus preserved may keep in good condition for weeks at a time, and its deterioration will be hardly noticeable; but as soon as the warm weather returns such cane rapidly deteriorates in quality. One may assume that cane which has remained in the field, unfrozen, is the best, and that cut cane which is kept under leaves is not of the same good quality, while cane in the field once frozen is the least valuable of all. This shows that "windrowing" is an excellent preventative against frost, but is not harmless in itself, so that it should only be resorted to in an emergency.

During the spring the stubble left in the ground is banked once more, and the cane is treated as in the first year; while after the first ratooning the land is sown with maize, and afterwards with peas for the sake of green manure.

As manual labour in Louisiana is very scarce and expensive, most of the work of digging furrows, cutting and banking is done by agricultural machinery, which leaves only the planting, trashing, and cleaning of cane to be done by hand.

Since the beginning of the cane cultivation in Louisiana the Purple and Striped sugar canes have exclusively been planted; but, chiefly as a consequence of the researches of the botanists of the sugar experiment stations, the seedling canes D 74 and D 95 obtained from Demerara have come in great demand. Besides an advantage in quantity of cane and sugar over the former types, the time of vegetation is also shorter, so that the canes ripen sooner, a feature which, on account of the short season allowed the Louisiana cane to ripen in, offers a great advantage. It has also been proved that the new cane is more resistant to damage done by storms, all of which goes far to make it likely that the new varieties of cane introduced from Demerara will supplant the older kinds.

The labour question still troubles Louisiana. After the abolition of slavery it was very difficult to find sufficient labour for the necessary treatment, so that the proprietors of land were obliged to lease parts of their ground to farmers. They still planted part of their land themselves, and as the farmers also had to employ hired labour it was by no means a way out of the difficulty. One of the first results of scarcity of labour is the general use of agricultural implements in order to do field work as much as possible by means of machinery requiring a minimum of labour. For the rest, the immigration of South Europeans, preferably Italians, viâ New Orleans, was promoted as much as possible as a means to procure a steady importation of white labour accustomed to a warm temperature.

In Texas a peculiar way of procuring labour prevails. The Government lends out convicts from the Penitentiary to the sugar planters for the tillage of the ground, and also under its own management plants cane with the help of convict labour. It is stated that in 1909 no less than 3,600 tons of sugar were prepared with the help of such labour, so that we may expect this system to be extended rather than be limited in the future.

The United States of America.

With the exception of one factory, that of Magnolia, which obtains its juice by means of diffusion, milling is universally employed. The Magnolia factory is one of the very few where cane is successfully treated by diffusion, a fact that may be attributed to the highly exceptional circumstances under which it works. The factory lies on the Mississippi, which at that very spot is a stream of such width and strength of current that all the bagasse may be thrown into it to disappear forthwith. Then there is mineral oil in the ground close to the factory, which oil furnishes all the fuel at a minimum of expense, so that bagasse is not needed as fuel. As the drying of the bagasse for fuel is the great drawback in cane diffusion, it is clear that where this obstacle does not exist, the diffusion process is more likely to be a success than where the fuel question demands full and constant attention. Although the factories were installed in a fairly primitive way up till a short while ago, they have much improved since centralization was introduced, and most of the installations now are on a par with the most modern plants. All the 214 factories working employ steam, 27 of them still use the open kettle system, but the rest are provided with vacuum pans. Of the 188,571 tons of Louisiana sugar produced in 1906–7, 3,093 tons were prepared with open kettles, 4,250 tons with open kettles and centrifugals, and 181,228 tons with vacuum pans and centrifugals. At the same time the factories produced 33,000,000 gallons of molasses.

It is chiefly raw sugar, basis 96° polarization, that is manufactured, the runnings of which, as a rule, are sold as table-syrup after being again clarified. Some factories produce white sugar for direct consumption, but as people in the United States are accustomed to very superior white sugar, it is not easy to find buyers for the somewhat yellowish or grey plantation cane sugar, and it is better to sell the raw sugar to the refiners of New York and New Orleans. The manufacturers selling on the New York market receive the market price of sugar, and those selling in New Orleans a price corresponding to the New York quotation, *minus* the approximate cost of transportation from the factory to New York.

In 1905–6 242,452 acres (99,000 hectares) were planted with cane in Louisiana, yielding 4,849,048 (short) tons of cane, or about 20 tons of cane per acre. Those factories that worked with open kettles did not realize more than 3·25 per cent. of sugar on the weight of cane ; those that used open kettles and centrifugals yielded 4·8 per cent ; while the up-to-date factories reached 8 per cent. With a cane yield of 20 tons to the acre, this does not amount to more than 5,322 lbs. (2$\frac{2}{3}$ tons) per acre. In the year 1910–11 6·9 per cent. was the average output of sugar calculated over all the factories. That of Plaquemines did best, extracting as much as 8·6 per cent.

The sugar production of Louisiana, beginning in 1827, and that of the other States from 1851 down to date, has been as follows, expressed in long tons of 2,240 lbs. :—

North America.

1823	15,401
1824	11,807
1825	15,401
1826	23,101
1827	36,452
1828	45,178
1829	24,640
1832	35,931
1833	37,482
1834	51,339
1835	15,401
1836	35,937
1837	28,925
1838	35,927
1839	59,049
1840	44,065
1841	46,257
1842	71,878
1843	51,347
1844	102,678
1845	142,723
1846	70,995
1847	123,214
1848	112,964
1849	120,465
1850	103,111

Year.	Louisiana. (Tons.)	Other States. (Tons.)	Total. (Tons.)	Molasses.		
				Louisiana. (Gallons.)	Other States. (Gallons.)	(Gallons.)
1851/52 ..	115,197	4,992	120,189	17,999,660	673,920	18,673,580
1852/53 ..	164,312	6,852	171,164	25,769,030	921,720	26,690,750
1853/54 ..	224,188	4,830	229,018	31,000,000	643,080	31,643,080
1854/55 ..	177,349	4,380	181,729	23,113,620	582,780	23,696,400
1855/56 ..	113,664	6,283	119,947	15,274,140	844,470	16,118,610
1856/57 ..	36,813	5,348	42,161	4,882,380	721,980	5,604,360
1857/58 ..	137,542	6,385	143,927	19,578,790	871,975	20,450,765
1858/59 ..	185,206	8,169	193,375	24,887,760	567,798	25,455,558
1859/60 ..	113,410	4,132	117,542	17,858,100	411,114	18,269,214

The United States of America.

Year.	Loui-siana. (Tons.)	Other States. (Tons.)	Total. (Tons.)	Molasses.		
				Loui-siana. (Gallons.)	Other States. (Gallons.)	(Gallons.)
1860/61	117,431	4,313	121,744	18,414,550	351,780	18,766,330
1861/62	235,856	5,138	240,994	36,982,505	3,502,000	40,484,505
1862/63	43,232	2,768	46,000	7,619,000	381,000	8,000,000
1863/64	39,690	250	39,940	2,303,000	217,000	2,520,000
1864/65	5,331	177	5,508	765,000	85,000	850,000
1865/66	9,287	348	9,635	1,128,000	172,000	1,300,000
1866/67	21,074	3,348	24,422	2,570,000	430,000	3,000,000
1867/68	19,289	4,518	23,807	2,800,000	570,000	3,370,000
1868/69	42,617	2,567	45,184	6,081,907	764,000	6,845,907
1869/70	44,382	2,829	47,211	5,724,256	2,004,544	7,728,800
1870/71	75,369	4,208	79,577	10,281,419	619,000	10,900,419
1871/72	65,635	4,217	69,852	10,019,958	681,000	10,700,958
1872/73	55,891	4,235	60,126	8,898,640	601,000	9,499,640
1873/74	46,078	2,410	48,488	8,203,944	507,000	8,710,944
1874/75	60,100	3,454	63,554	11,516,828	674,000	12,190,828
1875/76	72,958	4,045	77,003	10,870,546	1,380,000	12,250,546
1876/77	85,102	3,879	88,981	12,024,108	876,000	12,900,108
1877/78	65,835	5,330	71,165	14,237,280	913,000	15,150,280
1878/79	106,909	5,090	111,999	13,218,404	1,005,000	14,223,404
1879/80	88,836	3,199	92,035	12,189,190	4,877,025	17,066,215
1880/81	121,886	5,500	127,386	15,255,030	1,704,000	16,959,030
1881/82	71,304	5,000	76,304	9,691,104	2,308,896	12,000,000
1882/83	136,167	7,000	143,167	15,716,755	3,250,000	18,966,755
1883/84	128,318	6,800	135,118	15,277,316	3,118,000	18,395,316
1884/85	94,372	6,500	100,872	11,761,608	2,892,000	14,653,608
1885/86	127,958	7,200	135,158	17,863,732	3,645,000	21,508,732
1886/87	80,858	4,535	85,393	10,254,894	2,114,100	12,368,994
1887/88	157,970	9,843	167,813	21,980,241	4,651,260	26,631,501
1888/89	144,878	9,031	153,909	15,288,580	3,255,882	18,484,462
1889/90	128,343	4,089	132,432	18,431,988	11,068,147	29,500,135
1890/91	215,843	6,107	221,950	23,152,104	4,200,000	27,232,104
1891/92	160,937	4,500	165,437	16,429,868	4,200,000	20,629,868
1892/93	201,816	5,000	206,816	17,025,997	4,502,000	21,527,997
1893/94	265,836	6,854	272,690	18,469,529	8,439,197	26,908,726
1894/95	317,306	8,288	325,594	28,334,513	9,282,561	37,617,074
1895/96	237,720	4,973	242,693	21,663,411	5,569,547	27,232,958

Year.	Loui-siana. (Tons)	Other States. (Tons).	Total. (Tons).	Molasses.		(Gallons).
				Loui-siana. (Gallons).	Other States. (Gallons).	
1896/97 ..	282,009	5,570	287,579	20,820,130	6,886,927	27,707,057
1897/98 ..	310,447	5,290	315,737	22,241,510	7,093,634	29,335,144
1898/99 ..	245,511	5,266	250,777	24,952,188	1,768,250	26,720,438
1899/00 ..	147,164	1,510	148,674	13,628,840	10,838,903	14,467,743
1900/01 ..	270,338	2,891	273,229	31,419,689	6,144,102	37,563,790
1901/02 ..	321,676	3,614	325,290	23,727,735	7,680,127	31,407,802
1902/03 ..	329,226	3,723	332,949	28,069,571	9,216,152	37,285,723
1903/04 ..	228,476	19,800	248,276	18,247,038	6,912,114	25,159,152
1904/05 ..	355,530	15,000	370,530	33,302,854	8,640,142	41,942,996
1905/06 ..	336,751	12,000	348,751	21,604,869	6,048,100	27,652,969
1906/07 ..	188,571	13,000	221,571	33,000,000	3,628,860	36,628,860
1907/08 ..	302,855	10,200	313,055	20,351,900	4,717,518	25,069,418
1908/09 ..	273,178	10,368	283,546	29,970,750	7,360,000	37,330,750
1909/10 ..	269,431	6,126	275,557	29,660,500	7,470,000	37,130,500
1910/11 ..	263,308	5,004	268,312	28,862,400	5,594,700	34,457,100

It can easily be imagined that in a country like Louisiana, where labour is expensive, and where owing to the circumstances mentioned above the sugar production per unit area is less than in those neighbouring tropical countries in which cane cultivation is carried on in a rational way, the cane sugar industry could not possibly exist if not protected against foreign competition by heavy protective duties.

From the very beginning of the industry in the United States, the importation of raw and refined sugar has been subject to duties, while, with the exception of a short period about 1860, no excise has been levied on inland produce.

In 1789 the importation of raw sugar was taxed at 1 cent (American) per lb., which duty was gradually raised to amount to 3 cents in 1842. Later on it was continually changed ; at one time it was levied as a fixed percentage of the value, then again as a fixed amount for each kind of sugar according more or less to the patronage accorded by some class or other of people interested in it. In 1890, according to the McKinley tariff the importation of raw sugar was exempted, so that the price of sugar at once fell considerably, and but for other help offered, the Louisiana sugar industry would have been ruined by the importation of cheap foreign sugar. In order to counteract this, it

The United States of America.

was decreed in 1891 that the Government should give 2 cents premium per pound on sugar produced in the country itself, but this production was of a very short duration, as only during the first two years were the premiums paid in full and directly, while it was paid only six months in the year after the conclusion of the 1893–94 campaign. For the crop of 1894–95 Congress only allotted a certain amount corresponding to 0·8 cent per lb., while in the following year the import duty was restored and the premium abolished.

In 1897 the import duty on raw sugar was fixed at 0·95 cent per lb. for sugar polarizing 75°, and if more with an increase of 0·035 cent per lb. for each degree above 75. For sugars above No. 16 D.S. the duty amounted to 1·95 cent ; these amounts have remained the same since the last tariff revision, with the exception of the import duty on the last kind of sugar, which has been reduced to 1·90 cent per lb.

The raw sugar, basis 96°, consequently enjoys a protection of \$37.75 per ton, and the sugar in colour above No. 16 D.S. enjoys one of \$42.56 ; so that it is quite possible to manufacture cane sugar with profit in spite of less favourable circumstances as regards climate and wages. A disadvantage of this protection is, however, that as a matter of course the manufacturers are restricted to the inland markets for the sale of their produce and even if the prices of the inland market are low they cannot export to foreign countries but are bound to submit to those home prices. The closely united American buyers of raw sugar avail themselves of this opportunity to buy Louisiana sugar at a lower price than that ruling on New York market.

As the sugar buyers refine the greater part of the Louisiana crop at New Orleans and only a little goes to New York, this sugar involves hardly any expense for transport. In case the sellers should send their sugar to New York to be sold there this would amount to $\frac{3}{16}$ cent per lb. In consequence of this the refiners offer an amount that is on an average $\frac{3}{16}$ cent per lb. less than the New York quotation, and profit by this difference in price, as they do not send on this sugar, but refine it on the spot. The sellers still make the same profit as when they ship the sugar to New York, so that it is immaterial to them whether they sell the sugar in their own district or in New York, and they, of course, choose the easier method. As the greatest strength of the refiners lies principally in the impossibility of exporting raw sugar at a profit, the $\frac{3}{16}$ cent per lb. decrease in the sale price should be put to the account of the profit made by protection, which in the end would only come to 1·4975 cent per lb.

The buyers cannot exceed the $\frac{3}{16}$ cent per lb. as a difference in price, for should they make use of their power to fix too wide a difference between the price of raw and of refined sugar, it might lead to the sugar manufacturers producing white sugar themselves, as is done by all the beetroot sugar factories in the United States. This will involve some difficulties, which, however, seem to be of little moment, as the buyers content themselves with a margin of $\frac{3}{16}$ cent per lb., which, considering the great amount of sugar sold, comes to a good sum of money. The difficulties we refer to are of two different kinds: one technical, and the other commercial. First of all, the plantation sugar is not nearly so white and fine as the brilliant sugar from the refineries, to which the American consumer has become used. So it may involve much trouble to dispose of large quantities of white plantation sugar, especially in competition with the excellently organized sale system of the refined sugar manufacturers, which system is spread all over the United States by the Sugar Trust. This organization works so well and is under such strict supervision, that it would not be difficult for the Sugar Trust to harass any opponent who dared to compete with their refined white sugar.

The second drawback against the manufacture of white plantation sugar is this: the Louisiana sugar is sent to market during the months of November to February, consequently a little before or simultaneously with the Cuba sugar, and it is the buyers' policy to buy up the Louisiana sugar as quickly as possible, in order to prevent competition. After the month of March there is no uncontrolled stock of sugar left in the country, and should the refiners expect an increased manufacture of white plantation sugar they would be able at the beginning of the Louisiana harvest to reduce the margin between raw sugar and refined sugar to so small a sum that the entire profit on white sugar manufacture would disappear. But should the Louisiana sugar be sold and the danger be over, they can easily go back to the old margin, having suppressed all danger of competition at very slight expense.

The cane sugar industry of the United States is not likely to undergo any great changes. In 1909 the import duties reverted to what they used to be, and although some proposals have been made to considerably reduce and even to abolish the duty, it is not probable that these will pass into legislation. The great sugar buyers and refiners are more powerful than ever, and it has been their aim to keep conditions as stationary as possible by suppressing competition, so that the present state of affairs is not likely to change much for some years to come.

The sugar consumption in the United States increases both individually and through increase in population, and is quite capable of absorbing the increased production of Cuba, Porto Rico, Hawaii, and even that of the Philippine Islands, should they produce the 300,000 tons of sugar they are allowed to export free of duty, so that for the next ten years the inland consumer is not likely to be crushed to death by their more advantageously placed tropical competitors. It is difficult to say what may happen should Cuba sugar become altogether exempted from import duty through a change in the political condition of that country, as this would affect the whole complex of existing conditions, and make all conjectures useless. We might just as well leave this question undiscussed, as any such exemption from duty seems for the moment out of question.

Most probably the quantity of sugar produced within the continent of the United States will slowly increase, without developing to any unknown extent or experience any considerable decline. Should, however, the duty

TENANGO SUGAR FACTORY IN MEXICO.

on foreign sugar in the United States be abolished or considerably reduced, such important changes in the production and supply of all surrounding countries and in the United States would be the consequence, that it would be beyond the scope of this present work to deal with them here.

Literature :

Bouchereau's *Louisiana Sugar Report.*
Directory of Louisiana Sugar Planters.
Vogt. *The Sugar Refining Industry in the U.S.*

II.

MEXICO.

The Republic of Mexico, or the United Mexican States, lies in the Southern part of North America, between 14° 31′ and 32° 42′ N. Lat. and 86° 46′ to 117° 8′ W. Long   Its greatest length is 1,938 miles, and its greatest width 760 miles ; while its least width, near the Isthmus of Tehuantepec, only amounts to 134 miles.   The area of the republic is 750,000 sq. miles, and the result of the last census in 1900 gave 13,605,819 inhabitants, or 18 to the sq. mile ; 19 per cent. of the population are white people, 43 per cent. are of mixed race, and 38 per cent. are of Indian race.

The formation of the country is very curious.   Because of a succession of terraces it has a sudden rise from the low sandy eastern sea coast on towards the west to a central tableland, which slopes in a north-western and south-eastern direction, and rises from 4,000 to 8,000 ft. above sea level.   Above this plateau the snow-covered peaks of volcanoes, which for the greater part are extinct, stand out : the highest of these are Popocatepetl, Citlatepetl, and Ixtacihuatl, respectively 17,540, 17,362, and 16,076 ft. above sea level.

Two ranges of high mountains in Mexico run parallel with the coast, the one along the Gulf of Mexico and the other along the coast of the Pacific. The first runs at a distance of from 10 to 100 miles from the coast, and has a very gently sloping plain between its foot and the sea ; while the Cordilleras, on the Pacific side, are only separated from it by a very narrow strip of land. Then spurs branch off from this mountain chain, crossing the country in different directions and dividing it into valleys, which are covered with a fertile layer of earth of some considerable thickness, the result of the products of disintegration carried along by the rain.

The east coast of Mexico, on the Gulf of Mexico and the Caribbean Sea, is low, flat, and sandy, except at the mouth of the Tabasco River, where hills are found.   On the Pacific Coast the land, as a rule, is low, but in places it is broken by the spurs of the Western Cordilleras.   The principal gulfs are those of Mexico, California, and Tehuantepec ; and there are a number of important bays, including those of Guyamas, Santa Barbara, Topolobampo,

North America.

and Navachiste in the Gulf of California ; Conception, La Paz, and Muleje,
on the west coast of the same gulf ; San Quintin, Magdalena, and Amejas, on
the Pacific coast ; and San Blas and Valle de Banderas, on the coast of Tepic.

The principal rivers are the Rio Grande, which is 1,550 miles long, and
forms, from El Paso to the sea, the boundary between the United States and
Mexico ; the Lerma, or Santiago ; the Mescala, or Balsas ; the Yaqui, the
Grijalva, and many others. Through the terraced condition of the country
all these rivers form cascades, and, consequently, are not suitable for navigation ; but, on the other hand, are fit for power purposes. For the rest, many
of the rivers are used for irrigation, by damming up and draining off the water.
Owing to the great variation in height above the sea, the climate of Mexico
varies for different parts of the country. Tropical heat is experienced on the
sea coast, and in the low marshy regions near the Gulf of Mexico, and also
in the valleys shut in by high mountains, but on the plateaus where most
of the inhabitants live, the climate is much cooler, and is but moderately hot
all the year through. The year is divided into two seasons, namely, a rainy
season from June till November, and a dry time during the remaining months
of the year.

Meteorological observations for a number of places are as follows, the
names of the places engaged in sugar cane cultivation being italicized :—

1902. Locations.	Temperature in degrees Centigrade.			Average relative humidity.	Days of rain.	Total rainfall in inches.	Maximum rainfall in 24 hours.	Month of heaviest rainfall.
	Aver-age.	Maxi-mum.	Mini-mum.					
Colima	24·4	36·5	11·0	66	85	26·75	1·75	July
Chihuahua ..	18·5	37·0	− 3·0	46	74	18·41	1·69	July–Aug.
Guadalajara ..	20·0	34·7	5·0	55	94	31·66	2·28	July
Guanajuato ..	18·5	34·5	1·0	50	63	--	2·37	,,
Leon	18·6	34·5	− 0·9	60	104	22·55	2·15	,,
Mazatlán	24·7	33·3	13·8	74	70	16·27	1·60	,,
Mérida	25·4	40·8	8·9	70	69	32·27	3·54	October
México	15·9	30·6	0·5	55	131	17·78	5·66	July
Monterrey ..	22·7	38·5	1·2	64	97	15·66	1·89	September
Morelia	16·5	31·9	− 1·0	62	77	22·62	1·73	July
Pachuca	16·9	23·4	7·0	69	69	50·18	11·62	September
Puebla	15·5	28·6	− 1·4	64	110	36·04	2·94	July
Querétaro ..	18·3	34·8	0·6	54	79	23·12	2·14	,,
Zacatecas ..	15·0	30·6	− 2·0	55	86	18·94	1·13	September

Mexico.

The territory of the United Mexican States is divided into 1 Federal district, 27 States, and 2 Territories, the organization of which is almost the same as that of the corresponding parts of the United States of America. Its capital is Mexico, with 344,721 inhabitants (in 1905), situated 7,300 ft. above sea level; further important towns are Guadalajara, Puebla, Leon, Monterry, San Luis Potosi, Merida, Guanajuato, Pachuca, Morelia, Aguascalientes, Caxaca, Queretaro, Orizaba, Zacatecas, Durango, Chihuahua, and Vera Cruz.

Mexico's railway system covers 9,900 miles, most of the lines dating from twenty years ago. The railways connect the capital with the principal centres of population, trade, and industry, also with the seaports and with the United States. The Tehuantepec Railway connects the Atlantic with Pacific coast of Mexico viâ the Tehuantepec Isthmus, while a number of branch lines run from the harbours to the interior. Mexico has been estimated to contain 5,745 sq. miles of dense forests, 217,000 sq. miles of wooded land, and 490,000 sq. miles of uncultivated land.

It is difficult to say exactly how many acres are devoted to the sugar industry, which is carried on in the very fertile lower parts on the Gulf of Mexico and the Pacific coast, and chiefly flourishes in the States of Morelos, Vera Cruz, Puebla, Michoacan, Jalisco, Sinaloa, Guerrero, and Tepic.

This industry dates from a very early time, as Cortez is known to have possessed some sugar plantations in Izcalpam one year after the country was taken possession of. As early as 1553 sugar was exported from Mexico to Spain and Peru, and the sugar production continued to be profitable, and became increasingly important by the end of the eighteenth century, when through the desolation of San Domingo the greatest sugar producer disappeared from the scene, and other countries got a chance. During the nineteenth century the industry remained stationary, while for the last ten years it has gone up considerably owing to an increase in sugar prices.

Both the climate and the soil of many parts of Mexico are extremely well suited for the cultivation of sugar cane, but as the rainfall is not plentiful, irrigation is necessary to obtain a proper kind of cane. From seven to nine ratoons are produced without it being necessary to plant afresh, and even with such a lengthy continuation, and a most sparing manuring and tillage, a yearly product of forty tons per acre, and even of sixty tons, is expected in the States of Vera Crux, Oaxaca, and Chiapas.

The cane is rich in sugar, and very heavy, but the manufacture leaves so much to be desired that generally not more than 6 per cent. of the weight of cane is obtained in sugar. Most of the factories are extremely small, and produce only a few tons of sugar each year, while Mexico can boast of only a few big factories.

The number and the production of the sugar factories in the different States amounted in 1910-11 to the following figures in metric tons :—

North America.

State.	Number.	Tons of sugar.	Tons of molasses.
Campeche	6	265	595
Chiapas	68	485	602
Colima	4	1,550	775
Guerrero	16	2,812	2,070
Jalisco	28	4,850	2,356
Mexico	6	351	1,339
Michoacan	24	10,350	10,073
Morelos	35	49,747	16,673
Nuevo Leon	1	—	500
Oaxaca	33	3,217	1,796
Puebla	14	20,364	9,987
San Luis Potosi	16	4,768	4,880
Sinaloa	4	12,255	5,100
Tabasco	16	2,945	1,901
Tamaulipas	1	2,810	2,505
Tepic	2	3,500	1,200
Vera Cruz	39	40,868	21,341
Yucatan	16	465	260
Total	329	161,602	83,954

During the last few years this production was as follows :—

State.	1905/06.	1906/07.	1907/08.	1908/09.	1909/10.
Campeche	542	1,446	317	314	268
Chiapas	372	732	776	773	554
Colima	1,740	1,597	1,545	1,680	1,680
Guerrero	2,096	2,889	2,766	3,825	2,807
Jalisco	6,196	6,304	5,602	6,095	5,431
Mexico	158	190	210	301	323
Michoacan	6,659	7,493	8,482	9,187	9,310
Morelos	35,662	42,230	48,220	52,230	48,547
Nuevo Leon	914	924	1,206	800	260
Oaxaca	1,477	1,682	1,698	3,045	3,205
Puebla	16,549	16,739	18,157	20,207	21,063
San Luis Potosi	1,925	1,268	2,035	3,020	4,284
Sinaloa	8,540	8,785	6,347	8,393	10,462
Tabasco	1,967	2,005	2,045	2,205	2,480
Tamaulipas	1,694	1,578	1,412	600	2,786
Tepic	3,500	3,250	3,300	3,300	3,500
Vera Cruz	16,297	18,690	18,243	26,871	30,483
Yucatan	1,241	1,694	924	429	458
Total	107,529	119,407	123,285	143,179	147,905

Mexico.

The production of the States of Morelas, Oaxaca, Puebla, and Vera Cruz has greatly increased, while that of Yucatan has considerably decreased.

Besides this, about 50,000 tons concrete sugar (piloncillo or panela) are turned out yearly in a great number of small factories.

The total production of crystallized sugar has been for the last eleven years as follows :—

	Metric tons.
1889/1900	75,000
1900/01	95,000
1901/02	103,000
1902/03	112,000
1903/04	107,000
1904/05	107,000
1905/06	107,500
1906/07	119,000
1907/08	123,000
1908/09	143,000
1909/10	147,905
1910/11	161,602

Of this sugar the following quantities were exported :—

	Tons
1901/02	149
1902/03	8,258
1903/04	16,490
1904/05	39,270
1905/06	5,198
1906/07	31,380
1907/08	5,686
1908/09	4,212
1909/10	11,104

Since the 5th February, 1908, an import duty of 5 dollars Mexican (1 Mexican dollar = 2s. 0½d.) per 100 kg. (220 lbs.) of raw sugar has been levied on each kind. There used to be a duty of half that value, so that this increase has not a little contributed towards the rise in the inland price of sugar, which has made the manufacture of sugar correspondingly more profitable than it used to be.

The Mexican sugar industry promises much for the future; even now, in spite of its very primitive method of cultivation and manufacture, the industry is rapidly expanding, and it is difficult to tell how great a future may be in store when new capital is invested in the estates, and efforts are made to carry on the sugar industry in a more modern and rational way. Labour is abundant and cheap, a large extent of very fertile land is still uncultivated, and as soon as this is provided with an irrigation system there is no reason to doubt the prospect of a cane production and a sugar yield equal to any that Java or Hawaii yields.

The present political conditions of the country are not favourable for the extension of the industry, but as soon as order is restored, and a stable Government is master of the situation, Mexico will soon increase her sugar production.

Literature:

Mexico. A Handbook. Edited by the International Bureau of American Republics.
Revista Azucarera.
Sugar Report of the Hacendado Mexicano.

═══════════

III.

CUBA.

I.—Geographical Location, Population, Area planted with Cane, Total Sugar Production.

CUBA is a long narrow island, shaped somewhat like the arc of a circle, the convex side of which faces north. It lies between 74° and 85° Long. West from Greenwich, and between 19° 40' and 23° 33' N. Lat. Cuba's total area, including the adjacent islands, is 45,887 sq. miles; that of the island proper amounts to 43,319 sq. miles, and it is 730 miles long, while its breadth varies between 22 miles in the province of Habana and 160 miles in the province of Oriente.

The north coast is for the greater part steep and rocky, especially in the centre and eastern parts of the island, while it is flattest in the province of Pinar del Rio. The south coast is also steep and mountainous in the east, but low and marshy in many places beyond Cape Cruz. The part between Trinidad and Cienfuegos is again rocky. In accordance with this geographical condition, the seaport towns are found on the rocky coasts, most of them being situated on deep bays, which being narrow at the entrance provide a safe anchorage.

The middle part of the island, namely, the provinces Havana, Matanzas, Santa Clara, and Camaguey, consists chiefly of extensive plains and shallow valleys, without mountains of any importance. The country is mountainous only at its two extremities, in Pinar del Rio and in Oriente, but mountain tops of any importance it has none. The mountains generally do not exceed 2,000 ft. in height, though the highest peak, in Oriente, Pico Turquino, is reputed to be 8,320 ft.

Cuba.

The numerous rivers are not of any length, and for the greater part are not navigable. Only the Rio Cauto in Oriente is navigable for vessels of any considerable draft. So far river water in Cuba has not been applied to irrigation purposes.

The average annual temperature in Havana amounts to 24·2° C., with a maximum temperature of 37·5° and a minimum temperature of 10° C.; in the centre and the south the temperature is higher, which is shown by the following tables of yearly average temperatures for the several provinces :—

Province.	1906	1907	1908	1909	1910	1911
	°C.	°C.	°C.	°C.	°C.	°C.
Pinar del Rio ..	24·3	25·2	25·6	25·8	25·0	26·7
Havana	24·1	24·2	24·1	24·0	23·6	24·8
Matanzas	—	24·4	24·4	—	23·5	24·6
Santa Clara	25·1	—	—	25·9	25·3	25·0
Camaguey	25·5	—	25·8	25·2	24·8	25·9
Oriente	25·2	25·4	25·5	24·9	25·8	24·9

The warmest months are from May to October, while the lowest temperature prevails in the months of December to March. The warm season is at the same time the rainy season, which generally happens to be from May to October, although it may come later or earlier.

The quantity of rainfall and the number of rainy days has been on an average for the last five years as follows :—

Province.	1907 Mm.	Ins.	Days	1908 Mm.	Ins.	Days	1909 Mm.	Ins.	Days	1910 Mm.	Ins.	Days	1911 Mm.	Ins.	Days
Pinar del Rio ..	1009·8	39·75	80	1606·0	75·39	118	2·153	84·96	109	2097·0	82·55	94	1997·0	78·61	96
Havana .	686·2	25·05	70	1247·2	49·10	100	1·332	52·44	1?1	1183·1	46·60	81	1059·4	41·76	93
Matanza ..	1113·7	43·85	106	1348·7	53·12	106	1·873	73·74	115	1158·2	45·60	92	1482·1	58·36	86
Santa Clara ..	1049·8	41·37	71	—	—	—	1·460	57·48	100	1278·9	50·37	111	1419·7	55·91	126
Camaguey ..	—	—	—	1183·4	44·62	148	1·582	62·28	164	1056·3	41·50	117	915·2	36·02	114
Oriente	871·5	34·31	63	1457·5	57·84	92	1·420	55·91	93	552·0	21·75	74	926·1	36·88	85

The prevailing wind is north-east ; it is not a violent, but a steady wind. Then there are hurricanes that now and then come from the Caribbean Sea and sweep over the island, leaving a good deal of damage in their wake. These hurricanes are formed east of Cuba, and go first westward and then bend to the north ; and the later in the season they come the larger the circle to which they extend, and the more to the west they strike Cuba. In the beginning of the season—in July—East Cuba is more subject to damage from hurricanes, which are then distinguished by heavy rainfall and a fairly strong wind. Western Cuba comes in for them when, later in the season, they blow harder and are not accompanied by much rain ; while, as a rule, hardly any hurricanes are encountered after October. In 1906 a considerable quantity of cane was destroyed by a hurricane in the district between Matanzas and Havana.

As the results of the census of 1908 show, the population of Cuba amounted to 2,048,980 people, who were divided over the different provinces as follows :—

Pinar del Rio	240,372
Havana	538,010
Matanzas	239,812
Santa Clara	457,431
Camaguey	118,269
Oriente	455,086
	2,048,890

1,428,176 of these are whites, 620,804 coloured, and 228,741 are of foreign origin ; while 1,074,882 of the total population are men and 974,098 women.

While nowadays the population amounts to more than 2,000,000, that is about 46 to the sq. mile, previous censuses have resulted in the following figures :—

1774	172,260
1792	272,301
1817	553,028
1827	704,487
1841	1,077,624
1861	1,396,530
1887	1,631,687
1899	1,572,727

This table points to a considerable increase during the past ten years, if the census of previous years was as trustworthy as the last one. There is, however, much reason to suppose that the late Spanish authorities gave too low a figure on each occasion, so that we cannot make sure of this apparently large increase.

The exact figures of the number of immigrants have been known only since 1890, and up to 1902 they amounted on an average to 20,000 per annum. The years during the war 1896—1898 are left out, as immigration then came to a stop.

Classified according to the different nationalities, the immigration for the last nine years has been as follows :—

CENTRAL STEWART IN CUBA.

Cuba.

Nationalities.	1902/03	1903/04	1904/05	1905/06	1906/07	1907	1908	1909	1910
Spanish	9,716	16,276	35,161	44,672	22,178	24,792	21,305	24,662	30,913
N. Americans	1,066	1,263	1,849	2,384	1,709	1,528	1,841	1,903	1,572
British	375	354	374	615	2,204	1,438	1,667	1,575	993
Italians	228	374	255	339	215	215	223	194	200
French	147	194	333	369	281	257	272	240	259
Germans	64	104	162	176	80	83	134	103	113
Turks	23	88	86	228	264	231	190	277	210
W. Indians	144	233	479	1,550	953	1,610	758	553	1,427
Porto Ricans	79	223	413	738	717	619	471	578	595
Mexicans	140	173	235	254	132	188	233	185	160
Syrians	192	168	372	332	294	322	289	366	466
Arabs	51	39	51	207	182	85	50	49	38
S. Americans	169	113	250	221	143	140	121	184	155
Scandinav'ns	41	69	105	126	100	101	85	40	103
Other Nationalities	216	146	435	341	200	238	360	377	560
Total	12,651	19,817	40,560	52,652	29,572	31,227	27,999	31,286	37,764

During the years 1906—1910 the immigration at the different ports was as follows :—

	1906	1907	1908	1909	1910
Havana	21,947	23,618	20,930	23,477	29,244
Santiago de Cuba	6,334	6,678	6,157	7,096	7,791
Nuevitas	392	397	309	291	252
Caibarien	191	144	229	4	—
Cienfuegos	99	188	211	113	155
Puerto Padre	311	81	87	204	—
Guantanamo	300	60	9	26	239
Other Ports	98	61	67	75	21
Total	29,572	31,227	27,999	31,286	37,764

It is not known how many of those described as immigrants have left the country again, but this number no doubt must be rather considerable, as many of them only come for a single season at the end of which they return home.   Consequently, the number of immigrants given here should by no means be considered as an acquisition to the population.

Up to a short time ago the roads in Cuba were in a very deplorable state, and almost the entire transportation from town to town took place by sea. The rivers are not suitable for navigation, while when the Americans took over the administration of Cuba the main roads, except in the immediate vicinity of Habana and Santiago de Cuba, were either totally wanting, or were in an extremely bad condition.   It was therefore of great importance to the development of the country that the extension of the railway system was taken energetically in hand, so that, apart from the numerous narrow-gauge railways which connect the sugar factories with the main lines, about 1,000 miles of public railway are in operation.   The map shows the now existing railways, which connect the harbour towns with the interior, and which, since the connection of Santa Clara with San Luis in 1902 established direct communication between the western and eastern systems, are combined into one coherent and continuous railway system.   The construction of cart roads has also made great strides in the different provinces since the emancipation of the republic from Spain.

The sugar cane is cultivated in all the provinces of the island, and especially in Santa Clara, Matanzas, and Oriente.   The places where cane cultivation is carried on are represented by shading on the map.

The proportion between the area planted with cane for the years 1904-05 and 1908-09 in the different provinces, and their total area, and also with the area of arable land, is classified in the table underneath.

When considering this table we must bear in mind that the area set forth as planted with sugar cane is not measured, but obtained by calculating back the probable area from the weight of cane, in which calculation 50,000 arrobas, or 506·63 tons of cane, are supposed to be equivalent to 1 caballeria, or $33\frac{1}{3}$ acres, thus supposing a yield of 15·5 tons of cane per acre.

Calculated in this way, the crop of 1910–11, which has yielded 1,158,985,514 arrobas of cane, has come from 23,179 caballerias, or 772,657 acres of land, or from 2·84 per cent. of the area of the whole island.

Provinces.	Area.		Area fit for agriculture.		Cane Planted Area. 1904/05.				Cane Planted Area. 1908/09.			
	Hectares	%	Hectares	%	Hectares	% of the total area	% of the arable land	% of the total	Hectares	% of the total area	% of the arable land	°/₀ of the total
Pinar del Rio ..	1,295,900	11·4	882,848	68·1	6,844	0·52	0·76	4	7,271	0 56	0·82	2·16
Habana	717,948	6·3	620,420	86·4	10,602	1·47	1·73	6	39 814	5 55	6·42	11 86
Matanzas	959 300	8·4	599,659	60 6	46,366	4·83	7·97	27	81,686	8·52	13·61	24·35
Santa Clara ..	2,746,047	21·7	1 496,706	60 4	68.778	2·77	4·58	39	113,062	4·11	7·54	33·70
Camaguey.. ..	2,719,500	23·9	1,172,894	43·1	8,857	0·32	0·47	5	22,311	0·82	1·91	6·66
Oriente	3,229,212	28·3	1,527,639	47·3	33,013	1·02	2 16	19	71,862	2 21	4·67	21·27
Total	11,396,000	100	6,300,166	55·2	174,460	1·53	2 78	100	335,506	2·94	5·53	100·00
Acres	27,160,000		15,568,000		481.091				829,085			

Cuba.

This figure is not, however, to be considered as the real one, as besides the area necessary for actual cane cultivation, allowance must be made for extensive pastures in use for draught cattle, arable land for the cane planters, and the barren tracts of land in between, which because of their position cannot be used for anything else, and consequently must also be reckoned as ground occupied for cane plantation. We can safely assume the actual cane planted area to be twice as much as the nominally planted area, which results in more than 1,605,500 acres, or nearly 6 per cent., of the soil area being required.

The land given out to sugar plantations is yet larger, as in many of these tracts forest land occurs, and none of the estates have used all the acreage at their disposal for cultivation. Thus, all things considered, about 2,500,000 acres belong to the sugar plantations. The figures of about 15½ million acres for arable land must be accepted with reserve. Although the entire amount is put down as plantation ground, all of it is not by a long way in actual cultivation, and is not likely to be so for some time yet.

No recent exact figures exist, as the last date from 1892, but it is taken for granted that the proportion of cultivated to uncultivated land has hardly changed at all. In 1892, 49 per cent. of the total cultivated area was covered with sugar cane; if the same proportion still exists the entire area actually planted with agricultural produce would amount to no more than 1,600,000 acres. If we add to this the ground occupied by towns, villages, houses, and the very extensive meadows, etc., all more or less destined for production if not exclusively planted with agricultural vegetation, we come to the figure of 15½ million acres already cited.

The following table gives a full report of the production of the different provinces in tons of 2,240 lbs. for each year since the revival of the industry, while the number of factories in each province is mentioned :—

Provinces.	1900/1.	1901/2.		1902/3.		1903/4.		1904/5.		1905/6.	
		Facto-ries.	Tons.	Facto-ries.	Tons.	Facto-ries.	Tons.	Facto-ries.	Tons.	Facto-ries.	Tons.
Pinar del Rio	13.963	7	21,063	7	23,199	7	20,627	6	21,828	6	25 334
Havana	60,832	18	89,139	20	104,091	20	130,450	21	155,346	21	164.230
Matanzas	206,551	52	264,262	51	521,236	50	312,859	50	341,716	53	344,898
Santa Clara .	248,955	62	328 761	63	391,761	66	385,746	70	452.488	69	479,634
Camaguey	20,573	3	22,579	3	26 837	3	27,928	4	30 173	5	38,145
Oriente	61,901	26	137,970	27	136,749	28	175,163	28	181,001	27	178,495
Total ..	612,775	168	863,792	171	1,003,873	174	1,052,273	179	1,183,347	181	1,229 736

Provinces.	1906/7.		1907/8.		1908/9.		1909/10.		1910/11.	
	Facto-ries.	Tons.	Facto-ries.	Tons.	Facto-ries.	Tons.	Facto-ries.	Tons.	Facto-ries.	Tons.
Pinar del Rio	7	33,651	8	22.333	8	31,570	8	30,470	8	22,281
Havana	22	188 655	18	113,501	18	183,197	18	195,034	17	140,538
Matanzas	55	397,194	45	217,726	44	363,196	47	453,968	43	299 568
Santa Clara ..	70	520 424	66	344,314	68	510.078	66	604,198	68	550,950
Camaguey ..	4	52,788	6	52,919	6	98 024	6	117,316	6	112 092
Oriente .	28	256,598	26	218,482	26	335,753	25	403,363	26	343,876
Total ..	186	1,444,310	169	969,275	170	1,521,818	170	1,804,349	168	1,469,250

II.—The History of the Cane Sugar Industry.

Soon after the discovery of Cuba by Christopher Columbus in 1492, the sugar cane was introduced. There it found an extremely fertile soil for its growth and development, but the Spanish Government of the sixteenth and seventeenth centuries did not allow any full scope for Cuba's infant sugar industry. Indeed, after a few years sugar cane cultivation was forbidden, and even after that interdiction was withdrawn, monopolies and privileges have had such a restrictive influence that up to 1772 any real progress was out of question. After that year, however, any Spaniard was free to produce sugar, and this led to such an increased production that the exportation, which in 1760 only amounted to 4,392 tons, realized in 1780 about 12,000, and in 1790 14,163 tons of sugar. The revolution and consequent ruin of the sugar industry in San Domingo in 1791 were responsible for the great impetus given to the development of the sugar trade in Cuba, as all the neighbouring countries were eager to fill the vacancies. Within ten years the number of factories increased from 473 to 870, and the exportation amounted for 1792, 1796, and 1802 to 14,600, 24,000, and 40,800 tons respectively. Owing to the unfavourable state of affairs in Europe during the first years of the nineteenth century, Cuba, like every other sugar producing country, suffered heavily ; but when, after Napoleon's fall, the former regular commercial intercourse was restored, Cuba's sugar industry was able to expand once more. During the years 1826—1836 the combined sugar exportation of the Caribbean Isles realized from 270,000 to 350,000 tons, 80,000 to 170,000 tons of which were yielded by the English colonies, while the Spanish and French Caribbean Isles contributed the rest.

Although the production had increased, the methods of cultivation and manufacture remained crude and primitive, and labour was difficult to procure. The aborigines had been exterminated soon after the conquest, and were replaced as a makeshift by African negro slaves.

As long as the sugar industry remained on a small scale, the number of workmen was sufficient, but after the rapid extension it did not come up to the increasing demand, and the deficit was felt keenly, till in 1834, when the Governor of Cuba, Miguel Tacon, contrary to the contracts with Spain and England, openly encouraged the slave trade, and consequently raised the African population of Cuba to a higher figure. It is due to these measures, as well as to Tacon's strong disapproval of all sorts of abuses which had become associated with the administration, that the sugar industry revived and entered upon a period of prosperity such as has not since been witnessed in the history of Cuba till the occupation of the United States in 1898. The sugar industry extended to unknown parts, and several fishing ports developed into well-frequented harbours. In spite of the heavy taxes, export duties, and special levies, which the Mother Country demanded of its colonies, the sugar experienced a great time of prosperity from 1835 till the first war against Spain.

Although from 1850 onwards the sugar production and the number of sugar factories in Cuba were recorded in statistics, it was not till 1882 that they began to be reliable, when the incidence of an export duty procured fairly accurate figures. We know for a fact, however, that in 1870 the yearly output realized 610,300 tons, which were obtained from no fewer than 1,200 small factories. This lucrative period was brought to an end by the abolition of slavery as much as through the first war against Spain, the so-called " Ten Years' War," from 1868—1878. In 1872 all the children born from women slaves were declared free, while 1880 witnessed the total abolition of slavery, for which the owners were not indemnified. This great change as regards the labour problem dealt the sugar industry a heavy blow. Instead of being able to dispose of reliable and cheap labour on the estate, they had to look out for free labour, which was both scarce and expensive. At the same time, the country was suffering from the terrors of the war with Spain, which was carried on with great bitterness on either side, and led to the devastation of much property. The competition with beetroot sugar at that time became much more threatening, as this alternative source of sugar was protected by all sorts of privileges and bounties, and gradually became a powerful factor in the supplying of the world's demands. After the war was over the annual output rose again, so that in 1890 it realized 625,000 tons, which had been produced in about 470 factories. As the number of factories decreased, the number of undertakings for cane planting steadily mounted up. For want of labourers of their own, the manufacturers, soon after the abolition of slavery, resolved to give plots of land on lease to farmers, and to buy and work up their crops of cane, as well as that of entirely independent landowners. Thus a separation between plantation and manufacture was gradually brought about in Cuba, and was carried on so far that in the end cane was almost exclusively obtained by acquisition. The period of rest, following the end of the rebellion against Spain, was most beneficial to the development of the sugar industry, and in consequence its produce steadily increased, to reach its maximum of 1,054,214 tons in 1894. In the following year, 1895, however, the last rebellion against Spain broke out ; after much calamity and devastation it ended in the Spanish-American War, and ultimately in the establishment of the Cuban Republic. This period of disturbance and strife is the worst in the entire history of Cuba ; on both sides much harm was done by killing cattle and burning and destroying property, all for the purpose of cutting off their opponents' means of livelihood. Owing to the destruction of the factories, the burning over of cane fields, and the extermination of draught cattle, it became almost an impossibility to carry on the sugar industry ; and in spite of the strict regulations issued by the Spanish authorities to go on grinding as long as it was feasible, the production in 1897 went down to as low a figure as 212,051 tons. It goes without saying that the industry recovered only slowly when the period of misery and destruction had come to an end, and was followed by a time of quiet. Numerous factories had been destroyed ; others had lost their cattle and seen their plantations devastated, their means of conveyance rendered unfit for use, and their working population reduced in number, and accustomed to an irregular life; so that it took much time and trouble and capital to recreate a healthy state of affairs. Many manufacturers failed to realize the necessary funds for rebuilding their factories or reinstalling them, so they turned their lands into pastures, or became cane planters themselves for the sake of neighbouring " central factories." Others, again, who were able to get the necessary money, although at a high interest, extended their estates; while most of them, unable to pay for the urgent factory repairs out of their own purse, turned their properties into joint stock companies, or sold them to fresh companies. Instead of the great number of semi-patriarchal owners at the head of small factories working on rather crude lines, there is now a smaller number of mostly very big factories (so-called *centrales*), which belong to companies and are founded on a much better commercial basis. This gradual conversion of small establishments into big ones still goes on, and whenever news from Cuba tells of a new company being created for the purpose of building a central factory, which is to produce 200,000 bags of sugar or more, it is in most cases not an entirely new enterprise, and the total production of the island will consequently not be raised by that amount; it is in many cases simply the conversion of two or three small estates into a big one, to work up the cane of the still existing plantations. Besides these conversions, however, entirely new sugar estates are started, especially by American capitalists, on the north and south coast, and further in the interior of the island along the newly erected railroad, which connects Santiago de Cuba with Santa Clara and Havana, and has brought large extensions of excellent cane land within reach of cultivation. Although it must have been most unpleasant individually for the planters who were unlucky enough to see their property slip away, the sugar production of Cuba itself has been benefited by the modern methods of working that ask for concentration of labour; and also by the fact that the cane sugar industry nowadays is being increasingly carried on by powerful companies, which through their greater access to all sorts of resources can better turn to account the natural advantages of soil and climate than the small planters would ever be able to do.

The owners of the sugar factories working from 1906 till 1911 belonged to the following nationalities :—

	1906	1907	1908	1909	1910	1911
Cubans	78	73	67	67	67	64
Americans	30	31	36	38	38	41
English, Spaniards, etc.	73	82	66	65	65	63
Total	181	186	169	170	170	168

Cuba.

Of the 170 factories in operation in 1911,

57 belonged to individual owners,
54 belonged to private firms,
26 belonged to joint stock companies established in Cuba, and
33 belonged to foreign joint stock companies.

Closely connected with the diminution in the number of factories and the increase in the planted area, the average capacity of the factories has also greatly increased. We saw that in 1870 the average production of a factory was only 500 tons, or 3,500 bags; in 1880 this figure had gone up to 1,300 tons; while in 1907, 1908, 1909, 1910, and 1911 the proportion expressed in bags of 325 Spanish pounds was as follows :—

	1907	1908	1909	1910	1911
More than 500,000 bags	—	—	—··	1	—
More than 400,000 bags	—	—	1	1	1
More than 200,000 bags	3	2	3	4	3
Between 150,000 and 200,000 bags ..	4	—	4	5	1
Between 100,000 and 150,000 bags ..	25	6	16	22	19
Between 50,000 and 100,000 bags ..	61	36	55	62	54
Between 25,000 and 50,000 bags ..	51	48	50	51	38
Less than 25,000 bags	42	76	41	24	52
	186	168	170	170	168

In 1909 the average production of each factory amounted to 56,803 bags for all the existing plantations; for those under Spanish and European management, 44,497 bags; for those belonging to Cubans, 49,858 bags; while for American estates it was 99,830 bags.

In spite of the difference in the number of estates of each category (Cuban, American, and other nationalities), each of the three produced during the years 1907, 1908, and 1909 about one-third of the total sugar output.

In 1910 the proportion was no longer the same, chiefly owing to the gigantic production of the larger factories (such as Chaparra, Preston, Boston, and others), so that the output of the American factories in 1910 amounted to 35 per cent. of the total, and stayed at that figure in 1911 too.

The total sugar production of Cuba has been in the years following 1850 as below (but only the figures after 1882 are fully trustworthy) :—

Year.	Tons.	Notes.	Year.	Tons.	Notes.
1850	223,145		1883	460,327	Internal disturbances.
1851	263,999				
1852	251,609		1884	558,932	
1853	322,000		1885	631,000	
1854	374,000		1886	731,723	
1855	392,000		1887	646,578	
1856	348,000		1888	656,719	
1857	355,000		1889	560,333	
1858	385,000		1890	632,368	
1859	536,000		1891	816,980	
1860	447,000		1892	976,000	
1861	446,000		1893	815,894	
1862	525,000		1894	1,054,214	
1863	507,000		1895	1,004,264	
1864	575,000		1896	225,221	Rebellion against Spain.
1865	620,000		1897	212,051	
1866	612,000		1898	305,543	Spanish-Amer. war.
1867	597,000				
1868	749,000		1899	335,668	
1869	726,000		1900	283,651	Great drought.
1870	726,000		1901	612,775	
1871	547,000	Hurricane.	1902	863,792	
1872	690,000		1903	1,003,873	
1873	775,000	10 years' war.	1904	1,052,273	
1874	681,000		1905	1,183,347	
1875	718,000		1906	1,229,736	
1876	590,000		1907	1,444,310	Particularly favourable weather.
1877	520,000				
1878	533,000				
1879	670,000		1908	969,275	Great drought.
1880	530,000		1909	1,521,818	
1881	493,000		1910	1,804,349	
1882	595,000		1911	1,469,250	
			1912	1,800,000	Estimate.

III.—Cane Cultivation.

The price paid for land varies greatly for the different provinces. In Pinar del Rio a caballeria (33·16 acres) is to be had for $200, unless fit for tobacco cultivation or adapted for irrigation, in which case the price goes up enormously.

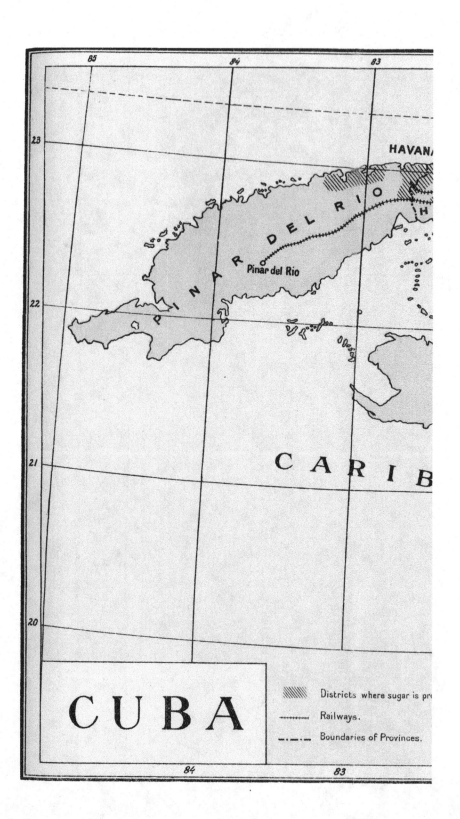

CUBA

Districts where sugar is pr[...]
Railways.
Boundaries of Provinces.

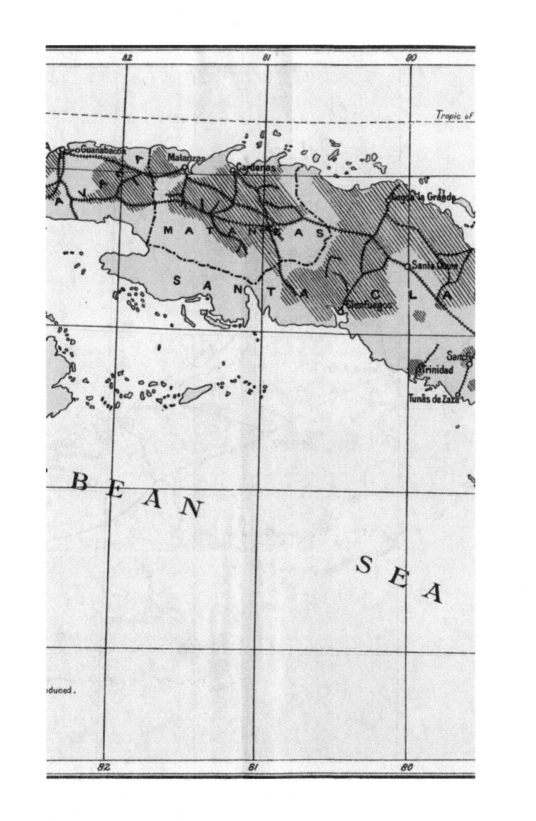

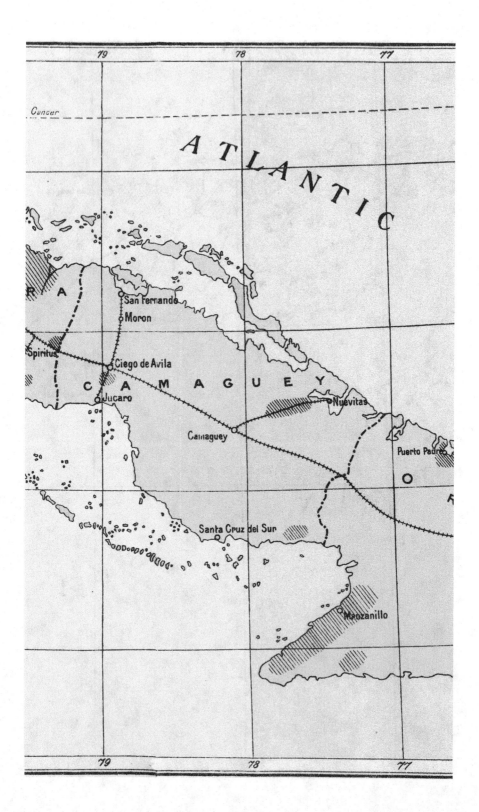

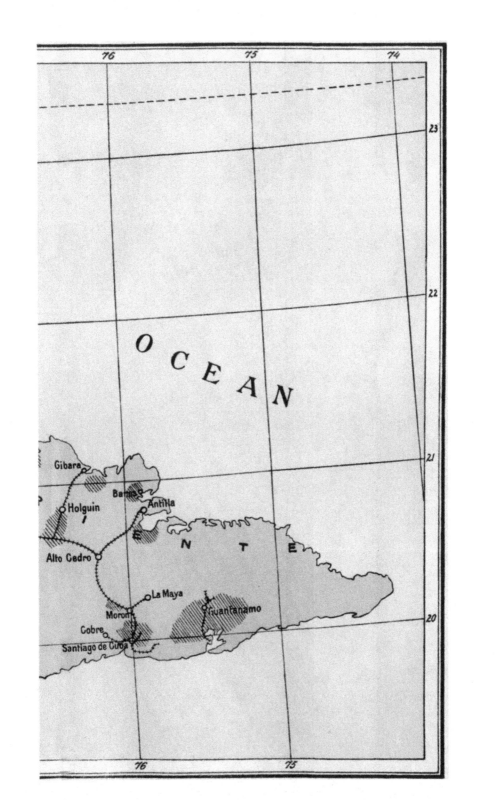

Cuba.

In Havana the cost of land is from $400 to $2,000 per caballeria, in Matanzas and Santa Clara from $300 to $800, and in Camaguey and Oriente the price is only from $100 to $300, while one can easily be suited for less than $100 per caballeria when buying larger tracts.

Only a very small part of the soil is fit for irrigation with water from wells; those parts occur in the provinces of Pinar del Rio and Havana. All the remaining ground is dependent on rainfall.

As has been mentioned before, the cane is partly planted by the factories themselves and partly by independent farmers (*colonos*). These again plant the cane either on their own ground or on ground they hire from the estates. In the year 1904-5 the different categories bore the following relation:

Province.	Total planted area.		Total.		Planted by the Estate itself.		Planted by colonos.				Number of Colonias.
							On ground of the Estate.		On their own ground.		
	Cabs*	Cords	Cabs	Cords	Cabs	Cords	Cabs	Cords	Cabs	Cords	
Pinar del Rio	576	198	†507	312	141	—	155	15	211	297	253
Havana ...	1,600	74	790	72	149	—	251	55	390	17	147
Matanzas ...	4,617	266	3 455	182	916	40	1,176	50	1 363	92	533
Santa Clara ...	9,275	276	5,125	161	1,206	243	1,297	285	2,620	261	1,923
Camaguey ...	2,924	81	660	—	366	—	287	—	7	—	—
Oriente	4,149	208	2,459	231	955	176	960	55	504	—	785
Total	23,594	131	12,998	319	3,774	135	4,127	136	5,097	19	3,641

But little care is bestowed on the planting, and yet the sugar cane once planted yields ample crops for years, and that without any manuring or tillage to speak of. When in the end the cane is considered too old for a further crop, and the old stubbles are removed, the same soil when planted anew will yield again very satisfactory crops for years, and that without any rotation of crops, till finally being exhausted it will be abandoned and used as pasture land.

When cane is planted on new soil, the jungle is first cut, the valuable logs are carried away and the rest is burnt, only the royal palms being left standing, as they are of great value, because their leaves can be used as thatch and their seeds serve as food for pigs. The cane tops are planted in the moderately levelled and ploughed ground at 6 ft. distance from each other, covered with earth, and left to grow.

* 1 caballeria = 342 cordeles = 13·42 hectares = 33·16 acres.

† Here, too, the planted area has not been measured, but calculated from the obtained weight of cane, in which case 50,000 arrobas cane are taken for 1 caballeria.

North America.

If the weather is favourable, *i.e.*, rainy and warm, the cane will grow well, but should drought follow the planting it will stop the growth, and the young cane is sure to die, thus making fresh planting necessary.   In Cuba one distinguishes spring and autumn planting.   The first falls before or during the first months of the rainy season—that is in April, May, and June ; and should the rain come in time the cane can be reaped in March and April of the following year.   Should the rain set in later, the cane will have no time to ripen, and as the grinding season will be broken by new rains, the spring cane cannot be ground till December in the following crushing season.

The autumn cane planted at the end of the rainy season in the soaked soil does not get ripe till December of the following year, or in the beginning of the year after, so that it may be cut by March.

Grinding is undertaken exclusively in the dry weather, so that it must be put off till the ground is well dried.   Hard roads are of rare occurrence in Cuba, and the cane, as a rule, has to be carried by ox carts from the fields to the weighing bridge, from whence it is further transported by train to the factory.   As long as the soil is dry the heavy carts, with a load of 300 arrobas (7,500 lbs.) of cane drawn by three pairs of oxen, can easily do the work ; but comparatively light showers, *i.e.*, of two inches, cause the ground to become so soft that the vehicles get stuck deeply in the earth, transportation becoming an impossibility. Consequently, grinding should be begun immediately rain is over, *i.e.*, in December, as the work has to be stopped when the next showers come, which may happen either as early as April or not before July.   Further on, when discussing the future of the cane industry in Cuba, it will be shown of how much importance this uncertainty as regards the duration of the rainy season may be for the sugar production of that island.

The cane is cut close to the ground with a *machete*, a kind of cutlass, then stripped of its tops and cut into pieces two or three feet in length.   These are bound into bundles and piled up on ox carts, which are driven to the factory or to the weighing stations in the fields, where they are weighed and laden into railway trucks for transportation to the mills.   Very often the cut cane is left lying in the field for some time before it is carried away.   Frequently no hurry as regards the transportation of the cut cane is shown, and this often causes the extremities to dry up to some extent.   But as cutting and grinding is usually done during the cold months of the year, the deterioration of cane thus neglected is far less than might be the case should cane be thus treated in hotter countries.   Even if there was thought of improving this state of affairs, it would soon be realized how difficult the matter is, as labour is scarce, and a regular supply of cane is all that can be expected ; so things are best left as they are.

After the cane is cut, the stumps are covered with dry leaves to prevent too great an evaporation, and owing to the natural moisture of the ground and the occasional showers the cane will soon shoot up again, and, as a rule, is once more ripe twelve months after the cutting.   The sugar content of first and second ratoon canes is supposed to be highest, while after the second ratoons the yield of cane becomes less. Generally five to six ratoons are grown, but very often this number is exceeded as circumstances require. A good crop should yield at least 80,000 arrobas per caballeria (62,000 lbs. or 27·8 tons per acre), although sometimes 100,000 and even 160,000 arrobas are obtained. The average crop is 50,000 arrobas per caballeria (17·33 tons to the acre). As soon as a plot promises no larger a crop than 20,000 arrobas per caballeria (say seven tons to the acre) it is usual to plant anew, providing there is no lack of labour. But when labour is scarce, and it is too late in the season to expect a timely harvest from the cane by the following crushing season, it is better to keep on the same cane for another year as this is more profitable in the end. The same field may happen to yield a crop exceeding 20,000 arrobas, in which case it is kept again for further ratoons, so that at the best of times fields may still yield quite satisfactory crops without requiring any fresh planting, after having been cut uninterruptedly for 30 seasons.

Field treatment does not amount to much; on some modern estates it simply involves cutting and weeding the grass regularly, and going with a plough, drawn by oxen, between the rows in order to loosen the soil after the cutting is done; but even this loosening of the earth is often neglected, so that reaping the crop is the only treatment the cane plantations regularly witness besides that of planting and weeding.

The cane varieties which are most in vogue in Cuba are the caña blanca and the caña cristallina; they are pale green and soft varieties, and easy to crush. Another kind found there is the caña rojo or red cane, a very inferior and hard kind which is difficult to grind. The latter is chiefly planted along the edges of the plots, in order to give stray cattle the impression that the entire plot is planted with this unpalatable kind of vegetation.

The cost of planting new cane depends greatly on the quality of the soil, on the wages to be paid, etc., but may be reckoned to amount to $1,000 to $1,400 per caballeria—$1,200 (£7 4s. 9d. per acre) on an average. The cost of first and following ratoons, of course, is much less, as it simply involves loosening the soil, cutting the grass, and weeding. It is to be estimated at $340 per caballeria, or £10 2s. 2d. per acre.

$400 is paid for cutting and cleaning the cane, $200 for loading, and $200 for transportation. The cost of a caballeria of planted cane from the time of planting till it is brought to the mill thus comes to about $1,900 to $2,000 per caballeria (£12 1s. 4d. per acre), and under the best conditions may drop to $1,700 (£10 4s. 8d. per acre).

If we take for granted that the once planted cane only yields five crops, the total expense of the planting will amount to $2,760, plus cost of cutting, loading, and transportation ($4,000); that is, altogether, $6,760 per caballeria. For the rest, we take as an average production 50,000 arrobas, or 250,000 arrobas altogether, so that each aroba of cane will have cost $0·207— 6d. per cwt.—including conveyance to the mill. While ground is to be got for

$100 per caballeria, which, when half of it is planted, comes to $200 net, it will not cost more than $20 per caballeria each year, even at the rate of 10 per cent., that is about 1d. per 50 arrobas, which only imperceptibly raises the cost price of sugar cane.

If the cane can be cut more than five times, the heavy cost of first planting will be distributed over more crops, so that the cost of cane goes down, and as in most cases more than four ratoons are reaped, the figure of 10s. per ton cane delivered at the mill will be rather too high than too low an estimate.

When buying cane from the colonos the price is not expressed in money value, but in per cents of sugar on 100 parts of cane. The seller generally gets an amount of 5 per cent. of the weight in cane paid in sugar, or, if desired, its equivalent in money calculated at the Havana quotation on the day of delivery. This figure of 5 per cent. is no fixed amount ; it may be less when the colonos have had much money advanced, or may increase when there is lack of cane, so that the planters are able to claim what price they wish. These prices are based on clean cane in bundles delivered on the scale, and have nothing whatever to do with the sugar content of the raw material, so that the manufacturer does not gain much profit from this compromise should the sugar content be low.

Cane diseases are hardly ever met with in Cuba, which is a very good thing for that country, for should a serious infectious disease make its appearance, it would be almost impossible to stamp it out, so that the harm done would be widespread. The plantations being close together, any isolation of fields that are attacked by the disease is out of the question ; moreover, labour is too scarce to weed out the infected plants and to plant new fields. For this reason it is to be considered a great advantage for the Cuban sugar industry that the fertility of the soil allows the sugar cane to be treated as though it were a weed, which once planted wants hardly any further care or treatment, and is proof against attacks from fungoid and other diseases.

Mice are the only animal enemies ; these in dry years get in great numbers into the sugar cane fields and gnaw the canes. At the approach of the rainy season they disappear as quickly as they come. Then stray cattle are a nuisance, for they make short work of fences, and invade the cane plantations. Borers, both the *Scirpophaga* and the *Chilo*, are of frequent occurrence, and sometimes cartloads of cane show traces of being infested on each stick by borers. In not one case are the attacks followed by infection through fungi, so that the financial loss caused by the borers may be estimated at very little. Far greater damage is done by cane fires, which here, like everywhere else, are mainly due to incendiarism. This crime is so often at the bottom of cane fires in Cuba that such a fire goes by the name of " candela " (candle), in consequence of the trick of putting a burning candle among the dry cane leaves.

Meteorological conditions are of much more importance for the cane production than any of the above-mentioned sources of loss. The cane depends on rain for its water supply, and, therefore, a long spell of drought may have a very disastrous effect on the growth of the young cane, so that the cane production in Cuba greatly depends on weather circumstances. Further, hurricanes may cause damage either by laying low the erect cane or by tearing it from its roots ; and in consequence of this it will be in poor condition the following year. It is estimated that cane swept by hurricanes, and consequently fallen cane, yields 1 to 1½ per cent. less sugar than would have been the case if there had been no storm, which when one has to give 5 per cent. of the weight of cane in sugar as cost price, while it realizes 10 per cent., means a decrease of 20 to 30 per cent in the profits. A further consequence of the damage by hurricanes is that the roots, as a rule, will not have got over their strain by the following year, so that the yield of sugar in the next crop still experiences the bad effects of the hurricane.

IV.—Sugar Manufacture.

It is the custom to convey the cane from the fields to the mills by the estate railways, for which purpose extensive tracks with sidings run in all directions, along which the cane, when cut into lengths, is steadily conveyed to the factory. Close to the sugar works is the railway yard, in which the trains on arrival can be shunted till the trucks can be taken to the mill elevator. Most of the Cuban factories have double crushing, with or without maceration, and some of them use a crusher as well. The biggest and best-arranged are those with triple crushing and a crusher applying maceration ; while it is quite an exception for a factory to have four or five mills in tandem.

The juice is limed with a mixture of lime and water prepared on the spot, as most of the manufacturers are of opinion that the success of clarification entirely depends on the use of milk of lime that has been mixed immediately before, and not some time in advance. The limed juice when exactly neutral goes through heaters, and is clarified either by simple clarification, or through superheat clarifiers according to Deming's system. The clarified juice on being syphoned off goes through Danek or similar filters, while the scum is filtered through filter-presses. The clarified juice is concentrated in a number of triple effects of very small dimensions ; quadruple effects are very rare, yet if the factories would go in for a considerable extension of their evaporating plant, a much more economical use of steam in the evaporation might be obtained, which would greatly diminish the amount of additional fuel required in most cases.

In the boiling process the returning of molasses is much in vogue, and in modern factories they often succeed in obtaining exhausted molasses of 30° purity directly after the second strike, which molasses is sold to alcohol distillers.

In the more ancient factories first and second sugars are made, in which case molasses of 50° purity is obtained, to be chiefly sold in America, where it is consumed as table syrup. The sugar in the centrifugals is not " covered," but the molasses is spun off as far as possible, and the sugar is packed in bags of 325 Spanish pounds without being dried artificially, and therefore in a somewhat sticky condition. In a great many factories the sugar of the second strike is mixed with that of the first, either in the crystallizers or in the centrifugals, or even after the centrifugalling is done, whereas others sell their second product separately. Hence, in some cases, second sugar is mentioned in statistics as first sugar, while it is mentioned separately in other cases, so that the quantities of first and second sugar (*azucar de guarapa* and *azucar de miel*) do not always bear the same relation to each other.

The first sugar is sold on basis of polarization 96°, plus $\frac{1}{32}$ cent per lb. for each degree higher than that figure, and less $\frac{1}{16}$ cent per lb. for each degree under, with fractions in proportion. Second sugar is sold on basis of polarization of 89°, plus $\frac{1}{32}$ cent per lb. for each degree higher than 89, and less $\frac{3}{32}$ cents for each degree lower.

The price of exhausted molasses is 3 to 4 cents per gallon (of 3·78 litres) delivered at the factory, while molasses of about 50° purity fetches 8 cents.

At one time rum and alcohol were distilled from the molasses, but since the Government has levied an excise on distillery products, this branch of the industry has been given up on the sugar plantations, and only a few distilleries are found in the island. By far the greater part of the exhausted molasses is sold to the so-called " Whiskey Trust " in the United States ; but some is sent to Europe, and some is distilled on the island itself, while the remainder is thrown away as useless ; the rich molasses is sold to the United States as an article of food.

Bagasse is used as fuel, and the cane trash is left in the field as a protection for the planted cane against drying up by the sun. The production of steam is not economically regulated, and the furnaces work with a great excess of air, in consequence of which the quantity of bagasse, notwithstanding a fibre content of 10 or 11 per cent. in cane, is insufficient as fuel (and this while maceration is only sparingly applied, and only one sort of raw sugar is manufactured), so that wood as extra fuel is everywhere much used.

The capacity of the factories, of course, varies greatly. There are very small installations as well as very big ones ; the new American factories, for instance, can grind as much as 3,600 short tons (of 2,000 lbs.) per 24 hours in three sets of mills, each of which consists of one crusher and three 3-roller mills—11 rolls in each.

In spite of this great capacity of the mills, the juice extraction is not so large as is the case in Java or in Hawaii. This may be accounted for in two ways ; in Cuba the crop greatly depends on the weather, and grinding is exclusively done in the dry season, for should the rainy season set in before the crushing is finished, the cane that is still in the field would be past reaping, which would mean a complete loss for that harvest. One can imagine that those engaged in grinding are simply and exclusively intent on getting the greatest quantity of material ground in the shortest time, and pay minor attention to the quantity of sugar to be obtained from the crushed cane, a quantity that slow and careful treatment might, of course, increase.

Then the wages paid in Cuba are very high, and amount to $1 or $1.50 a day ; the same wages are paid to labourers for working up a large vessel of juice as for treating the contents of a smaller vessel, so that it becomes advisable to make the quantities of cane to be worked as large as possible, and let the inevitable wages cover as much output as possible.

It is for these two reasons that the Cuban manufacturers working with very powerful American mills and machinery do not extract the same amount of sugar from the cane as do, for instance, the Hawaiian manufacturers with the same type of plant. Consequently, the loss of sugar in the bagasse exceeds that in other countries, while the loss of sugar in filter-presses, molasses, and unaccounted for in those factories where the loss is noted down shows nothing abnormal compared with factories in other centres.

Chemical control is still but little applied in the Cuban factories ; however, a number of estates belonging to American and Spanish firms have introduced a well-arranged system of control corresponding to that in Java and Hawaii, the production figures of which would allow of comparison. It would, however, be of little avail to quote these figures here, as only the best arranged and managed estates would be considered, and therefore no light would be thrown on the general condition of the average factory in Cuba.

The increase in the quantities of sugar obtained from 100 parts of cane during the several seasons shows an improvement ; the quantities amount to the following percentages for the different provinces :—

PROVINCE.	1902/03	1903/04	1904/05	1905/06	1906/07	1907/08	1908/09	1909/10	1910/11
Pinar del Rio	9·77	10·03	10·47	9 54	10 33	11·14	10·44	11·08	11·73
Havana	9·13	10·26	10·94	9·60	10·10	11·45	10·06	11·14	11·47
Matanzas	9·47	9·71	10·18	9·60	9·62	10·56	10·69	11·23	11·39
Santa Clara	9·68	10·22	10·15	10·01	10·28	10·84	10·84	11·32	11·58
Camaguey	9·47	9·51	10·02	10·40	10·63	10·68	10·56	11·03	11·94
Oriente	9·43	9·59	9·91	9·79	10·74	10·20	10·31	11·07	11·83
Gen. average ...	9·54	9·88	10·22	9·81	10·16	10·66	10·90	11·21	11·62

Although the yield of sugar depends first of all on the sugar content of the cane and the purity of the juice, and only secondly on the manufacture, the constant increase of the figure representing the yield of sugar points to a steady improvement, though no figures are given representing sugar content and purity. Little is known about the sugar content of cane ; the only thing we know is that at the beginning of the crushing season it is rather low and corresponds to 8 per cent. of sugar obtained in bags from 100 parts of cane, but gradually it increases, and finally allows of a yield of 12 per cent. or more if the weather is favourable and dry. Should it begin to rain again at the end of the grinding season, the cane starts growing again, and the sugar content, the purity and the yield of sugar drop. However tempting it may be to put off grinding till the cane is richer in sugar content, it must not be carried too far for fear of running the risk of not being ready by the time the dry season is over and the rainy season sets in again, thereby making the cane transport almost impossible.

The cost price of sugar depends primarily on that of the raw material and on the percentage it yields ; and, finally, on the expense of manufacture, packing, and transportation to the harbour. Suppose 100 arrobas of cane have cost the mill $2.70, and yield 10 per cent. of sugar, the cost of 1 arroba of sugar in raw material would be $0.27 ; suppose the cost of manufacture to amount to $0.10 per arroba, and that of transportation to $0.05, then the cost price of sugar delivered in the warehouses on the coast will come to 42 cents per arroba—7s. 6d. per cwt., not including interest on amortisation, capital and loans, renewal of machinery, etc. Should all these items be taken into consideration, the total cost price will be from 2 to $2\frac{1}{4}$ cents per lb., being equivalent to 9s. 4d. to 10s. 6d. per cwt., according to a number of data obtained in 1907, by the Committee of Ways and Means in the United States.

Doubtless there are estates in which the cost price is far less, owing to a favourable situation near the sea, which decreases the transportation expenses. Willett and Gray quoted in 1910 as cost price of Cuba sugar at average f.o.b. Cuba 1·85 cent per lb., and at average c.i.f. New York 1·95 cent. They fixed 2 cents per lb. as maximum f.o.b. Cuba cost price, and 1·5 cent per lb. as the minimum. Their figures, consequently, are lower on the whole than those quoted by the manufacturers in 1907.

The transport cost by railway sometimes forms a considerable part of the expense ; it amounts, for instance, to 60 cents a bag of 325 Spanish pounds —that is about 0·2 cents per lb., or about $11\frac{1}{4}$d. per cwt.—for all factories which have goods conveyed to the coast by the Cuba Railway Co., irrespective of distance.

Since March, 1911, the Cuban Republic has levied an import duty of $1 per 100 kg. of raw, and $0·75 per 100 kg. of white sugar, which duties are in accordance with the surtax stipulated by the Brussels Convention.

V.—Exportation of Sugar, Prices, Reciprocity Contract.

The greater part of the sugar produced in Cuba is exported to foreign countries, while only a very small portion, not exceeding 60,000 or 70,000 tons a year, is refined in the island itself, in two or three small sugar houses in Cardenas. Of late years the sugar exported has been sent chiefly to the United States, only a comparatively small quantity going to Europe. This preference is accounted for by the fact that owing to a reciprocity treaty the import duties into the United States for Cuban goods have been reduced by 20 per cent. of the general tariff. While the general import duty of sugar of 96° polarization is 1·685 cents per lb., only 1·35 cents have to be paid on Cuban sugar, which means no small preference for this kind of sugar. Through the active co-operation of the American buyers this preference does not altogether go to the Cuban producers, but chiefly falls to the organized American refiners. As in most years the Cubans have no option but to go to the American market, the refiners make the most of it by bidding less for Cuban sugar than for Java or other foreign sugar of the same quality, which being unprotected corresponds in price with free sugar, and consequently can fetch the world's price. They can easily do this as long as they take care to bid so much below the world's price as will keep it within 20 per cent. of the import duty, in which case their price would still be a little higher than the net world's price. Only when their margin exceeds the 20 per cent. will it become more profitable for the Cuban planters to offer their sugar in the open market ; but the buyers take good care to prevent this till their wants are provided for, so that so long as the refiners want the raw sugar Cuban sugar must needs go to America, and the full preference fall to the share of the buyers.

A single instance may suffice : at the beginning of November, 1908, the price of Java refining crystals, 96° polarization, was 3·98 cents per lb., including import duty, while Cuba ditto fetched 3·86 cents. As 1·68⁵ cents is paid as import duty on Java sugar, the importer would receive 3·98 — 1·68⁵ = 2·29⁵ cents ; whereas the Cuba importer, because of his reduced duties, only paid 1·35 cents duty, and consequently would receive 3·86 — 1·35 = 2·51 cents. At the same time the parity in England was 4·16 cents, or 4·16 — 1·685 = 2·475 cents, not including duty. The price realized in that country only just exceeds the world's parity, and that is why the Cuban producer, as a rule, would not entertain the thought of taking his sugar to any other market than America ; it becomes clear, too, that he only receives 0·04 cent of the preference of 20 per cent. on the duties, which amounts to 0·33⁵, while the remaining 0·29⁵ cent swells the pockets of the buyers.

When, however, as was the case in 1910 and 1911, the price of beetroot sugar is exceedingly high in Europe, and the American refiners are amply provided with sugar, then it cannot matter to them to keep the American parity for Cuban sugar just above the European ; and, in consequence, part of the Cuban crop will go to Europe. As soon as the shortage in Europe is over, the European parity will be lower than the American, and Cuban sugar will again go to the United States.

The sugar exported is chiefly raw sugar, both first and second sugars, while the exportation of refined sugar to Spain, Uruguay, and the United States is of little importance, and does not exceed two to three thousand tons yearly.

The shipments from the ports during the last six years have been as follows :—

Ports	1904/05	1905/06	1906/07	1907/08	1908/09	1909/10	1910/11
Havana	118,705	163,162	159,843	132,173	197,846	198,902	107,762
Matanzas	124,974	199,249	207,182	96,357	172,727	218,812	168,690
Cardenas	139,625	167,831	183,815	111,799	192,929	236,462	174,047
Sagua	73,841	94,252	106,980	54,086	102,677	140,555	116,123
Caibarién	65,924	95,055	91,093	81,915	98,982	123,204	119,299
Nuevitas	9,642	19,897	35,044	16,608	27,863	36,308	23,925
Puerto Padre ...	24,810	28,744	47,880	79,219	141,385	166,847	138,870
Gibara	25,804	13,902	10,893				
Banes	24,785	23,996	40,252	30,713	33,743	36,308	36,816
Nipe	—	329	41,711	17,909	40,796	64,101	41,291
Guantanamo ...	38,731	33,009	55,870	43,978	61,971	79,014	69,511
Santiago de Cuba	7,678	17,288	12,471	7,591	8,543	11,101	14,585
Manzanillo	40,168	44,468	49,393	48,490	67,791	68,074	74,994
St. Cruz del Sur ...	9,438	9,423	9,053	12,426	15,287	17,355	18,157
Tunas de Zaza ...	5,333	4,650	1,480	2,219	2,964	3,443	2,564
Trinidad	4,727	10,451	9,495	5,030	88,443	11,458	8,116
Cienfuegos	165,318	254,901	233,623	150,733	234,488	277,232	248,303
Jucaro	—	—	—	9,743	35,221	43,500	49,123
Total exportation	878,911	1,180,623	1,296,088	908,989	1,443,876	1,733,164	1,412,173

The distribution of the exportation has been for the last years as follows :—

	1907	1908	1909	1910	1911
United States, 4 ports north of Hatteras ..	1,213,389	878,624	1,330,215	1,428,271	1,218,335
United States, New Orleans, Galveston, and Charleston	131,534	27,389	113,347	177,761	192,552
Europe and Canada ..	864	—	—	127,132	1,286
	1,345,787	906,013	1,443,562	1,733,164	1,412,173

VI.—Future.

The fact that the very considerable sugar production of Cuba, now amounting to almost two million tons, is only reaped from a very small area of ground, has more than once given rise to predictions as to the further possibility of Cuba providing the entire world with sugar, or at least trebling its present production, if only it were given the chance. Although this prospect at first sight may seem not unlikely, circumstances will always be against it. Trebling the production is as yet out of the question, though the future may prove otherwise. We have noticed before that, in spite of statistical reports that quote 6 per cent. of the land as planted with cane, the cane producing the 1,800,000 tons of sugar is drawn nowadays from land equal altogether to half Cuba's entire area. This moiety, however, has been planted so extensively, and so much ground still lies uncultivated, that some further area of cane is likely to be planted, which, however, cannot amount to much.

We should not forget the circumstance that the Spanish were born agriculturists, and were wide-awake when selecting their lands. One may be sure that the stretches of land which yield twenty to thirty cane crops without replanting are of the very best, and that large extents of land which are left barren, or are used as pasture land for draught cattle, would never have yielded more than three crops without replanting. While now for lack of labour the profit of later ratoons may make up for the loss on first ratoons, it is clear that such ground in Cuba is altogether unfit for cane cultivation, so that the land at present in cultivation most likely contains a maximum of cane land, or at any rate would not offer scope for extension. This, however, need not prevent all extension of the cane planted area, for as long as the proportion of suitable cane lands to less suitable soil is the same for cultivated and still uncultivated ground, there will be some 750,000 more acres to dispose of, which might augment the present production.

There are still large extents of virgin soil which may be used for cultivation, and would not be inferior to the best cane soil that Cuba possesses. Even if the land is a little out of the way, the present facilities for conveyance are quite equal to overcoming distances as long as enough capital is invested in the enterprise. Those established by American capitalists on the north-east coast, for instance, show what money can do, for gigantic sugar factories, the most important of which produces in one year more than 480,000 bags, or about 70,000 tons, of sugar, have sprung up on entirely new and uncultivated land. The three largest of the new factories in the north-east in combination produced in 1909 no less than 1,135,000 bags of sugar. For the rest, the greater part of the province of Camaguey, formerly shut off from the world's commerce, has been put into communication with the coast through the Cuba Railway, in consequence of which some big sugar works have been erected, existing factories extended, and new ones put under construction. A glance at the following table of sugar production in the parts through which the new line goes will show how within a few years after the completion of the railway the sugar production of that neighbourhood has gone up, while large new undertakings are contemplated.

Production of sugar estates situated on the Cuban Railroad in bags of 325 Spanish pounds :—

North America.

	1902	1911
Jatibonico	—	124,258
Stewart	—	210,412
Tuinicu	25,000	71,500
S. Antonio	25,000	55,255
Hatillo	5,000	9,252
Santa Anna	25,000	52,461
Union	30,000	53,681
	110,000	576,809

Moreover, the increase in production need not exclusively be the outcome of the extension of planted area, but may also be caused by an improvement in the cane and sugar obtained per unit of area, both of which are open to improvement ; and this may easily be effected by turning a number of badly installed small factories into a single well-arranged large one, as in many cases has already proved a success. The juice extraction, although still nothing great, is in much better condition than it used to be, while the different losses experienced in the well-managed and controlled factories are not greater than in any other model factory in the world. There are still a number of concerns where they work in the old style, but these are gradually becoming fewer, and will continue to decrease as the advantage of modern methods of working becomes more and more evident. The next thing to be done is to prepare a better kind of sugar, viz., a dry kind that will keep, instead of the moist and sticky sugar that requires to be refined at once if it is not to lose its good qualities in the warehouse. No doubt this improvement will be carried out in a few years' time, in which case Cuba by then will produce the same output of sugar of a similar quality on 100 parts of indicated sucrose in juice as, for instance, Java does.

An increase of the cane production per acre will not, however, be so easily obtained. Importation of foreign cane species capable of a better product or of seedling cane varieties, is not welcome in Cuba, because the people there are familiar with the varieties now in use, while new kinds have to be tried first. Such a trial means no great risk in countries where planting is done every year, for should the crop be a failure, it only affects that year, and means no further loss ; but in Cuba they plant once every seven years, so that planting the wrong kind of cane involves ruin. But it is not only the kind of cane that matters so much, for the production might also be greatly improved through a better method of tillage, maintenance, etc. The Cubans are aware of this fact, and it is much to their regret that cane is being treated in such a primitive way, and is never transported till some time after the cutting is done. Scarcity of labour is at the bottom of this, and prevents a rapid and wide extension of the Cuban sugar industry.

Cuba, as we know, is very thinly populated; the native race is far from strong, and multiplies only at a slow rate. The only way to secure a considerable increase of labour is through immigration, and, as we said before, this source, too, is of little effect. After the years 1904-05 and 1905-06 had seen an immigration of some 50,000 men, that number has gone down since to 30,000, and it is difficult to reckon those who returned that same year. The immigrants are mostly Spanish people, and are reckoned to be the best workers by far. The fair, strongly-built, and sober immigrants from Galicia, in the north of Spain, work hard and steadily, and many of them settle in Cuba for good, or return every year after they have been home; but the immigration of these excellent workers tends to decrease rather than increase. People are doing better in Spain itself, so that many a Spaniard who formerly had to look for work outside his own country, nowadays can stay at home and earn his livelihood in Spain itself, which he of course, prefers to do. Then there are also many who have settled in Cuba, but on hearing of the better state of affairs at home are glad to go back—all of which means a decrease in the number of labourers in Cuba. Finally, the Spanish Government does not encourage the emigration of its industrious country people to a foreign land, and rather stops the progress of emigration by demanding of the steam navigation companies a contribution on each exported passenger, which means an increase in the cost of emigration, and indirectly a decrease in emigration itself. North Americans do not like to go and work in Cuba; they are much better off in their own country, where the climate is cooler, and better fit for manual labour. The immigration of Italians, once looked upon as a certainty, has resulted in nothing.

The difficulty as regards the supply of labourers is much against a rapid development of the industry, yet a steady improvement is to be expected, and considering what causes brought about a decrease in former times, we see that they were chiefly of a political nature, or were the result of climatic circumstances, so that it is interesting to examine how far these influences are to be feared in the future.

After the Spanish-American War was over, the United States, on 20th May, 1902, restored Cuba's independence, and when in 1906 President Palma failed to prove a match for his rebellious political opponents, the American troops came again in September, 1906, and restored peace in a very short time. During the time of the American intervention the authorities worked hard to bring about the consolidation of the affairs of the republic, and on 28th January, 1909, Cuba was again proclaimed as an independent State by the United States of America. There are two possibilities in the future: either that no repetition of the revolutionary outbreaks occurs, or that the recurrence of hostilities demands the return of the Americans, who in that event will settle in Cuba for good, so as to maintain order. Still, in the future there is little fear of further serious disturbances such as might impair the steady development of the cane sugar industry.

It is quite a different thing with the climatic conditions. It is quite possible that Cuba may be devastated by hurricanes, or that a lengthy period of drought may prevent the growth of cane, or that the rainy season may set in earlier than is usual, and put an end to the crushing much before the usual time, thus yielding a smaller crop. The remarkably small crop of 1907-8 was chiefly due to a long spell of drought in 1907, which stunted the growth of the then planted cane. All these climatic circumstances, however, only affect the crop season of that particular year, or else the following year. The cane itself, however, is not any the worse for it, and may later on produce a far better crop if the weather is favourable. Consequently, the influence of meteorological conditions may cause the Cuban crop to fluctuate greatly, making it difficult to estimate a crop beforehand; but these fluctuations cannot have any disastrous effect on the steady progress of production, which in 1912 is sure to amount to more than 1,800,000 tons, and may even increase, so long as the reciprocity treaty with the United States remains in force, and high import duties on foreign sugar are raised in the United States.

BOOKS OF REFERENCE.

Handbook of Cuba.
Industria Azucurera y sus derivados.
Riqueza agricolo-industrial y riqueza forestal.
Estadística general. Comercio exterior.
Boletin official de la Secretaria de Agricultura Industria y Comercio.
Immigracion y movimiento de pasageros en Cuba.
Santiago Dods. *Glimpses of the History of Cuba.*
Theo. Brookes. *Review of the Condition, Progress, and Future Outlook of the Sugar Industry in Cuba.*
E. O. v. Lippmann. *Geschichte des Zuckers.*

IV.

SAN DOMINGO.

THE Isle of Hayti, of which San Domingo forms the eastern part, lies in the Caribbean Sea, between 17° 37′ and 19° 57′ N. Lat. and 68° 21′ and 74° 30′ W. Long. It is separated from Cuba by the Windward Passage and from Porto Rico by the Mona Passage, and is the largest but one—namely, Cuba— of the Caribbean Isles. Its greatest length amounts to 390 miles, its least width to 25, and its greatest width to 164 miles. The area is 77,253 sq. miles, and the population amounts to 1,900,000 inhabitants.

San Domingo.

The island is very mountainous, and contains three separate mountain ranges, which extend in an east to west direction, and are separated from each other by wide, fertile plains. Hayti is watered by a great many rivers, all of which are silted up with sand, and therefore unnavigable. The climate is moist and hot; there are periodical wet and dry seasons that vary in time and duration in the different parts of the island. In the district of San Pedro de Macoris, the most important for sugar cane cultivation, the dry time is from December till May, and the rainy season from June till December. The annual rainfall amounts to 60 ins., which is not sufficient for the growth of cane, so that artificial irrigation is necessary. The average yearly temperature is 26·5° C. (79·2° F.); the average monthly temperature for July, 28·8° C. (84° F.), and for January, 24·1° C. (75·4° F.). The country suffers much from earthquakes and hurricanes, while volcanic eruptions are of frequent occurrence.

Hayti was discovered by Columbus in 1492; he called it Española, which in course of time was latinized to Hispaniola. At the time of the discovery the population amounted to about one million people, but the Spanish conquistadores compelled the physically weak population to undertake such heavy labour in the mines that it soon became extinct. In 1505 the Spaniards began to import negro slaves in order to overcome the lack of labour, but the supply was limited to a maximum of 4,000 per annum by a royal decree dated 1517, which, however, was not always fully maintained.

In 1630 a number of buccaneers, driven out of St. Kitts, conquered the western part of the island, and retained possession till 1697, when, on the occasion of the peace of Rijswijk, it fell to France. This territory was called Saint Domingue, while the rest remained Spanish and went by the name of San Domingo.

The flourishing state of the colony dated from this time, and was chiefly due to the extension of the sugar industry. In 1790 the number of factories was no fewer than 800, while during the years before upon an average 65,000 tons of sugar were exported, to be increased in 1789 to 53,000 tons of brown and 27,000 tons of white sugar. Unfortunately, such an enormous production implied great exertion on the part of the slaves. Many thousands of negroes were employed at heavy labour in order to produce such large quantities, and as only a few white people lived among these blacks this unequal proportion in the end led to a catastrophe, which ultimately ruined the prosperity of the island for good. The fact was, a large mulatto population had sprung up, which, as the children or descendants of white fathers, wanted to be privileged above the pure black Africans. These privileges were granted them during the first years of the French revolution. Yet a spirit of unrest and fermentation persisted, and resulted in a terrible insurrection of the coloured people on 23rd August, 1791, which, after the seizure of Cap Français, spread all over the island. A chapter of horrors and a general destruction followed in its train; more than 2,000 white people were massacred, while the rest fled, leaving their possessions behind. More than a thousand sugar and other plantations were

191

destroyed, and the entire sugar industry was ruined, so that the once important sugar trade came to a sudden standstill. In 1793, when the Spanish and English combined attacked the colony, the French Government declared the slaves in San Domingo free. The French by thus ameliorating the lot of the black population hoped to retain the island ; they not only succeeded in this purpose, but at the Peace of Basel, in 1795, they also obtained the eastern or Spanish territory, and consequently the entire island became French. This state of affairs was, however, not to last long. as the commander-in-chief, Toussaint de l'Ouverture, appointed by the Directory, tried to establish an independent government. Napoleon, then First Consul, embarked an army to San Domingo for the purpose of reconquering the island. In this he succeeded, but when the French tried to restore slavery another rebellion broke out, and led to the whites abandoning the island in 1803, since when it has remained under negro dominion. Dessalines, the leader of the insurrection, gave the island its old name of Hayti again, and turned it first into a republic, and afterwards into an " empire." Since that time the country has been subject to all sorts of disturbances, which are not over yet, and may last tor some time to come. In 1844 the eastern part separated and formed the Republic of San Domingo, while the western part is still called the Republic of Hayti.

In Hayti the sugar industry is of hardly any consequence, and what cane is cultivated there is used for chewing, or its juice is worked into an alcoholic beverage, tafia, and only seldom into sugar.

The greater part of the island of San Domingo, possessing an area of 24,300 sq. miles, is but scantily populated, there not being more than 500,000 people. Cane is planted in the south, near San Pedro de Macoris, in the plains of Arua and Romana, and in the river valleys near San Domingo, i.e., only on the south coast ; while the interior is devoid of sugar estates. The factories, as a rule, have their own ground, but grow only part of the cane themselves, while the rest is planted by " colonos." The latter receive their ground without having to pay rent for it, on condition that they plant cane ; they also get money advanced to them, while agricultural implements and draught cattle are lent them. They are supposed to find their own labourers, and have to deliver the cane at a price, stipulated beforehand, at the loading places of the railroads laid out by the estates, which railroads convey it to the factory. They employ as labourers the Dominicans, or negroes from the neighbouring islands, who come to stay for a season at the employers' expense. They come from St. Thomé, St. Eustatius, St. Kitts, St. Martin, and other islands in December, and leave again in May. Their wages are 50—75 cents (American) per day of twelve hours.

The soil of the sugar districts is of limestone formation, which through volcanic action has been raised and broken in places. Here and there the soil is covered with a thin layer of vegetable earth, 3 ins. to 1 ft. in thickness, while in some places $1\frac{1}{2}$ and sometimes even 2 ft. of good black or red soil covers the hard limestone subsoil. Water easily penetrates this limestone, so that the arable earth rapidly dries up. Irrigation when necessary is not carried on with river water, but with water out of artesian wells, which may be bored anywhere in these limestone mountains.

The cane variety that is most planted is the " caña cristalina," a yellowish-green coloured type of cane with green stripes ; then follows to a much smaller extent the " caña blanca," a pale-yellow cane with a high sugar content. These two kinds are the same as are exclusively found in Cuba. Soil treatment amounts to very little, while manuring is altogether neglected. When virgin ground is planted, cuttings are put into the ground two or three of them together, in a slanting position, and are partly covered with earth ; this is when the bush is cut and burnt. Planting is done at distances of 7 × 7 ft., or 6 × 7 ft., or even of 9 × 9 ft. in the level ground, without furrows or holes having been made beforehand. At the end of fourteen to sixteen months the cane is considered ripe, and is cut ; first and subsequent ratoons are kept and cut every year till the yield gets too small to make it worth while retaining the ratoons any longer. When they begin planting afresh, which is sometimes done at once, and sometimes after some years' interval, the old plants are removed with a plough, furrows are dug 4 to 6 ins. deep and 5 to 6 ft. apart, in which the new cuttings are planted at 4 to 5 ft. distance from each other. Only plant-cane is banked ; and after it is cut the stubbles are covered with trash and the soil between is levelled, but no more banking is done. The plant cane or virgin soil yields an incredibly high cane crop, while the cane is exceptionally tall and heavy, and can produce as much as ninety tons cane per acre. The quality, on the other hand, is poor, and it is the sort of cane that yields more syrup than sugar. The ratoons yield a much lighter crop, but of a far better quality, and ratoons are cut till the figure representing the production has gone down to eighteen tons per acre, when planting is recommenced. One can only expect such good first results in districts where the layer of arable earth rich in humus is very thick, in which case it is quite possible to reap crops for fifteen or twenty years before the yield will have gone down to its lowest efficiency. One does not get such satisfactoiy results from less fertile soil, where it is necessary to plant afresh after five to ten years.

The average cane yield of an estate which plants from 3,000 to 4,500 acres of cane is estimated at 23·8 tons of cane per acre, which, of course, varies according to the condition of the soil and the relation between the quantity of plant cane and ratoon. Planting, as a rule, is carried on in June as well as in October, while reaping takes place from December to April.

The factories are still installed in a rather old-fashioned way. In most cases cane is only crushed once, and even should it be crushed more often, maceration is dispensed with. The juice is purified by clarification and by subsiding ; filter-presses are seldom used, and for want of them the mud is simply caused to run off. The juice is evaporated and treated in triple-effects and vacuum pans. The sugar, a first product of 95—97 polarization, is packed in bags :

while the seconds of 86° polarization are sometimes remelted. The exhausted molasses is used either for the manufacture of rum or is thrown away.

In spite of the primitive installation of the factories, the cane yields 9—11 per cent. of sugar, as the raw material in San Domingo is of very good quality, and often contains juice exceeding 20° Brix, with a purity of 85—90°. This is when the cane is crushed only once.

The farmers, as a rule, get 3¼d. per cwt. cane, so that, including railway freight, it comes to about 4d. per cwt.

The cost price of sugar prepared in the old-fashioned factories amounts to about $36 per ton (8s. 3d. per cwt.), and that of sugar prepared in the more modernized factories comes to $25 per ton (5s. 9d. per cwt., or 11s. 5d. per 100 kg.).

The sugar is sent to the United States or to Great Britain, according to the current market quotation, while part of the production is consumed in San Domingo or Haiti, either as raw sugar or as white sugar, after it has been washed in the centrifugal.

Sugar used to be taxed with an export duty of $0·25 per 100 kg., but this tax has been abolished, and sugar is nowadays exempted from all duties and excise. An import duty on a scale approved of by the Brussels Convention acts as a bar to the importation of sugar, but as sugar is not imported at all it has no need to be enforced. The production of San Domingo during the last few years has amounted to the following quantities in long tons :—

Year.					Tons.
1903/04	..	..	..	..	47,000
1904/05	..	..	..	..	47,000
1905/06	..	..	..	..	55,000
1906/07	..	..	..	..	60,000
1907/08	..	..	..	..	62,235
1908/09	..	..	..	..	69,483
1909/10	..	..	..	..	93,003
1910/11	..	..	..	..	76,296

The greater part of this production is exported to the countries enumerated below (expressed in long tons) :—

Countries.	1905.	1906.	1907.	1908.	1909.	1910.
United States .. .	46,345	52,452	40,483	61,996	66,740	89,896
Great Britain	529	788	7,606	—	714	623
Germany	57	358	174	—	2	—
France	—	136	—	—	1,007	—
Italy	—	—	66	—	—	—
Cuba	—	—	7	—	—	—
Porto Rico	—	—	—	—	51	—
Other countries	478	150	968	151	969	926
Total	47,400	53,884	48,304	62,057	60,483	91,445

San Domingo.

The names, areas, and localities of the concerns are as follows :—

Name.	Area.		District.
	hectares.	acres.	
Angelina	8,000	20,000	San Pedro de Macoris.
Consuelo	8,500	21,250	,,
Porvenir	6,600	16,500	,,
Santa Fé	6,000	15,000	,,
Christobal Colon	7,000	17,500	,,
San Luis	1,600	4,000	Santo Domingo
San Isidor	5,000	12,500	,,
Italia	5,200	13,000	Azua.
Ocoa	3,500	8,750	,,
Azuano	4,000	10,000	,,
Ansonsa	3,000	7,500	,,
	58,700	146,750	

With the exception of the Christobal Colon factory, which belongs to Cubans, all these sugar factories are under American management. In the district of Romano an American company, which has also great interests in Porto Rico, plants cane for the purpose of transporting it to their Porto Rican mills, to be crushed there, so that the product may enter the United States free of duty. The same company also purchases cane from colonos for 5 per cent. sugar value; also for transporting it to their Porto Rican mill.

Not the entire area of 146,750 acres is, of course, planted with cane, for part of it lies fallow or is used as grazing land. The ground in most parts of the southern plains is most fertile, and yields an excellent cane crop, so that it seems extremely well fitted for cane cultivation.

Owing to lack of funds, the installations are behind the times, and the combination of an unstable government and everlasting internal troubles tends to keep foreign capitalists away. Although there seems to have been some inclination of late to instal factories on a more modern system, which may be looked upon as some improvement, the industry is not likely to extend much so long as the native political state of affairs does not change for the better, which seems, as yet, an impossibility.

V.

PORTO RICO.

THE island of Porto Rico is the most easterly of the large Caribbean Isles, and lies at the entrance to the Caribbean Sea, between 18° 30′ and 17° 55′ N. Lat., and 68° and 65° 10′ W. Long. It is in the shape of a rectangle, 100 miles in length, and 36 in width; and has an area of 3,140 sq. miles.

The island is very mountainous, and with the exception of a narrow border of flat coast land, it consists of rows of hills and a great many valleys. A larger chain of hills stretches from east to west, right through the centre of the island, which, however, is broken up to such an extent that any coherence hardly exists. Its highest peak is El Yunque, in the north-east, at a height of 4,900 ft. above sea level. Numerous rivers run through the valleys; there are about fifty of them, varying in size between shallow little streams in dry weather to wild mountain torrents in the rainy season.

Although the Porto Rican coast can boast of a great many harbours, all of them are more or less shallow, and only navigable for small craft. Those of San Juan, Guanica, and Jobos are partly land-locked, while the harbours of Arecibo, Aguadilla, and Mayaguez and Ponce are simply open roads. The climate of Porto Rico is uniformly warm, the yearly temperature varying between 66 and 86° F., but the daily differences are barely noticeable. The month of January has the lowest average temperature, and that of August the highest, but the maximum temperatures occur in the month of May. The highest maximum ever observed at the meteorological observatory at San Juan was 34·4° C. (94° F.) in May, 1903, and the lowest minimum 17·2° C. (63° F.) in March of the same year.

The year is divided into two seasons: a wet one from April till November, and a dry one from December till March. About 47 ins. of rain falls during the first season, and about 10 ins. during the rest of the year. The rainfall. however, is not equally divided all over the island; more rain is experienced on the northern side than on the southern coast, as the trade winds coming from the east drop most of their moisture north of the hill slopes, and lose much of their moisture by the time they have reached the southern half of the island. Like the other West Indian islands, Porto Rico is much subjected. to hurricanes. The one of August 8, 1899, did a tremendous amount of damage, both in loss of life and property, and destroyed great numbers of plantations, factories, houses and crops.

The soil is very fertile, and in the north may be cultivated without irrigation, but in the south, where the sugar cane chiefly grows, recourse must be had to artificial irrigation.

The population of Porto Rico amounted to 953,243 inhabitants, according to the census of 1899, 589,426, or 61·8 per cent., of whom were put down as whites ; but many of these were doubtless of mixed extraction. The census return of 31st December, 1909, gave the total of 1,118,017.

The two big towns of the island (San Juan, in the north, and Ponce, in the south) have each a population of about 30,000 inhabitants, and there are besid s other towns of lesser importance. A railway running by a circuitous route through the west along the flat coast connects the two, while the sugar plantations have made railroads which, later on, when connected up with the main line, may be converted into public lines.

Porto Rico was discovered by Columbus in 1493, and in 1505 Pinzon was allowed to build a fortress on the spot. The name Porto Rico dates from 1521, when discoveries of gold were made, while San Juan got its name from its founder, Juan Ponce de Leon. Both country and inhabitants were divided among the Spanish conquerors, who proved such tyrants that when, in 1544, the King of Spain ordered the inhabitants to be set free the population, originally estimated at 600,000 people, had dwindled down to some few hundreds. Many of them had died, and others had emigrated to Peru and Mexico ; but the Spaniards did not take long to fill the vacant places by a supply of slaves from Africa.

For years Porto Rico was involved in constant war. At one time it was the English who came to harass the country ; at other times independent pirates and buccaneers caused trouble ; now and then a rebellion among the slaves occurred, or Dutch fleets tried to take possession of the colony, so that Spain, during the sixteenth, seventeenth, and eighteenth centuries had to be constantly on the alert in order to hold her own among her envious neighbours.

The population, of course, could not thrive in the midst of all this strife, and at the beginning of the nineteenth century the island was still very thinly populated, containing only 155,426 inhabitants. The country could not pay the cost of its own government, so that a considerable deficit had to be made up by the Mexican surplus. Up to 1778 only Spaniards had been allowed to settle in Porto Rico, but after that the privilege was extended to people of other nationalities, on condition that they were Roman Catholics, while in 1815 immigration became possible for anyone. Foreigners were encouraged to come to Porto Rico, where privileges of Spanish citizenship were held out to them, and where land belonging to the dominion was offered them as free property.

These foreigners were promised exemption from export duty on their produce, and exemption from import duty on their implements and necessaries ; while they would be free to import as many slaves as they wished.

These liberal inducements tempted a great many planters from the French and British Caribbean Isles, who came to Porto Rico supplied with knowledge, capital, and a number of slaves ; and they had a great and beneficial influence on the development of the island.

Later on the population was swelled by immigrants from Hayti, San

Domingo, and Venezuela, who had been driven away from their homes through war and insurrection.

The rapid increase of the population in the nineteenth century is evident from the following table, which gives the various census returns :—

1802	163,192
1812	183,014
1820	230,622
1827	302,672
1830	323,838
1836	357,086
1860	583,308
1877	731,648
1887	798,565
1897	980,911
1899	953,243
1909	1,118,017

In 1873 a most important event for the colony was the resolution of the Republican Spanish Government to abolish slavery in Spanish possessions, so that 34,000 slaves in Porto Rico were declared free.

During the years following on 1880 the Spanish Government was most arbitrary in its decrees, and carried on a system of persecution which roused a feeling of aversion against Spain. Owing to remonstrances on the part of foreign nations more liberal laws were promulgated in 1896, and autonomy was even granted to the colony in 1897, but this reform came too late. On 21st April, 1898, the Spanish governor declared the island to be at war with the United States, and it ended in the incorporation of Porto Rico into the States on 25th July of the same year.

During the Spanish dominion hardly anything was done on behalf of the island ; the roads were in a very bad condition, and the population was deprived of all instruction, being kept in a state of mental incapacity. The owners of the plantations were poor, and were harassed by debts and mortgages, so that the economical conditions of the island left much to be desired.

Once annexed to the United States, conditions changed for the better. Although the sugar exportation had remained an important feature, it had dropped considerably, while the cultivation of coffee was considered of primary importance. It had been sent to Spain, being imported there free of duty, and was privileged by the protective duties levied on foreign coffee. When, however, Porto Rico was taken over by the United States, this privilege ceased, full duty having then to be paid on Porto Rican coffee imported into Spain. The United States gave no import duty on coffee, hence Porto Rico was in this respect not benefited through her cession to the States. Finally, the hurricane of 1899 caused extensive damage among the coffee plantations ;

this, of course, had a disastrous effect on the coffee cultivation. On the other hand, the incorporation of Porto Rico had a very favourable influence on the sugar industry. As early as 1899 the United States allowed a reduction of 85 per cent. on the import duty on sugar, while in 1891 the importation of sugar became free altogether, so that Porto Rico has since profited by the full protection of 1·68⁵ cents per lb. of raw sugar.

In order to prevent capitalists from availing themselves of this favourable opportunity to buy land on a large scale for the cultivation of sugar cane, and thus to deprive the native owner of his property, a law was passed in 1900 (that is, previous to the date of absolute exemption from duty) called the Forraker Act, which stipulated that no company should be allowed to possess more than 500 acres (or 200 hectares) of land, and that no shareholder of any one agricultural company should be entitled to have shares in any other similar partnership.

This restriction, no doubt, was meant to benefit the Porto Rican peasant proprietors through the advantage of duty-free sugar, and to prevent large foreign companies from pocketing the profits ; nevertheless, this stipulation had not the desired effect. The big owners lived outside the island, while the small farmers lacked money and energy to carry on their industry vigorously. Foreign capital, which was kept back through this restricting law, was the very thing wanted for the establishment of a flourishing sugar industry. So, later on, this law was deviated from in spirit, though not in letter, and of late years extensive sugar estates have been started in Porto Rico with American, British, and French capital, which have more than trebled the sugar production since 1902.

About 400,000 acres, or 20 per cent., of the 2,000,000 acres Porto Rico covers, are used for cultivation, half of which are taken up by sugar cane cultivation. The sugar cane grows on the alluvial plats along the coast ; on the south coast there is still plenty of space for more cane than has yet been planted. Should it eventually be utilized, it would involve expensive irrigation works, as in that event it is intended to conduct water from the northern part of the country, where the rainfall is abundant, to the south by means of aqueducts tunnelling through the hills.

The big sugar factories buy the cane from the colonos, who plant it either on their own land, or on ground hired from the factory, while each company, at the same time, plants about half of the cane under its own management. The price of cane generally amounts to 5 per cent. sugar of the weight in cane, though it varies at times.

Before planting is begun the land is ploughed twice, after which the furrows are dug, and these depending on the nature of the soil are from 400 to 800 ft. in length. On heavy soil exposed to much rain they plant in furrows, which are 2 ft. in depth and 8 ft. apart ; the cuttings are planted in a double row at a distance of 4 ft. from each other. The plant holes are 1½ ft. square and half a foot in depth. The tops and sometimes the entire upper part of the stalk are used as seed, while each plant hole contains two or even more of them.

When the soil is dry and sandy they plant in shallower holes, and in one row ; according to the fertility of the soil, the distance between these rows varies from 4½ to 6 ft.

The fields are kept in a clean condition, and are banked by means of hoes after the plants bud, and during the growth of the cane. Manure is hardly ever applied, neither is the cane trashed.

Cane is generally planted during the months of September to December, and is crushed in the following grinding season, which begins in January—that is, after an interval of 14—18 months. Such cane is called " caña de frio " or " de gran cultura " ; it yields the largest crop. Then another kind of cane, called " caña de pequeña cultura " or " caña de medio tiempo," is planted from January till March, and is crushed the next season, when it is about one year old. Finally, there is a kind called " caña de primavero," which is planted from March till June. In case of a very favourable season, it is also crushed in the following season—that is, when it is 10—12 months old ; but should it not be rich in sugar, it is kept over and opens the following crushing season, that is a year later. After the cane is cut, first, second, and third ratoons are grown, and then the cane is planted anew. The first and second ratoons yield the best results, plant cane comes next in productiveness, while third and subsequent ratoons give inferior results. Ratoons are cut every year, and formerly these were kept for twelve years, but this is now known to be bad policy, so nowadays after four or five years the fields are planted afresh.

Most of the cane diseases and parasites found in other countries are of frequent occurrence in Porto Rico, but as cultivation is only in its elementary stage, little attention is paid to these pests.

With the exception of a few years rich in sugar production, the average yields have amounted to 20 tons per acre, which, assuming them to be American tons of 2,000 lbs., is equivalent to 44,730 kg. per hectare.

The cane is cut with a *machete* as close to the ground as possible, and carried to the factory or to the railway depots by ox-carts, from which it is conveyed to the mill by rail.

The factories have been but recently installed, and so are provided with the best and latest machinery, while the operations are carried on according to scientific methods. The juice extraction is obtained by triple crushing with maceration, while the only factory in Porto Rico—La Fortuna—which tried the bagasse diffusion process after Naudet's system, has given it up entirely. Almost the only Porto Rican product is raw sugar, basis 96° ; only about 10,000 tons of the crop is muscovado, and about 14,000 tons after products. The exhausted molasses of about 40° purity is partly worked up to rum, and partly exported to be used for consumption.

The principal factories are the following, the production of which during 1910-11 is given in short tons :—

Guanica	..	..	..	..	..	57,251
Aguirre	..	..	..	..	..	25,639
Fajardo	..	..	..	..	..	25,015
Plazuela	..	..	..	..	..	16,600
Cambalache	..	.	..	..		14,135
Juncos	..	..	..	.	..	12,750
San Vincente	.	..	..	..		12,592
Coloso	..	..	..	..	..	11,096
Lafayette	..	..	..	..		8,933
Mercedita I.	..	..	..	..		8,797
Machete	..	..	..	..	..	8,623
Monserrate	..	..	..	..		8,050
Juanita	..	..	..	..		7,401
Canovanas	..	..	..	..		7,546
Constancia	..	..	..	..		7,194

The remaining central factories, 29 in number, are all much smaller, and the smallest, Santa Isabel, produced in 1910–11 only 34 tons of sugar. Then there are 24 smaller factories with steam power, and 72 driven by oxen, which produce muscovado ; while still other sugar enterprises are planned or already under construction.

As Porto Rican sugar may be imported into the United States free of duty, all sugar not wanted for local requirements is sent to America as a matter of course.

In 1853 the sugar exportation of Porto Rico amounted to 112,000 tons ; it dropped to 70,000 tons in 1854, and neither increased nor decreased during the following twenty years. In 1870 and 1871 the production realized once more 105,000 tons, to drop to 89,000 tons in 1885, and to 65,000 tons in 1886. During the past twenty years it has been as follows, in long tons :—

1891/92	..	..	..	..	..	70,000
1892/93	..	..	..	..	..	56,000
1893/94	..	..	..	..	..	43,000
1894/95	..	..	..	..	..	48,500
1895/96	..	..	..	..	..	55,000
1896/97	..	..	..	..	..	54,000
1897/98	..	..	..	..	..	55,000
1898/99	..	..	..	..	..	54,000
1899/1900	..	..	..	..	..	35,000
1900/01	..	..	..	..	..	62,000
1901/02	..	..	..	..	..	82,000
1902/03	..	..	..	..	..	104,000
1903/04	..	..	..	..	..	130,000
1904/05	..	..	..	..	..	145,000
1905/06	..	..	..	..	..	210,000

1906/07	.		..	..	194,000
1907/08	..	.	..	..	214,489
1908/09	..		..	..	258,363
1909/10	..	.	..	.	308,000
1910/11	..	..	..	..	295,000

Great things are anticipated for the sugar industry in Porto Rico. Labour is cheap and abundant, and the people employed are willing. The climate is favourable, and when a greater water supply is available in the southern part of the island, on the completion of the irrigation works which have just been planned, and for which a 4 per cent. loan of $3,000,000 has been raised, still larger tracts of ground that used to be too arid for cultivation may be turned into cane growing areas.

Enterprising and powerful American companies have already started large central factories in the plain of Ponce and Juana Diaz, and have bought up other already existing sugar works, and plant sugar cane on a very large scale in that part of the country. The profit is considerable, as Porto Rican sugar is admitted into the United States free of import duty, and consequently has a great advantage over the Cuban, Javanese, and West Indian sugar. It is difficult to say to what extent the output may increase, but one may be sure of an important extension in the near future, commensurate with the progress that has been experienced since 1902.

VI.

BRITISH WEST INDIES.

I.—Historical Survey of the Sugar Industry.

THE British West Indies vary so much as regards climate, character of the soil, population and history that it is not possible to discuss these separately. For this reason we must confine ourselves now to a general survey of the history of the industry, indicating the points in common, while further on some details relating to each of the islands or group of islands will be given.

All, or at least the principal, of these islands were consecutively discovered by Columbus, and the names then received have been mostly kept, only a few having since been changed.

Some of the islands were colonized at once by the Spanish, while others were only invaded after a time, while the French, the English, and Dutch were responsible for many conquests. All through the seventeenth and eighteenth centuries continual war was waged in the Caribbean Sea, and a great many of the islands were repeatedly captured and lost again, or kept in common possession to be restored at the next declaration of peace, so that most of them in course of time have changed hands several times. After the wars between France and Great Britain at the beginning of the nineteenth century things settled down, and with the exception of some unimportant changes, the possessions of the different powers have remained as they were in 1814.

The British West Indian Possessions are grouped as follows :—

1. Bahama Islands.
2. Barbados.
3. Jamaica, with Turk's and Caicos Islands.
4. Trinidad and Tobago.
5. The Windward Islands, St. Lucia, St. Vincent, Grenada, and the Grenadines.
6. Leeward Islands, Antigua with Barbados and Redonda, St. Kitts, Nevis and Anguilla, Montserrat, Dominica and the Virgin Islands.

The sugar industry was immediately introduced after the islands had been taken possession of, and this necessitated the importation of negro slaves. In 1562 Sir John Hawkins began to import them, and in 1568 Sir Francis Drake followed his example. At the end of the sixteenth century Dutch slave-traders supplied a great many blacks, while the formation of two English-African companies for the purpose of providing British colonies with slaves date from 1662 and 1672 respectively. In consequence of this, at the end of the sixteenth century some 25,000 negroes were yearly imported to British colonies on British vessels.

Although at this time the people on the British islands knew how to prepare sugar, the sugar industry did not attain any importance till after 1654, when the Dutch colonists driven from Brazil with their capital, knowledge, and slaves settled on several French and British islands, where they soon produced a good and marketable kind of sugar. Barbados and Jamaica especially were soon largely planted with sugar cane, and exported large quantities of sugar to the Mother Country. They suffered much, however, from French competition, as the inhabitants of the French islands of Saint Domingue, Martinique, and Guadeloupe far excelled in the manufacture of sugar at a lower cost price. From an investigation carried out by the British Government, it soon appeared that it was not only the methods of cultivation and manufacture among the British colonists that were inferior to those of the French, but that, in addition, heavy taxes and an export duty of 4½ per cent. of the value on all exported goods greatly injured the industry. Then sugar refining was forbidden, so that there was no inducement to try and improve the manufacture ; and last, and not least, the British Government levied heavy import duties on all sugar and syrup imported from the Antilles to the North American colonies, which caused the natural market of the West Indian colonies to be closed. In spite of all these untoward circumstances, the production increased, especially when in 1791, through the destruction of the sugar plantations in San Domingo this formidable competition disappeared from the scene.

North America.

Besides the loss of this great rival, the West Indian Islands experienced another unexpected piece of luck, when at the end of the eighteenth century a newly imported species of cane proved to be heavier in weight and richer in sugar content than the cane variety hitherto planted. This new kind was the Otaheite or Bourbon cane that had been conveyed from the Malabar Coast to the Isle of Bourbon, and was sent to Cayenne, Martinique, and Guadeloupe by the French Government. It was introduced from the French Antilles to British Guiana and the British Antilles, and we know that William Firebrace took it to Barbados in 1796. Sir John Palfrey, at the end of the eighteenth century, imported it straight from Otaheite into Antigua, while Captain Bligh introduced it from the same country into Jamaica in 1796.

According to von Humboldt, the sugar exportation of the British West Indian colonies amounted to the following figures between 1698 and 1806 :—

1698—1712	20,000 tons
1727—1733	50,000 ,,
1761—1765	75,000 ,,
1771—1775	92,000 ,,
1781—1785	79,000 ,,
1791—1795	101,000 ,,
1801—1806	169,000 ,,

This prosperity ended, however, when slavery was abolished in the British possessions, as we have already had occasion to mention (see pages 19 and 20).

The sugar production did not, however, all at once drop through the abolition of slavery ; it was a gradual downfall. The once well-tilled fields kept yielding good crops for years after they had been deprived of regular maintenance, but they began to diminish gradually, so that in consequence the new measures did not show themselves forcibly till some twenty or thirty years after.

It was a great grievance of the sugar planters that slavery was still in full force with their neighbours—for the French colonies did not follow Great Britain's example till 1840, the Dutch not until 1863, Porto Rico not until 1873, St. Thomas only in 1876, while Cuba brought up the rear in 1880. It is true that Great Britain levied an import duty on sugar produced by slave labour, but in 1846 this penalty became greatly reduced, to disappear altogether a few years later, so that cane sugar produced by slaves was taxed the same as sugar coming from colonies where slavery was abolished, when imported into Great Britain.

When in 1834 labour was urgently wanted, an effort was first made to import free labourers from Madeira, St. Helena, Rio, and Sierra Leone into the West Indies, but these efforts proved ultimately futile. In 1845 they began to import coolies from British India on a small scale ; and this importation, under the supervision of the British Indian Government, has since taken place continuously on a large scale, except during the years 1849 and 1850, when it was temporarily stopped.

The coolies are recruited in British India by an Immigration agent in Government employ, with headquarters at Calcutta. They are sent to the West Indies, and distributed among the different applicants, to whom they are to be indentured for five years at 1s. 1¼d. a day for men, and 8d. a day for women. Those who have entered the colony before the 5th of August, 1898, are entitled to their passage back to India on payment of a quarter of the fare in case of men, and of one-sixth of the fare for women, while the rest has to be paid by the planter. Nowadays a ten years' stay in the country entitles them to a free passage home on paying half of the fare for men, and one-third for women. Besides these, a great many regulations are made for the benefit of the immigrants, while special officials called " Protectors of Immigrants " see to the strict enforcement of these rules.

In 1845 the first immigrants arrived in Trinidad and Jamaica, and in 1849 came to St. Lucia ; but only Trinidad affords a case of negroes having been successfully replaced by British Indian labourers. In the two last-mentioned islands immigration has been as irregular as in the other British West Indian islands.

Slavery had hardly been abolished in Cuba in 1886, by which time all the West Indian possessions had come to the same position in this respect, when a new difficulty cropped up in the way of competition. The European beet-root sugar industry had been bolstered up by bounties and privileges to such an extent that it steadily expanded, and had to fall back more and more on its export trade in order to maintain its flourishing condition.

In the first part of this volume it was shown how the bounties and cartels, which the European beetroot sugar manufacturers enjoyed, tended to lower the price of sugar to such an extent that sugar was to be had below cost price in the world's market. The manufacturers in protected countries, where the sugar consumption amounted to a considerable figure, could easily stand this state of affairs, but those in unprotected countries, where the loss on exported sugar could not be made good by the home consumption, were hard put to make ends meet. This was still more so the case with the inhabitants of the West Indian Islands, whose sole occupation for centuries had been to plant and manufacture sugar, and who now found this industry disappearing.

The West Indian sugar manufacturers constantly complained, but the British public could not disabuse their minds of the picture of sugar magnates surrounded by a halo of extravagant splendour, and so would not take these complaints seriously. The British Government, however, was fain to see the West Indian colonists content and well at ease, for fear they should otherwise wish to be incorporated into the United States. At this very time the States were negotiating with Denmark for the sale of the Danish Antilles, and if it had not been for one adverse vote, the Danish Parliament would have agreed. All this shows how much more America had become interested in the Antilles than it used to be. It was apparent, too, through the internal troubles in Cuba and Porto Rico, how the Americans had made their influence felt in these parts, so that there was every reason to fear that these colonies would be lost to Great Britain if the United States Government seriously wanted to annex them.

Consequently, the British Government had to study the West Indian question, and secure their loyalty by having all their grievances removed. It meant quick and thorough help, for the interests at stake were considerable enough to make great sacrifices necessary. No sacrifice was deemed too great for the conquest of the West Indian possessions in the flourishing time of the sugar industry. All through the seventeenth and eighteenth centuries war had been waged for its supremacy, and at each treaty of peace that concluded a war between European powers the restitution or retention of some West Indian islands always afforded important discussions during the negotiations, which shows how much importance was attached to the possession of these fertile regions. It was not till after many heavy wars and bloody sea-fights against the Spanish, French, and Dutch, and expeditions against buccaneers and filibusters, that Great Britain got the ascendency in the Caribbean Sea, and the name of each British naval celebrity was at some time or other connected with a West Indian victory.

Although the West Indian possessions had decreased in wealth, their glory was still vividly remembered by the British, and it would have meant a severe blow to Imperialism and the devotion of the Colonies and Dominions beyond the Seas for the Mother Country if the oldest colonies which through blood and strife had become theirs should have been lost at this crisis. During the last years of the nineteenth century, more than at any other time, British Imperialists felt that nothing should be left undone to bring Mother Country and Colonies together, and to strengthen the bond of union, even if the British West Indies were never to revert to their old prosperity. But this supposition was not in accord with the facts, and the far-seeing British statesmen were well aware of the possibility that another time of prosperity might be in store for these colonies. By the time of the completion of the Panama Canal, the new trade route would go through the Caribbean Sea, in which case a flourishing island-colony with magnificent harbours and gulfs and fertile soils would be a valuable possession for Great Britain. With this prospect in view, it was realized that the West Indies should be made into a prosperous and flourishing possession at whatever cost. Money temporarily spent by the Mother Country on its colonies could not be wasted, and in case of neglect the government of these islands should be open to appeal to the Treasury at home.

In consequence of these considerations, help was granted, in 1898, in the following manner :—

1. By establishing farmers as owners, especially on the Crown lands in St. Vincent.

2. By promoting industries other than the sugar industry : (*a*) by establishing a special agricultural department under the supervision of a competent expert for the purpose of studying the cultivation of useful plants in the islands, the headquarters being at Barbados, while experimental stations and laboratories were to be established on the other islands as well. The cost was to be £4,500 for the first year, and £17,500 for the following years. Were results to prove satisfactory, they intended to go on with this Department till the colonies could afford to defray the expenses themselves. (*b*) By improving the existing steamship connections by a direct route to Canada, an improved service between Jamaica and Great Britain, and a fortnightly steamboat communication between the Islands. The expenses were to come to £5,000 for the first year, and to £20,000 for the following years.

3. By the Government guaranteeing a 3 per cent. loan of £750,000 during ten years for the foundation of central factories in Antigua, St. Kitts, and Barbados.

The Department of Agriculture was not long in starting ; it comprises a head department with laboratory and station in Barbados, and branch botanical stations in Antigua, Tobago, Grenada, St. Vincent, St. Lucia, Dominica, Montserrat, St. Kitts, and British Honduras. There are also independent Agricultural Departments in British Guiana, Trinidad, and Jamaica.

The institutions in Barbados, Jamaica, Trinidad, Antigua, Demerara, St. Kitts, and Montserrat are devoted mainly to the sugar industry, and have done most useful and important work by investigating the best means of manuring cane and establishing the best cane varieties, and by cultivating seedling canes and combatting the numerous diseases and pests.

The other measures adopted by the Government on behalf of the sugar industry did not have the results that were expected.

Canada had allowed 25 per cent. discount off its import duty on all produce from the British colonies, but this deduction was not enough to tempt the planters to send their sugar to Canada instead of to New York. The United States levied besides their uniform import duty on sugar an additional so-called " compensating duty " on all bounty-fed sugar, amounting to the value of the bounty. As all European sugar was bountied, in contrast to the free West Indian sugar, the latter when imported into the United States enjoyed an advantage greater than when imported into Canada, where no countervailing duties were known, and where the British colonial sugar only enjoyed a rebate of 25 per cent., which deduction in most cases was less than the countervailing duty on European sugar when imported into the United States.*

* In 1900 for instance the advantage of 25 per cent. on the import duty in Canada amounted to 18 cents per 100 lbs. sugar of 96 polarization while the countervailing duty on German sugar in the States was 27 cents.

North America.

Again, the capitalists were afraid of risking their money in the British West Indian sugar industry, and did not participate in loans for the erection of central factories, so that the proposed 3 per cent. loan of £750,000 was not achieved. In the first place, the complaints about the decline and unsatisfactory condition of the industry in the West Indian Islands had drawn attention to these parts, but at the same time had frightened capital away, so that all efforts to raise money for the establishment of central factories proved a failure. Secondly, the fierce competition of the bounties was in full force for the sake of encouraging the exportation of the beetroot sugar from the several producing countries. Each measure taken by a government to further the exportation of its produce was sure to be followed by a corresponding measure on the part of other governments, which resulted in a steady fall of the world's price of sugar, and made it an impossibility for unprotected countries to make any profit out of the manufacture of sugar. One can imagine that in such circumstances even Great Britain's offer to guarantee during ten years 3 per cent. interest on the loan for central factories did not tempt anyone to take an interest in the sugar industry of the West Indian Islands.

Chamberlain was well aware of this fact, and as the West Indies and Mauritius, together with the British Indian sugar refiners, wanted help urgently, he carried through the Brussels Convention, when the negotiations over the abolition of bounties threatened to result in failure again.

In addition a grant of £250,000 was made by Parliament to cover the pressing needs of the sugar planters for the year immediately preceding the coming into force of the Brussels Convention.

In consequence of this Convention, the compensating duties on European sugar in the United States were no longer levied, and sugar from the West Indies was admitted into the States on the same basis of duty as European beetroot sugar ; thus it was no longer privileged in that country. In Canada, however, it still enjoyed this advantage ; consequently, the importation of West Indian sugar into that country began to increase, especially as, in 1900, the rebate on the duty on British colonial sugar had gone up to 33⅓ per cent.

To give an idea of the extent to which the importation of sugar from the West Indies into Canada has increased, while that from other countries has dropped, we quote the following table, where *general tariff* means full import duty, *preferential tariff* the decreased duty on sugar from the British Empire, and *surtax tariff* the duty on German sugar raised by a surtax since 1903. The sugar from the British Empire was almost exclusively West Indian and Demerara, with small quantities of refined sugar from England and raw sugar from British India, British Africa, and Fiji.

VERE FACTORY, JAMAICA.

Year.	General tariff.	Preferential tariff.	Surtax tariff.	Total.
	lbs.	lbs.	lbs.	lbs.
1902/03 ..	326,824,196	43,251,261	—	370,075,457
1903/04 ..	288,150,338	100,091.559	128,935	388,370,832
1904/05 ..	100,128,451	290,414,865	1,344	390,544,660
1905/06 ..	71,740,809	274,863,036	148,753	346,752,598
1906/07 ..	77,919,591	371,042,486	446	4 8,962,528
1907/08 ..	51,867,068	393,584,054	—	45,451,122
1908/09 ..	51,158,971	392,802,583	—	443,961,554
1909/10 .	149,538,843	348,249,538	—	497,788,481
1910/11 ..	183,518,288	390,589,876	—	74,108,164

The West Indian sugar industry not only benefited by the Brussels Convention, but also by other advantages as mentioned in the first part of this volume, such as a better and more regular world's price of sugar and a greater stability and certainty for the industry, which can now proceed uninterruptedly and need not fear fresh changes as regards bounties or further privileges to the beetroot sugar industry.

After the Convention was brought into force the necessary funds for establishing central factories in Antigua and St. Kitts were found ; the Government central factories in Barbados are still hanging fire in consequence of peculiar difficulties, although private central factories are being established without Government assistance. A central factory has also been established in St. Kitts, while great and important additions have been made to the working of factories in Trinidad. Although, as may be gleaned from the following pages, the condition of the sugar industry in the West Indian Islands is far from brilliant, yet the feeling of despondency belongs to the past, and the efforts of the British Government to make the West Indian population contented British subjects at any cost have had satisfactory results.

II.—Cane Cultivation and Sugar Manufacture

The sugar cane cultivation varies in the different islands as regards condition of the soil and available labour ; cane must be treated differently in low-lying, marshy regions from that in hilly, undulating country ; while in islands such as Barbados, where properties are small and the population dense, cane can be grown much more intensively than in islands where the inhabitants are few and far between.

Sugar cane used to be cultivated in fields belonging entirely to the sugar plantations, but when the difficulties about insufficient labour became increasingly stringent, the planters took refuge in a system of cane farming in many of the islands. Pieces of ground were allotted or sold to small planters who, supported by loans of money or other help, grew cane at their own risk for the purpose of selling it to the factory. Opinions differ as to the wisdom of thus separating the planting from the manufacturing interests ; there are people who emphasize the advantages, while others, on the contrary, show up the faults of the system. The great advantage, of course, is that cane is now obtained by free labour and without any risk from land that under other circumstances would yield nothing. But a drawback of the regulation is that farmers who are short of capital cannot or will not spend much money on manuring and soil improvement, and only try to get as much out of the land as possible, which, of course, has a bad influence on the fertility of the soil. Then the manufacturer has little or no control over the planting and maintenance compared with what he has under his own management, and although it is by far the best plan for a regular establishment to have a certain quantity of cane brought daily to the mill, cane farming does not allow this quite so well as planting by the estate does. Finally, it is not possible for the manufacturers to exercise sufficient control over the quality of the cane delivered, so that it is often unripe cane and cane with impure juice that they receive to grind.

However bad conditions may be, their own labourers are not capable of cultivating and harvesting any sufficiently large quantity of cane ; so as they wish to produce a sufficient amount of raw material to keep the factory working at its proper capacity, they are obliged to let ground to independent farmers. They have to take both the advantages and the drawbacks of this system into consideration.

Up to a few years ago Bourbon or Otaheite cane was almost the only variety planted in the West Indies, but during the years 1892 and 1895 and 1896 this cane variety was all at once generally affected by a disease, which considerably diminished its power of production, and caused its cultivation to be abandoned in most of the islands. It has been supplanted in Barbados by the White Transparent cane, and there and elsewhere by several of the seedling varieties grown at the experimental stations in Barbados and Demerara, especially B 208, B 147, D 145, and D 625.

In Jamaica the Bourbon cane was never very popular ; White Transparent or Mont Blanc cane was chiefly planted. Bourbon cane is still found in Trinidad and St. Lucia, but in Barbados, Antigua, and St. Kitts other kinds have replaced it.

In most of the islands the ground is treated according to the Reynoso system, with furrows 18 ft. in length and 5 to 7 ft. apart from centre to centre. In Barbados, where the hard coral cliffs are only covered with a thin layer of arable soil, the cane is not planted in rows, but in plant holes which are from 15 to 18 ins. in length, from 6 to 12 ins. deep, and from 8 to 12 ins. wide. In one acre, as a rule, 3,000 of such holes occur.

The cane is cut after twelve to fifteen months, when ratoons are kept ; the leaves are worked under the soil with forks to provide the necessary humus, and the cane is left to grow and be cut again a year later. This is sometimes repeated five times, or even more, after which new cuttings are planted in rows between the places of the former ones, so that the part of the soil that had not been used is given a turn. As long as the cane is still short, weeds are carefully removed, and the soil is manured with stable dung, superphosphate, basic slag, sulphate of ammonia, chili saltpetre, or guano, or mixtures of any of these manures. While the cane is still young the dead cane shoots are replaced by new ones, which are obtained by chopping off a piece of cane stool from the same plot and replanting it.

Among the pests that harm the cane, rats and the borers come first, while most of the known fungous diseases occur in the West Indian Islands. The most important among them are the " rind " and the " root " disease, which have caused a decrease in the area of Bourbon cane. Pineapple disease, red smut, and *Marasmius sacchari* are found in all the islands, and often cause great damage.

Although most of the factories in the West Indies are up-to-date, there are still many, especially in Barbados, that work in the old style, with open pans, and produce the old-fashioned muscovado sugar.

The preparation of this sugar is accomplished as follows :—The cane juice heated to boiling point is put in clarifying pans, where it is tempered and subsided ; then the clarified juice flows into the so-called " copper walls," a series of three or more big open copper vessels, called " tayches," in which it is concentrated. Under these vessels is an open fire, fed by sun-dried bagasse, cane trash, and wood. The juice enters the first pan, and as it concentrates it is scooped out into the second, and so on. There are factories where the last percentage of water is not evaporated above an open fire, but in a separate pan with steam, called the Aspinall pan.

When the concentrated juice has reached the requisite degree of density, it is scooped out into big square tanks, in which the sugar crystallizes. There is sometimes a stirring apparatus inside which keeps the massecuite moving, but generally the latter is allowed to crystallize at rest.

When the crystallization process is complete, the boiled mass is filled into big wooden barrels or hogsheads with perforated bottoms. These barrels stand in racks over drainage troughs, and remain there two or three weeks, till the molasses between the sugar crystals has drained off as much as possible. Then the holes are closed with wooden plugs, and the hogshead is fit to be transported.

The analysis of the sugars prepared in this way is approximately as follows :

	1	2	3	4
Polarization	88·6	86·2	83·9	83·0
Glucose ..	5·30	4·40	5·92	6·98
Ash	0·47	2·66	2·12	1·02
Water ..	3·42	3·72	4·66	3·84
Undetermined ..	2·21	3·02	4·30	4·26
Total ..	100·00	100·00	100·00	100·00

Analyses of some of the syrups drained off from the muscovado are as follows :—

	A	B	C	D	E	F
Sucrose	55·7	51·6	56·2	49·8	46·9	50·7
Glucose	10·3	8·1	11·4	14·4	24·2	6·8
Organic non-sugar	5·4	5·3	4·8	8·2	2·7	10·4
Ash	3·2	4·2	2·8	2·9	8·1	5·0
Moisture	25·4	30·8	24·8	24·7	22·9	27·1
Total	100·00	100·00	100·00	100·00	100·00	100·00

III.—Survey of the Industry in the different Islands.

(a) BARBADOS.

Barbados, the most western of the West Indian Islands, lies at 13° 4′ N. Lat. and 59° 37′ W. Long. ; it is 21 miles in length and 14 miles in width, has an area of 166 sq. miles, and possessed in April, 1911, a population of 171,982 inhabitants, that is 1,036 to the sq. mile.

The island is of coral formation, covered with a very thin layer of fertile soil, which, it is said, is derived from volcanic ash from La Soufriére, of St. Vincent, that has been driven there by the wind after eruptions. Only the north-eastern district, Scotland, is at all hilly. Not only does the Barbados subsoil consist chiefly of coral, but the island is surrounded by coral reefs, which at some places stretch far into the sea, and are dangerous to navigation. The island is very flat and only rises in the parish of St. Andrews in terraces to a height of 1,105 ft.

Barbados does not possess any natural harbours, though the open road of Carlisle Bay, on the west coast, is well sheltered, and offers a safe anchorage for ships. There are not any rivers of importance in the island ; rainwater rapidly penetrates the porous coral, to collect in subterranean wells and springs. The climate of the island is pleasant and favourable. The temperature, as a rule, varies between 24° and 30° C. (75° and 86° F.), while the minimum night temperature in the coolest season is occasionally as low as 63° F.

North Point

59°30′ W.Gr.

BARBADOS

Scale of English Miles

0   1   2   3   4   5

Cliffs

Flatfield

Crab H.

Cuckold's

Harrison Pt

St.Lucy's Ch.

Gay's Cove

Pico Teneriffe

Lambert's

Woodbury

Boscobelle

Colleton

Nicholas Abbey

Cherry Tree Hill

Farley Hill Ch.

Cleland

St.Andrew's Ch.

POLICE STA.

Speights Town

Prospect

Richmond

St.Andrew's Sta.

Chalky Mount

St.Peter's

Mullins

Swanns

Joe's R.

Sun Hill

Turner's Hall Wood

Bathsheba Sta.

Westmoreland

Spring

Mt.Hillaby 1140

Hackleton's Cliff

Martin's Bay

Porters

Mt.Misery

Chimborazo

St.Joseph's

St.Margaret's

Sta.

CODRINGTON COLLEGE

Consett B.

St.James' Ch.

Lewis

Highland

St.Thomas's Ch.

Clifton Hill Ch.

St.John's Ch.

Bath

Consett Pt

Holetown

Welchman Hall

St.And's Ch.

Sherborne

St.Mark's Ch.

Bell Pt

Whitehaven

Bennetts

Andrew

13°10′
N.Lat.

POLICE STA.

Rugby

St.Jude's Ch.

Mt.Pleasant

Ragged Pt

LIGHT HOUSE

The Chair

Thorpes

Hanley

POLICE STA.

Three Houses

Kitridge Pt

Husbands

Dayrell's

Gun Hill

Rowans

St.George's Ch.

Busby

St.Philip's Ch.

Sunbury Sta.

Crawford

Lord's Castle

Cobbler Reef

Lazaretto

NEW LUNATIC ASYLUM

Windsor

Carrington Sta.

Hopeland

Belle Vue

POLICE STA.

Bulkeley Sta.

Sta.

Crane

Pelican I.

Gov.House

Fort George

Rowen Sta.

POLICE STA.

Yorkshire

Oldbury

Foul Bay

BRIDGETOWN

Kent

Carlisle Bay

Highgate

Needham Pt

St.Ann's Fort

Worthing

Light

Hastings

St.Lawrence Ch.

Valencia

Christ Ch.

Oistin's Town

Long Bay

Oistin Bay

Light

South Point

Reproduced, by kind permission, from "The Pocket Guide to the West Indies" by Algernon E. Aspinall   Stanford's Geographical Estab.

British West Indies.

The rainfall for the last twelve years amounted to the following quantities, expressed in mm. and inches :—

				Mm.		Inches
1897	..	..	..	1826	..	71·75
1898	..	..	..	1735	..	68
1899	..	..	..	1270	..	50
1900	..	..	..	1549	..	60·5
1901	..	..	..	2297	..	90·5
1902	..	..	..	1401	..	55
1903	.	..	..	1681	..	66
1904	..	..	..	1484	..	58·5
1905	..	..	..	1362	..	53·6
1906	..	.	..	1780	..	70
1907	..	..	..	1192	.	47
1908	..	..	..	1110	..	44

Bridgetown (of 16,648 inhabitants in April, 1911) is the capital of the island, while the other towns are of little consequence. A narrow-gauge railway connects the capital in the south-west with St. Andrew's Church, on the north-east coast, a distance of twenty-four miles, which journey is covered in two hours.

Barbados was discovered by the Portuguese in 1536; they named the island Barbados after the trees with long parasitical drooping plants which they found there.

In 1605 Barbados was taken possession of by the English, but was not colonized by them till 1626. At first it was the private property of some English noblemen, but later became a possession of the British Government on payment of an indemnity to the last possessor, Lord Carlisle, which was raised by an export duty of 4½ per cent. *ad valorem* on all articles exported from Barbados. This unusual indemnification, which was paid by the Barbados traders for a transaction in which the British Crown did benefit, was in force in spite of much opposition from 1686 till 1838, when its payment was abolished.

Barbados was the first island under British rule to plant sugar cane. Under Philip Bell's governorship the sugar industry was established there, and slaves were introduced; but not till the Dutch colonists, who had been driven away from Brazil, came and brought their knowledge and experience with them did the sugar industry begin to flourish. During the seventeenth and eighteenth and the beginning of the nineteenth centuries, Barbados became one of the principal sugar-producing countries. The island delivered exclusively muscovado sugar in hogsheads, and not in white loaves as the French Antilles used to do.

In consequence of the dense population on this small island, it is entirely cultivated, and as the inhabitants had not exclusively to rely on the sugar industry, they were not so stricken by the consequences of the abolition of slavery and by the decreased profits as other British colonies were.

On the emancipation of slaves, in 1834, the Barbados plantation owners got an indemnity of £1,720,345 for no fewer than 83,176 slaves, and as there are no great distances to cover in the island, which made it unnecessary for the emancipated blacks to withdraw from the interior, a great many of them began to work as free labourers in the plantations, so that after all the abolition of slavery was not detrimental to the sugar industry.

In 1898 the British Government decided to make Barbados the headquarters of the Imperial Department of Agriculture, which latter has since done so much good by its scientific investigations, by giving expert advice, and by experimenting with manures, seedlings, etc. At the same time, a sum of money was found as a 3 per cent. loan for the establishment of a central factory, but in spite of the proposal being kept to the front ever since, the plan has not yet been carried out.

In Barbados the land is divided into very small estates, and up to recently each plantation had its own mill. At the present time there are no fewer than 335 sugar factories, 221 of which are driven by windmills. In recent years, however, plans have been executed for the improvement of the factory installations, and some ten factories are equipped now with modern machinery.

The area planted with cane is estimated at 60,000 acres. The cane planted used to be exclusively Bourbon, but this variety, that at one time yielded most satisfactory crops, steadily dropped in quality, and has been practically abandoned. Its place has been taken by seedlings raised in the island, and by the White Transparent.

The cultivation is done thoroughly, as labour is abundant and cheap. There is, of course, the possibility of drought and hurricanes having a bad influence on the crop, while the cane diseases of general occurrence—such as root disease, red smut, rind disease, cane borers, and grubs—do considerable harm at times. Only a very few factories in Barbados possess a vacuum pan, while most of them prepare muscovado in the old way. This is not a case of headstrongness or conservatism, but simply the result of the great value the molasses of the so-called " open kettle " sugar has, and for this very reason it is transhipped in large quantities to the United States, Canada, and Newfoundland.

The introduction of the vacuum pan process would produce a larger quantity of sugar, but molasses of an inferior and unsaleable kind. The present price of molasses of about 55° polarization is £2 10s. per ton, while there were times when it fetched as much as £5 to £6 per ton.

The sugar content of the cane, on an average, amounts to 13·5 per cent.; about 7½ per cent. muscovado sugar, and some 3·5 per cent. molasses are obtained from it.

It is difficult to state the cost price of sugar, as it depends greatly on the proportion between sugar and molasses derived from the same juice. One generally reckons £8 per ton of muscovado of about 84° polarization, which covers the value of the syrup produced simultaneously.

The production of Barbados has been as follows during the fifty years 1860 to 1910, expressed in long tons :—

1860	..	..	..	37,350	1886	 40,047
1861	..	..	..	43,614	1887	 60,263
1862	..	..	..	40,355	1888	 63,882
1863	..	..	..	36,996	1889	 57,106
1864	..	..	..	31,675	1890	 74,606
1865	..	..	..	41,307	1891	 44,226
1866	..	..	..	50,105	1892	 51,849
1867	..	..	..	46,725	1893	 58,765
1868	..	..	..	50,960	1894	 57,967
1869	..	..	..	29,465	1895	 33,331
1870	..	..	..	34,363	1896	 45,170
1871	..	..	..	47,166	1897	 51,275
1872	..	..	..	34,372	1898	 46,878
1873	..	..	..	32,669	1899	 40,442
1874	..	..	..	41,377	1900	 44,250
1875	..	..	.	56,875	1901	 56,912
1876	..	..	..	32,676	1902	.. .: .. 45,576
1877	..	..	..	43,545	1903	.. .: .. 33,795
1878	..	..	..	38,073	1904	 55,785
1879	..	..	..	50,001	1905	 41,210
1880	..	..	..	47,439	1906	 50,630
1881	..	..	..	45,073	1907	 33,033
1882	..	..	..	48,269	1908	 31,353
1883	..	..	..	46,242	1909	 15,571
1884	..	..	..	54,263	1910	 36,389
1885	..	..	..	52,694	1911	 32,514

Since 1903 a large and increasing amount of syrup was transhipped, besides sugar and molasses. Bovell assumes 315 gallons of syrup of 41° Beaumé to correspond in sugar value to one hogshead of sugar and 80 gallons of molasses, and it is according to this basis that he reckons the total sugar production for the years 1904—1908 to be as follows :—

Year.	Sugar.	Molasses.	Total.
1904	55,785	151	55,936
1905	41,210	2,239	43,449
1906	50,630	7,296	57,926
1907	33,033	12,462	45,495
1908	31,353	10,248	41,601

North America.

Barbados sugar is chiefly exported to England, but is also sent to the United States and Canada. No export duty is levied on sugar leaving the island, but there is an import duty of 2s. per 100 lbs.

A considerable increase in production is not to be expected. All the available ground has already been used for cane cultivation, and the growing of other agricultural crops and cotton takes up so much land that any extension of the cane-planted area is out of the question. The sugar estates are mostly in the hands of small owners, who have already mortgaged their property heavily, and would never be able to raise capital for the purpose of working on a larger scale, and of reaping better crops. Besides, the owners cling to their land, and only reluctantly entertain offers from British capitalists to buy the land in Barbados for the establishment of central sugar factories which would turn to account the Governments' loan. From all this we may gather that radical changes are not likely to occur in the sugar industry in Barbados for some time to come.

Literature :

G. Washington Eves. *West Indies.*
The West India Committee Circular.
J. R. Bovell. *Comparison of the Bourbon sugar cane with other varieties.*
Publication of the West India Imperial Agricultural Department.
G. Hughes. *Natural History of Barbados.*
H. R. Schomburgh. *History of Barbados.*
West Indies in Canada 1910.
A. E. Aspinall. *Pocket Guide to the West Indies.*
Sinckler. *Handbook of Barbados.*

(b) TRINIDAD.

The Island of Trinidad lies in the southern part of the Caribbean Sea, between 10° and 10° 50′ N. Lat. and 61° and 62° W. Long. It is separated from the Venezuelan coast by the Gulf of Paria and the two narrow straits of Bocas, one the Dragon's Mouth, north of, and one, the Serpent's Mouth, south of the gulf. The area of the island is 1,754 square miles, its greatest length being 53 miles and its greatest breadth 40 miles. The coast is flat, and extensive lagoons or marshes are found all over the island. The ground rises in the centre and in the north, so that from there a number of rivers flow into the sea in all directions. The principal harbours, Port of Spain and San Fernando, are situated on the west coast, where navigation is commonest.

The climate of Trinidad is very even ; the temperature varies between 21° and 30·5° C. (70° and 87° F.). In 1905 the average temperature was 25·5° C. The rainfall of that same year amounted to 70 ins., while the average annual rainfall was 56·75 ins. during the years 1862—1905 ; in the tracts given to cane cultivation they can reckon on 80 ins. The rainy season commences in June and lasts five or six months ; August is generally the wettest month. The island is out of the path of hurricanes, so that the terror of the

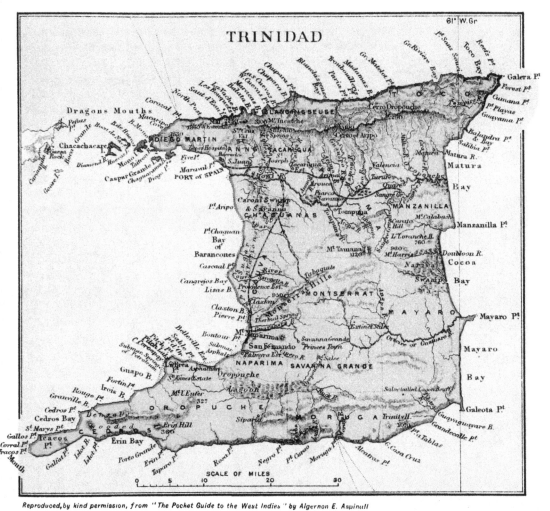

TRINIDAD

61° W. Gr

Reproduced, by kind permission, from "The Pocket Guide to the West Indies" by Algernon E. Aspinall

other West Indian Islands does not trouble them. Neither earthquakes, volcanic eruptions, nor long spells of drought afflict this island, so that as regards climate and geographical position it has much to be thankful for.

Trinidad was discovered by Christopher Columbus in 1498; he called the island Trinidad in consequence of a hill-top branching off into three ridges which caught his eye at a distance. About ninety years after the discovery of the island the Spaniards took possession of it, and founded the town of San Jose de Aruna, at some distance from the coast; this now goes by the name of St. Joseph. In 1797 the English took the island from the Spanish, and since then it has remained a British colony.

The Indian aborigines were soon exterminated by their Spanish conquerors, and have since been replaced by repeated supplies of African negro slaves. In 1780 a Frenchman from the neighbouring island of Grenada visited Trinidad, and was so struck with the fertility of the soil that he asked permission to settle there with a great number of colonists of French and Creole origin. Later on, in 1845–46, the population was strengthened by Portuguese who were driven from Madeira on account of religious persecutions, and took refuge in Trinidad. The population was also very considerably swelled by British Indian immigrants, who some years after the abolition of slavery, in 1834, were imported into Trinidad under contract, and now form one-third of the whole population. When the English took possession of the island the number of inhabitants amounted to 17,718; in 1838 it had increased to 39,328, in 1891 to 200,028, and in 1906 to 315,000, about 100,000 of whom were of British Indian origin. This works out at 181 inhabitants per square mile, a very high figure for this part of the world.

The capital of the island, Port of Spain, is situated on the Gulf of Paria, and contains about 60,000 inhabitants. Other towns are San Fernando, Princes Town, Arima, St. Joseph, and Couva, the principal of which has a population not exceeding 7,600 inhabitants, and, consequently, is of little importance.

A railway runs from Port of Spain in an eastern direction to Sangre Grande, 5½ miles east of Port of Spain. St. Joseph lies on the railway, and from there another line runs in a southern direction, which near Cunupia, 7½ miles from St. Joseph, branches off into two lines. One goes due south as far as San Fernando and Princes Town, while the other runs in a south-eastern direction to Tabaquite. The whole length of the railway is about 100 miles. Then there is a regular steamboat service between Port of Spain and San Fernando and the smaller seaport towns of the west coast and the islands in the Bocas Straits.

The soil of Trinidad is very fertile, and is very suitable for sugar cane, cacao, coffee, tobacco, and lemon cultivation, while the woods produce excellent timber. The sugar industry is only carried on in the western centre of the island, namely, in the districts of Tacarigua, Caroni, Couva, Naparima, and in a small portion of the Savannah Grande. The soil here consists of a dark clay, which is considered excellent for sugar cane ; while the sandy soil of the westernmost tracts produces numerous coconuts, and the cacao grown on the hill slopes in Montserrat in the north thrives well. It is chiefly due to this fitness of the soil for such various kinds of staple products that Trinidad has not suffered like most of the British West Indian possessions from the consequences of low sugar prices since 1890. While others had to depend exclusively on the sugar cultivation, and became destitute when this branch of industry failed to bring them profit, Trinidad was much more able to endure these bad times, and has even known prosperity in spite of untoward circumstances.

In the years following 1895 many owners of plantations were forced, through bad times, to let part of their land to farmers, who used it for growing cane, which cane they sold to the factories. This system has gradually spread, so that nowadays about one-fourth of the sugar produced is derived from purchased cane, while the rest is grown by the plantations themselves.

The crushing season begins with the dry season, that is in January, and lasts till May or June.

There are 16 sugar factories in Trinidad that in 1909 produced 52,972 tons of sugar, obtained from 606,464 tons of cane, which means a yield of sugar of 8·74 per cent. 451,801 tons of this cane, yielding 39,553 tons of sugar, were planted by the estates themselves, and the balance, 154,663 tons of cane, yielding 13,419 tons of sugar, was bought from cane farmers. Altogether, 11,401 of those planters took part in the production, 6,077 of whom were East Indians and 5,324 West Indians.

For the ten preceding years these figures were as follows :—

Year.	Tons of Cane Ground.			Sugar Produced.	Yield of Sugar.	Number of Farmers.	
	On their own Estate.	Bought Cane.	Total.			East Indians.	West Indians.
1900 ..	364,355	105,996	470,351	41,269	8·80	2,826	3,591
1901 ..	434,003	169,918	603,921	51,077	8·45	3,829	4,737
1902 ..	337,911	184,867	522,778	44,913	8·56	4,506	4,850
1903 ..	337,632	166,590	504,222	46,029	9·13	4,443	4,440
1904 ..	385,015	171,947	556,962	50,744	8·95	4,646	4,685
1905 ..	244,418	144,868	389,286	38,240	9·82	5,424	5,462
1906 ..	397,912	237,844	635,756	62,975	9·91	6,127	5,446
1907 ..	373,577	169,709	543,286	50,564	9·30	6,557	5,777
1908 ..	380,334	139,442	519,756	48,933	9·42	5,922	5,619
1909 ..	451,801	154,663	606,464	52,972	8·94	5,912	5,488

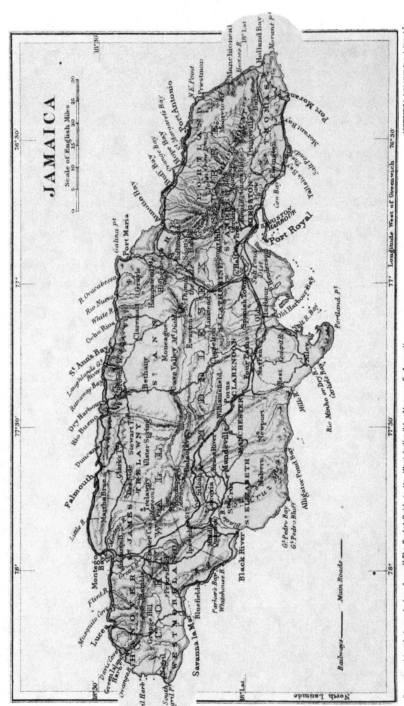

JAMAICA

Scale of English Miles
0 5 10 15 20 25 30

North Latitude

Railways —— —— Main Roads

Reproduced, by kind permission, from "The Pocket Guide to the West Indies" by Algernon E. Aspinall

Stanfords Geographical Estab.

British West Indies.

The following amounts of sugar have been exported from Trinidad :—

1906	.. .. 56,455 tons.	1909	.. .. 44,413 tons.
1907	.. .. 45,631 ,,	1910	.. .. 44,139 ,,
1908	.. .. 41,626 ,,	1911	.. .. 36,645 ,,

In the years before 1898 one-third of the Trinidad sugar was sent to Great Britain, and the rest to the United States ; but that did not long continue, as from 1st August, 1897, Canada yielded a rebate of 25 per cent. in import duty on sugar produced in all the British West Indian possessions increased later to a preferential duty of 31½ cents per 100 lbs. 96° crystals. In consequence of this, Canada, in conjunction with Great Britain, and the United States, has become one of the regular consumers of Trinidad sugar since 1899, while a small amount is sent to neighbouring South American States and other West Indian Islands.

(c) JAMAICA.

The Island of Jamaica lies in the northern part of the Caribbean Sea, 90 miles south of Cuba, between 17° 43′ and 18° 32′ N. Lat. and 76° 11′ and 78° 2′ 50″ W. Long. The greatest length of the island amounts to 144 miles, its greatest width to 49 miles, its narrowest part (from Kingston to Annotta Bay) 21½ miles. Its total area is 4,207 square miles, and its population in 1911, 831,123 inhabitants, or 198 to the square mile.

The island is very mountainous, the mountain chains running chiefly from east to west, with spurs to the north-west and south-east, the latter ending in the well-known Blue Mountains, the highest top of which rises 7,360 ft. above sea level.

Jamaica has a greatly indented coast-line, with many bays and harbours, the best known of which are Port Antonio, at the eastern extremity of the north coast, and Old Harbour and Kingston, both on the south coast. Kingston Bay is a deep and wide sheet of water, protected against the waves of the Caribbean Sea by a long isthmus called the Palisades. Port Royal is situated at its extremity.

Jamaica possesses many rivers and streams, most of them with a rapid current. In the south-west is the Black River, which is navigable for 130 miles, while in the north-east there is the Rio Grande. The Rio Cobre, which falls into Kingston Harbour, the Plantain Garden River, the Martha Brae, and others are of much less importance.

In consequence of the great variations in height above sea level, the climate varies greatly for the different parts of Jamaica. Close to the sea the temperature fluctuates between 20° and 30° C. (68° and 86° F.) but in the mountains the thermometer in the coolest nights goes down to 7° C. (45° F.).

Though rain may occur all through the summer, there are two months, May and October, when rain falls in greater quantities than usual. The total rainfall amounts to about 40 ins.

Jamaica lies in the route of hurricanes, and these sometimes do immense damage, while the island is also subject to earthquakes.

North America.

Jamaica is intersected by excellent roads, which, as the mountain slopes are far from steep, make easy intercourse possible between the different parts of the island. For the rest, a railway connects Kingston with Montego Bay *via* Spanish Town, while a branch line runs from Spanish Town to Port Antonio. The total length of the railway runs to 180 miles.

Jamaica was discovered by Columbus in 1494, and was named by him San Jago ; it however soon reverted to its original name, Jamaica.

The Spanish colonized the island as early as the beginning of the sixteenth century, and in 1523 founded a town, San Jago de la Vega on the south coast, which now goes by the name of Spanish Town.

The country has suffered much from wars—it was often a scene of hostilities between English, Spaniards, and runaway slaves (Maroons), the latter siding either with the Spaniards or the English, or were sometimes against both. Jamaica for some time was the centre and headquarters of the buccaneers who infested the West Indian seas and robbed whoever it suited them. The town of Port Royal was their headquarters, on the isthmus near Kingston Bay, which town was destroyed by an earthquake in 1682. After having been conquered several times, and as often recaptured, Jamaica was finally ceded to England at the peace concluded at Madrid in 1670, and has remained ever since a British possession.

As soon as the civil wars were subdued, the sugar industry of Jamaica entered upon a flourishing period, to which not only the sugar, but also the secondary product, rum, contributed greatly.

The emancipation of slaves hit Jamaica a severe blow ; the liberated negroes left the solitary plantations, which went to decay at once. The low prices of sugar in the years between 1890 and 1900, too, were fatal to this colony, and had it not been for its special product, Jamaica rum, which always commands a high price, the island would have been ruined altogether.

When Chamberlain, in 1898, proposed to give financial support to the West Indian islands at the expense of the Mother-Country, he was specially mindful of Jamaica. We may consider the improved mail service between Jamaica and Bristol an outcome of this proposition, through which fruit, especially bananas, was quickly transported to the centres of consumption in temperate climates.

In 1890 some bunches of bananas had been transhipped to London, but not until 1898 did this importation become of any moment. At the present day the export of bananas amounts to about 15,000,000 bunches, and has exceeded in value both that of sugar and rum, as the following table for the 1907 returns shows :—

			£	£
Exportation of Fruit	..	..		972,273
,,	bananas	..	842,689	
,,	citrus fruits..	..	90,468	
,,	of Sugar	..	..	122,328
,,	of Rum	..	..	98,923

British West Indies.

Of the planted area of 750,000 acres in 1906, 26,180 acres were planted with sugar cane, 60,000 with bananas, and 27,170 with coffee, while the rest was occupied with coconuts, cacao, pimento, vegetables, and pasture land.

The cane-planted area is not in proportion to the quantity of sugar produced, but we must remember that cane is not exclusively used for the manufacture of sugar. A considerable quantity of cane juice is directly worked up into rum, while the boiled massecuite is purposely made to yield little sugar, for the sake of getting a large quantity of a pure kind of material for the production of rum.

There are 83 (chiefly small) sugar factories in Jamaica, of which only three are so-called central factories; only 12 of the remaining 80 sugar works have vacuum pans, the others prepare muscovado and rum.

The cost price of sugar cannot be fixed with certainty, as it is greatly influenced by the proportions of sugar and rum prepared from the same quantity of cane.

The production during the last twenty years has amounted to the following quantities, expressed in long tons :—

1892	23,654
1893	21,872
1894	24,149
1895	23,452
1896	22,995
1897	16,331
1898	14,462
1899	18,326
1900	19,823
1901	16,083
1902	20,323
1903	13,574
1904	9,903
1905	11,935
1906	21,823
1907	13,971
1908	24,000
1909	18,823
1910	19,960
1911	19,414

Literature :

B. Pulley Burry. *Jamaica as it is.*
Algernon E. Aspinall. *Pocket Guide to the West Indies.*
The West India Committee Circular.
Beckford. *A descriptive Account of the Island of Jamaica.*

(d) WINDWARD ISLANDS.

Among the islets comprising the Windward group only two occur that used to have a sugar industry of any importance, viz., St. Lucia and St. Vincent.

Their location, dimensions, and population are given in the following table :—

Island.	Latitude	Longi-tude	Greatest Length Miles	Greatest Width Miles	Area Sq. miles	Popula-tion.
St. Lucia	13° 50′	60° 58′	40	21	233	48,637
St. Vincent	13° 10′	60° 57′	18	11	140	41,877

Both the islands are mountainous and of volcanic origin, and craters abound that quite recently have been in violent eruption. The climate is rather damp and hot ; the rainfall amounts to 80 to 100 ins. ; the wet season lasts from August to November ; February is the coolest and July the hottest. The temperature varies between 15° and 34° C., and at night it is cool, as a rule.

These islands not only suffer from volcanic eruptions and earthquakes, but also from hurricanes, the approach of which is generally indicated by the meteorological stations, so that the damage done by them has grown considerably less of late.

Both these islands were discovered by Columbus, respectively on St. Vincent's Day, 1498, and St. Lucia's Day, 1502. Like all the smaller Antilles, they were involved in much struggle during the seventeenth and eighteenth centuries, and have repeatedly changed possession, to be annexed by England in the end.

The sugar industry used to flourish in St. Vincent from 1805 to 1829 ; 18,000 to 20,000 hogsheads of sugar were exported. After the abolition of slavery this prosperous trade at once came to an end ; in 1873 the exportation was no more than 8,491 tons of sugar, in 1883 9,255, in 1887 5,088, in 1890 6,176, and in 1897 2,896 tons, to drop since to about 600 tons muscovado sugar.

In St. Lucia the sugar industry is in a somewhat better plight ; there are four central factories that produce vacuum pan sugar, while the exports have amounted to an average of about 5,000 tons during the last five years. This amount is not likely to increase, so that the two islands together contribute no more than some 5,000 tons a year to the world's supply.

The exports of these two islands during the last seventeen years have amounted to the following quantities in long tons :—

	St. Lucia.	St. Vincent.
1894	4,485	2,727
1895	3,627	2,585
1896	3,548	2,555
1897	3,859	2,772
1898	3,751	1,865
1899	3,989	361
1900	4,018	587
1901	4,772	887
1902	4,278	645
1903	3,884	262
1904	5,161	930
1905	4,834	350
1906	5,795	549
1907	5,365	298
1908	4,977	224
1909	5,518	288
1910	5,220	280

(e) LEEWARD ISLANDS.

The Leeward Islands group consists of the islands of Antigua, Montserrat, St. Kitts, Nevis, Anguilla, Dominica, and the Virgin Islands. They lie in the Caribbean Sea, between 15° and 19° N. Lat. and 61° and 65° W. Long. The total area of the islands covers 600 square miles, while their population amounts to about 125,000 inhabitants.

Location, dimensions, and population of the different islands are given in the following table :—

Island.	North Latitude.	West Longitude	Area in Sq. Miles.	Greatest Length in Miles.	Greatest Width in Miles.	Population.
Antigua	17° 6′	61° 45′	170	20	—	32,265
Montserrat	16° 45′	61°	33½	10	7	12,196
St. Kitts	17° 18′	62° 46′	65	23	—	26,283
Nevis	17° 10′	62° 33′	50	—	—	12,945
Anguilla	18°	64°	35	30	3	4,075
Dominica	15° 25′	61° 15′	305	28	15	33,863
Virgin Islands ..	—	—	58	—	—	5,562

North America.

All the islands are volcanic, and most of them are surrounded by coral reefs. Antigua is volcanic in the south and south-west, but it is composed of coral in the north and north-east. The island has many natural harbours, of which that of St. John is the most important. The capital, St. John, with 9,000 inhabitants, is situated there.

Montserrat is also mountainous; it consists of a row of circular hills that have developed into a mountain chain.

St. Kitts, or St. Christopher, has a mountainous centre, consisting of rows of hills which run from south-east to north-west, with Mount Misery of more than 3,280 ft. as the highest peak.

Nevis is nothing more than a large volcanic cone, 3,900 ft. high, the sides of which are well wooded.

The Island of Anguilla is only a narrow ledge of rock rising from the sea.

Dominica, the largest of the group, shows all the characteristics of a volcanic island, and is the only one where rivers are found. In all the others the rain water immediately penetrates into the ground without forming streams.

The Virgin Islands form a group of about fifty small islets and reefs, many of which attain to a considerable height above the sea level. Tortola, Virgin Gorda, Anegada, Salt Island, and St. Peter are the principal ones.

All these islands generally suffer more or less from drought; the yearly rainfall in Antigua is about 40 ins; that in St. Kitts a little more, viz., between 50 and 60; that in Nevis from 43 to 80 ins.

All these islands were discovered and named by Columbus on his second voyage in 1493 and 1494.

Antigua got its name from a church at Seville, St. Maria la Antigua; Montserrat from a convent in Spain where Loyola planned the Order of the Jesuits; St. Kitts, a corruption of the name St. Christopher, received its name from Columbus' patron saint; and Nevis is derived from the mountain Neives, near Barcelona, since the volcanic cone wrapped in clouds resembled a snow-cap at the time of the discovery. Anguilla got its name from its snake-like shape. Dominica was discovered on a Sunday; while the Virgin Islands are said to have been called after the 11,000 legendary virgins.

All these islands have been taken possession of and colonized by the British, Spanish, Dutch, and French. During the frequent wars they changed hands every now and then; under a certain treaty of peace they were ceded to France, but under another they became English, which they have remained. Since 1871 they have formed a Federation, with Antigua as the seat of government, and they are divided into different presidencies.

Although all these islands produced sugar for export during the eighteenth and the beginning of the nineteenth centuries, the sugar industry dwindled greatly after the abolition of slavery. As a matter of fact, it is now only carried on in Antigua, Montserrat, St. Kitts, and Nevis, and of these only in Antigua and St. Kitts to such a degree that exportation is possible.

In Antigua there are two central factories, one of which was founded with the financial aid of the British Government in the form of a 3 per cent. consolidated loan ; in St. Kitts there are also two central factories working, while a number of small muscovado factories are in operation in the other islands that go to swell the sugar industry.

For want of rivers in these islands, irrigation is a matter of difficulty, and the long sustained drought causes the sugar production to be an uncertain factor, which leads to greatly varying annual output.

The exportation of Antigua alone has been for the last thirty years, expressed in long tons, as below :—

1881	..	..	8,645	1896	.. ..	13,714
1882	..	.	12,769	1897	.. ..	12,766
1883	.	..	10,518	1898	.. ..	6,968
1884	..	..	13,721	1899	.. ..	10,084
1885	..	..	11,848	1900	.. ..	7,622
1886	..	..	12,271	1901	.. ..	9,125
1887	..	..	14,052	1902	.. ..	12,611
1888	..	..	14,925	1903	.. ..	10,494
1889	..	..	14,413	1904	.. ..	11,940
1890	..	..	16,120	1905	.. ..	7,829
1891	..	..	12,091	1906	.. ..	13,238
1892	..	..	15,302	1907	.. ..	10,806
1893	..	..	14,562	1908	.. ..	13,451
1894	..	..	12,342	1909	.. ..	12,075
1895	..	..	6,685	1910	.. ..	18,145

The exportation of St. Christopher, Nevis, and Montserrat, etc., has amounted to the following figures for some of the last few years :—

Year.	St. Kitts and Nevis.	Montserrat.	Dominica.
1890	17,409	1,442	2,349
1891	13,149	1,131	1,662
1892	18,156	2,540	2,251
1895	13,360	711	762
1896	15,037	1,778	609
1897	14,681	813	559
1903	13,511	870	225
1904	14,190	513	130
1905	12,345	239	181
1906	15,898	652	82
1907	12,346	60	107
1908	11,044	89	24
1909	12,321	84	—
1910	8,671	54	—

This table shows that only St. Kitts, Nevis and Antigua are still of any importance as regards the sugar industry, and even they are not likely to extend their trade as the years go by, but will, no doubt, remain stationary.

VII.

FRENCH ANTILLES.

I.—Geographical Location, Climate, etc.

(a)—GUADELOUPE.

GUADELOUPE comprises two islands divided by a strait six miles long and thirty-six miles broad. These two islands situated on either side of the Rivière Salée, are called Basse Terre and Grande Terre. The islands lie north of Martinique, between 15° 59′ and 16° 14′ N. Lat. and 63° 51′ and 61° 4′ W. Long.

The island Grande Terre has an area of 220 sq. miles ; Guadeloupe, or Basse Terre, an area of 365 sq. miles ; while some lesser islands which belong to the group, among which is Marie Galante, together cover an area of 115 sq. miles.

The island Grande Terre is of triangular shape, and has a coastline of 164 miles ; while Basse Terre is oval in shape, and has a compass of 112 miles.

The population of this group amounted to 182,000 inhabitants on 1st January, 1892 : that is, 264 per sq. mile. In 1903 14,862 of these were immigrants.

Basse Terre is of volcanic origin, and was the product of four volcanic centres, namely, the Soufrière, the Morne-sans-toucher, les deux Mamelles, and the Grosse Montagne. Besides these big craters, there are still a number of lesser ones, while several hot wells are to be found.

Grande Terre, however, is a limestone rock, which rises only a short distance above sea level, and is covered with a layer of disintegrated calcareous earth, very porous to water. The soil of Basse Terre is a stiff clay, the result of the disintegration of volcanic trachytes and basalts.

The climate of both these islands is the same—moist and warm. On account of the great porosity of the soil no rivers or streams occur in Grande Terre, while the firm clay soil of Basse Terre causes the abundant rain-water to run into the sea by a number of brooks. The average temperature of Guadeloupe is as follows for the different months :—

French Antilles.

	°C.
January .	24·52
February	24·17
March	24·74
April	25·72
May	26·55
June	27·02
July	27·21
August	27·62
September	27·58
October	26·87
November	26·26
December	25·28
Total	26·13

while the rainfall in millimetres is distributed as follows :—

Month.	1897.	1898.	1899.	1900.	1901.	1902.
January	77	58	104	55	169	35
February	73	53	41	59	28	20
March	141	47	41	51	25	31
April	73	15	44	64	8	109
May	300	98	55	108	129	79
June	108	65	121	142	393	114
July	186	296	174	199	327	68
August	179	153	16	223	219	245
September	188	395	141	97	139	191
October	64	139	245	234	154	300
November	155	241	305	101	48	181
December	303	70	71	76	100	215
Total	1,747	1,630	1,358	1,389	1,739	1,588

or an average of 59 ins.

The principal towns are Pointe a Pitre in Grande Terre, and Basse Terre in Guadeloupe ; besides these there is the town Grand Bourg, in the island of Maria Galante.

Guadeloupe was discovered by Columbus in 1493 ; he named it after the convent of the same name in Estramadura. In 1635 it was taken possession of by a number of Frenchmen, and remained French till the English captured it in 1759. Since that time it has been alternately under English and French dominion, but it fell to Sweden in 1810. In 1814 the French reconquered it, but had to give it up to England in 1815, though only for a very short time, for it was returned to France that same year.

(b) MARTINIQUE.

The Island of Martinique lies in the Caribbean Sea, between 14° 52' N. Lat. and 63° 16' and 63° 31' W. Long. It has an area of 3,820 sq. miles; its greatest length is 50 miles; its greatest width 19 miles; and its circumference, not including the capes, amounts to 217 miles. On the 1st January, 1902, its census was 204,000, or 535 inhabitants to the sq. mile, but since the Mount Pelé catastrophe, occurring that same year, in which 35,000 persons lost their lives, the number has been greatly reduced.

Martinique is by no means flat; the northern volcanic part consists of pumice-stone and lava, while the southern part is clay soil. During the dry season the numerous streams dry up, to change into wild mountain torrents during the rains. The well-known volcano, Mount Pelé, lies at the northernmost point of the island.

The climate is hot and moist, and shows the following characteristics :—

	Aver. temp.	Hygrometer.	Barometer.	Rain monthly in mm.
Dry Season.				
1. Nov.—Feb.	25·7	87·2	757·4	148 in 18 days
2. Mar.—April	26·9	85·0	758·5	100 in 15 ,,
				792 mm.
Wet Season.				
1. May—half of July ..	28·0	86·8	758·9	201 in 19 days
2. Half of July—Oct. ...	29·3	94·8	757·6	233 in 19 ,,
Yearly average ..	27·2	88·4	758·1	2·158 in 197 days per y'r

The rainfall may vary considerably according to the locality, and in some years it will amount to more than 275 ins. in Port de France, the greater part of which falls during the period July to September.

The coast is deeply indented, but the bays are almost inaccessible through the numerous coral reefs. The best harbours are those of Port de France and of Saint Pierre, on which towns of the same name are situated.

Martinique was discovered by Columbus in 1493, and was colonized in 1635 by a number of French people from St. Christopher. In 1664 the French Government bought the island from these colonists, and kept it in spite of the frequent wars. Then the English conquered it, and returned it several times in the course of time, but it was ultimately restored to France by the Treaty of Paris in 1814.

II.—History of the Sugar Industry.

Immediately after the French took possession of these islands, a start was made in the planting of sugar, but the first plantation of any importance dates from 1655, when the Dutchmen driven from Brazil settled in Martinique with their capital and slaves. The industry soon grew in importance, so much so that the sugar exportation to France formed a considerable part of the French overseas trade in the seventeenth century.

Owing to decrees promulgated by Colbert, it had become impossible to import foreign sugar into France, as the differential import duties of 1664 protected the importation of raw sugar from French colonies so far above that of raw sugar of foreign origin that it almost meant prohibition for the latter On the other side, the import duty on white sugar so much exceeded that on raw sugar that importation of white sugar from their own colonies, and especially that of refined sugar into France, likewise became an impossibility. Although the colonial planters really possessed a monopoly of the raw sugar trade, they lost the chance of selling refined sugar, with the result that the sugar refineries established in Martinique had to cease operations. In 1669 the refining of sugar was prohibited in the colonies, as was the export of raw sugar to foreign ports, and an export duty was levied amounting to 3 per cent. of the value of sugar sent to France. In 1682 this prohibition was removed as regards raw sugar ; on the other hand, the import duty on refined sugar was increased so much above that on raw sugar that it would have been impossible for the refiners to compete with the French. Afterwards the planters took up the preparation of clayed sugar (which will be fully described in the following pages), and exported it to North America and to the Mediterranean ports, so that the French refiners did not attain their object, viz., to refine the sugar produced in their own colonies exclusively in the mother country.

It was for this reason that in 1717 all restrictions on the imports were repealed, and import duties on French goods were actually abolished in the colonies, thus establishing almost complete free trade between the mother country and colonies. All this caused the sugar industry in the French colonies to flourish, and Martinique, Guadeloupe, and San Domingo, in the end, produced larger quantities of sugar than France was able to refine or consume—the remainder was then allowed to be exported to other countries.

At the end of the eighteenth century conditions were no longer so favourable. San Domingo was devastated, and the other islands suffered much from the frequent wars between France and England, as a great many of these were fought in the Caribbean Sea, thus creating no little uncertainty in trading circles.

After the treaty of peace signed in Paris, both these colonies were restored to France; whereupon the sugar industry began to flourish once more, its production steadily increasing, till in 1848 the abolition of slavery caused the quantity of sugar produced to drop considerably.

As soon as slavery was put an end to, and the colonies were deprived of their customary labour, everything was done to supply them with free labourers from other parts. In 1852 a ship's captain was permitted to recruit 4,000 labourers in British India within six years at a premium of 500 francs for each immigrant. Part of the indemnification that was granted to the slave-owners by the Government at the time of the emancipation of slaves was destined for this purpose, while the Government added a yearly subsidy of 100,000—150,000 francs. When 1,191 Indians had arrived, this undertaking ceased to work, but not long afterwards a company resumed the business, and imported 9,158 Indians to Martinique between 1855 to 1862, all but 200 of whom stayed in the island when their five years' contract had expired.

In 1861 France and England came to an agreement regarding the regulation of the immigration of British Indians to the French Antilles. These immigrants were recruited in the French towns of Pondicherry, Yanaon, Karikal, and in Calcutta under the superintendence of a British official, and were sent to Martinique; and in this way 25,509 labourers arrived in the island between 1862 and 1884, 4,041 of which returned home at the end of their term of indenture. At the request of the General Council of India, official immigration was abolished in 1885, and since then the immigration of Indians has ceased altogether.

Besides the British Indians, free negroes from the West Coast of Africa used to be imported, but this, too, did not last because of the great difficulties encountered. Then the buying of negro slaves from the Congo and Loango and the exportation of them to the Antilles was commenced. On arrival at the Antilles they were liberated, and were allowed to go back to their native country when the time of their indenture had expired. This brought 9,090 negroes to the Antilles.

Then some hundreds of Chinese from Canton were imported, not to mention some Annamites; but since 1889 all immigration has come to an end.

Between 1854 and 1889 the following foreign labourers were imported into Guadeloupe :—

Indians	..	..	..	..	42,595
Africans	..	..	..	..	6,600
Chinese	..	..	..	..	500
Annamites		..	..	..	272
					49,967

But on 1st January, 1874, only 15,947 Indians were left, the remainder having either returned home, migrated to other islands, or died.

In 1901 the foreign population in Martinique only amounted to :—

Indians	..	..	..	..	3,764
Africans	..	..	..	..	5,345
Chinese	..	..	..	..	430
					9,539

This shows how far the labour problem is still from solution, and the fact that all enjoy the same privileges, including franchise, and spend far too much time in discussing politics, does not improve conditions. In 1910 serious disturbances of a political nature occurred again in Guadeloupe, which had an injurious effect on the quiet development of the sugar industry. There is no sign of extension of this industry in either of the islands ; the production of Martinique remains stationary at 36,000 tons, like that of Guadeloupe,while fifty years ago their outputs were respectively 32,000 and 25,000 tons of sugar.

III.—Sugar Cane Cultivation, Sugar Manufacture, Duties, Production, and Costs.

In Martinique sugar cane cultivation is carried out on the narrow strip of alluvial land along the coast, and on the hills in the interior, where heavy showers wash away the arable soil and thus hinder the cane's growth. In Guadeloupe, also, the sugar estates are on flat coastland, though a few estates are found in the small island of Maria Galante.

North America.

Formerly sugar was manufactured in a number of small factories, but since 1865 larger houses have been built, and cane is cultivated by the smaller planters for sale to the central factories.

The ground used for cane is first stripped of its existing vegetation, and is then ploughed. Then shallow furrows are dug by means of a plough 4½ ft. apart and 20 ins. deep. As much rain falls in the islands during the wet season, it is necessary to prevent stagnant water remaining in the fields by an adequate system of drainage. During the period from October to January the cuttings are planted in holes which have been dug 5 ins. deep in rows at a distance of 3 to 5 ft. from each other. After three weeks the cane is banked up and manured with stable dung, filter-press mud, sulphate of ammonia, Chili saltpetre, super-phosphate, basic slag, or mixtures of these. Further, the soil between the plants is repeatedly loosened and the cane trashed* several times to be cut about a year after it is planted. Generally no more than two ratoon crops are grown, and these are cut once a year. Then the land is left to lie fallow for some years, when the whole process as described above is repeated.

Otaheite or Bourbon cane is chiefly planted ; it was first imported from Réunion to the Antilles at the end of the eighteenth century. But this cane variety is supposed to have degenerated, and consequently is inferior to what it used to be ; hence seedling varieties from Demerara and Barbados, especially the types B 147, B 109, D 208, and D 145 have since been utilized.

Rats and several kinds of borers are great enemies to the cane in the French Antilles, while the universal fungous leaf-and-stalk diseases are also found here.

The quantity of cane reaped per unit of planted area very much depends on the age of the cane after planting. While a yield of 24 tons per acre (60,000 kg. per hectare) is expected from plant cane, it drops to 16 tons for first ratoons, to 8 tons for second ratoons, and even to 4 tons for third ratoons. These figures, of course, do not hold good for all kinds of land, but they are the average at which the different crops work out.

The cane is carried by men or mules from the fields to the large carts which convey it along the hard roads to the factories.

Railways with locomotives, or narrow-gauge lines with mules pulling the trucks are often employed.

It was in these islands that sugar manufacture was first carried on in a rational scientific way, and the methods invented there have gradually been copied by most of the other sugar-producing countries. For this reason we venture to give the following description of the manufacture of raw and refined sugar as Père Labat records it in his book on the American islands, written in 1722 :—

---

* Trashing means removing the dried cane leaves.

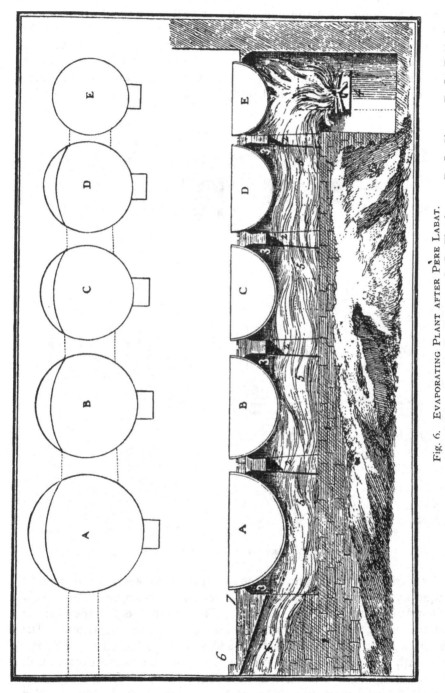

Fig. 6. Evaporating Plant after Père Labat.

1. A, B, C, D, & E, the open pans. A—La Grande. B—La Propre. C—Le Flambeau. D—Le Sirop. E—La Batterie.
2. Masonry to separate the pans from each other. 3. Support for the pans. 4. Furnace. 5. Channel for the flue gases.
6 & 7. Reservoir for the mill juice.

North America.

The cane juice is evaporated in a series of five, or sometimes six, open copper pans standing in a row over a furnace heated with bagasse and wood. Each succeeding vessel is smaller than the preceding one, and each is placed a little higher than the one before, so that when boiling over it is impossible for juice of less density to flow into the further concentrated mass. All vessels go by different names, and, beginning at the biggest, these are: la grande chaudière, la propre, la lessive, le flambeau, le sirop, and la batterie.

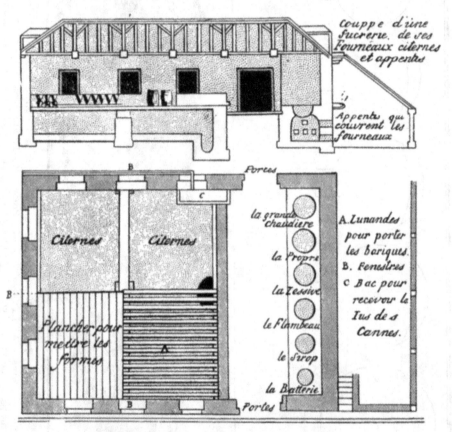

FIG. 7. SUGAR FACTORY AS DESCRIBED BY PÈRE LABAT.

For clarification a mixture of lime and a solution of wood ash is used; consequently, nothing but impure caustic potash to which, in some cases, a little powdered crude antimony is added. The juice first enters the "grande chaudière" when the clarifying medium is added and is boiled with it. The froth forming is constantly scooped off and as soon as the juice has become clear enough it is rapidly poured into the "propre" and, after a little alkali has been added, is again boiled and skimmed off. Then the juice is scooped out into the "lessive," when potash lye and an extract of salt herbs is added

234

to it, and it is skimmed in turn. The juice subsequently passes through the " flambeau," the " sirop," and at last finds itself in the " batterie," where it is concentrated as much as possible.

The temperature is highest here, and the syrup foams up through the intense heat, but is prevented from boiling over by adding small quantities of oil; the syrup is boiled string-proof, and the concentrated mass is scooped out into the cooling vessels, where it is stirred slightly till grain begins to form. After the latter has been thoroughly stirred into the mass in order to divide it evenly, the crystallizing mass is poured into the moulds where it is to cool. When sufficiently cooled, it is put into hogsheads, the bottoms of which are provided with three holes at least. The hogsheads stand on a frame of lattice-work above a receptacle for the treacle, and pieces of sugar cane or banana-stalk are put into the holes so that it can drain off but sugar cannot come through them. The molasses contained in the mass trickles slowly through the holes, leaving crystallized sugar amounting to about 50 per cent. of the total weight. The holes are filled up with wooden plugs, and the cask with its contents is sent out as raw sugar. The molasses is not boiled any further, but is used for the manufacture of rum.

Besides this raw sugar much white sugar, called *sucre terré*, was prepared. The best and ripest cane was taken for this purpose and was clarified with as little lime as possible, no antimony being used, for although the latter makes the juice clear, it also causes a dark colour. Then the juice is not simply scooped from one pan into another, but is strained through cloth each time: first through coarse cloth, and later on through some of a finer texture. The juice that is concentrated string-proof in the battery is ladled into earthenware sugar-loaf moulds, which are capable of holding 30—35 lbs of massecuite or 20—21 lbs. of white sugar. These moulds are provided with holes at the bottom, which have to be plugged before the moulds are filled.

The latter are first filled one quarter full, then to the middle, next three-fourths full, so that filling is done in four stages. A quarter of an hour after the last instalment of massecuite is added, a layer of crystals appears on the top of it, which should be stirred carefully into the mass, after which the contents of the vessel are left to cool. After a day or so, the plugs are pulled out of the holes, and the mass is pierced with a hard piece of wood, to let the treacle run freely from the mould. Each pot fits into another one, so that the molasses running out may be collected without loss. Now and then attention is paid to the way the molasses trickles down, *i.e.*, whether it goes evenly or not; should this not be the case, and should it adhere to the crystals, the massecuite is remelted and poured in a second time; but should it proceed satisfactorily claying is proceeded with. The top part of the loaves when not even and smooth, and when showing dark stains, is scratched off and returned to the pans. Then a few good specimens of loaves are crushed to powder and used for covering the scraped loaves, and after the mass is pressed together with a hammer a level and smooth surface remains. Further, an exceedingly fine mixture is got by mixing a special sort of clay coming from Rouen with water, for the purpose of pouring it on the top of the sugar in the moulds, to fill them full to the brim. The water must trickle evenly from the clay through the sugar, and windows and doors are shut to prevent evaporation, the moulds being left like this for nine or ten days. The now fully dried-up clay is then removed, the sugar loaf is cleaned on the surface, and given a fresh amount of clay and water, then left for another nine or ten days. The clay is removed, the loaves are taken out of the mould and left to dry in the air. Then they are dried in a special drying room, which is gradually heated, after which the dry sugar is crushed to powder with wooden pestles.

The fine sugar is packed into barrels of 600 to 700 lbs. net weight and dispatched. The first syrup is worked up into rum, or is turned into a second product sugar, while the covering syrup is always worked up to a second kind of sugar, the so-called *cassonade*.

At the present day this old-fashioned method of sugar manufacture has been quite abandoned, and sugar is being produced in the French Antilles in as modern a manner as elsewhere. The cane is generally crushed twice, mostly in two different mills, sometimes twice in the same mill. In the first case maceration is often applied, varying between 10 and 30 per cent. of the weight of cane. In front of the mill a *défibreur Faure* is found in these islands, an apparatus corresponding to the Krajewski crusher, but less powerful and not giving the same results.

The quantity of bagasse is generally not sufficient to supply all the fuel necessary for the factory, and therefore wood and coal have to be used in addition. The latter is rather expensive, and comes to 37 to 50 francs per ton, according to the freight charges. It is sometimes imported as ballast by sailing vessels, which are to take the sugar away, in which case the price is considerably lower than if a journey were made specially to convey the coal. The juice is sulphitated cold, and pumped into defecation pans, where it is heated. Fifty to sixty grams of fine powdered quicklime are added to each hectolitre of juice, after which the juice is heated till the scum begins to crack, and at this point the steam is shut off. By syphoning off the juice is divided into clarified juice and mud : the first goes to the evaporators, while the latter is subsided once more or filtered in filter presses. The filter-press-cakes are considered a favourite food for cattle, horses, and mules.

The juice is next concentrated in double, triple, or quadruple effects, but all of these are old-fashioned in construction, and lack the latest devices for saving steam. The very primitive juice evaporation in Guadeloupe and Martinique no doubt accounts for the extremely heavy consumption of fuel in the sugar factories, which, of course, leads to the cutting down of timber, and, by the devastation of forest, causes the continuous drought that the planters have every cause to complain of.

The pans are small and old-fashioned in construction ; crystallization-in-motion is not in use ; the centrifugals, too, are very out-of-date and slow in their manipulation. In Martinique the massecuite falls from the vacuum pans into large receptacles placed under them, while in Guadeloupe it falls into waggons. It flows from these into pug mills, after which it is centrifugalled ; later on, the sugar is packed in barrels of 16 cwt. net or in bags of 100 kg. The molasses are boiled string-proof, and are cooled and centrifugalled again ; as a rule, three or four products are turned out, after which the molasses is sent to the distillery to be worked into rum.

When the law of 1882 was in full force, sugar from the French Antilles enjoyed a handsome bounty when imported into the mother-country, because 13 per cent. tare was allowed for sugar in barrels, while the actual tare was really much less. It was accepted, for instance, that a barrel of sugar weighing 1 metric ton gross contained 870 kg. of sugar, while the actual contents were as much as 925. The duty at the time amounted to 60 francs per 100 kg., so that no less than $55 \times 0.60 = 33$ francs of the duty were exempted per ton. Now that the duty is reduced to 25 francs, this profit has become much less—so much so that it does not pay to apply the more expensive method of packing in barrels since the consumption duty was lowered.

E. Légier quotes a few figures as regards the manufacture which follow here :—

	Average Case. Per Cent.	Unfavourable Case. Per Cent.
Yield of sugar on 100 cane	9·70	8·00
Loss in bagasse	2·15	3·45
,, ,, molasses	1·75	1·75
,, ,, manufacture	0·90	1·40
Sugar in cane	14·50	14·60
Yield of juice on 100 cane	75·	66·
Litres of juice on 100 kg. cane	69·70	61·40
Density of juice	1·0770	1·0750
Fibre on 100 cane	12·	12·
Sucrose on 100 juice	16·47	15·70
Purity of juice	86	84
Molasses on 100 cane	4·15	4·15

In 1865 the first central factories, La Pointe Simon and Lareinty, were built, but were shut down after some time. Others, however, were added, so that at the present day there are 18 sugar factories in Guadeloupe and 15 in Martinique.

They are divided over the districts as follows :—

In Guadeloupe				
In Grande Terre.	Pointe a Pitre	.. ..	1
	Sainte Anne	.. ..	2
	Saint Francois	.. ..	2
	La Moule	.. ..	2
	Port Louis	.. ..	1
	Petit Canal	.. ..	1
	Morne à l'eau	.. ..	1
In Basse Terre.	Sainte Rose	.. ..	1
	Baie Mahault	.. ..	1
	Capesterre	.. ..	2
In Marie Galante.	Grand Bourg	.. ..	1
	Marie Galante	.. ..	2
	Capesterre	.. ..	1

18

In Martinique.			
Lamentin	.. .. ..	2
Petit Bourg	.. ..	1
Rivière Salée	.. ..	1
Trois Rivières	.. ..	1
Marin	.. .. ..	1
Vauclin	.. .. ..	1
Francois	.. .. ..	1
Robert	.. .. ..	1
Trinité	.. .. ..	2
Sainte Marie	.. ..	1
Mariget	.. .. ..	1
Grand' Anse	.. ..	1
Basse Pointe	.. ..	1

15

The cost price of cane depends on various circumstances, so that it is rather difficult to quote any average figure. At any rate, it is no lower than 12 francs per 1000 kg., while a great many manufacturers are not able to produce cane for less than 13 to 14 francs per 1,000 kg.

The following table gives an instance of the prices of cane and of the data that contribute to it. It is quoted in francs per metric ton :—

	Plant Cane.	1st Ratoon
Salaries	6·96	5·28
General Expenses	3·	3·
Manuring	3·	3·86
Transportation costs	0·35	0·40
Cutting	0·80	1·
	14·11	13·54

The manufacturers do not plant the sugar cane themselves, but buy it from the small farmers, and their method of fixing the price is most intricate, but seems to be approved by all parties concerned.

Before the central factories were established, sugar used to be prepared according to Père Labat's method, and sugar called " Bonne quatrième," considered to be of first importance, influenced the price quotation. The factories at first paid for cane 5½ per cent. of the weight of cane in " bonne quatrième" sugar, according to the market price at Saint Pierre. In 1876 a premium was paid above that price, should the profit have been more than 14 per cent.; consequently, the cane growers shared the extra profit. When the price of sugar went steadily down, the cane (in 1884) was paid for on the basis of 6 per cent. of the weight of cane in "bonne quatrième" sugar, and a share of all excess above 14 per cent. was out of the question, as the manufacturers, owing to the low sugar price, had so considerably run into debt that their profit went entirely towards payments of interest. Later on they decided not to fix a price depending on that of the sugar, but to fix a minimum of what the cost price of cane would come to, and to pay a premium, called "majoration," above that price should more profit be made. The minimum was fixed at 32 francs for 100 kg. sugar, or at 6 per cent. at 19·20 francs per ton cane.

In 1884 a law was passed to establish the "détaxe coloniale," which was a kind of premium on crystal sugar from the French colonies, the amount of which was to be fixed every year, but which actually always amounted to 20 francs per 100 kg., and allowed of a decrease in import duty on French colonial sugar over sugar of other origin. So it became increasingly profitable to export to France, and as raw sugar was not in demand in that country, the "bonne quatrième" gradually disappeared from the market, and no quotation of it was kept, which made the standard for the estimation disappear.

A way out of the difficulty was devised by taking the price of sugar 88° on the Paris market as basis, and by supposing the trade yield of "bonne quatrième sugar to amount to 70°. Consequently, the price of this kind of sugar was fixed at 70/88 of the price of beetroot sugar in Paris, but as the latter is quoted in that city while the "bonne quatrième" is at Saint Pierre, there was a deduction for cost of freight at 5 francs per 100 kg. for Martinique, and 6 francs for Guadeloupe. As, however, the colonial producer enjoyed the "détaxe coloniale," the price was increased by 70 per cent. of this profit, which discount disappeared when France joined the Brussels Convention.

The present quotations are as follows:—

MARTINIQUE.—The basis of payment is 6 per cent. of the weight of cane in "bonne quatrième" sugar, including a premium, in accordance with the profit of the factory. Should, for instance, the price of "bonne quatrième" be quoted at 22·61 francs, 5 francs is to be deducted for freight, but 1·71 francs must be added for the still valid "détaxe de distance," so that the price comes to $22.61 - 5 + 1.71 = 19.32$ francs. This at 6 per cent. raises it to $19.32 \times 60 \div 100 = 11.59$ francs, as the price of 1,000 kg. of cane. To this is added the "majoration" which is found by taking 28 francs as the price of sugar under all circumstances—even should it actually be less, and fixing the price of cane at $28 \times 60 \div 100 = 16.80$ francs. When the crushing season is over the net profit of the factory is decided on, and the extra profit is divided among the shareholders and the cane producers.

At the present moment the following method is under consideration:

The cane growers receive 6 per cent. of sugar for every 100 parts of cane paid according to the market price; next 3 per cent. of the profit is given to the shareholders as interest on their capital. For the rest, the cane suppliers get a first " majoration " by taking 24 francs as basis of the sugar price and paying in excess whatever they might have lost. In our example of 11·59 francs, it would be 14·40 — 11·59 = 2·81 per ton. The rest of the profit is divided as follows : the manager gets 5 per cent., and the balance of 95 per cent. is equally divided among shareholders and cane producers, the latter in proportion to the quantity of cane supplied. In this way cane may fetch 20 to 25 francs per ton.

GUADELOUPE.—As basis of payment, the average price of sugar, 88° on the Paris Exchange, is taken for the month in which the cane is delivered. This calculation again depends on a trade rendement of 70 per cent. of the " bonne quatrième," so that, when the price of sugar in Paris is 27 francs, the basis of Guadeloupe becomes $27 \times 70/88 = 22·61$. From this 6 francs for freight is deducted, which leaves 16·61 to be diminished by 0·35 francs as exchange charges, by 1·66 francs as export duty, and 0·20 francs for a statistical duty (altogether 2·21 francs), leaving in the end 14·41 francs. As cane is paid for on the basis of $6\frac{1}{2}$ per cent. of this sugar, the planter, consequently, will receive $14·41 \times 65 \div 100 = 9·36$ francs per ton of cane, to which should be added : the " détaxe de distance " at 2·25 francs per 100 kg. sugar of 92, and the exchange, which together come to 1·92 francs per ton of cane ; so that the final price will amount to $9·36 + 1·92 = 11·28$ francs per ton.

All this shows that when reckoned according to this system, the price of cane in Martinique is better than that in Guadeloupe. In Guadeloupe one of the large sugar manufacturers would much rather do away with this method of calculation, and from 1910 would give the fixed price of 12 francs per metric ton, independent of prices on the Paris exchange.

We saw how difficult it was to produce cane at a price lower than 13 to 14 francs, so that should the planter only get 12 francs for it, he cannot be accused of piling on profits. It is not to be wondered at that the small planter loses through sugar cane cultivation, and has to sell his ground or let it lie fallow, should his neighbours be unable to pay a certain price to buy it. At the best he starts on the cultivation of other crops ; but all this points to a diminution in the cane cultivation and a decrease in importance for these islands as regards the sugar industry.

As long as the factories are installed in such a primitive way that cane with 14 per cent. sucrose does not yield more than 8·20 commercial sugar, it is impossible to pay more for cane. Should, however, more capital be spent on buying machinery, etc., the yield of cane would be improved, and cane could be bought at a far higher price, while the manufacturers would make more profit than they do at present. Yet this prospect is still far from being realized, as the French spirit of enterprise is at its best when not far from home, and shrinks from experimenting in remote regions.

French Antilles.

On the other hand, the planter by exerting himself a little more might asily reap a better crop of cane, in which case the price of 12 francs would pay im equally well, as it does his neighbours in the other Antilles. There, too, t is lack of enterprise, capital, and industry that are chiefly against the French lanter, while he cherishes greater expectations from political speculations han from actual labour and exertion, which, of course, do not make for im-rovement in the present state of affairs.

There is no excise on sugar in the French Antilles, but an export duty of ·20 francs per 100 kg. is paid, for Martinique with 10 and for Guadeloupe with .o per cent. addition on account of local Government charges ; an export duty f 0·50 francs is paid on treacle from Martinique, and of only 0·10 francs on reacle from Guadeloupe. Then there is a statistical duty of 0·15 francs per ollo.

Sugar from the French colonies, however, enjoys a discount on the import luty of 2·25 francs per 100 kg. sugar of 92 as " détaxe de distance " when im-orted into the mother-country. The import duties are in accordance with he Brussels Convention—that is, on sugar from countries adhering to the onvention 6 francs is paid per 100 kg. of refined sugar and 5·50 francs for aw sugar, while it is prohibited to import sugar from countries not belonging o the Convention, though it may be stored as bonded goods. Then an " octroi le mer " of 20 francs per 100 kg. is paid on sugar when imported into Martinique, vhich is a kind of municipal excise. When imported into Guadeloupe this ' octroi de mer " only amounts to 10 francs per 100 kg. As, however, no oreign sugar is imported into these islands, these regulations are never enforced.

The future of the sugar industry in the French Antilles is far from promis-ng. There is always lack of labour, for although there are inhabitants enough, hese do not wish to work for any time at a stretch ; hence there is no relying n them for carrying out work promptly. Moreover, the local councils are gainst the immigration of British Indians, because their members are coloured eople who are afraid of losing their preponderance by that influx, and are ncertain to obtain any more work, even if they choose to ask for it. It is bvious that nobody would think of employing unwilling negroes when it is ossible to obtain the more reliable immigrants.

This shows how little chance there is of reaping a better crop of cane, nd one can easily imagine that capitalists are not eager to risk their money 1 the improvement of the factories, however necessary these may be. As oon as the immigration of British Indian coolies is made possible, the sugar ndustry will enter upon a period of prosperity, but the present political eelings both of the white and of the coloured people in these islands are sure to e against such a measure.

The sugar exportation for the two islands has been since the first quarter f the nineteenth century up till now as follows in metric tons :—

North America.

Year.	Martinique	Guadeloupe	Year.	Martinique	Guadeloupe	Year.	Martinique	Guadeloupe
1816	—	5,305	1848	18,153	20,453	1880	38,592	41,322
1817	—	17,895	1849	19,522	17,709	1881	42,090	42,276
1818	16,068	21,126	1850	15,069	12,832	1882	47,887	57,501
1819	18,160	18,737	1851	23,408	20,046	1883	46,857	51,619
1820	21,447	22,300	1852	26,116	17,292	1884	49,370	55,257
1821	22,078	23,019	1853	22,358	16,679	1885	38,786	41,131
1822	20,173	23,477	1854	24,929	23,558	1886'	30,199	36,678
1823	20,587	24,324	1855	20,790	22,158	1887	39,582	54,940
1824	20,294	30,645	1856	28,181	22,506	1888	30,434	48,354
1825	26,477	24,015	1857	26,371	22,462	1889	35,965	45,173
1826	28,425	34,330	1858	28,048	28,494	1890	33,598	47,438
1827	24,576	28,266	1859	29,706	27,666	1891	32,376	30,329
1828	33,339	35,810	1860	32,954	28,800	1892	19,528	46,016
1829	29,083	38,812	1861	31,837	17,316	1893	32,737	41,158
1830	28,282	22,898	1862	32,101	31,312	1894	36,937	43,732
1831	27,846	35,056	1863	30,458	30,266	1895	29,329	29,866
1832	22,493	33,279	1864	24,161	15,906	1896	34,430	43,300
1833	20,059	30,827	1865	30,491	24,457	1897	34,734	40,127
1834	26,258	37,928	1866	34,657	33,942	1898	31,469	37,136
1835	24,379	32,097	1867	29,403	22,759	1899	31,665	39,889
1836	22,447	34,994	1868	37,671	30,792	1900	33,767	28,342
1837	20,458	25,057	1869	37,330	28,600	1901	39,749	38,697
1838	26,161	35,124	1870	38,314	34,216	1902	39,530	40,637
1839	28,723	36,672	1871	41,821	38,434	1903	29,036	38,499
1840	21,681	29,944	1872	39,700	31,508	1904	23,939	35,916
1841	24,948	29,136	1873	37,515	35,844	1905	30,187	27,336
1842	27,989	35,137	1874	43,441	34,855	1906	42,233	43,217
1843	25,479	27,169	1875	50,526	48,032	1907	36,924	38,961
1844	33,110	34,555	1876	38,845	35,470	1908	35,937	36,055
1845	30,031	33,748	1877	40,502	43,215	1909	37,757	25,211
1846	25,580	26,372	1878	44,218	48,118	1910	39,940	45,000
1847	31,338	37,894	1879	46,869	47,635	1911	35,438	39,000
						1912	40,000*	40,000*

Emile Legier. *La Martinique et la Guadeloupe.*
Emile Legier. *L'industrie sucriere à la Martinique et la Guadeloupe.*

* Estimate.

VIII.

ST. CROIX.

THE Island of St. Croix, which belongs geographically to the Virgin Islands and politically to Denmark, lies at 18° N. Lat. and 65° W. Long., and has an area of 77 sq. miles and a population numbering 19,683 people. A range of hills runs parallel to the coast on the west side, the highest summit of which is the Blue Mountain. The principal towns are Bassin and Christiansted, on the north coast, and Frederiksted, on the west coast. The island was discovered by Columbus in 1494, and was colonized by the English and Dutch in 1643. Since that time it has alternately been English, Spanish, and French, to fall to the Maltese knights, who sold it to the King of Denmark in 1733. During the first years of the nineteenth century it was repeatedly taken by the English and renounced, till in 1814 it became a Danish possession. In 1901 the Danish Antilles would have been ceded to the United States if it had not been for the Danish National Assembly, who refused to give their consent.

About 10,000 of the 50,000 acres which form the area of the island are cultivated, chiefly with sugar cane. The Island of St. Croix was the first of the West Indian Islands in which sugar cane was planted, and the sugar industry was in a flourishing state there during the time of slavery, as it was in the neighbouring Island of St. Thomas, also a Danish possession.

When in 1848 slavery was abolished in the Danish colonies, the sugar industry began to decline, and has revived only recently, when the landowners divided the ground into plots of 250 acres each to lease to cane farmers. Originally each plantation had a little cane factory of its own, in which muscovado sugar was prepared, but nowadays there are only seven small sugar works left, and the other planters sell their cane to central factories.

The latter number four, namely :—

Lower Love	..	Working 600 tons of cane daily.			
Bethlehem	..	,,	500	,,	,,	,,
Central ..	..	,,	600	,,	,,	,,
La Grange	..	,,	250	,,	,,	,,

In 1908 the cane suffered much from a period of intense drought, and the crop was a failure; but 1910 yielded an improved crop.

The sugar factories do not, as a rule, make much profit; only during the last few years, while sugar prices have been high, has the cultivation paid.

243

North America.

The sugar, chiefly raw vacuum pan sugar, basis 96, is sent to the United States and to Great Britain. The production has been for the past sixteen years, in long tons, as follows :—

1895/96	..	..	..	..	.. 8,000
1896/97	..	..	..	..	.. 13,000
1897/98	..	..	..	..	.. 13,000
1898/99	..	..	..	..	.. 12,000
1899/00	..	..	..	..	.. 12,000
1900/01	..	..	..	..	.. 13,000
1901/02	..	..	..	..	.. 13,000
1902/03	..	..	..	..	.. 13,000
1903/04	..	..	..	..	.. 13,000
1904/05	..	..	..	..	.. 11,000
1905/06	..	..	..	..	.. 13,000
1906/07	..	..	..	..	.. 13,000
1907/08	..	..	..	..	.. 13,000
1908/09	..	..	..	..	.. 14,000
1909/10	..	..	..	..	.. 15,000
1910/11	..	..	..	..	.. 13,000

Central America.

GUATEMALA.

The Guatemala Republic lies in Central America, at 30° 42' to 17° 49' N. Lat. and 88° 10' to 92° 30' W. Long.   Its area amounts to 48,600 sq. miles, and its population numbers 1,991,261 inhabitants.

In Guatemala about 6,000 acres are planted with cane, half of which belong to large estates that go in for the preparation of centrifugal sugar, while the other half is taken up by smaller concerns that produce panela or dolce (evaporated cane juice).

Of the latter there are about 40, and of the former 11, all of which are situated in the district Guatemala.   The principal of these, Pantaleon, produced 2,000 tons of sugar in 1908-09, while Concepcion had an output of 1,500 and Chocola of 1,000 tons; the others are still smaller, and the smallest, Torolita, did not produce more than 100 tons of sugar and 50 tons of molasses that very year.   The total production of the big sugar factories was for :—

1901/02	..	9,618 tons sugar and	1,964 tons molasses		
1902/03	..	8,524 ,,	,,	,, 1,901	,,	,,
1903/04	..	7,640 ,,	,,	,, 1,824	,,	,,
1904/05	..	7,502 ,,	,,	,, 1,600	,,	,,
1905/06		6,795 ,,	,,	., 2,256	,,	,,
1906/07	..	7,412 ,,	,,	,, 2,513	,,	,,
1907/08	..	7,521 ,,	,,	,, 2,616	,,	,,
1908/09	..	7,260 ,,	,,	., 2,835	,,	,,
1909/10	..	7,110 ,,	,,	,, 2,715	,,	,,
1910/11	..	7,110 ,,	,,	,, 2,715	,,	,,

The production, as shown by the above table, keeps fairly stationary.

Besides this quantity of centrifugal sugar, an equal amount of brown sugar (" panela ") is being produced, so that the entire crop amounts to some 15,000 tons of sugar.

The yearly consumption accounts for about 11,500 tons ; and the balance of 2,500 tons, or about one-fifth of the total production, is exported.   The last few exportation figures have been :—

1907	..	..	..	..	..	2,117 tons
1908	..	..	..	..	..	2,771 ,,
1909	..	..	..	..	..	2,278 ,,
1910	..	..	..	..	..	2,232 ,,

Both centrifugal sugar and "panela" are exported; the "panela" exported to England amounted to 1,472 tons in 1907, and to 690 tons in 1908. It is used for brewing stout.

Up to 1st October, 1910, an import duty of 0·23 pesos per kg. sugar was raised; but since then it has been free from duty when imported.

II.

SALVADOR.

The Salvador Republic is the smallest of all the Central American States. Its area only covers 8,150 sq. miles, but, on the other hand, it has the densest population among the countries forming the American Continent—1,707,000 inhabitants, or 209 per sq. mile.

Two mountain chains with numerous branches, which sometimes attain to considerable height, cross the country for almost its entire length.

Nearly everywhere in Salvador there are cane plantations yielding the native brown sugar called "panela." There is also a number of sugar factories where crystallized sugar is prepared; this is partly consumed in the country itself, and partly exported to other countries.

The total production has been during the last few years as follows, expressed in metric tons. The number of factories is included in the table :—

Year.	Number of Factories.	Sugar.	Molasses.	"Panela."
1901/02 ..	6	6,086	1,369	12,000
1902/03 ..	6	6,604	1,875	11,000
1903/04 ..	7	6,300	2,070	10,000
1904/05 ..	6	5,588	1,540	10,000
1905/06 ..	6	5,994	1,238	10,000
1906/07 ..	6	6,048	1,118	10,000
1907/08 ..	6	5,490	1,098	10,000
1908/09 ..	6	6,242	1,248	10,000
1909/10 ..	6	6,356	1,248	10,000
1910/11 ..	6	7,380	2,373	10,000

III.

HONDURAS.

The Honduras Republic extends from 13° 10' to 16° N. Lat. and from 83° 20' to 89° 30' W. Long. Its greatest length is about 400 miles, and its greatest breadth 186 miles. Its total area amounts to about 46,250 sq. miles, and its population numbers about 745,000 inhabitants.

Sugar cane is cultivated all over the country, as it grows well in the uplands and on the mountain slopes to a height of 10,000 to 13,000 ft. It is worked in a number of small factories scattered all over the country, in which the mills are driven by oxen, a kind of raw sugar, or rather evaporated cane juice, being prepared. We cannot light upon any exact figures representing the amount of sugar produced, but approximately the yearly sugar production is estimated at 1,500 tons of raw.

The cane-planted area is supposed to be 12,500 acres. The import duty on sugar is 5 centavos per half kilo, or 8s. 4d. per cwt.

IV.

BRITISH HONDURAS.

British Honduras lies in the Caribbean Sea, at 18° 29' to 15° 54' N. Lat., and 88° 10' to 89° 9' W. Long. Its greatest length is 174 miles, and its greatest width 68 miles, while its area covers 8,598 sq. miles. Its population numbers about 40,500 people.

In spite of many an effort to promote its sugar industry, the latter has never come to anything much, most probably owing to lack of labour. In 1909 there were 49 sugar factories working, two of which used oil motors, 11 worked with steam, while 36 were driven by cattle. One factory prepares white sugar, another brown sugar, while sometimes molasses is worked up into alcohol. The sugar production from 1894 to 1910 was as follows :—

1894	..	.. 586 tons	1902	..	.. 792 tons
1895	..	.. 633 ,,	1903	..	.. 504 ,,
1896	..	.. 687 ,,	1904	..	.. 519 ,,
1897	..	.. 312 ,,	1905	..	.. 570 ,,
1898	..	.. 606 ,,	1906	..	.. 630 ,,
1899	..	.. 215 ,,	1907	..	.. 616 ,,
1900	..	.. 484 ,,	1908	..	.. 605 ,,
1901	..	.. 633 ,,	1909	..	.. 410 ,,
			1910	..	.. 400 ,,

The import duties amount to 3 cents per pound of refined sugar, and 1½ cents per pound of raw

V.

NICARAGUA.

The Nicaragua Republic lies in Central America, between 10° 45′ and 15° 6′ N. Lat. and 83° 10′ and 87° 35′ W. Long. It has an area of 47,880 sq. miles, and a population of 430,000 people.

In all the western districts of the country sugar cane is planted, especially in the Chinandega and Leon districts, which contain the biggest factories. No sugar undertakings are found on the Atlantic coast.

The area of the plantations expressed in hectares is as follows :—

					1906/07.	1907/08.
Chinandega	..	..	..	..	1,282	1,707
Leon	..	..	..	..	585	791
Other districts	..	..	..	..	2,533	2,379
Total .. { Hectares					4,400	4,877
{ Acres					10,870	12,500

Owing to the high sugar prices in San Francisco, where part of the Nicaragua sugar is sent, more cane was planted in 1907 than ever had been grown before, but as soon as the prices dropped the planted area decreased in extent.

It soon appeared that it was of little profit to ship to the United States, so this exportation did not continue long. Cane, as a rule, is reaped ten to fourteen months after it has been planted, which generally is done during the dry months, December to the end of April. In the crop year, 1907/08, there were 1,203 small sugar plantations in Nicaragua, each of them having a small mill of its own, besides five big factories : 964 of the smaller factories worked with wooden mills, 1,184 were driven by cattle, 14 by steam, and 5 by water. About one-third of the smaller factories are found in the north and the sequestered departments Nueva Segovia and Matagalpa, where about one-tenth of the entire cane cultivation is planted. The smaller factories, or " trapiches," make only brown sugar (" dolce " or " panela ") : this is " concrete " sugar, or evaporated cane juice, and is also consumed at home.

The large factories all belong to the Nicaraguans ; they are well-installed, and prepare a kind of crystallized sugar, which is destined both for refining purposes and for direct consumption.

The crushing season generally lasts 100 days. In Chinandega a yield of 40 Spanish hundredweights (of 101 lbs.) of sugar is expected from each manzana (1·7 acres), that is 2,340 lbs. per acre. All the important sugar works lie near the railway, which conveys the sugar to Corinto harbour. The molasses is sold to the brandy distillers, who have cane plantations of their own. In Nicaragua brandy distilling is a Government monopoly; the Government have, however, leased the distilling business and the trade in spirits to a company. All the alcohol produced in Nicaragua has to be sold to that company, which places the product on the market. The total sugar production is about 5,000 tons of refined and 1,500 tons of raw sugar, or " dolce " ; some of it is exported to the neighbouring republics, but this trade is of little importance and amounted to but 600 tons in 1899 and to 180 tons in 1901, to 300 tons in 1903 and to 206 tons in 1905. The wages paid are low: a field labourer, for instance, earns 2½ pesos paper (1 peso = 6d.) for a seven-hours' day ; a factory labourer earns 3 pesos for 12 hours' work daily, and so on. But there is a lack of labour, and the production is not likely to exceed the consumption for some time to come, remaining 6,000 to 7,000 tons a year.

During the last few years the total production has been as follows :—

1902/03	..	..	..	4,640 tons
1903/04	..	.	.	4,235 ,,
1904/05	..	..	.	4,235 ,,
1905/06	..	..	..	4,400 ,,
1906/07	..	..	..	3,905 ,,
1907/08	..	..	..	4,175 ,,
1908/09	..	..	..	3,950 ,,
1909/10	..	. .		3,450 ,,
1910/11	..	..	..	3,450 ,,

All this is centrifugal sugar ; for the rest, the country produces yearly on an average 700 to 800 tons of evaporated cane juice (" panela " or concrete sugar) and 1,200 tons of molasses, which is worked up into alcohol.

====

VI.

COSTA RICA.

Costa Rica lies in Central America, between Panama and Nicaragua, between 81° 40' and 85° 40' W. Long. and 8° and 11° 16' N. Lat. Its area amounts to 23,000 sq. miles, and in 1909 its population was 368,780 people, most of whom are Creoles ; there are some thousands of Indians, a few negroes, and 6,000 foreigners. The population is densest in the highlands of San José and Carthago, and in the valley of the Rio Grande. It is in the first-mentioned plateau that the capital, San José, with its 25,000 inhabitants, is situated.

Central America.

The cane planted area was for :—

1905	..	..	..	..	25,900 acres
1906	..	..	..	..	27,670 ,,
1907	..	..	..	..	27,950 ,,

Two-thirds of the planted area is in San José and Alajuela, consequently in the hills, and the remaining one-third is on the Pacific coast. In the latter plain the cane is reaped 1½ years after it has been planted, but it takes two years on the plateau before the cane has sufficiently ripened.

Costa Rica has a great many small factories in which raw brown sugar, or rather concentrated cane juice, is manufactured ; then there is also a number of larger factories preparing crystallized sugar. The figures of these two categories were as follows up to two years ago :—

Year.	Small factories.	Metric tons sugar per day.	Large factories.	Metric tons sugar per day.
1904	770	130	4	4
1905	1,660	307	16	23
1906	1,769	264	16	25
1907	1,711	230	15	27

In 1909, 13 of the 15 large factories worked and produced in all 2,466 tons of sugar ; the biggest of these turned out 407, and the smallest only 10 tons. Some 2,000 tons out of the 2,466 consisted of brown sugar, or " dolce," while the balance was composed of white sugar.

The molasses, like part of the brown sugar, is worked up into brandy in the Government factories, and over and above the entire quantity of molasses the following amounts of brown sugar were sold :—

1905	..	..	..	..	1,591 tons
1906	..	..	..	..	1,047 ,,
1907	..	..	..	..	955 ,,

But not all the sugar was fermented, for when sugar went up in price and became scarce in the country, the administration sold 218 tons of sugar in 1907, and imported alcohol from Cuba for the inland market. The sudden increase of sugar factories after 1904 is due to the law of 18th August of that same year, according to which an import duty of 0·02 colon (colon = 2s.) is raised per kg. of white sugar, and 0·03 colon per kg. of brown sugar.

The price of white sugar, which used to be 10 colons for a Spanish hundred-weight of 101 lbs., has gone up to 18, and the price of brown sugar has increased from 4 to 10 or 12 colons, and as the difference in price between these two kinds of sugar is only very slight, the consumption of white sugar has increased. In spite of high protecting duties, the cane-planted area does not extend: first of all, because they cannot be sure of these duties remaining in force which makes it a great risk putting money in this sugar industry; and, secondly, because the roads are bad and impassable in the rainy season, and make the transportation of cane and sugar very difficult. Finally, there is no capital to be found in the country itself, and foreign capitalists are loath to risk money in Central American undertakings; besides, the inhabitants lack a spirit of enterprise, and wages are excessively high, *i.e.*, 1·80 colons for a field labourer working ten hours daily, which exceeds the wages in the neighbouring country of Nicaragua. The production of all kinds of sugar, taken together, does not exceed 4,000 tons, and any change for the better is not likely. The sugar produced is not sufficient to supply the wants of the country, so that small quantities of sugar have now and then to be imported from neighbouring states.

1901/02	..	..	.. 3,912	tons of sugar
1902/03	..	..	.. 3,856	,, ,,
1903/04	..	..	.. 3,275	,, ,,
1904/05	..	..	.. 2,306	,, ,,
1905/06	..	..	.. 1,377	,, ,,
1906/07	..	..	.. 2,365	,, ,,
1907/08	..	..	.. 2,415	,, ,,
1908/09	..	..	.. 2,466	,, ,,
1909/10	..	..	.. 2,245	,, ,,
1910/11	..	..	.. 2,275	,, ,,

together with, on an average, 1,500 tons of molasses.

In 1910 a decree was issued, according to which all sugar for twenty years to come was to be exempted from duty when imported into Costa Rica; this exemption included harbour dues as well.

<hr>

VII.

PANAMA.

The Panama Republic, which lies between Costa Rica and Colombia, covers an area of 31,650 sq. miles, and has a population of 361,000 people. A great amount of sugar cane is already being planted to serve in the preparation of brown sugar or to be used as a dainty, and the Government has begun to start large sugar undertakings for the sake of supplying what sugar is wanted in the country itself, for up to now there has been considerable importation of sugar from Peru, Salvador, and Costa Rica. A contract has been drawn up with an American for the purpose of establishing a small sugar factory on Government property, while plans for the installation of a second factory in the capital, Panama, are under consideration. This concession involves the disposal of large tracts of land, exemption from import duties on necessary machinery and material, exemption from Government and municipal taxes on produced sugar, while $2·50 has to be paid per 100 lbs. when imported from abroad.

With so much protection the sugar industry in Panama cannot fail to become successful, as the soil is fertile and the climate is favourable for cane cultivation. So it will not be long before Panama is able to supply its own want of sugar, and to dispense with all foreign importation.

South America.

I.

COLOMBIA.

The Republic of Colombia lies between 12° 35' N. Lat. and 2° 40' S. Lat., and between 68° and 79° W. Long. on the Pacific Ocean and the Caribbean Sea. It has an area of 488,500 sq. miles, and its population only numbers four millions.

Several small sugar mills are found all over the country for the purpose of crushing cane. The juice is either consumed as it is, or is worked up to brown sugar, which latter occasionally is purified to white sugar by "claying." The brown sugar (" panela ") is chiefly consumed by the lower classes, at such a low price that it is an impossibility for foreign sugar to compete with it. We cannot say for certain what the total production is, as the sugar is manufactured in so many small factories. A big factory, however, has been built in Sincerin, near Carthagena, which works up the cane grown on 1,850 acres, and is said to have produced in 1909 6⅓ tons per acre, or 16,000 kg. sugar per hectare. It, however, seems to us an exaggeration to credit Colombia with any such production. But as soon as transportation facilities allow of it more sugar factories will spring up. Colombia at the present time does not produce enough sugar to supply her own wants ; the gap is filled by a small importation of refined sugar from Germany.

II.

VENEZUELA.

The Republic of the United States of Venezuela is situated on the north coast of South America, between 1° 40' S. Lat. and 12° 26' N. Lat., and 57° 2' and 73° 29' W. Long. Its area is 450,000 sq. miles ; the greatest distance from north to south is 770 miles, and that from east to west 1,037 miles.

According to the most recent census, Venezuela had a population of 2,633,671 inhabitants, or about 6 to the sq. mile.

Venezuela is a very mountainous country, and contains three important mountain chains. The first is a spur of the Andes, which breaks off into two ridges. The first of these runs from Pamplona in a northern direction to Ocana and gradually slopes down, while the other, running in a north-easterly direction,

253

forms a chain of high mountains, which have summits covered with eternal snow in spite of the tropical climate. The second mountain range runs parallel to the Caribbean Sea from east to west ; while the third range covers the entire territory of Venezuelan Guiana, and forms a convex tableland of wide area. Owing to the considerable difference in altitude above the sea level, the climate in Venezuela varies for the different parts, and this makes it possible to divide the country in three belts. The highest summits of the Merida mountain chain are 18,000 ft. above sea level ; there, where the thermometer on an average registers 2° to 3° above zero, vegetation ceases to exist, and just above is the eternal snow. Between 2,000 and 7,000 ft. above the level of the sea is the eternal temperate zone, with a temperature varying between 18° and 20° C. It is here that the agricultural districts are found and most agricultural crops are grown. In the still lower regions from the sea level up to 2,000 feet, the climate is tropical, and the temperature fluctuates between 25 and 33° C. (77—92° F.)

In Venezuela there are, properly speaking, only two seasons—a dry and a wet one. The first commences as soon as the sun enters the tropic of Capricorn, and the second begins when it enters the tropic of Cancer ; so that the rainy season is from April to October, when the temperature is highest. During the dry season the temperature is cool and pleasant.

At Caracas the average yearly temperature is 66·2° F. ; the highest maximum temperature was 84·2° F. (29° C.), and the lowest minimum 48·2° F. (9° C.) during the years 1891 to 1902. The rainfall for these years according to the Cajigal Observatory at Caracas amounted to the following quantities, in millimetres :—

Year.	January.	February.	March.	April.	May.	June.	July.	August.	September.	October.	November.	December.	Total.
1891	18·7	4	16·1	48·6	154·2	45·3	165	69·3	96·6	112·1	82·3	42·8	755
1892	33·2	33	36·9	95·9	185·5	159·9	194·3	122·9	95·7	138	88·6	19	1,202·9
1893	4	8·6	0·7	29·3	136·7	71·2	213·2	43	146	151·8	79·4	92·3	976·2
1894	23·6	15·5	5·1	0	42·3	30·6	60·9	127·8	99·3	64·8	78·9	53·2	602
1895	60·9	3·6	13·7	17·7	45	136·8	56	65·4	93·9	117·3	134	40·1	784·4
1896	13·2	0·2	4·8	115·3	110	118·4	36·6	69·8	33·2	64·5	128	54·2	748·2
1897	40·7	3·8	0	5·4	79	99·1	126·1	92·4	38·6	139·2	80·3	78·2	782·8
1898	15·9	0	68·3	17·7	23·9	78·8	107·2	150·9	103·3	79·4	105·2	12·3	762·9
1899	15·5	4·4	2·1	0	0	116	63·5	88·5	101·3	113·9	58·8	47·7	611·7
1900	22·2	4·7	49·6	19·7	14·4	88·3	185·2	140·5	38·1	141·3	109·5	0	863·5
1901	16·4	0·4	1·1	0·9	38·6	76·9	186·9	118·2	75·4	141·4	129·1	38	823·3
1902	61·6	0	0	15·3	84·4	124·9	94·7	75·4	178	52·5	27	68·3	782·1

Venezuela.

Sugar cane grows in all parts of Venezuela, with the exception of the mountainous regions, as irrigation cannot be obtained there. Both climate and soil are well fit for cane cultivation, and where irrigation can be applied success is certain.

Four different kinds are planted: the Criolla or native cane, the Otaite or Otaheite, the Batavia, and the Salangore. The first kind contains the highest sugar content, and is used most for sugar manufacture; while Batavia cane is generally used for the production of rum. Planting and reaping of cane are done in such a way that grinding is possible all the year through, and consequently any definite crushing season is not necessary, as with most cane sugar producing countries. The cane cultivation is seldom carried on by the owners of the land themselves. The ground is mostly divided among " medianeros," who plant and look after the cane and cut it when ripe, after which they take it to the mill. Half of the profit goes to the landowner, the other half to the planter. The " medianeros " can plant beans, maize, or wheat on their soil in the time between two cane crops, which products they can consider their own. Still, as a rule, they keep their ground constantly planted with sugar cane, with as little rotation of crops as possible.

The plantation producing the largest quantity of crystal sugar is situated in the State of Zulia, close to Maracaibo, and not far from the large lake of the same name; the sugar which is produced in that place is delivered as white sugar, and sold in packets of half a pound, which are sent all over the country in chests of 100 Spanish pounds (101 lbs. avoird.). Other large factories producing white sugar lie close to La Guira, and near Guatire in the State of Miranda.

For the rest, much brown sugar ("papelon") is manufactured; this, again, is the same concentrated cane juice we have come across under various names in Central-and South American countries. The most important plantation for this article is near the capital, Caracas; its production is 400 to 475 tons yearly. Then there is another factory close to the first-mentioned, but in the province of Libertador, while a great many smaller factories are spread all over the country. The form in which the sugar appears varies for the different parts of the country. In this Federal district, and in the States of Miranda and Aragua, sugar is sold in cylindrical lumps of $3\frac{1}{2}$ lbs.; in the State Carabobo it is sold in the same shape, but the pieces weigh only $1\frac{1}{2}$ lbs.; while in the States Merida, Trujillo, Tachira, Zulia, Falcon, and Lara the sugar is delivered in squares of $3\frac{1}{4}$ lbs.

Finally, much alcohol is distilled from cane; the best district for it is in the neighbourhood of Caracas, where a factory is capable of turning out more than one million bottles of brandy in addition to 300 tons of brown sugar.

The sugar production of Venezuela slightly exceeds its sugar consumption, so that it allows of some being exported. The sugar manufacturers have agreed to set aside 20 per cent. of their produce for export in order to prevent a surplus in the country itself, and by so doing to keep the price of sugar up. In consequence of this, February, 1910, saw 500 tons of crystal sugar find its way to the London market, while two or three hundred tons of "panela" were exported to Germany and Holland. In 1909–11 the exportation of papelon amounted to 2,255 tons.

Venezuela raises an import duty of 0·25 bolivar* per 101 lbs. avoird. of muscovado or raw sugar, burnt or granulated sugar for beer manufacture, and an import duty of 0·75 bolivar on white or refined sugar, while the importation of molasses and honey is prohibited.

Since 1910 an export bounty has been granted on sugar when exported in larger quantities than 100 Spanish hundredweights (of 101 lbs.) ; this bounty was started at 0·50 bolivar per 100 lbs., but is to decrease 20 per cent. each year, so that in 1915 it will have disappeared altogether.

In spite of this export bounty, and the agreement between the manufacturers to divert a certain part of their product for export, Venezuela is not likely soon to belong to the leading sugar exporting countries.

Literature :
Handbook of Venezuela.

III.

BRITISH GUIANA.

British Guiana lies on the north-east coast of South America, between 1° and 9° N. Lat. and 57° and 62° W. Long. ; it has an area of 90,500 sq. miles, and a population of only 296,041, or about 3 per sq. mile should the population be spread over the whole area. But this would not be a fair comparison, as, apart from the comparatively small gold area, only the coast and the country along the rivers are inhabited.

In the interior there are numerous mountain chains, and among them extensive savannahs or grassy plains and thick woods. Roraima is the highest mountain peak ; it is 8,740 ft. above sea level, and its summit is difficult of access owing to its peculiar formation. The sea-coast is marshy, and consists of mud and clay, which is carried by the Amazon from the Brazilian interior and deposited in the sea. The width of this alluvial ground varies greatly, being widest near Berbice. The clay is sometimes many feet deep, and in some places there are reefs of sand, lime, and shell. These reefs, sometimes forming a regular series of dunes, generally run parallel to the coastline.

The principal rivers of British Guiana are the Essequibo, the Demerara, the Berbice, and the Corentyne, the latter forming the boundary between British and Dutch Guiana. The Essequibo rises in the Acarai mountains, not far from the Equator, and traverses about 620 miles, including the bends.

* Bolivar = 10d.

British Guiana.

It has a great many tributaries, and it widens in the flat lowland so considerably that it forms a stream 18 miles broad, with numerous islands, some of which are 12 to 15 miles in length. Rapids in its upper course cause the river to be navigable only up to 50 miles from its mouth. The much smaller Demerara River, the source of which is not yet known, is navigable up to 75 miles from its mouth; this river, too, widens in the low reaches, and at its junction with the sea has a width of 1¼ miles. The Berbice is navigable for small craft up to 186 miles above its mouth, and on reaching the sea it has a width of 2½ miles; while the Corentyne—which, like the Essequibo, has its source near the Equator and forms numerous big cascades—is navigable for more than 150 miles, and has a width of 10 miles when entering the sea. In consequence of its flat and low coast, British Guiana has no natural harbours, but the very broad estuaries form excellent anchorages for fairly big ships. The climate is warm and moist, and very even, without sudden changes to cold or hot weather. There is only one rainy and one dry season in the interior—that is from the end of April to the middle of August, but near the coast, where the sugar estates are located, two wet and two dry seasons are experienced. The chief rainy season begins about the middle of April and lasts till August— the winds are westerly during that time; this period is followed by a lengthy dry period up to November, when the short rainy season begins and lasts till the end of January, after which the short dry period prevails till April. During the dry season the wind is always from the sea. Hurricanes do not occur in Guiana, and even the equinoctial gales are not violent, and cause very little damage.

The average annual temperature in Georgetown amounts to 80° F. (26·7° C.); it seldom exceeds 89·6° F. (32° C.) or is lower than 75° F. (24° C.). The average rainfall is about 90 ins. yearly.

The principal towns are Georgetown, on the Demerara, with 49,000 inhabitants, and New Amsterdam, on the Berbice, with a population of 7,500; while, besides, there are a few unimportant villages. A railway runs from Georgetown to Rossignol in an eastern direction, and westwards from Georgetown to Greenwich Park, for some 75 miles in all. The first journey takes 3½ hours, the second only 45 mins.

Some 125,000 acres of the entire area of this colony are used for cultivation, 39,000 of which are planted with sugar cane.

Columbus, in 1498, caught sight of Guiana from the sea, but Alonso de Ojeda was the first actually to visit it in 1499; while Pinzon, in 1500, went up some of the rivers. When trying to find the wonderland " Eldorado," which was supposed to exist in those regions, Sir Walter Raleigh came to Guiana in 1595, and met with his death afterwards in that place. Some years previously Dutch pirates had settled on the banks of the Essequibo river; they were driven away by the Spanish and Indians in 1596; the Dutchmen, however, came back to the same spot, and in 1613 built a fortress called " Kijk over Al " on a little island at the mouth of that same river. The colony Essequibo joined the Dutch West Indian Company as soon as this was founded, and was under its management up to its dissolution in 1791.

In 1624 Abraham van Peere founded a colony on the Berbice river, which, in 1732, came under the protection of the States-General of the United Provinces. Demerara used to be a subdivision of Essequibo, but in 1765 it got a Governor of its own, and through the immigration of colonists from the British West Indian Islands it increased in importance till this colony gradually became the leading one of the three.

In 1781 the three colonies were conquered by British freebooters, who handed them over to an expedition sent out by the Governor of Barbados. Later on the country was returned to its former owners, only to be reconquered, whereupon, in 1815, it became a British possession for good and all.

For some time the colonies were under separate managements, but in 1831 Berbice, Demerara, and Essequibo were united into one colony, called British Guiana, while their own names only survived as the names of counties of which the new colony consisted. The population, which at the time of the union, in 1831, had amounted to 98,000 people, has increased in course of time, as will be shown by the following table :—

1841	..	..	98,154	1881	..	..	252,186
1851	..	..	135,994	1891	..	..	278,328
1861	..	..	155,907	1904	..	..	301,923
1871	..	..	193,491	1911	..	..	296,041

The considerable increase is due to British Indian indentured labourers ; the number of British East Indians amounted to 21,045 in 1861, to 32,681 in 1871, to 65,161 in 1881, and to 122,824 in 1891.

During the Dutch occupation the colonies of Essequibo and Berbice, and later on Demerara, produced rather considerable quantities of sugar, which came from the drained swamps along the sea coast and along the banks of the rivers ; that is why a great many of the existing sugar plantations still have Dutch names, these dating from the time preceding the British occupation.

Since the Otaheite or Bourbon cane was introduced, in 1795, into this colony, the sugar industry had first a prosperous time, then remained almost stationary, to enter gradually upon a period of greater importance, which, however, had its fluctuations.

Like the West Indian Islands, Demerara also suffered from the consequences of the abolition of slavery ; but as the introduction of British Indian coolies proved to be a great success, the lack of labour has never been felt so keenly here as it was in many of the neighbouring islands.

In 1808 the trade in African slaves was prohibited, notwithstanding which slaves did enter the country. When, in 1817, a census was taken for the first time, the slaves numbered 101,712, but gradually their number decreased, and in 1834 it only amounted to 82,824, which was the number coming in for compensation. After the abolition, they tried to get free labourers from the neighbouring West Indian Islands and from Madeira. In this latter island much harm was caused to the cultivation of the vine by disease, and many people who had lost their means of livelihood in that way emigrated to British Guiana, where they settled. In 1840 the British Government allowed the importation of free African immigrants from the British possessions in Africa ; moreover, the number of immigrants was swelled by negroes imported from Africa, by Brazilians, Cubans, and other slave traders, who were captured by British men-of-war, which set the slaves free. In the years 1840 to 1865 this number amounted to no less than 13,355 emancipated blacks, who arrived in British Guiana and worked there as free labourers.

When Brazil, as well as other countries, also abolished slavery, the slave-trade and the setting free of slaves came to an end, and this supply of labour ceased to exist. In 1867 even the importation of free black people from the British African possessions was forbidden. In 1853 two shiploads of Chinese immigrants landed, and since 1859 Chinese labourers were systematically supplied up to 1866, when the Chinese Government wished the immigrants to be sent back to the mother-country at the end of this indenture at the expense of the colony. But as it was not the aim of the immigration to send the people back again, the immigration of Chinese labour soon came to an end. Later on it was agreed that the immigrants should receive a sum of $50 at the end of their five years' service, which would enable them to pay their own passage if they wished to go back to China. This stipulation brought new immigrants : in 1874 388 left China, in 1878 another 515 came, but since then this source of labour has ceased. The immigration of British Indians proved a far greater success ; once they gave it a trial in 1838, these immigrants have come regularly to the country from 1845 down to the present date. They are indentured for five years, and only at the end of the five years following the expiration of their contract are they entitled to a journey home free of charge. During these extra five years, and even after, they can work as free labourers, while they can easily become owners of small plots of land. Of this last opportunity a great many Indians have availed themselves, so that the number of Indian settlers in British Guiana increases yearly. From the very beginning of this immigration up to now 225,231 British Indians have been sent to British Guiana as indentured coolies, 57,554 of whom have gone back to their country. Then there are also a great many Indians who after a short stay in India come back to Demerara at their expense as free labourers ; but these, of course, are not mentioned in the statistical lists. In 1908 there were 12,539 indentured British Indian coolies and 58,388 free labourers, or 70,927 in all, including men, women, and children.

By far the greater part of the sugar plantations lies along the sea shore, all of them in drained marshes which are protected by massive dykes, and are drained into the sea either by pumping out with steam pumps or by sluices. The plantations on the banks of the rivers are also " empoldered " and drained through sluices into the rivers. On March 31st, 1911, the entire amount of drained marshes of the colony was 160,000 acres, no less than 81,000 acres of which were used for cane cultivation. The sugar plantations are of oblong shape lying side by side, having one of the short sides facing the sea or the river. They originally had each an area of 500 to 1,000 acres, but many have now been amalgamated. A massive dyke is built at the front facing either river or sea, while the dykes at the side and at the back are, as a rule, much less elaborate. A broad main road generally runs in the middle of the plantation, having a navigation canal on either side. This canal contains fresh water, sea-water being carefully kept out by a sluice, which can be opened at the time of ebb in order to carry off any surplus of fresh water, and can be closed in times of flood. In addition, there are short feeding canals running at right angles to these. They, however, are not put in communication with the drainage canals, so they can, if need be, contain salt water. When a drainage canal passes a navigation canal, it is conducted underneath by means of a syphon. The cane fields lie between these navigation canals, and are separated by smaller drainage canals; their size, as a rule, varies between 10 and 20 acres. The canals in British Guiana are generally of the following dimensions: the larger navigation canals have a width of 16 to 20 ft. at the top, and 12 to 16 ft. at the bottom, and a depth of 4 to 5 ft. The smaller navigation canals have a width of 12 ft. above and of 9 ft. below, and are from 4 to 5 ft. deep. The larger drainage canals are 15 ft. wide at the top and 4 ft. deep. The dimensions of the lesser irrigation canals are: 2 to 3 ft. wide at the top, $1\frac{1}{2}$ to 2 ft. at the bottom, and 3 ft. deep. In the fields the beds are between 24 and 36 ft., and the furrows running across them are at 6 to 7 ft. distance from centre to centre.

To prepare new land for cane cultivation, the trees are cut down, the grass and weeds are removed, canals and furrows are dug, and the cane tops are planted. Weeding is carried out after a month's interval, and in case of a sufficient rainfall the cane will have grown high enough by that time to prevent any further growth of weeds, so that further weeding will no longer be necessary. Then the young cane is banked, and the soil between the furrows is loosened by means of forks, in order to leave space and air to the cane plants and to promote their root development. Five months after planting, the cane is trashed and the weeds are removed, if necessary; the whole proceeding being repeated three months later. When the cane is about one year old it is trashed for the last time, and is reaped a fortnight later. Once it is cut the soil is again loosened with forks, the dry leaves are put underground in the spaces between the rows, and the cane plants bud out afresh, to be cut again after a year's time. In British Guiana ratoons are kept two or three years on the same land; as soon as the crop gets too scanty, however, the plot of land is left fallow, and another plot is chosen. Up to a short time ago it was only Bourbon cane that was planted in British Guiana; but recently they have been planting a great many seedling cane varieties, of which the D. 625,

British Guiana.

D. 145, D. 100, and D. 208 are the principal. One may state for certain that more than half of the present-day plantations consist of the progeny of seedling canes. Basic slag and superphosphate, guano, potash manures, and sulphate of ammonia are mostly used as manure, together with all disposable stable dung from the cattle.

The cane is exclusively transported by water, along the navigation canals in flat-bottomed punts. The factories are, on the whole, well-fitted out, all having powerful mills, and using vacuum pans. Besides the ordinary raw sugar polarizing 96° and second sugar, a kind of coarse-grained yellow-coloured raw sugar, the so-called " Demerara crystals," is also manufactured. The colour is produced by working with acid juice throughout ; chloride of tin being added in the vacuum pan to preserve the yellow tint. From 1 to 5 per cent. is lost by inversion. The bulk of the molasses is converted into rum, while a considerable proportion is mixed with dry fine bagasse, and is sent to the United Kingdom under the name of " molascuit," as a patent dry cattle fodder containing sugar.

When the ground is virgin soil, fresh plantations yield in Demerara at their best 60 to 70 tons of cane per acre (150,000 to 160,000 kg. per hectare), but the average crop is much less, and will just attain to 20 tons per acre (or 50,000 kg. per hectare), while the yield of sugar does not exceed $8\frac{1}{2}$ per cent. on 100 cane.

The number of sugar factories has decreased considerably of late, a fact chiefly due to the amalgamation of many small ones into a few large enterprises. A large number of estates were abandoned on account of the emancipation of slavery, chiefly on account of the heavy expenses involved in reclaiming and digging.

In 1891 the cane-planted area covered 78,777 acres, in 1895 it was only 68,000, and in 1908 it covered 73,471 acres occupied by plantations, and 2,500 acres by cane farmers. The number of sugar plantations amounted to 64 in 1895, but has since gone down to 42. According to their size they are and have been divided as follows :—

			1895		1908
More than 7,000 acres	..	..	—	..	1
,, ,, 3,000 ,,	..	..	—	..	4
,, ,, 2,000 ,,	..	..	4	..	6
,, ,, 1,000 ,,	..	..	23	..	25
Less than 1,000 ,,	..	..	37	..	6
			—	..	—
			64	..	42
			—		—

South America.

The yield of sugar has been since 1826 as follows, in long tons :—

1826	43,378	1869		66,598
1827	62,272	1870		75,075
1828	55,752	1871		92,178
1829	58,586	1872		77,094
1830	59,790	1873		83,391
1831	58,058	1874		86,578
1832	54,962	1875		82,195
1833	54,588	1876		104,667
1834	47,155	1877		97,261
1835	57,577	1878		75,316
1836	48,999	1879		92,436
1837	54,666	1880		95,370
1838	47,983	1881		89,844
1839	33,680	1882		120,654
1840	35,619	1883		113,396
1841	29,925	1884		121,840
1842	31,685	1885		93,390
1843	32,271	1886		108,748
1844	34,125	1887		131,127
1845	34,681	1888		105,118
1846	22,935	1889		112,376
1847	41,307	1890		102,553
1848	40,784	1891		113,719
1849	29,672	1892/93		112,880
1850	32,692	1893/94		107,771
1851	37,655	1894/95		102,502
1852	48,737	1895/96		101,059
1853	38,802	1896/97		107,073
1854	48,632	1897/98		100,839
1855	48,447	1898/99		96,648
1856	45,156	1899/00		84,783
1857	51,420	1900/01		94,745
1858	51,552	1901/02		105,694
1859	48,072	1902/03		120,127
1860	54,423	1903/04		125,949
1861	63,305	1904/05		106,716
1862	56,875	1905/06		125,217
1863	67,462	1906/07		120,334
1864	64,248	1907/08		99,730
1865	75,356	1908/09		117,176
1866	80,132	1909/10		115,842
1867	72,385	1910/11		100,954
1868	78,776	1911/12 (estimate)		86,000

What has been said about sugar in the West Indian Islands also holds good for Demerara sugar; part of that sugar is sent to Great Britain and part to Canada, while the rest is exported to the United States.

The quantities have been as follows during the last seven years :—

	1905.	1906.	1907.	1908.	1909.	1910.	1911.
United Kingdom ...	19,311	16,411	23,921	23,921	29,505	29,191	12,103
United States... ...	28,608	40,454	5,372	17,856	13,726	20,263	27,099
Canada	65,328	62,895	70,642	68,880	72,458	56,249	59,249
Total	113,247	119,760	99,207	110,657	115,689	106,439	98,451

No great changes are expected in the condition of the sugar industry of British Guiana in the near future. As we have just pointed out, an increase of cane-planted area is not likely, on account of expensive labour ; a decrease is more probable instead, as the British Indian immigrants seem inclined to apply themselves increasingly to rice cultivation. Further, in Demerara proper, the land available has become restricted. The labour distribution is well organized, the exports of sugar to Canada and Great Britain leave nothing to be desired, so that the sugar industry in Demerara is still a remunerative business, and most likely will continue to be so, although it is no longer in the flourishing state it used to be.

Books of Reference :

British Guiana Directory.
West Indian Bulletin.
Algernon E. Aspinall. *Guide to the West Indies.*
Noel Deerr. *Cane Sugar.*
J. Sibinga Mulder. Mededeelingen betreffende de Suikerindustrie in Suriname en Demerara.

IV.

DUTCH GUIANA.

Dutch Guiana or Surinam lies on the north coast of South America, between 2 and 6° N. Lat. and 54 and 57° W. Long., between British and French Guiana, from which it is separated respectively by the Corentyne and the Maroni rivers. Its area covers 49,800 sq. miles, and the census returns on 31st December,

1909, gave it a population of 89,906 people, of which 862 were Europeans, 7,442 were Dutch Indians, and 16,203 British Indians, while 65,000 were aborigines.

The country near the coast and the immediate neighbourhood of the rivers is inhabited, while the rest, 99·9 per cent. of the entire area, is still wilderness. The climate is moist and warm, which the following Paramaribo observations show :—

RAINFALL IN MILLIMETRES.

Year	January	February	March	April	May	June	July	August	September	October	November	December	Total
1897 ..	47·2	99·8	38 3	227 4	377·4	337·7	208·3	136·4	122	74·3	399·3	198 6	2266 7
1899 ..	171·6	39 4	177·2	36·3	120 8	313 7	144·1	59·1	21 5	46·5	64	45 9	1240·1
1900 ..	235·1	328	322 1	223·4	371·8	210·4	87·3	129·8	82·6	156 2	134·8	114·4	2395·4
1901 ..	176·9	106·7	257	271·5	816.9	234 2	179·7	205 2	101·1	117 7	203	220 9	2290·8
1902 ..	182·4	558·3	222·3	522·4	522·4	406·6	314·1	150·8	57·9	57 8	194·6	171 9	3091·5
1903 ..	158·3	144 7	450·1	434·3	819 7	413·3	171 3	191·1	59 9	41·4	25 0	171·1	2456·2
1904 ..	163 7	166·8	540 4	241·5	362·5	262·5	274·0	41·8	52 5	105 5	165 0	278·1	2654·3
1905 ..	120·4	145·1	748	366 8	385·0	453 9	318·1	65 9	38·6	68 3	122·0	318 5	2421·9
1906 ..	159·3	26 2	173·4	358·7	307 3	182 4	171·4	180·1	71·0	102·0	145·1	118 6	1945·5
1907 ..	178·5	238.0	321 2	584·3	453·8	802 4	252·2	89·7	103 9	74·8	59 8	260·7	2918 4
1908 ..	145 4	321·4	133·0	145 1	347·1	262·2	291·0	219·4	62 7	24·6	125 0	173·0	2251·0
Average of 41 years ..	221·1	176·3	223·9	240·9	313·6	257·0	229 8	214 7	66·4	72·9	198·4	232 9	2851 0

Temperature in degrees C. :—

Month.	8 a.m.	2 p.m.	6 p.m.	Maxi-mum.	Mini-mum.
January..	24·3	29·1	26·0	30·3	21·5
February	23·8	27·9	25·9	29·4	22·2
March	24·9	28·7	26·2	29·3	22·8
April	25·1	28·3	26·1	29·5	22·8
May	25·1	28·2	26·2	29·3	23·2
June	24·6	28·5	25·5	29·8	22·8
July	24·9	29·4	26·6	30·5	22·8
August	25·4	30·4	26·7	31·5	23·1
September	26·4	32·7	28·2	33·2	23·9
October	26·1	31·7	27·3	32·8	22·8
November	25·5	28 9	26·2	31·1	22·4
December	24·6	28·4	25·9	30·3	22·4

In the south there are the high Tumua-Humac and Acarai Mountains, where the large rivers, which form the boundaries between the neighbouring colonies derive their source. Then there are the Nickerie, Coppename, Sara-

Dutch Guiana.

macca, and the Surinam Rivers, as well as the Commewyne, a tributary of the Surinam. The Surinam is navigable up to 100 miles from its mouth.

The capital, Paramaribo, has 32,600 inhabitants, Nickerie has 1,700 inhabitants, and there are some smaller towns. A railway runs in an almost southerly direction from Paramaribo to Kadjoe, and covers some 82 miles; otherwise transportation of goods and people is generally done by water, and occasionally along country roads.

Surinam was discovered in 1499 by Amerigo Vespucci, but it was not before 1603 that the English colonized it. Later on, French emigrants from Cayenne settled in the place, where they established a few sugar plantations on a small scale. The Dutch conquered Surinam in 1667, and in 1683 sold it to the Dutch West India Company, which later on disposed of a part of it to the town of Amsterdam, and to Aersen van Sommelsdyk, who became governor of this Colony.

The sugar industry was greatly extended by the introduction of slaves, who were supplied in large quantities as a monopoly of the West India Company. In 1712 the French invaded the country and destroyed several sugar plantations, causing the slaves to run away and never return. These maroons, continually reinforced by runaway slaves, remained in the woods, and kept attacking the settlements. Their guerilla warfare lasted for fifty years, till in 1758 they gave it up, whereupon the so-called "bush-negroes" were emancipated. Then a better time began for that colony, but if the owners were able to make money, they also knew how to spend it, for they got more and more into debt. In 1799 Surinam was conquered by the English, and after several phases of restoring and reconquering, it in the end became a Dutch possession, and has remained so ever since. In 1858 the trade in slaves was forbidden, and in 1863 slavery was abolished altogether on the Dutch West Indian colonies, while the owners of slaves got some slight compensation.

The liberated slaves were put under State supervision for ten years, after which they were considered free citizens. The abolition of slavery here, as in other countries, caused a great desertion of labour, so that work could not be done properly in the plantations. An effort has been made to improve that state of affairs by importing indentured British Indian coolies, and also Javanese. In spite of this resort, the supply does not fill the gap, and lack of labour is still the general complaint.

The sugar industry is carried on on drained marshes in exactly the same way as it is in British Guiana. At the present time there are five sugar factories which make molasses and rum as well as sugar, but are far from flourishing. Some years ago the possibility of founding a central factory, which was to work up the sugar cane cultivated by small farmers on ground allotted to them by the Government, was considered. It, however, soon appeared that there would not be people enough before long to get a sufficient quantity of cane to keep a sugar factory of any considerable capacity going, so that this plan was never carried out. The cane variety chiefly planted in Surinam is Bourbon, while there are also small plantations of other varieties.

On virgin soil the cane yields 5 tons of sugar per acre (or 12,500 kg. per hectare) ; on ground having been used in cultivation for some time the cane yields from 3 to 5 tons (7,500 to 12,500 kg. per hectare). The average yield is supposed to be 39 tons of cane and 3·8 tons of sugar per acre. The sugar, for the greater part, is sent to New York, and only a little is exported to the Netherlands. The total production has been during the last years as follows (expressed in metric tons of 2,200 lbs.) :—

1900	..	..	12,950	1906	..	..	12,635
1901	..	..	12,721	1907	..	..	11,930
1902	..	..	13,147	1908	..	..	11,999
1903	..	..	12,073	1909	..	..	10,938
1904	..	..	11,001	1910	..	..	12,055
1905	..	..	10,790	1911	..	..	14,459

The exportation has been as follows since 1715 :—

1715	..	..	9,766	1855	..	..	15,409
1725	..	..	11,095	1865	..	..	8,222
1735	..	..	8,585	1875	..	..	10,393
1745	..	..	11,427	1885	..	..	5,497
1750	..	..	12,302	1895	..	..	8,152
1755	..	..	8,208	1900	..	..	10,142
1765	..	..	10,062	1901	..	..	10,080
1775	..	..	10,128	1902	..	..	8,748
1784	..	..	7,171	1903	..	..	7,443
1794	..	..	12,142	1904	..	..	9,380
1805	..	..	5,862	1905	..	..	8,405
1816	..	..	5,784	1906	..	..	11,014
1825	..	..	11,908	1907	..	..	10,372
1835	..	..	18,887	1908	..	..	9,018
1845	..	..	14,894	1909	..	..	7,352

Surinam's sugar industry does not look promising. It is always the inevitable lack of labour that retards progress. The production will most likely keep stationary at 10,000 to 15,000 tons ; any increase is not to be expected.

V.

ECUADOR.

Ecuador is situated on the west coast of South America, between 1° 23′ N. Lat. and 4° 45′ S. Lat., and between 73° 10′ and 81° W. Long. It has an area of 118,650 sq. miles, and a population of 1,272,000 citizens, and about 200,000 wild Indians.

The country is very mountainous, and is traversed in a north and south direction by two mountain-chains, with a number of high volcanoes, partly active and partly extinct. There are lowlands near the coast, while vast high-lands, the so-called Inter-Andes territory, are found between the two mountain ranges. There are on the coast only two gulfs of any importance, the Guayaquil and the Ancon Bays. The rivers flow from the Andes either to the Pacific or to the Amazon. The climate in the lowlands along the coast is hot and damp, while in the highlands it is cool and even. The sugar industry is exclu-sively carried on in the lowlands, near the coast in the Province of Guayaquil. The cane crop is reaped in the months from July till November, and even as late as December.

Till a short while ago it was difficult to transport sugar to the exterior from Guayaquil, as the high cost for carriage viâ the Andes added too much to the price. Part of the sugar used to go by sea to Chile and Colombia, while Colombia used to send sugar to Quito and other market towns in the Andes. Since 1902, when a railway was constructed which runs to Riobamba, this drawback has ceased, and all the sugar prepared in Ecuador is consumed in the country itself, and some sugar is imported. Up till 1907 Ecuador used to raise an import duty on sugar of 4 cents per kg. (16s. 8d. per 100 kg.), but this duty has been abolished since, so that sugar can be freely imported into that country now. This, of course, first of all caused a drop in the price of sugar of $2 to $3 per 200 lbs., which is equivalent to the amount of the import duty. The sugar production for the last few years has been as follows, ex-pressed in metric tons :—

1904	..	..	6,400	1908	..	..	7,000
1905	..	..	5,900	1909	..	..	7,600
1906	..	..	6,900	1910	..	..	8,750
1907	..	..	7,100				

The production does not supply the local wants altogether, so that some sugar has still to be imported.

VI

PERU.

Peru lies on the west coast of South America, between 3° 30' and 18° 45' S. Lat. and 70° and 81° 40' W. Long. It has an area of 690,000 sq. miles, and a population of 4,500,000.

At some distance from the coast the high Andes mountains run parallel with it, leaving a narrow streak of land near the sea, intersected by several little rivers.

South America.

There are a great many good seaport towns on the Pacific coast, Lima and Callao being the most important. Owing to the very mountainous character of the country, the climate naturally varies. While little rain falls on the Pacific side of the Andes, that is, the part where most of the sugar industry is carried on, there is much rain, as a rule, on the eastern side, and that is why the latter consists of well-wooded country, while the western part has hardly any forest. Although Peru lies absolutely within the tropics, its temperature is seldom very high, as the following figures will show :—

Average Temperature observed on the Cartavio Estate in degrees C.

Months.	1904.	1905.	1906.	1907.
January	22·22	23·33	22·90	25·04
February	22·00	24·44	24·56	26·93
March	22·22	21·11	24·26	24·93
April	20·12	22·78	22·00	21·37
May	20·20	21·11	19·32	18·98
June	18·89	20·55	17·26	17·77
July	19·44	19·11	17·12	18·44
August	20·00	19·20	17·54	18·88
September	18·89	18·93	18·70	18·87
October	20·00	19·43	19·22	19·15
November	20·00	19·81	20·66	20·57
December	21·11	21·48	22·12	21·55

During the same years the highest maximum temperature was 35·3° C. (95·5° F.), and the lowest minimum was 11·1° C. (52·0° F.).

Sugar cane cultivation is exclusively carried on along the narrow strip of land between the Andes and the Pacific Ocean, and in the valleys which stretch from the seacoast to the mountains. This territory covers the entire coast between 6° and 16° S. Lat., while estates lie in the valleys of the following mountain streams : Lambayeque, Pacasmayo, Chicama, Santa, Huama, Lima, Cañete, and Tambo ; with their haibours : Eten, Pacasmayo, Huanchaco, Salaverry, Chimote, Jamanco, Supe, Huacho, Callao, Cerro Azul, and Mollendo. In addition, there is a number of small plantations spread all over the interior having small factories, which crush the cane by means of wooden rollers, and work up the juice to " chancaca " or " panela " (evaporated cane juice), or to " jonque " (brandy).

As was mentioned above, the cane plantations coming in for regular sugar manufacture are all found on the west coast. The rainfall is of little consequence in these parts, and it would be impossible to get a good cane crop without irrigation. So irrigation on a large scale is applied by damming up and distributing the numerous mountain streams which flow from the Cordilleras to the Pacific Ocean. These mountain streams contain much water when heavy rains fall on the mountains, but their outflow is small in the dry season, so that it is necessary to be careful with the irrigation supply, for which purpose a special irrigation service is appointed by the Government, who see to the water being equally divided among the different applicants. As the cane cultivation tracts in Peru have no special periods of rainy and dry weather, planting and reaping can be done at any time of the year ; there are instances of factories not having had to stop for years together for any longer period than is necessary for cleaning and carrying out repairs.

The land devoted to cane cultivation is first treated by a Fowler steam-plough, then it is harrowed and rolled. After that it is time to dig the ditches for irrigation and drainage, and the furrows ; the latter cannot be dug till the land is divided up by roads and footpaths into plots of 330 ft. in length and 160 ft. in width. The irrigation and drainage canals are dug alongside these roads and footpaths ; afterwards the furrows are hollowed out by a wooden plough ; these, according to the state of the soil, being dug at a distance of 9 to 15 ft. apart from centre to centre.

The cane tops put into the furrows are cut from the healthiest looking stalks, and are planted in a sloping direction, so that their top ends stick out of the soil. As soon as the plants are a foot high, weeding the fields is begun, which weeding is repeated till the danger of the cane getting smothered by weeds is past. About five months after the cane has been planted it is banked, and manured with guano from the neighbouring islands, or a mixture of guano and ashes from the factory, or potassium sulphate. Sometimes lime, saltpetre, or other suitable fertilizer is added to the manure ; but guano, which is cheap in Peru, is the chief component of the sugar cane manure.

During the vegetation period, cane is now and then irrigated; on soil which is moist on account of the abundance of subsoil water so that it wants little irrigating, only once every season, while other kinds of soil require supplying with water as many as twenty-four times during the same period. On an average, five applications is supposed to be sufficient. The wet ground is drained by open canals, and sometimes by pipes ; dry ground does not need drainage, the water which had run into the field by irrigation being left to penetrate the soil.

It takes twenty to twenty-four months for the planted cane to ripen, depending on local circumstances and the disposable supply of irrigation water. After the first crop, ratoons are grown several times, and these ripen in a much shorter time than the first crop does. Five ratoons of cane are cut, and sometimes this is extended to ten, which, of course, covers a space of fifteen to twenty years. This, however, is an exception ; five ratoons taking up nine years are of general occurrence, during which time a single planting yields successive crops.

The cane very seldom flowers; still, it does so enough to enable the experiment station at Lima to cultivate seedling cane varieties on a large scale, in order to procure better cane varieties for agriculture. Up to now none of these kinds have been introduced for cultivation on a large scale, but considering the great use these seedling varieties have been to other cane cultivating countries, they may contribute greatly to the cane production in Peru before long. At the present time the average yield of the varieties now cultivated—the white, the yellow-green, and the red—is 34 tons per acre, or 85,000 kg. per hectare, after a vegetation of 22 months; but as soon as a better organized treatment of the soil and of irrigation and manuring is applied, and a better type of cane is obtained, there is no reason why a yield equal to that obtained by the cane cultivators in Java and Hawaii should not be obtained in Peru, as the ground and the climate are very well suited to cane cultivation.

The cane does not suffer much from disease and pests; rats, which have such an injurious effect in neighbouring countries, do little damage in Peru. The only insect pests which do any considerable harm are the borers, though these are indirectly combatted by choosing only uninfected cane tops for planting.

When reaping the cane, it is cut close to the ground by the machete; the top part is removed, and the cane, either as it is or cut in two, is put on railway wagons and conveyed to the factories. These factories, as a rule, are not installed in modern style; in most cases this is due to lack of capital, which prevents the gradual substitution of the old mills and machinery by new inventions, but as the general condition of Peru is improving and sugar fetches higher prices than it used to do, this country will doubtless not lag behind, but will eventually instal most of the factories with modern plant, which will make the low yield of sugar rise considerably.

The sugar cane in Peru has a high fibre content, through its lengthy vegetation in a dry climate, and consequently little juice; but the latter is rich in sugar, and at the same time particularly pure. Consequently, 15 per cent. fibre on cane and 20° Brix at 92·5 purity and 0·46 per cent. glucose in first mill juice often occurs. Through the combined influence of a high fibre content, a high sugar content in juice, and weak mills, the loss of sugar in bagasse is exceedingly great, and on an average amounts to 3 per cent. on 100 cane. In spite of the high sugar content of cane juice, the yield of sugar is not particularly high for these very reasons, and amounts to 10 per cent., 7·5 per cent. of which is first, 2·5 per cent. second, and 0·5 per cent. third product.

When planted on virgin soil, plant cane has yielded crops of 8 tons of sugar per acre, or 20,000 kg. per hectare, but the average amount is 3 tons, or 7,500 kg. per hectare, a figure that may soon increase thanks to the improvement in machinery. By far the bulk of the sugar production in Peru is a brown raw kind of 96·5° polarization; but they also manufacture white sugar for local consumption, which is obtained by washing the brown sugar in the centrifugals. Part of the raw sugar, called " Peruvian crystals," is sent to the United States; the rest, together with part of the molasses, goes to Liverpool. What is left from the second and third products is exported to a refinery in Chile, while alcohol is distilled from the molasses, chiefly in Bolivia.

There used to be a refinery in the Cañete district, and one in the district of Lambayeque, but these are no longer working, so that no refinery is at present to be found in Peru.

A short time after Peru was conquered by Francisco Pizarro, sugar cane was imported into that country, and in 1570 the first sugar was commercially manufactured there. The sugar industry at first suffered from the competition of Mexican sugar, but it was not long before their own sugar supplied their wants. As in all American countries, the sugar industry was carried on by negro slaves, but after the abolition of slavery they endeavoured to procure labourers from other countries. No fewer than 90,000 Chinese were imported from Macao between 1849 and 1874, who were not treated any better than slaves; in consequence of this, so many died that the Macao Government prohibited all further recruiting. There are still some 25,000 Chinese residing in Peru, but no longer engaged in the sugar industry; they have settled as tradespeople in the towns. The field and factory work is done by native Indians of the country, so that foreign labour is no longer required.

In 1860 a great change took place in the primitive condition of the Peruvian sugar industry. Much capital, including foreign money, was put into the sugar undertakings, factories were installed with the most modern machinery, and Peru became a sugar-producing country that could compare with the very best. Large profits were made, and much money was spent, too, though not on the maintenance or the improvement of installations. When, in 1875, the period of low sugar prices came, the sugar estates had not got stamina enough to bear up under the stress of competition, and gradually they ran deep into debt. The industry also suffered from the fatal war against Chile in 1878, while afterwards sundry revolutions disturbed the peace of the country. But since the disturbances in 1895 Peru has had peace and quiet, and the sugar industry has greatly extended, chiefly owing to the rise in sugar prices through the Brussels Convention. In 1906 a sugar experiment station was established near Lima, which has made a point of studying the manuring and irrigation problems thoroughly and diligently, and is trying to get a more profitable cane variety than the one at present used. In addition, the cultivation and manufacturing methods are being improved upon, all of which points to a revival of the Peruvian cane sugar industry.

At the present moment Peru possesses 47 modern sugar factories, the principal of which are: Patapo, Tuman, Cayalti, Pomalca, and Pucala, all round Eten harbour; then there is Lurifico, near the Pacasmaya harbour; Casa Grande, Sausal, Roma, Laredo, Cartavio, and Chiguito, near Salaverry port; Tambo Real, San Jacinto and San Jose, near Chimbote; Paramonga, San Nicolas, Humaya, and Andalusia, nor far from Huacho harbour; La

South America.

Estrella, Caudivilla, Chacra Cerro, Infantes and Monte Rico, St. Clara and Narranjal, near Callao ; and the British Sugar Estates, near Cerro Azul.

The factory of Casa Grande, in the Chicama Valley, the yearly product of which is, on an average, 25,000 tons of sugar, is considered the most important. The others are of less capacity, still are of such a size that they cannot plant the full amount of the cane needed, but have to buy some of it from farmers. There are cases in which these farmers get 65 per cent. of the value of sugar and alcohol manufactured from the cane which they have planted, cut and delivered at the factory door ; in other cases the factory pays the expenses of cutting and transportation, and then only pays 50 per cent. of that value. A third agreement is that the value of the cane is to be estimated by the degrees Bé. of the juice and according to the sugar quotations ruling in Liverpool.

About 125,000 acres are planted with cane, which area may be extended in the near future.

The production for the last few years has amounted to the following quantities, expressed in metric tons, while the export figures are also given in the list :—

Year.	Production.	Exportation.
1894	74,690	65,000
1895	78,541	75,000
1896	75,735	71,735
1897	111,080	108,080
1898	110,373	105,713
1899	109,070	103,707
1900	118,173	112,223
1901	119,956	113,956
1902	123,906	117,362
1903	147,123	127,620
1904	156,500	131,957
1905	160,366	134,234
1906	169,418	136,729
1907	141,193	121,932
1908	157,294	137,670
1909	150,000	138,177
1910	190,000	160,000
1911	187,000	—
1912	195,000 (estimate)	

Besides the sugar manufactured in the modern way, some nine to ten thousand tons of evaporated cane juice or " chancaca " are produced and consumed in the country itself.

Since July, 1910, the import duty on sugar in Peru has been as follows :—

For sugar from countries belonging to the Brussels Convention ;

Refined or its equivalent	.. ..	per 100 kg. :	2·44 Sol*
Other kinds	.. ..	,, 100 ,,	2·23 ,,

For sugar from other countries .

Candy	.. ..	per kg. :	0·20 Sol
White or other sugars ..	.. ..	,,	0·13 ,,

As we said above, the cane sugar industry in Peru may be greatly extended. Both soil and climate allow of expansion, and should the irrigation works now being planned be carried out, a considerable extension of ground will be disposable for cane cultivation. Besides that, improvements in manuring, in the treatment of and the kind of cane used, may increase the product per acre, while an improvement in the mechanical installations of the factories should lead towards obtaining a better product from the raw material. Now that the political circumstances are favourable, and sufficient labour is to be found in the country itself, we may expect great things from Peru's sugar production.

Books of Reference :

Memoria de la Estación Experimental y Laboratorio para caña de azucar en Lima.
La Cultivation du sucre dans le Perou par M. César Broggi.
The Sugar Industry in Peru, by Thomas F. Sedgwick.
Zuckerindustrie in Peru, von Alfredo Solf.
The Cane Sugar Industry in Peru, by F. Zerban.

VII.

BOLIVIA.

The Republic of Bolivia is situated in the centre of South America between 57° 30′ and 73° 47′ 30″ W. Long. and 6° 30′ and 26° 52′ S. Lat. Its area covers 567,000 sq. miles, its greatest length being 1,280 miles from north to south, and its greatest width 865 miles from east to west. According to the returns of the last census of September, 1910, the population amounted to 1,816,217 people, including the nomadic tribes on the northern and eastern frontiers, which means about three inhabitants to the sq. mile. About 250,000 are white people, 550,000 are half-bred, 1,100,000 are Indians, and 4,000 are negroes.

Bolivia is very mountainous ; in the west are found the Cordilleras, which divide into two branches, and enclose an extensive tableland of 40,000 sq. miles at a height of about 13,000 ft. The mountains that surround this plateau have a great many high peaks covered with eternal snow, so that all climates are represented in this country, although Bolivia lies within the tropics.

* 1 Sol @ 100 centavos = 2s.

In the lowest parts, where the vegetation is tropical, the average yearly temperature varies between 66° and 72° F., but some days may be subject to differences of 36° F. in consequence of cool southern winds ; this uneven climate is experienced chiefly in the southern plains. In the north they experience a heavier rainfall than in the south ; the average rainfall amounts to 31½ ins. yearly over the whole country, with a maximum of 33½ in the north and one of 29½ in the south. The sugar industry is chiefly carried on in the Province of Santa Cruz; the people of Potosi, and the eastern and north-eastern part of Chuquisaca are engaged in it, but to no great extent. Altogether there are about thirty little factories, each of which produces from 50 to 500 tons of sugar yearly, all consumed in the country itself. The production does not, however, cover the demand for sugar, so that some importation of sugar from adjacent countries is necessary. The sugar industry in Bolivia is still in an early stage of development ; there are no good roads, and the small factories are installed in a most primitive manner, which makes the manufacturing cost very high. Departmental and local excises very much affect the industry, for sugar being exported from Santa Cruz to another province in Bolivia is first taxed by a provincial excise of 4s. 2d. per 100 kg., and then is subject to a local tax at the place of destination. The total amount of raw sugar exported from Santa Cruz to the other provinces does not exceed 700 tons, while the entire production of the country seldom exceeds 1,000 tons.

VIII.

BRAZIL.

The only parts of the gigantic Brazilian Republic where sugar cane is cultivated, and where cane sugar is manufactured, are States on the coast, namely, Pernambuco, Alagoas, Sergipe, and Parahyba in the north, and Bahia, Rio de Janeiro, and Sâo Paulo in the centre of the huge territory. All these places lie between 4 and 21° S. Lat., consequently in the tropics, and being on the east coast of South America within reach of the moist eastern winds, they get sufficient rainfall for the proper cultivation of the sugar cane. The big harbours of Pernambuco, Bahia, Rio and Santos lie in the same territory, and make the exportation of sugar to foreign countries by sea quite an easy matter ; on the other hand, the transport of sugar to the several States of the Union is attended with great difficulties, as the roads are bad and the distances considerable.

Brazil was discovered in 1500 by Pinzon, one of Columbus' companions, and the same year it was taken possession of by Cabral in the name of the King of Portugal. It was not till 1531 that any colonizing of this possession was attempted, as her Indian possessions at that time required all the attention and resources of Portugal. One of the first things done by the colonists was the founding of a sugar factory in the Isle of St. Vincent, occupying that part of the territory which is now taken up by Sâo Paulo. Both soil and climate of Brazil is exceedingly fit for cane cultivation, and this made the factories increase in number; in 1580 there were already as many as 120, and in 1590 there were 36 sugar mills in Bahia and 66 in Pernambuco. In 1580 Portugal and all the Portuguese possessions were annexed by Spain, and this made Brazil a Spanish colony. Thereupon an opportunity presented itself of which the numerous enemies of the King of Spain availed themselves to attack this rich country. In 1621, at the end of the twelve years' truce, the Dutch West Indian Company planned the conquest of Brazil, and carried it out by taking Bahia in 1624; but the following year the Dutch were driven away again by the Spaniards. The Dutch, however, settled in Pernambuco in 1629, and succeeded not only in extending their territory as far as Maranhão in the north and Rio Real, near Bahia, in the south, but also in conquering the West African outposts, Sâo Thome and Angola, and diverting the supply of negro slaves quietly to their own territory, thus dealing a great blow to their enemies. Joan Maurits van Nassau, who was appointed Governor in 1637, tried his very best to revive the sugar industry, which had greatly suffered from the wars and marauding expeditions, and actually achieved what he intended, for, when in 1644 he had to relinquish his post, Brazil had regained its former importance as a sugar producing colony. In 1640 Portugal had shaken off Spain's supremacy, whereupon the Portuguese, being proud of their nationality, keenly resented the loss of Brazil, their most important colony, and so made plans to recapture it. In 1642 the Dutch were driven away from Maranhão, in 1645 from Tabocas and Casa Forte, and, finally, they had to give up Recif after a long siege. Although Brazil had become Portuguese once more, the Dutch were still living there, and carried on their sugar industry undisturbed till, in 1655, when they were forced to leave owing to a Government decree. This resolution, of course, dealt a heavy blow to the sugar industry, as the manufacturers took their slaves, their capital, and their knowledge with them, and settled in the Antilles, to continue their occupation there. Although Brazil had been the principal sugar producing colony which supplied the wants of the entire world, the establishment of the Dutch in the Antilles led to competition which, in the end, got the better of Brazil. As early as the beginning of the eighteenth century the Antilles had forged ahead of Brazil, and gradually became the great sugar producers; while Brazil began to lose much of its former importance.

In 1825 Portugal acknowledged Brazil's independence, and at one time the latter became an empire under the Emperor Don Pedro I; but the country suffered continually from rebellions and agitations caused by partisans from the different provinces. Later on, from 1851 to 1854 and 1865 to 1870, Brazil waged bloody and expensive wars with the neighbouring republics, which ended in her acquisition of free navigation on the tributaries of the Plata River and on the Paraguay River, and put the Brazilian provinces in communication with each other and with the outer world.

South America.

The abolition of slavery was a question that greatly influenced the internal state of affairs. In accordance with a contract entered into with Great Britain in 1826, Brazil had bound herself to prohibit and to suppress the trading in African negro slaves from 1830 onwards. When, however, Brazil did not act up to this contract, the British Parliament passed the Aberdeen Bill in 1845, which authorized the English men-of-war to capture all slavers met in Brazilian waters, to liberate the slaves, and to summon the dealers to British law-courts. This action on the part of Great Britain was humiliating to the Brazilian Government, who thereupon took good care to suppress the importation of slaves altogether. In 1871 a bill was passed which decreed that any child that should be born of a slave woman was to be considered free ; it also led to funds being raised for the emancipation of slaves. Besides these measures taken by the Government, a great many private individuals and societies took it upon them to emancipate and redeem slaves, thus reducing their number to a minimum. The year 1888 chronicled the total abolition of slavery without any indemnification to the former owners. The latter joined the republican party and a great many other malcontents, and in 1889 succeeded in over-coming the monarchy and founding a republic. After some further disturbance, in which the army and the navy took part, and which had for its object the restoration of the monarchy, peace ensued, and has prevailed up to now.

There are two kinds of sugar factories in Brazil : the " usines," or recently installed factories, where crystal sugar is manufactured ; and the " engenhos," or small sugar mills, which produce evaporated cane juice.

In 1904 the factories were divided over the several States as follows :—

State.	Usines.			Engenhos.	Total.	Production.	
	Diffu-sion.	Single Crushing	Double Crushing			Metric Tons.	Sacks of 60 kg.
Pernambuco	1	40	6	1,500	1,547	156,000	2,600,000
Alogoas	—	4	3	850	857	36,000	600,000
Sergipe	—	15	1	650	666	30,000	500,000
Bahia	—	2	21	200	223	18,000	300,000
Parahyba Norte	—	2	—	100	102	4,000	70,000
Rio Grande Norte	—	1	—	150	151	4,000	80,000
Maranhâo	—	2	1	60	63	3,000	50,000
Rio de Janeiro	1	35	5	30	71	27,000	460,000
Sâo Paulo	1	6	5	20	32	15,000	250,000
Minas	—	3	—	50	53	2,000	40,000
Other States	—	5	—	230	235	3,000	50,000
Total ..	3	115	42	3,840	4,000	298,000	5,000,000

Brazil.

Although Pernambuco produces by far the greatest quantity of sugar, the Bahia industry is much more up-to-date, as 21 of the 23 usines work with double crushing, while most of the other States use usines with but single crushing.

When studying the Brazil sugar industry, it is apparent that it is carried on in three different centres, namely, in the North, in the Middle, and in the South. The cultivation methods, both in the north and in the centre, are practically the same, and show but little difference from the usage of by-gone days in Brazil. Holes 8 ins. deep are dug 5 ft. apart, in which pieces of cane 8 ins. in length are put. These are covered up with earth without any manure ; after five weeks the soil is loosened, and the cane is left to grow for fifteen months, at the end of which time it is ripe and very often has a high sugar content. In the third sugar belt, the State of Sâo Paulo, the cane is better looked after, and modern cultural methods are followed. Here, in the months September to April, the cane is planted in the following way : Whenever new land is to be cultivated, all the trees and shrubs are cut down and burnt, and the soil is treated with a plough or a spade. Afterwards furrows 8 ins. deep are dug about 4 ft. distant from each other, in which the tops, 1 ft. long, are put in a row at 4 ins. distance from each other. In the case of ratoons, the land to be planted is first weeded and covered with compost manure, whereupon the ground is well ploughed up, furrows are dug, and cuttings are planted in the same way as described above.

After about twenty days the cane has appeared, and when it has reached a height of about 8 ins., the soil between the cane plants is loosened with spades, a treatment which is repeated four to six times, according to the nature of the soil. Irrigation is not applied, as rainfall is exclusively relied upon. In the case of a sufficiency, the cane will ripen in fourteen to sixteen months after planting, and it is cut from June till the middle of November, when the rainfall is so heavy that harvesting has to be abandoned. After the cane is cut, the dry cane leaves left in the fields are burnt, as a preventive against borers, beetles, and other injurious pests. Then the plough goes as close as possible to the old plants and cuts off part of the roots, thus forming a stimulus to a new growth. The eyes bud out again, new cane stalks appear, and the earth is loosened again, as was done for the plant cane. After twelve to fourteen months the cane is cut again, and four to six ratoons are generally grown, after which the cane is dug out, the land manured, ploughed up, provided with fresh furrows, and planted anew.

The type of cane planted will greatly depend on the nature of the soil and the situation of the estate. In the north we find Cayenne, Cristallina, Salangore, Bamboo, etc., all varieties that require a warm and dry climate ; while we find Louziers or Bois Rouge cane is planted in Sâo Paulo. Seedling varieties are much experimented with, although they are very seldom taken up for cultivation on a large scale.

The yield of cane depends on the variety, the nature of the soil, the rainfall, etc., and varies between 20 and 30 tons per acre (or 50,000 to 70,000 kg. per hectare) for first ratoons, and a smaller quantity for further ratoons. The sugar content is often very high, and attains to 18 per cent. Cane is planted by *colonos* on land belonging to the estate, and sold to the factory. The *colonos* get a free house, pasture land for their cattle, wood for fuel and timber for sheds and storehouses. In addition, each group receives 6 to 24 quarteis* of land, depending on the number of persons, this land being already planted with cane, so that the contracting party is only responsible for further labour of maintenance and the crops, for which the *colono* gets 60 milreis† per quarteis or £2 10s. per acre. Supposing the yield to be twenty tons, the cane would cost to the manufacturer £2 10s. ÷ 20 = 2s. 6d. per ton for maintenance and harvesting.

Besides this class of workmen, there are also indentured labourers, who receive untilled soil, together with houses, pasture land and cane tops ; but they have to look after the tilling of the soil and the cultivation of the cane. When the cane is ripe it is cut and put on carts, and it fetches the following market price in Sâo Paulo per bag (of 60 kg.) of sugar :—

Price per bag of sugar.	Price per ton of cane.
18 milreis or less	7 milreis
18—24 ,, ...	8 ,,
24—35 ,, ...	10 ,,
Over 35 milreis	12 ,,

In Bahia 5 milreis is paid for a ton of cane when the price of sugar is 200 reis per kg., and for every difference of 10 reis, 300 reis is paid above or under the standard price.

Most of the sugar is produced in small factories, " enghenos " or " banques," and only a comparatively small part is manufactured in the usines. The mode of preparation in the first is as follows : The cane is pressed between a pair of hard wooden rollers, and the strained juice is boiled string-proof in copper pans. Then the massecuite is poured into big wooden moulds which taper off like cones toward the bottom, which is perforated. When the mould is being filled the holes are stopped up, but as soon as the substance has got cold, the stoppers are taken out and the treacle runs through the holes into a kind of gutter to the distillery, to be worked up into alcohol. Then a thick mixture of water and clay is carefully spread on the sugar in the moulds. The water slowly trickles through the sugar, washes the crystals clean, and after some time the contents are taken out of the moulds. The top layer of sugar is white, or almost white ; the middle is yellow, and the bottom one is brown. The two first kinds are dried on mats, and the third on the floor in the sun, after which they are packed in calico bags containing 60 kg. or 132 lbs. each.

* 4 quarteis = 1 aliquare, or 6 acres.
† 1 Brazilian milreis of paper = 1s. 4d.

Brazil.

Although the cane sometimes contains 15 per cent. of sugar, the sugar obtained in this way is not more than 5 to 6 per cent. on the weight of cane. Even sugar prepared in usines only stands for 9 per cent. of the weight of cane, which is generally due to the unsatisfactory mill pressure. In these factories the juice is strongly sulphitated, neutralized with lime, boiled, settled, and then boiled to grain. After being cooled in wagons or tanks, the massecuite is centrifugalled, and the runnings are boiled once more. The molasses obtained from this process is used for the preparation of alcohol or brandy.

The output is distinguished as follows :—

Cristaes blancos (white sugar washed in the centrifugals).

Cristaes amarellos (" Demerara " sugar, yellow, first product).

Mascavinhos (fine-grained, light-coloured, second product).

Mascavos (very dark-coloured after-product).

The raw sugar produced in the sugar factories is only partly consumed as such, and most of it undergoes a refining process before it goes into consumption. Attempts have repeatedly been made in Brazil to purify sugar in large refineries, as is done in Europe, but they have never been a success. In Pernambuco a large factory was built which was supposed to work according to Steffens' washing process, and to make cubes and granulated, but after a year's working they had to stop. A second refinery was built in Campos, but no longer exists, and has sold its machinery to raw sugar factories ; while about eight years ago another factory was opened in Rio de Janeiro, with no better results. These failures can only be accounted for by the high wages, excessive prices for coal and transport charges, and the restricted demand for sugar refined after European fashion.

The so-called " area " or sand sugar prepared in very small refineries is much more in demand with the Brazilians, and consequently finds a readier sale. This kind of sugar is a smooth, moist, fine-grained product, strongly smelling of molasses, and which contains about 2 per cent. of reducing sugars and 1 to $1\frac{1}{2}$ per cent. of ash, and has a polarization of 91°. The white sort is prepared by dissolving the crystal sugar in water to form a syrup of 31° Bé, by clarifying with blood, and then filtering it over animal charcoal. Then the clarified syrup is boiled to a water content of about 4 per cent. over the open fire at 130° C., after which it is taken off the fire, a little crystallized sugar is put into it, and it is stirred with a wooden trowel till the mass has become cold, dry, and powdery. In the same way yellow sugar, the so-called " terzira," is obtained by dissolving the " Demerara " crystals in water, and by turning the fluid into a dry, fine-grained product, in the same way as described above, but this time without any clarifying or filtering. The caramel taste and smell make this sugar a favourite sweetening agent, for which the public is quite willing to pay a better price than for the fine sugar refined in European fashion. While the daily sugar consumption of Rio de Janeiro is supposed to be 1,200 bags of sugar of 132 lbs., the consumption of " terzira " is estimated at 800 to 900 bags, which proves the popularity of this kind of sugar.

South America.

It does not take much skill or large well-installed factories to prepare "terzira," and that is why it is so well fitted for the native industry, especially carried on by shopkeepers and confectioners, who can sell their goods direct to the public. As a large refinery cannot possibly prepare "terzira" in a mechanical manner, and as it wants a go-between to bring it into contact with the consumers, and finally, owing to the heavy transport expenses, can only reach a restricted number of consumers, it is no use starting a big sugar refinery in Brazil, as the failure of earlier results has shown.

Of late years the Brazilian Government has done what it could to promote the sugar industry, but its efforts have been of very little avail up to the present time. In 1875 the Government guaranteed an interest of 7 per cent. on the capital spent in the building of central factories. The maximum number of factories was fixed for each State, and the period was appointed when interest and capital had to be returned. In 1881 this law was modified, and although the guaranteed interest dropped to 6 per cent., the latter regulation had better results than the earlier one, as the repayment was divided over a larger period. All at once twenty concessions were granted, and a foreign company was also started. In 1889 the provinces having become States got their own Governments, and the State of Pernambuco granted an allowance of 250 million reis gold (according to legal currency, £28,125) to forty factories that were to be capable of crushing 200 tons of cane a day. This allowance was to be paid back by the factories concerned after the third grinding season in twenty instalments, one each year. The allowances were increased by later laws, but they led to nothing tangible ; in fact, some factories they had started to build were never finished.

Sugar cultivation and manufacture in Brazil have remained of little consequence, and the exceedingly high costs of transportation make it impossible for Brazil to compete successfully with other sugar producing countries. In 1908 a kind of sugar trust was established, the "Coligaçao Assucareira," the members of which pledged themselves to take 20 per cent. from their production for a combined exportation. In January, 1909, this amount was increased to 40 per cent., but after a year it appeared impossible to carry out this plan of keeping up the sugar prices by a large exportation, to such a height that the losses suffered through the exportation might be made up for by the greater profit the home trade would obtain. In 1906 an import duty of 200 reis per kg. was levied, and when, owing to the above-mentioned increase in prices, beetroot sugar could be successfully imported from Germany, the Government, on 27th March, 1908, raised the import duty to 400 reis per kg., and this prevented all further import of foreign sugar. In consequence of this, Brazil has to rely on its own sugar production exclusively, and as the bad roads make carriage expensive, and some States levy high export duties, whereas others raise import duty on goods imported from other States, it is extremely difficult to get a clean insight into the sugar trade and sugar prices of Brazil, and still more so to give an adequate survey of it. This also refers to the production and the exportation. Sugar is being manufactured on so many small farms and estates to be retailed to the native consumers, that all we can do is to guess at the quantity of sugar produced.

It is just the same with the " export trade." It sometimes implies exportation to foreign countries, while in other instances it includes exportation to neighbouring States, which dual definition makes statistics most unreliable. So it is only under every reserve that the following figures are given as regards the export trade from Brazil since 1820. Those of the years before 1889 may be considered more reliable than those of the years following :—

1820	75,000 tons
1831	83,000 ,,
1832	91,000 ,,
1833	99,000 ,,
1834	83,000 ,,
1839—1844 yearly average	82,500 ,,
1846—1857 ,, ,, ...	132,400 ,,
1869—1874 ,, ,, ...	153,300 ,,
1875	123,000 ,,
1876	88,400 ,,
1877	133,000 ,,
1878	170,540 ,,
1879	187,540 ,,
1880	246,461 ,,
1881	161,258 ,,
1882	246,769 ,,
1883	223,865 ,,
1884	329,376 ,,
1885	274,312 ,,
1886	112,340 ,,
1887	226,010 ,,

Production in Pernambuco.

1888	186,750 tons	1896	159,460 tons
1889	129,525 ,,	1897	124,428 ,,
1890	111,675 ,,	1898	131,820 ,,
1891	156,750 ,,	1899	109,650 ,,
1892	137,625 ,,	1900	128,475 ,,
1893	133,200 ,,	1901 . .	139,441 ,,
1894	178,100 ,,	1902	178,977 ,,
1895	208,275 ,,		

Production in Brazil.

1891	185,000 tons	1897	205,000 tons
1892	200,000 ,,	1898	151,500 ,,
1893	275,000 ,,	1899	175,000 ,,
1894	275,000 ,,	1900	256,460 ,,
1895	225,000 ,,	1901	312,957 ,,
1896	210,000 ,,	1902	254,693 ,,

South America.

1903 .. .. 187,500 tons	1908 .. .. 197,000 tons
1904 .. .. 197,000 ,,	1909 .. .. 248,000 ,,
1905 .. .. 195,000 ,,	1910 .. .. 253,000 ,,
1906 .. .. 275,000 ,,	1911 .. .. 270,000 ,,
1907 .. .. 260,000 ,,	1912 .. .. 348,000 ,,
	(estim.)

The sugar exports of Brazil were destined for the following countries the last few years, and amounted to the following quantities, expressed in long tons—

	1910/11.	1909/10.	1908/09.	1907/08.
From Pernambuco to:				
Europe	6,941	35,864	36,006	380
United States	—	1,408	11,011	458
Argentina	—	15,955	6,666	3,630
Brazilian harbours	144,270	93,964	118,934	89,841
Total	151,211	147,191	172,617	94,309

	1909/10.	1908/09.	1907/08.
From Maceio to:			
Europe	17,311	10,329	12
United States	200	1,238	—
Argentina	434	783	—
Brazilian harbours	25,008	28,673	20,145
Total	42,953	41,023	20,157
From Bahia to:			
Europe	110	2,975	1
United States	—	—	—
Argentina	—	29	62
Brazilian harbours	16,967	11,601	6,974
Total	17,077	14,605	7,037
Total Exportation to:			
Europe	53,285	49,310	393
United States	1,608	12,249	458
Argentina	16,389	7,478	3,692
Total to foreign countries ..	71,282	69,037	4,543
To Brazilian harbours	135,939	159,208	116,960
Grand total	207,221	228,245	121,503

Brazil.

Opinions are divided as to the future of Brazil as a sugar producing country. In the north the sugar industry may still be called profitable on account of the low wages, especially as a sugar estate in that part makes a profit the very first year. The conservative nature of the population, however, is against the introduction of modern methods of working, as they require more labour.

Exports decrease steadily as the United States can get as much sugar as they wish for from Cuba and Porto Rico, and consequently can do without Brazilian sugar. The sugar prices in the country can only be kept high by an artificial export trade; as soon as the latter ceases, the sugar prices will go down to such an extent that any profit will be out of the question. Not until the cultivation and, especially, the manufacturing methods are greatly improved, which would cause the price to fall considerably, can any extension of the sugar industry be looked for without an artificial export trade. On the other hand, everything is done to supplant the sugar industry by the more profitable cotton and cacao cultivation, and this makes the near extension of the Brazilian cane sugar industry an improbability.

Books of Reference:
United States of Brazil. A Geographical Sketch.
P. Stolle. *Zeitschr. f. d. Ruben Ind.* 1907, 107.
Reports of the British Consulate in Pernambuco.
Reese. *Geschiedenis van den Amsterdamschen Suikerhandel.*
Report of Vice-Consul Rhind of an Inquiry into the Sugar Industry in Brazil.

IX.

ARGENTINA.

The extensive Argentine Republic in the south-east of South America stretches from 22° to 56° S. Lat., has an area of 1,135,485 sq. miles, and according to the last census has a population of 5,410,028 inhabitants, including the half-wild nomads. As only the most northern part of Argentina lies in the tropics, and as that part happens to be very mountainous, only a very small portion of the country is fit for cane cultivation, 28° S. Lat. being the limit for its production. It is only found in the Provinces of Tucuman (8,950 sq. miles), Salta (62,254 sq. miles), and Jujuy (19,000 sq. miles), and in the territories Formosa (4,140 sq. miles), Chaco (55,600 sq. miles), and Missiones (11,300 sq. miles), all of which are situated in the northern part of the Argentine Republic.

The western part of the Provinces of Tucuman and Salta, and the whole of Jujuy are mountainous, the mountains having tops covered with snow and slopes decked with a luxurious vegetation. The north-west portion of this province is a plateau over 10,000 ft. above sea-level, in part fertile and in part barren. The eastern part of Tucuman and Salta is composed of fertile, well-watered plains, exceedingly well suited for sugar cane cultivation. The three mentioned territories consist chiefly of flat country, marshy in some places, and covered with extensive forests in other parts. It is very thinly populated, and rivers are the only means of transportation, as roads are still lacking.

The average temperature and rainfall of the cane-planted area in Argentina are as follows :—

District.	Yearly Average in the Period.	Temperature in Degrees C.			Rain in Millimetres.		Days of Rain.
		Average	Maximum.	Minimum.	Average	Maximum in a month.	
Tucuman	1855—1896	19·56	40·6	— 3·2	935·3	328·0	65
Salta	1882—1893	17·47	35·0	— 4·3	551·4	408·0	46
Formosa ..	1879—1892	21·87	40·0	— 0·5	—	—	—

The atmospheric moisture, as a rule, is low, which makes the heat quite bearable in the warm season ; the nights, moreover, are cool. During September and October a scorching north wind will all at once be followed by a cold south wind, so that the people there may experience in one day changes in temperature of 27° F. (15° C.). In winter time the temperature at times falls below zero, much to the detriment of the cane, which it affects in weight and sugar content, but although it makes the leaves wither and brown, the frost never kills the cane outright.

In the cane cultivating districts, the rainy season is from October to March, and the dry one from April to September.

In 1901 some 8,350,000 acres of the area of Argentina were cultivated, 115,000 of which formed cane areas. These figures have not undergone any material change since.

The Argentine cane sugar industry has only recently sprung up. In 1871 the total sugar production only amounted to 1,000 tons, but since then it has developed rapidly, owing to several causes. First of all, the Government levied a high import duty on foreign sugar, so that the price of sugar in the interior went up, thus encouraging production ; secondly, there was a considerable margin between the inland silver currency with which the cane was paid for, and the foreign gold currency after which foreign countries fix the world's price. In consequence of these advantages, the sugar production increased so much that in 1894 it exceeded the requirements of consumption, and imported sugar was no longer necessary ; some sugar was even left unsold. This led to an excess of production in the Argentine Republic, to get rid of

Argentina.

which the Government granted an export premium, with the result that a considerable amount of sugar was exported, chiefly to Great Britain. At the same time, the manufacturers formed a cartel to limit the amount of sugar produced, and this actually led to a much smaller annual output than was realized during 1894 and 1896. This decrease had become necessary, as exportation did not run as smoothly as was desired ; the neighbouring South American States, for instance, barring their frontiers to Argentine sugar. The United States levied compensatory duties over and above their ordinary import duty ; and Great Britain, too, was expected before long to put a stop to the importation of bounty-fed sugar. It was therefore resolved to limit the production in the following manner : A fixed quantity of 71,500 tons was contingented over all the then existing factories in Tucuman, so that every one of the twenty-one smaller factories was allowed to produce a quantity of 1,000 to 4,500 tons exempted from duty. while the two biggest factories respectively came in for 8,500 and 20,000 tons. A duty of half a peso (paper) had to be paid on every 100 kg. in excess, while factories not yet in operation when this law was enacted would have to pay this duty on a quarter of their produce. Part of this money was to go towards a fund for indemnifying such planters as would abandon the planted cane or destroy it, or do anything except work it up to alcohol or sugar. The indemnification was 60 pesos per acre for a successful plantation, and less for an unsuccessful one. Then some of the money was used for the payment of an export bounty to the amount of 16 centavos (paper) per kg., while the rest went to the Exchequer.

Through the Brussels Convention this export bounty was rendered futile, as all the countries adhering to the Convention pledged themselves to levy a special duty on bounty-fed sugar amounting to the sum of the bounty ; hence offering a premium was useless, and sugar receiving a bounty was on neither a better nor a worse footing than sugar without one. In 1905 both premium and sugar duty were abandoned, and only an import duty of 9 centavos (gold) per kg. sugar of 96° and of 7 centavos per kg. brown sugar was maintained.

From 1st June, 1912, the import duty is fixed at 0·088 pesos (gold) per kg. on refined sugar or sugar polarizing over 96°, to be diminished each year by 0·002 till 1st July, 1921, when it will be 0·070 pesos. Sugar under 96° pays 0·068 pesos per kg., with a decrease by 0·002 till a minimum of 0·05. In case the sugar prices rise over 4·10 pesos per 100 kg., these duties will be reduced. Over and above these duties, Argentina levies additional duties from bounty-fed foreign sugar, in accordance with the stipulations of the Brussels Convention.

Nowadays the production covers the consumption ; a little sugar is sometimes imported or exported, but within recent years Argentina has supplied its own wants. No excise is levied, no export duty is paid ; consequently, the inland manufacturer enjoys all the protection of the import duty, which now amounts to 18sh. 3d. per cwt. of sugar of 96° polarization, and to 16sh. per cwt. of brown sugar.

South America.

The production during the last twenty-two years has been as follows, in metric tons :—

1890	.. ..	40,000	1901	158,154
1891	.. ..	40,000	1902	123,081
1892	.. ..	75,000	1903	142,895
1893	.. ..	75,000	1904	128,104
1894	.. ..	103,000	1905	130,596
1895	.. ..	130,000	1906	114,000
1896	.. ..	163,000	1907	91,488
1897	.. ..	111,617	1908	161,772
1898	.. ..	75,538	1909	124,811
1899	.. ..	90,268	1910	143,000
1900	.. ..	117,208	1911	180,092

Generally only one cane variety is planted, *i.e.*, a hard, dark-coloured kind which the Spanish brought from Peru or Mexico years ago. There are other kinds on trial, among which are some good varieties from Java, but these are not yet in general use. The furrows are dug about 3 ft. distance from each other, in which the pieces of cane are put in a row. Tops are not made use of, and the cane to be planted is neither selected nor disinfected. Planting is generally done in September or October, that is at the beginning of the rainy season. On most of the estates the cane is irrigated by water from the Rio Sali or other streams ; artificial manure is hardly ever applied, and stable manure not at all. The cane is weeded, banked, and cut as low down as possible as soon as it is ripe. When they are not afraid of frost, first and second ratoons are kept as many as five times ; but in places where the cane is apt to be frost-bitten the planter prefers to plant afresh every year. The cane suffers from borers and fungous diseases, but no measures are taken to protect them from these. One can hardly wonder at the poor crops this kind of cane yields, considering the unfavourable condition of the soil and the small amount of care taken. They reap 9 to 15 tons of cane per acre if the soil is bad, 11 to 17 tons from average soil, and fully 18 tons on selected land. Though the cultivation may be in a poor state, the factories are in very good condition, being large and well installed, and equipped with the newest inventions.

The cane is taken to the factories by rail, and thrown on the mill-carriers by means of mechanical dischargers. All the mills are driven by steam ; there is triple-crushing with maceration, sulphitation of the juice, crystallization-in-motion, in short everything that is newest and best. The sugar that is prepared is chiefly white sugar of 98° polarization, while the molasses are worked up to alcohol. Some factories manufacture pure white sugar for consumption, but most of them send their produce to the sugar refineries in Rosario.

As the cane is very poor, the yield of sugar is small, even if the manufacture of the sugar from the cane is as thorough as possible. In 1907 the yield was 6·50 per cent. of the weight on cane, and in 1908 it was on an average 8·15 per cent. ; while the maximum for a factory was 10·03 per cent., covering the whole crop, and the minimum 5·61 per cent.

In Tucuman there are 29 sugar factories, 27 of which worked in 1911. The 27 combined ground 2,008,805 tons of cane in that year, and obtained 152,965 tons of sugar, or 7·65 per cent.

In the other provinces there are thirteen factories, which have a total production of :—

Tucuman	152,965	tons in	27 factories.
Jujuy	23,026	,, ,,	3 ,,
Salta	1,176	,, ,,	2 ,,
Chaco	1,907	,, ,,	4 ,,
Other provinces ..	1,019	,, ,,	4 ,,
Total	180,092	tons in	40 factories.

One can easily imagine that, considering the low price cane fetches, the cost price of sugar, even for well-installed factories, must be very high, being, for instance, £18 per ton of sugar. Therefore, but for the fiscal protection the Argentine sugar industry would soon come to an end ; with these duties, it is a profitable business so long as the production does not exceed the home consumption, for if the production can supply the country's wants, as happens to be the case now, the sugar manufacturers enjoy the protection of these high import duties. Even in case of a slight surplus the manufacturers need not be alarmed, for the profit made on sugar for home consumption would be considerable enough to make up for any possible loss on the export of the surplus sugar. Only when the production appreciably exceeds the home consumption shall we have a repetition of the 1895 experience, and export premiums have to be resorted to in order to get rid of the sugar.

These export premiums, however, could not have existed any longer, according to the Brussels Convention, if Great Britain in 1908 had not got herself exempted from the regulation that bounty-fed sugar if imported should be specially taxed to an amount equivalent to the bounty ; but now Great Britain again allows bounty-fed sugar from countries where the difference between excise and import duty exceeds 6 francs per 100 kg. of white sugar and 5·50 francs per 100 kg. of raw. Any considerable export trade from the Argentine Republic is out of the question just now ; the production just covers the consumption, and this condition is not likely to change.

Books of Reference :

Revista Azucarera.
Handbook for the Argentine Republic.
Revista Industrial y Agricola de Tucuman.

X.

PARAGUAY.

Paraguay is a republic, entirely surrounded by land, and lies in the centre of South America, between 22° 4' and 27° 30' S. Lat., and between 54° 32' and 61° 20' W. Long. It has an area of 112,000 sq. miles, and its population in 1889 amounted to 636,571 inhabitants, 100,000 of whom are Indians.

The climate may be described as pleasant; it rains through all the year, so that no long spell of drought can cause harm to vegetation. The average temperature of the capital, Asuncion, is 22—23° C. (72° F.), and the average difference between summer (October to March) and winter (April to September) temperatures is about 6° C. (11° F.). The maximum reading of the thermometer in Asuncion has been 41° C. (105°8· F.), but for years at a time the temperature has never been higher than 37° C. (98° F.), while the minimum temperature is 2 to 3° C. (37° F.), and is consequently never below zero.

The average rainfall during the period 1877 and 1891 has been as follows (expressed in mm.) :—

Month.	Total.	Maximum.	Minimum.
January	146	390	46
February	140	610	32
March	190	321	53
April	174	445	37
May	134	288	11
June	85	232	14
July	70	121	16
August	56	131	5
September	99	167	29
October	162	204	42
November	135	253	25
December	153	262	64
Total	1,554 mm. or 61·2 ins.		

Sugar cane is planted in all parts of the Republic, and the sugar cane cultivation is by far the most profitable of all the crops, as owing to the favourably moist climate and the absence of periods of drought, cane can grow with great ease without any trouble or expense, and may be reaped regularly for five to fifteen years from the same stools. It does not need any other treatment, but that of planting and reaping and occasional weeding and loosening of the soil after each crop. Up to some time ago, the canes were exclusively crushed in wooden mills driven by oxen, and the juice was not concentrated beyond a thick syrup, which was stored in bags of cowhide ; but now even on small estates there are iron mills, while much sugar in crystallized form is cured by centrifugalling.

In 1901 the cane-planted area in Paraguay amounted to 26,000 acres, and one acre of cane land is expected to yield on an average twelve tons of cane, of which a greater or smaller amount of sugar may be gained according to the power of the mills. Besides sugar and syrup, brandy is made from the cane juice. Apart from innumerable small factories, there are several big ones in Paraguay, the biggest of which is on the Tebicuary River, near Villa Rica, with an output of 350 to 400 tons of sugar yearly. The production of the country is, however, much below its requirements ; hence, the importation of about 250 to 300 tons of sugar each year.

A duty of 70 per cent. of the value is paid on sugar when imported into Paraguay, while raw sugar in bags, imported viâ Villa Encarnacion, to be used on the Paraguay tea or " maté " estates, enjoys a reduction of 25 per cent., and when imported viâ San Jose a reduction of 10 per cent. on the duty.

Africa.

I.

MADEIRA.

The Isle of Madeira lies in the Atlantic Ocean, about 450 miles from the African coast, between 33° 37' and 32° 51' N. Lat., and between 16° 37' and 17° 16' W. Long. It has an area of 286 sq. miles, its greatest length being 38 miles, and its greatest width 15 miles. It is a very mountainous country, rising steeply from the sea and forming a lofty ridge, the highest point of which is 5,500 ft. above sea level. Its climate is uniformly warm : the average yearly temperature on the south coast is 18·8° C. (65° F.), and that on the north coast a little less. There is no greater difference between winter and summer temperatures for any given place than 6° C. (11° F.). The average rainfall amounts to 28 ins. The population, amounting to 132,000 people, consists chiefly of Portuguese ; there are also Italians, Moors, and descendants of the negroes formerly imported as slaves.

Funchal is the only place of importance. Madeira was known to exist as early, or earlier, than the Middle Ages ; but it did not attain any importance till the Portuguese colonized it on one of their exploring voyages to the west and south. It was taken possession of by them in 1410, to become Spanish in conjunction with Portugal in 1580. In 1640 it was restored to Portugal, as soon as the latter became an independent country again ; save for a short period of English occupation, 1807 to 1814, it has been, and still is, a Portuguese possession.

The first Portuguese colonists took sugar cane from Sicily to Madeira, where the fertile disintegrated basalt soil was excellent ground for the cane to thrive in, promoted by the mild and lovely climate. After the Portuguese had penetrated more southwards, and had settled in Guinea, they used to send negro slaves from this part to Madeira to till the ground. The cane sugar industry rose to a then unknown height, in consequence of which the centre of this branch of industry was moved from the Mediterranean coast to the Portuguese colonies in West Africa. This was not to last long, however, for as soon as America was discovered the Spanish and Portuguese colonists took sugar cane to the tropical countries, which proved to have a still better soil, and the cultivation of cane there yielded such a plentiful supply of sugar,

290

sold at a very low price, that this industry soon got ahead of that of Madeira. In course of time the sugar cultivation has more than once been wrecked by diseases and pests. In 1502 the cane was ruined by borers, after which it was planted afresh. As such calamities caused repeated harm, the status of the cane cultivation naturally fluctuated. As a rule, cane cultivation and vine growing were alternately of first importance. During the years 1846 to 1852 the vineyards were damaged by *Oidium* (a fungous disease), in consequence of which they were turned into cane fields by their owners. In 1864 the cultivation of the vine was taken up again, but was attacked by the *Phylloxera* in 1873 ; but later on it became increasingly important, and now again forms the principal factor of the export trade. Since a law was promulgated, in 1903, for the promotion of the sugar industry, the state of affairs has been as follows : The planting of sugar cane is free, so is the manufacture of brandy from it, but the manufacture of sugar and the strong class of alcohol so necessary for Madeira wine is a monopoly only granted to two factories. One of these two only makes alcohol, but the other both alcohol and sugar. The fact is, there are a great many cane planters in the island who sell their cane, as it is, to the factories, or crush it themselves and work the juice up into brandy. They sell retail as much brandy as they like ; while the rest is taken to the factories, where it is worked up to alcohol of high strength. The factories are obliged to buy all the cane and brandy offered them. Against the obligation of buying the cane at the extremely high price of £3 6s. 8d. per ton, there is the monopoly they have in the manufacture of sugar and of alcohol, large quantities of which are wanted for wine making, and the reduction allowed them in the import duty of £1 5s. per ton on imported foreign molasses, which can be used for distilling alcohol, and often is of such a good quality that it still yields a fair amount of sugar first. Another privilege of the factory is the right to introduce sugar exempt from duty into Portugal, while foreign sugar is heavily taxed when imported into that country. This duty amounts to 120 reis* per kg. (£1 4s. per cwt.) for sugar below No. 20 D.S. and 145 reis per kg. (£1 9s. per cwt.) for sugar above No. 20 D.S., which shows that Madeira sugar enjoys a good premium, and accounts for the sugar industry existing in that island. But for this protection the industry could not possibly be carried on, for, as it is, it is far from being an important one, as will be shown further on.

The regulation mentioned above had its drawbacks, as the small planters began to grow great quantities of cane, and supplied the factories with such large amounts of cane and brandy that the latter could easily get sugar and alcohol enough from this source to supply Portugal's whole demand for sugar, and to furnish Madeira with alcohol. The importation of beet sugar molasses from Hamburg was therefore no longer necessary. This did away with the advantage of a reduced import duty which the monopolists were to enjoy on molasses imported from abroad, and consequently upset their calculations. Every now and then the quantity of sugar to be imported free into Portugal

* 1,000 reis = 4s.

has to be fixed, as the literal regulation about free importation, dating from the time when the total production was about 1,000 tons of sugar, may become a great tax on Portugal's Exchequer, should the sugar production and importation from Madeira increase too much.

For some years the hard British Indian cane variety, the Uba, has been planted in order to prevent attacks of disease among the canes, and has proved a success. Sugar cane is planted on the lowest levels near the coast, and is generally taken to the factory in carts when the crushing season begins in March. The factory is installed with mills, and the bagasse diffusion system of Naudet gives satisfaction here, though in other places, *e.g.*, in Cuba and Porto Rico, it was not satisfactory, chiefly on account of the heavy expense for fuel. This seems strange, but this apparent contradiction may be explained by the fact that cane in Cuba and Porto Rico need not cost more than 10s. per ton, whereas in Madeira it never costs less than £3 6s. So it is in the latter country quite worth while to spend some money on trying to extract from this costly raw material as great a percentage of sugar as possible ; while in other countries, where cane is cheap, it pays better not to go to any great expense, and to leave some sugar in the bagasse than to incur the heavy cost of total extraction.

During the last eleven years the production of cane and the use made of it have been as follows (expressed in metric tons) :—

Year.	Total Cane.	Cane for Sugar.	Cane for Alcohol.	Year.	Total Cane.	Cane for Sugar.	Cane for Alcohol.
1900	30,000	12,000	18,000	1906.. ..	33,000	20,000	13,000
1901	21,000	6,000	15,000	1907.. ..	45,000	21,000	24,000
1902	25,000	8,000	17,000	1908.. ..	50,000	24,000	26,000
1903	19,000	6,000	13,000	1909.. ..	60,000	33,000	27,000
1904	20,000	8,000	12,000	1910.. ..	68,000	36,000	32,000
1905	28,000	14,000	14,000				

The yield of sugar in 1906 amounted to 1,800 tons, or 9 per cent. ; in 1907 to 1,840 tons, or 8·8 per cent. ; in 1908 to 2,125 tons, or 9·1 per cent. About 700 tons of this sugar were exported to Lisbon and Oporto in 1908, while the rest was used for home consumption. The export to Portugal was 1,650 tons in 1909.

This all shows that while the conditions are unnatural, and a monopolist has to pay ten times as much for his cane as many of his fellowmen in tropical countries have for theirs, the sugar industry can only be carried on on a small scale, and should be considered rather in the light of a relic of a greater past, than as a vital branch of present-day industry.

II.

THE CANARY ISLANDS.

The Canary Isles, lying in the Atlantic Ocean, between 27° 30′ and 29° 30′ N. Lat., and 13° 17′ and 18° 10′ W. Long., form a Spanish province, and consist of seven large and five smaller inhabited islands. Their total area amounts to 3,000 sq. miles, and they have a population of 360,000 inhabitants.

After the voyages of exploration at the end of the fifteenth and the beginning of the sixteenth centuries, these islands were colonized, and from that time dates the introduction of the sugar industry, which soon began to flourish, so that Canary sugar was known as a good commercial product as early as the sixteenth and seventeenth centuries. But competition with American cane, and later on with European beetroot sugar, caused the Canary industry to decrease in importance, till gradually it became of no consequence. Grand Canary is the only island where some cane is still cultivated; everywhere else its production is nil. The soil once utilized for cane cultivation is gradually being used for the banana export trade. The amount of sugar these islands yield does not supply the wants of the small population; as a matter of fact, beetroot sugar has to be imported every year in increasing amount. About 1900 the sugar imported from England and Germany only amounted to 200 to 300 tons, but in 1909 it had risen to 600 tons.

III.

ANGOLA.

Only a little sugar cane is cultivated near the harbour of Benguela, in the Dombe Grande District, belonging to the large Portuguese colony of Angola, which stretches along the south-west coast of Africa, between 6° and 17° S. Lat. and 12° and 25° W. Long., and has an area of 509,000 sq. miles and a population of 4,180,000 inhabitants. An extensive plain is found running from the sea to Lobita, through which will pass the projected railway to Katanga, in the Congo.

The principal sugar estate of Angola is the Parceria Santa Theresa do Luracho; it does not, however, produce sugar, it simply works up the cane juice to rum, to be sold to the natives. More recently the duty on the manufacture of spirits has been increased so much on account of the Alcohol Convention that profit is out of the question, and for this reason cane cultivation on those estates has been supplanted by that of cotton and oil palms.

The "Companhia do Dombe Grande" used to occupy itself exclusively with the preparation of rum, but it has recently begun to work up cane to sugar. Further, there are some smaller estates where cotton, tobacco, and oil palms are grown instead of cane, so that the cultivation of sugar cane in this colony is very restricted.

Great things were expected from the privilege Portugal held out to its African colonies, namely, a reduction of 50 per cent. in the import duty into Portugal for a maximum of 6,000 tons for each colony, which is equal to a premium of £11 17s. per ton of raw sugar, as the full duty is 120 reis per kg. on raw, and 145 reis per kg. on white sugar. But in spite of this handsome preferential treatment, the manufacture and export of sugar in Angola have remained insignificant, and there is no present indication of a revival.

IV.

LIBERIA.

A little sugar cane is cultivated and a little cane sugar manufactured in the Liberian Republic, lying between 8° and 12° W. Long. and 4° and 9° N. Lat. on the west coast of Africa. This cane is chiefly found on the banks of the St. Paul, Cavalla, and other rivers, the soil of which seems exceedingly well fitted for canes and capable of producing very tall and heavy types.

When virgin soil is to be planted with cane, the shrubs are cut in January and the trees in February, and two or three weeks afterwards the rubbish is burnt and cane tops are planted in shallow furrows in the untilled soil. After the cane is banked and the weeds are removed between the rows, the cane is left to grow undisturbed, to be finally cut a year after the planting time. Then first, second, and third ratoons are kept, after which fresh tops are planted.

Only syrup, as a rule, is made from the cane, the juice being concentrated and sold in tins of 5 gallons or 25 litres. Sugar is also made by evaporating the juice a little further, and by pouring it into barrels when sufficiently concentrated, where it is left to cool and crystallize. After being boiled the crystallized massecuite is scooped into barrels with a perforated bottom, which allows the molasses to trickle through, and leaves behind crystals that are sold locally. Cane juice, as well as treacle and molasses, is worked up to rum, which is easily sold.

White sugar is not manufactured in Liberia, being only imported from Europe. The industry is only of very recent date. Both capital and enterprise are lacking in Liberia, and this prevents the industry from becoming important ; and in spite of an import duty of a little more than 3d. per pound of brown sugar and 1d. per pound of white sugar, the home production is not sufficient to supply the consumption, however little this may be. Exact figures as regards the sugar production are not to be obtained, and the data that are given only refer to isolated cases, and not to the conditions in general.

V.

EGYPT.

Only that part of Egypt stretching along the banks of the Nile is devoted to the cane sugar industry, that is from a little south of Cairo up to Assouan, near the Sudanese frontiers. This tract covers a distance of 4° to 30° N. Lat., but although this stretch of land is of considerable extent as regards length, it is only of restricted width, being limited by the narrow Nile Valley, which is only a few miles broad at its narrowest part, and twelve miles at its widest, the desert stretching away from it on both sides. The ground fit for cane cultivation is chiefly situated on the left bank of the Nile, as on the right bank the desert mountains reach to the river in many places. For this very reason all the factories have been built on the left bank. Rainfall is very scanty in these parts. There are years in which there is no rain at all, so that the humidity of the air falls to a very low figure. Indeed, were it not for irrigation, cane cultivation would be impossible; but on the big estates it is splendidly carried out and large pumping stations exist to pump up the river water and by means of canals to irrigate the cane throughout the year with the necessary water. Small fields are irrigated by means of water-wheels, which are moved by buffaloes or by hand-power. In order to increase the irrigated area, the Government in 1902 had a large dam erected across the Nile, near Assouan, through which large reservoirs are filled at the time of the annual rise of the Nile (in the months of June and September), to be drawn from during the dry months. In the cane districts the temperature varies between 28° and 43° C. (82° and 110° F.) during the summer months, and between 10° and 30° C. (50° and 86° F.) during the winter. The nights generally are cool; in winter sometimes they are so cold as to have the sugar canes nipped by frost, an inevitable loss to the planters. While Egypt in the Middle Ages was known for the extent of its cane plantations and the skilfulness of its inhabitants in manufacturing sugar of all sorts therefrom, the industry ceased altogether in 1517, when Egypt was conquered by the Turks, who ruined the country outright. As a matter of fact, some sugar cane was still planted and a little sugar was manufactured subsequently, but it was no longer an industry worthy of the name, and not till the beginning of the nineteenth century was the manufacture resumed on a practical scale. In 1850 Ismael Pasha ordered sugar cane to be brought from Jamaica, and in 1855 the Government began to encourage the manufacture of sugar; but it was not till 1877 that a well-established national sugar industry began to exist. The factories no longer belonged to the Khedive, but fell to a Government Committee, the Dariah Sanieh, which was not long in building several factories, and in 1896 it could boast of an output exceeding 75,000 tons of sugar. At that time cotton only fetched very low prices, so that sugar cane was the most profitable plant for the fellahs to grow; but when the price of cotton went up and better profits were promised, they no longer planted sugar cane exclusively. In 1893 a French Society, called the " Société Générale des Sucreries d'Egypte," began to manufacture sugar, and for this purpose built three large factories, which as early as 1900 produced as much as 30,000 tons of sugar. In 1903 the Darieh Sanieh sold its nine factories (not the planting area) to the " Société Générale," which thus almost got the monopoly of sugar manufacture in Egypt. There are still a few small factories that occasionally work, but their sugar production is not worth mentioning. The " Société " shut up some of the newly-acquired factories, and kept cn working with the others, but the amount of cane that was brought to the mills was not sufficient to make them run at their full capacity, and so their profits were almost nil. In 1905 there was a big financial crisis also affecting the business, but all this seems now to belong to the past, and the company expect soon to extend their cane-planted area, and to increase the quantity of cane to be crushed.

In 1898—1899 Egypt had an area under cane of 88,000 acres ; in 1903 —1904 it had gone down to 50,000 ; and in 1907—1908, the worst year on record, it only touched 40,000 ; but at present the area seems to be increasing.

In 1905—1906 685,000 tons of cane were worked up, yielding 63,634 tons of sugar ; in 1906—1907 the figures were 415,000 and 41,664 ; in 1907—1908 they were 253,459 and 28,541 respectively ; while in 1908—1909 359,360 tons of cane were brought to the mill, and 34,844 tons of sugar were produced ; and in 1909—1910 553,376 tons of cane were worked up, which yielded 59,279 tons of sugar. The figures for 1910—1911 were 472,344 tons of cane, and 49,403 of sugar.

The present existing sugar factories and their capacities are as follows :—

Factories of the " Société Générale."
a   Group Ibrahimieh :
    Bibeh .. ..   1,800 tons of cane per 24 hours (closed).
    Mattai .. ..   1,800 ,,   ,,   ,,   ,,
    Abou Kourgas .. 2,000 ,,   ,,   ,,   ,,
    Rodah .. .   1,800 ,   ,,   ,,   ,,   (closed).
    Cheick Fadl .   1,500 ,,   ,,   ,,   ,,
b. Southern Group :
    Nag Hamadi ..   2,500 ,,   ,,   ,,   ,,
    Ernant .. ..   1,000 ,,   ,,   ,,   ,,
    Motana .. ..   500 ,,   ,,   ,,   ,,
    Kom Ombo .   3,000 ,,   ,,   ,,   ,,
Factories belonging to other owners :
    Tarchont ..   (closed).
    Beni Kora ..   ,
    Belianeh .
Egyptian Sugar and Land Co. (closed).
    Demeus ..   2,000 tons of sugar yearly.

In addition, the " Société " possesses a very big refinery at El Hawamdieh, which deals with not only the raw sugar from its working factories, but also raw sugar imported from other countries. This refinery is capable of working up 230 tons of sugar daily ; in 1909 it worked up 49,354 tons of sugar, 20,040 tons of which came from its own factories, while 29,314 tons were raw Java sugar. In 1910 the amount of raw sugar worked up was 60,000 tons.

The manufacturers buy the cane from the planters, who are either big estate owners or small farmers who rent a few acres and plant cane on them. The ground destined for cane growing is ploughed up in the autumn, and afterwards is tilled two or three times in February of the next year. In the same month the furrows are dug with a spade or a plough, 8 ins. deep, and soon after pieces of cane 16 to 20 ins. long are planted in two rows in the furrows. Not only are tops used for this purpose such as are employed in most of the other sugar-producing countries, but all of the cane is cut into lengths. Large quantities of cane are used as seed, namely, 6 700 lbs. per acre. This is done in the months of March and April, the planted cane is covered with earth and watered. Then they start to irrigate ; ten days later they irrigate once more, and keep this up till the end of October, after which the intervals are fourteen to twenty days, according to the appearance of the cane, while irrigation is stopped after October in order to give the cane opportunity to ripen. Reaping is begun at the end of December, and kept up till the beginning of April, at the end of the grinding season. The cane variety most in use up to a short time ago was a red kind very much like Bourbon cane, which will thoroughly ripen in the short time allowed it. The " Société Générale " has recently ordered cane from Java, and has had the cuttings distributed among the cane farmers. This kind of cane is said to yield 25 to 30 per cent. more cane than the old types. It is nothing extraordinary that on growing these improved tops the quantity of cane obtained should increase, considering that the Arabs, who have to supply their own sets, were formerly in the habit of having the attacked, diseased, damaged, or fallen stalks, which they could not sell to the factory, for this very purpose. The manure they use is stable dung and " ruins " manure ; but pigeons' dung from caves, and, recently, artificial manures have also been used

When the cane is cut, camels convey it to the railways, by which it is carried to the factory ; as a rule, one ratoon crop is grown after a crop of plant cane ; then the land is sown with cotton or beans, and lies fallow a whole year ; after which period it is planted with cane again, so that once every four years cane is planted in the same field.

The yield of cane very much depends on the kind of soil and the disposable quantity of irrigation water ; while the temperature during the vegetative period also influences the yield. On an average 24 tons of cane per acre are expected from plant cane and 16 tons from ratoons.

The factories buy the cane at 15·75 frs. per ton, so that for a production of fifty tons of cane per hectare, it realizes 787·50 frs. and 15·50 frs. for dry leaves, amounting altogether to 803 frs.

Africa.

The " Société Générale's " greatest trouble is want of cane, their factories being so vast and well installed that they might easily work up much larger quantities than they have done lately. The " Société " therefore does its very best to encourage cane cultivation. Owing to the high price of land, it is not possible to plant its own cane, but it is willing to advance money to planters to improve the roads, and is disposed to give a better price for cane coming far, and consequently having to pay heavier transportation charges. All these measures seem to have taken effect, and the once steadily decreasing quantity of cane to be worked up has changed into an increasing amount.

As has been said before, the factories are established on a good basis, and are installed throughout with the newest machinery. For want of sufficient cane brought to the mill, this modern installation does not show to advantage, but should the factories ever work at full capacity they would deal with tremendous quantities of cane most economically and with a minimum of loss. They generally manufacture but one kind, that is raw sugar for the refinery, and occasionally white sugar for direct consumption. The molasses is distilled to alcohol.

The average yield amounts to :—

1st product	..	..	9·80 per cent. on	100 cane	
2nd ,,	..	..	0·45 ,,	,,	100 ,,
3rd ,,	..	..	0·17 ,,	,,	100 ,,
In all ..	..		10·42 per cent. on	100 ,,	
Molasses	..	..	2·25 per cent. on	100 ,,	
Total production		12·67 per cent. on	100 ,,		

In the last years of the working of the Dariah Sanieh, the yield was :—

1895 ..	..	.. 9·60	1899..	..	.. 9·32
1896 ..	..	.. 10·23	1900..	..	.. 9·95
1897 ..	..	.. 11·02	1901..	..	.. 10·39
1898 ..	..	.. 8·79			

In the year 1906—1907 the statistics of the five factories belonging to the " Société Générale de Sucreries and de la Raffinerie d'Egypt " were as follows :—

Factory	Tons of Cane Worked.	Sugar Content of Cane.	Yield.			Production in Tons.	Cost of Production in frs. per 100 kg.
			First Product	Second Product.	Total.		
Mattai	40,671	12·75	9·56	0·75	10·31	3,891	28·42
Aboukourgas	73,590	12·91	10·37	0·21	10·58	7,633	23·62
Nag Hamadi	147,520	12·49	9·86	—	9·86	14,597	28·42
Cheikh Fadl	97,180	12·66	10·22	—	10·22	9,934	24·81
Ernant	55,905	13·18	10·03	0·95	10·98	5,609	24·47
Average and total	414,866	12·73	10·03	0·13	10·16	41,664	26·14

Egypt.

In 1910 the average yield was 10·71 per cent. of sugar of 96·4 per cent. polarization. Since November 1st, 1909, the following regulation about import duties and excises has been issued for the ensuing ten years :—

1. On all foreign sugar imported by the Société Générale up to 31st October, 1910, a duty of 5 per cent. *ad valorem* was to be paid, while 20 piastres (4s.) is to be paid on home produce (this duty used to be 7s. on the first 40,000 tons and 6s. for the rest).

2. The import duty was to be 6½ per cent. *ad valorem* from 1st November, 1910, till 31st October, 1911.

3. It is now 8 per cent., dating from 1st November, 1911, till the end of the agreement, while the rate of excise duty will rest at 4s. per ton.

4. The total amount of the excise should not be less than 10,000 Egyptian pounds* ; while, on the other hand, nothing should be paid in excess to what it used to be at the time of the 7s. and 6s. tariff.

5. Beginning with 1st November, 1909, the paid excise was to be returned in case sugar should be exported, namely, in such a manner that the returned excise should never exceed the excise of the preceding year.

The total production of Egypt has been for the last fifteen years, expressed in metric tons :—

1897	101,000	1905..	60,000
1898	80,000	1906..	63,634
1899	88,000	1907..	41,664
1900	98,500	1908..	25,541
1901	95,000	1909..	34,844
1902	98,000	1910..	55,330
1903	70,000	1911..	49,403
1904	60,000		

Besides this quantity of locally produced sugar, Egypt imports a considerable amount of sugar, which is shown by the following table :—

Sugar Imports into Egypt in tons.

Origin.	1904.	1905.	1906.	1907.	1908.	1909.	1910.
England	10	12	20	11	8	—	
Germany	35	22	11,751	245	191	368	125
Austria	43	8,860	13,012	16,837	4,155	7,815	10,927
Belgium	28	555	3,279	81	—	—	—
Java	6,227	17,416	6,415	3,093	11,108	18,584	19,790
France...	3	168	1,041	10	10	—	—
Russia	11,540	11,973	—	4,610	37,792	22,404	1,371
Total	20,794	39,409	34,419	24,890	53,255	49,171	32,213

* 1 £E = 20s. 6d.

In 1911 Egypt imported 25,493 tons of sugar.

Egypt used to export much sugar to Turkey and Asia Minor, and candy to the champagne vineyards in France. The latter buy their candy from Egypt because they think cane sugar the only sugar that will not interfere with the taste of the champagne. In 1906 the exports came to £45,000, in 1907 to £38,250 ; in 1908 some 11,377 bags of sugar of 100 kg. were exported to Djeddah, and 5,284 bags to Rheims, which showed a great decrease. In 1909 the total export of sugar was 5,868 tons, chiefly to Turkey and Arabia ; in 1910, 6,384 tons, of which 5,828 went to Turkey ; while the 1911 exportations amounted to 10,821 tons. The increased consumption of Egypt and the Sudan takes up nearly all the sugar produced and refined in Egypt, and allows of a considerable amount being imported into those countries as well. In 1908—1909 the consumption for Egypt and the Sudan was 78,457 tons of sugar, 61,740 of which were provided by the " Société Générale," while the rest was imported. The consumption in 1910—1911 amounted to 80,527 tons. Egypt can easily produce a larger quantity of sugar than it does at present without having to be afraid of over-production in its own country ; and since the " Société Générale " does what it can to improve the quality of the cane, and to advance money to the farmers, and to encourage them to grow cane, the cane production is likely to exceed the crops of the last few years ; the factories are quite capable of working up much more cane than they have done, which shows that the Egyptian sugar production has dwindled solely for lack of cane. As the cotton industry has not been the success they expected it to be, the farmers, no doubt, will take up cane cultivation once more, and by so doing will remove the only obstacle to the further development of the Egyptian sugar production.

Books of Reference :

Walter Tiemann. *The Sugar Cane in Egypt.*
La Culture de la Canne à Sucre en Egypte (Journ. de l'Agric.).
Bouricius and Cohen. *Een en ander over de rietsuikerindustrie in Egypte.*

VI.

MOZAMBIQUE.

The Portuguese colony of Mozambique lies on the east coast of Africa, between 10° and 27° S. Lat. and 30° and 41° W. Long. Its area covers 300,000 sq. miles, and its population is estimated at 800,000 inhabitants. Only along the banks of the Zambesi and the Limpopo rivers is sugar cane cultivated and cane sugar manufactured. This industry is of very recent date, as it was only in 1896 that the " Companhia d'Assucar de Mozambique " was founded, which built a factory near Mopea. In 1897 the Companhia Assucareira da Africa Oriental Portuguese was established, which in 1900 started a sugar factory in Marromeu. In addition an English company, the " Sena Sugar

Factory Company," was responsible for a factory started at Chimbue, so that sugar is now being produced by three factories. Then others were constructed, so that we may expect a considerable extension of the sugar industry in Portuguese East Africa before long.

The production of these three factories has been from the beginning as follows, in long tons :—

	1898	1899	1900	1901	1902	1903	1904	1905	1906	1907	1908
Mopea ...	1,000	1,630	2,560	1,250	1,792	2,050	3,700	3,625	3,165	1,820	6,000
Marromeu	—	—	1,310	300	2,970	1,200	3,750	2,470	700	1,300	1,500
Chimbue	—	—	—	—	—	—	-	—	—	—	5,165
Total ..	1,000	1,630	3,870	1,550	4,762	3,520	7,450	6,095	3,865	3,120	12,665

In 1909 the total production amounted to 17,362 tons, while that of 1910 was 15,714, and that of 1911 27,700 tons. Rum used to be distilled from molasses, which rum could be imported into the Transvaal free from duty, as Mozambique enjoyed trade privileges with that country when importing goods viâ Delagoa Bay. After the war, and since the Confederation of the South African colonies, this advantage has ceased to exist, and the profit on the manufacture of alcohol has disappeared.

In 1909 the area under cane was as follows :—

Mopea	..	..	.. 4,000 acres
Marromeu	..	..	.. 5,139 ,,
Chimbue	..	..	.. 3,100 ,,
Total	..	..	.. 12,239 ,,

Owing to the extension of these, and the establishment of other estates we may put down the area under cane in Mozambique at the present date as 30,000 acres.

The climate of Mozambique is generally warm, but very changeable. From November till March it is very warm and rainy; the rest of the time it is dry and cooler. During the months May to July the temperature often drops to 20° C. (68° F.), and the day and night readings are apt to vary considerably. The soil is a rich clay, sometimes mixed with sand ; on the banks of the Limpopo River the cane lands stretch along the banks at a gentle slope, so that irrigation with river water is available by a process of damming-up. The banks of the Zambesi River, however, are high and steep, and for that reason, the irrigation water has to be raised by powerful pumps, to be distributed over the country through a network of canals.

Nowadays *Uba* cane, imported from India, which seems to be a success all over South Africa, is planted. The planting season begins with the rainy period in December or January, and the cane is irrigated if necessary till May or June of the following year, when the harvesting commences, to end in November. As the cane fields depend for their success on irrigation, they are laid out in long strips along the banks of the rivers or at the side of lagoons, from whence the irrigation water can be obtained by damming or pumping.

Ratoon is kept for fifteen months or longer, after which the cane is cut every year. A cane production of 36 tons to the acre, yielding 10 per cent. sugar or 3·6 tons, is generally expected, but we very much doubt whether this average yield is really attained. The plants often suffer from drought or from grasshoppers, which, of course, affect the crops for the worse, as may be seen from the above-mentioned irregular figures of production from the different estates.

The newer factories are of modern construction, and are kept up-to-date by the purchase of the most perfect kind of machinery.

On sugar exported a duty of 1 per cent. *ad valorem* is levied, but when it is imported into Portugal and into the States of the South African Union it enjoys great privileges. In 1902 a reduction of 50 per cent. was allowed on the import duty on sugar sent to Portugal from Mozambique, and from Portuguese East India and Timor for fifteen years up to a maximum of 6,000 tons for each of the two colonies. As this duty amounts to 120 reis per kg. or 2½d. per lb. of raw sugar, and 145 reis per kg. or 3d. per lb. of white sugar, the first 6,000 tons of raw sugar from Mozambique enjoy a drawback of £11 13s. per metric ton. All quantities above 6,000 are fully taxed, which explains why in 1908, when Mozambique exported almost twice 6,000 tons, the excess was not sent to Lisbon, but to Antwerp and the Transvaal. Besides this very considerable protection accorded the Mozambique sugar when imported into Portugal, it, up to June, 1912, also enjoyed privileges in the colony itself. An import duty amounting to £16 per ton was levied on foreign sugar, while an excise of 20 reis per kg., or about £4 per ton, is paid on sugar consumed in the country itself. The surtax was, consequently, no less than £12 per ton ; but in the middle of 1912 the import duty was lowered to 30 reis per kg., doing away with the privilege. At the present time the sugar consumption in Mozambique and the interior is not very considerable, and is not likely to extend, as there are but few white people, and the natives have not acquired the habit of using sugar as a food.

When Mozambique sugar is imported into the Transvaal it is exempted from import duty, which means £5 per ton of white and £3 10s. per ton of raw sugar ; hence the Portuguese colony is privileged above other foreign importers. Moreover, the sugar enjoys a rebate of 40 per cent. in railway rates. The unification of the British South African colonies threatens to put an end to this state of affairs, as the Governments of Cape Colony, Orange River Colony, and Natal have put an extra duty on Mozambique sugar of 4s. 8d. per

100 lbs. of refined and 4s. 10d. per 100 lbs. of raw above the ordinary import duty just referred to. At the present time, however, Mozambique sugar is imported free of duty into the Transvaal, and as there are no longer any inland customs barriers in British South Africa this sugar also goes untaxed from Transvaal into the other States of the South African Union.

The Mozambique sugar industry may be considered a promising one. There are extensive stretches of fertile soil, with great facilities for irrigation, to be obtained for little outlay. Labour is near at hand, but there is not enough of it. The expensive transportation of sugar is a great drawback. It might be sent by water, if the transport did not happen to coincide with the time of great drought, which reduces the Zambesi to a low level, and prevents the boats carrying more than a very little cargo at a time, so that the cost of carriage would be heavy.

On the whole, sugar can be prepared in Mozambique at very low cost, and the recently established new plantations will doubtless lead to a considerable increase in the sugar production.

VII.

NATAL.

In Natal the sugar industry is carried on along the coast between Durban and the mouth of the Tugela River ; and likewise in Zululand, between 28° and 30° S. Lat., that is outside the tropics. Natal's sugar industry only dates from 1850, when a few planters began to crush a little cane in small mills, and to work the juice up to sugar. Not till 1878 was the first modern sugar factory driven by steam founded at Mount Edgecombe by sugar manufacturers from Mauritius. Since that time the sugar industry has steadily improved ; more factories have been built, while the existing ones have extended their cane production, till at the present time there are no fewer than thirty-four in operation, their output being estimated to amount to 92,000 tons in 1911–12. Besides the land originally given up to sugar cultivation, viz., the tract on the coast north of Durban, much cane has lately been planted successfully in Zululand, and the sugar industry will no doubt extend considerably in that territory, as the founding of a great many large and well-installed sugar factories is being considered.

As Natal lies outside the tropics, it takes longer for cane to ripen there than in most of the other sugar-producing countries. It takes plant cane two years, and first and second ratoons eighteen months, which means three crops from one single planting within five years. At the end of the five years the cane is planted over again. The cane variety most in vogue nowadays is the *Uba*, the hard, yellow cane from British India, which, as we have already had occasion to remark, proves a success wherever it is planted in South Africa.

For manure stable dung and cane ash are used, while phosphatic manures have also been tried. The cut cane is taken by means of railway trucks to the factories, which used to be most primitively installed, but are now being improved by the owners. The raw sugar is refined in the country itself, except the amount of raw sugar that is consumed as it is. There is one refinery at South Coast Junction belonging to a firm of raw sugar manufacturers, which delivers 100 tons of sugar daily, and before long may be capable of twice this output. Then there is another refinery to work up the sugar coming from the four central factories belonging to Sir Liege Hulett & Sons. As soon as all these refineries are fully employed, Natal will be able to provide the South African Union with white sugar, and will not require any from abroad. At the present moment it cannot do without imported sugar, as the consumption of British South Africa is about 90,000 to 100,000 tons per annum.

The labourers are Kaffirs and British Indian immigrants ; but the planters are better satisfied with the work of the latter, as they work more steadily.

The British Indians are indentured for five years, at the end of which time they have to sign for two more years or have to return to India, unless they should be able to pay a yearly contribution of £3, which enables them to stay in the country and become landowners. During the time of indenture they receive 10s. per month the first year, which is increased by 1s. each subsequent year ; over and above this they get food, quarters, and medical attendance free, so that they have only to find clothes.

The Indian Government has now prohibited Indians going to Natal, because they are alleged to be ill-treated ; so that the labour problem in Natal has entered on a new and less favourable phase, which may greatly retard progress.

The trade among the different South African States used to be very complicated, as everyone of them had their own import duties, and granted different kinds of privileges to different countries. Mozambique sugar, for instance, was exempted from duty when imported into the Transvaal, while Natal sugar was taxed, and this state of affairs remained in force a couple of years after the former Boer Republics had come under British rule.

In 1906, however, a Convention was drawn up, according to which the British South African colonies guaranteed each other free trade, while import duties on sugar from abroad were fixed as follows :—

		£	s.	d.
For adherents to the Brussels Convention :				
Candy, loaf, castor, cubes, etc. .. .. per 100 lbs.		0	5	0
,, ,, ,, ,, ,, ... per ton		5	0	0
Other sugar, golden syrup, maple syrup, molasses sac charum, treacle, etc. .. .. .. per 100 lbs.		0	3	6
,, ,, ,, ,, .. per ton		3	10	0
Saccharin and the like .. .. .. per lb.		1	0	0

Bounty-fed sugar is taxed with additional duties according to the stipulations of the Brussels Permanent Committee.

TINLEY MANOR FACTORY, NATAL.

Natal.

The sugar production of Natal has amounted for the last seventeen years to the following quantities, in long tons :—

1894	19,369
1895	20,508
1896	20,651
1897	20,245
1898	29,186
1899	Boer War
1900	16,689
1901	36,662
1902	21,095
1903	33,944
1904	19,238
1905	26,158
1906	21,479
1907	24,223
1908	31,999
1909	77,491
1910	84,437
1911	92,000
1912	106,000 (estimate)

Besides this production, a good deal of sugar is imported from abroad. Natal sends much of its own sugar and that from foreign countries to the neighbouring States. The figures of imports and exports vary for every year, and those representing exports seem to us to be unreliable, as the values appear to be out of reason in a great many instances.

The sugar industry of Natal is likely to flourish before long. There is land and labour enough to judge from the present state of affairs for good and extensive cane cultivation ; the factories have been, or are being, well installed. Finally, the British South African Union has done away with interstate customs boundaries, in consequence of which sugar may be transported all over the extensive territory free from duty ; while a rather high import duty of about 5s. per cwt. levied on foreign sugar makes outside competition impossible. Then sugar is transported at a low rate by the railways, so that it is easy for Natal to compete with tropical cane sugar-producing countries, although Natal itself does not lie within the tropics. After the labour problem is fully solved, it will not be long before this colony will be capable of producing all the 100,000 tons of refined sugar that South Africa needs for her home consumption ; but as things are at present, some sugar has still to be imported.

VIII.

MAURITIUS.

I.—Location, History, Cane-planted Area, Total Production.

Mauritius is an island lying in the Indian Ocean, between 19° 58′ and 20° 32′ S. Lat. and 57° 17′ and 57° 57′ E. Long., and is separated from Madagascar by a strait 560 miles wide. Its area covers 742 sq. miles, its greatest length being 13½ miles and its greatest width 22 miles.

Mauritius is of volcanic origin, and is surrounded by a coral reef which is submerged at high tide. Only in three places does the land rise steep from the sea, where there are openings in the coral reef. There are only two good harbours to be found on the highly indented coast, namely, Port Louis, the capital, on the west, and Port Bourbon on the east coast.

A low-lying coastland extends around the entire island, with the exception of the south-west; this coastland widens in the north, and forms the flat districts of Pamplemousses and Rivière du Rempart. A central tableland covers more than half of the entire area, and rises from 800 to 2,000 ft. above the level of the sea. Rows of steep hills of peculiar shape separate this highland in the north, west, and north-west from the lowlands, save in places where an opening affords access, as, for example, from Plaines Wilhems to the Black River district and to Port Louis.

In the east three parallel rows of well-wooded hills run from east to west, and form a transition from highland to low coastland. A mountain ridge which runs across the highlands from north-east to south-west forms the principal watershed of the island. Owing to their enormous affluence, the numerous rivers are of no use for navigation; they generally run through deep, densely overgrown ravines. As, however, the forests on the slopes have been cut down, they are capable of becoming raging mountain streams in the rainy season

There is only one big lake, the Mare aux Vacoas, 1,950 ft. above sea level, which has an area of 1½ sq. miles. This used to be a marsh, but the Colonial Government has turned it into a reservoir by damming up its out-flowing canal, which reservoir provides the towns of Plaines Wilhems with water.

The temperature of Mauritius is not particularly high; at the Observatory at Pamplemousses an average year temperature of 21—22·5° C. (70—72° F.) was observed during the years 1897 to 1902. December, January, February, and March are the warmest months, while the temperature falls during the period April to June, to rise again from June till December. In December, 1900, a maximum temperature of 34·8° C. (94·5° F.) was recorded, while the minimum temperature in May was 10·4° C. (50·7° F.). The average maximum is 25·6° C. (78° F.), and the average minimum 17·5° C. (63·5° F.). The average yearly rainfall was for the ten years period 1893 to 1902 79 ins. over the island.

Mauritius.

With the exception of a few very dry years—such as 1897 and 1900, with a rainfall of 63·2 and 59·8 mm. respectively—the fluctuation in rainfall records does not amount to much. The month of March is the wettest, and that of October the driest ; while the wet months, as a rule, come during the warm season, and the dry months belong to the cold spell. More rain is observed to fall on the windward or eastern side than on the lee-side or south and west part of the country ; the difference in height above the sea level likewise influences the rainfall ; and, as will be pointed out later on, Mauritius is subject to a great many cyclones, which generally occur between December and April ; as a rule, they are accompanied by rain, so that the cyclone period is at the same time the wettest period.

According to the 1901 census, the population of Mauritius, not including the garrison, amounted to :—

People of European, African, or mixed origin ..	108,428
People born in Mauritius from Indian parents ..	198,878
Immigrants born in India	60,208
Chinese	3,509
	371,023

The inhabitants who are not of Asiatic extraction are either the descendants of the original French colonists or of the slaves who were imported from Madagascar and the African Continent. These two races have mixed together, or have mixed with the later British Indians, so that the coloured Creole population consists of the mixture of three types of people. The Indian population dates from the abolition of slavery, 1834 to 1839. As the liberated slaves, numbering 49,365 according to the 1841 census, did not choose to work after their emancipation, coolies were imported from India, a proceeding that has been kept up save for a few intervals till the present day, although in 1908 and 1909 no indentured coolies were recruited. The Chinese, as a rule, are shopkeepers, and the Arabs are very often merchants of some importance.

During the decade 1891 to 1901 the total number of inhabitants had only increased by 435 ; the original population was 2,731 fewer than it used to be, while the Indian population increased by 3,166 inhabitants. The number of deaths is balanced by that of births ; but this proportion was less favourable with the old Mauritian population, which points to a steadily increasing British Indian majority. The sanitary conditions leave much to be desired and the death rate is high : in 1903 it was 35·9 per 1,000 inhabitants.

Owing to the steep and mountainous country, Mauritius does not possess any waterways, but it has 130 miles of public railway viz., two lines from Port Louis to Grande Riviere Sud Est, one along the north and one right across the island. Then there is a line from Port Louis to Mahebourg, with a branch line to Souillac, in Savanne ; and, finally, there is a line to the Black River district. All these railways are single line, and are intersected by a number of stations and passing places.

In connection with these main lines, there is a number of private railway lines, while tram-lines were laid in 1902, when the *surra* disease had made a gap among the bullocks and mules, and the Government helped to have these lines constructed for the transport of cane.

Port Louis is the capital of the island ; it is rather unfavourably situated, as being surrounded by mountains it cannot get the benefit of the south-east trade wind. Since a malaria epidemic in 1866, its population has steadily decreased, for though Port Louis numbered 74,426 inhabitants in 1861, this had dropped to 52,740 in 1901, and can hardly be more than 50,000 at the present day. Many of the well-to-do inhabitants preferred to live near the railway stations in the district of Plaines Wilhems. The second town in size is Mahebourg, with 20,000 inhabitants. What other towns exist are smaller still.

Mauritius was discovered by Mascarenhas, a Portuguese, in 1505, and remained Portuguese or Spanish till 1598. Afterwards it remained unattached, till in 1644 it was taken possession of by the Dutch, who gave it the name of Mauritius. After being abandoned by the Dutch in 1712, it fell to the French in 1715, when it was called Isle de France. It continued a French possession till 1810, after which it fell to the British, who have held it ever since, and who restored the old name of Mauritius. It used to be of greater strategical value to the English than it is now, and that is why it was called " the Malta of the Indian Ocean " or " Star and Key to the Indian Ocean."

In 1650 the Dutch took sugar cane from Java to Mauritius, but this branch of cultivation was not a success ; in 1747 sugar cane was imported once more while Governor Mahé de la Bourdonnais was in office. In 1750 a sugar estate was in operation in the most northern district of the island, named Pample-mousses, which undertaking belonged to the Governor's brother, Mahe de la Villebague. The industry soon extended, and for a long time it was the only profitable one. The production of 1816 amounted to 4,000 tons, prepared in 68 mills, but in 1825 it was extended and improved when Mauritian sugar, on being imported into Great Britain, enjoyed similar or equal rights as did the West Indian sugar. Another cause of improvement was the success of the importation of British Indian coolies after the abolition of slavery, when the sugar exportation of 1855 rose to 120,000 tons. This was a stationary figure during the following forty years, till in 1895 the production all at once rose again considerably, thanks to improvements in the cultivation and manufacturing methods.

At the present day 173,958 out of the total area of 472,750 acres are cultivated, but a considerable part of the country lies fallow owing to the slight rainfall and the lack of irrigation works. Another part is given up to woods, and towns and villages take up some space.

Mauritius.

The 173,958 acres of cultivated area are divided as follows :—

Sugar cane	151,134
Aloe fibre	20,709
Other vegetation	2,115
	173,958

which shows that sugar cane is the staple crop.

Sugar cane is planted all over the island where soil and water conditions allow*. It is met with from the coast up to a height of 1,400 or 1,500 ft., but higher than 1,500 ft. it is too cold for profitable cultivation ; 600 to 800 ft., or even less, is considered the most suitable. There are four different belts as regards fitness of soil for cane cultivation ; the first, including the districts of Pamplemousses and Rivière du Rempart together with the coast of Flacq, is very dry, and does not get more than 40 to 50 ins. of rain yearly, which is not at all evenly distributed, so that there are lengthy dry periods to be recorded. Owing to the regular cutting down of forest, irrigation supplies yield less and less water, in consequence of which this belt has a great many estates fewer than formerly.

The second belt surrounds the central highland ; the latter gets sufficient rain, even as much as 200 ins., but the low temperature that prevails in this district prevents heavy crops from being reaped here. The third belt is in the southern part of the island ; it does not exceed 600 ft. in height, and gets enough rain. The district of the Black River, on the western coast, on the contrary suffers continually from drought, and hardly ever gets more than 20 ins. of rain a year. The three sugar estates in that district are for this reason all well irrigated, and if the irrigation plants were improved and extended, that part of the country would be capable of producing yet more cane.

The total production and the exportation of sugar and molasses have been as follows for the last twenty-eight years, all the figures being expressed in metric tons :—

Year.	Production.	Exportation of sugar.	Exportation of molasses.
1884/85†	126,347	127,784	310
1885/86	117,615	115,299	1,195
1886/87 . ..	100,381	102,376	3,450
1887/88	121,024	124,073	6,060
1888/89	130,337	132,173	3,905
1889/90	127,714	124,565	5,893

* The cane-planted area is shown *shaded* on the Map.

† The statistical year is from August 1st to July 31st.

Africa.

Year.	Production.	Exportation of sugar.	Exportation of molasses.
1890/91	126,483	130,220	4,690
1891/92	114,583	113,813	5,621
1892/93	69,044	68,519	3,359
1893/94	138,965	139,752	7,415
1894/95	116,874	113,793	9,808
1895/96	142,857	142,646	8,553
1896/97	150,749	152,678	13,636
1897/98	121 772	121,694	12,967
1898/99	183,624	186,487	12,681
1899/1900	157,404	157,025	14,929
1900/01	183,433	175,025	19,613
1901/02	153,639	147,828	15,378
1902/03	141,684	150,350	11,412
1903/04	215,697	218,532	18,404
1904/05	142,253	137,899	11,095
1905/06	186,007	191,765	18,597
1906/07	214,699	211,464	14,000
1907/08	163,911	169,161	11,838
1908/09	195,897	191,271	——
1909/10	252,905	235,184	——
1910/11	222,837	217,413	——
1911/12	169,145	160,000	——

The figures of production and of exportation do not always tally ; in most cases the latter exceed the former, in spite of a slight home consumption. This difference can only be accounted for by the fact that the quantity of the production is expressed in bags estimated to contain 170 lbs. These bags, no doubt, do not always contain the same weight, so that the total weight does not quite come to 170 times the number of bags. The sugar when exported is invariably weighed, so we must take the export figure to be the correct one, and as the sugar consumption is estimated at 27 lbs. per head of population, we get to the probable figure of production by adding about 4,000 tons to the export figure.

II.—Cane Cultivation, Cane Varieties, Diseases and Pests, Sugar Manufacture, Output of Sugar, Production per Acre and Cost Price.

The soil of Mauritius is, on the whole, a very light clayland, through which water easily penetrates, so easily indeed that the soil soon dries up, to which the presence of big holes covered with a thin layer of crust at a little distance under the surface greatly contributes. In some places the layer of clay is even and rather thick, while in other places the soil is full of big pieces of lava, which prevent the land from being ploughed. The cane is generally planted in holes, 2,800 to the acre, which is supposed to be better than planting in rows ; especially because cane in holes is much more sheltered from storms.

The holes are placed 3 ft. apart in rows 3 or 4 ft. from each other. They plant two top ends in each hole, cover them slightly with earth, water them, and leave them to sprout. When the young shoots are well developed, manure in the form of sulphate of ammonia, saltpetre, superphosphate, and potash fertilizers or mixtures of them, is put on the plants, and when the cane has grown to some height a quantity of rotten stable dung is added. In addition, the fields are weeded and trashed, and as soon as the cane is ripe it is cut.

The time the cane takes to ripen depends very much on the locality, the kind of cane, and whether it is plant cane or ratoon. The planting in the high and colder districts begins in September, and goes on till May or June ; while at warmer levels the planting season lasts till July or as late as August. In temperate regions the chief planting is done from December to February. Grinding is begun in August, which gives the cane in cool regions two years to grow before it is reaped, the cane of warm tracts a little more than one year, and the cane in temperate regions 18 to 20 months. When ratoons are grown they are manured with guano or other manurial mixtures and stable dung. The ratoon cane is cut after one year, if possible. In the higher parts of the country, where it takes ratoons two years to ripen, a makeshift is to cut the cane late in the crushing season, to keep ratoons for another year, and to cut them at the beginning of the third year, that is after 20 to 22 months of vegetation. Formerly fourth or fifth ratoons were cultivated, but as the quantity of cane reaped was found to decrease gradually on account of the exhaustion of the soil, nowadays only second and third ratoons, taking up about five years, are grown. After this the cane is dug out, and the soil is sown with leguminosae (*Phaseolus lunatus*) and Pois Mascate (*Mucuna utilis*). After a few years these are pulled out and forked under in the planting holes, in order to increase the fertility of the soil with the humus and the nitrogen absorbed from the atmosphere.

A great many cane varieties are grown in Mauritius, some of which were thought much of at one time, to be abandoned subsequently when they were found to be prone to disease. In 1856 a great many borers occurred in the cane ; in 1864 it was a louse, the " pou-à-poche blanche," which played such havoc among the then prevalent cane variety, that they resolved, in 1866 to 1870, to import new cane varieties from Java, Trinidad, British Guiana, Queensland, Hawaii, and other countries. In 1862 the Louzier cane was discovered as a sport of an existing type, and was planted almost all over the island from 1862 to 1875. As it has since been subject to disease, it has now been discarded ; while the White and Striped Tanna species from Java seem now to be popular. Besides these, there are the Port Mackay, the Iscambine, and other well-known varieties ; while some years ago seedling canes were suddenly adopted with great enthusiasm, though the step was of doubtful wisdom. Having heard about the success of West Indian and Java seedling varieties, it was consequently thought any seedling cane would have better results than their existing types. For this reason fields were planted with some kind or other of seedling cane without making sure whether that kind would answer the purpose. But the chaos thus brought about was not to last long, for at the present time, besides the ordinary plant cane, only a few seedling cane varieties are thriving in Mauritius. These came from Barbados and Demerara, especially D. 145, D. 130, and B. 208.

The sugar industry of Mauritius is, as we observed, subject to many difficulties. First, there is prolonged drought from which the cane often suffers, especially on that side of the island furthest from the prevailing winds which does not experience their influence till after the rain has fallen. As the cane cultivation takes up a considerable amount of land, the woods have been cut down, and this has interfered with the equal distribution of the rain. Pamplemousses and Rempart, which used to be the richest districts, are now the poorest, and many of their irrigation canals have become useless because the water that was to fill them is wanting. Moreover, Mauritius is in the route of cyclones, which now and then rage in great force and damage both buildings and crops. The cyclone season is from December to April or May, and as the crushing season begins in August, a late cyclone may just strike it when it is full-grown and least able to resist the force of the wind.

The cane itself is attacked by all sorts of diseases and pests, the borers, the *Sesamia nonagrioides* in particular, doing a lot of harm. These insects were imported from Java years ago together with the grass (*Panicum*) that was to be used as fodder for cargoes of ponies when transported to Mauritius. The caterpillars were hidden among the grass, appeared as moths and laid their eggs on the sugar cane, which ever since has been infested with them. A method of combatting the pest is to search the newly-planted fields and cut off the shoots still containing caterpillars, and use the former as fodder, but it does not succeed in exterminating the pest. Another insect much found among the canes is the shot-borer beetle (*Xyleborus perforans*). According to the opinion of some people, it is found on living canes, while others think it is only found on the dead plant. Most of the diseases known in other countries— such as Smut, Black Rot, Red Smut, and Root Disease, etc.—are found here,

Mauritius.

too ; also a so-called Gum Disease, discovered in 1894, which, according to some investigations, is due to bacteria, and is apt to do much damage.

In 1901 the stock of cattle in Mauritius suffered severely from the *Surra* disease, which carried off one-third of the draught bullocks and two-thirds of the mules, and also affected the cane industry indirectly by disorganizing the cane transportation through want of cattle, lack of stable dung being another effect.

Several estates through lack of capital have been forced to give up planting cane themselves, and lease large pieces of land to British Indian immigrants, who grow cane on it, and sell the cane to the factories. Other estates have been divided and sold piecemeal to British Indian immigrants, who when living close to the factory can easily have the cane carted there, but should they live at some distance away the cane is transported by the State railways. The small planter is never sure of his business, for should there be an abundance of cane the manufacturers might not want to buy the whole lot, in which case the planter does not know what to do with it ; on the other hand, should the crop turn out insufficient for the estates, the small planter can charge a high price for his cane, and consequently make some profit. But for this industrious and numerous class of British Indian cane planters, the sugar industry of Mauritius would soon come to a stop, for which reason a system of planting by independent farmers is to be recommended in a way, although it likewise has its drawbacks. The old Mauritian planter used to spend much money and labour in manuring and in the maintenance of the fertility of the soil in general ; while the Indian, who only thinks of immediate profit, is too economical as regards manuring and tillage, and robs the soil on a large scale.

During the years 1894 to 1898, on an average 3,500 to 4,000 tons of sulphate of ammonia were imported into Mauritius, together with 100 to 120 tons Chili saltpetre (sodium nitrate), 1,000 to 1,100 tons of superphosphate, 500 to 350 tons of other phosphates, 1,800 to 1,900 tons of saltpetre (potassium nitrate), 120 to 130 tons of sulphate of potash, 6,000 to 8,000 tons of guano from the Seychelles and other islands, which means in all 14,000 tons of imported manure. Supposing that 75,000 acres are yearly manured, we come to the average of 420 lbs. artificial manure per acre. But we cannot in practice speak of an average manuring, as the Indian is not likely to add any artificial manure to his stable dung. This shows how large a quantity of manure the old Mauritian uses to give to his land ; and that, at the same time, should the land become Indian property the ground would soon be the poorer for it and have a bad effect on the sugar production.

The old planters maintain that thirty or forty years ago they used to reap from their plantations sown with the old kind of cane 5 to 6 tons of sugar per arpent*, or 10 to 12 metric tons of sugar per hectare ; while now they have to be content with 2 to 2½ tons per arpent (4,000 to 5,000 kg. per hectare).

* 1 arpent = 1·04 acres.

The crop the Indian plantations yield is far less than this, as 14½ tons of cane seems to be their average crop per acre.

It is difficult to say how far these old-time stories are true, but it is a fact that the production of planted cane nowadays amounts to 30 tons of first and 20 tons of second ratoons, the yield being 9 per cent. ; hence on an average 2 to 2½ tons of sugar are obtained from an acre of cane that takes twelve to twenty-two months to ripen.

The proportion between the quantity of plant cane and that of ratoons is for the following districts as follows :—

District.	Plant cane.	Ratoons.
Pamplemousses	23·3	76·7
Rivière du Rempart	22·1	77·9
Flacq	24·4	75·6
Grand Port	22·4	77·6
Plaine Wilhems	24·0	76·0
Black River	27·5	72·5
Moka	22·5	77·5
Savanne	26·4	73·6

The proportion is hence about 1·3 ; from this and the preceding figure we can easily assume a cane production of 50,000 lbs. (or say 22⅓ tons) per acre.

We cannot tell for certain how many plantations are engaged in sugar cane cultivation, as there are a great many whose yearly output amounts to but a few cartloads. The estates which have more than 100 acres of cane planted are divided as follows :—

More than 1,000 acres	31
Between 500 and 1,000	44
Between 100 and 500	68

The planted area of the big undertakings amounts to 83,900 acres, while the area under cane belonging to the Indians is estimated at 47,500 acres.

The labourers for field and factory work are recruited in British India. The planters enter into a contract with the coolies for five years, at the end of which time the agreement may be renewed from year to year. There is no lack of labour, so that in Mauritius they are not troubled by that stock complaint of most cane sugar producing countries. Once or twice a year the planters apply to the Immigration Bureau, and state the number of labourers required. When the coolies arrive they are distributed by the Bureau among the different plantations, the owners of which have to pay 170 rupees* towards the transportation expenses of the coolies. The wages of the latter vary according to the work done. The newcomers are employed for field work ; after a year or two they get more important work in the field or in the factories. The wages which vary from 8 to 9 rupees per month are paid every week, and above this they get each 5 rupees' worth of rice, oil, and salt every month. They have free medical attendance and medicine from the employers. Most free day-labourers receive 0·60 to 0·75 rupees per day in case of men, and 0·30 to 0·50 rupees for women, in which case there is no question of all the above privileges, such as free medical treatment, etc., being granted. After the end of their indenture, a great many of the imported British Indians remain in the country, or come back after having returned for a short time to their native land, and as their immigration dates from the abolition of slavery in 1834, it is clear that by now several generations of Indians have lived in Mauritius, and have made this island their permanent home. This, of course, has solved the labour difficulty, in so far that since 1908 no more indentured coolies have had to be imported.

The cane which the sugar manufacturers cannot themselves plant is bought from European or Indian planters, and then crushed. In this transaction two different systems may be followed, according to the quantity of cane offered. In the case of big transactions, the planter receives 6·5 or 7 per cent. of the weight in cane paid in sugar or in money equivalent at the average market price. This refers to the delivery of cut cane to the weighing bridge or to the tram halt. When cane is bought from smaller planters they simply pay 8 to 10·50 rupees (9 rupees on an average) per ton, also for cane delivered at the factory. In most cases the cane is laden into carts of 2 to 2½ tons capacity, and conveyed to the factory in a train of ten to twelve wagons, the load and the number of carts depending greatly on the slope of the ground. In many places with steep slopes, and where the roads are traversed by deep ravines, they transport by cable carriers. Some estates transport their cane by the State railways, in which case they pay very low rates ; but one of the drawbacks of this mode of transportation is that these wagons are run in the ordinary train service, so that the cane does not get worked up till a long time after it is cut.

The number of sugar factories gradually decreases : between 1875 and 1881 there were 171 ; in 1891, 131 ; in 1901, 115 ; and in 1910 the number had gone down to 64. As, however, the total sugar production is not any less, the average capacity of the factories must have increased considerably. In many places they have turned two or three small factories into one, and the old machinery they have combined into one bigger plant ; but this does not always mean modernizing the old installations.

Up to some time ago the factories were not at all modernly installed ; the mills were of but low power, and the whole installation was old-fashioned, and far from economical. Since 1900, however, matters have been much

* 1 rupee @ 100 cents. = 1s. 4d. Rs. 170 = £11 6s. 8d.

improved, and double and triple crushing, with maceration, is found everywhere, together with evaporation and boiling in vacuum, crystallizers, etc. ; in short, all the most modern apparatus. But not a single factory is altogether up-to-date ; it always has some old-fashioned item among its machinery. This of course, is due to the fact that by turning small estates into big ones use is made of the old material as much as possible ; while some new odd pieces are bought to complete the plant. The furnaces do not seem altogether a success, and consume a good deal of fuel, consisting of bagasse as well as cane trash and wood. Six factories manufacture over 50 tons of sugar per 24 hours, while the others produce something between 20 and 50 tons.

The kinds of sugar which Mauritius produces are distinguished as follows :—

	Polarization
Vesou or white first product	98·5
First after-product sugar, white crystals ..	97·5—98
Second ,, ,, ,, yellow ,, ..	88·0
Third ,, ,, ,, dark yellow crystals	84—86

In addition, there is brown sugar, while the remaining molasses, polarizing about 40°, is also sold.

The average polarization of the total production of Mauritius sugar is estimated at 96·7 per cent.

As regards the chemical control, Mauritius is still behind the times. Only 23 out of the 64 factories, consequently a little more than one-third, possess a proper chemist of their own ; and when chemical control is exercised, the methods of analysis are obsolete, and no unity exists in the application and calculation of the data obtained, so that the figures representing sugar losses and sugar yield are far from exact.

With this reservation, we can place the average sugar content of cane at 13·77 per cent., which in 1911 yielded the following quantities of sugar of 96·7 per cent. on an average.

Number of factories.	Per cent. of the total.	Yield.
3	4·68	below 9·5
7	10·94	9·5—10
14	21·87	10—10·5
17	26·56	10·5—10·75
7	10·95	10·75—11
10	15·62	11—11·5
6	9·38	above 11

The maximum was 12·26 per cent. yield on cane with 15·13 sucrose, and the minimum 9·24 per cent. on cane with 13·13 per cent. sucrose.

Mauritius.

As may be seen from the figures given for a number of factories during the period 1904 to 1909, a great improvement is to be noticed :—

Year.	Yield on 100 cane.	Yield on 100 sucrose in cane.
1904/05	9·92	73·5
1905/06	10·00	74·1
1906/07	10·12	75·0
1907/08	10·41	77·1
1908/09	10·56	78·2
1909/10	10·56	78·3
1910/11	10·63	78·5

The quantity of sugar for each of the districts is given in the following table ; we have, however, to add that the total exceeds the figure of production given on page 310, which may be due to the conversion of bags into kilograms.

District.		1910/11	1909/10	1908/09	1907/08	1906/07	1904/05
Savanne	12	42,475·9	46,267·5	35,859·1	29,946·2	39,720·8	22,613·8
Grand Port ...	12	41,192·9	46,135·3	35,431·7	30,234·2	41,925·5	26,096·5
Flacq	8	38,494·4	42,995·8	32,907·3	34,227·9	47,209·4	33,517·6
Moka	7	35,496·8	40,469·1	32,763·5	25,617·1	30,875·5	21,983·5
Riviére du Rempart	8	27,188·4	31,197·8	23,705·6	15,675·6	23,807·5	17,096·7
Pamplemousses ...	9	20,921·5	26,699·8	19,291·8	15,461·2	20,600·9	13,908·9
Plaines Wilhems...	4	13,375·0	15,007·	11,875·8	9,680·	11,699·5	5,191·4
Riviére Noire ...	2	3,692·1	4,222·3	4,062·3	3,241·	4,292·8	3,250·
Total	62	222,837·0	252,994·6	195,897·1	164,083·2	220,131·9	143,658·4

Four factories state the following as the average cost of production for the years between 1893 and 1907—the prices at which the sugar is sold being also given.

Year.	Average cost of production per 50 kg. Rs.	Market price per 50 kg. Rs.	Gain or loss. Rs.
1893	6·71	10·21	+ 3·50
1894	9·74	9·69	− 0·05
1895	7·26	9·75	+ 2·49
1896	7·61	8·24	+ 0·63

Year.	Average cost of production per 50 kg. Rs.	Market price per 50 kg. Rs.	Gain or loss. Rs.
1897	7·46	8·15	+ 0·69
1898	5·44	7·12	+ 1·68
1899	5·89	8·15	+ 2·26
1900	5·78	8·75	+ 2·97
1901	7·52	7·25	− 0·27
1902	8·14	7·25	− 0·89
1903	6·58	6·75	+ 0·17
1904	6·67	9·70	+ 3·03
1905	5·97	7·00	+ 1·03
1906	5·52	6·60	+ 1·08
1907	6·41	7·60	+ 1·19

A report on ten other factories gives for 1908 the cost price at Rs. 6·94 per 50 kg., and a market price of Rs. 7·85, which means a gain of Rs. 0·91 per 50 kg. A calculation of another factory comes to Rs. 6 per 50 kg., as follows :—

Raw material	4·50	Rs.
Manufacture	1·20	,,
General expenses	0·15	,,
Transport to the harbour	0·15	,,
	6·00	,,

Import and Export Duties, Government Assistance, Financial Affairs, and Place of Destination of Sugar Exported.

Mauritius levies an export duty of 32 cents per 100 kg. of sugar ; of this 2 cents goes towards the maintenance of the Experiment Station. The export duty on molasses is 40 cents on a barrel of about 6 cwt. The import duty amounts to Rs. 2 per 100 kg. of raw sugar, while that on refined sugar and candy is Rs. 4·50.

Although the idea of levying export duty on the principal article of the export trade is not in accordance with modern economical points of view, this export duty is a means of making the sugar industry contribute towards the financial affairs of the State, and considering the help the Government have given to the sugar industry, it is only fair they should in their turn get something out of it.

The financial position of the Mauritius sugar industry is far from favourable, and in times of great stress the owners of the estates would have been bankrupt but for the timely help of the Mother country. In 1892 a violent hurricane caused much damage to buildings and to vegetation ; it was on this occasion that the British Government lent Rs. 5,868,450 to the planters, and Rs. 700,500 to the owners of the factories at 5 per cent., with regular redemption up till 1924. On 30th June, 1909, Rs. 3,101,673 and Rs. 668,701 had been paid up respectively, while only Rs. 22,255 were still in arrears, Rs. 14,355 of this being due to the non-payment of one borrower. Then the Government had to purchase two estates in order to realize Rs. 6,500 and Rs. 100,000 which were owing to the Government ; but further losses it has not suffered.

In 1898, when the Mauritian planters had got into a fix again, the Government was considerate enough to lend Rs. 1,491,000 for one year, which sum has also been paid back. In 1902 another bad time, brought about by a lowering of prices, a hurricane, and an infectious cattle disease, was experienced—all of which causes had an injurious effect on the cane production. The Government was ready again to help, and in 1908 loaned an amount of £185,185 to planters, in order to enable them to construct narrow-gauge railways and other transport systems and £197,732 to forty-three sugar factories and three small planters in order to secure a better cultivation.

The first loan, known as the " Mechanical Transport Loan," was to be repaid, together with 5 per cent. interest, in twenty half-yearly instalments, and this has been done so far without any difficulty ; in 1909 as much as £102,354 was repaid. The second loan, called " Advance in Aid Loan," had to be reimbursed with 6 per cent. interest by June, 1903, or in two instalments by June, 1903 and 1904. This, however, did not work quite so smoothly, but at the end of 1906 all the money had been paid in, so that the Government has not been out of pocket on account of these loans, except in the case of the Rs. 22,255.

Encouraged by this success, the Department of Agriculture in 1907 asked for another loan of £600,000 in order to enable the sugar manufacturers to modernize their machinery ; and another £100,000 in order to buy land for reforestation ; while, later on, £200,000 was asked for raising a fund for the sugar planting, with an eye to better cultivation. Before consenting to this, the British Government sent a Commission to Mauritius, for the purpose of examining thoroughly into the condition of the island, and of the industry, and to propose measures for their improvement should these be required.

This Commission visited Mauritius from 22nd May to 29th September, 1909, and presented their Report in April, 1910. The conclusion arrived at was that the condition of Mauritius as a sugar-producing country was, on the whole, not unsatisfactory. Though the soil may be less fertile than the soil of many another country, still it is capable of good crops if manuring and tillage are properly carried out. Labour in Mauritius is cheap, abundant, and reliable; the railway system is extensive, and forms a connection with the excellent country roads and narrow-gauge lines, so that all the conditions that make for success are fulfilled. One weak point is that sugar is Mauritius' only industry, so that fluctuations in prices or a disease amongst the canes or draught-cattle must of necessity affect the whole island. This is the more so in that the financial position of planters and manufacturers is not strong, and one year's adversity will be enough to make them dependent on State assistance, as the Commission has forcibly pointed out. First of all, most of the sugar estates are heavily mortgaged at 7 to 9 per cent. interest. Next, 34 of the 65 sugar factories have contracted other debts-besides those with the Government; 55 factories being under a combined debt of Rs. 12,000,000 (that is including the loans); the other 11 factories have no debts whatever, but the numerous cane planters who have no factories are badly off in this way.

But it is not only these mortgages on land and factories they have to pay off; most of the planters have also borrowed floating capital. About April they have generally used up all the money received from the last year's crop, and new money has to be borrowed from lenders under the security of the crop for the completion of the harvest in the field, and for the planting of new cane. These money-lenders are generally merchants or brokers who have something to do with British Indian sugar merchants, and consequently can influence the sale-price of the product. The interest, as a rule, amounts to 10 per cent., and the commission on the goods sold 2½ per cent.; these rates vary, of course, according to the financial position of the party borrowing money.

Besides having to pay a large sum as interest on mortgages and floating capital, the manufacturer is also handicapped through his debts by having to depend on the sugar merchants, who choose their time for selling sugar, however inconvenient this may be for the planter. Then the manufacturer has to buy his implements and necessaries through his money-lender, and consequently has not much to say as regards the choice of goods, which, again, may mean financial loss to him. The planters' and manufacturers' dependence as described above is considered a great drawback by the Commission, and is at the bottom of the present unsatisfactory condition of the sugar industry in Mauritius; and for this very reason the Commission recommended, besides an improved railway system and a campaign against malaria, the necessity of granting a loan not exceeding £115,000, £15,000 of which should go towards assisting the small planters in their periodical troubles. Moreover, a Department of Agriculture would have to be created similar to that in British India, while the irrigation problem must be studied thoroughly. The authorities have not yet resolved on anything, but the British Government, no doubt, will grant the loan.

The exportation of sugar for the last twelve years has been destined for the following countries, the figures representing tons of 2,240 lbs. —

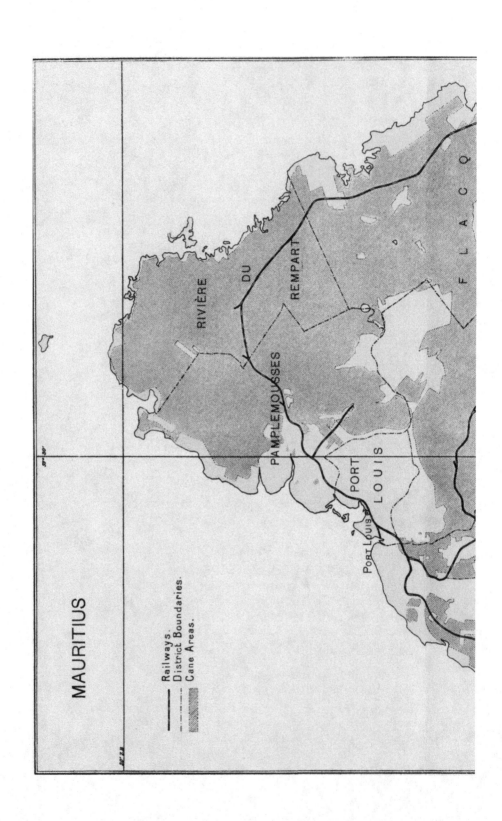

MAURITIUS

Railways.
District Boundaries.
Cane Areas.

RIVIÈRE DU REMPART

PAMPLEMOUSSES

PORT LOUIS

Port Louis

F L A C Q

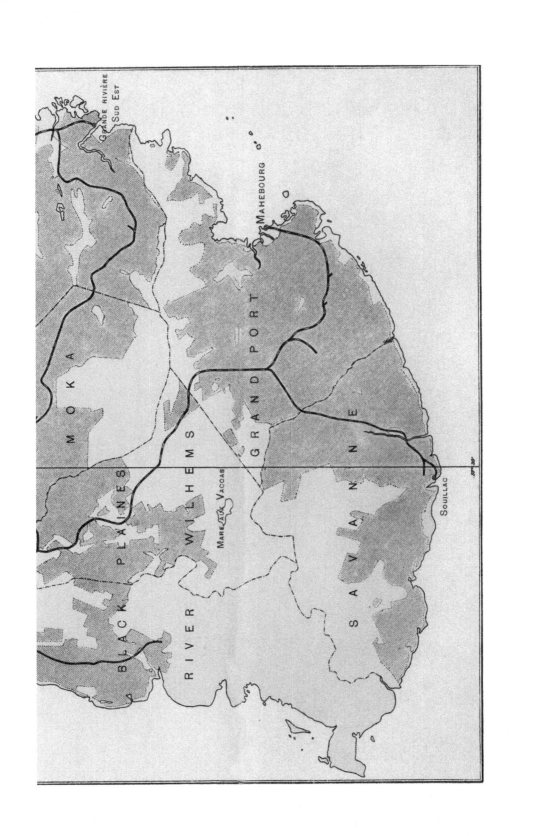

COUNTRY.	1899/1900	1900/01	1901/02	1902/03	1903/04
Europe	9,785	16,728	16,587	15,778	28,602
British India	82,055	109,274	103,675	89,398	140,112
Australia	14,252	9,290	3,735	8,416	6,231
South Africa	29,578	31,860	21,190	28,589	37,314
America	16,032	6,415	—	—	—
Other countries	2,227	1,701	2,641	8,065	3,731
Total ..	153,929	175,268	147,828	150,306	215,031

COUNTRY.	1904/05	1905/06	1906/07	1907/08	1908/09	1909/10	1910/11
Europe	9,349	7,304	24,249	21,188	22,791	46,699	52,485
Bombay	66,294	90,587	101,767	86,162	96,086	97,621	106,454
Calcutta	6,620	11,695	15,350	8,905	8,151	21,596	5,404
Kurachi	3,468	4,460	16,650	14,271	21,892	28,743	24,614
Australia	1,216	5,348	4,324	3,334	2,462	3,108	2,159
South Africa	39,010	43,342	34,836	23,486	18,089	16,066	20,879
America	5,498	4,824	3,392	7,959	15,208	9,526	—
Hong Kong	} 4,272	19,079	6,611	345	8	6,517	867
Other countries			931	846	3,572	1,604	4,551
Total ..	135,727	186,639	208,133	166,496	188,259	231,480	217,413

Most of the molasses is sent to British India, the rest to South Africa ; hence the total export of sugar products is chiefly directed to the neighbouring British Indian peninsula, with which Mauritius has many points in common, e.g., as to currency. Bombay is the Indian port to which Mauritius sugar is chiefly shipped, then comes Calcutta. South Africa also buys Mauritius sugar, although the amount dwindles every year, as South Africa itself tends to produce her own sugar, especially in Natal, Zululand, and Mozambique ; in the end she may not want any more sugar from Mauritius, so that British India and England will eventually be the sole buyers of the Mauritian product.

Apart from the high interest the manufacturers have to pay to the sugar merchants, they are also dependent on them in having to put up with lower prices than the sugar might fetch in a free market, if it was not for the sugar merchants' interference. Then Mauritius cannot always rely on British India as a buyer, for during the years 1898 to 1903 Austrian and German sugars flooded the British Indian markets, because of the low prices at which they could be sold owing to the Cartel bounties. This was a severe blow to both the Mauritius sugar industry and the British Indian refineries. In 1899 a compensating duty equal to the amount of the bounty paid on sugar when exported from the producing country was levied in India ; this was done by way of compensation to those affected branches of industry, and when this measure did not prove adequate, the import duty on Austrian and German sugars was again raised in 1903 by a sum corresponding to the surplus profit made by the Cartels in those countries. This duty, of course, made it impossible for German and Austrian sugar to be imported, and not till all bounties on European beetroot sugar were abolished, and the Cartel profit disappeared through the provisions of the Brussels Convention, did this unequal competition cease to exist. Mauritius, however, has another powerful competitor on the British Indian market in Java, which exports white sugar to India in larger quantities every year. But these supplies are readily absorbed in India, so that this does not affect the price of the sugar, nor does it supplant Mauritius sugar in any way.

To judge from the present state of affairs, the sugar industry of Mauritius is not likely to expand, even should the proposals for ameliorating the existing conditions, as given above, become law ; it will retain its present position for some time to come.

Books of Reference :

Report of the Mauritius Royal Commission, 1909.
James Forrester Anderson. *The Sugar Industry of Mauritius.*
Noel Deerr. *Some Notes on the Sugar Industry of Mauritius.*
Deutsche Consulatsberichte.
Rapports annuels de la Station agronomique de l'île de Maurice.

IX.

RÉUNION.

The Island of Réunion lies in the Indian Ocean at 20° 51′ S. Lat. and 53° 10′ E. Long. Its area is estimated at 970 sq. miles, its population being 173,315. Its greatest length amounts to 44 miles, its greatest width 31 miles. Réunion is of volcanic formation, and may have been the result of consecutive eruptions, the main crater having shifted in a north-west south-east direction. At the present time it lies in the south-east of the island, and forms an isolated moun-

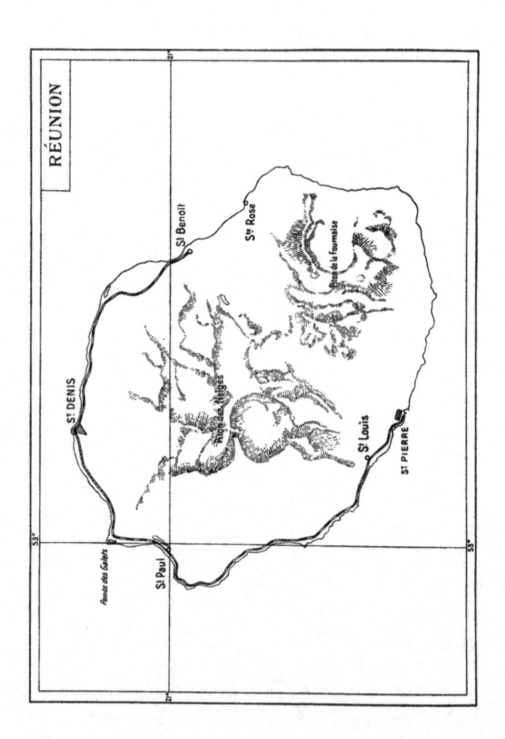

tain, in the midst of the mountainous tract bearing traces of former volcanoes now extinct. The whole island is a mountainous cone, the highest peak of which, the Piton des Neiges, is 10,000 ft. high. Then there are the summits of Piton de la Fournaise, still an active volcano, 8,600 ft. high, and the Piton du Petit Bernard, 8,330 ft. high. A great many rivers flow from the mountains into the sea in all directions ; they have no length to speak of, and are of no use to navigation. The climate of the island is tropical, and varies according to the locality, *i.e.*, the lee or windward side. From April to November a south-west wind blows steadily and with great force, and after touching the high mountain-chain splits into two. One branch follows the coast from the south-east in a northern direction, then bends to the west, as far as the capital, St. Denis, where it reaches the sea ; the other branch follows the coast in a south to west direction, and joins the first branch a long way out at sea.

The cyclones that infest these parts approach the island from the north-east, and do not make themselves felt till they come to the seaport of Sainte Rose. As the mountains block the path of the wind, it is not till twelve hours after that the cyclone penetrates to the western side of the island ; this leaves the authorities time enough to warn by telegraph the people on the lee side of the coming danger, so that they may take measures to minimize the damage.

It is the high mountains, again, that make the clouds discharge their moisture on the east and south-east sides, and leave the north and west coast drier than the windward side of Réunion. Owing to the frequent gales and cyclones, the roads form no safe anchorage for ships ; consequently, an artificial harbour has had to be built near Pointe de Galets as a shelter to navigation.

Along the west and north coast a narrow-gauge railway has been constructed from St. Pierre to St. Benoit viâ Saint Paul, Pointe des Galets and St. Denis— totalling in length 78 miles. This line, covering two-thirds of the entire circumference of the island, runs along the coast all the way except between St. Denis and St. Benoit, where it goes inland for some distance. As a great many streams from the mountain ranges running into the sea are crossed by the railroad at right angles, a comparatively large number of bridges and other artificial works had to be built for the mileage ; there is one 6-mile tunnel in the mountainous district between Possession and St. Denis, which tunnel is only broken by the valleys of the Ravine à Jacques and of the Grande Chaloupe. The Southern districts, Sainte Rose, Saint Philippe, and Saint Joseph, being very mountainous, have no railway connections whatever.

Besides the railway mentioned there are wide, metalled roads, a main road all around the island, and other smaller ones that connect the towns ; altogether, they cover 322 miles.

The Portuguese discovered Réunion and called it Santa Appolina, but the island changed its name to Mascareigna, after Pedro Mascarenhas, who visited the place in 1505, as well as Mauritius and Rodriguez.

Africa.

The Portuguese had to leave the island in 1638, when it was taken possession of by Salomon Goubert in the name of the French King Louis XIII. The latter used it as a sort of convict colony for prisoners from Madagascar, but it was not a success as a colony till in 1665 the French East Indian Company took the island in hand, to which they gave the name of Isle Bourbon, and turned it into a flourishing colony. In 1764, however, it fell to the French Government, as the French Indian Company had experienced bad times ; and in 1776 it was united to Mauritius, then called Isle de France, and formed into one colony. In 1790 the island was renamed Réunion, and from that time it sent its delegates to the National Assembly.

In Napoleon's time it changed its name again, this time for Ile Bonaparte ; in 1810 it was taken by the English, and in 1815 it was returned to France and was then called Ile Bourbon again. Finally, the Second Republic changed Ile Bourbon to Réunion once more, which name it has kept ever since.

In 1848 slavery was abolished, the owners were indemnified, and the slaves themselves changed into French citizens, who in 1870 obtained the franchise. After the abolition of slavery it was made clear here as well as everywhere else that emancipated slaves cannot be turned into steady labourers, so that the gap in the labour had to be filled by indentured immigrants from British India, who were such a success that in 1870 no fewer than 62,000 Indian immigrants were employed in Réunion, and the sugar production amounted to 60,000 to 70,000 tons. The coffee plantations were also in a flourishing state ; so were agriculture, commerce, and navigation.

In 1882 the immigration from India came to an end, England being opposed to it, and from this time we notice a gradual deterioration in many respects. The lack of labour soon became critical, and at the present time not more than 16,000 British labourers are employed in the island, too small a number to be adequate, so that the sugar cane plantations had to be limited, and this, of course, affected the yearly output of sugar, and reduced it to half the amount it had once been. Attempts were made to get labourers from the East African coast, but without success, as these labourers were unsuitable, and the competition with Natal meant too much. It was no use either to endeavour to obtain immigrants from Tonkin and Java ; so that the sugar industry of Réunion is retarded by a constant lack of labour in both field and factory.

Still the cane production per acre in 1895 was double the amount it used to be in 1880, and the sugar yield has increased from 9 per cent. to 10 per cent. in that time ; but the planted area has gone down 40 per cent., so that nevertheless the total increase does not amount to much.

The sugar industry dates from 1806, when terrible cyclones played havoc among the coffee and clove plantations, and made the people look for an annual plant that, when destroyed, would not mean the loss of many years' trouble and expense.

The improvement in both the industry and the population of the island may be seen from the following table referring to the years 1815 to 1860 :—

Year.	Number of Inhabitants.	Number of Immigrants.	Cane planted hectares.	Sugar Exportation in tons.	Kg. sugar per hectare.
1815	68,400	—	—	21	—
1820	71,700	—	—	4,500	—
1825	81,800	—	6,500	7,607	2,341
1826	87,100	—	8,200	10,000	2,439
1829	100,000	3,100	—	12,506	—
1833	—	2,400	11,500	19,622	2,963
1836	108,800	1,900	14,500	18,218	2,759
1837	106,000	1,400	15,100	18,275	3,298
1840	104,700	1,400	16,000	19,783	3,625
1842	105,000	1,350	24,000	28,186	2,459
1843	104,500	1,350	24,100	28,479	2,505
1846	106,200	2,400	25,300	23,184	1,833
1849	120,000	12,100	26,000	18,540	1,520
1851	135,000	23,400	27,000	23,749	1,755
1855	176,000	49,100	56,500	56,905	1,802
1856	181,600	50,200	58,000	56,211	1,934
1857	185,800	53,200	59,000	51,954	1,930
1858	194,300	60,800	60,500	58,655	1,939
1859	199,400	64,700	61,300	62,599	2,042
1860	200,000	64,400	62,000	68,464	2,208

Since 1860 the sugar production has amounted to the following quantities, expressed in metric tons :—

1861/70 (average)	..	48,413		1884..	..	..	37,972
1870 ..	..	..	23,533	1885..	..	..	34,732
1871 ..	..	..	33,100	1886..	..	..	31,389
1872 ..	..	..	30,419	1887..	..	..	35,031
1873 ..	..	..	36,353	1888..	..	..	25,418
1874 ..	..	..	32,176	1889..	..	..	36,165
1875 ..	..	..	35,449	1890..	..	..	38,410
1876 ..	..	..	34,262	1891..	..	..	38,949
1877 ..	..	..	40,380	1892..	..	..	35,971
1878 ..	..	..	33,031	1893..	..	..	39,829
1879 ..	..	..	21,175	1894..	..	..	37,748
1880 ..	..	..	27,373	1895..	..	..	44,747
1881 ..	..	..	24,709	1896..	..	..	40,447
1882 ..	..	..	33,020	1897..	..	..	31,488
1883 ..	..	..	37,799	1898..	..	..	37,781

1899 ..	..	..	35,000	1905..	..	..	38,000
1900 ..	..	..	42,631	1906..	..	..	44,689
1901 ..	..	..	30,120	1907..	..	..	39,380
1902 ..	..	..	39,624	1908..	..	..	41,187
1903 ..	..	..	41,617	1909..	..	..	41,087
1904 ..	..	..	30,000	1910..	..	..	45,549

At the present moment it is accepted that 62,000 to 70,000 acres are planted with cane, 26,000 of which are cut every year. The cane is planted from July till March, according to the location of the estate and to custom. The soil is first ploughed up, and then rectangular holes are made 1 ft. deep, 22 to 24 ins. long and 5 to 8 in. wide, at 3 ft. distance from each other in rows also 3 ft. apart, so that 2,400 plant holes are dug on one acre. They put one or two tops with at least three buds in each hole, and as soon as the cane has sprung up it is banked, weeded, and manured with stable dung or with artificial manure ; while green manure with leguminosæ is applied at the time when the ground is not planted with cane.

The cane, both plant and ratoon, is reaped about 14 to 20 months after planting.

The following table gives a clear insight into the consecutive crops of planted cane, and it shows that they only plant once on the same soil during eight to twenty years :—

	Low-lying ground from 1—100 feet above sea level.	High-lying un-irrigated land 100—2,000 feet above sea level
First year ..	Planting done in July and August	Planting done Oct.—Nov.
Second year ..	First crop in November ..	——
Third ,, ..	Second crop in December	First crop
Fourth ,, .	——	
Fifth ,, ..	Third crop in July, lying fallow, green manure	Second crop
Sixth ,, ..	Maize	
Seventh ,, ..	Manioc	Third crop in July, lying fallow, green manure
Eighth ,, ..	Cane planting	Maize, manioc, and cane again the tenth year

In Réunion a great many cane varieties are in vogue, as each planter seems to affect a special type. In addition to the old varieties, there are also some descendants of seedling canes, although one never comes across a specimen of this kind that excels in any way.

Among animal pests of the cane we may mention the borers and aphis; while smut, yellow spot disease, gum disease, and sereh are among the parasitical diseases. The greatest obstacle to the development of the sugar industry is scarcity of labour, as has been pointed out above. Although the number of immigrants in Réunion amounted to 68,469 in 1860, it went down to 41,045 in 1881, and to 13,578 in 1902, who belonged to the following races :—

	31 Dec., 1881	31 Dec., 1902
Indians	27,034	6,636
Africans	13,518	5,934
Chinese	493	1,008
	41,045	13,578

These figures also include servants, and persons who are not employed by the cane cultivators; and for want of fresh supplies the amount has considerably decreased since.

Réunion had twenty-four sugar factories in 1909, distributed over the different districts as follows :—

Sainte Marie	3
Saint André	3
Bras Panot	2
Saint Benoit	1
Sainte Rose	1
Saint Joseph	1
Saint Pierre	4
Saint Louis	1
Saint Leu	2
Trois Bassins	1
Saint Paul	5
	24

It is almost impossible to state the exact figures of production, but those at our disposal show how the cultivation suffers from want of proper labour, which has a bad effect on the cane weight. The following table, giving the production of fifteen factories, will demonstrate this fact :—

| | Kg. cane per hectare. | |
	Plant cane.	Total amount of cane.
1882	——	29,852
1883	——	34,064
1884	——	36,330
1885	——	37,182
1886	——	37,233
1887	——	39,052
1889	——	50,596
1890	——	50,649
1891	70,000	49,263
1892	63,213	45,719 (cyclone)
1893	72,550	51,382
1894	75,371	56,927
1895	83,913	60,937
1896	74,665	60,495
1897	67,699	54,229
1898	65,923	55,729
1899	56,403	44,179 (cyclone)
1900	68,215	52,059
1901	58,018	45,326
Average	68,724	52,385
Tons per acre	27·390	21·485

The cost price of cane delivered on the factory scales is calculated at 20 frs. per ton, although it may be more or less according to the weather, the distance between the factory and the fields, and to the labour supply.

During the last few years cane has fetched from 15 to 18 frs. per ton, or 5·6 to 6·2 per cent. of the weight of the cane, in first sugar or its equivalent in money. The planters have not made much profit, but can just keep things going, for, including everything, we may put down 12 to 22 frs. as the price cane costs the planters when employing hired labour, and 12 to 15 frs. for planters who do all the work themselves.

The princ pal manufacturing concern is the Crédit Foncier Colonial, which owns the best estates, numbering seven. It plants one-seventh of the cane produced in the is!and, and adds so much bought cane to it that the amount of cane worked up and sugar exported by the company comes to one-third of the entire production. As it has got plenty of capital, it can itself export its sugar to France, and enjoy the " détaxe de distance," a discount which is allowed on cane sugar when imported from French colonies into the Mother-country.

Réunion.

The smaller manufacturers who do not possess any capital have been the recipients of money advances from British Indian merchants, and consequently they are obliged to sell their sugar at a lower price, and any profit is out of the question. In 1906 no fewer than 9,000 tons of sugar went to Bombay in payment for rice sent to Réunion ; but in other years almost the entire exportation of sugar was destined for France.

They tried, as in Mauritius and some of the Antilles, to let out small plots of ground for cane cultivation, but there was no demand for them, and the whole project was a failure. The topography of the island does not allow of central factories being founded amidst a large extent of soil tilled by farmers. It may be tried on the windward side, where the factories should lie on the coast ; but on the lee side the roads would be far too bad, the transport too difficult, and the distance to the railway too great to carry on the industry on such a large scale.

On the sugar exported 2 per cent. of the value is levied as an export duty, in addition to an extra duty of 8½ centimes per 100 kg. and a statistical duty of 3 centimes per 100 kg. When Réunion sugar is imported into France it enjoys a reduction on the import duty, a *détaxe de distance* equal to the actual freight of sugar from the colony to the Mother-country up to the maximum of 2·80 francs per 100 kg. white, and 2·33 francs per 100 kg. raw sugar.

As the actual freight cost always exceeds this maximum, the *détaxe de distance* on Réunion sugar may be estimated at this maximum amount.

The Brussels Permanent Commission does not look upon this rebate as a premium, as the sugar is simply put on the same footing as sugar originating in the Mother-country. The amounts of sugar imported from Réunion into France have been as follows for the past ten years, expressed in metric tons :—

1901/02	..	..	23,364	1906/07	..	..	29,190
1902/03	..	..	32,080	1907/08	..	..	38,194
1903/04	..	..	44,147	1908/09	..	..	41,917
1904/05	..	..	27,912	1909/10	..	..	38,558
1905/06	..	..	18,883	1910/11	..	..	39,000

As to the prospect of the sugar industry in Réunion, it depends largely on the labour problem. Should the immigration of British Indians be re-established, then there is not a single reason why this sugar industry should not flourish like that of the neighbouring island of Mauritius. Both climate and soil are favourable, and as long as there are enough labourers to till the soil at the proper seasons, to look after the cane, and to keep the factories going, the sugar industry will soon double its output. Should, however, immigration not be available—as is very likely—Réunion will not regain any of her old prosperity, and her sugar production will remain as it is now.

Books of Reference :
A. G. Garsault. *Notice sur la Réunion.*
Léon Colson. *Culture et Industrie de la Canne à Sucre aux Iles Hawaii et à la Réunion.*

Australasia.

I.

THE COMMONWEALTH OF AUSTRALIA.

In the Commonwealth of Australia, cane sugar cultivation is only met with in the northern states, and along the coast of New South Wales, and also in the sub-tropical parts of Queensland. In the first-mentioned territory the sugar industry is carried on in the districts which are watered by the Richmond, Tweed and Clarence rivers, and have a soil and climate fit for this cultivation.

At one time sugar cane was planted on the Mackay River, but as it suffered much from frost this has been given up and other vegetation cultivated instead, or the breeding of cattle and the production of dairy products have been substituted.

The southern border line of cane cultivation in Australia is 30° S. Lat., and the entire slip of land used for cane cultivation stretches obliquely between 147° and 153° W. Long.

In Queensland the principal sugar districts are Bundaberg at 25° S. Lat., Mackay at 18°, and the rainy region on the Hubert River at 19° S. Lat. up to Port Douglas at 16° S. Lat.

One part of the sugar cultivating area of Australia still lies within the tropics, but the southern part falls outside, thus causing the yearly production and the sugar content of the cane to differ very greatly even for states so close together as Queensland and New South Wales. As the cane area comprises only a very narrow strip of land which stretches lengthwise over a vast mileage from north to south, it is almost impossible to lay down figures as to temperature and rainfall. Figures and data relating to the meteorological condition of a number of places do exist, but they vary so much that they cannot be a true representation of the weather or temperature of the entire sugar producing area. It may suffice to say that frost is observed occasionally in the south of Queensland and in New South Wales, and does much harm to the cane. In the north of Queensland, on the other hand, the temperature never drops to freezing point, although the changes in temperature are great, and the difference between summer and winter is rather considerable. The northern tropical part is distinguished by two seasons—the north-west monsoon prevails from October to April, and the dry south-east monsoon from April to October. The climate is very changeable, and the country now and then experiences long spells of drought, which even affect the moist regions on the east coast, and occasion a great deal of loss of sugar cane.

The yearly rainfall decreases from north to south ; in the most northernly sugar district it amounts to 80 ins. ; in Mackay it just comes up to 40 ins. ; while the neighbourhood of Brisbane is noted for its scanty rainfall, and this part, properly speaking, cannot be considered fit for cane cultivation.

The sugar cultivation in Australia is of very recent date ; the first cane was planted in Queensland by Captain Louis Hope, near the Logan River ; while in 1863 a few pounds of sugar were prepared in the Botanical Gardens at Brisbane by Mr. Bunot by way of experiment, to show that Australia could yield crystallized sugar, though most people were then of a different opinion. In consequence of this successful experimentation, a great many small factories on the streams south of Brisbane began to take up this new cultivation, while a sugar manufacturer called Porter went round with a floating mill, the " Walrus," to all the planters living near the rivers to work up their cane to sugar. Brisbane soon appeared to lie too much in the southern latitude to make cane cultivation a profitable business, and that is why the sugar industry begun in South Queensland was transferred to the neighbourhood of Mackay and carried on there on a larger scale. The first cane was planted in 1864, and the first sugar factory, Alexandra Mill, produced 230 tons of sugar, in 1868, in addition to 148 hogsheads of rum. Since 1870 the sugar industry has gone up considerably in extent, so that in 1879 the Mackay district was capable of producing as much as 10,000 tons of sugar.

In order to obtain the necessary labour in the warm climate of tropical Queensland, natives of the South Sea Islands, so-called Kanakas, were imported in 1866, and in 1868 the recruiting and distributing of labourers was taken over by the Government. The ship-owners who shipped the Kanakas were authorized by the Government, and had to carry an official whose duty it was to see that the natives enlisted of their own free will, and were aware of the conditions to which they bound themselves. They were indentured for three years, received a house, food, and clothing, and £7 to £8 in money yearly. At the end of the three years they were entitled to a free passage home, but many of them preferred to stay where they were when their time was up, and to get employment as free labourers. These Kanakas worked in the fields only, for which labour they were exceedingly well-fitted, much more so than for the factories, where white labour was employed.

This plan of procuring labour had very good results ; a great many cheap and efficient labourers came to the country and helped to extend the sugar industry. But the latter is only carried on in a very small part of Queensland, as the rest of the country has nothing whatever to do with this trade, and its interests lie in quite a different direction. Although the white labourers could find ample work in the factories, they were, however, so much opposed to the employment of coloured labour that they succeeded in getting a Royal

Commission appointed in 1884 for the purpose of studying the Kanaka question. In consequence of the Report returned by this Commission, the then Premier, Sir Samuel Griffith, proposed to prohibit all further Kanaka immigration from 1890. But the sugar industry soon felt the injurious effect of this resolution of their Government. Capitalists became unwilling to invest money in Australian sugar estates, and the general opinion was so much against these proposals that the Government were obliged to withdraw them and allow fresh supplies of Kanakas to enter the cane districts. But in order to promote the sugar industry with white labourers exclusively, and to prove that their idea could very well be carried out, the Government of Queensland in 1889 advanced money to two groups of farmers to the amount of £25,000 and £20,000 respectively at 5 per cent. interest and 3 per cent. yearly redemption. These two groups founded two sugar factories, " North Eton " and " Racecourse Mill,"which were to work up the cane which would be cultivated by white farmers on their own land with the help of white employees. Five years afterwards, in 1893, the Sugar Works Guarantee Act was brought into force. This act authorized the Colonial Minister of Finance to enable companies to borrow money for defraying expenses which the building of sugar factories would entail, but not until they were certain of a sufficient amount of cane-planted area to guarantee a profitable working up of the cane in a large size factory.

The Queensland Government guaranteed the redemption of the capital in fifteen years, and an interest of 5 per cent. for the rest of the capital. The Exchequer, on the other hand, was entitled to a first mortgage on the ground and factories, and should the companies not be able to pay interest and redemption regularly, the Minister of Finance would have the right to fix the price of cane, and to take possession of and manage the factory and cane-planted area till arrears should be paid. The Exchequer would be entitled also to sell the factory by public auction. According to an amendment to this law dating from 1895, the Government had also a right to buy up all the shares in sugar factories that were put up for sale at the Government's expense, which made the Government become a shareholder in the particularly subsidized sugar factories. A number of factories were immediately founded in consequence of this regulation, and the two factories already existing were turned into joint stock companies having the same rights as the newly-founded ones.

Altogether twelve factories and a tramline were conducted by this Guarantee Act, which did away with a great many factories that, up to that time, had got cane from the lands now reserved for the new undertakings. It soon appeared that it would take more than capital and modern installations to carry on a sugar concern well ; and that experience, knowledge, and ability were indispensable factors to making it a success.

To procure the Government's guarantee they had only to build a sugar factory and to leave the management to a Committee formed by shareholders, who were mostly cane planters, without having to submit to Government supervision. The management, it is true, rested with cane planters, but not with sugar manufacturers or directors of large financial firms ; so that it was not to be wondered at that the financial part of the business turned out a failure and neither redemption nor interest were paid in time. Not till this unsatisfactory state of affairs had lasted for some years did the Government appoint an inspector to supervise the factories, and see what was wrong with them, and find out how to remedy the defect.

On 30th July, 1902, £514,000 had been spent on the thirteen companies £90,855 had since been paid as interest and redemption, while £70,090 was still in arrears.

The estates in question may be divided into three groups, for which the following measures were proposed to be taken :—

A. Factories which were well managed, and had never fallen short of their indebtedness towards the Exchequer. There was no reason to interfere and it sufficed for the Government to tender advice if necessary.

B. Factories that are well arranged and in good condition, but have not acted up to their obligations towards the Exchequer. For this category a co-operation of company and Government was proposed, which might be granted under the following terms :

1. The management of the estate, together with the Government, were to take measures to promote a sufficient supply of cane.

2. The technical control and the management were to be superintended by an expert appointed by the Government.

3. The machinery was not to be extended or added to unless the Government approved of the plan.

4. The price to be paid for cane was fixed by the Minister of Finance (at any rate, not without his knowledge).

5. No price was to be accepted for sugar unless the Government approved of it.

6. No loan was to be contracted unless the Government consented to it.

After the price of the cane should have been paid and after the expenses of maintenance and manufacture would have been defrayed by the sale of the sugar, the remainder was to go to the Exchequer till arrears of redemption and interest were made good. When, however, it was agreed that the company should pay a certain fixed sum, every amount that was earned in excess to this sum would go towards a reserve fund, which would be used for paying the redemption money in bad times to come.

C. Factories which had once been negligent and could not guarantee better management in the future were simply taken possession of by the Government.

These resolutions were accepted : three factories fell under A, four under B, while the Government took possession of five factories that had been absolutely in arrears and managed them at its own risk. Dr. Maxwell was appointed as expert to assume the management ; this he did with great energy, and soon after his appointment, in 1903, he succeeded in bringing about better results as far as these inefficient factories were concerned. The principal reason why these undertakings were a failure at first, and later on a success, lay in the quantity of cane planted. The shareholders were not in a condition to plant enough to keep the factories going, and the managers did not offer non-shareholders such prices for their cane as to enable them to take up this branch of cultivation. But as soon as it became a Government business there was no longer any distinction made between shareholders and outsiders, and only one price was paid by one and all.

Within three years' time the quantity of cane delivered at these factories increased by 72 per cent., and is still increasing, so that the industry can be carried on much more economically, and all but three factories have become free again from the Government's control. The " B " factories have been returned to their former owners, while the " C " factories were changed into new joint stock companies, which carried on the business.

Besides the twelve factories which were founded under the Sugar Works Guarantee Act, Queensland possesses a number of free factories, which up to now have been working and providing for themselves, and have had nothing to do with Government assistance. It is not likely that the Government will embark again on another extension of assistance of the sugar industry, for although a great many maintain that the quantity of sugar that Australia imports yearly might be supplied by Queensland, if it was not for want of factories, the Government turns a deaf ear to these representations, and does not propose anything in the way of more guaranteed factories.

Although after 1901 the sugar industry had been founded on a more solid basis by Government support, the planters had to complain ere long of some act of Government legislation. In 1901 the Australian colonies had united to form the Commonwealth of Australia, and one of the first resolutions passed by the new Parliament was the so-called Pacific Island Labourers' Act. At the time of the foundation of the Commonwealth, the Labour party had become very powerful, and insisted that Australia be occupied by white people only, and that all coloured races should be barred from entering. In 1901 about 12,000 coloured labourers were working in the cane fields, 10,000 of whom were Kanakas or inhabitants of the South Sea Islands, while the rest were British Indians, Japanese, or Chinese. For the rest there were about 50,000 other coloured people in Australia, chiefly Asiatics (Chinese) ; but these were merchants and joiners, cooks, pearl-divers, and other types of artizans, who entered the country at their own risk and could not be barred. The bill dealing with the Kanakas, which was passed in 1901, prohibited all immigration from 31st March, 1904. All agreements with Kanakas were legally annulled on 31st December, 1906, and any Kanaka who was found in the country after 1906 was to be sent back to his native island.

Notwithstanding strong opposition on the part of the Queensland Premier, the bill became law, and accordingly more than 9,000 Kanakas were expelled

The Commonwealth of Australia.

in the years 1906, 1907, and 1908 from Australia, very often against their wish, in order that it might become a " white man's land."

This act on the part of the Labour Party had serious consequences for the Australian sugar industry, however proud the partisans of this policy may be of the fact that 92 per cent. of the total sugar production in Australia is obtained by white labour.

The following tables state the quantity of sugar produced by white and by coloured labourers ; they also give the amount of premiums and excise.

Year.	Tons of sugar produced			Percentage of sugar produced with		Quantity of bounty-fed cane, in tons.	Amount of premium in £.
	White labour.	Coloured labour.	Total.	White labour.	Coloured labour.		
1902..	12,254	65,581	77,835	15·7	84·3	105,364	24,493
1903..	24,406	65,456	89,862	27·2	72·8	222,537	50,652
1904..	39,404	105,616	145,020	27·2	72·8	378,885	85,301
1905..	50,897	101,362	152,259	33·4	66·6	502,061	111,872
1906..	127,539	54,619	182,158	70·0	30·0	1,195,673	285,420
1907..	162,480	22,583	185,063	87·8	12·2	1,452,400	499,068
1908..	132,078	18,322	150,400	87·8	12·2	1,273,762	436,403
1909..	118,364	14,452	132,816	89·1	10·9	1,048,166	365,297
1910..	187,956	19,384	207,340	90·7	8·3	—	590,879
			NEW SOUTH WALES.				
1902..	19,434	1,526	20,960	92·7	7·3	181,665	36,333
1903..	19,236	2,561	21,797	88·3	11·7	200,847	40,154
1904..	17,812	1,838	19,650	90·7	9·3	180,535	36,107
1905..	18,019	1,964	19,983	90·2	9·8	181,170	36,234
1906..	21,805	1,613	23,418	93·1	6·9	205,797	42,790
1907..	28,247	934	29,181	96·8	3·2	260,271	78,080
1908..	14,351	964	15,315	93·7	6·3	135,652	40,687
1909..	13,839	815	14,654	94·4	5·6	122,781	36,834
1910..	17,010	990	18,000	95·1	4·9	160,311	45,731

The opponents of the present policy take a different view of the matter, and say that one should not lose sight of the fact that a sugar crop takes four to five years to mature, and that when they plant from September till April of one year they do not reap any crop till April to December of the next year.

When the great drought of 1902 was over, every available Kanaka was set to work to till as much land for the cane cultivation, and plant as much cane as they were capable of in order to get as much labour out of them before

1904 arrived.　They anticipated the time when the Kanakas would have gone, and the remaining white labourers would just be able to manage the crop, and would be none too many for the labour of planting.　We notice a considerable increase in the cane-planted area while the Kanakas were still being employed, and a temporary decrease after they had gone.

I.　Acres of cane planted during the last Kanaka years :—

1902/03	1903/04	1904/05	1905/06
85,338	111,516	120,317	134,107

II.　Acres of cane planted after they had gone :

1906/07	1907/08	1908/10	1910/11	1911/12
133,284	126,810	123,902	128,178	141,779

One should not overlook the fact that fields planted in 1905 were not abandoned till 1909, so that the influence of a decreased amount of labour would not be fully felt till 1910.

The white labourers who were employed instead of the coloured race had higher wages and did less work, while they kept bothering the planters by repeated strikes and their constant demands for better payment.　The labour problem in Queensland has just entered upon a critical stage ; in the tropical regions fit for sugar cultivation white labour cannot be used, while employing coloured labour raises trouble, and in southern parts where white labour would come in useful the climate is such as to prevent any cane cultivation flourishing. So in order to promote cane growing by whites they hit upon another expedient.

The import duty on sugar into the Commonwealth of Australia amounts to £6 per ton, while only £4 excise is levied on sugar produced in the country itself, which means a protection of £2 per ton.

Sugar grown by white labourers only enjoys a decrease in excise amounting to £3 ; consequently only £1 is paid per ton, and the protection enjoyed amounts in this case to £5.　But to come in for this they have to be able to prove that none but white labour was used, and that these labourers were paid according to regulations issued by the Government.　As the Labour Party in Australia has great influence, and is much in favour of rigorous measures, both planters and manufacturers are forced to pay exorbitant wages in order to get hold of the rebate on the excise.　As circumstances are at present, we cannot call the condition of the Australian sugar planter and sugar manufacturer satisfactory, owing to a rather unfavourable climate, to the Government regulations as regards coloured labour, and to the preposterous demands of the white employees, so that we are not surprised that the sugar production has been decreasing for the last few years, and most likely will continue to do so, though the sugar consumption of that country is steadily increasing.

At the present moment the system of central factories extends over the entire Australian sugar industry, including both free factories and those under Government supervision.　A great many of the big estates are divided up into small plots, on which cane is grown and sold to the factories at a price calculated according to the density of the juice.　The factories sell their sugar to a large company, the Colonial Sugar Refining Company, which has the monopoly of the sugar and fixes the prices. This company lets a good deal of land to the cane planters, who supply the factories with cane, and has caused the number of planters to increase enormously during the last few years. However advantageous this system may be, it has this drawback that the smaller planter cannot possibly give the necessary attention to the cane all the year through, nor can he apply regular manuring and tillage.

There is not much to be said about the cane cultivation itself. Irrigation has been carried out more than formerly, because the advantages of a regular water supply have been recognised. When irrigation cannot be arranged by damming up the rivers and streams and distributing the water all over the fields, pumping stations which supply the necessary amount of water have been constructed. The cane is planted from September to April, and is reaped between 1st July and 31st December of the following year. In New South Wales the cane is left two years before it is cut, while in Queensland part of the cane is cut after fourteen months, and the rest left on the fields. Second and third ratoons are always grown, especially when they have not enough labour for planting afresh.

The number of factories, the acres of cut cane, and the quantity in tons of sugar have been for Queensland since 1876 as follows :—

Year.	Number of factories.	Acres of cut cane	Tons of sugar produced.
1876/77	70	7,245	8.214
1877/78 . ..	59	8,043	12.243
1878/79 . ..	68	10,702	13,525
1879/80	70	11,409	18,714
1880/81	83	12,306	15,564
1881/82	103	15,550	19,051
1882/83 . ..	120	16,874	15,702
1883/84	152	25,792	36,148
1884/85	166	29,951	32,010
1885/86	166	40,756	59,225
1886/87	160	36,104	56,859
1887/88 . ..	118	34,821	57,960
1888/89	106	30,821	34,022
1889/90	125	31,239	44,411
1890/91	110	39,435	69,983
1891/92*	68	36,821	51,209
1892/93	72	40,572	61,386
1893/94	61	43,670	76,146

* Since 1892 only estates that ground their own cane.

Year.	Number of factories.	Acres of cut cane.	Tons of sugar produced.
1894/95	62	49,839	91,712
1895/96	64	55,771	86,255
1896/97	81	83,093	109,774
1897/98	62	65,432	97,916
1898/99 .	62	82,391	163,734
1899/00 ..	58	79,435	123,289
1900/01 . .	58	72,651	92,554
1901/02 .	52	78,160	120,858
1902/03	43	59,102	77,835
1903/04	39	60,375	89,862
1904/05	53	82,741	145,020
1905/06	53	96,093	152,259
1906/07	53	98,194	182,188
1907/08	54	94,384	185,063
1908/09	54	92,219	150,400
1909/10	54	80,095	132,816
1910/11	54	99,634	207,340
1911/12	54	96,396	176,076

Since 1882 the sugar production has been as follows, in tons per acre :—

1882	0·98
1883	1·38
1884	1·11
1885	1·45
1886	1·69
1887	1·65
1888	1·07
1889	1·36
1890	1·69
1891	1·39
1892	1·51
1893	1·74
1894	1·84
1895	1·55
1896	1·51
1897	1·50
1898	1·99
1899	1·55
1900	1·28

1901	1·55
1902	1·67
1903	1·52
1904	1·78
1905	1·59
1906 .. , ...	1·59
1907	1·88
1908	2·00
1909	1·64
1910	2·08
1911	1·86

Although the sugar production per unit of area has increased a little during these last thirty years, it is still of small amount compared with that of tropical countries, being but 1·5 tons per acre, and this figure is especially unsatisfactory, because it may refer to the acres reaped in one year, and because the number of acres planted with cane in one year is much more, as all the cane in the fields is not reaped annually. A comparison between the figures of the planted and the cut area is given in the following table :—

Year.	Planted acres.	Cut acres.	Cane in tons.	Sugar in tons.
1904/05	120,317	82,741	1,326,989	145,020
1905/06	134,107	96,093	1,415,745	152,259
1906/07 . ..	133,284	98,194	1,728,780	182,158
1907/08 . ..	126,810	94,384	1,665,028	185,063
1908/09 ..	123,902	92,219	1,433,315	150,400
1909/10 . ..	128,178	80,095	1,163,591	132,816
1910/11	141,779	99,634	1,564,993	207,340

This shows at the same time that the sugar yield from cane has been about 10·95 per cent.

The corresponding figures of New South Wales are as follows :—

Year.	Productive acres.	Non-Productive acres.	Tons of cane.	Tons of sugar.
1870/71	1,475	2,607	—	—
1871/72	1,995	2,339	—	—
1872/73	3,470	2,001	—	—

Australasia.

Year.	Productive acres.	Non-Productive acres.	Tons of cane.	Tons of sugar.
1873/74	3,565	3,105	—	—
1874/75	4,087	4,453	—	—
1875/76	3,654	2,800	99,430	—
1876/77	3,524	3,231	99,978	—
1877/78	3,331	3,735	104,192	—
1878/79	2,949	4,489	126,119	—
1879/80	3,676	4,102	121,676	—
1880/81	4,465	6,506	128,752	—
1881/82	4,983	7,184	169,192	—
1882/83	6,362	7,176	204,547	—
1883/84	7,583	7,401	105,323	—
1884/85	6,997	10,520	239,347	—
1885/86	9,583	6,835	167,959	—
1886/87	5,915	9,202	273,928	—
1887/88	8,380	6,907	110,218	—
1888/89	9,997	10,284	168,862	—
1889/90	7,348	11,382	277,252	—
1890/91	8,344	12,102	185,258	—
1891/92	8,623	13,639	264,832	—
1892/93	11,560	15,191	252,606	—
1893/94	11,750	16,357	264,254	—
1894/95	14,204	18,705	207,771	—
1895/96	14,398	18,259	207,771	—
1896/97	18,194	12,859	120,276	—
1897/98	12,936	12,929	269,068	—
1898/99	14,578	10,181	289,206	—
1899/00	9,435	13,082	170,500	—
1900/01	10,472	11,642	199,118	—
1901/02	8,750	12,019	187,711	—
1902/03	8,899	11,402	183,105	21,612
1903/04	10,405	9,814	227,511	21,812
1904/05	9,772	11,753	199,640	19,650
1905/06	21.205		201,998	19,983
1906/07	20,601		221,560	23,418
1907/08	9,916	8,037	277,390	29,181
1908/09	6,957	10,024	144,760	15,315
1909/10	6,480	8,457	131,081	14,654
1910/11	5,596	8,005	160,311	18,828

The Commonwealth of Australia.

The quantity of cane and sugar per acre reaped is higher here than in Queensland, being in 1907–08, 1908–09, and 1909–10 respectively 27·97, 20·88, and 20·23 tons of cane, and 2·93, 2·20, and 2·28 tons of sugar. One should not forget the fact that this cane is two years old, and that the quantity of sugar per planted acre amounts to a very small percentage, as it very seldom attains to 1 ton per acre on the average, and is very often below that figure.

As to the cost of production of cane, we give the following figures from an article in the *Australian Sugar Journal*, which figures represent the average, and are by no means exceptional :—

Field 12.

1906. 1,408 tons 18 cwt. cane	Wages	..	£192 13 3
	Rent ..	..	220 0 0
	Own salary ..		50 0 0
1907. 1,316 „ 17 „ „	Wages	..	283 14 0
	Rent ..	..	220 0 0
	Own salary ..		50 0 0
1908. 955 „ 6 „ „	Wages	..	290 17 0
	Rent ..	..	220 0 0
	Interest	..	56 4 2
	Own salary ..		50 · 0 0
			————£1,633 8 7

Field 8a.

1906. 1,221 tons 8 cwt. cane	Wages	..	£138 3 2
	Rent ..	..	140 0 0
	Own salary ..		50 0 0
1907. 1,363 „ 17 „ „	Wages	..	142 7 0
	Rent ..	..	140 0 0
	Own salary ..		50 0 0
1908. 1,061 „ 8 „ „	Wages	..	175 2 0
	Rent ..	..	240 0 0
	Own salary ..		50 0 0
			————£1,025 12 2

Field 8b.

1906/07. 1,162 tons 9 cwt. cane	Wages	.	£644 10 11
	Rent ..		200 0 0
	Own salary ..		100 0 0
1908. 1,057 „ 13 „ „	Wages	..	149 16 6
	Rent ..	..	100 0 0
	Own salary ..		50 0 0
			————£1,244 7 5

Value of installation £400, 20 per cent. of which is redeemed yearly £240 0 0

Taxes in one year 90 0 0

Total cost for 9,452 tons 16 cwt. cane £4,233 8 2

or 8s. 10½d. per ton ; to which has to be added the cost of reaping at 4s. 9½d. per ton, so that the total cost per ton amounted to 13s. 8½d.

The factories pay for the cane according to different rates, but on an average about 11s. to 13s , while the planter receives a premium of 6s. per ton when the cane is cultivated by white labour.

The calculation of price was for one factory as follows : For cane with 9 to 12 per cent. sugar content 11s. is paid ; for cane of 12 to 13 per cent., 12s. ; and for cane of 13 per cent. or more sugar content, 13s. ; while cane containing less than 9 per cent. of sugar can be refused or paid less for according to the analysis. For burnt cane 1s. less per ton is obtained.

During the first five years of Federal Tariff, the following prices were paid for cane by the central factories and by the factories of the Colonial Sugar Refining Company :—

Year.			Central factories.		C. S. R. Co.	
1901/02	..	..	301,811 tons	14/6¾	336,396 tons	13/7¾
1902/03	..	..	202,421 ,,	15/6¼	230,852 ,,	16/9¾
1903/04	..	..	285,070 ,,	15/4½	250,130 .,	15/10
1904/05	..	...	448,318 ,,	16/3	337,335 ,,	17/1½
1905/06	..	..	449,727 ,,	15/6½	383,885 ,,	14/8½
			1,687,417 tons	15/6½	1,588,598 tons	15/7½

The sugar realized on an average the following sums :—

1906/07 ..	..	..	..	£10	14	8 per ton
1907/08 ..	..	..	..	10	9	1 ,,
1908/09 .	..	..	..	11	3	5 ,,
1909/10 ..	..	..	..	12	2	5½ ,,

and was bought by the Colonial Sugar Refining Company (the only sugar buyer) exclusively at these average prices.

The sugar industry in Australia is thus far from satisfactory. The inhabitants of the districts where no sugar is cultivated complain because an import duty of £6 per ton makes sugar too expensive, while the sugar manufacturers, on the other hand, are not pleased either that they have to do without proper legal protection. They maintain that an excise of £4, with an import duty of £6, only leaves them a protection of £2 per ton, and that they have paid for their bounty of £3 on cane cultivated by white labour too dearly, by having had to expel their black labourers, and by having become dependent on white labour which is not always reliable.

While their neighbours in Hawaii are benefited by a protection in the form of an import duty of £9 per ton on foreign sugar entering the United

States, and are themselves exempted from import duty and excise, the Australian sugar planters, on the other hand, come to the conclusion that their industry, far from deriving money from the Exchequer, rather helps to swell the latter.

In 1906–07, for instance, excise brought in £741,929, and £567,248 was paid as premium, which left £164,781 for the Exchequer; in 1907–08 these figures were respectively £751,163, £477,090, and £274,773. In 1908–09 the premium, however, cost £402,131, and in 1909–10 £579,133, so that the Exchequer's share in comparison with that of the planters is decreasing. The prospect the proposals of the premium held out, namely, that Australia would soon supply her own sugar wants, has not been realized. With a consumption of more than 200,000 tons, about 50,000 tons, or 25 per cent., is being imported chiefly from Java, Hong Kong, Fiji, and Mauritius; and as the consumption increases and the production goes down—with the exception of the production of 1910—this proportion is likely to become increasingly unfavourable.

In New South Wales the more profitable industry of dairy products is preferred; while cane is simply cultivated for the sake of the factories which otherwise would be rendered useless. In the north of Queensland there is the difficulty of getting enough labourers who can stand the climate; while in the south unfavourable climatic circumstances reduce the cane area. At the beginning of 1910 a Commission was appointed to investigate the condition of the sugar industry, and to ascertain whether the present protection given by the Government was adequate, and if not how to extend it successfully. As long as the result of these investigations is unknown, we cannot say much on the prospect of the Australian sugar industry in the near future, which, as it is, looks far from promising.

Literature:

The Australian Sugar Journal.
Yearbook of Australia.

II.

THE HAWAIIAN ISLANDS.

I.—Geographical Location, Climate, Population, Cane-planted Area, Total Sugar Production.

THE group of the Hawaiian Islands lies in the northern part of the Pacific Ocean, between 18° 54′ and 22° 14′ N. Lat. and 154° 18′ and 160° 13′ W. Long. from Greenwich. It consists of eight inhabited islands, forming one group, with scme smaller uninhabited islets at some distance to the north. The total area amounts to 6,455 sq. miles, divided among the different islands as follows :—

Island.	Sq. miles.	Sq. kilometres.
Hawaii	4,015	10,360
Maui	728	1,879
Oahu	598	1,514
Kauai	547	1,412
Molokai	261	674
Lanai	139	359
Niihau	97	251
Kahoolawe	69	171
Uninhabited islands	6	15
Total	6,455	15,635

All these islands are the result of volcanic upheavals of the soil, dating from fairly recent periods.

The largest island, Hawaii—from which the entire group derives its name—is of recent date, and covered with lava not long since formed by the extensive volcanoes of the island. The coast, especially on the north-west, rises steeply from the sea, and gradually slopes up towards the mountain tops, so that no level seashore is to be found here. There are not any harbours to speak of except H lo Harbour, which is not a safe anchorage at all. The highest mountain peaks are Mauna Kea, 13,900 ft., Mauna Loa, 13,600 ft., Hualalai, 8,300 ft., while the extensive volcano of Kilauea only measures 5,500 ft.

The island Maui is of much older geographical formation than Hawaii, and can boast of extensive plains. Its highest mountain peak is that of Haleakala, 10,000 ft. high. The scantily populated Molokai and the two smaller islands, Lanai and Kahoolawe, are grouped together—the latter two being almost uninhabited, and are used as pasture land for cattle.

Oahu is likewise of ancient formation, and has already gone through so many upheavals of the ground that the exact site of the volcano crater which created the island is difficult to trace. Owing to these changes in the level of the land, it is interspersed with coral cliffs, which seem to be pushed between the original layer of lava, and the subsequently formed products of disintegration. Instead of a few craters, as are found in the other islands, Oahu possesses two nearly parallel mountain ranges, between which a plateau is found that slopes down to the sea both in a northern and a southern direction.

On the south side the capital of the Hawaiian group, Honolulu, is situated on a very fine bay excellently suited for navigation.

The Hawaiian Islands.

Kauai is the oldest island of the group, consisting of a peak, Waileale, 5,250 ft. high, and its disintegration products. This mountain rises from the sea as a deeply grooved mass of rock, while a great many of its spurs run out to sea. Between these spurs the disintegration products carried along by the rain have settled and formed a number of valleys, which lead on the coast into some small harbours.

Niihau, lying close to Kauai, is of some importance. In consequence of the mountainous nature of these smaller islands, they do not possess any navigable rivers—with the exception of Kauai, which can boast of several streams which, flowing from the mountains, run through the alluvial ground to the sea, and are to some extent navigable near their mouths.

The climate of the Hawaiian Islands varies little all the year through, and all over the island group. The north-east trade wind is the prevailing one which blows 264 days out of the 365 every year, and carries along quantities of moisture. The high mountains keep the wind back, force it to rise, and in this way bring on a heavy rainfall on the north-east and eastern slopes of the mountain ; while the rainfall on the lee side is very slight, and is sometimes lacking altogether. Some parts of the island group have as much as 200 ins. yearly of rainfall, while other parts are stated at 2 ins. ; and others, again, derive some rain from south-west gales, which are very rare. So it is impossible to quote any average rainfall for Hawaii, as the position of the different localities is the greatest factor for obtaining rain and sunshine. As, however, this factor is the same all the year through, the climate of each place is fairly steady during the twelve months, and a succession of cold, warm, dry, and wet seasons is not experienced here.

The average temperature in Honolulu has been for a period of fifteen years 22·7 to 23·3° C. (72° to 74° F.) ; for the same period the observed maximum temperature was 31·7° C. (88·3° F). ; while the minimum temperature was never lower than 11·1° C. (52° F.), which was observed for a few hours. On climbing the mountains one will find a lower temperature, of course, and the highest mountain tops, even in this tropical climate, are covered with snow all the year round. The temperature on the windward side is generally lower than on the lee side, while the humidity of the atmosphere is higher, though it is still comparatively low.

The wind is seldom violent, and hurricanes, though prevailing in other tropical parts, do not occur here.

Though the following meteorological data, collected in 1908, only refer to Honolulu, and cannot be looked upon as characteristic of the Hawaii group as a whole, we think it worth while to quote them :—

Month.	Average Temperature in degrees °C.	Average Maximum Temperature.	Average Minimum Temperature.	Total Rainfall in Mm.	Maximum amount of Rain in 24 hours.	Per cent. of possible Sunshine.	Cloudiness 1—10.	Days with				
								0·2 Mm. Rain or more.	1·0 Mm. Rain or more.	6·5 Mm. Rain or more.	25 Mm. Rain or more.	Thunder Storm.
January ...	22·0	24·9	19·1	12·7	6·3	77	4·1	8	4	0	0	0
February ...	22·2	24·9	19·5	86·9	42·9	75	5·8	11	10	5	1	1
March	22·4	25·0	19·8	205·5	130·0	59	6·5	14	11	6	2	0
April	22·6	25·3	19·9	15·0	4·0	70	6·0	13	5	0	0	0
May	23·9	26·6	21·3	9·8	5·4	72	5·5	5	2	0	0	0
June	24·1	26·7	21·5	9·9	5·6	68	5·6	11	2	0	0	0
July	24·7	27·2	22·2	4·1	2·2	68	5·6	6	2	0	0	0
August	25·1	27·8	22·4	23·1	13·9	74	4·8	9	5	1	0	0
September ...	25·0	27·6	22·6	19·0	12·1	67	5·1	10	4	1	0	1
October ...	24·6	27·2	21·9	5·6	2·2	67	4·5	7	2	0	0	0
November ...	23·1	26·0	20·3	27·9	12·7	73	3·6	5	4	2	0	0
December ...	22·2	24·7	19·7	68·1	31·2	68	5·5	13	8	4	0	0
Average ...	23·5	25·1	20·6	488·6		70	5·2	112	59	19	3	2

According to the census returns of January, 1908, the population of the Hawaiian Islands amounted to 218,462, distributed over the several islands as follows :—

Hawaii	..	..	..	..	59,621
Maui and surrounding islands ..		..		..	39,980
Oahu	..	..	..	..	95,398
Kauai and adjacent islands		..		..	23,463
Total ..		..		..	218,462

The census returns of 1st January, 1910, only gave 191,909 inhabitants for all the islands ; 45,000 of these inhabit the capital, Honolulu ; while the second town, Hilo in Hawaii, accounts for 4,500. The aborigines number only 35,000, which number is steadily decreasing, as the race is dying out. The other nationalities consist of white people born in the island and half-breeds, American, Portuguese, Chinese, and especially Japanese, the latter of whom number some 85,000. The Portuguese hail principally from the Azores, but as the state of affairs in their own country is improving, their number decreases, because they return home ; but a great number of them have done well in the Hawaiian Islands, and prefer to remain there.

With the exception of Honolulu and Hilo, there are hardly any towns, and the centres of population are seldom any better than villages ; while the population is densest on the sugar estates. There is regular communication between the several islands by means of steamers of the Inter-Island Steam

Navigation Co., plying from coast to coast ; while the islands themselves have excellent roads, which, of course, follow the coast line where possible.

Over and above the many railroads on the sugar estates that are used for cane transportation, there are five railway companies. These are the Oahu Railway, 70 miles in length, connecting Honolulu with the extreme north point of Oahu, where it joins the shorter Koolaua Railway ; the Hilo Railway, running from Hilo to a point nine miles distant from the Kilaue volcano ; the Kohala Railway, running from the sugar estates near Kohala to the sea, and joining the Kahului Railway connecting this harbour town with several sugar estates in Maui.

Sugar cane is only grown in the four large islands, Hawaii, Oahu, Maui, and Kauai, for which cultivation the following areas have been planted with cane :—

Island.	1904 Acres.	1905 Acres.	1906 Acres.	1907 Acres.	1908 Acres.	1909 Acres.	1910 Acres.
Hawaii ..	47,058	45,002	44,984	47,907	46,896	49,672	52,447
Maui ..	13,949	15,116	15,971	16,724	16,778	18,501	18,864
Oahu ..	15,832	18,783	18,178	18,995	20,497	20,329	20,543
Kauai ..	14,959	15,542	17,096	16,289	17,209	17,626	18,392
Total ..	91,798	95,443	96,229	99,915	101,380	106,218	110,246

As, however, the crop from the entire planted area is not reaped every year, the canes taking a much longer vegetative period than twelve months, it cannot be far wide of the mark to estimate the entire cane-planted area of the Hawaiian Islands at 225,000 acres, although higher figures are sometimes quoted.

The sugar production of the last nineteen years has been in the several islands as follows, expressed in long tons :—

Island.	1892/93	1893/94	1894/95	1895/96	1896/97	1897/98	1898/99	1899/00	1900/01
Hawaii	50,962	64,484	55,038	98,602	113,157	81,791	104,678	102,878	120,194
Maui...	29,170	30,080	24,764	25,054	36,649	40,208	48,562	51,203	52,097
Oahu	17,736	16,788	15,566	31,948	25,829	30,518	40,911	47,879	88,869
Kauai	38,400	37,248	38,228	46,123	48,584	52,355	58,356	56,561	60,301
Total	136,268	148,600	133,596	201,727	224,219	204,832	252,507	258,520	321,461

Island.	1901/02	1902/03	1903/04	1904/05	1905/06	1906/07	1907/08	1908/09	1909/10	1910/11
Hawaii ...	108,299	152,379	109,701	112,861	122,991	128,474	160,856	153,875	142,728	172,729
Maui ...	50,648	75,693	69,630	89,693	91,928	93,546	109,490	120,183	124,513	89,883
Oahu ...	96,312	108,094	91,088	109,906	101,562	106,493	122,333	123,592	114,864	118,869
Kauai ...	62,250	54,896	57,684	68,136	66,744	64,358	72,609	80,167	80,508	124,514
Total ...	377,509	391,062	328,103	380,576	383,225	392,871	465,288	477,817	462,613	505,995

II.—History of the Cane Sugar Industry in the Hawaiian Islands.

Although we have some reports of a Japanese junk touching at Maui in the thirteenth century, and of a Spanish ship calling in 1550 on the south coast of Hawaii on its way from Mexico to the Philippines, our knowledge of the Hawaiian Islands really only dates from 1778, when Captain Cook discovered them. He found sugar cane already growing, and the natives using the product as a dainty ; still, it was not till 1837 that the exportation of sugar from those islands is mentioned, an exportation amounting to only 4,286 lbs., or less than two tons. This exportation, however, soon increased considerably, and in 1876, the year the reciprocal treaty with the United States was entered upon, it realized as much as 11,600 tons

The real beginning of the Hawaiian sugar industry dates from the time of this reciprocal treaty, which turned the Hawaiian Islands into a vassal state of the United States. As this treaty and its effects have influenced the entire sugar industry, it may be as well to touch on this subject somewhat fully here.

In 1855 negotiations were opened with a view to drawing up a reciprocal treaty between the United States and the Kingdom of Hawaii ; but although the Foreign Secretary at Washington was much in favour of the proposal, it was not ratified by the Senate. In 1867 it was again approved of by the Hawaiian Government and the President of the United States, but again voted down by the Senate, till in 1875 the treaty was signed to take effect from September, 1876. According to this treaty, the principal products of the Hawaiian Islands, rice and raw sugar (known in San Francisco as " Sandwich Islands Sugar "), were altogether exempted from import duty in the United States ; while nearly all kinds of agricultural produce and goods from the United States enjoyed a similar privilege when imported into Hawaii. This treaty was to hold good for seven years, with the option at the end of that time of renewing it indefinitely, unless one of the parties should wish it to terminate, and gave twelve months' notice.

The principal reason for entering upon this agreement was not so much the commercial advantage for the United States as political considerations and State interests. The measure was recommended by both political parties in the Congress as a means of obtaining ascendency in the affairs of the Hawaiian Islands, and to make the Hawaiian Islands virtually part of the United States, both commercially and industrially, and so prevent foreign powers from getting any footing there—a most dangerous possibility for the west coast of the United States in case of war.

Before this treaty was signed the population of the Hawaiian Islands was rapidly decreasing, and the trade of the islands was deteriorating also in consequence of the bad times the whale fishery encountered. Although the soil was very well fitted for cane cultivation, it was no fit place for the sugar industry, as labour was scarce and expensive, and the import duties in the United States, their only market, were too high to make any profit possible.

In 1875 there was a proposal to get Hindoos from British India to come and live on these islands, in order to supply the lack of labour cheaply and abundantly, for which Great Britain's acquiescence was sought. Moreover, the Australian colonies were gaining in importance commercially, so that they were looked upon as the market for Hawaiian sugar, instead of the United States. An attempt was actually made to send the entire crop of 1876–77 to Australia, in the hope that Hawaii might one day become independent of the United States, both politically and economically, and might be turned into a British colony. As soon as the United States became aware of this move, they readily seized the opportunity, and entered into the above reciprocal treaty, which allowed raw sugar to be imported into the United States free from any duty whatever. At that time the duty used to amount to 40 per cent. of the value, so that the value of the sugar all at once increased by 40 per cent., and became on that account a highly profitable product.

The first sugar factory in the Hawaiian Islands dates from 1835, when a mill was built in Koloa, driven by oxen, which crushed the cane. In 1861 the number of factories had expanded to 22,—9 of which were driven by steam, 12 by water, and 1 by animal power. Just before the agreement was drawn up, the factories numbered 33 ; while fifteen months later the number had increased to 46. The table at the end of this chapter shows clearly how the sugar industry has developed since 1877.

This reciprocal agreement was not only a boon to the sugar industry, but also to every trade connected with it, such as manure and machinery manufacture, navigation, etc., so that America benefited by it indirectly, although Hawaii, of course, derived most direct financial profit. This consideration, and the advantage that the only possible basis of operation for a hostile fleet belonged to a friendly disposed nation, caused this agreement to be retained *sine die*, in spite of the many attacks made on it in Congress. We need not be surprised at these attacks when we think of the envy with which both the American sugar producers and the Exchequer looked upon this ever-increasing Hawaiian sugar importation into America, which threatened the home industry and the public revenue.

In 1891 King Kalakaua died, and was succeeded by his sister, Liliuokalani, but the latter was not equal to suppressing the revolutionaries ; in consequence, Hawaii was created a republic in 1893, to be incorporated into the Union in 1898—after the sovereignty had already once been offered in vain to the United States.

This incorporation, as might be expected, led to a flourishing increase in the sugar industry. As long as the exemption from import duties in America was guaranteed by a treaty between the two powers which was exposed to all sorts of attacks and might be cancelled at any moment, the sugar industry could not rest on a firm footing. All this changed when the republic was incorporated into the

349

United States, and Hawaiian sugar, as a matter of course, was admitted free from any duty into San Francisco and New York. A great many new sugar companies with large capital were founded, while the existing ones extended their capital in order to increase their sphere of activity. Other companies shared this desire for extension, and as most of the capital was found by men of limited means—citizens of the Hawaiian Islands—it ended in bankruptcy or in straightened circumstances for the people who had procured the money. But these consequences of excessive speculation soon disappeared, after a period of judicious management, and it was not long before the sugar industry was placed on a firmer footing, with a bright prospect in store for it. In 1897 to 1898—that is, a little time before the annexation—the production only amounted to 229,000 tons, while in 1901–02 it had gone up to 360,000 tons—that is 60 per cent. increase in four years' time. Besides these political and economical causes, there was another that greatly contributed to the improvement of the sugar industry, and will continue doing so in future, namely, the application of irrigation from the rivers and artesian wells. As was stated at the beginning of this chapter, the rainfall is unevenly distributed over the different parts of the islands. Whereas the north-east and east coast get plenty of rain, the rainfall in the west and south-west is so slight that it cannot bring about the ripening of the cane. In consequence thereof the area fit for sugar cultivation was very restricted, so that, still, in 1882, competent experts estimated the disposable cane-growing land for the combined island group at 72,500 acres, of which only 34,000 acres per annum were available for reaping. As a matter of fact, irrigation works were started in 1887 to collect the water of the mountain streams and distribute it over the land ; but owing to the uncertainty of the reciprocal contract and the subsequent vissicitudes of the sugar industry, they shrank from spending much money on supplying the estates with extensive irrigation works. Previous to the annexation, the Lihue waterworks were built in the Island of Kauai in 1882 ; those at Hamakua in 1876 ; the Hawaiian Commercial and the Waihea works in 1878 ; and the Makaweli works in 1890. When after the annexation of the Hawaiian Islands by the United States the sugar industry obtained a firmer footing, capitalists invested larger sums in irrigation works, and numerous gigantic systems for the distribution of water over the barren land date from this time. It was not only the diversion of mountain streams through tunnels, ditches, and syphons, but large reservoirs were constructed to collect the effluence of rivers which water was led through artificial canals and distributed all over the estates by aqueducts. A third mode of water supply is the artesian wells, which, especially in Oahu, supply a large quantity of water. Part of the rainfall does not reach the sea by the rivers, but penetrates into the porous soil and flows to the sea through subsoil rivers, which can be reached by means of artesian wells, and brought to the surface again by pumping. At the present moment there are about 1,500 miles of irrigated canals in the Hawaiian Islands, 70 miles of which are tunnel ; then there are 250 reservoirs, containing altogether 8,000 million gallons and 428 artesian wells capable of 500 million gallons daily; and besides these there are some subterranean sources which carry 100 million gallons of water daily. All this water from subterranean sources is pumped up by steam pumps of a total of 27,000 horse-power to a height of some 500 ft., and flows through 70 miles of iron pipes 16 to 54 ins. in diameter. Part of this water is transported across ravines, sometimes 650 ft. deep, by suspended syphons. All this shows what great energy and what large sums of money have been expended on the irrigation works in anticipation of great returns. One of the consequences of this broadly conceived irrigation system has been a considerable increase in the planted area ; another has been an increase in the production of these irrigated plantations. The quantity of acres irrigated and not irrigated, and the quantity of reaped cane during the years 1895 to 1910 were as follows :—

Year.	Acres of Irrigated land.	Acres of non-irrigated land	Acres of area reaped.
1895 .	23,454	23,945	47,399
1896 .	25,950	29,779	55,729
1897 .	23,101	30,724	53,825
1898 ..	24,507	30,728	55,235
1899 ..	27,380	32,928	60,308
1900 ..	27,090	39,628	66,718
1901 ..	34,740	43,878	78,618
1902 ..	38,987	41,966	80,953
1903	42,097	51,253	93,392
1904 ..	42,810	48,987	91,797
1905 ..	48,668	46,775	95,443
1906 .	50,112	46,117	96,329
1907 .	50,624	49,292	99,916
1908 ..	53,104	48,276	101,380
1909 ..	54,896	51,232	106,127
1910 ..	55,973	54,273	110,246

While at first the non-irrigated land was most in evidence, after 1904 it has been the other way about, and irrigated land forms the greater proportion of the cultivated soil.

Simultaneously with the introduction of irrigation, the methods of cultivation and the factory installations were improved upon, and a rational method of manuring tried, so that we may say that the Hawaiian sugar industry began to flourish after 1898, and it will most likely continue to do so for years to come.

The number of sugar estates in the Hawaiian Islands at the present time amount to 53—26 of which are found in Hawaii, 10 in Kauai, 10 in Oahu, and 7 in Maui. Not all of them, however, possess a sugar factory, as the factories number 48 ; and 5 estates have to leave the grinding of their cane to neighbouring sugar mills.

Australasia.

The figures representing the exportation of sugar from the Hawaiian Islands were from its first year, 1837, up to 1867, as follows, expressed in long tons :—

1837	..	..	..	2	1857 ..	.. ..	311
1838	..	..	..	40	1858 ..	.. ..	540
1839	..	..	..	45	1859 ..	.. ..	815
1840*	..	..	..	161	1860 ..	.. ..	644
1841†	..	..	..	27	1861 ..	.. ..	1,149
1842‡	..	..	..	—	1862 ..	.. ..	1,340
1843	..	..	..	511	1863 ..	.. ..	2,360
1844	..	..	..	229	1864 ..	.. ..	4,780
1845	..	..	..	135	1865 ..	.. ..	6,840
1846	..	..	..	134	1866 ..	.. ..	7,920
1847	..	..	..	265	1867 ..	.. ..	7,740
1848	..	..	..	223	1868 ..	.. ..	8,170
1849	..	..	..	282	1869 ..	.. ..	8,168
1850	..	..	..	334	1870 ..	.. ..	8,385
1851	..	..	..	10	1871 ..	.. ..	9,720
1852	..	..	..	312	1872 ..	.. ..	7,690
1853	..	..	..	286	1873 ..	.. ..	10,300
1854	..	..	..	257	1874 ..	.. ..	10,970
1855	..	..	..	130	1875 ..	.. ..	11,200
1856	..	..	..	248	1876 ..	.. ..	11,640

The total production of sugar, dating from 1876 until now, is expressed in the following table, also in long tons . :—

1877	..	..	11,410	1894 ..	..	..	148,000
1878	..	..	17,240	1895 ..	..	..	134,500
1879	..	..	21,870	1896 ..	..	..	202,000
1880	..	..	28,400	1897 ..	..	..	223,000
1881	..	..	41,800	1898 ..	..	..	204,000
1882	..	..	51,000	1899 ..	..	..	253,000
1883	..	..	51,000	1900 ..	..	..	258,000
1884	..	..	64,500	1901 ..	..	..	321,000
1885	..	..	77,500	1902 ..	..	..	317,000
1886	..	..	96,500	1903 ..	..	..	391,000
1887	..	..	95,000	1904 ..	..	..	328,000
1888	..	..	105,000	1905 ..	..	..	381,000
1889	..	..	108,000	1906 ..	..	..	383,000
1890	..	..	116,000	1907 ..	..	..	393,000
1891	..	..	123,000	1908 ..	..	..	465,000
1892	..	..	110,000	1909 ..	..	..	478,000
1893	..	..	136,000	1910 ..	..	..	463,000
				1911 ..	..	..	505,995

* These figures indicate the period January till August.
† For 1841 the figures are given for the time August, 1840, to August, 1841.
‡ There are no separate data for 1842, but they may be included in those of 1841.

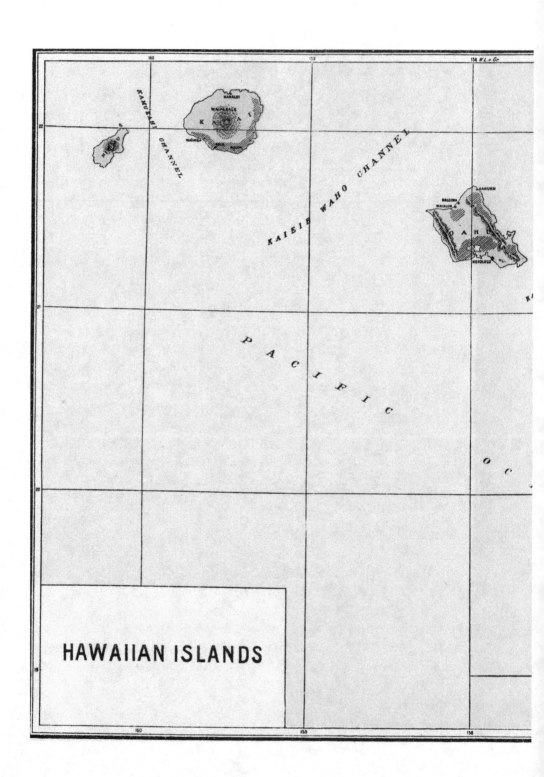

HAWAIIAN ISLANDS

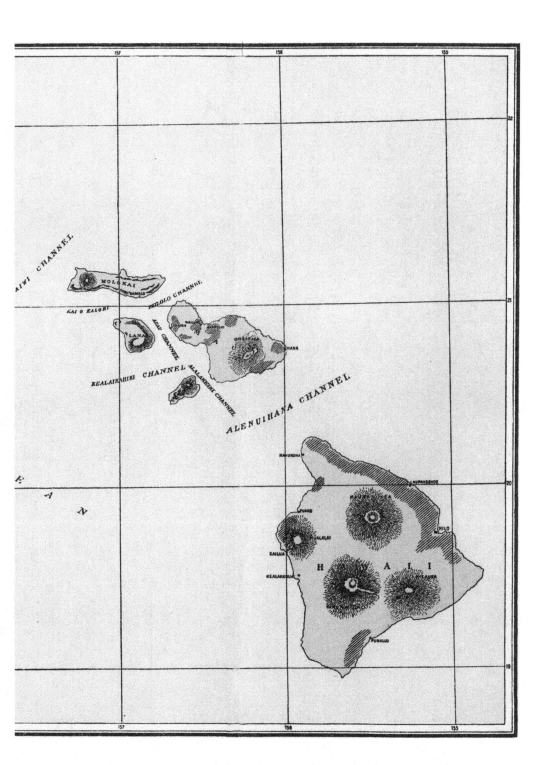

III.—Cane Cultivation.

The land necessary for agriculture may be obtained from the Government either on perpetual lease or freehold. As the soil in these islands is intersected in many places by large extents of wild and hard rocky tracts, nicely bordered plots of arable land cannot be expected, barren as well as fertile ground being intermingled. For this reason the ground is classified under three kinds of arable land, two kinds of pasture land, and in woodland.

The Government land is exclusively sold by auction at a minimum price fixed by the officials. Pasture land is sold at $2 to $5 per acre, land for the cultivation of vegetables at $5 to $25, while land for cane cultivation may fetch from $28 to $60 per acre. These are exceedingly easy terms for the smaller farmers to obtain land, and are made so in order to create a class of smaller farmers. who are protected against land speculators. These terms simply amount to the possibility of buying land at about 25 per cent. of the estimated value ; while the payments may be made in instalments, and no interest has to be paid during the first five years. Five per cent. of the sale price has to be paid cash down, 5 per cent. after two years, and 5 per cent. every following year, which means that the sum has to be paid over within twenty years. The buyer is obliged to have at least 20 per cent. of the arable land cultivated within two years' time, and 10 per cent. more every following year, till a minimum is reached of 50 per cent., while the land not fit for cultivation has to be planted with trees; five trees per acre during the first two years, and five trees more per acre for each following year, till the obligatory minimum of twenty five trees per acre shall be reached. All these regulations tend to make it easy for Americans to settle in Hawaii without being obliged to have recourse to money in advance or other obligations in order to get a plot of land as their property ; while they, at the same time, form a colony of Americans in the Pacific as an advance guard and protection on the west side for the great republic.

The total amount of arable land is 568,000 acres (or 228,000 hectares) which is distributed as follows :—

    12,000 acres used in rice cultivation.
    225,000   ,,   planted with cane.
    15,000   ,,   fit for cane cultivation.
    326,000   ,,   fit for small agriculture.

The big sugar estates became at once owners of the ground, and were, at the same time, entitled to use the water from the subsoil, of which, as we saw, they made excellent use. Their position is indicated on the map by *shading ;* they occupy the wide strips and slopes on the sea coast and up the mountain spurs.

The principal valley for sugar cultivation is that round Pearl Loch near

Australasia.

Honolulu, in Oahu, where an area of less than 40 sq. miles, cultivated by three companies, yields about 100,000 tons of sugar.

Before planting is begun the land is thoroughly ploughed up by steam ploughs wherever the depth of the loose arable soil allows of it ; after which it is levelled down and furrows 30 ft. long, 1½ to 2 ft. wide, and 1½ ft. deep are cut 5 ft. apart. In these furrows tops are planted, which are cut 12 ins. long and put in one or two rows close together, lengthways of the furrows ; after which these are covered with earth and then watered. At first this is done every two days, and afterwards it is repeated at increasing intervals, till the cane is ripe. After some time they manure, bank, and weed occasionally ; and by the time the cane ripens it has been trashed once or oftener. The months from May till August are best for planting ; by this time the cane may have attained to a sufficient height to endure the winter cold, which often causes stagnation of growth ; while, at the same time, it is not then old enough to begin flowering, which it does in November. Should the planter for want of labour be obliged to start earlier in order to get all the cane planted, he would run the risk of seeing the cane when only slightly grown, in flower at the time when the winter cold commences ; this, of course, would involve the loss of the still immature cane. In order to prevent this, the cane planted in March or April is cut off close to the ground in July, and then left to bud out and grow up together with the cane that was planted at the most favourable planting season. During the winter it will grow slowly, and during the following summer will shoot up tremendously, and finally fall down ; but it will keep growing till it is 20 to 30 ft. in length, and begin flowering in the second November of its existence, and be full-grown eighteen months after it was first planted.

Here the crushing is not regulated by the time of lowest rainfall, because the weather all through the year is subject to great changes, but by the state of ripeness of the cane and quantity of the expected crop. Only very few planters begin to crush on the 1st of November, some start in December ; but in January the crushing season ought to be in full swing all over the sugar belt.

After the crop is reaped, ratoons are generally cultivated. For this purpose the trash left in the field is removed and burnt, the soil is levelled and irrigated, then manured and banked. In case the field is reaped early—for instance, in December or January—ratoons will grow up so well that in November they will flower again, and will be ready to be cut by the following harvest time. These ratoons being ripe one year after they are cut are called " short ratoons." Should, however, the harvest be left till late, preventing the ratoon cane from reaching the stage of flowering in November, it is left to grow till the following crushing season, in which case it will be cut after twenty-two to twenty-four months' vegetation. This is called " long ratoons," and the long duration of the growing process easily explains why such fluctuations occur between the cane-planted areas and crops reaped every year. It goes without saying that the crops from the " short ratoons " are much smaller than those from long ones and from plant cane. After having kept on ratoons for several crops, that is about six to ten years after first planting, the soil is ploughed up and planted anew immediately afterwards.

The cane varieties most prevalent in the Hawaiian Islands are Lahaina, Yellow Caledonia, and Rose Bamboo cane ; while a few seedling cane varieties from Demerara are cultivated too, or are on trial at the experiment stations.

In Oahu and Maui, Lahaina cane is exclusively cultivated, and Yellow Caledonia is in evidence in Hawaii, while the Kauai plantations plant both these kinds together with Rose Bamboo.

The Lahaina cane got its name from an estate in Maui, where it was first planted. It is said to have been imported there from Otaheite, where it seems to have been indigenous, although we cannot state this as a fact.

The Rose Bamboo cane somewhat resembles the Cheribon cane of Java ; while Yellow Caledonia is said to be identical with the White cane grown in Cuba.

Much trouble is taken as regards manuring ; sulphate of ammonia, Chili saltpetre, potash and phosphate are used, and the total sum of money spent on manures is estimated at 22 million dollars, or an average of $4·65 for each ton of sugar produced, or $22·20 for each acre harvested. It seems to take a heavier manure each time to keep the cane production up to the same standard.

The former director of the Hawaiian Experiment Station has shown repeatedly that it is quite easy to wash out the soil of the Hawaiian Isles, and that a heavy rate of irrigation can soon do away with the content of available potash and lime from the soil, so that an alarming decrease in these constituents in the land is even now noticeable, although the irrigation installations have only been in use for a very short time. This property indeed proves to be a great drawback to the otherwise successful application, and it seems that the remarkably favourable effect it had in the beginning is partly due to using up what stock of necessary plant food there was to be obtained from the subsoil. As soon as this food ceases to be found, it will take a still larger amount of manure to keep the sugar production up to the old standard.

Cane is generally transported from the fields by narrow-gauge railways, of which 840 miles of fixed and moveable railroad exist in the different islands, together with 120 engines and 8,500 wagons. Besides this mode of transportation, there are 370 miles of water-gutters, the so-called " flumes," and 40 miles of suspended aerial ropeways for the transportation of cane from the more highly situated fields to the factories. The flume system is often applied, especially in Hawaii ; there are even factories that get their whole supply conveyed in this way—whereas in Oahu, where no river water is obtainable, this system could never be applied.

These flumes are shallow and boarded on each side, slightly sloping down from the fields to the factory, and ending in a kind of grate close to the mills. In the fields the cane is cut in pieces of 4 to 5 ft. long, and thrown into the gutter, so that a constant stream of cut cane keeps flowing to the factory.

When the cane has come to the grating it is retained there, while the water streams through the bars and is used later on for condensing the vapour of the evaporators and vacuum pans, or is pumped up again for transport purposes.

The cane from the fields not lying along the railway or water-flumes is taken to the mill by carts drawn by mules. As the temperature of the islands is not very high and the humidity of the atmosphere never gets excessive, cut cane keeps much longer without deteriorating, than it does in hotter countries, so that people are not in such a great hurry to get the reaped cane crushed as they are in Java and Cuba.

In 1910 43,131 hands were working on the sugar estates, 25,808 of whom were engaged on field work and 7,060 in the factory; while the rest were acting as managers, foremen, and clerks. The 7,060 factory labourers are subdivided into 1,200 artizans, 2,522 skilled labourers, and 4,388 unskilled hands. The labour problem is still a difficult one to solve in the Hawaiian Islands. The natives, who are not numerous and are far from industrious, as a rule fill the places of carmen, but do no regular field or factory work. In order to supply the want of labour everything has been tried: Germans, Scandinavians, Portuguese from Portugal and the Azores, Spaniards, Chinese, Filipinos, Japanese, Russians from Vladivostok, West Indians, and even negroes have been imported; but the European nationalities, with the exception of the Portuguese, could not endure the heavy field work in a tropical climate.

The economical conditions in the Azores are steadily improving, and consequently lessen the inducement for Portuguese labourers to try their fortune in Hawaii; Portuguese immigration is therefore uncertain, and at the same time expensive. In 1909 as many as 874 Portuguese—men, women, and children—immigrated from the Azores, costing on an average $90 a head; adult males cost $235, and adult females $145; but children (of whom there were many) were much less.

As long as Hawaii was still a kingdom and an independent republic, the immigration of indentured European labourers was quite an easy matter, and in this way South Europe provided a good deal of comparatively cheap labour.

Once annexed, Hawaii came under American laws, which consider indentured immigration as a sort of slavery, and consequently forbid it. As European labourers do not like to risk leaving home in such circumstances, and very often have not the means to pay their passage, the American immigration law has actually put a stop to this easy way of procuring labour, and has dealt a nasty blow to the Hawaiian planters, which should be considered over and against the advantages of this annexation. Another clause of this law forbids further immigration of Chinese into the dominion of the United States, consequently into Hawaii; so a second source of immigration is excluded.

At the present time the Japanese is the only nation that comes to Hawaii in large numbers to work in the fields and stay on for some time with the intention of earning a handsome sum of money, and then departing either for Japan or for the United States when the language has been mastered. Thanks to the restricting regulations, the Japanese immigration has decreased much of late, as more Japanese leave the country than enter it, and this, of course, has led to the immigration of other races. Then they tried to get Russians from Manchuria and Siberia to settle in Hawaii, their numbers having risen to 1,300 the last two years. It is cheaper to send these people to Hawaii than Portuguese immigrants, as the fare of a Russian on an average amounts to $70, namely, $165 for a man, $100 for a woman, and a much smaller sum for a child. Up to now the results of this type of immigration may be called very satisfactory, but we cannot be certain yet of their wish to stay on or of their enduring power to stand the work in tropical fields. They have also tried to get some thousand labourers from the Philippines, but though the mode of working of this people leaves much to be desired, the Hawaiian planters readily put up with their drawbacks, being glad of the help obtained.

In order to save labour, several field operations have already been abandoned : for instance, trashing the cane, which means saving much manual labour, has been given up. Then the cane plots that are to be cut down are now burnt over, as this greatly diminishes work, for it is much easier to cut the burnt down cane than the green cane leaves full of sharp edges and hairs.

Rats are among the greatest enemies to the Hawaiian cane. Attempts have been made to exterminate them by introducing a sort of weasel, but this has not had satisfactory results. Then the borers do a great deal of harm. They are not caterpillars in this case, but black beetles, called *Sphenophorus obscurus*. This beetle deposits its eggs in the higher nodes of the cane, where the leaf-sheaths stand out from the stalk, and when the eggs are hatched the larvæ get into the cane, where they turn into grubs and destroy the entire inner tissue of the cane. The harm they do is considerable, and, according to an article in a magazine the truth of which we cannot altogether vouch for, is estimated at $2,000,000 a year.

The Entomological Division of the Hawaiian Experiment Station has tried to find parasites of this beetle and cultivate them in hopes of being able to exterminate the pest, as they once were able to exterminate the " leaf-hopper " (*Perkinsiella saccharicida*). This insect, a kind of very small bug, sucks the middle nerve of the leaves, and causes so much damage that, small as it is though large in number, the sugar crop of some estates is said to have been diminished by 10 per cent. The same bug occurs in many other sugar-producing countries, such as Java, but never does so much harm there as parasitical enemies, especially ichneumon flies, are also found there, and impede too rapid a multiplication of this insect. The *Perkinsiella*, unfortunately, seems to have come to Hawaii from Queensland enclosed in a parcel of cane, but the parasite, worst of all, was left behind, and here in a new country, without its usual enemies, it multiplied at an incredibly quick rate, and did much harm. The Experiment Station of the Hawaiian Sugar Planters appointed a number of practical entomologists, who set about searching for the accompanying parasites wherever the bug was found. When found they cultivated them, and sent them to Honolulu to attack their natural enemies. As the ichneumon flies, however, could not travel the distance from Java to Honolulu, for instance, without a break, an intermediate station was founded in Hong Kong, where a great number of them were cultivated on sugar cane under a gauze cover, in order to enable the parasites to give birth to a new generation before their span of life should terminate. In this way they succeeded in conveying a number parasites, the principal of which are the *Paranagrus optabilis* and *Paranagrus perforator*; there are also the *Anagrus frequens* and *Ootetrastichus beatus*. A few years after the introduction of the parasites, an experiment showed that 87 per cent. of the eggs of the leaf-hopper were infested with larvæ of the ichneumon fly, so that we may consider this danger as past.

Further, *red smut* and *marasmius* are of frequent occurrence, as well as other less important diseases, all of which, however, are combatted by disinfecting the cuttings with Bordeaux mixture, which is highly recommended for this purpose by the Experiment Station.

IV.—Sugar Manufacture, Sugar Production per Acre, Cost Price, Kind of Sugar and its Destination.

The manufacture of sugar from sugar cane in the Hawaiian Islands is carried on in the very best possible way; this may be partly due to the fact that the owners of the factories live in the islands, and can see for themselves what their concerns require. Their factories are installed with the best machinery to be had, and work under fairly good chemical and technical control. Then the cane here is of excellent quality, and produces far richer and purer juice than in other cane-growing countries. Peru alone can boast of having an equally good kind of cane, but, on the whole, the cane of other countries is much inferior to the Hawaiian cane in sugar content and purity. Some factories crush from March till May cane of 17 per cent. sugar, and the highest average figure on a weekly statistical list was for April, 1909—no less than 17·81 per cent., the crusher juice having a density of 23·23° Brix. The highest monthly averages for 1909 were 16·81 per cent., 15·89, 15·87, and 15·85 per cent. on a 100 of cane. All these figures refer to Lahaina cane in rainless regions, but planted under irrigation. It was planted in June, 1907, flowered in November, 1908, and was crushed from March to May, 1909; so that it stood in the field for almost twenty-two months.

Ratoons from one-year-old cane grown in parts dependent on rain never realize so high a juice content. The juice nowadays is exclusively expressed by means of mills; diffusion has been tried in some factories, but these shared the common lot of diffusion plants in cane sugar factories, being soon superseded by mills. In many cases one crusher and three or four 3-roller mills have been combined into one system with one or two engines, maceration with water and with last mill juice, and hydraulic pressure on the rollers. The extraction results thus arrived at are never met with elsewhere, nor have they been surpassed. With so high a sugar content as the Hawaiian cane possesses, the sugar content of the bagasse is reduced to 3 per cent., and the loss of sugar on extraction to 0·65 on 100 cane ; while the extraction of sugar on 100 of sugar in the cane reaches 95 per cent.—but not without maceration of sometimes more than 30 per cent. This is not only due to the excellent way of working of the American mills, but also to the hardness of the cane through having ripened in a dry climate, and to the fact that in Hawaii they need not hurry to such an extent as they have to in other countries, and can take their time over the crushing operations. In Cuba, for instance, where the mills are equally powerful, work has to be expedited to get the cane crushed before the rainy season sets in, and harvesting cane would be out of the question ; while in Java work has to be carried out quickly, too, in order to get the grinding season over before the cane dies or loses in sugar content. In Hawaii the cane in the field keeps in good condition long after it is full-grown, while no early rainy season is to be feared, so that there is not a single reason for hurrying over the grinding, but everybody can work carefully, and try to get as much sugar as possible out of the canes. The manufacture calls for no special mention. The juice is limed ; clarifying is generally done in Deming's superheat or similar installations, and the juice is evaporated in triple or quadruple effects. The syrup, without being further clarified, is evaporated to a well-concentrated massecuite, which, when centrifugalled, produces a raw sugar of about 97° polarization (so-called " A " sugar) and first molasses of about 70° purity. This is boiled to grain and the massecuite is cooled and then yields a sugar of about 95° polarization (the " B " sugar), and exhausted molasses of about 30 apparent purity. Only one factory, the Honolulu Plantation Company, makes exclusively crystallized and crushed white sugar to the amount of 20,000 short tons a year, to be exported to San Francisco as well as for home consumption. The exhausted molasses is used partly as cattle fodder or as fuel for the furnaces in conjunction with a special burner ; while a considerable part is thrown away as waste, as excise regulations forbid working up the last molasses to alcohol.

Owing to the high sugar content of the cane, as well as to the high purity of the juice and the high juice extraction by the mills, the sugar yield on 100 cane is extremely high in Hawaii. In 1908 the maximum amount of one factory during a whole year was 14·36, while the minimum still came up to 10·78 ; 12·61 per cent. could be taken as an average figure, so that one may conclude that in 1908 8·18 tons of cane were needed for one ton of sugar. For 1909 and 1910 these figures have respectively been 7·67 and 7·99 tons of cane for one ton of sugar, being equal to yields of 13·04 and 12·52 per cent. The yield from irrigated cane is higher than that from non-irrigated. The chemical control of the sugar house work is generally well managed, and analyses and calculations have been uniformly conducted for the last few years, according to methods adopted by the Hawaiian Sugar Chemists' Association, which are founded on the same system as those applied in Java and Cuba ; the results obtained in the different islands can therefore be accurately compared. The fibre content of the cane is generally very high—on an average 12·8 per cent., with a maximum of 15 and a minimum of 10 per cent. ; as the bagasse is pressed quite dry, and the manufacture of raw sugar crystals does not require much steam, it can stand ample maceration and a lot of extra water to be evaporated without the attendants having to have recourse to additional fuel. Moreover, the factories are still new, and generally installed in a practical manner as regards steam production and application, so that most of them can make their bagasse suffice. Those which are short of fuel fall back on molasses as additional fuel, or on crude oil, which is imported in tank steamers and is sprayed into the furnace by means of injectors.

The sugar production per area was during the years 1897 to 1907 for the different islands as follows, expressed in short tons per acre and kg. per hectare :—

Year.	Oahu.		Kauai.		Maui.		Hawaii.	
	Short Tons per acre.	Kg. per hectare.	Short Tons per acre.	Kg. per hectare.	Short Tons per acre.	Kg. per hectare.	Short Tons per acre.	Kg. per hectare.
1897	5·38	12,069	5·60	12,547	4·72	10,576	4·21	9,429
1898	6·36	14,249	5·39	12 081	5 45	12,198	2·98	6,677
1899	7·35	16,466	5·88	13,179	5·85	13,106	3·48	7,799
1900	7·38	16,531	5·34	11,963	5·50	12,320	3·36	7,533
1901	7·29	16,335	5·21	11,674	5·12	11,465	3·30	7,401
1902	7·09	15.799	4·89	10,947	4·74	10,640	3·03	6,792
1903	7·26	16,254	4·26	10,362	5·80	12,984	3·50	7,845
1904	6·44	14,435	4·32	9,373	5·56	12,514	2·64	5,915
1905	6·55	14,680	4·61	10,234	6·64	14,882	2·83	6,347
1906	6·24	13,670	4·37	9,799	6·44	14,440	3·09	7,134
1907	6·28	14,067	4·43	9,928	6·26	14,032	3·02	6,766
1908	6·68	14,970	4·73	10,618	7·31	16,362	3·83	8,616
1909	6·61	14,795	5·03	11,280	7·27	16,201	3·46	7,745
1910	6·26	14,023	4·90	10,964	7·39	16,538	3·03	6,788

The Hawaiian Islands.

The production all over the territory was as follows, *on the whole*, and sub-divided into *irrigated* and *non-irrigated* land :—

Year.	On the whole land.		Irrigated land.		Non-irrigated land.	
	Tons per acre.	Kg. per hec-tare.	Tons per acre.	Kg. per hec-tare.	Tons per acre.	Kg per hec-tare.
1895..	3·24	7,249	3·83	8,589	2·65	5,947
1896..	4·07	9,126	4·52	10,116	3·68	8,276
1897..	4·66	10,451	5·08	11,369	4·35	9,755
1898..	4·15	9,303	5·63	12,622	2·97	6,646
1899..	4·69	10,503	6·08	13,616	3·53	7,936
1900..	4·54	10,164	6·12	13,724	3·13	7,013
1901..	4·57	10,232	6·19	13,874	3·28	7,348
1902..	4·37	9,793	5·84	13,083	3·00	6,737
1903..	4·69	10,511	6·19	13,862	3·86	7,759
1904..	4·00	8,966	5·60	12,557	2·60	5,827
1905..	4·48	10,030	6·08	13,614	2·81	6,309
1906..	4·47	10,018	5·76	13,009	3·07	7,077
1907..	4·41	9,885	5·57	12,552	3·02	6,778
1908..	5·14	11,488	6·33	14,123	3·83	8,588
1909..	5·03	11 227	6 48	14,447	3·48	7,746
1910..	4·69	10,503	6·27	14,035	3·06	6,875

This shows that the irrigated plantations yield much better results than those depending on rain, and that the Island of Hawaii, where most of the plantations are not irrigated, produces much less sugar per area than the well irrigated Island of Oahu does. It also shows that the soil of the Hawaiian Islands, on the whole, does not yield that high sugar production such as is often mentioned in journals or current talk. These favourable reports are due to the fact that a few sugar estates are found in the neighbourhood of Honolulu, which are favoured by a deep layer of fertile soil, are well sheltered, and pro-vided with an excellent irrigation installation, all of which, of course, leads to extremely high cane and sugar yields. As most travellers do not get any further than the neighbourhood of Honolulu, the things seen there are apt to be taken as in the ordinary run—and so reports such as of Hawaii yielding 12 tons of sugar per acre get afloat. Under favourable circumstances some field or other may yield such a production, but this figure has never been attained all through a crushing season. The famous Ewa plantation in Oahu near Honolulu yielded in 1908 275.145·175 tons of cane from 3,795·74 acres, or 69·88 tons per acre, and made 34·340 tons of sugar out of these or 8·8 tons per acre. The planted area was as follows :—

Plant cane	544·04
Long first ratoons	537·24
Long second ratoons	1,285·48
Long third ratoons	215·54
Long fourth ratoons	558·91
Long fifth ratoons	38·38
Short ratoons	616·15
Total	3,795·74 acres

The cost price of sugar, of course, depends on several circumstances, so that it is absolutely impossible even to give an approximate figure for it. Van Hoorn mentions in the *Archief voor de Java Suiker Industrie*, 1909, page 579, that the cost price of sugar from Oahu delivered in Honolulu in 1908 amounted to $34 per ton, or 7s. per cwt. Oahu, as a matter of fact, is very well situated, and this accounts for the much lower cost price here than at any other factory in the Island of Hawaii, which yields us the following data : 2,810 acres of cane-field yielded 11,953 tons of sugar, or 4·25 tons per acre.

The cost of production was :—	Per ton
Planting	19·57
Cutting	2·18
Transport	2·47
Loading	1·14
Manufacturing cost	6·30
Carriage to the seaport	1·50
General expenses	7·50
Freightage to the U.S., Commission, etc.	14·40
Total	$55·06

This cost included no less than $30 per acre for artificial manure.

With the exception of about 20,000 short tons of white sugar produced by the Honolulu Plantation Company, all Hawaiian sugar is raw sugar destined for refining purposes. It is sold by contract to the American Sugar Refining Company at San Francisco and to the Californian and Hawaiian Sugar Refining Company, also established in San Francisco. During the last few years about three-fifths of the exported sugar was shipped to the Atlantic coast, and the rest to the Pacific ports of the United States.

In 1909 San Francisco received 161,236 out of the 393,000 tons from Hawaii ; in 1908 200,534 out of the 465,000, in 1909 208,661 out of the 478,000, in 1910 201,317 out of the 463,000 tons, and in 1911 227,690 out of the 505,995 tons. The sugar is sold at New York prices, basis 96° Cuban centrifugal sugars *plus* import duty. For sugars destined for New York or Philadelphia one-tenth of a cent is deducted from that price per pound ; while for those destined for San Francisco the deduction is three-eighths of a cent. Apart from this the ordinary custom is followed ; for instance, the price applies to 96° polarization, with an increase of $\frac{1}{32}$ cents per pound for each degree above and a decrease of $\frac{1}{16}$ cent for each degree below 96.

Consequently, should the price of duty-paid Cuba 96° centrifugals be 4·05 cents, Hawaiian sugar of 97° polarization would realize in San Francisco 4·05 $-\frac{3}{8}+\frac{1}{32}=3\cdot70\frac{5}{8}$ cents ; and in New York 3·98$\frac{5}{8}$, or respectively 74·12^5 and 77·62^5 dollars per short ton

This shows that in being dependent on American buyers the Hawaiian producers do not enjoy fully the protection given to foreign sugars of 1·685 cents per pound on 96° polarization by the high import duty. First of all, the Cuban price, as has been stated before, is always lower than the world's price owing to the working of the Trusts ; hence free Java sugar, for instance, fetches a higher price in the American market than Cuban sugar would do. As the world's price quoted by New York is not taken as basis, but the price paid for Cuban sugar, Hawaii first of all shares the same lot, and then makes less for its sugar than sugar from free countries does. Again they most arbitrarily deduct respectively 0·10 and 0·375 cents per pound, and, worst of all, the Hawaiian producer is compelled as an American citizen to send his goods in American bottoms, which brings about a monopoly that naturally drives up the prices to no small extent. So while we should not make light of the fact that Hawaiian sugar enjoys a protection of 1·685 cents per pound, or 7s. 10d. per cwt., there is the disadvantage of freight cost being extremely high, and of sugar fetching less in America than free sugar, and that in addition something is deducted from the already low price. The first of these drawbacks must be put up with, but these other disadvantages are already neutralized to some extent by the fact that Hawaiian planters themselves have founded a refinery of their own at Crockett, near San Francisco, the Californian and Hawaiian Sugar Refining Company, which works up 80 per cent. of the Hawaiian crop transported to the Pacific coast ; hence the lower price received for raw sugar comes to the good of their own refinery, and, finally, neutralizes the deficit. The only disadvantage left is the higher freight cost, but as the protection amounts to $33·70 per ton, and the entire cost of freight does not come to more than $11 to $14, citizenship of the United States must, on the whole, be advantageous for Hawaii, and be looked upon as a matter of life or death. Where sugar fetches $80 per ton without including deductions, and costs $55 to deliver it in America, it goes without saying that Hawaii could not possibly keep up her sugar production if it was not for the $33 protection in the $80, or in other words, if it did not continue to enjoy the same protection the United States grant now to their own producers.

V.—The Future.

From the foregoing we may conclude that the future of the cane sugar industry in the Hawaiian Islands, first of all, depends on the fiscal policy of the United States. Should the Americans decide to abolish or considerably diminish the import duties on sugar, thus placing the consumption price of sugar in the United States on a level with the world's price that free sugar fetches, this would deal a heavy blow to the Hawaiian sugar industry, and almost destroy it. Although the duties on sugar in the United States have been almost untouched by the action of the Payne tariff, the discontent prevailing in American circles as regards the heavy protective tariff has become increasingly strong of late, and it is an open question whether the first Cabinet change will not lead to a modification in the import duties on sugar, to Hawaii's immediate detriment.

In the Hawaiian Islands there are still large tracts of land that might be turned into sugar cane plantations; while there is also ground that could be made more productive if irrigation were applied. Where some estates make six tons per acre and others three, there is still the possibility of increasing this lower production by improving the cultural methods and selecting suitable cane. Where irrigation is prone to wash out and eliminate the mineral constituents of the soil which have collected for ages, this shortage can be made up by applying artificial manure, so that it need not lead to any decrease in returns. If more American small farmers would settle in these islands, the most necessary articles of food might be supplied by farmers instead of by China or Japan, which would mean a reduction in the price of nearly all articles of consumption, and make life out there a little less expensive. Scarcity of labour, however, is the greatest obstacle to further extension of the sugar industry, and as long as the laws on immigration are not modified a further noticeable increase in production will be out of question for the present. Proposals have already been made to issue exceptional regulations on the immigration laws, either by allowing Portuguese to be accepted by contract and with money advanced, or by admitting a limited number of Chinese manual labourers into the islands. In order to prevent their invading the United States, or competing with American workmen in the Hawaiian Islands, stipulations might be made that they should only come in for field work, and that they are not to be allowed into the United States, the latter stipulation also being enacted against Chinese living in Hawaii.

364

When the Government of the United States will allow and promote the immigration of field labourers in one way or other, the sugar industry of Hawaii will, no doubt, enter upon a period of greater extension, as this would be the last factor to ensure complete success.

Books of Reference

Royal D. Mead. *A History of the Progress of the Sugar Industry of Hawaii since the Reciprocity Treaty of 1876.*
British Consular Reports.
The Climate of Hawaii.
Hawaii and its Agricultural Possibilities.
Maps, Guides, and Pamphlets issued by the Hawaii Promotion Committee.

III.

THE FIJI ISLANDS.

The Fiji Islands lie in the Pacific Ocean, between 15° 47′ and 21° 4′ S. Lat., and between 176° 51′ W. Long., and 175° 38′ E. Long. They consist of six groups, composing in all two big and 253 small islands. Their total area is 8,054 sq. miles, and their inhabitants amounted to 116,684 in 1901. The two bigger islands have respectively areas of 4,550 and 2,500 sq. miles ; about eighty of the smaller islands are inhabited, while the rest have no population at all.

The bigger islands are of volcanic formation and mountainous, while the smaller ones are coral islands. The climate is warm and moist, and the soil of the big islands is fertile and suitable for all sorts of tropical vegetation.

Suva, in Viti-Levu, is the capital, possessing a good harbour ; what other towns there are are of no importance.

The Fiji Islands were discovered by Tasman in 1643 ; in 1773 Cook visited them, and after him came other travellers. Its king in 1853 offered Great Britain the sovereignty of his island kingdom, in order to escape punishment at the hands of the United States, but the offer was not accepted. In 1858 it was renewed and declined once more ; but finally, in 1874, the islands became a colony of the British Empire.

Sugar is the principal article produced, and is cultivated in the Islands of Viti-Levu and Vanua-Levu ; while the Island of Taviuni also possesses land fit for sugar cultivation, which may be turned to account later on. About 1880 the Colonial Sugar Refining Company began to grow cane, and a few years afterwards the Fiji Sugar Company followed its example, but the first-named company had the greatest interest by far in the industry. The early factories were at first most primitive, but soon improved, and as early as 1883 an exportation of 5,232 tons of sugar was recorded. The labour difficulty at first retarded developments. The aborigines could not be got to do regular work, and when the inhabitants of neighbouring islands, like Tonga and the Solomon Islands were tried for this purpose, they proved better workers ; still the importation of this type of labour was no success in the end. Finally, the British Colonial Government came to their succour, and allowed British Indian coolies to immigrate on the same terms as prevailed in the West Indian colonies. The coolies are recruited by Government officials in the districts round Calcutta, as required by the planters, and conveyed to Suva by the Government. On arriving there they are distributed among the plantations for five years' indenture, and have the option to renew after that time is expired. The coolies are generally provided in the proportion of two men to one woman. The planters return the money advanced to the Government, and pay the coolies the following wages : 25s. per month for an indentured male labourer, and 20s. for an indentured female worker. A man can usually make 1s. a day, and a woman 9d. a day when engaged on piecework. Lodging, medical treatment, and medicine are provided by the estate, but the workmen have to find their own food, which does not come to much, and they are soon able to put by some money, which they convert into silver ornaments, an investment easy to transport and to keep possession of.

In order to be able eventually to do away with the necessity of having to import and keep indentured coolies at great expense and under legal difficulties, the sugar manufacturers have tried to keep on the British Indians as free labourers after they have served their indenture, and to give a group of labourers the usage of plots of land—some sixty acres in extent—for cultivation. The land is first prepared for the cane, and the latter planted before the British Indians assume possession under the superintendence of the factory staff. During the time it takes the cane to grow, each indentured labourer gets 1s. for each 9-hour working day by way of payment in advance, which money, together with tillage expenses, is deducted later on when they settle the money the cane crop has fetched.

We give an example of the mode of settling this payment for a plot 60 acres in size, yielding 1,843 tons of cane, which cane was sold at 4s. per ton (standing) in the field :—

	£	s.	d.	£	s.	d.
1,843 tons at 4s.				368	12	0
Wages in advance at 1s. per day	141	19	11			
Cutting wages advanced by the factory	66	0	0			
Cleaning and loading expenses paid in advance	8	18	11			
				216	18	10
				£151	13	2

The Fiji Islands.

So the planters get a sum of £151 13s. 2d. at the end of the harvest, and as it had taken 2,595 days of work, it means an extra daily premium of 1s. 2d., which, together with the 1s. advanced as wages, comes to 2s. 2d. ; consequently, quite a little sum accrues for the planter.   And then this is not a specially good piece of land, as there are instances of 3s. for a day's work.   We should remember that this 2s. 2d. a day only refers to the work done in planting the cane, and does not refer to the daily wages during the time the cane is ripening.

It will happen, of course, that cane does not want any attention when growing, thus leaving the farmers time to occupy themselves with other work, such as the laying out of new fields, the cutting and transporting of cane, etc. This is sometimes classed as day work, but more generally as contract work ; this latter arrangement being a better one in that it leaves the planter free to shelve his work for the time, and give his whole attention to his own cane when it needs his special care.

It is clear that it takes a good deal of management and tact to see to the several interests—those of the factory, of the planters, the Indians' interests, and the planting on ground under lease ; for all these various conditions make it necessary for the land to be planted and tilled at different times, so that the labourers should have work all through the year.   As all these difficulties seem to have been overcome, this system of cane planting in instalments is much in vogue—the Indians being rather partial to the system, and it leads to an increasing amount of production, which at the present moment is estimated at about 80,000 tons. In spite of the large profits the planters make, the cane when delivered at the mill does not cost too much for the manufacturers.

According to the following specification, the net cost of cane comes to 7s. per ton.   The expenses of working the same plot of ground of 60 acres, yielding 1,843 tons of cane were as follows :—

						£	s.	d.
Ploughing	..	..	..	..	..	5	2	9
Harrowing	..	..	..	..	..	1	4	0
Making of furrows	..	..	..	..	..	9	8	3
Making ready for planting		..	..	..	1	14	0
Actual planting	..	..	..	..	..	18	8	9
Supplying	..	..	..	..	..	5	1	0
Ploughing between the rows		..	..	..	2	12	6
Banking	..	..	..	..	..	1	7	9
Portable railway and transport	..	..	..	5	2	0
Implements	..	..	..	..	..	6	12	0
866 coolies at 5d. per task		..	..	..	18	0	10
289 hours at 1s. 7¼d.		..	..	..	23	18	0
466 mules at 1s. 0¾d.		..	..	..	24	15	1
898 oxen at 2½d.	..	..	..	..		9	7	1
Survey, administration : 60 acres at 30s.		..	..	90	0	0

	£	s.	d.
2 595 coolies for planting at 5d. per task ..	54	1	2
Paid for 1,843 tons of cane at 4s.	363	7	3

£645 7 3

which for 1,843 tons of cane is 7s. per ton.

One disadvantage of this system of having the planting done by contract is that the planters are no longer in close touch with the farmers, but lose their hold over them, and cannot compel them to work intensively, nor can they let them share irrigation expenses. Much ratoon is grown, little money is spent on manuring or irrigation ; hence the sugar production seldom exceeds three tons to the acre.

The factories, on the other hand, are excellently installed, and supplied with triple crushing and maceration and gieen bagasse furnaces ; in short, with all modern machinery. The Colonial Sugar Refining Company possesses four big sugar factories, three of which are in Viti-Levu, and one at Labasa, in the Island of Vanua-Levu.

In addition, there are a few smaller factories, which either belong to the Colonial Sugar Refining Company, or sell their production to them. Nearly all Fiji sugar is sent to Auckland, New Zealand, where it is treated in the refinery of the Colonial Company.

The sugar exportation from the Fiji Islands has amounted to the following quantities in tons :—

1883	..	..	5,232	1902	..	..	35,901
1886	..	..	11,887	1903	..	..	46,438
1889	..	..	13,411	1904	..	..	52,138
1892	..	..	19,202	1905	..	..	65,517
1895	..	..	23,571	1906	..	..	38,487
1896	..	..	27,788	1907	..	..	66,596
1897	..	..	27,432	1908	..	..	66,149
1898	..	..	34,540	1909	..	..	68,942
1899	..	..	31,210	1910	..	..	68,900
1900	..	..	32,098	1911	..	..	75,000
1901	..	..	31,751	1912	..	..	80,000

(estimate).

IV.

TAHITI.

Tahiti, a French possession, belongs to the Society Islands in the Pacific Ocean, in 180° W. Long. and 17° S. Lat. It is mountainous and scantily populated. Attempts have been repeatedly made to introduce the sugar industry, but so far in vain.

The native population are disinclined for steady work, and as Tahiti is a French colony, working with indentured British Indian coolies is out of the question here. Sugar when imported is very heavily taxed, and so cannot be introduced from other countries with any profit. The population is not considerable enough to carry on a flourishing sugar industry.

Up to 1892 not more than 40 tons of sugar was its yearly production; in 1894 a big plantation close to the capital, Papeete, which had been abandoned, was started again, and about 25 acres were planted, and yielded 67 tons of sugar. The next year 40 acres yielded 94 tons; while in 1897 124 tons were produced. In 1898 the crop attained to 83 tons, and in 1899 it was 207 tons; the industry has since developed to such an extent that two factories together produce 400 to 450 tons of sugar yearly, which amount just supplies the home consumption. Hence, only a very little refined sugar has to be imported from France and the United States; and raw sugar is no longer imported from New Zealand at all.

Appendix.

I.

___

International Convention relative to Bounties on Sugar.

___

Signed at Brussels, March 5th, 1902.

___

His Majesty the German Emperor, King of Prussia, in the name of the German Empire ; His Majesty the Emperor of Austria, King of Bohemia, &c., &c., and Apostolic King of Hungary ; His Majesty the King of the Belgians ; His Majesty the King of Spain, and, in his name, Her Majesty the Queen-Regent of the Kingdom ; the President of the French Republic ; His Majesty the King of the United Kingdom of Great Britian and Ireland, and of the British Dominions beyond the Seas, Emperor of India ; His Majesty the King of Italy ; Her Majesty the Queen of the Netherlands ; His Majesty the King of Sweden and Norway ;

Desiring, on the one hand, to equalize the conditions of the competition between beet and cane sugar from various countries, and, on the other hand, to promote the consumption of sugar ;

And considering that this twofold result cannot be attained otherwise than by the abolition of bounties and by the limitation of the surtax ;

Have resolved to conclude a Convention to this effect, and have appointed their Plenipotentiaries ;

Who, having exchanged their full powers, found to be in good and due form, have agreed on the following Articles :—

ARTICLE I.

The High Contracting Parties engage to suppress, from the date of the coming into force of the present Convention, the direct and indirect bounties by which the production or exportation of sugar may profit, and not to establish bounties of such a kind during the whole continuance of the said Convention. For the application of this provision, sugar-sweetened products, such as pre serves, chocolates, biscuits, condensed milk, and all other analogous products containing, in a notable proportion, artificially incorporated sugar, are assimi-lated to sugar.

Appendix.

The preceding paragraph applies to all advantages derived directly or indirectly, by the several categories of producers, from State fiscal legislation, and in particular to—

(*a*) Direct bonuses granted on exportation ;

(*b*) Direct bonuses granted to production :

(*c*) Total or partial exemptions from taxation which profit a part of the products of manufacture ;

(*d*) Profits derived from excess of yield ;

(*e*) Profits derived from too high a drawback ;

(*f*) Advantages derived from any surtax in excess of the rate fixed by Article III.

ARTICLE II.

The High Contracting Parties engage to place in bond, under the continuous supervision, both by day and by night, of Revenue officers, sugar factories and sugar refineries, as well as factories for the extraction of sugar from molasses.

For this purpose, the factories shall be so arranged as to afford every guarantee against the surreptitious removal of sugar, and the officers shall have the right of entry into all parts of the factories.

Check registers shall be kept respecting one or more of the processes of manufacture, and finished sugar shall be placed in special warehouses affording every requisite guarantee of security.

ARTICLE III.

The High Contracting Parties engage to limit the surtax—that is to say, the difference between the rate of duty or taxation to which foreign sugar is liable and the rate of duty or taxation to which home-produced sugar is subject —to a maximum of 6 fr. per 100 kg. on refined sugar and on sugar which may be classed as refined, and to 5 fr. 50 c. on other sugar.

This provision is not intended to apply to the rate of import duty in countries which produce no sugar ; neither is it applicable to the by-products of sugar manufacture and of sugar refining.

ARTICLE IV.

The High Contracting Parties engage to impose a special duty on the importation into their territories of sugar from those countries which may grant bounties either on production or on exportation.

This duty shall not be less than the amount of the bounties, direct or indirect, granted in the country of origin. The High Contracting Parties reserve to themselves, each so far as concerns itself, the right to prohibit the importation of bounty-fed sugar.

In order to calculate the amount of the advantages eventually derived from the surtax specified under letter (*f*) of Article I, the figure fixed by

Article III is deducted from the amount of this surtax ; half of this difference is considered to represent the bounty, the Permanent Commission instituted by Article VII having the right, at the request of a Contracting State, to revise the figure thus obtained.

ARTICLE V.

The High Contracting Parties engage reciprocally to admit at the lowest rates of their tariffs of import duties sugar the produce either of the Contracting States or of those Colonies or possessions of the said States which do not grant bounties, and to which the obligations of Article VIII are applicable.

Cane sugar and beet sugar may not be subjected to different duties.

ARTICLE VI.

Spain, Italy, and Sweden shall be exempted from the engagement which forms the subject of Articles I, II, and III, so long as they do not export sugar.

Those States engage to adapt their sugar legislation to the provisions of the Convention within one year—or earlier if possible—from the time at which the Permanent Commission shall have found that the above-mentioned condition has ceased to exist.

ARTICLE VII.

The High Contracting Parties agree to establish a Permanent Commission charged with supervising the execution of the provisions of the present Convention.

This Commission shall be composed of Delegates of the several Contracting States, and a Permanent Bureau shall be attached to it. The Commission elects its President ; it will sit at Brussels and will assemble at the summons of the President.

The duties of the Delegates will be :—

(a) To pronounce whether in the Contracting States no direct or indirect bounty is granted on the production or on the exportation of sugar.

(b) To pronounce whether the States referred to in Article VI continue to fulfil the special condition foreseen by that Article.

(c) To pronounce whether bounties exist in the non-signatory States, and to estimate the amount thereof for the purposes of Article IV.

(d) To deliver an opinion on contested questions.

(e) To prepare for consideration requests for admission to the Union made by States which have not taken part in the present Convention.

It will be the duty of the Permanent Bureau to collect, translate, arrange, and publish information of all kinds respecting legislation on, and statistics of, sugar, not only in the Contracting States, but in other States as well.

In order to insure the execution of the preceding provisions, the High Contracting Parties shall communicate, through the diplomatic channel, to the Belgian Government, which shall forward them to the Commission, the Laws, Orders, and Regulations on the taxation of sugar which are or may in the future be in force in their respective countries, as well as statistical information relative to the object of the present Convention.

Each of the High Contracting Parties may be represented on the Commission by a Delegate, or by a Delegate and Assistant Delegates.

Austria and Hungary shall be considered as separate Contracting Parties.

The first meeting of the Commission shall be held in Brussels, under arrangements to be made by the Belgian Government, at least three months before the coming into force of the present Convention.

The duty of the Commission shall be limited to findings and investigations. It shall draw up a report on all questions submitted to it, and forward the same to the Belgian Government, which shall communicate it to the States interested, and, at the request of one of the High Contracting Parties, shall convoke a Conference, which shall take such decisions or measures as circumstances demand.

The findings and calculations referred to under letters (b) and (c) must, however, be acted on by the Contracting States ; they will be passed by a vote of the majority—each Contracting State having one vote—and they will take effect in two months' time at the latest. Should one of the Contracting States consider it necessary to appeal against a decision of the Commission, the said State must, within eight days of notification to it of the said decision, require a fresh meeting of the Commission ; the Commission will immediately hold a meeting, and will pronounce its final decision within one month of the date of the appeal. The new decision shall take effect, at latest, within two months of its delivery. The same procedure will be followed with regard to the preparation for consideration of demands for admission provided for under letter (e).

The expenses incurred on account of the organization and working of the Permanent Bureau and of the Commission—excepting the salaries or allowances of the Delegates, who shall be paid by their respective countries—shall be borne by all the Contracting States, and shall be divided among them in a manner to be determined by the Commission.

ARTICLE VIII.

The High Contracting Parties engage, for themselves and for their Colonies or possessions, exception being made in the case of the self-governing Colonies of Great Britain and the British East Indies, to take the necessary measures to prevent bounty-fed sugar which has passed in transit through the territory of a Contracting State from enjoying the benefits of the Convention in the market to which it is being sent. The Permanent Commission shall make the necessary proposals with regard to this matter.

Appendix.

ARTICLE IX.

States which have not taken part in the present Convention shall be admitted to adhere to it at their request, and after concurrence has been expressed by the Permanent Commission.

The request shall be addressed through the diplomatic channel to the Belgian Government, which shall undertake, when occasion arises, to notify the adhesion to all the other Governments. The adhesion shall entail, as of right, acceptance of all the obligations and admission to all the advantages stipulated by the present Convention, and will take effect as from the 1st September following the dispatch of the notification by the Belgian Government to the other Contracting States.

ARTICLE X.

The present Convention shall come into force from the 1st September, 1903.

It shall remain in force for five years from that date, and in the case of none of the High Contracting Parties having notified to the Belgian Government, twelve months before the expiration of the said period of five years, its intention of terminating the effects thereof, it shall continue to remain in force for one year, and so on from year to year.

In the event of one of the Contracting States denouncing the Convention, such denunciation shall have effect only in respect to such State; the other States shall retain, until the 31st October, of the year in which the denunciation takes place, the right of notifying their intention of withdrawing as from the 1st September of the following year. If one of these latter States desires to exercise this right, the Belgian Government shall summon a Conference at Brussels within three months to consider the measures to be taken

ARTICLE XI.

The provisions of the present Convention shall apply to the oversea Provinces, Colonies, and foreign possessions of the High Contracting Parties. The British and Netherland Colonies and possessions are excepted, save as regards the provisions forming the object of Articles V. and VIII.

The position of the British and Netherland Colonies and possessions is furthermore regulated by the Declarations inserted in the Final Protocol

ARTICLE XII.

The fulfilment of the mutual engagements contained in the present Convention is subject, as far as necessary, to the completion of the formalities and requirements established by the Constitutional laws of each of the Contracting States.

Appendix.

The present Convention shall be ratified, and the ratifications shall be deposited at the Ministry for Foreign Affairs at Brussels, on the 1st February, 1903, or earlier if possible.

It is understood that the present Convention shall become binding, as of right, only if it is ratified by those at least of the Contracting States who are not the subject of the exceptional provision of Article VI. Should one or more of the said States not have deposited their ratifications within the period stipulated, the Belgian Government shall immediately take steps to obtain a decision by the other Signatory Powers as to whether the present Convention shall come into force among them alone.

In faith whereof the respective Plenipotentiaries have signed the present Convention.

Done at Brussels, in single copy, March 5, 1902.

Final Protocol.

On proceeding to the signature of the Sugar Convention concluded this day between the Governments of Germany, of Austria and of Hungary, of Belgium, of Spain, of France, of Great Britain, of Italy, of the Netherlands, and of Sweden, the undersigned Plenipotentiaries have agreed as follows :—

As regards Article III.

Considering that the object of the surtax is the effectual protection of the home markets of the producing countries, the High Contracting Parties reserve to themselves the right, each as concerns itself, to propose an increase of the surtax, should considerable quantities of sugar produced by one of the Contracting States enter their territories · this increase would only apply to sugar produced by that State.

The proposal must be addressed to the Permanent Commission, which will decide, at an early date, by a vote of the majority, whether there is good ground for the proposed measure, as to the period for which it shall be enforced, and as to the rate of the increase ; the latter shall not exceed 1 fr. per 100 kg.

The assent of the Commission shall only be given when the invasion of the market concerned is the consequence of real economic inferiority, and not the result of a factitious increase in price brought about by an agreement among producers.

As regards Article XI.

(A.) 1. The Government of Great Britain declares that no bounty, direct or indirect, shall be granted to the sugar of the Crown Colonies during the continuance of the Convention.

2 It also declares as an exceptional measure, and reserving in principle entire liberty of action as regards the fiscal relations between the United Kingdom and its Colonies and possessions, that, during the continuance of the

Convention, no preference will be granted in the United Kingdom to Colonial sugar as against sugar from the Contracting States.

3. Lastly, it declares that the Convention will be submitted by it to the self-governing Colonies and to the East Indies, so that they may have an opportunity of giving their adhesion to it.

It is understood that the Government of His Britannic Majesty has power to adhere to the Convention on behalf of the Crown Colonies.

(B.) The Government of the Netherlands declares that during the continuance of the Convention no bounty, direct or indirect, shall be granted to sugar from the Netherland Colonies, and that such sugar shall not be admitted into the Netherlands at a lower Tariff than that applied to sugar from the Contracting States.

The present Final Protocol, which shall be ratified at the same time as the Convention concluded this day, shall be regarded as forming an integral part of the Convention, and shall have the same force, value, and duration.

In faith whereof the Plenipotentiaries have drawn up the present Protocol. Done at Brussels, the 5th March, 1902.

II.

List of Countervailing Duties to be levied by every Country adhering to the Brussels Convention (except Great Britain) on importation of bounty-fed Sugar from the following sources. As fixed by the Permanent Commission at Brussels in August, 1911.

Origin.	Description of Sugar.	Countervailing Duty in francs per 100 kg.
Argentina	Refined, or polarizing 96° and more	19·90
	Unrefined or polarizing under 96°	15·05
	Candy	10·50
Commonwealth of Australia	Raw..	0·94
	Refined	5·62
Brazil	Raw..	36·00
	Refined	35·00
British South Africa	Raw..	2·05
	Refined	3·89
Chile	Refined whole or crushed..	13·51
	White, crystallized or crushed	10·86
	Crystallized, first product or moscobada (cassonade)	6·45
	Crude (chancaca or con-creto)	5·98
Costa Rica	White	20·50
	Other kinds of refined	15·00
	Raw..	15·25
Japan	Refined, candy	2·61
Canada	Refined	3·63
Mexico	Raw and refined ..	3·00
Nicaragua	Raw..	34·75
	Refined	34·50
Mozambique	Raw..	13·50
	Refined	13·00
Rumania	Raw..	15·15
	Refined	20·00
Spain	Raw and refined ..	19·50

III.

Table of Measures, Weights and Currency, with their sub-divisions and their British equivalents.

A. MEASURES.

Foot = 12 inches = 0·304794 metre.

Inch = 0·02539954 metre.

Kilometre = 3,280 feet 10 inches = 0·62137 mile.

Metre = 39·37 inches.

Mile = 1,609·315 metres.

Yard = 3 feet = 0·9144 metre.

Acre = 4,046·71 square metres.

Aliquiere (Brazil) = 4 quarteis = 5·98 acres = 2·42 hectares.

Are = 100 metres = 119·6 square yards.

Arpent (Mauritius) = 1·043 ⸱cres = 4,221 square metres.

Bouw (Java) = 500 square Rhineland rods = 1·747 acre = 7,096·5 square metres.

Caballeria (Cuba) = 342 cordelas = 33·16 acres = 13· 2 hectares

Hectare = 10,000 square metres = 2·471 acres.

Koh Formosa and Japan) = 2·45 acres = 0·9915 hectare.

Mananza (Nicaragua) = 1·70 cre = 0·69 hectare.

Square Metre = 1,550 square inches.

Orlong (Straits Settlements) 1⅓ acre = 0·535 hectare.

Square Rhineland Rod (Java) = 17·21 square yards = 14·39 square metres.

Gallon (Imperial) = 4 quarts = 4·545963 litres.

Gallon (American) = 0·832 Imperial gallon = 3·785 litres.

Hectolitre = 100 litres = 22 Imperial gallons = 26·417 American gallons.

Litre = 0·88 quart.

Hogshead (*see under ' Weights.'*).

Sack (*see under ' Weights '*).

B. WEIGHTS.

Arroba = 25·3175 lbs. avoird. = 11·5 kg.

Hundredweight (Great Britain and British Colonies) = 112 lbs. = 50·80235 kg.

Hundredweight (Spain and Spanish countries) = 100 Spanish pounds = 101·27 lbs. avoird. = 46 kg.

Hundredweight (Old German) = 100 German pounds = 114·44 lbs. avoird.

Hogshead (British West Indies) = ⅞ ton = 889 kg.

Kilogram (kg.) = 2·2046 lbs. avoird.

Maund Bazar (British India) = 40 seers = 100 pounds Troy = 82·30 lbs avoird. = 37·3242 kg.

Picul (China) = 133·27 lbs. = 60·453 kg.

Picul (Japan) = 133·33 lbs. = 60·5 kg.

Weights.

Picul (Java) = 125 Amsterdam pounds = 136·16 lbs. = 61·761302 kg.
Picul (Philippine Islands) = 139·44 lbs. = 63·25 kg.
Picul (Straits Settlements) = 133·33 lbs. = 60·5 kg.
Pood (Russia) = 36·112 lbs. avoird. = 16·3805 kg.
Pound (Great Britain) = 0·4535925 kg.
Pound (American) = 0·45304 kg.
Pound (Spa n and former colonies) = 1·0143 lbs. avoird. = 0·46 kg.
Ton (United States and territories) = 2,000 lbs. = 906·08 kg.
Ton (English and statistical) = 2,240 lbs. avoird. = 1,016·047 kg.
Ton (metric) = 1,000 kg. = 2,204·60 lbs. avoird.
Sack (Brazil) = 132·27 lbs. = 60 kg.
Sack (Cuba) = 325 Spanish pounds = 330 lbs. = 149·5 kg.   (This is sometimes
    reckoned to be one-seventh of an English ton or 320 lbs. avoird.
Sack (France) = 220 lbs. = 100 kg.
Sack (Mauritius) = 170 lbs. = 77 kg.
Ton (Spanish, for cane only) = 100 arrobas = 2,531·75 lbs. = 1,150·24 kg.

C. CURRENCY.

Bolivar Venezuela) = 100 centimos = 10d.
Colon (Costa Rica) = 100 centavos = 2s.
Dollar (Mexico) = 100 centavos = 2s. 0½d.
Dollar (Straits Settlements) = 100 cents. = 2s. 4d.
Dollar (United States) = 100 cents = 4s. 2d.
Franc (France and colonies) = 100 centimes = 9½d.
Gulden (Netherland) = 100 cents = 1s. 8d.
Krone (Austria) = 100 heller = 10d.
Mark (Germany) = 100 pfennig = 1s.
Milrei gold (Brazil) = 1,000 reis = 2s. 3d.
Milreis paper (Brazil) = 1,000 reis = 1s. 3d.
Milreis (Portugal and colonies) = 1,000 reis = 4s.
Peseta (Spain) = 100 centimos = 9½d.
Peso gold (Argentina) = 100 centavos = 4s. 1d.
Peso paper (Argentina) = 1s. 8d.
Peso (Guatemala) = 100 centavos = 4s. 1d.
Peso (Honduras) = 100 centavos = 4s. 1d.
Peso (Nicaragua) paper = 100 cent vos = 6d.
Peso (Philippines) = 100 centavos = 2s. 1d.
Pound (Egypt) = 100 piasters = 19s. 10d.
Rouble (Russia) = 100 kopecks = 3s. 2d.
Rupee (British India) = 16 annas = 192 pies = 1s. 4d.
Rupee (Mauritius) = 100 cents = 1s. 4d.
Rijksdaalder (Netherland) = 4s. 2d.
Sol (Peru) = 100 centavos = 2s.
Yen (Japan) = 100 sen = 2s. 1d.

IV.

ADDENDA.

At Page 61 :—

Sugar imported into India in 1911–12 :

BEET SUGAR.

From Austria-Hungary	..	241,433 cwt.
,, Germany	..	9,821 ,,
,, United Kingdom..	..	——
,, Other countries ..	..	2,506 ,,
Total	..	253,760 cwt.

CANE SUGAR.

From Mauritius	..	1,709,773 cwt.
,, China .. .	..	12,656 ,,
,, Java	..	8,190,469 ,,
,, Straits Settlements	..	767 ,,
,, United Kingdom..	..	—
,, Other countries ..	..	4,408 ,,
Total	..	9,918,073 cwt.
Grand total ..	..	10,171,833 cwt.

At Page 68 :—

Exportation of sugar from British India in 1911–12 : 175,895 cwt. raw sugar ; 25,388 cwt. refined sugar.

At page 209 :—

	General Tariff.	Preferential Tariff.	Total.
1911/12 ..	208,969,811 lbs. ..	375,831,681 lbs. ..	584 801,492 lbs.

At Page 104 :—

Sugar Production and Area Planted with Sugar Cane in the different Provinces of the Philippines in the year 1911.

Provinces.	Sugar Production.		Hectares planted with Cane.	Kg. of Sugar per Hectare.	English Tons of Sugar per Acre.	Island.
	Piculs.	Metric Tons.				
Albay	1,146	72	141	514	0·205	Luzon.
Ambos Camarines	3,081	195	367	531	0·212	,,
Antique	53,186	3,364	1,580	2,129	0·849	Panay.
Bataan	7,491	474	341	1,389	0·554	Luzon.
Batangas	190,955	12,078	5,183	2,330	0·934	,,
Bohol	1,941	123	166	739	0·296	Bohol.
Bulacan ..	54,442	3,443	2,935	1,173	0·4	Luzon.
Cagayan	2,154	136	281	484	0·190	Mindanao.
Capiz	6,729	426	385	1,105	0·439	,,
Cavite	24,910	1,576	1,198	1,315	0·523	,,
Cebu	33,007	2,008	1,866	1,118	0·445	Cebu.
Ilocos Norte ..	41,443	2,621	2,338	1,121	0·447	Luzon.
Ilocos Sur	101,116	6,396	3,412	1,874	0·748	,,
Iloilo	124,564	7,879	3,308	2,311	0·919	Panay.
Isabela	475	30	42	715	0·289	Basilan.
La Laguna	23,880	1,510	741	2,038	0·812	Luzon.
La Union	24,934	1,577	1,018	1,549	0·616	,,
Leyte	10,854	687	815	843	0·336	Leyte.
Mindoro..	177	11	19	589	0·245	Mindoro.
Misamis	726	46	34	1,350	0·537	Luzon.
Moro	1,620	102	119	861	0·345	,,
Montañosa	2,274	144	175	821	0·326	,
Nueva Ecija ..	10,055	636	527	1,206	0·481	Luzon.
Nueva Vizcaya ..	617	39	60	650	0·264	,,
Occidental Negros	973,231	61,557	26,820	2,295	0·915	Negros.
Oriental Negros ..	48,266	3,053	1,410	2,165	0·863	,,
Palawan	60	4	5	759	0·308	Palawan.
Pamparga	454,264	28,732	16,551	1,735	0·691	Luzon.
Pangasinan	35 338	2,235	2,794	800	0·317	,,
Rizal	30,345	1,919	1,752	1,095	0·435	,,
Samar	8,622	545	667	818	0·342	Samar.
Sarsogon	7,292	461	398	1,159	0·462	Luzon.
Surigao	425	27	47	572	0·238	Mindanao.
Tarloa	115,810	7,325	4,427	1,654	0·659	Luzon.
Tarebas	15,148	958	1,005	953	0·380	,,
Zambales ..	2,692	170	141	1,207	0·481	,,
Total	2,413,270	152,639	83,168	1,836	0·734	

General Index.

383

S PAGE

Sugar manufacture   50, 98, 130, 146
    155, 163, 173, 174, 181, 183, 194, 210
    232, 233, 234, 235, 236, 237, 263, 265
    266, 276, 277, 286, 289, 295, 304, 315
        316, 359, 360
Sugar producing countries in early
    ages 6
Sugar production and rendement . 18
    21, 22, 39, 46, 47, 53, 59, 73, 82, 83
    114, 115, 120, 128, 129, 131, 132, 133
    134, 135, 142, 148, 153, 155, 156, 157
    158, 164, 165, 171, 172, 173, 174, 175
    176, 183, 188, 194, 201, 215, 217, 218
    221, 231, 237, 244, 245, 246, 247, 249
    251, 255, 261, 262, 263, 266, 272, 276
    281, 282, 286, 287, 289, 292, 293, 296
    298, 299, 301, 304, 310, 311, 316, 317
    325, 328, 335, 337, 338, 340, 341, 342
        347. 352, 360, 361, 368
Sugar schools 16
Sugar Works Guarantee Act   332, 334
Surtax   17, 24, 27, 28, 34, 35, 64, 146
        302

T

Tables on :
    Additional Duties 29
    Amount of Rain   70, 93, 112, 151
    162, 167, 212, 227, 228, 255, 263, 284
        288, 289, 346
    Analyses 57, 211
    Areas of some factories . . . 195
    Cartel profits 28
    Exports 11, 68, 75, 77, 79, 89, 104
    105, 186, 195, 202, 204, 223, 224
    225, 243, 283, 321, 325, 352, 368
    Factories 90, 103
    Factories in the French Antilles 239
    Humidity 111
    Imports 62, 67, 77, 78, 79, 146, 209
        210, 329

T PAGE

Import duty . . . 65, 272
Irrigated land 351
Location, dimensions, population
    of some West Indian Islands . 224
Number of slaves 8
Production of beetroot sugar . 18
Prime cost   61, 102, 130, 136, 138
        317, 318, 362
Planted area   44, 45, 114, 170, 177
        248, 325, 347, 362
Relation of the quantity of assort-
    ments 137
Relation between newly planted
    cane and ratoons . . . 314
Shipment of Java sugar . 140, 141
Sugar duty in Germany . . . 23
Sugar production and rendement   21
    22, 39, 46, 47, 53, 59, 115, 120, 128
    129, 131, 132, 133, 134, 135, 148
    156, 157, 158, 164, 165, 171, 175
    176, 183, 188, 194, 201, 215, 218
    221, 237, 244, 245, 246, 247, 249
    251, 261, 263, 266, 286, 272, 276
    281, 282, 286, 287, 292, 296, 298
    299, 301, 304, 310, 311, 316, 317
    325, 328, 335, 337, 338, 340, 341
        342, 347, 352, 360, 361
Temperature   109, 110, 111, 151, 162
    167, 227, 228, 265, 267, 284, 346
World's sugar production   21, 39
Temperature   93, 109, 110, 111, 151
    162, 167, 191, 196, 212, 220, 221, 227
    228, 254, 265, 268, 273, 284, 288, 296
        307, 331, 346
Trianon decree 13
Twelve years' truce 275

W

Want of sugar 13, 30
World's production of sugar . 21, 39
Wilson Tariff 30

Geographical and Proper Names.

Index.

Index.

Index.

389

Index

Index.

Index.

Index.

Index.

Index.